Phonology

Phonology
A Formal Introduction

Alan Bale
Charles Reiss

The MIT Press
Cambridge, Massachusetts
London, England

For information about special quantity discounts, please email special sales@mitpress.mit.edu.

This book was set in Times by the authors.
Printed and bound in the United States of America.

Library of Congress Cataloging-in-Publication Data

Names: Bale, Alan. | Reiss, Charles author.
Title: Phonology : a formal introduction / Alan Bale and Charles Reiss.
Description: Cambridge, MA : The MIT Press, 2018. | Includes bibliographical
    references and index.
Identifiers: LCCN 2017057051 | ISBN 9780262038386 (hardcover : alk. paper)
Subjects: LCSH: Grammar, Comparative and general–Phonology.
Classification: LCC P217 .B25 2018 | DDC 414–dc23 LC record
    available at https://lccn.loc.gov/2017057051

10 9 8 7 6 5 4 3 2 1

This book is dedicated to the memory of Morris Halle.

Contents

Acknowledgments

Authorship of any sort is a fantastic indulgence of the ego. It is well, no
doubt, to reflect on how much one owes to others.

John Kenneth Galbraith, *The Affluent Society*

We are grateful to the many colleagues who have influenced this book, either through
conversation or through our familiarity with their work, including other excellent in-
troductions to phonology. Eric Baković must be singled out for his interest and en-
couragement over the course of this project. Some of the material here derives from
research developed over many years with Mark Hale, so he too deserves special thanks.
Brendan Gillon and Dana Isac offered sympathetic ears and good advice during the
long thinking and writing process. Péter Siptár's careful reading of a late draft saved
us from a lot of embarrassing mistakes. Our copy editor, Mary Calvez, caught errors
and helped us clarify the writing in many parts of a long and difficult manuscript.

A number of younger scholars and former students—Maxime Papillon, Bridget
Samuels, David Ta-Chun Shen, Frédéric Mailhot, Sigwan Thivierge, Veno Volenec,
September Cowley, Ollie Sayeed, Thomas Graf, and Karthik Durvasula—have influ-
enced our thinking. Dariia Dziuba created a bank of html exercises and also pro-
vided useful suggestions and corrections over the course of many revisions. Hisako
Noguchi's acumen, both linguistic and stylistic, has improved the book considerably.

A reviewer commented on an unsuccessful grant application for an early stage of
this work that "Students won't be inspired to study linguistics through set theory, but
rather through hip-hop music." Over the years, many students who like both set theory
and hip-hop music have assured us that it was the former that kept them in linguistics.
We appreciate the vindication.

Part I

Preliminaries

Unit 1

Phonology and Theoretical Neuroscience

Perhaps you have no idea what the words *pangolin* and *maypop* mean. However, if we told you that both words are nouns—the first is a kind of animal (also called a *scaly anteater*) and the second a kind of flower (also called a *purple passionflower*)— you would have no problem creating plural forms for each word. In writing, you would probably guess *pangolins* and *maypops*. One noteworthy fact about these words is that the plural markers, written as *-s* in both forms, sound different. If you say *pangolins*, you will notice that the sound at the end of the word sounds like the beginning of *zinc*, whereas if you say *maypops*, the sound at the end of the word sounds like the beginning of *sink*. This distinction is an example of a phonological fact about your language. In this book we take the position that the study of such facts, the study of phonology, is a branch of cognitive science that ultimately can serve as a form of theoretical neuroscience.

This suggestion, that *phonology* is relevant to theoretical neuroscience, might strike you as outrageous. However, once we consider that you had to use your mind to come up with the plural forms for those previously unknown words, and that the mind is somehow closely related to the brain, our apparently controversial characterization of phonology becomes a platitude: our linguistic behavior, like all of our behavior, is highly dependent on our mind/brain and thus ultimately has to be compatible with the correct theory of our brains.

This is not to say we will be talking about neurotransmitters or networks of cells

3

in this book. We wish we could; we wish phonology were at a stage where we could link our phonological knowledge to neurological states. Unfortunately it is not. No one has identified correspondences between linguistic "sounds" and neurological patterns. No one yet understands the correlations between a specific set of neurons firing and the representation of syllables, stress patterns, or tone, and it is not even clear that this is the right kind of correlation to look for. The study of the relationship between activity in the brain and language, or in fact any other kind of cognition, is in its infancy. However, our ambitious goal in this book is to introduce you to phonology as a useful step toward a future unification of cognitive science and neuroscience. As Gallistel and King (2009, p. vii) put it, "The truths the cognitive scientists know about information processing, when integrated into neuroscience, will transform our understanding of how the brain works."

Prior to figuring out how the brain works at the (sub-)neurological level, we must first understand what the brain does: What kind of information does it store and process, and what kind of operations does it perform on this information? Our focus will be on the information structures that are stored—the *representations*—and the operations that are performed—the *rules*—in the domain of phonology.

As phonologists interested in unifying our field with other branches of cognitive science, our job is to formulate theories using terms and concepts that are accessible to specialists in fields like psychology and neuroscience. With this in mind, we have attempted to build phonological theories out of a general logical and mathematical toolbox containing functions, sets, set operations, and variables. Theories built with these tools can be easily translated to precise algorithms. Precise algorithms, in turn, should ultimately make it easier to associate neurological states and activity with phonological cognition.

It is important to note that pursuing phonological theory in this way opens the door to making connections between phonological processes and other kinds of cognition. Once we state our phonological patterns in such general terms, neuroscientists can try to figure out how functions, sets, set operations, and variables can be implemented in biological systems more generally. This basic mathematical toolbox can describe a variety of cognitive behavior, from higher level concept formation to insect navigation systems. This generality could mean that studying the neurology of a wasp making her way home might tell us something about what goes on in your brain when you say *pangolins*. This is an exciting possibility and one that a cognitive science should strive for.

Hopefully, outlining these lofty goals will help you, the reader, understand why we made the choices we did in our introduction to phonology. However, emphasis should be put on the word *introduction*. This book is intended for a broad audience and does not assume any prior knowledge of mathematical concepts or cognitive science. In fact, not only do we use basic math and logic to understand phonology, but we also use basic phonological patterns to teach some math and logic. By the end of this book, we hope the reader has a better grasp of fundamental notions such as *function*, *variable*, and *set*.

Exercises

1.1. On his blog *Faculty of Language* (http://facultyoflanguage.blogspot.com/) the syntactician Norbert Hornstein paraphrases his friend the phonologist Elan Dresher saying that "if describing how a bunch of bees dance is biology so too is describing how a bunch of Parisians speak French." Hornstein cites this in the midst of a discussion of Karl von Frisch's Nobel prize-winning research on the waggle dance that bees use to communicate the direction, distance, and quality of a food source to hive-mates. So, Hornstein and Dresher think it is self-evident that linguistics is ultimately biology, and that it is useful to think of linguistics as a natural science.

In contrast, Jan Koster, who works on syntax and semantics, says:

> [I am] committed to a version of the traditional view that language is in the first place a cultural phenomenon, crucially depending on a supra-individual, external record. I furthermore believe that the mind, unlike the brain, cannot be seen in isolation from the shared, external memory with which the brain lives in symbiosis [reference omitted–ab & cr]. This external, cultural record determines how our biologically given resources are applied. A good example is playing the piano. It is of course based on our biological capacities: tone perception memory, the physiological and neurological aspects of finger movement, etc. Nevertheless, piano playing is primarily seen as a cultural activity. It involves a tradition of musical composition and, crucially, the invention of an artefact, the piano, which allows us to integrate our biological capacities with the culture we participate in. ...We can only speak of language because of the invention of cultural artefacts, *words*, which are comparable to the piano. ...As for the relation between biology and culture, I see no logical difference between playing the piano (and the rest of our culture) and the use of language. (2006:351-2)

As you see, even professional linguists can disagree greatly concerning the nature of their field. Which of these positions do you find more convincing? Are your own beliefs somewhat compatible with both positions? Which position do you think the average person would be more sympathetic to? Answer one of these questions in a brief essay.

1.2. Go to the webpages of five university linguistics programs and try to find out how linguistics is classified at each university—humanities, social science, natural science, engineering, or computer science—and in which other departments the professors in linguistics programs have affiliations. If you were an administrator of a university planning to open a new linguistics department, how would you classify it? Do you think this choice would matter? Answer in a brief essay.

Unit 2

Language as Knowledge

2.1 A Grim Scenario: Introducing I-Language

Suppose you wake up and find that you are the only person alive after a nuclear holocaust. Suppose further that all books have been incinerated in the conflagration that you alone have miraculously survived. As you wander, dazed, through the post-apocalyptic world you talk to yourself. Since you presumably know what you are thinking and what you are going to say, it is not clear that any communication is occurring when you talk to yourself. You are pretty bored all alone in the world, and after a while you notice that you can feel vibrations on your throat at the beginning of the word *zinc*, but no vibrations at the beginning of the word *sink*. (Take a moment to put down this book and put your fingers on your throat to confirm that this is true.) Let's say that you conclude that there is some physiological correlate to your sense that these words begin with different sounds.

Next, you discover that when you pronounce certain plural words like *dogs, frogs, pigs* and *hogs* you also feel the funny vibration on your neck at the end of the word, but when you pronounce *picks, frocks, shacks, locks, socks* and *snacks* you don't feel the vibration. Now, you had always known that *sink* and *zinc* began with different sounds, but if you hadn't been fortunate enough to read our discussion of *maypops* and *pangolins* from Unit 1 or otherwise study linguistics before nuclear Armageddon, you probably would have thought that *frogs* and *frocks* ended with the same sound, the sound of the plural ending common to these two words.

One way to understand your discovery about the pronunciation of plurals is to

7

decide that in your mind, *pigs* and *picks*, say, in some sense do have the same ending, but that the process of pronouncing this ending involves changing it in some cases, depending on the preceding sound. This is all very vague, and a goal of this book is to make such vague ideas more concrete. However, an important thing to note is that this supposed ending, and this supposed process, are properties of *you*. They are not shared properties of a group of people, because in our grim scenario, there are no other people. They are not parts of a communication system, since in our scenario, there is nobody for you to communicate with.

We want to focus on three aspects of the posited plural ending and the process that selects its variant realizations:

- They are properties of you and nobody else, since there is nobody else, so they belong to you as an *individual*. In our current scenario you appear to be the only individual in the world.

- These properties you have are not in the air or the water or in books, since books don't contain sounds, and since, in our post-Armageddon world, all books have been incinerated. Instead of you, we could have chosen as our lone survivor an illiterate person whose spoken language is just like yours, a person with no access to information stored in books. In any case, the English writing system actually *obscures* what is going on, since it spells the plural marker the same in *frogs* and *frocks*, despite the difference in sound. The properties relevant to these patterns must be encoded in your brain, somehow, as stored information. So the properties are *internal* to you.

- These properties apply in a vast number of situations, and in fact the pattern you noted of pronouncing the plural with vibration after nouns ending in *g*, but without vibration after nouns ending in *k*, appears to generalize. If you were to invent new words for your lonely self, you would detect that you pluralize them just as you pluralize words you have known all your life. The process of adjusting the pronunciation conforms to a pattern or principle. For reasons that will be clearer later, we call such a system *intensional*.

The status of these three characteristics of your language—that it is *individual, internal* and *intensional*—would not be affected if it turned out that others had survived the nuclear holocaust, say somewhere in Hungary, Chechnya, and Cameroon. Of course, the people in these places speak languages that are not called English, but still each of them could discover patterns somewhat analogous to what you discovered.

Once we grant this last point, it becomes clear that the status of the three characteristics would not change, even if other speakers of what we might call English had survived, whether or not you actually interacted with them. Obviously, the existence of others who have the same pattern of plurals does not bear on the *intensional* nature of the system. Whether others exist or not does not affect your ability to generalize to new contexts, say. Similarly, this ability of yours is still *internal* to you, since it is still encoded somehow in your nervous system, presumably in your brain. Finally, despite the fact that other individuals share systems that are very much like your own, this does not bear on the fact that the system is a property of *you* as an individual, just as your visual system is a property of you, despite being similar or identical to that of other humans. Both your visual system and your phonological system are *your* properties as an individual.

We are finally ready to leave our grim scenario and return to the world we live in. Despite the fact that we *do* communicate with others who appear to be similar or identical to us in terms of our speech patterns, it remains true that each of us is characterized by an *I-language*, a system that is *individual, internal* and *intensional*.[1]

2.2   Innateness and Universal Grammar

Another word beginning with *i* that is often discussed in linguistics is *innate*. The *I-language* concept is logically independent of the question of whether there is a significant innate component to the language faculty determined by the human genome. In principle, one could accept the intensional, internal, individual view of language without accepting the *nativist* view that there is an innate language faculty. However, we believe that there are strong arguments to accept the existence of a non-trivial innate component to human phonology and other aspects of language. The existence of this component, sometimes called *universal grammar* (UG) is considered by some to be a controversial hypothesis. Our own position is that UG is a logical necessity. Arguments for UG stem from the work of Noam Chomsky (e.g., 1965) with influences from Lenneberg et al. (1967). See the suggested readings in Unit 5 for some accessible discussions of why UG is better thought of as the definition of a research topic, rather than as a hypothesis.

---

[1] In fact, many of us have several I-languages. In everyday terms we might refer to such a person as *multilingual*, that is, having I-languages that we categorize in everyday terms as, say, Albanian, Berber, Nepalese, Xhosa, and Yiddish.

2.3   Abstract Knowledge

How do children learn a language? Well, that question might be too hard to answer since everyday notions of language appear to require various skills, each of which might be learned in a different manner. So, let's focus on one aspect of language, and ask "What must a child learn in order to pronounce words?" A simple answer would be that kids learn some information that gets stored in their brains, and they have some way of transforming that information back to pronunciations, so that they can speak the words they have heard.

This simple answer already abstracts away from lots of detail—kids don't learn to pronounce words they first heard from their grandmother with a voice that sounds like an old lady and words they first heard from their brother with a voice that sounds like a little boy, for example. They also don't necessarily scream words that they heard first from another kid having a tantrum, and whisper words that they first heard from a mother calming down a baby for a nap. And they don't try to imitate a diesel engine every time they pronounce a word they first heard when a bus was passing.

There is a lot of abstraction that takes place in the process of encoding the information that gets stored. Since that information is stored in the mind of the child, we refer to it as "knowledge." This knowledge somehow arose from, or is related to, the child's experience, and for linguists[2] it is this knowledge, this information stored inside the child's brain, that we consider to be our object of study. We sometimes refer to this as the child's "knowledge of language" but we don't mean that it is knowledge of something out in the world. We mean instead that it is this knowledge that *constitutes* language. Put more simply, a language *is* knowledge in a person's head. We sometimes refer to a language in this sense as a *mental grammar*.

It is interesting to note just how abstract the information is that gets stored in the child's brain. Consider a pair of utterances like the following.

(1)   a. You went to the store.

        b. You went to the store?

In such pairs, it is typical for most speakers to have a difference in intonation. The declarative sentence in (1a) usually has a falling pitch at the end, whereas the pitch rises at the end of the question in (1b).

This small fact has dramatic consequences for how the pronunciation of words is represented inside our head. For example, the word *store* in the two sentences is

---

[2]We use *linguist* and *linguistics* to talk about the study of *I-language*. Some more specific terms that distinguish this kind of linguistics from others are *theoretical linguistics*, *generative linguistics*, and *biolinguistics*. For our purposes, these are equivalent.

pronounced differently compared to the preceding words—in (1a) with a relatively low pitch and in (1b) with a relatively high pitch. And the word *store* is not unique. This difference can be illustrated with any noun you put into such pairs of utterances.

(2)   a.   You went to the shore.

      b.   You went to the shore?

(3)   a.   You went to the mountain.

      b.   You went to the mountain?

It seems plausible to assume that speakers have not heard a low pitch version and a high pitch version of each noun. In fact it turns out that being a noun is not really relevant—we get parallel differences no matter what words are involved.

(4)   a.   You went up.

      b.   You went up?

(5)   a.   You danced.

      b.   You danced?

(6)   a.   You dance gracefully.

      b.   You dance gracefully?

The pitch variation occurs whether the final word is an adverbial particle like *up*, a verb like *danced*, or an adverb like *gracefully*. So, it appears that even when you abstract away from individual voice quality (grandmother versus screaming child) and background noise (passing buses), the information that relates to specific word pronunciation must be combinable with a knowledge about intonation patterns (and other factors) to create actual pronunciations. We'll refer to the individual word information and the intonational information as *linguistic* aspects of pronunciation. Other factors, like whether you are whispering, have a sore throat, or have peanut butter in your mouth, are non-linguistic.

Why is this interesting? These observations demonstrate that what a speaker has stored as the pronunciation of a word can *never* correspond directly to an actual pronunciation. Learning a language is *never* a matter of imitation since kids do not store words with intonation—they abstract away from intonation and store something that they *never* hear. Even this basic aspect of language learning, namely learning the pronunciation of words, is massively abstract. Learners have to factor out all kinds of non-linguistic information (grandmotherly voice creak and passing bus noise), but also some kinds of linguistic information, like the intonation pattern that can distinguish a statement from a question.

In our discussion of English intonation, it was perhaps comforting that the same string of segments of a word like *store* always appeared in the linguistic pronunciation, whatever intonation it was combined with. In other words, all the information that the child ultimately must store in his lexicon was contained in each pronunciation. Unfortunately (for those with a simplistic view of language learning) this is not always the case. For some words, the form stored in a speaker's mind, and thus the form "learned" in the course of constructing a grammar, may be a sequence of segments that the learner *never* has heard and in fact never *could* hear.

Our student Sigwan Thivierge found an example of this situation while studying a grammar of Anishinaabemowin, the traditional Algonquian language of her community in Québec. The verb meaning 'walk' appears with different combinations of prefixes that lead to differences in syllable structure, which in turn, result in the deletion of vowels in certain positions. So we get forms like *gii-bmose* 'he walked' and *n-bimse* 'I walk'. Analysis of the language leads us to posit a root *bimose*, but in the first form the *i* does not appear, and in the second form the *o* does not appear. One or the other of these vowels always fails to appear, but a speaker has to store a form that contains both, a form that is never pronounced. The rules of the language *compute* the correct output form by deleting one or the other of the stored vowels. Such examples have been found in many languages—try to find some in your own dialect of English by looking for related words with different stress patterns.

Again, note that we have made the shocking claim that a child constructing an I-language infers and stores strings of segments that he or she has never heard! A language develops in the child's mind on the basis of what he or she hears other people saying, but this "imitation" encodes information in a form that is never manifested directly in what the child hears. Even after years and years of studying language, we still find this fascinating.

Unit 3

Apologia

> As concepts and principles become simpler, argument and inference tend to become more complex—a consequence that is naturally very much to be welcomed.

Noam Chomsky, *Some Concepts and Consequences of the Theory of Government and Binding*

The word *apology* has a formal meaning somewhat removed from the everyday sense of an excuse or admission of guilt with a request for forgiveness. We are following an inconsistent tradition of using *apologia*, which is closer in form to the Greek original, to provide an explanation for a position taken or a course of action. Plato's work from around 400 B.C.E. known in English as the *Apology of Socrates* is the most famous example of an *apologia*. In the dialogue, Socrates is not *apologizing*, not asking for forgiveness, for corrupting the youth or being an atheist or disobeying authority, but rather he is explaining his actions and actually arguing that they have entailed none of those sins. The putative sin we are about to commit is much less serious than the charges against Socrates: we have written a phonology textbook based mainly on made-up datasets from so-called toy languages.

We expect that many phonologists will find our use of toy languages odious— "How can you do *real* phonology with *fake* data?" they may wonder. There are several points to discuss in this regard. First a practical matter: we refer to our toy languages with fake names. If you haven't heard of the language, or if we don't tell you where it

is spoken, then you should assume it is made up. Don't cite it in a research paper as a
real language!

To justify our toy languages, we'll begin with an appeal to authority, which is always a suspect form of justification, but, as you'll see, our authority is fairly convincing
in *his* justification. Here is how Kenneth Pike (1947, p. 68) introduces his use of toy
grammars, which he calls dialects of 'Kalaba':

> The illustration of the analytical procedures will be given by means of
> sample problems. Certain of the problems are hypothetical and will be
> called dialects of KALABA. These hypothetical problems have the ad-
> vantage of allowing complete control of the data, and the admission of
> only those data which illustrate the procedures. With this method, the dif-
> ficulties and the complexity of the procedure may be increased gradually.
>
> Other problems are comprised of data from actual languages. Here,
> however, there is not space to present all of the information available for
> any one specific language, and even if space did so permit, the problems
> would be too complicated for solution by the first procedures given to the
> student, and they would take too much time for solution. RESTRICTED
> LANGUAGE problems, then, give actual language material. Such exer-
> cises give valuable practice. At the same time they are presented to the
> student so that he may see that the theoretical procedures are applicable to
> actual language situations. . . .
>
> Furthermore, in handling those problems the student is to consider that
> *the data presented constitutes the entire material for the language.* Any
> statement therefore which he can make about the material so presented are
> pertinent to the entire "language," whether the problems represent data
> from the hypothetical Kalaba dialects or from artificially restricted but
> actual languages.

Like Pike, we see pedagogical value in using toy languages to isolate various issues that
are independent from each other for demonstration and discussion. We also expect that
the reasoning that you master will be applicable to "real" languages. However, even
the pedagogic reasoning leads quickly to more philosophical considerations.

Consider the practice in physics teaching. When you start studying mechanics in a
physics course, you learn about the behavior of perfectly spherical balls rolling down
perfectly straight, smooth ramps, with no friction between the two. This situation has
never been observed, since the rolling of balls down ramps always involves friction. A
pedagogic reason for idealizing a description of ball-rolling is that the teacher wants

to get you to understand one aspect of the world, gravity, not a whole messy complex situation that might include, say, even the presence of bubblegum stuck to the ball. Related to this pedagogical idealization are two fundamental ideas of science. The first idea is that actual events observed in the world are the result of multiple interacting factors, say, gravity and friction and maybe the distorting effect of bubblegum on the almost spherical ball. The second idea is that these factors are isolable in principle. In other words, science gives us the means to understand the contributions of gravity and friction to the behavior of balls on ramps separate from each other; but every "real" ball-rolling event involves both of them (and maybe some bubblegum); there is no ball-rolling data that is unaffected by friction.

Lawrence Sklar, a philosopher of science, makes the point that without such isolability, science itself would probably be impossible:

> [W]ithout a sufficient degree of isolability of systems we could never arrive at any lawlike regularities for describing the world at all. For unless systems were sufficiently independent of one another in their behavior, the understanding of the evolution of even the smallest part of the universe would mean keeping track of the behavior of all of its constituents. It is hard to see how the means for prediction and explanation could ever be found in such a world. ... [I]t can be argued that unless such idealization of isolability were sufficiently legitimate in a sufficiently dominant domain of cases, we could not have any science at all. (2000, p. 54-55)

By working through our toy languages, you are committing to at least tentatively trusting that we have constructed datasets that isolate for study real, independent aspects of phonological representation and computation. Of course, as you get more sophisticated you will want to reconsider whether our "idealizations of isolability were sufficiently legitimate."

Notice that you are probably willing to accept the idealizations of a physics textbook, because you have some preconceptions about what "counts as physics." In the case of a "real" ball rolling down a real ramp, one could in principle ask all kinds of questions that the physics book chooses to ignore:

- Which trucking company delivered the ramp to the lab? What was the gender of the driver?

- What color is the ball?

- What phase was the moon in when the ball was ordered by the lab technician?

- Is the ramp's high end toward the west?

- Does the ball smell like the sweat of the grad student who held it in his/her hands?

Nobody worries about such questions, which are not relevant to the ball-rolling problem. However, in the case of linguistic data, there are all kinds of questions whose status is either unclear or up for debate among different researchers, such as the following:

- Did one speaker produce all the listed forms?

- Are all members of the speech community consistent in their judgments of these forms?

- Did speakers accept any forms as acceptable alternatives for the forms they produced?

- How frequently does that form occur in normal speech? How frequently do related forms occur?

Under the perspective we have outlined, some of these questions can be dismissed since they are about speech communities, not individual, internal, intensional mental grammars (I-languages), but difficulties remain. For example, your transcription of a speaker's words may differ significantly when the person is drunk or tired or is missing a tooth. Or the person may try to talk "fancy," perhaps using a pronunciation that reflects a dialect that's more prestigious than their own, if they know that they are being recorded by a university professor. It is really hard to avoid this kind of problem when you record speakers in a soundbooth or with a microphone mounted on their head. Such data can be very "fake." [1]

Let's turn to a simple example of phonetic transcription. Silently mouth the English words *hip* and *hop* and pay attention to what your lips and tongue are doing at the beginning of each word. You will notice that when you mouth the two *h*'s, your mouth is in a completely different position, basically the position for the vowel in the middle of each word. The first would typically be transcribed phonetically as [hɪp]

---

[1] "Fake" in the sense of not reflecting well the output of the grammar. However, we do not want to suggest that speech recorded in a more natural setting, for example, utterances produced while the speaker is chewing gum, feeding a baby, cooking dinner, and watching who is walking past the window, will necessarily give an accurate sense of what is in the grammar either. Using speech data to figure out what is in the grammar is a difficult task.

with an initial consonant followed by a vowel, then a final consonant. The second would typically be transcribed phonetically as [hɑp], also with the same initial consonant followed by a vowel, then a final consonant. However, for someone who has no knowledge of English, upon first hearing, say, *hip*, it would be perfectly reasonable to transcribe it as [ɪ̥ɪp], with a voiceless vowel, followed by a voiced version of the same vowel. Similarly, *hop* could be transcribed [ɑ̥ɑp]. In other words, in terms of the physiological properties of your mouth, there is no difference between an *h* followed by a vowel and a sequence of voiceless and voiced versions of the same vowel.

So, what is the correct transcription? The correct transcription cannot be determined by paying attention to the physiological properties of the utterances,[2] but instead our choice is made on the grounds of certain assumptions. For example, we might conclude that since we say *a hip*, like *a shoe*, and not *an hip* like *an imp*, the word "acts like" it begins with a consonant, and we want our transcription to reflect that inference.

What does all this have to do with our toy languages? Well, our point, following Hammarberg (1981) and others, is that there is no such thing as raw, "real" data. Even if we stuck to published datasets from the phonological literature and even if we made the implausible assumptions that these datasets contain no errors of transcription; do not reflect performance errors by speakers; and reflect the output of a single grammar, and are thus consistent with the I-language perspective; it would *still* be the case that the data embodies many conscious and unconscious artefacts of analysis (including the exclusion of intonational information of the kind discussed in the previous unit). Even at the level of deciding on which segments are present, there is a tremendous amount of decision making that must happen—consider that there are phoneticians (e.g., Port, 2007) who reject the existence of symbolic mental representations such as segments (like [p,t,k,i,a,u]) and features (like VOICED) altogether, who see segmentation as a *consequence* of alphabetic writing.[3]

So, once you accept that there is no pure, objective, "real" data, you are liberated to go along with our idealizations. In the end, it is up to you to decide if you find them useful and enlightening. In plain words, our apologia reduces to "Give us a chance— everyone's data is fake, but we hope to have made ours fake in useful ways. In the end, the proof is in the pudding."

---

[2] For a related point, see footnote 1 in Unit 12

[3] We reject this view, but this just reinforces our point that theoretical perspective plays a large role in determining what one takes to be 'the facts'. The status of segments as mental representations will be discussed in Part III. Features are not introduced in this book until Part VIII.

Exercises

For the following exercises, you might want to use the free acoustic analysis program Praat available from *praat.org* to record, analyze, and transcribe sound files on a computer. You can also record on a different device, then import the file into Praat. Record in mono and save in .wav format. There is a manual on the program's homepage and there are help files available from within the program. There are also some basic instructional videos made by our former student Jesse Lawrence on the Rational Phonology YouTube channel.

3.1. Record three minutes of conversation of your family or friends around the dinner table. Based on this 'real' data corpus, provide a description of the structure of noun phrases, including the position of determiners, adjectives, prepositional phrases, and other modifiers. Comment on some problems you encounter.

3.2. Using the first thirty seconds of the same three-minute corpus, provide a transcription in a phonetic alphabet. Comment on some problems you encounter.

3.3. Using the first ten seconds of the same corpus, use an acoustic analysis program (such as Praat) to locate the boundaries between speech segments. For example, for the word *dog*, you would find the boundaries between the initial consonant, the vowel and the final consonant. Comment on some problems you encounter.

3.4. Repeat the previous exercise using a recording from a language you are unfamiliar with. You can find recordings online or find a speaker and make your own recordings. Compare your results with a classmate who uses the same recording. Comment on some problems you encounter.

Unit 4

Formalism with Sets

Mathematics, rightly viewed, possesses not only truth, but supreme beauty—a beauty cold and austere, like that of sculpture, without appeal to any part of our weaker nature, without the gorgeous trappings of painting or music, yet sublimely pure, and capable of a stern perfection such as only the greatest art can show. The true spirit of delight, the exaltation, the sense of being more than Man, which is the touchstone of the highest excellence, is to be found in mathematics as surely as poetry.

Bertrand Russell, "The Study of Mathematics"

4.1 Formalisms: A Justification

Variables, functions, quantifiers, power sets, and generalized intersections for linguistic analysis—why should semanticists have all the fun? This book adopts the pedagogic position that the fundamental logical and mathematical notions that in linguistics curricula are typically taught explicitly only in semantics courses, can be introduced profitably, and should be, in a basic phonology course.

There are two reasons for this. First, it will be good for students to study the formal tools behind linguistic theories more than once. Second, in our view phonology is grammar, and grammars are formal systems. Since the study of formal systems requires an understanding of formalism, you need to know the mathematics behind such

19

formalisms to do phonology. So, our position is not only about pedagogy, but also about how we conceive of the science of phonology. In fact, we think that you need to know the mathematics behind formal systems at least as much as you need to know basic phonetics. We think that the logic of phonology is an interesting and useful domain of study which can be largely divorced from considerations of phonetics—from how phonological representations map to the input (auditory) and output (articulatory) systems that they interface with.[1]

One more thing about our unorthodox attitude toward phonetics: many phonology texts begin, perhaps after a quick overview, with a review of phonetics. We follow Hammarberg (1976) in rejecting the notion that you need phonetics to do phonology. In fact, Hammarberg goes further in pointing out that you can't do *phonetics* without *phonology*—"phonology is logically and epistemologically prior to phonetics." Hammarberg's argument is basically that we can't ask simple phonetic questions like "Does the *k* in *Kool-Aid* involve more lip rounding than the *k*'s in *Kiss me, Kate*?" if we don't have the abstract phonological category of "the segment *k*." Such categories are not definable in purely phonetic terms, and we need the phonological categories to even formulate the phonetic questions. We will come back to phonetics in our discussion of features in Unit 47, but for now, we assume that the intuitive phonological notion of *segment* will suffice for our entrée into phonological reasoning.[2]

To a student, this may all seem very complicated already, but our goal is to simplify your mastery of phonological reasoning by isolating the various analytic techniques that typically form part of a phonological education. We aim to help you see that the apparently complicated structure that is phonological theory is actually a combination of simple, isolable ideas.

If you are reading this book, you probably have done some phonology in a phonetics course or in a general introduction to linguistics, and you will be familiar with at least some of the items on this list:

- The logical structure of the derivational model—how phonology relates to the lexicon, morphology, and phonetics.

- The logic of rules—what form rules have and how they are applied.

- The logic of rule interaction—the possible effects of rule ordering.

[1] If this position is correct, it supports the legitimacy of "substance free phonology" (Hale and Reiss, 2008; Reiss, 2017b).

[2] We will introduce phonetic symbols to represent segments as we proceed. Their precise phonetic value is not important, but we will sometimes indicate the phonetics by reference to English examples. Transcribed words will sometimes be presented in phonetic brackets like this: 'thin' [θɪn], with each segment corresponding to a symbol (more or less).

- The logic of natural classes of segments and of phonological environments.

By using very restricted datasets from actual linguistic corpora and our toy language artificial data, we will teach you about each of these "logics" separately, instead of throwing them at you all at once. The intention is that a better understanding of each will help you to gain insight into how they interact.

However, before we discuss any of this in detail, we first review some very basic mathematical notions that we will draw on as we proceed. Our discussion here will not be complete, and we will leave some of the more complicated concepts to be discussed later as they are needed to illuminate phonological issues. If you have never encountered set theory before, or if you have not done so since grade school, the following sections should serve you well for the rest of the book. However, if you are already familiar with sets, functions, variables, and related topics, feel free to skip the rest of this unit, or go directly to the exercises.

4.2   Sets

Much of the foundation of logic, mathematics, and other formal systems can be understood using set theory. Fortunately, sets and set operations have the benefit of being intuitively accessible. So, set theory is probably the quickest and easiest way to get accustomed to formal systems. There is some terminology that you need to remember, and a few symbols that you need to get familiar with, but otherwise all of the important operations are based on the idea of collections and membership in those collections.

Naively defined, sets are collections of things. The *things* in the collections are often called *elements* or *members* of the set. The central idea behind sets is the notion of *membership*. Sets are defined only by what belongs to them.

We will sometimes represent sets using capital letters like S or A, but we will also represent sets using the members themselves. For example, let's suppose there is a set S that has the elements a, b, and c as members. We could talk about this set using its name S, but we could also talk about this set using the members along with special symbols that indicate the boundaries of the collection. Mathematicians do this in the following way:

$$\{a, b, c\}$$

The pair of curly brackets, { }, can be thought of as a *container* symbol. If we informally think of a set as a container for its members, then the symbols between the brackets indicate what is in the container, the members of a set. The members of a set are listed with commas between them.

4.3   Sets and Relations

A *relation* is a concept that involves two or more things. Thus, fatherhood is a relation, one that holds between men and their children. Similarly, sisterhood is a relation that holds between females and their siblings. Statements involving relations can be evaluated as true or false. The statement *Steven Tyler is the biological father of Liv Rundgren Tyler* is true, whereas the statement *Todd Rundgren is the biological father of Liv Rundgren Tyler* is false. The statement *Steven Tyler is the biological father of Mia Tyler* is also true. Relations can hold between any kinds of entities. We will see examples of relations that hold between elements and sets, and also relations that hold between sets.

4.3.1   Set Membership

Membership is a relation between elements and a set. This relation lies at the heart of what it means to be a set, and hence many (if not most) other relations, operations, and functions depend on this fundamental relation.

   The idea of membership is best understood through an example. Consider the set consisting of the collection of the elements a, b, and c, that is, $\{a, b, c\}$. Members of a set appear between curly brackets, thus the element a is a member of the set, as are b and c. However, the element d is not a member of the set $\{a, b, c\}$.

   Mathematicians often use the membership symbol ($\in$) and its counterpart, the non-membership symbol ($\notin$). The character '$\in$' can be read as "is a member of," whereas the symbol '$\notin$' can be read as "is not a member of." With this convention in mind, the facts mentioned above can be symbolized as follows:

(7)   a. $a \in \{a, b, c\}$

      b. $b \in \{a, b, c\}$

      c. $c \in \{a, b, c\}$

      d. $d \notin \{a, b, c\}$

Statements of this form are either true or false. For example, all the statements in (7) are true; however, the statement $d \in \{a, b, c\}$ is false.

   It is important to note that when we list the elements in a set, the order in which they appear does not matter. Thus $\{a, b, c\} = \{a, c, b\} = \{b, a, c\} = \{b, c, a\} = \{c, a, b\} = \{c, b, a\}$. This is because sets are defined by membership alone. Saying "a and b and c are members of the set" is equivalent to saying "c and b and a are members of the set." Each enumeration of the three elements defines the same set.

Another important point is that repetition does not matter when we list the members of a set. Thus $\{a, b, c\} = \{a, b, c, a\} = \{a, b, b, c\} = \{a, b, b, c, a\} = \{a, b, c, c\} = \{a, c, b, a, c, b\}$. Once again, this is due to the fact that sets are defined by membership. Saying "a is a member, b is a member, c is a member, and a is a member" is equivalent to saying "a is a member, b is a member, c is a member." The first statement is just a bit repetitive, but conveys the same information.

We have not put any restrictions on what can be a member of a set. So far, our examples have involved simple elements such as a, b, and c. However, sets themselves can also serve as members of sets. For example, the set $B = \{a, b, c\}$ is a member of the set $A = \{e, f, \{a, b, c\}, g\}$, and we describe A also as $\{e, f, B, g\}$. However, A does not have a, b, or c as members. These elements are members of a member of A but not members of A itself. Here are some true statements involving the set A:

(8)   a. $\{a, b, c\} \in \{e, f, \{a, b, c\}, g\}$

       b. $a \notin \{e, f, \{a, b, c\}, g\}$

       c. $e \in \{e, f, \{a, b, c\}, g\}$

       d. $a \in \{a, b, c\} \in \{e, f, \{a, b, c\}, g\}$

The concept that sets can be members of other sets, and that elements that are members of members of a set are not members of the set themselves, can be a bit confusing. In some ways, this is due to the container analogy—the idea that sets contain their elements much like boxes contain their contents. If I am storing a child's rubber ducky in a small box and then I put this small box into a bigger box, intuitively speaking both the bigger box and the small box contain the rubber ducky. However, containment of this sort is not a good analogy for membership.

A better analogy would be "what you can grab." By reaching into the smaller box, you can grab the rubber ducky. However, you cannot grab the rubber ducky by reaching into the bigger box. You can only grab the small box that contains the rubber ducky. The same holds for set membership. Suppose we had a set $\{b, c, d\}$ contained within the set $\{a, \{b, c, d\}, e\}$, where d is the rubber ducky. By reaching into the set $\{a, \{b, c, d\}, e\}$ I can "grab" a, e and the set $\{b, c, d\}$. These are the members of the set. I cannot "grab" d because it appears within another set of brackets (i.e., it is in a smaller box). These other brackets "block" me from grabbing d. In contrast, by reaching into the set $\{b, c, d\}$ I *can* retrieve d (or b or c).

Note that although repetition does not matter with respect to simple membership, repetition of a symbol does matter when there are sets contained within sets. For example, the sets in (9) are all different.

(9)   a. $\{a, \{b, c\}, c\}$

    b. $\{a, \{b, c\}\}$

    c. $\{a, \{b\}, c\}$

    d. $\{a, b, c\}$

With (9a), you can reach in and "grab" c, but you cannot do this with (9b). The inner brackets "block" you. In symbols, $c \in \{a, \{b, c\}, c\}$ but $c \notin \{a, \{b, c\}\}$. With (9a) and (9b), you can reach in and "grab" $\{b, c\}$. You cannot do this for (9c) and (9d). In symbols, $\{b, c\} \in \{a, \{b, c\}, c\}$ and $\{b, c\} \in \{a, \{b, c\}\}$, but $\{b, c\} \notin \{a, \{b\}, c\}$ and $\{b, c\} \notin \{a, b, c\}$. With (9c), you can reach in and "grab" $\{b\}$, but you cannot do this with (9d). In contrast, with (9d) you can "grab" b but you cannot do this with (9c). In symbols, $\{b\} \in \{a, \{b\}, c\}$ and $b \in \{a, b, c\}$, but $b \notin \{a, \{b\}, c\}$ and $\{b\} \notin \{a, b, c\}$.

It will turn out that having sets as members of sets is particularly useful when we discuss the representation of phonological segments as sets of properties or features. For example, the set of oral labial stops (in English) can be represented as the set $\{p, b\}$. However, if we represent p as a set of features, such as {LABIAL, VOICELESS, STOP}, and in the same way b as {LABIAL, VOICED, STOP}, then we would represent the labial stops as a set of sets: {{LABIAL, VOICELESS, STOP}, {LABIAL, VOICED, STOP}}. We will formalize the idea that the two segments p and b form the *natural class* of "labial stops" by virtue of being the only two segments that have as elements certain properties (namely, both LABIAL and STOP).

4.3.2   Subset and Proper Subset Relations

Once set membership has been defined, other types of relations and operations can be defined as well, such as the subset and superset relations. These relationships will be particularly useful when we discuss the interpretation of phonological rules.

The subset relation is symbolized as $\subseteq$, and its counterpart, the *not-a-subset* relation is represented as $\nsubseteq$. These relations hold between two sets. The statement $A \subseteq B$ is read as "A is a subset of B" and the statement $A \nsubseteq B$ is read as "A is not a subset of B," where A and B are both sets. These relations are defined as follows:

(10)   **Definition of the subset relation:** If A and B are sets, then A is a subset of B if and only if every member of A is also a member of B. ($A \subseteq B$ if and only if for every $x \in A$, $x \in B$.)

(11)   **Definition of the not-a-subset relation:** If A and B are sets, then A is not a subset of B if and only if there is some member of A that is not a member of B. ($A \nsubseteq B$ if and only if for some $x \in A$, $x \notin B$.)

For example, the set $\{a, b, c\}$ is a subset of $\{a, b, c, d, e\}$ since a, b, and c are members of $\{a, b, c, d, e\}$. This fact can be stated as follows:

(12) $\{a, b, c\} \subseteq \{a, b, c, d, e\}$

Statements of this form are either true or false. In the case above, it is true. The following is a false statement since e and d are members of the first set but not the second.

(13) $\{a, b, c, d, e\} \subseteq \{a, b, c\}$

Note that by definition, every set is a subset of itself. This holds due to the fact that for any given set X, every member of X is trivially a member of X. Hence $\{a, b, c\} \subseteq \{a, b, c\}$, $\{1, 2, 3, 4\} \subseteq \{1, 2, 3, 4\}$, $\{b, c\} \subseteq \{b, c\}$, and so on.

The line underneath the horseshoe symbol represents this potential equality in the subset relation. However, there is another relation, called the *proper subset* relation, that is a bit more strict and forbids equality. It is symbolized using the horseshoe symbol without the line underneath, namely $\subset$.

(14)   **Definition of the proper subset relation:** If A and B are sets, then A is a proper subset of B if and only if A is a subset of B but A does not equal B. ($A \subset B$ if and only if $A \subseteq B$ and $A \neq B$.)

Note that by definition, every set A that is a proper subset of a set B is also a subset of B (but critically not vice versa). For example, $\{a, b, c\}$ is both a proper subset and a subset of $\{a, b, c, d\}$.

(15)   a. $\{a, b, c\} \subset \{a, b, c, d\}$
       b. $\{a, b, c\} \subseteq \{a, b, c, d\}$

However, although $\{a, b, c\}$ is a subset of itself, it is not a *proper* subset of itself.

(16)   a. $\{a, b, c\} \subseteq \{a, b, c\}$
       b. $\{a, b, c\} \not\subset \{a, b, c\}$

Note that an alternative way of defining the subset relation is to specify that it is the opposite of the not-a-subset relation, as in (17).

(17)   **Alternative definition of the subset relation:** If A and B are sets, then A is a subset of B if and only if there is no member of A that is not also a member of B. ($A \subseteq B$ if and only if there is no $x \in A$ such that $x \notin B$.)

In other words, a set A is a subset of B if and only if $A \not\subseteq B$ is false. Although technically equivalent to the definition in (10), this way of wording the subset relation will be helpful when we discuss the empty set, below.

Since the subset relation is established through membership, the interaction between members, sets, and sets containing sets is relatively straightforward. For example, $\{a, \{b, c, d\}\}$ is a subset of $\{a, \{b, c, d\}, e, \{f, g\}\}$ since a and $\{b, c, d\}$ are members of $\{a, \{b, c, d\}, e, \{f, g\}\}$. Similarly, the set $\{\{b, c, d\}\}$ is a subset of the set $\{a, \{b, c, d\}, e, \{f, g\}\}$ since $\{b, c, d\}$ is a member of $\{a, \{b, c, d\}, e, \{f, g\}\}$. However, $\{b, c, d\}$ is not a subset of $\{a, \{b, c, d\}, e, \{f, g\}\}$ since neither b, c, nor d are members of $\{a, \{b, c, d\}, e, \{f, g\}\}$. These facts can be represented symbolically thus:

(18)   a. $\{a, \{b, c, d\}\} \subseteq \{a, \{b, c, d\}, e, \{f, g\}\}$

      b. $\{\{b, c, d\}\} \subseteq \{a, \{b, c, d\}, e, \{f, g\}\}$

      c. $\{b, c, d\} \not\subseteq \{a, \{b, c, d\}, e, \{f, g\}\}$

It is important to keep in mind the difference between the subset relation and the membership relation. Often when first learning about these concepts, people confuse or confound the two relations. Make sure you understand that $\{a\} \notin \{a, b\}$ and $\{a\} \subseteq \{a, b\}$ are both true.

4.3.3   Superset and Proper Superset Relations

The *superset* and *not-a-superset* relations, like the *subset* and *not-a-subset* relations, also track whether or not all the members of one set are in another set. The only difference is that the containment relation holds in the opposite direction and hence is symbolized by reversing the symbol used for the subset relation (i.e., $\subseteq$ = subset and $\supseteq$ = superset).

(19)   **Definition of the superset relation:** If A and B are sets, then A is a superset of B if and only if every member of B is also a member of A. ($A \supseteq B$ if and only if for every $x \in B$, $x \in A$.)

(20)   **Definition of the not-a-superset relation:** If A and B are sets, then A is not a superset of B if and only if there is some member of B that is not a member of A. ($A \not\supseteq B$ if and only if for some $x \in B$, $x \notin A$.)

By definition, it holds that $A \supseteq B$ if and only if $B \subseteq A$, and similarly $A \not\supseteq B$ if and only if $B \not\subseteq A$. In (21) and (22), we give some examples of the relationship between supersets and subsets.

(21)   Some relationships between $\{a, b\}$ and $\{a, b, c\}$

      a. $\{a, b, c\} \supseteq \{a, b\}$

      b. $\{a, b, c\} \nsubseteq \{a, b\}$

      c. $\{a, b\} \subseteq \{a, b, c\}$

      d. $\{a, b\} \nsupseteq \{a, b, c\}$

(22)   Some relationships between $\{\{a, b\}, c\}$ and $\{a, b, c\}$

      a. $\{a, b, c\} \nsupseteq \{\{a, b\}, c\}$

      b. $\{a, b, c\} \nsubseteq \{\{a, b\}, c\}$

      c. $\{\{a, b\}, c\} \nsubseteq \{a, b, c\}$

      d. $\{\{a, b\}, c\} \nsupseteq \{a, b, c\}$

We can use this connection between supersets and subsets to also define the *proper superset* relation.

(23)   **Definition of the proper superset relation:** If A and B are sets, then A is a proper superset of B if and only if B is a proper subset of A. ($A \supset B$ if and only if $B \subset A$.)

(24)   Some more relationships between $\{a, b\}$ and $\{a, b, c\}$

      a. $\{a, b, c\} \supset \{a, b\}$

      b. $\{a, b, c\} \not\subset \{a, b\}$

      c. $\{a, b\} \subset \{a, b, c\}$

      d. $\{a, b\} \not\supset \{a, b, c\}$

(25)   Some relationships between $\{a, b, c\}$ and itself

      a. $\{a, b, c\} \supseteq \{a, b, c\}$

      b. $\{a, b, c\} \subseteq \{a, b, c\}$

      c. $\{a, b, c\} \not\subset \{a, b, c\}$

      d. $\{a, b, c\} \not\supset \{a, b, c\}$

The superset versus subset distinction is really just a matter of direction, much like the less-than versus greater-than relations among numbers—if it is true that A is a subset of B, then it is true that B is a superset of A.

4.4   Set Operations and Special Sets

Operations are similar to relations in that they can apply to two elements, such as two sets, but they are different in that they do not necessarily result in a statement that is true or false. Operations always result in elements that are identical in type to the elements they applied to. So for example, $+$ in contrast to $=$ is an operation. It applies to two numbers and does not yield a statement that is true or false (e.g., $2 + 1$ is not a true or false statement, unlike $2 = 1$, which is false). The operator $+$ applies to two numbers and maps them to another number (e.g., $2 + 1$ maps to 3). In this section we will discuss operations that apply to two sets and yield another set. Specifically, we will discuss set intersection, set union, and set subtraction. Relevant to our discussion will be the definition of the empty set. This set has a special relationship with set intersection.

4.4.1   Set Intersection

Set intersection is an operation on two sets that results in another set. This operator is symbolized as '$\cap$'. Set intersection operates on a set to its left and a set to its right. The expression $A \cap B$ is pronounced "the intersection of A and B." The resulting set can be defined as follows:

(26)   **Definition of Set Intersection:** If A and B are sets, then $A \cap B$ is the smallest[3] set that contains every element that is both a member of the set A and a member of the set B.

For example,

(27)   a. $\{a, b, c, d\} \cap \{b, c, e\}$ maps to $\{b, c\}$

b. $\{a, b, c, d\} \cap \{a, b, c\}$ maps to $\{a, b, c\}$

c. $\{a, b, c, e\} \cap \{e, f, g\}$ maps to $\{e\}$

As in mathematics, we can turn statements with operators into statements that are true or false by using the equality relation, symbolized by $=$. For example, the statements in (28) are all true, given the mappings specified in (27).

(28)   a. $\{a, b, c, d\} \cap \{b, c, e\} = \{b, c\}$

---

[3]Obviously, there are an infinite number of sets that contain every element that is both a member of the set A and a member of the set B. The *smallest* such set is the one that is a subset of all the others. The idea is to get a set that has all the desired elements and nothing else.

b. $\{a, b, c, d\} \cap \{a, b, c\} = \{a, b, c\}$

c. $\{a, b, c, e\} \cap \{e, f, g\} = \{e\}$

Note that, like the subset relation, this operation has at its roots the notion of membership. The set intersection operator tracks shared membership.

4.4.2 The Empty Set

It may be the case that two sets do not share any members. For example $\{1, 2, 3\}$ does not have any members in common with $\{a, b, c\}$, nor does $\{e, f\}$ share any members with $\{g, h, i, j, k\}$. An interesting question is what would happen if we intersected these sets.

(29)   a. $\{a, b, c\} \cap \{1, 2, 3\}$ maps to ?

        b. $\{e, f\} \cap \{g, h, i, j, k\}$ maps to ?

Following the definition given above, the result of each intersection should be a set that contains all the members that the two sets have in common. However, since there are no members in common, the result would be a set that contains no members.

This set is often called the *empty set*. It is symbolized as '$\emptyset$' or '$\{\ \}$'. Thus, the results of the intersections above can be written as follows.

(30)   a. $\{a, b, c\} \cap \{1, 2, 3\}$ maps to $\emptyset$

        b. $\{e, f\} \cap \{g, h, i, j, k\}$ maps to $\emptyset$

Note that by definition, any set intersected with the empty set results in the empty set:

(31)   For all sets X, $X \cap \emptyset = \emptyset$.

Since the empty set has no members, it trivially follows that the empty set does not share any members with another set. Since the result of intersecting a set A with another set B is the smallest set that contains all the shared members, it follows that if anything were intersected with the empty set, the result would be a set with no members. But this is just the empty set itself!

Another fact about the empty set is that it is a subset of all other sets, and of course it is a subset of itself:

(32)   For all sets X, $\emptyset \subseteq X$.

This follows from the nature of the empty set and the definition of the subset relation. Recall that a set A is a subset of another set B if and only if there are no members of A that are not in B. (This wording reflects the second, "alternative" definition of the subset relation.) Since the empty set has no members, it trivially follows that there are no members in it that are not members of another set.

4.4.3   Set Union

Unlike set intersection, which takes two sets and yields a set that is the same size or smaller, set union takes two sets and yields a set that is the same size or larger. In this respect, set intersection and union are opposites, or what are sometimes called "duals" of one another.

Set union creates sets by combining all the members of one set with all the members of another. Since—like set intersection—it is a function on two sets that results in another set, this function is also an operator. Set union is symbolized as '∪'. The function operates on a set to its left and a set to its right. The expression $A \cup B$ is pronounced "the union of A and B." The resulting set can be defined as follows:

(33)   **Definition of Set Union**: If A and B are sets, then $A \cup B$ results in the smallest set that contains all the elements of A and all the elements of B.

For example:

(34)   a. $\{a\} \cup \{b, c\}$ maps to $\{a, b, c\}$

       b. $\{a, d\} \cup \{b, c, e\}$ maps to $\{a, b, c, d, e\}$

       c. $\{a, b, c, d\} \cup \{b, c, e\}$ maps to $\{a, b, c, d, e\}$

       d. $\{a, b, c, d\} \cup \{a, b, c\}$ maps to $\{a, b, c, d\}$

       e. $\{a, b, c\} \cup \{e, f, g\}$ maps to $\{a, b, c, e, f, g\}$

Note, that any set unioned with the empty set results in the original set:

(35)   For all sets X, $X \cup \emptyset = X$.

Since the empty set has no members, it follows that it has nothing to contribute in the formation of the new set. Often, due to this property, the empty set is called the *identity element* with respect to set union. This behavior of the empty set in union is paralleled by the number 0 in normal addition: 0 is the identity element for addition since for any number n, $n + 0 = n$. What's the identity element for normal multiplication?

4.4.4 Set Subtraction

Set subtraction, or set difference, is another operation on sets. Like set union and intersection, it takes two sets as arguments and yields another set. The operation can be defined as follows:

(36) **Definition of Set Subtraction**: If A and B are sets, then $A - B$ results in the set that contains all and only the elements of A that are not elements of B (i.e., the largest subset of A, call it A', such that $A' \cap B = \emptyset$).

For example,

(37)   a. $\{a, b\} - \{b, c\}$ maps to $\{a\}$

         b. $\{a, b, c, d\} - \{b, c\}$ maps to $\{a, d\}$

         c. $\{a, c, d\} - \{b, c, e\}$ maps to $\{a, d\}$

         d. $\{a, b, c, d\} - \{a, b, c\}$ maps to $\{d\}$

         e. $\{a, b, c\} - \{e, f, g\}$ maps to $\{a, b, c\}$

By definition, it follows that the set subtraction of any set with the empty set ends up being the original set:

(38)   For all sets X, $X - \emptyset = X$.

Recall that part of the definition of set subtraction specifies that $A - B$ maps to the largest subset of A that when intersected with B yields the empty set. Suppose that set B were the empty set. Since every set intersected with the empty set yields the empty set, it follows that "the largest subset of A" would be A itself.

    Unlike set union and intersection, the order in which the sets appear matters for set subtraction. For example, $\{a, b\} - \{b, c\}$ does not map to the same set as $\{b, c\} - \{a, b\}$, even though $\{b, c\} \cap \{a, b\} = \{a, b\} \cap \{b, c\}$ and $\{b, c\} \cup \{a, b\} = \{a, b\} \cup \{b, c\}$.

(39)   a. $\{b, c\} \cap \{a, b\} = \{a, b\} \cap \{b, c\} = \{b\}$

         b. $\{b, c\} \cup \{a, b\} = \{a, b\} \cup \{b, c\} = \{a, b, c\}$

         c. $\{a, b\} - \{b, c\} = \{a\}$

         d. $\{b, c\} - \{a, b\} = \{c\}$

         e. $\{a, b\} - \{b, c\} \neq \{b, c\} - \{a, b\}$

Set union and set intersection are called commutative operators, just like normal addition and multiplication of numbers: $A \cup B = B \cup A$; $A \cap B = B \cap A$; $n + m = m + n$; and $n \times m = m \times n$. However, set subtraction is not commutative, just like subtraction of numbers: in general, $A - B \neq B - A$ and $n - m \neq m - n$.

4.5 Intensional versus Extensional Definitions

Sets can be defined in two ways: *extensionally* and *intensionally*. Extensional definitions characterize a set by listing its members. Thus far, we have only used extensional
definitions. Intensional definitions are a little more interesting. They define a set by
giving a rule or criterion for collecting members. To understand the difference between
the two types of definitions, consider the following sets.

(40)   a. $\{a, b, c\}$

       b. $\{2, 3, 5\}$

Both of the sets in (40) have been defined extensionally by giving a list of members.
However, we could easily define these sets with some instructions about how to collect
these members:

(41)   a.   The set containing the first three letters of the alphabet.

       b.   The set containing the three smallest prime numbers.

These descriptions define the exact same sets as in (40), but they do so by giving a
recipe to make the collection. This can have consequences if circumstances change.
For example, consider the following extensional and intensional definitions.

(42)   a. $\{b, h, s\}$

       b.   The set containing Seymour's favorite letters of the alphabet.

Suppose that in 2010, Seymour's favorite letters were b, h and s. Thus, in 2010, the
two sets described in (42) have the same members, and thus correspond to the same set.
However, in 2013, Seymour changed his mind. He no longer likes h, and his favorite
letters are now b, e, and s. Because Seymour changed his mind, the members of the
two sets are different.

    Defining a set extensionally can be very useful. With an extensional definition, the
membership of the set remains constant even if circumstances and opinions change.
However, sometimes intensional definitions are more appropriate. For example, if
we are more concerned with Seymour's feeling about letters than with the letters b,
e, and s in and of themselves, then the intensional definition is more useful. Under
such condition, our intensional definition remains constant, but the extension of the set
changes according to Seymour's feelings. This property of intensional definitions will
play a role in later chapters, such as Units 45 and 60 when we define what are called
natural classes of speech segments. The same intensional definition can have different

extensions for different I-languages, or even in different situations relevant to a single language.

Mathematicians have a special way of writing intensional definitions. Inside the set brackets, they use a symbol called a variable, followed by a colon, then a list of one or more statements attributing properties to the variable. For example, consider the intensional definitions in (43).

(43)   a. $X = \{x : x$ is one of Seymour's favorite letters$\}$
       b. $Y = \{y : y$ is a natural number and $y \leq 3\}$
       c. $Z = \{z : z$ is an even number and z is a prime number$\}$

The variables in the definitions—x, y, and z—are used the same way as variables in mathematics—they are place holders used to talk about potential set members. The nature of the definitions can be understood in the following way. The bracket symbols $\{\ \}$ indicate that a set is being defined. The first instance of the variable represents the potential members. In theory, one calculates the members of the set by letting the variable temporarily name each possible member of the set and then reading the sentence to the right of the colon with the variable picking out that member. If the sentence is true, then the entity temporarily named by the variable belongs to the set. If the sentence is false, then the thing/person is not a member.

The descriptions in (43) define the sets in (44), assuming that b, e, and s are currently Seymour's favorite letters.

(44)   a. $X = \{b, e, s\}$
       b. $Y = \{1, 2, 3\}$
       c. $Z = \{2\}$

The first set is $\{b, e, s\}$ since it is only when x temporarily names b, e, or s that it is true that "x is one of Seymour's favorite letters." The second set is $\{1, 2, 3\}$ since it is only when y temporarily names 1, 2, or 3 that it is true that "y is a natural number and $y \leq 3$." The third set contains only 2 since it is only when z temporarily names 2 that it is true that "z is an even number and z is a prime number."

Another way to think about the characterization given in an intensional definition of a set is that the members of the set are *all* and *only* the entities that meet the conditions of the definition. So, for example, in (43a), the set defined contains *all* the letters that are one of Seymour's favorites, and *only* such entities are in the set.

If the number of elements in a set is very large, it becomes unwieldy to list all the members and give an extensional characterization of the set. For example, you probably wouldn't want to define extensionally the set of all registered voters in Mexico City.

It is simple to define the set intensionally: $\{x : x$ is a registered voter in Mexico City$\}$. You *might* be able to get a computer printout of all the members of this set and have an extensional definition. However, there are situations when an extensional definition is completely impossible: you can give an *intensional* definition, but not an extensional definition, of a set that has an infinite number of members. Examples of such sets are the set of integers, the set of even positive integers, and the set of sentences generated by your grammar. Note that given any finite list of sentences generated by your grammar, you can always characterize another sentence, not in the original list, by linking the original members by *and*. So, if you start with a set like {*It is raining, I dance well, I like pie*}, you can create another sentence like *It is raining and I like pie and I dance well*, and then you can get *I like pie and it is raining and I like pie and I dance well*, and so on.

This property of human language syntax ensures that the set of sentences generated by a human language is unbounded—there are an infinite number of sentences generated by a human grammar. Therefore, it is necessary to characterize the set of sentences *intensionally*, and that's why we included *intensional* as one aspect of the *I-language* approach we adopt in Unit 2. Your grammar can't consist of an infinitely long list of sentences stored in your finite brain, so the grammar must characterize sentences using rules or patterns or procedures or templates, in other words, it must characterize them *intensionally*.

We have mentioned the fact that sentences have to be paired with an intonation pattern, so the unboundedness of syntax leads us to an unboundedness of phonology as well. Since each sentence is not listed, the intonation of each sentence cannot be listed. Intonation has to be mapped onto sentences by a procedure.

4.6 Functions

You are probably quite familiar with the concept of functions. Functions are defined with respect to a set called the *domain* and a set called the *co-domain*. The domain is the set of input values to the function, and the co-domain is the set of possible output values of the function. The set of values in the co-domain that are actually realized as output values is called the *range*. Functions map every element in their domain to a unique element in their range. An example should clarify how this works.

We can define a function m that maps members of a group of children (the domain) to each child's biological mother (the range). If the set of children is {*Mary, Kanguq, Rolf, Axochitl, Öner, Taha, Giang*} and the set of mothers is {*Ludmilla, Sigwan, Umakashte*} we can define this function by listing each child with his or her mother:

(45) Extensional definition of a function

m :

Mary	$\longrightarrow$	Ludmilla
Kanguq	$\longrightarrow$	Ludmilla
Rolf	$\longrightarrow$	Ludmilla
Axochitl	$\longrightarrow$	Ludmilla
Öner	$\longrightarrow$	Sigwan
Taha	$\longrightarrow$	Sigwan
Giang	$\longrightarrow$	Umakashte

This is an example of an extensional definition of a function, with the obvious parallel to an extensional definition of a set. Notice that each child corresponds to just one mother—that is a crucial property of a function. However, more than one child may correspond to the same mother. This possibility for functions will be important when we introduce NEUTRALIZATION in Part IV.

An intensional definition of the same function would just be this:

(46) $m(x) = x$'s mother

With functions in which the domain and range are small, it is a trivial matter to define a function extensionally. A function with an infinite set as its domain cannot actually be defined extensionally since that would require an infinitely long list of pairs from the domain and range. However, there is a practice of suggesting a function over an infinite domain by showing enough examples to illustrate the pattern of relationship between inputs and outputs, and then using ellipsis dots to suggest that the pattern continues indefinitely:

(47) Pseudo-extensional definition of a function

f :

0	$\longrightarrow$	1
1	$\longrightarrow$	2
2	$\longrightarrow$	3
3	$\longrightarrow$	4
4	$\longrightarrow$	5
$\vdots$		$\vdots$

This notation assumes that the reader can figure out the pattern that would appear in a traditional intensional definition, so it is really a version of an intensional description. Here is a more traditional intensional version of the same function.

(48) **Intensional definition of function in (47)**:

Let f be a function from natural numbers to natural numbers such that for each natural number n, $f(n) = n + 1$.

With the intensional definition, we do not specify a list explicitly containing any individual mappings.

For our purposes, the relevant functions will map members of a set of strings to members of a set of strings. Phonological rules will be analyzed as functions mapping a string to a string. We won't be concerned with functions mapping numbers to numbers. Thus, a more relevant example is the function g with a pseudo-extensional definition in (49) and an intensional definition in (50).

(49) Pseudo-extensional definition of a function mapping strings to strings

$$
\begin{array}{lll}
g : & c & \longrightarrow & d \\
    & d & \longrightarrow & c \\
    & cac & \longrightarrow & dad \\
    & cad & \longrightarrow & dac \\
    & aadcb & \longrightarrow & aacdb \\
    & aetdd & \longrightarrow & aetcc \\
    & cdccdc & \longrightarrow & dcddcd \\
    & abeeeeab & \longrightarrow & abeeeeab \\
    & ekz & \longrightarrow & ekz \\
    & ceababdc & \longrightarrow & deababcd \\
    & \vdots & & \vdots
\end{array}
$$

(50) **Intensional definition of the function in (49)**:

Let g be a function from strings of letters to strings of letters. For each string X, $g(X) = Y$, where Y is the same length as X, and for each segment position in X, if that position is a c, then the corresponding position in Y is a d, and if that position is a d, then the corresponding position in Y is a c.

This function g maps each string of letters (or segment symbols) to a corresponding string by switching each input c to d and each input d to c. Note that no other symbols are affected. It follows therefore that a string that contains neither c's nor d's will be mapped to itself—the function has no effect on some kinds of inputs. When we analyze phonological rules as functions in laters units, this kind of identity mapping will be called *vacuous rule application*.[4]

---

[4]There is a tradition of saying that "The rule does not apply" in such cases. We prefer not to use that

4.7 Set Cardinality

In mathematics, the most interesting results involve sets with infinitely many members, like the set of integers, or the set of prime numbers. In phonology, we will mostly be dealing with sets that have a finite number of members, like the set of segments in a given language, or the set of segments made available by *UG*. For such finite sets, the size of a set is just the number of members that the set has. In set theory discussions, set size is typically referred to as a set's *cardinality*.[5] We can think of cardinality as a function that applies to sets and yields the number of members of that set. This function is defined as follows:

(51) **Definition of Set Cardinality**:

Let $|\ \ |$ be a function that maps finite sets to natural numbers (integers from 0 and up). For every finite set X, $|X| = n$, where n is the exact number of members in X.

For example,

(52) a. $|\{a, b\}| = 2$

b. $|\{b, c, d, e\}| = 4$

c. $|\emptyset| = 0$

d. $|\{\emptyset\}| = 1$

e. $|\{a, \{b, c, d, e\}, f\}| = 3$

f. $|\{a, a, b, c, b\}| = 3$

Since the set-cardinality function involves counting members, it is critical to remember the intricacies of membership. For example, the set being counted in (52e) has only three members (a, f and the set $\{b, c, d, e\}$) even though one of its members, namely $\{b, c, d, e\}$, has four members. When counting cardinality, you only count the members and you ignore the members of members. Also, keep in mind the difference between the empty set and the set that contains the empty set. Although the empty set has no members, as shown in (52c), the set that contains the empty set has one member,

---

expression, since we assume that all strings are in the domain of each rule in a language. A rule, like a mathematical function, may map an input to an identical output.

[5]Here's why things are complicated for non-finite sets: The set of integers and the set of positive odd integers have the same cardinality (by a slightly different definition from what we have given for finite sets); however, the latter set is a subset of the former (as you can confirm, since every member of the latter is a member of the former) and thus is called the smaller of the two sets. For finite sets, a smaller set has to have a lower cardinality.

namely the empty set itself, as shown in (52d). Note also that repetition does not affect the cardinality of a set. For example, the cardinality of $\{a, b, c\}$ is 3, but so is the cardinality of $\{a, a, b, c, b\}$ in (52f). This is because $\{a, b, c\} = \{a, a, b, c, b\}$. The result of the cardinality function is always defined by membership. It is not defined by the number of symbols that occur in between the set brackets.[6] Understanding set cardinality will be critical to our discussion of combinatorics at various points in the book.

4.8   Ordered Sets

As we have mentioned, the order in which elements are listed is irrelevant to the characterization of a set. Two sets are identical if each element in one is in the other, and vice versa. So {a, b, c} and {c, a, b} denote the same set.

Sometimes, however, it is useful to present elements in a particular order. For example, the *ordered set* $\langle a, b \rangle$ contains the elements a and b in that order. That ordered set differs from $\langle b, a \rangle$, in which the element a is in the second position and the element b is in the first position. So, the ordering of ordered sets is important.

Ordered sets with two elements are called *ordered pairs*. The coordinates of points in a Cartesian coordinate system are typically given as ordered sets, typically ordered pairs in an alternative notation like (3,2) when dealing with a two-dimensional system. This refers to a point that is 5 units to the right of the origin and 2 units above the origin. Obviously, this is a different point than (2,3). Because ordering is relevant, repetition in ordered sets is relevant: each '2' in (2,2) means something different. One is an x-value, and the other is a y-value.

So, ordered sets are different from sets in that *uniqueness* of elements does not hold. Thus, from a set $\{a, b\}$ with just two elements, we can construct the following four ordered pairs:

(53)   Ordered pairs from the set $\{a, b\}$

   - $\langle a, b \rangle$
   - $\langle a, a \rangle$
   - $\langle b, a \rangle$
   - $\langle b, b \rangle$

---

[6]Note that the cardinality function must take a set as its argument, and the cardinality of a set is an integer. So, $|\{a, b, c\}|$ is 3, and not $|3|$. The symbol for cardinality is identical to the symbol for absolute value, but we will not be concerned with absolute value in this book.

Of course, the idea of ordered pairs can be generalized to ordered triples like $\langle a, b, a \rangle$, ordered quadruples like $\langle a, b, a, a \rangle$, and so on. An ordered set of length n is called an n-tuple. In Unit 18.1, we will make use of ordered sets to formalize the notion of a string or sequence of segments. We will introduce more set-theoretic concepts as we proceed.

Exercises

Note: A collection of self-grading exercises is available from the MIT Press website.

4.1. Are these the same or different?

     (a) $\{1, 2, 3, 4\}$ and $\{4, 3, 2, 1\}$

     (b) $\{1, 2, 3, 4\}$ and $\{a, b, c, d\}$

     (c) {John Lennon, Paul McCartney, Ringo Starr, George Harrison} and {George Harrison, John Lennon, George Harrison, Paul McCartney, Ringo Starr, George Harrison}

     (d) {Mike's guitar, Hisako's drum} and {Hisako's guitar, Mike's drum}

     (e) $\{a, b, c, d\}$ and $\{b, c, a, a, a, a, a, a, d, a, a, d \}$

     (f) $\langle a, b \rangle$ and $\langle b, a \rangle$

     (g) $\langle a, b \rangle$ and $\langle a, b, b, b \rangle$

     (h) $\langle a, b \rangle$ and $\{b, a\}$

     (i) $\langle a, b \rangle$ and $\langle \{a\}, \{b\} \rangle$

     (j) $\{\langle a, b \rangle, \langle c, d \rangle\}$ and $\{\langle c, d \rangle, \langle a, b \rangle, \langle c, d \rangle\}$

     (k) $\{\langle a, b \rangle, \langle c, d \rangle\}$ and $\langle \{c, d\}, \{a, b\} \rangle$

4.2. Change from an intensional to extensional characterization or vice versa. Say which is which.

     (a) Ex: $\{6, 9, 12, 15\}$ (extensional) $\Rightarrow$ "Whole number multiples of 3 from 6 to 15" OR $\{x \colon x = 3 \times n$, where n is an integer from 2 to 5$\}$ (intensional)

     (b) The set of letters of the English alphabet

     (c) $\{x \colon x = 6\}$

     (d) $\{ \{ 6 \} \}$

4.3. Give examples of the following kinds of sets:

   (a) S_1 with an infinite number of members

   (b) S_2 with a finite number of members, and each member is an individual object

   (c) S_3 with a finite number of members, and each member is a type of object

   (d) S_4 with a finite number of members that are described by a shared property

   (e) S_5 with a finite number of members with no obvious shared property

   (f) S_6 with an infinite number of members with no obvious shared property

4.4. Answer the following questions about the set $S = \{a, b, c, d\}$:

   (a) Is $a \in S$?

   (b) Is $a \subseteq S$?

   (c) Is $\{a, c\} \in S$?

   (d) Is $\{a, c\} \subseteq S$?

   (e) Is $\{a, b\} \subset S$?

   (f) Is $\{a, b, c, d\} \subseteq S$?

   (g) Is $\{a, b, c, d\} \subset S$?

   (h) Is $\emptyset \in S$?

   (i) Is $\emptyset \subseteq S$?

   (j) Is $\emptyset \subset S$?

4.5. Answer the following questions about the set $T = \{a, \{a, b\}, \{a, c\}, d\}$:

   (a) Is $a \in T$?

   (b) Is $b \in T$?

   (c) Is $\{a, c\} \in T$?

   (d) Is $\{a, c\} \subseteq T$?

   (e) Is $\{\{a, c\}\} \subseteq T$?

   (f) Is $\{a, b, c, d\} \subseteq T$?

   (g) Is $\emptyset \in T$?

(h) Is $\emptyset \subseteq T$?

4.6. Let $P = \{w, x, y\}$, $Q = \{v, w, x\}$, $V = \{v, w, x, y, z\}$. Complete the expressions below:

   (a) $P \cap Q =$

   (b) $P \cup Q =$

   (c) $Q \cap P =$

   (d) $Q \cup P =$

   (e) $P - Q =$

   (f) $Q - P =$

   (g) $V - Q =$

   (h) $V - P =$

   (i) $P - V =$

   (j) $\emptyset - P =$

   (k) $\emptyset - Q =$

   (l) $\emptyset - V =$

   (m) $\emptyset \cap Q =$

   (n) $\emptyset \cup Q =$

   (o) $P - \emptyset =$

   (p) $|P| =$

   (q) $|V - Q| =$

4.7. More cardinality:

   (a) $|\{a, b, c, d, a, d\}| =$

   (b) $|\{a, \{a\}, \{\{a\}\}\}| =$

   (c) $|\emptyset| =$

   (d) $|\{\}| =$

   (e) $|\{\emptyset\}| =$

   (f) $|\{\emptyset, a\}| =$

(g) $\left|\{\{\emptyset, a\}\}\right| =$

(h) True or false: $\left|\{1, 2, 3, 4\}\right| = \left|\{a, b, c, d\}\right|$

(i) $\left|\Big\{\{\{\}\}\Big\}\right| =$

(j) $\left|\{\{\}, \{\}\}\right| =$

(k) $\left|\{a, b, c, \{a\}\}\right| =$

Unit 5

Suggested Reading

This book introduces phonology very differently from other texts. The list of books and papers below are sources you can start with to better understand our discussion of linguistics and neuroscience, the concept of I-language, fundamental set theory, and the relationship between phonetics and phonology. Each of these will lead you to many more excellent scholars. We also recommend that you spend a few hours browsing the shelves of the linguistics, cognitive science, and math sections of your university library. We provide titles, dates and authors here; you can find full publication information in the bibliography at the end of the book.

- CONNECTIONS BETWEEN COGNITIVE SCIENCE AND NEUROSCIENCE:

    1. Pylyshyn, Zenon. 1999. What's in your mind?

    2. Poeppel, David. 2012. The maps problem and the mapping problem: Two challenges for a cognitive neuroscience of speech and language.

    3. Gallistel, C. R., and King, Adam Philip. 2009. *Memory and the computational brain: Why cognitive science will transform neuroscience.*

    4. Marr, David. 1982. *Vision: A computational investigation into the human representation and processing of visual information.*

- I-LANGUAGE AND UNIVERSAL GRAMMAR:

    1. Jackendoff, Ray. Jackendoff (1994). *Patterns in the mind: Language and human nature.*

43

2. Pinker, Steven. 1994. *The language instinct.*

3. Isac, Daniela, and Reiss, Charles. 2013. *I-language: An introduction to linguistics as cognitive science.*

4. Chomsky, Noam. 1965. *Aspects of a theory of syntax.*

5. Chomsky, Noam. 1986. *Knowledge of language.*

- SET THEORY:

1. Halmos, Paul. 1960. *Naive set theory.*

- PHONOLOGY AND PHONETICS:

1. Sapir, Edward. 1949. The psychological reality of phonemes.

2. Sapir, Edward. 1925. Sound patterns in language.

3. Hammarberg, Robert. 1976. The metaphysics of coarticulation.

- ONLINE RESOURCES:

1. Some material related to this book is presented on the Rational Phonology YouTube Channel.

2. Self-grading exercises in html format and a format for use in Moodle are available from the MIT Press website. There were developed by our student Dariia Dziuba.

Part II

The Motivation for Phonological Rules

Unit 6

Segmentation: Sound and Meaning

6.1 Do We Need Phonology?

Communication with spoken language involves the production of a variety of sounds which determine the message that is communicated. As shown in (54), the difference between an [s] and an [m] can have consequences for choices you make in life.

(54) a. Your spouse is very sad.

b. Your spouse is very mad.

Do you choose to go home (to provide comfort) or do you stay out for one more drink (letting hot emotions cool down)? This all might depend on an [m] versus an [s].

This example demonstrates the importance of sound in linguistic communication. However, just because sound is important, this does not necessarily mean that it requires an independent module of grammatical *computation*—maybe all the relevant aspects of pronunciation are encoded in the mental lexicon, the list of meanings and associated pronunciations stored in your mind. Under this view, you just memorize the pronunciation of words, and, when you use a word, your brain somehow sends the appropriate commands to the vocal organs for converting that memory into speech. In this unit, we'll first assume that there is *not* a separate component of grammar dedicated to computations involving sound patterns.[1] Rather, we begin by assuming only

---

[1] Other than what we discussed earlier concerning intonation.

47

simple correspondences between sounds (or other types of signs) and meanings. Our goal is to build an empirical foundation that motivates the study of phonology as a module of grammar.

We know that a great deal of memorization is required when learning a language. One of the first things you do in a second language class is memorize a few words, like simple greetings. Part of this memorization involves storing what words mean, but the other part involves remembering how they sound (or in the case of languages like American Sign Language, how they are signed). In the next few sections, we will develop two different methods for analyzing the link between sound and meaning. We will then explore some consequences for the organization of our grammar based on these methods.

6.2   Methods of Segmentation

Suppose you are a teacher and your students have developed a secret language, or rather, an encoding of English. You want to crack the code, but all you have are a few symbol sets with their translations, as shown in (55). (A snitch has provided you with the translations.) Before reading on, stop for a second and take a careful look at the code with the translations. Take out a piece of paper and a pen, and try to figure out some of the words in this secret language.

(55)   Secret Code

	Code	Meaning
a.	$\diamond + \nabla \infty -$	'Teacher is rude'
b.	$\diamond + \nabla \triangle \star$	'Teacher is stupid'
c.	$\square \clubsuit \nabla \triangle \star$	'Earvin is stupid'
d.	$\square \clubsuit \heartsuit \# \diamond +$	'Earvin likes Teacher'

It probably only took you a couple of minutes to figure out that $\diamond +$ means 'Teacher', ∇ means 'is', $\infty -$ means 'rude', $\triangle \star$ means 'stupid', $\square \clubsuit$ means 'Earvin', and $\heartsuit \#$ means 'likes'. But how did you figure it out?

Although not all of us are able to formulate them as explicit instructions, we typically use two methods to solve a problem like this. These methods are also useful for analyzing linguistic data for which we have a translation in a language that we know.

In one method, which we will call the *comparison method*, we compare symbol sequences that share a meaning and then examine which symbols they share. We look for a consistent set of symbols for a given meaning. This method allows us to identify the symbols for 'Teacher', 'Earvin', 'is', and 'stupid'. For example, the only part of the meaning of (55a) that is the same as the meaning of (55d) is 'Teacher'. The only part of the symbol sequence that is the same between the two is ◇ +. Thus it is a reasonable hypothesis that ◇ + means 'Teacher'. Similarly, the only part of the meaning of (55a) that is the same as the meaning of (55c) is the copula 'is'. The only part of the symbol sequence that is the same is ∇. Thus it is a reasonable hypothesis that ∇ means 'is'. Similar comparisons can be made to determine the symbols for 'Earvin' and 'stupid'.

Another method for determining the association between symbols and meaning involves the subtraction of known symbol sequences: we will call this the *subtraction method*. For example, we have already determined that ◇ + means 'Teacher' and that ∇ means 'is' and thus we also know that ◇ + ∇ means 'Teacher is'. We also know that ◇ + ∇ ∞ − means 'Teacher is rude'. If we substract the symbols for 'Teacher is' (◇ + ∇) from the symbols for 'Teacher is rude' (◇ + ∇ ∞ −), we are left with the symbols ∞ −. It is a reasonable hypothesis that these leftovers are the symbols for 'rude'. Similar methods can be used to determine the symbols for 'likes'.

The idea behind each methodology is to establish consistent correspondences between symbols and meaning. In other words, we attempt to individuate the vocabulary items in a secret code by paying attention not only to the symbols that are used, but also to the meaning associated with these symbols.

In linguistics, we use these same methods to analyze natural languages. For example, suppose we were investigating a language that has the following three words, with the meanings given in (56).

(56)   Issanoan[2] data

	Noun Phrase	Meaning
a.	nale	'some hat'
b.	nalo	'the hat'
c.	pike	'some frog'

Even with this small dataset, we will be able to develop some reasonable hypotheses concerning the symbols for what is translated as 'some', 'the', 'hat', and 'frog'.

- By comparing (56a) and (56c), we can conclude that [e] means 'some'.

- By comparing (56a) and (56b), we can conclude that [nal] means 'hat'.

- By subtracting [nal] from [nalo] we can conclude that [o] means 'the'.

- By subtracting [e] from [pike] we can conclude that [pik] means 'frog'.

---

[2]This is our first made-up language name.

Note that unlike secret codes, which tend to model the symbol order of the language they are encoding, in natural language the order of elements can often differ from one language to another. So, just as there are languages where the definite and indefinite article appear as a suffix (as mimicked by Issanoan in 56) there are also languages where the definite and indefinite article appear as a prefix, as in Oreallan in (57):

(57)   Oreallan

	Noun Phrase	Meaning
a.	enal	'some hat'
b.	onal	'the hat'
c.	epik	'some frog'

There are even natural languages that mix prefixes and suffixes, as mimicked by Koriaboan in (58):

(58)   Koriaboan

	Noun Phrase	Meaning
a.	nale	'some hat'
b.	onal	'the hat'
c.	pike	'some frog'

To complicate things even further, it is also possible that some meanings are associated with a form and others are not. This is demonstrated with the language in (59).

(59)   Kangaruman

	Noun Phrase	Meaning
a.	nale	'some hat'
b.	nal	'the hat'
c.	pike	'some frog'
d.	pik	'the frog'

Kurmanji Kurdish, like this toy language Kangaruman, sometimes uses a bare noun for the definite form and a suffixed noun for the indefinite: *mirovek* 'a/some man', *mirov* 'the man'.[3]

---

[3]You might wonder why we don't just provide examples of real languages for each pattern above, and the answer is that there are always complications. For example, Romanian uses a separate word, not a prefix, before a bare noun to express indefinite but a suffix to express definite. A bare noun with no article is usually considered to be indefinite; however, after a preposition, a bare singular noun is interpreted as *definite*, whereas a bare plural noun is (still) interpreted as indefinite. Modifying the nouns with adjectives or relative clauses adds even more complications. Such issues, which crop up in all languages, are irrelevant

In this unit, we will not dwell on the different complexities introduced by this type of cross-linguistic variation. Rather, a more critical point for the present discussion is that order does not matter with respect to our methodologies. Despite the variation in the placement of nouns like *hat* and *frog* with respect to determiners like *some* and *all*, the methods for discovering sound-meaning correspondences remain the same.

- By comparing utterances that share one aspect of meaning, we can isolate the sound associated with that meaning (*comparison method*).

- By subtracting known sound sequences from an utterance (while also subtracting the corresponding meaning), we can isolate the sound associated with the residual meaning (*subtraction method*).

- Order does not matter.

It is important to note that the results of applying this methodology are not final and irrevocable. The method only yields plausible hypotheses that can be revised or rejected as more data is considered—this is just normal scientific practice. For example, suppose we are presented with the Turkish word *eller* which is translated as 'hands'.

(60)   Turkish I

Noun Phrase	Meaning
eller	'hands'

With just this one form, there is no way of knowing if the word consists of various isolable parts or what the parts might be. Is the word an unanalyzable atomic unit, like the English plural *people*, or can it be separated into a noun root plus a plural marker like the English plural *cats*? Is the plural marker a prefix which has the sound *e*? Is the noun *ller*? We cannot tell.

However, if this form is compared to the Turkish word *evler* 'houses', the situation changes.

---

to our main points that suffixes and prefixes occur in various combinations, and that a meaning marked by an affix in one language may have no correlate form in another. There are two possible explanations for why the meaning has no associated form. It could be that there is no element in the language that corresponds exactly to a given meaning in the translation, or it could be that there is such an element, but that element does not contain any phonological segments. Both of these logical possibilities seem to arise in real languages, but this is more a topic for morphologists and semanticists to study, and we will mostly put it aside in this book, after some discussion in Unit 15.

(61)   Turkish II

	Noun Phrase	Meaning
a.	eller	'hands'
b.	evler	'houses'

With this additional information, it becomes reasonable to hypothesize that the (non-contiguous) part *e--ler* means plural and that the *l* vs. *v* corresponds to the difference between 'hand' and 'house'. However, this idea becomes less palatable when we look at the Turkish word *ipler* 'ropes'.

(62)   Turkish III

	Noun Phrase	Meaning
a.	eller	'hands'
b.	evler	'houses'
c.	ipler	'ropes'

It is now more promising to suppose that the meaning 'plural' corresponds to *ler*, and that the meanings 'hand', 'house', and 'rope' correspond to *el*, *ev*, and *ip*, respectively. Looking at more data, we could compare words meaning 'at a house', 'from a house', and 'of a house': *evde*, *evden*, and *evin*, respectively.

(63)   Turkish IV

	Noun Phrase	Meaning
a.	eller	'hands'
b.	evler	'houses'
c.	ipler	'ropes'
d.	evde	'at a house'
e.	evden	'from a house'
f.	evin	'of a house'

This confirms the hypothesis that *ev* means 'house'. The more data we consider, the more refined and solid our hypotheses get. Each time we compare different meanings we are performing a small experiment that allows us to adjust our hypotheses.

The subtraction and comparison methods of analyzing words into component parts is sometimes called *segmentation*. This can be confusing in light of our use of the term *segment* to refer to individual speech sounds or phones, denoted by phonetic symbols like *a, p, ʃ, t*. The kind of segmentation we have demonstrated is segmentation of words into units of meaning traditionally called *morphemes*. Each morpheme consists of a string of segments, in the sense of speech sounds.[4]

---

[4]Phoneticians sometimes use the term *segment* in yet another sense, referring to an even smaller entity,

6.3 The Lexicon

Scientific linguistics studies language as an aspect of the natural world. We believe that our word segmentation method works so well because words really are structures created from simpler parts by our mental grammars. In this section, we discuss more explicitly some properties of our minds that are presupposed by our analytical techniques. In particular, we describe what our minds must be like for our technique of segmentation to yield sensible results.

The main assumption behind our methods is that of *compositionality*. We assume that the sound of the whole (word, phrase, or sentence) is a concatenation of the sounds of the parts, and likewise the meaning of the whole is a combination of the meaning of the parts. Furthermore, we assume a relation between the smallest parts that contribute meaning and those that contribute sound. This relation is one of identity: the smallest contributor of sound is also the smallest contributor of meaning, an entity that has traditionally been called a *morpheme* within the linguistics literature:[5]

(64)   MORPHEME:
       The smallest unit of sound that is associated with a unit of meaning.

By the smallest unit of sound, we do not refer to the individual speech segments that are referred to in a phonetic alphabet, for example. Sometimes a morpheme contains only a single segment, as with the plural morpheme *-s* in English, but more typically we'll see morphemes that contain sequences of segments, as in the root *cat*.

These morphemes, by definition, cannot be broken down into subcomponents of meaning and associated sound, and hence cannot be built or constructed like phrases and sentences. Linguists propose that there is a mental storage system called a *lexicon* that encodes these basic sound-meaning correspondences.

(65)   THE LEXICON: Humans need some kind of memory system to store the information corresponding to the sound-meaning relations uncovered by the comparison and subtraction methods. In other words, they need the capacity to store a set of morphemes. This memory system is called the lexicon.[6]

"defined by relative distinct changes in the speech wave structure" (Fant, 2006, chapter 4).

[5] It should be noted that this assumption is by no means innocent. Many theories propose that the smallest unit for sound contribution is distinct from the smallest unit for meaning. In fact, this one of the basic tenets of Distributed Morphology (see Marantz, 1997; Halle and Marantz, 1993, 1994).

[6] In Distributed Morphology, sometimes the term *Encyclopedia* is used to describe the memory system on the meaning side and the term *Vocabulary* to describe the system on the sound side. In such a system, there is also a third memory system that is used to store syntactic roots.

The lexical items, or morphemes, are traditionally described as a minimal sound-meaning correspondence, an entity containing information relating to sound and information relating to meaning. We call the information relevant to a morpheme's pronunciation its *phonological representation*, and we call the information relevant to its meaning its *semantic representation*.

Besides sound and meaning, there is a third aspect of a morpheme presupposed by our methods of segmentation. Recall that our methods assume that words, phrases, and sentences are composed of parts. This means that speakers must somehow combine morphemes to create larger linguistic units. When the output of such a process is a word, for example, when a root and a suffix are combined, the process is usually called MORPHOLOGY. When the output is a phrase, for example, when an adjective and a noun are combined, the process is usually called SYNTAX. There is much debate about whether there is a difference between morphology and syntax (see Sadock, 1985; Baker, 1985; Anderson, 1992; Marantz, 1997); however, such a debate lies beyond the scope of a phonology textbook. More relevant for the present discussion is that morphemes likely encode some kind of information that informs the syntactic and morphological systems about combinatoric properties (like the fact that the English plural morpheme -*s* only combines with nouns, whereas the past tense morpheme -*ed* only combines with verbs). We will call this type of information the morpheme's *syntactic representation*.

Given our discussion, we can graphically represent a morpheme as a set of linked representations as in (66):

(66)   A morpheme, m_i, as a set of linked representations

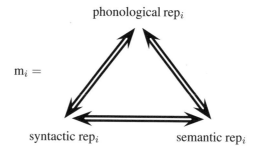

We will refer to this tripartite (three-part) structure of morphemes at various points in the book.

6.4   What's Ahead?

The subtraction and comparison techniques have been around for a long time, although they have not always been seen as providing explicit evidence of our mental capacities. Our discussion of the segmentation techniques in the context of the I-language approach leads to some concrete discoveries concerning the nature of the human mind, including the insight that mental representations like morphemes must contain three independent components. We can see this as a small contribution to the challenge of defining the kinds of data structures that are relevant to human (and non-human) cognition (Gallistel and King, 2009; Poeppel, 2012; Matamoros and Reiss, 2016). However, in the rest of the book, our primary goal will be to demonstrate that our methods of segmentation are actually insufficient to account for a great number of phenomena in the structure of words in human languages. What can we say about this? How can we justify teaching you something that so clearly does not work? Here are a few answers:

Pedagogy: It is, we think, good pedagogic practice to introduce a simple, "clean" model in order to allow students to understand certain key concepts before confronting them with the latest results of linguistic research. Of course, we assume that the basics of the earlier models will be useful in understanding what lies ahead—in the simplest case, the earlier models would be incomplete and we could just add to them to get closer and closer to the current state of knowledge.

Heuristics vs. principles: We overstated somewhat the relationship between our analytic technique and the model we build. Morphological segmentation using the comparison and subtraction methods will turn out to give us good hypotheses about the construction of words, but it will not guarantee the truth—we will need a much richer model to explain even basic patterns.

The incompleteness of scientific knowledge: All scientific knowledge is subject to change and elaboration. There are many things we don't know, and for some of these, we know we don't know, but for others we don't. We could not give you "the truth" at any point, even if we wanted to. We do, however, think we can provide you with a conceptual framework for approaching the truth.

Exercises

These are pure morphology problems. There is no phonology involved. Just segment the words into component morphemes. Answer questions, list the morphemes, and describe the structure of words in the language in terms of prefixes, roots, suffixes, and so on.

6.1. Michoacán Nahuatl (Mexico):

nokali	'my house'	nokalimes	'my houses'
mokali	'your house'	mokalimes	'your houses'
ikali	'his house'	ikalimes	'his houses
nopelo	'my dog'	nopelomes	'my dogs'
mopelo	'your dog'	mopelomes	'your dogs'
ipelo	'his dog'	ipelomes	'his dogs'
nokwahmili	'my cornfield'	nokwahmilimes	'my cornfields'
mokwahmili	'your cornfield'	mokwahmilimes	'your cornfields'
ikwahmili	'his cornfield'	ikwahmilimes	'his cornfields'

- List the three possessive markers. Where do they occur?
- How is the difference between singular and plural marked?

6.2. Isthmus Zapotec (Mexico)

žigi	'chin'	kažigi	'chins'
žigibe	'his chin'	kažigidu	'our chins'
žigiluʔ	'your (sg.) chin'	kažigitu	'your (pl.) chins'

- List the four possessive markers. Where do they occur?
- How is the difference between singular and plural nouns marked?

Unit 7

Rules: Yet Another Module of Grammar

7.1 Two Forms, One Meaning

Unfortunately, our comparison and subtraction methods do not always yield consistent results. They may work perfectly for restricted natural language data, and it is interesting to note that they work perfectly for all formal artificial languages, such as computer and logical languages;[1] when it comes to raw data from real languages, however, we often end up with more than one hypothesis about how certain meanings are associated with sounds. The data in (67) illustrates the kind of complexity that we often come across in analyzing data from natural languages.

---

[1] Presumably, when we create languages consciously, we intentionally make the symbol-meaning correspondences one-to-one, without any variation. This makes sense for the intended purpose of these languages, namely interaction with computers or with other mathematicians. Natural languages do not share this property of "one meaning, one form" with artificial languages, probably because they were not designed to serve any purpose.

(67)   Paramecian: A language with two forms for one meaning

	Noun Phrase	Meaning
a.	ɢoli	'some dog'
b.	ɢola	'the dog'
c.	posi	'some foot'
d.	pota	'the foot'

Let's use our methods from Unit 6.2 to analyze this dataset and see why it is problematic.

Using our comparison method, we come to a variety of reasonable hypotheses. For example ...

- By comparing (67a) and (67b), we can conclude that [ɢol] means 'dog'.

- By comparing (67a) and (67c), we can conclude that [i] means 'some'.

- By comparing (67b) and (67d), we can conclude that [a] means 'the'.

However, once these hypotheses are established, the subtraction method yields somewhat contradictory results.

- By subtracting [i] from [posi] we can conclude that [pos] means 'foot'.

- By subtracting [a] from [pota] we can conclude that [pot] means 'foot'.

The same meaning, 'foot', is associated with two different forms, *pos* and *pot*. A linguist would find this very suspicious. The two forms have the same meaning and share some of the same sounds in the same order. Now, it is not impossible that this is a mere coincidence: there might be two different lexical items that happen to have the same meaning and also happen to be similar in form. A central topic in phonology is to decide when such a coincidence is unlikely, and to provide a principled alternative account.

To give you a sense that (67) is representative of a common linguistic pattern, we discuss two examples below from our own dialects of English in which a single meaning appears to correspond to two different forms. One striking aspect of these examples is that they are quite simple, drawn from accessible data from widespread dialects of English, but you may be completely unaware of them, unless you have learned about them in an introductory linguistics class.

Consider the sentences in (68):

(68)   a. Mark is trying to say what?

          b. What is Mark trying to say?

It is clear that the morphemes *what* at the end of (68a) and the beginning of (68b) are the same word: they have the same basic meaning and great similarity in form. In fact, the sentences themselves are almost the same except for a rearrangement of the word order. The sentences contain the same words and have pretty much the same meaning.

      The obvious identity of the two words spelled *what* is reflected in their identical orthography, the way they are written. Despite this obvious identity, many people (including the present authors) pronounce *what* differently in these two sentences. For example, in many North American dialects of English, the *what* in (68a) is pronounced with a glottal stop at the end. This is the same sound that is in the middle of the expression *uh-oh* for people who speak these dialects, symbolized by ʔ in the International Phonetic Alphabet (IPA). In contrast, the *what* in (68b) is pronounced with a so-called flap or tap at the end. This is the same sound that is in the middle of *madder* and *mutter* for people who speak these dialects, symbolized by ɾ in IPA. Thus, if the writing system reflected pronunciation, the form of *what* would be as in (69). (Recall that w represents the sound at the beginning *wedding* and that ə represents the sound in the middle of *but*.)

(69)   a. Mark is trying to say [wəʔ]?

          b. [wəɾ] is Mark trying to say?

For the speakers of these dialects, the change in the pronunciation of the word is completely unsurprising and does not prevent them from recognizing [wəʔ] and [wəɾ] as *what*. Furthermore the change is conditioned by the surrounding environment. For example, the people who speak these dialects of English cannot pronounce the *what* in (68a) as [wəɾ] nor the one in (68b) as [wəʔ].[2] Note that the asterisk symbol denotes the fact that the sentence is unacceptable for native speakers of these dialects.

(70)   a. *Mark is trying to say [wəɾ]?

          b. *[wəʔ] is Mark trying to say?

The pronunciation of the letter *t* in *what* depends on its phonological context, in particular on the sound at the beginning of the next word, if there is a next word. A full explanation of this inter-word phenomenon is quite complex. For now, we leave it aside in the hope that you see that there *is* definitely something to be explained here.

---

[2] Actually, a glottal stop is possible here if the sentence is uttered with an intonation break after *what*, but for now we are ignoring such complexities.

Words like *what* are not the only type of morpheme that demonstrates a variation in form. Subcomponents of words, like prefixes and suffixes, may also change in pronunciation in different contexts. Consider again the English plural morpheme, which we discussed in Part I.

(71) PLURAL IN ENGLISH

	Form	Gloss
a.	dog	'(one) canine'
b.	dogs	'more than one canine'
c.	lake	'(one) large, enclosed body of water'
d.	lakes	'more than one large, enclosed body of water'

Unlike words such as *what*, the plural marker cannot be moved around by syntactic rules. However, it can be attached to different noun roots. For example, the words *dog* and *lake* are generally used to talk about single individuals.[3] When these words are concatenated with the plural morpheme, they can be used to talk about groups of individuals.

Similar to our examples with *what*, the addition of the plural affix is consistently marked orthographically by the same letter, namely '*s*', which appears at the end of the words. However, as is often the case in English, the orthography is misleading. If you listen carefully to how most English speakers[4] pronounce the plural morpheme in (71b) versus (71d), you will notice that there is a slight difference in the form of the affix—recall our discussion of *pangolins* and *maypops*, and the explanation that the plural in (71b) is pronounced as a [z] sound—the same sound that is at the beginning of the word *zinc*; whereas the plural form in (71d) is pronounced as an [s] sound—the same sound that is at the beginning of the word *sink*.

(72) a. *dogs* [dag**z**] with [z] as in *zinc*

b. *lakes* [lejk**s**] with [s] as in *sink*

Futhermore, the plural affix on *dog* cannot be pronounced as an [s]; nor can the one on *lake* be pronounced as [z]. The asterisks in (73) indicate that the forms are not possible outputs of an English grammar.

---

[3]One of us (Alan) does research on the semantics of number — believe us, we are simplifying greatly in our presentation of what *singular* and *plural* mean.

[4]Remember, we are assuming the I-language perspective, so we are not actually interested in how "most" people pronounce English. There are people we call "English speakers" who do not have the segment [z] at all, and they produce [s] in *dogs*. We are being informal in talking as if there were a thing called English that we can analyze. For the most part, we will try to avoid being too tedious by glossing over this fact unless it is crucial to the point under discussion. If this makes no sense to you, see the references mentioned at the end of Unit 1 on I-language.

(73)   a.   *dogs* *[daɡs]

      b.   *lakes* *[lejkz]

Just like the two pronunciations of *what* in (68), the plural morpheme changes its form in different environments.[5]

This variation in form of the plural marker also cries out for an explanation. Is it plausible that the [s] and [z] versions are unrelated, that they reflect two different morphemes, distinct items in the mental lexicon? We will see later that their distribution is quite systematic, not at all random, and thus subject to some kind of generalization. Like the variation of *what*, we also want to explain why naive speakers[6] tend to be completely oblivious to these facts about their own language.

7.2   In Search of an Explanation

It is natural to ask *why* the patterns and correlations discussed above exist. In what follows, we attempt to justify a certain type of explanation: PHONOLOGICAL RULES. As we will see, linguists' justification for positing phonological rules is often based upon two types of evidence: SYSTEMATICITY and PRODUCTIVITY.

In the beginning of this unit, we used our two methods of segmentation (comparison and subtraction) to analyze the Paramecian dataset in (67), repeated in (74).

(74)   Paramecian (repeated)

	Noun Phrase	Meaning
a.	ɡoli	'some dog'
b.	ɡola	'the dog'
c.	posi	'some foot'
d.	pota	'the foot'

As a result of applying these methods we came to two seemingly contradictory conclusions about the morpheme meaning 'foot': either it has the form [pos] or the form [pot]. We proposed that their similarity in form and meaning suggested that they might not really manifest two different lexical items.

---

[5]To be clear, the placement of *what* depends on the syntax, whereas the pronunciation of the *t* depends on the phonology and the syntactic relations among adjacent elements. In *What can Mark sing?* the pronunciation is [wɔʔ] in the relevant dialects—you only get the form with a flap before an unstressed vowel. This example is useful for pedagogic purposes, but in the remainder of the book we restrict discussion to phonology within words, and ignore effects that occur between words. A fuller treatment of phonological theory will have to deal with such issues of the interaction of phonology and syntax.

[6]This is a technical term meaning 'speakers without linguistics training'.

There are three situations to consider. The first is that we are just wrong, and that our data collection was incomplete. It might turn out that in fact it is possible to say *poti* to mean 'some foot' and it is possible to say *posa* to mean 'the foot'. We would realize, if we collected such data that we were in the same position as someone who had elicited from English speakers the forms *some couch* and *the sofa* and decided that the noun in question changes form depending on whether it is used in the indefinite or definite. That's the wrong conclusion. Or, perhaps our original hypothesis reflected some now-obscure historical relationship, like that between *raise* and *rise*, which synchronically, in a given I-language, are independent forms.

The second possible relationship between *pot* and *pos* is that there *are* two separate forms stored, two separate phonological representations, with some rule of grammar that determines when each form is used—say, *pot* in the definite and *pos* in the indefinite. Such a solution is referred to, confusingly, as either *lexical* or *morphological*. The relationships between *foot* and *feet* or between *go* and *went* in English are examples of this second type of relationship.

A typical property of this kind of relationship is its idiosyncratic nature. Consider the case of *go* and *went*. This is not a general pattern, so we don't find alternations such as *tow* vs. *tent*: *They will tow your car tomorrow* vs. **They tent your car yesterday*. Furthermore, the variation does not generalize to new forms—so if someone coined the verb *to ko*, meaning 'to date someone virtually', people would not reflexively generate *kent* as its past tense.

In a phonology book we are not responsible for explaining how cases like *go*/*went* work. We are only concerned with a third situation, where we do get lots of parallel alternations in the data, and where we are able to predict how speakers generate forms they have never heard. These two properties, systematicity and productivity, may suggest that a *phonological* analysis is warranted to explain the relationship between multiple pronunciations for a single meaning. We now illustrate how to make an argument for a phonological analysis by referring to systematicity and productivity, and then we show how these properties arise from a model with phonological rules that generate the observed patterns.

7.2.1 Systematicity

Let's suppose that we suspect that *pos* and *pot* are two forms of the same morpheme. This means that we are ready to accept a more abstract notion of identity than, say, "pronounced the same". We might want to investigate the language further to see if there are other, parallel variations. Suppose we look at some other nouns in Paramecian and we discover the pattern in (75).

(75)   Some more Paramecian noun forms

	Noun	Meaning		Noun	Meaning
a.	nesi	'some fish'	g.	mogi	'some duck'
b.	neta	'the fish'	h.	moga	'the duck'
c.	bodi	'some bowl'	i.	zasi	'some horse'
d.	boda	'the bowl'	j.	zata	'the horse'
e.	fusi	'some plate'	k.	gisi	'some frog'
f.	futa	'the plate'	l.	gita	'the frog'

As demonstrated in (75), the alternation between [t] and [s] is not unique to the morpheme meaning 'foot'. Using our methods for segmentation (in particular, the substraction of *-i* and *-a*), we discover the same pattern for the morphemes meaning 'fish' (*nes* vs. *net*), 'plate' (*fus* vs. *fut*), 'horse' (*zas* vs. *zat*) and 'frog' (*gis* vs. *git*). Furthermore, the alternation occurs in the exact same environment (before *-i* as opposed to before *-a*).

We could even deepen our investigation by looking at verbs instead of nouns. Consider the words in (76).

(76)   Verb forms from Paramecian

	Verbs	Meaning
a.	pokin	'we work'
b.	pokap	'you work'
c.	budin	'we love'
d.	budap	'you love'

Using our segmentation methods, we can compare (76a) to (76c) and come to the reasonable conclusion that *-in* is a suffix signaling that the subject of the verb is *we* (first person plural). Similarly, we can compare (76b) to (76d), reaching the reasonable conclusion that *-ap* is a suffix signalling that the subject of the verb is *you* (second person). With this analysis in mind, suppose that we discover the following data:

(77)   Some more Paramecian verb forms

	Verbs	Meaning
a.	kisin	'we kick'
b.	kitap	'you kick'
c.	dusin	'we hate'
d.	dutap	'you hate'

Using the subtraction methodology (subtracting *-in* and *-ap* from the verbs), we discover that there are two forms for 'kick' (*kis* vs. *kit*) and 'hate' (*dus* vs. *dut*). This is the same pattern exhibited in the nouns—sometimes we get [t] and sometimes we get [s]. The environments where the variants appear is also the same as what we saw in the nouns: the version of the morpheme with [s] always appears when there is an affix starting with [i] and the version of the morpheme with [t] always appears when there is an affix starting with [a].

This is an example of systematicity. The pattern is general. It occurs with a variety of different morphemes in a variety of different grammatical contexts, for example, both in nouns and verbs. In fact, the pattern would be completely systematic if no exceptions could be found, if we could never find [t] to the left of [i] in any word in the language.[7] This kind of systematicity should pique your curiosity: *Why does this pattern show up again and again in the language?*

7.2.2 Productivity

We can perform an experiment to try and answer this question. Suppose we have a native speaker of Paramecian; call him Xerxes. What happens if we introduce novel words or morphemes to Xerxes? These would be words that Xerxes does not have stored in his mental lexicon. For example, suppose that we show Xerxes a new kind of object with a funny shape and tell him that we call it a *widget* in English, and that 'the widget' is *gata* in Paramecian. We might then ask Xerxes, or indirectly prompt him, to produce the form for 'some widget'.

What would Xerxes say? Well, it all depends on whether the new form would be consistent with the pattern established by our observation of other nouns (and the verb forms as well). If he produces an inconsistent form such as *gati* then we might conclude that the *t/s* alternation we had observed is a non-productive pattern. However, if Xerxes produces the form *gasi*, which is consistent with what we have seen, this suggests that the pattern is productive.

The purpose of this type of experiment is to find out how a speaker would produce a complex expression (say, a noun root plus a suffix) using a piece (the new noun meaning 'widget') that he or she has never heard in that combination. In our example, we have just given Xerxes *gata*. He has never heard the indefinite form of the new noun (whether it be *gati* or *gasi*). Whatever answer Xerxes gives about how to say 'some widget', it cannot be based on memorization of the form. In the fields of psychology and linguistics, this is often called a *wug test*, based on a famous experiment by Jean

---

[7]Speech sounds are, of course, ordered in time, not from left to right; so strictly speaking, we should say that that we never find [t] *before* [i]. However, we often talk about sequences of speech sounds by referring to the strings of symbols that they correspond to in our left-to-right writing system.

Berko Gleason described in Berko (1958) in which she tested how English-speaking children would pluralize a made-up noun like *wug*.

7.3 Phonological Rules and Morphemes

Rules generally produce systematic and productive patterns.[8] For example, it is a rule in the game of chess that bishops can move only diagonally. Thus, it is unsurprising that in each game of chess bishops move diagonally, nor is it surprising when a new bishop enters the game (through pawn promotion) that it also moves diagonally.

Linguists hypothesize the existence of phonological rules that are part of a speaker's I-language, a speaker's mental grammar. Speakers typically are not conscious of the existence or nature of these rules, yet the rules account for the kind of systematic and productive patterns observable in their behavior. Such a hypothesis requires a greater degree of abstraction than we have discussed so far. Let's consider a (simplified) potential phonological rule to see why. Given the [t] vs. [s] alternation in Paramecian, many linguists would hypothesize a rule similar to the one in (78).[9]

(78) Rule P:
      The sound *t* becomes *s* when appearing immediately to the left of the sound *i*.

We think of rules such as (78) as applying to the sounds inside of words and phrases. However, there is a slight nuance in that it applies to a *mental representation* of words *prior* to production (or comprehension) of a sentence. It is best to illustrate this idea with a concrete example. Suppose that the morpheme meaning 'foot' in Paramecian was memorized with the form *pot*. In forming a noun phrase meaning 'the foot', Xerxes's morphology combines the morpheme for 'the' with the one for 'foot', creating the form *pota*. So far, this is just *morphology*.

Next, the *phonological* rule in (78) applies—"turn any *t* appearing to the left of an *i* into *s*." The application of the rule is VACUOUS; it does nothing since there are no *t*'s appearing to the left of an *i* in *pota*.

---

[8]You might wonder why we don't say that rules *always* have this effect—it almost seems like it follows from the meaning of *rule* in a formal system. We will see later that the regular effects of rules can be obscured by other factors. The rule can be regular, but the resulting pattern may not appear regular. Finding the more abstract regularities in a rule system constitutes the challenging fun of linguistics. We are heading in that direction.

[9]Another possible rule would be one that converts *s* to *t* when appearing immediately to the left of *a*. We will discuss later the various considerations used in selecting among alternative rules.

Now contrast the formation of 'the foot' with 'some foot'. In forming this word, Xerxes's morphology combines the morpheme for 'some' with the one for 'foot' creating the form *poti*. Next, the rule in (78) applies. This time, the application of the rule changes the *t* to an *s*. Thus the output of the rule is *posi*.

In positing this type of rule, we also hypothesize a more abstract notion of words with different levels of representation. For instance, notice that the rule has an input (the mental object it applies to) and an output (the mental object it yields). As a result, words like the one meaning 'some foot' in Paramecian have two different levels of representation. They have an input representation /poti/ and an output representation [posi]. The input representation is typically called the *underlying representation* (UR), and the output representation is called the *surface representation* (SR). The difference between 'the foot' and 'some foot' is that the word meaning 'the foot' has a UR that is the same as its SR (*pota* at both levels). It is important to emphasize that *pota* is not missing a level of representation: it still has two (the input and the output) even though the two are identical.[10] The model we have just sketched is called a *derivational* model. In a first step, URs are derived from morphemes by morphological rules. In the next step, SRs are derived from URs by phonological rules. To reiterate, words are not stored in lists or look-up tables; they are derived by morphological and phonological rules. In this book, we will assume that the morphological rules precede all the phonological rules.

Before proceeding, we need to clarify some terminological issues. First, we will use the terms MORPHEME, LEXICAL ENTRY, and LEXICAL ITEM interchangeably. Morphemes are the items in the lexicon. Since we are doing phonology, we will be concerned only with the phonological part of these items. Second, the variant forms in which a morpheme shows up in surface representations are called the morpheme's AL-TERNANTS. We can say that the various alternants *alternate* with each other depending on phonological context, by virtue of the effects of rules. Third, we will use the terms *underlying form*, *underlying representation*, and *UR* in two ways. Sometimes these are synonymous with '(the phonological part of a) morpheme/lexical item'. However, sometimes *underlying form*, *underlying representation*, and *UR* refer specifically to a combination of morphemes that is fed to the phonology. So, we'll sometimes talk

---

[10]It is traditional to differentiate levels of representation by enclosing transcription in different brackets. Forward slashes (/) are used to denote either the phonological part of a morpheme, like /pot-/ or a combination of morphemes into a form that will come out as a word, like /pot-i/ and /pot-a/. The corresponding surface representations of these words are denoted in square brackets as [posi] and [pota]. In this book, we will not take the brackets too seriously, because we find that doing so obscures our discussion. We sometimes denote segments in square brackets, sometimes in forward slashes, and sometimes just in italics. Within datasets and diagrams, segments may appear without any special indication of level of representation.

about the UR of a word and sometimes the UR of a morpheme. This should not lead to any problems, since in both cases, the idea is just to refer to phonological material that is unchanged, by the effect of rules, from what is in the lexicon.

7.4   Derivation Tables

Phonologists who work with derivations typically present them in a table that makes it possible to trace the effects of rules on words as they pass from URs to SRs. For now our tables will be simple, because we have discussed only the possibility of languages with a single rule. Here is a derivation table for some of the Paramecian forms that we have been discussing.

(79)   Paramecian derivation table (first draft)

UR	/goli/	/gola/	/poti/	/pota/
Rule P	goli	gola	posi	pota
SR	[goli]	[gola]	[posi]	[posa]
Gloss	'some dog'	'the dog'	'some foot'	'the foot'

We will revise this table in four ways.

First, note that the first line of the derivation table contains the URs, which are the phonological strings that arise from the combination of morphemes by the morphology. Since we are assuming that phonology has no access to morphological structure, the URs do not contain any information about that structure. However, as a matter of convenience, it is standard to show the morphological structure in derivation tables, to show what the pieces are in each word. We will adopt this convention and thus replace the forms in the first line of the table with forms using hyphens to show morpheme boundaries. For example, we will replace goli with gol-i, and so on.

Second, we won't use brackets in tables to distinguish, say, underlying /goli/ from surface [goli], since the position in the table is sufficient to convey the relevant information.

Third, note that the effect of a rule is either to change the UR or not. We have shown this by writing the current form, the form at each stage in the derivation, into each box. As derivations become more complex, the tables become harder to read, so when a cell in a derivation table is the same as the one above it (because the current rule has had no effect on an input form), we will follow tradition and just write '—'. The exception to this convention is when we get to the bottom of the table. The SR will always be written. It will always be the same in value as the cell above it, which will represent the effect of the last rule in the grammar; later our rules will be ordered. The cell above the SR contain a string or a dash, '—', depending on whether or not the last rule had an effect on the input to that cell.

Fourth, we have called this rule of Paramecian 'Rule P', but if there is space in the table, it is preferable to write out the rule. This becomes important as our derivations increase in complexity. Since our rule is formulated in words, it takes up a lot of space, so here we use an abbreviation.

Given these four revisions, our model derivation table now looks like this:

(80)   Paramecian derivation table (revised)

UR	gol-i	gol-a	pot-i	pot-a
P: t → s before i	—	—	posi	—
SR	goli	gola	posi	pota
Gloss	'some dog'	'the dog'	'some foot'	'the foot'

It is important to highlight a few other properties of these tables. First, it is crucial to include the line for glosses/translations. This allows us to confirm that we have included the correct morphemes in the UR, and also to differentiate derived forms that may end up with the same SR, a phenomenon we will see in Part IV. Next, note that in the URs, each meaning always has the same form. So, 'foot' is always going to show up in Paramecian URs as *pot-*. If we were to put *pos-* into the URs where that form surfaced, there would be no point in having Rule P. Finally, note that the table encodes part of the Paramecian grammar, since every word of Paramecian is derived in the same way, by the application to particular URs of the same Paramecian rules.

This derivation table reflects the fundamental idea that a morpheme that has various forms on the surface (such as the morpheme for 'foot') has only one form as the phonological part of its lexical entry (say, the form for 'foot' is stored as /pot/, and variation arises due to the phonological rule).

(81)   The morpheme (lexical item) meaning 'foot' in Paramecian:

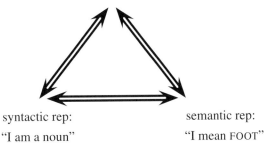

phonological rep:
"My phonological content is /pot/"

syntactic rep: semantic rep:
"I am a noun"   "I mean FOOT"

In other words, our model preserves the intuition that every meaning is (underlyingly) associated with one form.[11]

Another result is that we can now account for systematic patterns in a given language. For example, the rule in (78) can explain why nouns other than *pot* would exhibit the *t/s* alternation, and why verbs would as well. The rule, as it is written, is not specific to the noun morpheme *pot* nor to the class of nouns in general. It applies whenever a *t* appears before an *i* no matter what the grammatical status of the word is. Furthermore, these types of rules can explain why an alternation would appear for a novel word. We account for both systematicity and productivity. The rule does not check to see if its input has been stored in the lexicon for a long time or was just learned a moment before—it cares only about whether the UR contains a certain sequence of segments. For example, if Xerxes the Paramecian learns the noun root *gat* and combines it for the first time with the morpheme *-i*, creating the UR *gati*, the grammar would automatically apply the rule in (78), yielding the SR *gasi*.

In addition to accounting for the alternations in the pronunciation of morphemes, our posited rule also gives us insight into the distribution of segment sequences in the language. The rule provides insight into why we never find the sequence *ti* in the language. Once again, we must warn you that phonological life will become more complicated, but this is a good start.

---

[11]We know that this intuition ultimately can't be maintained, but one view of phonology is that it defines the cases where the intuition *can* be maintained.

Exercises

Using the template in (80), fill in the cells of the following derivation tables with forms
and dashes as appropriate. A rule and some URs are provided. In the first two tables the
SRs are provided. In the rest, you need to fill them in. Notice that the same principles
work whether there are prefixes or suffixes, and whether alternations arise on affixes or
roots.

7.1. Clostridian

UR	ʃkrer-qali	ʃkrer-nu	bat-qali	bat-nu
ɾ → w before q				
SR	ʃkrewqali	ʃkrernu	batqali	batnu
Gloss	'with a snake'	'over a snake'	'with a cake'	'over a cake'

7.2. Prevotellan

UR	zon-lopi	zon-fnak	bik-lopi	bik-fnak
f → x between two n's				
SR	zonlopi	zonxnak	biklopi	bikfnak
Gloss	'she chants'	'we chant'	'she codes'	'we code'

7.3. Kocurian

UR	wak-til	nom-til	wak-moɣ	nom-moɣ
m → b after k				
SR				
Gloss	'this taco'	'that taco'	'this wonton'	'that wonton'

7.4. Zymomonasian

UR	p-talupa	n-talupa	p-sowila	n-sowila
p → v before s				
SR				
Gloss	'will dance'	'has danced'	'will sneeze'	'has sneezed'

7.5. Neisserian: Given the list of morphemes and the rule, construct URs and provide derivations for the SRs corresponding to the glosses given in the table.

- Lexicon
  - vihil   'walk'
  - snuglap   'truck'
  - -ubika   CONTINUATIVE suffix, 'keep on doing something'
  - -walog   INCHOATIVE suffix, 'start doing something'
- Rule: *p* becomes *w* before *w*

UR				
Rule				
SR				
Gloss	'keep on walking'	'start walking'	'keep on trucking'	'start trucking'

7.6. Tularemian: Given the list of morphemes and the rule, construct URs and provide derivations for the SRs corresponding to the glosses given in the table. This one is tricky.

- Lexicon
  - kioako   'cactus'
  - oram   'camel'
  - zum-   DIMINUTIVE **prefix**, 'little'
  - -kit   AUGMENTATIVE **suffix**, 'big'
- Rule: *m* becomes *g* before *k*

UR				
Rule				
SR				
Gloss	'little cactus'	'big cactus'	'little camel'	'big camel'

7.7. Suppose that Xerxes the Paramecian speaker in section 7.2.2 produces *gasi* for the meaning 'some widget'. Discuss this example by relating these concepts: the *intensional* property of the I-language approach and *productivity*. You might want to mention notions like a *list* or the related computer science notion of *look-up table* in your answer. A look-up table is exactly what is sounds like—a table of information where you can look up answers to questions, instead of calculating them. Gallistel and King (2009) have a nice discussion of the problem of using look-up tables to model cognition generally.

Unit 8

Review

At this point, you should be asking yourself the following questions about our discussion of Paramecian in Unit 7:

- Why did we choose to put /pot-/ in the lexicon and not /pos-/?

- Why did we choose a rule that turns /t/ to [s] and not /s/ to [t]?

- Are these questions related?

- What is a possible rule?

- What does it mean for a rule to apply?

Answers to all these questions will be developed in the following pages. It is also worthwhile reviewing the components and concepts specific to the model we have presented thus far:

- MORPHEME: The smallest unit of sound that is associated with a unit of meaning; also called a LEXICAL ENTRY or a LEXICAL ITEM.

- THE LEXICON: The list of stored morphemes.

- COMPOSITIONALITY: There is a system that selects morphemes from the lexicon and *concatenates* them into *strings*.

- PHONOLOGICAL RULES: Some of the strings of segments that are the output of morphological composition are subject to changes.

These components relate as follows:

(82)   The derivational model: morphology precedes phonology

> - Compose *morphemes* from *lexicon*.
>   This is MORPHOLOGY!
>
> - Result is called an *underlying form* or *underlying repre-sentation* (UR).
>
> - Apply *phonological rules* to URs to derive
>   *surface forms* or *surface representations* (SRs).
>   This is PHONOLOGY!

We have presented the basics of a model of phonological computation. We will see, as we proceed, that even this simple model is capable of generating a rich variety of linguistic phenomena. In fact, one of our recurring themes will be the mismatch between the simplicity of the model and the "welter of descriptive complexity" (Chomsky, 2000, p. 122) that it can account for. This perspective is consistent with what Chomsky (2007, p. 4) calls a bottom-up approach to studying universal grammar that characterizes recent work in the Minimalist Program for syntax:.

> Throughout the modern history of generative grammar, the problem of determining the character of [the language faculty] has been approached "from top down": How much must be attributed to UG to account for language acquisition? The M[inimalist] P[rogram] seeks to approach the problem "from bottom up": How little can be attributed to UG while still accounting for the variety of I-languages attained...? The two approaches should, of course, converge, and should interact in the course of pursuing a common goal.

These issues will come up repeatedly as we proceed, developing ideas in work like Samuels (2011), Reiss (2012), and Matamoros and Reiss (2016).

Part III

A Formal Model for Phonological Rules

Unit 9

Formalization

By pushing a precise but inadequate formulation to an unacceptable conclusion, we can often expose the exact source of this inadequacy and, consequently, gain a deeper understanding of the linguistic data. More positively, a formalized theory may automatically provide solutions for many problems other than those for which it was explicitly designed. Obscure and intuition-bound notions can neither lead to absurd conclusions nor provide new and correct ones, and hence they fail to be useful in two important respects.

Noam Chomsky, Preface to *Syntactic Structures*

9.1   Smurfs and Science

The Belgian comic artist, Peyo, created a group of small blue imps called Smurfs. The Smurfs have their own language in which they often substitute the word *smurf* for random nouns, verbs, and adjectives. For example, as an insult a Smurf might say "Go smurf an egg," or in an attempt to regain order he might say "Now, now, we all need to smurf down." The word *smurf* ends up being a very useful and versatile term. However, there are drawbacks to this flexibility. For example, in the movie *The Smurfs and the Magic Flute* one character, Peewit, asks, "Can I have a smurf?" Each Smurf who hears him interprets his question differently. Peewit ends up with a variety of objects, none of which satisfy him. (What he actually wanted was a glass of water.) Sometimes smurfing inhibits communication. You may be surprised to learn that so-called "normal" languages, like English, are not that different from the Smurf variety. Both allow creative and versatile expressions, but sometimes they are suboptimal for communication.

The late philosopher, Julius Moravcsik, in his book *Meaning, Creativity, and the Partial Inscrutability of the Human Mind*, suggests that the vagueness, flexibility, and context sensitivity of natural languages can actually be an asset in the early stages of a science. This "smurfiness" can serve as a tool to explore and discuss inchoate, vague ideas and allow a new science to develop. Of course, as a field does progress, it becomes necessary to formulate hypotheses and claims more precisely and eradicate smurfiness by using a specialized formal language.

Before we develop such a formal language to model phonology, let's make more explicit some of the problems with natural language that can trick us into thinking that an idea is rigorously stated when in fact it is not. Consider the sentence in (83).

(83)   Tall men prefer black bats.

There are at least two types of "imperfections" in this statement: one involving the term *tall*, the other the term *bat*. Let's discuss *tall* first. Suppose we do a study and find that all men above 5′11″ do indeed prefer black bats. However, we find one man who is exactly 5′11″ and does not have such a preference. Is the statement in (83) false? Well, it could be, depending on how one thinks of the height 5′11″. Is it *tall*? Some people might think it is. Others might not. Still others might not even have an opinion. Unfortunately, there is no fact of the matter. There are certain heights, such as 5′11″, where we are not sure if the word *tall* applies or not. Even worse, a given person's use of the word might depend on whether the context of discourse is limited to Montenegrins or Pygmies, or on what historical period is under discussion.

Even if we correct this problem, another exists. What is meant by the term *bats*? Does the statement claim that tall men prefer black baseball bats? Or are we talking about flying mammals? Or perhaps both? The difficulty in interpreting the statement stems from the fact that *bat* has more than one meaning and it isn't clear which is the intended meaning in this sentence. These problems with natural languages must be avoided if we want to formulate statements with scientific rigor.

By developing an artificial language, we can rid ourselves of these kinds of "imperfections." For example, we can create a new word *shtall* and arbitrarily define it as the property of being exactly 5′11″ or taller. Furthermore we can define two other new words, *bat-one* and *bat-two*, reserving the first for application to baseball bats and the second for application to flying mammals. Hence, the statement in (84) is much clearer than the one in (83).

(84)   Shtall men prefer black bat-ones.

We have solved the problems of vagueness (with respect to *tall*) and ambiguity (with respect to *bat*) by creating new terms with precise, unambiguous meanings. Although this might not be the only solution (we could add additional natural language clauses to try and make the statement more precise), it is a relatively simple one.

Adding such precision to theoretical statements aids in the objective identification of predictions. Vague, ambiguous, and imprecise theories yield vague, ambiguous, and imprecise predictions, which is not acceptable for doing science.

9.2   Expressibility

Our goal in this book is not just to describe the phonology of particular languages, but to develop a model of the phonological component of the human language faculty. We end up using the term *language* in at least three distinct senses:

- Language$_1$: A particular I-language. We typically generalize when we talk about such things and refer to entities such as "English" or "Cree," even though we know that each I-language is slightly different. Since this is a phonology book, we are mostly interested in the phonological components of such I-languages. So for our purposes, a language$_1$ is a particular phonological system of a given I-language.

- Language$_2$: The human language faculty. Again, we are focused on phonology, so this basically means *phonological UG* for us.

- Language$_3$: The formal language we are developing to analyze language$_2$ as well as individual tokens of language$_1$. Here's the idea: language$_3$ is a scientific model of language$_2$, in a sense discussed below. Our goal is that everything in language$_2$ can be described in language$_3$, and nothing else can be described by language$_3$.

Each individual token language$_1$ manifests some of the possibilities provided by UG, language$_2$. For example, UG is the property of humans that determines what phonological rules humans *can* have, and a particular I-language has some subset of those rules, say the ones we call "the phonological rules of Réjean's French-like I-language," or informally, "the phonological rules of French." Phonological UG also determines a set of possible speech segments, and an individual phonology has some subset of those segments.

Since our model (language$_3$) should be able to express all and only the rules and symbols allowed by language$_2$ (UG), it can also be used to describe each particular language$_1$, each particular I-language. In fact, we *should* use our universal model to describe each particular phonology if we take seriously the idea that each particular phonology contains just some of what UG makes possible. It would be nonsensical to describe the segments of a particular language as segments that are *not* provided by UG and thus not accounted for in our model.

Since we are doing linguistics as natural science, we consider UG (language$_2$) and each I-language (each token of language$_1$) to be things in the world, instantiated in human brains. These are the *objects* of study for phonologists, just as planets, stars, and forces of nature are objects of study for astronomers. Language$_3$, our formal model, exists as a *result* of the theorizing of linguists like you and us. We are trying to make language$_3$ be a perfect match for, a perfect model of, isomorphic (having parallel structure) to language$_2$.[1]

Part of what make this so confusing is that we are using one particular language$_1$— call it "English"—to *discuss* all three kinds of "language." This is just an accident— the book could have been written in Berber or Ainu and made all the same theoretical claims. In general the most difficulty in discussion arises from the relationship between language$_2$ and language$_3$. But why not avoid all this trouble and just use a natural language like English as our language$_3$ instead of inventing a formal language?

The answer relates to the concept of *expressibility*, a notion common in discussions comparing various logical systems. The problem is that English has *too much* expressibility. This may seem like a strange problem—isn't the capacity to express a lot a good property for a language to have?

Let's first illustrate what we mean for a proposed model, a language$_3$, to have too little expressibility. Then we'll illustrate the excessive capacity of English, and see why it is a problem. Finally, we'll offer a solution for avoiding this problem as we construct a custom-made language$_3$ for phonological theory.

If our formal language has too *little* expressibility, it will not be able to describe the patterns that are observed in phonological systems. For example, suppose our formal language$_3$ could express the idea that *t* and *i* occur 'next to each other', but

---

[1]We feel obligated to point out that we have inherited the terminological mess apparent in these discussions. Chomsky (1965, p. 25) acknowledges a tradition of using both *grammar* and *theory* with "systematic ambiguity," overlapping with the uses of *language* used here. Such ambiguities arise in all fields—*history* is an academic discipline, but it is also what actually happened in the past, etc.

could not express the idea that *t* occurs before *i*. In such a case, we would not be able to differentiate rules like '*t* becomes *s* before *i*' from rules like '*t* becomes *s* after *i*'. Observation tells us that phonological systems do in fact distinguish the order of adjacent segments, because they differentiate such rules. So, we need to develop a formal model that has *enough* expressibility to describe precedence, what comes before what.

Since we don't know in advance the components and structures of the phonological faculty (language$_2$) that we are trying to match, we need a principled way to develop our model, the formal language$_3$ we are building.

That's all pretty obvious. But why would it ever be desirable to *limit* expressibility? Imagine adopting a bowdlerized version of a common expression as our language$_3$: *Stuff happens.* Yes, that is true, but it is too general to provide any insight for differentiating between what actually does or might happen as opposed to what can *never* happen. The expression has *too much* expressibility to be useful.

This is basically the situation we are in if we adopt English as our language$_3$. English can express phonological segment patterns that seem well beyond the types of things we see manifested in natural language. To give two ridiculous examples, consider statements such as "Change every third *t* to an *n*" or "Change every *t* to an *n* on every third Tuesday of the month." These statements are expressible in English but you know that they are not plausible candidates for phonological rules.

When Goldilocks was looking for the "just right" porridge to eat, she was able to test out each of the three available choices (Papa Bear's bowl, Mama Bear's bowl, and Baby Bear's bowl). Phonologists do not have the luxury of such a straightforward method of finding the logical language with exactly the right amount of expressibility. If we start out with too much expressibility, we can describe everything that is phonologically possible. We are never forced to change our model, but we also end up with a *stuff happens* kind of non-insight into what phonology is. The way we (and all scientists, basically) deal with this problem is to initially "lowball" the world. We offer an unrealistically conservative estimate of what will be needed. As we observe more phenomena that our formal model cannot describe, we enhance the language incrementally. In principle, this is the approach we will take in this book. We start with a formal language that is very restricted in both its vocabulary (it has segments like *p* and *u*, but not "Tuesday" or "red" or the concept *prime number*), and in its syntax, the way symbols can combine in statements. As we proceed, we will develop a model with greater and greater expressibility, ideally without ever overshooting. Things are never so simple, of course, so there will be a lot of back-and-forth to figure out which model is "just right."

Unit 10

Formalizing Phonological Rules

10.1 Functions on Strings

Recall from Unit 4.6 that functions map members of a set of inputs (the domain) to members of a set of outputs, (the co-domain). Each member of the domain maps to a single member of the co-domain. For some functions, like the successor function $f(x) = x + 1$, each member of the domain (let's say, the set of integers) maps to a unique member of the co-domain (also the set of integers). But this is not necessarily the case. For some functions, several, many, or even infinitely many members of the domain may map to the same member of the co-domain. For example, if we evaluate the squaring function $f(x) = x^2$, we get the same output value if $x = 5$ or $x = -5$. For the function that maps an integer to the remainder when the integer is divided by 17, there are an infinite number of integers that map to 3, such as 20, 37, 54, and so on. Finally, note that some functions map some, but not all, members of the domain to an output that is the same as the input. A mathematical example would be a function that rounds an integer to the nearest multiple of 10. Numbers like 7, 8, 9, 11, 12 all map to 10, but 10 also maps to 10.

This last possibility is particularly relevant when we think of the phonological rules that capture the segment alternations we discussed in Unit 7 as functions. There are inputs, the underlying forms (URs), and outputs, the surface form (SRs). The underlying form is a string of phonological segments from the morphemes that compose a word, potentially a complex word with several roots and affixes. For example, for the word meaning 'some foot' in Paramecian, shown again in (85), we hypothesized an underlying form /pot-i/ which consisted of the root *pot* and the suffix -*i*. We suggested that a phonological rule applies that changes the underlying /t/ to [s].

(85)   Basic Paramecian (once again)

	Noun Phrase	Meaning
a.	goli	'some dog'
b.	gola	'the dog'
c.	posi	'some foot'
d.	pota	'the foot'

In other words, the phonological rule mapped the input *poti* to the output *posi*. The underlying /t/ was changed to [s] because it appeared before the segment *i*.

It is important to emphasize two aspects of this rule. First, it applies to entire words and not single segments. Sometimes this can be confusing since potentially only a single segment changes in the string. This effect will be built into the rule formalism we develop below.

Second, if we define the domain of rules to be the set of all possible segment strings, then in the technical sense of function application used in math and logic, a phonological rule doesn't apply only to forms where a change occurs. It applies to every underlying form to produce a surface form. It just so happens that most surface forms in Paramecian look just like their underlying forms because there are no *t*'s occurring before *i* in most forms. In other words, some inputs map to a non-identical output, but some inputs map to an output identical to the input, just like the function that rounds to the nearest multiple of 10.

Unfortunately, there is a mismatch between the mathematical notion of applying functions and how phonologists typically talk about rules. Phonologists sometimes say that a rule "does not apply" to a given input when it applies in such a way that the input is identical to the output. We'll just have to live with this ambiguity and try to remember that "does not apply" really means "applies in such a way that there is no effect on the input."[1]

---

[1]The problem is not that phonologists are being sloppy; it's that they are using a conception of a rule in which the grammar first checks whether certain conditions are met, and then only effects the relevant change if they are met. In other words, one could think of the first step in using a rule being to restrict the domain of strings under consideration to those that contain the target in the right environment. We are giving priority to the mathematical and logical ways of talking about rule application, because one of our goals is to import insight from mathematics and logic into phonology, and because of the longer and richer formal traditions in these fields. This decision allows us to treat all rules as having the same domain, the set of strings. To make our approach more concrete, consider a set of rules that all have as their domain the set of positive integers. A rule that doubles an element of the domain if it is even applies (in our sense) to *all* integers. Such a rule maps 8 to 16, and it maps 9 to 9.

We can represent the "*t* to *s*" phonological rule with the following functional notation.

(86)   Phonological Rule for Paramecian

PHONRULE$_1$:	*goli*	$\longrightarrow$	*goli*
	gola	$\longrightarrow$	*gola*
	poti	$\longrightarrow$	*posi*
	pota	$\longrightarrow$	*pota*
	kitap	$\longrightarrow$	*kitap*
	kitin	$\longrightarrow$	*kisin*
	dutap	$\longrightarrow$	*dutap*
	dutin	$\longrightarrow$	*dusin*
	$\vdots$		$\vdots$

This is not the full function. If Paramecian were a real language it might be possible, but cumbersome, to list all the combinations of noun roots combined with the suffixes that start with -*i*. Since an I-language is somehow stored in a person's finite brain, each I-language has a finite lexicon. However, given our discussion of systematicity and productivity, and our I-language perspective, we want to reformulate the extensionally defined function with an intensional version. As we discuss in the following sections, intensional definitions express key generalizations (such as the fact that *t* becomes *s* only before *i* in Paramecian) while also helping us to address problems of precision and expressibility.

10.2   A More Constrained Approach to Phonological Functions

In the previous section we represented phonological rules as mappings from strings to strings. However, this broad characterization provides far too much expressibility: there is almost no limit on what type of mappings can be expressed in this way. As long as the item to the left of the arrow is a string and the one on the right is also a string (and for each input there is only one output), this would constitute a legitimate function from strings to strings.

Thus, such a system permits not only mappings like *poti* → *posi*, but also *poti* → *xyabgrtqaabaa*. Since our object of study, what we are modelling, is a component of the human language faculty, we want to build a theory that adequately characterizes this system, and not the phonological equivalent of *stuff happens*. If there is no evidence for rules allowing mappings like *poti* → *xyabgrtqaabaa*, then we don't want our theory to be able to express such mappings.[2] We will start on purpose with a system that is *too* restrictive, in that it is not powerful enough to model the human phonological system. Our strategy is to start with something simple and expand as necessary.

One formalization for representing phonological rules is based on a system used by Noam Chomsky and Morris Halle in the book *The Sound Pattern of English* (1968), which is usually referred to as *SPE*. Even though we diverge from *SPE* in many details, we will refer to our evolving model as the SPE system, in homage to *SPE*'s foundational role in the field. Our goal here is two-fold: first, to introduce you to a system for representing rules; second, to provide a framework for analyzing and understanding phonological processes as mental computations.

It might be useful to have some intuitive idea of what a phonological rule is before getting into the details of the formal rule systems. We already introduced one instance of such a rule in (78), repeated in (87).

(87)   The sound *t* becomes *s* when appearing immediately to the left of the sound *i*.

As mentioned above, the phonological rules we are concerned with apply to sound segments inside of words. The general structure of the rule in (87) states that one type of sound segment is replaced by another when it occurs in a certain environment. Furthermore, the environment is quite limited—the segments immediately adjacent to the one undergoing the change. Broadly speaking, the phonological rules that we will discuss initially have the following properties:

(88)   Properties of phonological rules

    i.   They apply to strings of segments in (potentially complex) words (the output of the morphology). These words are the *output* of the morphology, but the phonology has no access to anything but the concatenated segment string that is a component of this output. In other words, the morphological structure is not visible to the phonology.

    ii.   They replace one type of segment with another in particular environments.

    iii.   Their environments are restricted, defined by the segment to the immediate right or immediate left (or both).

---

[2]This is a bit overstated. We really can't argue from non-occurrence in such a simplistic manner, but we'll leave things like this for now. In brief, there can be non-linguistic reasons why certain linguistic patterns do not occur.

Although we ultimately discuss evidence that challenges some of these properties (in Parts IV to VIII), for the sake of exposition we adopt them as a basis for building our first formal rule system.

10.3   SPE System

In this presentation of our SPE system, rules will be encoded using a string of symbols, some of which represent sound segments (such as *a*, *d*, *ə*, *ð*, and so on) and others which represent phonological relations and conditions for rule application (e.g., the right arrow '→ ,' the slash '/' and the underscore '___ ').[3] The key to understanding the system relies on knowing how the non-sound-segment symbols interact with the sound-segment symbols.

The right arrow (→) symbolizes substitution: one sound segment replacing another.[4] Generally, sound segments appear on both sides of the arrow, the one on the left being the target segment (the one that will be replaced), the one on the right being the output segment (the replacement).

The slash symbol (/), unlike the arrow symbol, does not signify any kind of function or relation. Rather it only separates the specification of the change from the specification of the environment that triggers the change. The set of symbols to the right of the slash, which specifies the environment, consists of the underscore symbol (___), which indicates the position of the target segment, with optional sound segments on either side. At least one segment symbol must be present in the environment.[5]

Let's consider an example of how these symbols are used to express phonological rules by providing a translation of the rule in (87), which specifies that *t* becomes *s* before *i*. The formulation appears in (89).

(89)   t → s / ___ i

Since the *t* is to the left of the arrow with an *s* on the right, this rule specifies that it is *t* that will be replaced by an *s*. The symbols to the right of the slash indicate that this replacement only occurs when the *t* appears to the (immediate) left of an *i*.

---

[3]In the system of the *Sound Pattern of English* book, the symbol for a segment is an abbreviation for a set of features. However, we will not introduce features until Part VIII of this book. This is just one way in which our SPE rule system strays from the original. We reiterate here that we call our model "SPE" as a tribute to the foundational work that appeared in the book, not because we intend to present that model unchanged.

[4]Note that this is a different use of the arrow from our discussion of relations and functions.

[5]There is more to say about this in the context of so-called unconditioned redundancy rules, but we leave it aside.

To provide a better intuitive grasp of this format, let's consider a couple of other potential rules written in English with their translations in SPE.

(90)   • The segment *o* becomes a *u* when appearing immediately to the right of the segment ʃ.

    • o → u / ʃ ___

(91)   • The segment *s* becomes a *z* when appearing between the segments *e* (on the left) and ə (on the right).

    • s → z / e ___ ə

As shown in (90), when the trigger for the change is a segment to the left (instead of the right), the symbol for the trigger appears to the left of the underscore. When there are two segments constituting the triggering environment, one to the left and another to the right, as specified in (91), the symbols appear to the left and right of the underscore. The rules in (89) to (91) are specific examples of the three different rule patterns in our SPE system. A more general (and yet precise) way of outlining these three patterns is given in (92).

(92) **SPE rule syntax**

Let SEG be the set of segment symbols. Let ENV be the set of symbols that specify the environment. Let α and β be any member of SEG. Let γ and δ be any member of ENV. (It is possible for γ to be the same as δ.) The following are possible rules.

  a. $\alpha \rightarrow \beta /$ ___ γ
  b. $\alpha \rightarrow \beta / \gamma$ ___
  c. $\alpha \rightarrow \beta / \gamma$ ___ δ

Nothing else is a possible rule.

According to (92), every instance of an SPE rule must fit into one of the three sub-formats specified in (92a–c), where the Greek letters represent the possible segmental values chosen from the sets SEG and ENV.[6] As discussed in later units, it is useful to separate the symbols used to specify the environment (the set ENV) from those used to specify the change (the set SEG), even though there is typically significant overlap in the two sets.

---

[6]The letters α, β, γ, δ are the first four letters of the Greek alphabet: α is pronounced as "alpha," β as "beta," γ as "gamma," and δ as "delta." These Greek letters are used as variables over the set of symbols. Another, more common use of Greek letters as variables is introduced much later.

10.4   Expressibility in SPE

Our SPE system in (92) is a highly compact, well defined, and versatile system that can express a variety of different phonological rules. For example, consider an artificial language where the set of segments consists of only two members (let's call them *a* and *b*). For the purpose of the example, let the set SEG = ENV = {a, b}. According to (92), the following are possible SPE rules in this language:

(93)   Possible SPE rules where SEG = ENV = {a, b}

i.	a → b / a ___	xvii.	b → b / a ___
ii.	a → b / b ___	xviii.	b → b / b ___
iii.	a → b / ___ a	xix.	b → b / ___ a
iv.	a → b / ___ b	xx.	b → b / ___ b
v.	b → a / a ___	xxi.	a → a / a ___
vi.	b → a / b ___	xxii.	a → a / b ___
vii.	b → a / ___ a	xxiii.	a → a / ___ a
viii.	b → a / ___ b	xxiv.	a → a / ___ b
ix.	a → b / a ___ a	xxv.	a → a / a ___ a
x.	a → b / a ___ b	xxvi.	a → a / a ___ b
xi.	a → b / b ___ a	xxvii.	a → a / b ___ a
xii.	a → b / b ___ b	xxviii.	a → a / b ___ b
xiii.	b → a / a ___ a	xxix.	b → b / a ___ a
xiv.	b → a / a ___ b	xxx.	b → b / a ___ b
xv.	b → a / b ___ a	xxxi.	b → b / b ___ a
xvi.	b → a / b ___ b	xxxii.	b → b / b ___ b

Despite having only two sound segments in its inventory, there is a possibility of 32 different phonological rules. Each one contains only segments in ENV and SEG. Furthermore, each one fits into one of the patterns in (92a–c).

In contrast, the expressions in (94) are clearly not possible SPE rules, at least not in a system where SEG = ENV = {a, b}.

(94)   Impossible rules

    i. a → b / ab ___

    ii. a → / a ___ b

    iii. b → w / ___ a

    iv. b → a / ___ *nouns*

The symbol sequence in (94i) has two adjacent members of ENV to the left of the underscore. This does not conform to any of the patterns for environments set out in (92). The symbol sequence in (94ii) has no segment symbol after the arrow and before the slash, and thus this sequence also does not conform to any of the patterns in (92). The symbol sequences in (94iii) and (94iv) have symbols in them that are not members of SEG or ENV (the 'w' and '*nouns*' symbols, respectively), thus violating the conditions set out at the beginning of (92).

Notice that as we change and expand the sets ENV and SEG, we change not only the number of possible rules but also the character of the rules that can be expressed. If we allowed for syntactic categories (such as *adjective, noun, verb, suffix*) to be members of ENV, then we would have a system where segment changes are triggered by morphological or syntactic features.[7] If we restricted ENV to only phonological segments, then we would have a system where the possible triggers for segment changes would be purely phonological. One of our goals in developing a rule system is to restrict the definition of a possible rule to one that can capture all the facts we believe to reflect phonology but yet not overreach—we do not want to allow the formulation of rules whose structure will never be found in a natural language.[8] In other words, we don't want too much expressibility.

We can even take this exploration of expressibility one step further, not just asking whether a given symbol sequence is a rule or not, but also asking how many rules are possible. In (93), we listed all 32 possible rules for an SPE system where ENV = SEG = {a, b}.

Let's do some basic combinatorics to see why the number of rules comes out to 32. You might initially think the calculation is simple. First of all, the symbols '→ ', '/', and '___' appear in every rule, so they are not relevant to the calculation. Then, there are just two choices for each Greek letter: α can have the value a or b, β can have the value a or b, γ can have the value a or b, and δ can have the value a or b. Since $2 \times 2 \times 2 \times 2 = 2^4 = 16$, we end up with 16. But that is not quite right.

The easiest way to see what is going on is to look at (92c): $\alpha \rightarrow \beta / \gamma$ ___ δ. It is true that there are two choices for α and β, so there are $2 \times 2 = 4$ possibilities for the left side of the '/' symbol. But there are actually *three* choices for each segment in the environment. For the positions before and after the underscore, γ and δ can have the values a or b, or there can be no segment at all in those positions. For example, in (93 i) 'a → b / a ___' there is no symbol following the underscore. So, it looks like there

---

[7]The problem is a bit worse than this, since it is not clear how these non-phonological features can fit into a segment string representation.

[8]The interpretation of what is a *possible* rule is a complicated task. See Hale and Reiss (2008), Newmeyer (2005), and Isac and Reiss (2013) for discussion of possible *vs.* probable languages.

are $3 \times 3 = 3^2 = 9$ possible environments for rules. However there is a glitch. Our rule syntax makes it clear that we can't leave out both γ and δ in the same rule, which means that an expression like 'a $\rightarrow$ b / ___' is not a possible rule.[9] So, instead of 9 environments, there are only 8. Putting everything together, we have 4 possibilities to the left of the '/' and 8 to the right, so we get $4 \times 8 = 32$ different rules.

To ensure that you understand our reasoning, suppose that UG provides only one segment: SEG = ENV = {a}. How many rules are possible? List them all and explain your reasoning. See Exercise 10.4 at the end of this unit to check yourself.

10.5   Useless Rules

But what is the status of rules (93xvii–xxxii) in the second column of the table? These rules map every input string to an identical output string. Do we really want our model of phonological UG to allow for such *useless rules*?

Now, it is hard to imagine why a phonologist would posit the existence of *useless rules* in a particular I-language, since it is hard to imagine what evidence there could be that such rules exist. They would not be responsible for a morpheme having different surface forms, for example. In Paramecian, the morpheme meaning 'foot' shows up as *pos* because of the rule that changes *t* to *s* before *i*; but the form *pot* shows up when no rule has affected the segments.[10]

So, we will assume that no actual phonological grammar (no language₁) has such a rule that maps every string to itself, like those in (93xvi–xxxii). However, we will consider two views concerning whether or not phonological UG (language₂) allows for such possibilities. Before we begin weighing the alternatives, it is important to notice that the only reason we are considering the question is because the process of trying to develop a formal model of UG brought us here inadvertently. This is a benefit of explicit modeling; it makes us ask questions that we would not have otherwise considered.

Given our discussion of expressibility, it seems obvious that we should revise our SPE rule syntax to exclude rules that we will never find in any language. Why would we want a model that clearly has more expressibility than we need, given the assumption that *useless rules* are not part of any I-language whatsoever?

---

[9]This is just a working assumption, and we may want to give it up later—see Exercise 53.4.

[10]We should point out that there are phonological models like Optimality Theory (e.g., Kager, 1999) that explicitly model identity between inputs and outputs via so-called faithfulness or identity or correspondence constraints.

There is an alternative view, however. If we have a different explanation for why *useless rules* never occur in actual languages, then we don't want to redundantly build an explanation into our rule syntax. In other words, we could argue that our model, our language$_3$, should allow for useless rules even though such rules will never be found in any language$_1$. There can be factors other than UG that account for the non-occurrence of useless rules. The observational gap is perhaps due to the fact that particular I-languages have to be acquired, and no data would lead a learner to posit a useless rule. Think of it this way: if useless rules are compatible with the language faculty, then a mad neuroscientist of the future could potentially program them into a person's brain, and the brain's language faculty would not treat such rules as different from a non-useless rule. However, such rules will never arise through the normal course of events that lead to the encoding of a grammar in a brain, normal language acquisition. You can find further discussion of such matters in Kaplan (1987); Newmeyer (2005); Hale and Reiss (2008); Isac and Reiss (2013).

Although excluding half of the 32 possibilities seems fairly dramatic, the exclusion of *useless rules* does not affect the order of magnitude of combinatoric possibilities in general. Consider a language with around 35 segments, like English. There are 35 possibilities for the target of a rule (α); now if we allow useless rules, the number of combinations to the left of the '/' is $35 \times 35 = 35^2 = 1225$. On the right side of the '/' we get $36 \times 36 - 1 = 1295$ possibilities. Putting this all together, we get $1225 \times 1295 = 1,586,375$ different rules. The effect of excluding useless rules is to reduce the left side to $35 \times 34 = 1190$ possibilities. This is because once one of the 35 choices are made for α, there remain 34 non-identical choices for β. Then 1190×1295 yields 1,541,050 rules. We get less than a 3 percent reduction by excluding useless rules in this case. There is nothing principled about this argument, but it should at least weaken the impression that useless rules are an affront to the idea of limiting expressibility.

And of course, useless rules take on even less importance as the number of segments provided by UG increases. If we assume that the International Phonetic Alphabet represents all possible speech segments, then allowing useless rules yields over 133 million possibilities. Restricting our syntax to exclude useless rules only brings the number down to something over 132 million.

Whatever you decide you want to do about useless rules, whether to exclude them by constraining the SPE syntax to require that $\alpha \neq \beta$ or rather to account for their absence by appeal to other factors, you should appreciate that our humble SPE syntax can already generate quite a range of possible phonological rules, over 100 million if we let SEG = ENV = IPA (the set of all IPA segments).

Note that this sets up a potentially dramatic learning problem for a child trying to acquire phonological rules. In any given language there are only a small set of rules—let's say thirty or forty. How is it that the child searches through over one million possible rules to find the thirty or forty that are part of his or her parents' grammars? Obviously the search cannot be a matter of randomly testing candidates from an immense list of possibilities one by one to see if they yield outputs that are consistent with the parents' speech. There must be more to acquisition than merely searching through this large space. Or maybe we have mischaracterized the task the child faces.

We will discuss such learnability issues further in Unit 61. For now, it should be noted that the SPE system is not completely unconstrained. If children only considered rules that conform to (92), they would not need to consider rules that could be specified in other systems—for example, rules that look more than one segment to the right or left, or rules that refer to categories like *noun* or *verb*. The simple point to take away is this: although the system defines a tremendous space of possibilities, it is still an improvement over a completely unconstrained system that allows humans to acquire any mapping between segment strings as a rule. By narrowing the scope of possible rules, we define limits on the nature of the phonological system and thus constrain the search space for a learner. In other words, our (overly) simple SPE constitutes a useful initial hypothesis about phonological UG.

Exercises

10.1. Express the following in SPE rule format:

    i. "n becomes w when the segment to its immediate right is z"

    ii. "f becomes q when the segment to its immediate left is j"

    iii. "g becomes k between m and h"

    iv. "g becomes k between h and m"

    v. "q becomes t after b"

    vi. "c becomes y before r"

10.2. Express the following in words:

    i. $t \rightarrow q\ /\ b$ ___

    ii. $x \rightarrow h\ /$ ___ f

    iii. $v \rightarrow z\ /\ f$ ___ j

10.3. Explain why each of the following expressions is not a possible rule in our system, assuming SEG = ENV = {a,b}:

    i. a → b / ___ ab

    ii. b → f / a ___

    iii. ___b / a → b

    iv. b → a / b ___ in rapid speech

    v. b → a / a ___ optionally

    vi. → a / a ___ b

    vii. a → b / a ___ in frequently occurring words

    viii. b → a / b ___ from Latin to French

    ix. a → b

    x. a → b / ___

10.4. We showed that if UG provides SEG = ENV = {a, b}, there are 32 possible rules.
We asked you to consider the case where UG provides just one segment: SEG =
ENV = {a}. You should have found that such a system allows for exactly three
rules:

- a → a / a ___
- a → a / ___ a
- a → a / a ___ a

Now consider the case where UG provides three segments: SEG = ENV = {a,b,c}.
There are too many rules to write out. How many are there? Explain your
reasoning.

Unit 11

Interpreting Phonological Rules

How do you interpret this expression: $3 \times 5 - 4$. We assume your answer will be 11. Why is this your answer? Maybe you compute the multiplication before subtraction, because multiplication comes first in the expression. We can test this hypothesis by asking you to compute $7 - 3 \times 2$. If you always performed operations left-to-right, we would expect the output to be 8, but that is not what happens—the answer is 1. Both the expressions we gave you are well formed according to the syntax of arithmetic; however, the syntax is not enough to interpret the expression. There is a lack of precision in the syntax of arithmetic expressions concerning the order of application of different operations. You need to know that multiplication gets applied before subtraction in interpreting such expressions, but that is not part of the *syntax* of the expressions. The priority of multiplication over subtraction is a rule that must be followed to interpret well-formed arithmetic expressions.

A similar issue arises in the application of the SPE rules we developed. Despite our simple and clear characterization of SPE rule syntax, there are still imprecisions in our formalization. Consider again our first example of a rule from Unit 7.

(95) • The segment *t* becomes an *s* when appearing immediately to the left of the segment *i*.

• t → s / ___ i

In (95) we have an English statement and also an SPE formalization of a rule that takes a word as an input and yields a word as an output, one that is almost identical to the input except that all the *t*-segments before *i*-segments in the input have been replaced with *s*-segments in the output.

The rule in (95) appears to be easy to understand. For example, if the inputs were the sequences of segments in (96), the outputs would be the sequences in (97).

(96)   Input to the rule in (95)

     a. gotin

     b. butati

     c. katitin

(97)   Output from the rule in (95) where input is (96)

     a. gosin

     b. butasi

     c. kasisin

The t's in (96a) and (96c) and the second t in (96b) are all changed to s because they appear immediately to the left of an i. However, the first t in (96b) does not change since it appears before an a.

Despite our ease in determining the outputs for these examples, there is a hidden vagueness in our statement of the rule, a vagueness that actually makes the rule still imprecise, even if we refer to the SPE version.

11.1   Directionality in Rule Application

To clearly illustrate why these questions matter, it might be best to simplify our example a little. Let's consider an artificial language like the one we discussed in section 10.3, a language where there are only two types of segments, a and b. Consider the rule in (98):

(98)   •   The segment b becomes an a when appearing between two other b segments.

     • $b \rightarrow a / b$ ___ b

Just like (95), the application of this rule seems obvious at first sight: the rule takes a word as an input and yields an output that is identical to the input except all the b-segments appearing between two other b-segments are replaced by a-segments. Given the inputs in (99) one would expect the outputs in (100).

(99)   Input to the rule in (98)

    a. bbba

    b. abbabbba

    c. abbbabbba

(100)   Output from the rule in (98) where input is (99)

    a. baba

    b. abbababa

    c. abababababa

The second *b* in (99a), the fourth in (99b) and the second and fifth in (99c) are replaced by *a*-segments since they appear between two other *b*'s. However, the other *b*-segments do not change.

Despite the ease in which we apply the rule to the examples in (99), there are certain inputs where the method of application is not at all clear. Consider the input in (101).

(101)   Input to the rule in (98) : abbbba

What would be the output of (101)? Would the output be (102a), (102b), or (102c)?

(102)   Potential output from the rule in (98) where input is (101)

    a. ababba (*left-to-right*)

    b. abbaba (*right-to-left*)

    c. abaaba (*global*)

You might pick (102a) as the obvious answer, looking to apply the rule to neighborhoods of three segments by moving through the word from left to right, segment by segment ('abb, 'bbb', and so on). When you consider the third segment as the middle of a three-segment neighborhood, the rule applies and changes that segment from *b* to *a* since that third segment satisfies the rule conditions by being a *b* between two other *b*'s. Next, upon considering the fourth segment as the middle of the three-segment neighborhood, the rule would not apply, and the fourth segment would not change from *b* to *a* since its environment would no longer satisfy the conditions of the rule (because of the previous replacement, the third segment would be *a*, not *b*, i.e., the fourth segment is no longer between two *b*'s).

Another possibility, perhaps not as appealing intuitively, might be to choose (102b) as the answer, using the same strategy as specified above, but applying the rule segment by segment, moving from *right to left* instead of left to right.

Yet another possibility is to pick (102c) by inspecting the input as a whole and noting that the third and fourth *b*-segments match the conditions specified by the rule, and hence they both should be changed to *a*. Given these three reasonable choices, you might simply be confused and not know how to apply the rule.

There is no fact of the matter in our made-up example. The rule in (98) does not specify what to do in this type of situation. However, there must be a fact of the matter with respect to actual phonological rules, since these rules are part of the I-languages that humans have in their minds/brains. Do real human rules require a left-to-right interpretation, a right-to-left interpretation, or the "global" interpretation? Maybe all three interpretations occur in human languages, maybe different interpretations can occur within the same I-language. These are empirical issues that will have to be investigated, but whatever the outcome, our statements of the rules, even in our formal language, needs to make clear what we, as linguists, intend to express with our rules.[1]

11.2   A More Realistic Example

An artificial grammar with only two types of segments might seem very distant from natural language. You might wonder whether these issues really come into play in a language with more complexity. Let's consider another example with a greater variety of segments and more realistic morphemes such as the Esicherian data in (103). (Before reading further, take a couple of minutes and try to use the comparison and subtraction methods to analyze this data. It is always a good idea to practice using these techniques.)

---

[1]We have not exhausted the possibilities in this discussion. We intend our global interpretation of the rule to apply just once, whereas the other two options can be understood as applying the rule from one end of a string and then reapplying the rule to the output thus derived. In other words, the left-to-right and right-to-left applications can be understood iteratively, whereas the global application should not be understood in this way. Note that we say *can* rather than *must*. Mathematically speaking, the left-to-right and right-to-left applications can be represented as a single function as well, one that is the composition of all of the functions used in the iterative application. Also note that iterative global application—applying a "global" rule to its own output until such application causes no further changes—is another logical possibility, one that produces different results than the three possibilities discussed in this section.

(103) Esicherian

Noun	Meaning		Noun	Meaning
a. nusa	'the dog'		f. baps	'mice'
b. nustu	'some dog'		g. kita	'the finger'
c. nust	'dogs'		h. kitsu	'some finger'
d. bapa	'the mouse'		i. kits	'fingers'
e. bapsu	'some mouse'			

Using our comparison method, we can reach several reasonable conclusions.

- By comparing [nusa], [nustu] and [nust], we can conclude that *nus* is the phonological form of the morpheme meaning 'dog'.

- By comparing [bapa], [bapsu] and [baps], we can conclude that *bap* is the phonological form of the morpheme meaning 'mouse'.

- By comparing [kita], [kitsu] and [kits], we can conclude that *kit* is the phonological form of the morpheme meaning 'finger'.

- By comparing [nusa], [bapa] and [kita], we can conclude that *a* is the phonological form of the morpheme meaning 'the'.

So far there are no contradictions: each meaning corresponds to a unique sound. However, this situation changes when we employ the subtraction method.

- By subtracting *bap* and *kit* from [bapsu] and [kitsu] respectively, we can conclude that *su* is the phonological form of the morpheme meaning 'some'.

- By subtracting *bap* and *kit* from [baps] and [kits] respectively, we can conclude that *s* is the phonological form of the morpheme meaning PLURAL.

- By subtracting *nus* from [nustu], we can conclude that *tu* is the phonological form of the morpheme meaning 'some'.

- By subtracting *nus* from [nust], we can conclude that *t* is the phonological form of the morpheme meaning PLURAL.

There seem to be two phonological forms for the morpheme meaning 'some' and similarly two for the morpheme meaning PLURAL. As mentioned before, it is possible that this is a mere coincidence: maybe there are two lexical items with different forms that happen to have the same meaning. However, it is also possible that the morphemes meaning PLURAL and 'some' each have only one underlying phonological representation, namely /s/ and /su/ respectively. The change in surface form might be due to a phonological rule like the one in (104).

(104)   The segment *s* becomes a *t* when it appears to the right of *s*.[2]

If this hypothesis is correct, the UR of the word meaning 'some dog' would be /nussu/ (the concatenation of *nus* with *-su*). After applying the rule in (104), the SR would be [nustu]; the second *s* is replaced with a *t* since it appears to the right of another *s*. Similarly, the UR of the word meaning 'dogs' would be /nuss/ (the concatenation of *nus* with the plural marker *-s*), and after applying the rule in (104) the SR would be [nust].

    To see if this explanation is plausible, we would need to check to see if the alternation between *s* and *t* is systematic and productive. For the sake of this example, let's suppose we found evidence that the alternation is indeed systematic and productive, in support of the phonological account, the claim that there really is a rule like the one in (104) that is part of Esicherian grammar.

    Given this rule, we can ask how other words would surface. Of particular interest is the surface form of the word meaning 'some dogs'. This word involves concatenation of the noun root 'dog' followed by the morpheme meaning PLURAL followed by the morpheme meaning 'some':

(105)   /nus/ + /s/ + /su/

Hence the underlying representation would be /nus-s-su/. (We sometimes use hyphens in URs to mark morpheme boundaries, but we assume that these are invisible to the phonology.) If this UR serves as the input to the rule in (104), what would be the output? Would it be the form in (106a) or (106b)?

(106)   a. nusssu → nustsu

        b. nusssu → nusttu

If the rule applies left to right, the answer is (106a). When the string *nusssu* is scanned left to right, the second *s* occurs to the right of an *s* and changes to a *t*. The third *s*, thus, is no longer to the right of an *s*, so it does not change. However, if the rule applies right to left, the third and second tokens of *s* will both be changed to a *t*. In this case,

---

[2]This is not the only possible rule. It could be that *t* changes to *s* when it appears to the right of either *p* or *t*. We will discuss how to choose between different possible phonological rules in later units.

so-called "global" application yields the same result as right to left application (that is, two of the three interpretations yield the same output).

Which approach is correct? Again, there is no fact of the matter, since this is a made-up example and the rule in (104) does not specify how it applies to words. In the case of an actual language, there *is* a fact of the matter, which we can potentially discover. For now, we will *assume* that all rules in all languages apply globally, but we must be clear that this is an assumption we have not justified.

Exercises

As you work through these exercises, be sure to understand the difference between having an environment defined by a segment to the left or right (or on both sides) of the target, and the direction of scanning the input string, right to left, left to right, or globally.

11.1.   Let's consider three different rules and three different modes of application. For each of the nine combinations, apply the rule to the input string $k\,k\,k\,k$:

  - Rule 1: k → g / k ___
    - Left-to-right: $k\,k\,k\,k$ ⤳ _____
    - Right-to-left: $k\,k\,k\,k$ ⤳ _____
    - Global: $k\,k\,k\,k$ ⤳ _____

  - Rule 2: k → g / ___ k
    - Left-to-right: $k\,k\,k\,k$ ⤳ _____
    - Right-to-left: $k\,k\,k\,k$ ⤳ _____
    - Global: $k\,k\,k\,k$ ⤳ _____

  - Rule 3: k → g / k ___ k
    - Left-to-right: $k\,k\,k\,k$ ⤳ _____
    - Right-to-left: $k\,k\,k\,k$ ⤳ _____
    - Global: $k\,k\,k\,k$ ⤳ _____

11.2. For each of the three rules above , give a string that will yield the *same* output however the rule is applied. (You might be able to use the same string for different rules.)

- String that yields identical output for all modes of application of R1: _____
- String that yields identical output for all modes of application of R2: _____
- String that yields identical output for all modes of application of R3: _____

11.3. Consider the rule 'q → m / ___ m' and an input string *aqmbqqmcqqqm.*

- Assume that rule applies right to left through a string. What is the output?
- Assume that rule applies left to right through a string. What is the output?
- Assume that rule applies once globally to a string. What is the output?

11.4. Consider the rule 'x → y / y ___' and an input string *ayxyxxxyyxxyayxy.*

- Assume that rule applies right to left through a string. What is the output?
- Assume that rule applies left to right through a string. What is the output?
- Assume that rule applies once globally to a string. What is the output?

11.5. Consider the rule 'p → k / p ___ p' and an input string *apappapppappppappppppapppppppa.*

- Assume that rule applies right to left through a string. What is the output?
- Assume that rule applies left to right through a string. What is the output?
- Assume that rule applies once globally to a string. What is the output?

11.6. Consider the rule 'b → a / ___ a' and an input string *bbbba.* Contrary to what we assumed above, and to what we will assume for human phonology, suppose here that the rule applies globally to the whole string, and then reapplies to its own output, if reapplying the rule has an effect. What is the output?

Unit 12

The Semantics of SPE Phonological Rules

> Everything is vague to a degree you do not realize till you have tried to make it precise, and everything precise is so remote from everything that we normally think, that you cannot for a moment suppose that is what we really mean when we say what we think.

Bertrand Russell, "The Philosophy of Logical Atomism"

We have presented our SPE system by rigorously defining what is a possible rule and by discussing the meaning of those rules by comparing them to English translations. We have also demonstrated that the rules themselves do not specify the direction of application. In order to specify that rules apply globally (by assumption) we need to specify a *formal semantics* for phonological theory from an I-language perspective (i.e., a method for systematically interpreting the symbol systems used to express phonological rules). We note that this is an unusual step to take within phonology. Normally phonologists assume that the exact interpretation of their theoretical symbol system is clear, without the aid of formal semantics. However, we introduce a formal semantics, both to help you learn how to specify a precise interpretation that lacks vagueness and ambiguity, and also because we think that the informal practice in much of phonology obscures some important and interesting issues. Our discussion of a semantics for phonology will establish a platform for discussing issues about mental representations and metatheoretical use of symbols in later units.

As a starting point, let's reconsider the simple rule in (104) along with its SPE translation.

(107)   a. The segment *s* becomes a *t* when it appears to the right of *s*.

         b. s → t / s ___

Our ultimate goal is to provide a precise interpretation (rather than a loose translation) of the symbol sequences in (107b). To do this, we need a set of things that the symbols will be interpreted as. Taking an I-language perspective, we assume that the members of this set are in the mind: in other words, we assume that the phonological symbols are mapped either to mental representations or mental functions.

One possible way of presenting this perspective is to create a *model of the mind*, which we will label M. For the purposes of clarity, we will create this model M with a two-part structure, separated into a set of mental representations (labeled D for *Domain*) and a set of mental functions (labeled F for *Functions*). The functions (rules) are maps from one string of mental representations to another.

In our definition of a *mental model* in (108), we follow a mathematical convention of defining the *model* as an ordered pair: we put the set of mental representations first and the set of functions second.

(108)   Let M be $\langle D, F \rangle$ where D is a set of mental representations and F is a set of functions that map strings of mental representations to other strings of mental representations.

With this *model of the mind*, we can now specify how to interpret some of the symbols in our phonological theory.

12.1   Semantics for IPA Symbols

At this introductory stage, IPA symbols are being used to represent the members of the sets SEG and ENV. (In later units, we will introduce and interpret sets of phonological features.) With this assumption in mind, it is simple to provide an interpretation of the sound-segment symbols in the target, output, and environment of the SPE rules.

Although sometimes IPA symbols are used to talk about actual sounds and specific kinds of articulations (especially within the phonetics literature), within phonological theory they are (or should be) exclusively used to refer to mental representations.[1] For the purposes of our mental model, we assume that for each IPA symbol, there is a corresponding mental representation available to the human language faculty, and furthermore that the set D contains all of these mental representations. Thus the interpretation of an IPA symbol in the *model of the mind* will be the corresponding mental representation. We specify this formally by using the convention of superscripting the symbol with M to indicate the interpretation (what is signified). Thus, while æ is an IPA symbol, $æ^M$ is the mental representation associated with the IPA symbol.

Below we outline this general convention in a semantic rule. For ease of presentation, we use the Greek letter α as a (meta)variable that ranges over the IPA symbols so that we do not have to state an interpretation rule for each IPA symbol. Thus α serves as a stand-in for *k*, *b*, ð, and so on, and hence α^M serves as a stand-in for k^M, b^M, $ð^M$, and so on.

(109)   If α is a member of SEG or ENV, then α^M is the mental representation of α.

According to this semantic rule, the interpretation of the IPA symbol *b* is the mental representation of *b*—in symbols, b^M. The interpretation of the IPA symbol æ is the mental representation of æ—in symbols, $æ^M$. The same reasoning applies to each symbol.

In this book, we will use this superscript M in certain situations to clarify that we are talking about mental representations rather than IPA symbols (such as when we are specifying the interpretation rules with IPA symbols). However, to "save ink" we will often leave off the superscripts when it is obvious that the IPA symbol is being used to talk about mental representations, as when we use them to represent the input and output strings of phonological rules. It is implicit that inputs and outputs to phonological rules are mental representations.

Given this interpretation of the IPA symbols, it should be noted that the use of the term *sound segment* in the previous units, or for that matter any reference to *sound*, is misleading. Phonology is not in the business of dealing with actual sounds but rather is only in the business of mental representations. From now on, we will be a little more careful about our use of the term *sound*.

---

[1] In brief, consider the difference between hissing like a snake and pronouncing the segment *s*. We might sloppily describe the hiss as [s], because the physiological action is identical to pronunciation of the initial segment of *sing*, but as Edward Sapir (1949) pointed out, the distinction between the *s* and the hiss is a matter of *intention*. Speech is speech because it is meant as speech by a speaker, not because the vocal tract is in a particular configuration.

12.2   Semantics for SPE Rules

A semantics for rules with arrows and slashes is a bit trickier to characterize than a semantics for IPA symbols. Rules are not interpreted as mental representations but rather as functions on such representations: specifically, members of F, the set of functions that map sequences to other sequences. Specifying these functions can be difficult. For the sake of clarity, we follow a few mathematical and linguistic conventions.

i. We represent the phonological part of a morpheme as an ordered list of IPA symbols, a string. These strings have an implied left-to-right linear order and are equivalent in structure to ordered sets written with angled brackets, as we discussed above. For example, the mental representation of the word *man* will be $m^M \ae^M n^M$ which is equivalent to $\langle m^M, \ae^M, n^M \rangle$. The representation for *dog* will be $d^M a^M g^M$ which is equivalent to $\langle d^M, a^M, g^M \rangle$. Generally, we will leave off the superscripts since it is implicit that strings are mental representations. Thus, we will symbolize the mental representation of *man* and *dog* as mæn and dag. Note that we will often refer to the spaces occupied by the segments in a string as *positions*. Thus, for mæn, m is in the first position, æ is in the second position and n is in the third position.

ii. We use x and y as metavariables that range over mental representations. They are "metavariables" in that they are not part of the phonological system but rather are used (by us linguists) to specify an interpretation of the system. Thus, in the interpretation rules, x can serve as a stand-in for the mental representation of k (k^M), or b (b^M), or ð ($ð^M$), and so on.

iii. We use various numeral subscripts, or indexes, not only to distinguish between the variables but also to indicate their relative position in a string.[2] Thus, if $x_1 x_2 x_3 = m^M \ae^M n^M$, then $x_1 = m^M$ (the first member of the string), $x_2 = \ae^M$ (the second member of the string), and $x_3 = n^M$ (the third member of the string). Furthermore, the variable in the first position will always be x_1 or y_1 (but never x_2 or y_2), the variable in the second position will always be x_2 or y_2 (but never x_3 or y_3), and so on It is important to note that even though indexes distinguish between variables (e.g., x_1 and x_5 occupy different positions and hence are different variables), they could be assigned the same value. For example, x_1 could represent s^M, and s^M could also be the value of x_5.

---

[2]As with the use of metavariables, the use of numeral subscripts does not imply that the human phonological faculty makes reference to the natural numbers. The indices are part of our description, as linguists, of what phonological rules in human I-languages are computing, but they are not part of the phonological rule system itself.

Given these conventions, let's consider one possibility for interpreting rules where the environment to the left of any segment serves as a relevant environment that triggers segment replacement. For the sake of consistency, we indicate the interpretation of rules in the same way we indicated the interpretation of IPA symbols: the rules appear in brackets with a superscripted M to the right.

(110)   **Interpretation of the pattern '$\alpha \to \beta / \gamma$ ___'**

If α and β, are members of SEG and γ is a member of ENV, then $(\alpha \to \beta / \gamma$ ___$)^M$ is the function f (a member of F) that maps any (finite) string of mental representations $x_1 x_2 \ldots x_n$ to the string of mental representations $y_1 y_2 \ldots y_n$ such that for each index i that is greater than or equal to 1 and less than or equal to n ($1 \le i \le n$)...

(a)   If $x_i = \alpha^M$ and $x_{(i-1)} = \gamma^M$, then $y_i = \beta^M$.

(b)   Otherwise $y_i = x_i$.

This interpretation states that rules take a string and map the "target" to its "replacement" when it occurs in the right environment and leaves everything else alone. In other words, rules are interpreted as functions from strings to strings where the output string is identical to the input string, except for the replacement of the target with the replacement segment.

Perhaps it might be easier to understand this type of interpretation if we consider a specific instance of the pattern rather than the pattern in general. For example, let's consider the rule in (107b), s $\to$ t / s ___. With this specific rule, we would have the following interpretation.

(111)   **Interpretation of (107b)**

$(s \to t / s$ ___$)^M$ is the function f that maps any (finite) string $x_1 x_2 \ldots x_n$ to the string $y_1 y_2 \ldots y_n$ such that for each index i that is greater than or equal to 1 and less than or equal to n ($1 \le i \le n$)...

(a)   If $x_i = s^M$ and $x_{(i-1)} = s^M$, then $y_i = t^M$.

(b)   Otherwise $y_i = x_i$.

The interpretation of this rule is a function that searches the input sequence for mental representations of s that appear to the right of another mental representation of s. In the output, it replaces these mental representations of s with mental representations of t. For all other members of the input sequence, the ones that either are not mental representations of s or do not appear after mental representations of s, the corresponding slot in the output is the same mental representation as the slot in the input.

By interpreting the rules as a specific function, there is no uncertainty about how the rule would apply to any input. This kind of interpretation specifies that a change in the mental representation occurs for any slot whose environment in the input string satisfies the conditions for replacement. So for example, if the input were *nusssu*, the output would be *nusttu*. In the input string, the environments for both the fourth and fifth position match the conditions for the structural change specified by the rule. No other position matches this environment, hence their values in the output string are the same as their values in the input string.

In general, due to the way we have specified the functional interpretation of the rules, it is the input string that determines the triggers for a structural change. Hence, changes that become part of the output do not figure into how the rule is applied. For example, if the input to the rule in (111a) is *nusssu*, the output cannot be *nustsu*. The fact that the middle *s* gets mapped to *t* does not change the fact that the third *s* still appears to the right of an *s* in the input. In other words, changes in values due to the application of the function to a specific position in the string will not affect how the segment change applies to other positions in the string. This is how our semantics implements *global* application of phonological rules. Let's reiterate that this is an arbitrary choice.

12.3   Optional: Sketch of an Alternative Semantics

We have assumed without argument that rules apply globally, and that *nusttu* is the correct output of the rule 's → t / s ___' applied to *nusssu*. We could have interpreted the rules differently. For example, we could have mapped the rules to a function that checks and changes the mental representations of the input string segment by segment from left to right, allowing changes on the left to affect the conditions for functional application to the right.

It might help you to understand our global application semantics if you compare it to a left-to-right application semantics. Let's provide such an interpretation for the rule 's → t / s ___'. To do so, we first need to specify a function that applies to a specific position in a given input. This can be done by defining a function that maps strings to strings but only potentially changes the jth position, where j is a number that is greater than or equal to 1 but less than or equal to the size of the input sequence.

(112)   Let f_j be the function that maps any (finite) string $x_1 x_2 \ldots x_n$ to the string $y_1 y_2 \ldots y_n$ such that for each index i that is greater than or equal to 1 and less than or equal to n $(1 \leq i \leq n) \ldots$

(a)   If $i = j$, $x_i = s^M$ and $x_{(i-1)} = s^M$, then $y_i = t^M$.

(b)   Otherwise, $y_i = x_i$.

This function will change the element in the jth position as long as that position is a mental representation of *s* that has another mental representation of *s* to its left. For example, given the input *nusssu*, the output of f_4(*nusssu*) would be *nustsu*. The fourth position satisfies the conditions for making the symbol change, hence the input differs from the output. Critically, all segments not in the fourth position are unchanged. In contrast, the output of f_3(*nusssu*) would be *nusssu*, the same as the input. The third position does not satisfy the conditions for making the replacement, hence there is no change to the sequence.

To apply this function one position at a time, we would first apply the function f_1 to the input. We would then apply the function f_2 to this result. Next, we would apply f_3 to that result. And so on and so forth until we apply the replacement rule to the last position — the nth position.

With respect to the notation for this segment-by-segment application, note that the function f_j that applies first will be farthest to the right (closest to the original input). The function that applies last will be the one that appears farthest to the left (farthest from the original input). For example, if f_1 applies to *nusssu* and then f_2 applies to its output, then this would be represented as $f_2(f_1($*nusssu*$))$.

With this in mind, consider the following possible interpretation for 's → t / s ___.'

(113)   **Left-to-Right Interpretation of (107b)**

(s → t / s ___)^M is the function that maps any (finite) string $x_1 x_2 \ldots x_n$ to the string $y_1 y_2 \ldots y_n$ such that
$$y_1 y_2 \ldots y_n = f_n(f_{(n-1)}(f_{(n-2)} \ldots f_1(x_1 x_2 \ldots x_n) \ldots)).$$

The use of the triple dots and the n and $n - 1$ in this semantic interpretation are needed since the function is sensitive to the size of the input (n represents this size). Applying the above rule, in the table below, consider the potential inputs on the left with their corresponding applications on the right.

Input	Functional Application
nus	$f_3(f_2(f_1(\text{nus})))$
nuss	$f_4(f_3(f_2(f_1(\text{nuss}))))$
nusss	$f_5(f_4(f_3(f_2(f_1(\text{nusss})))))$
nusssu	$f_6(f_5(f_4(f_3(f_2(f_1(\text{nusssu}))))))$

When the input has three positions in it, three different functions apply to it (first f_1, then f_2, and finally f_3). When it has four, four different functions apply to it (f_1 through f_4). The number of slots in the input determines how many f_j functions apply.

Critically, the result of applying this function to the input *nusssu* would not be *nusttu*. It would be $f_6(f_5(f_4(f_3(f_2(f_1(\textit{nusssu})))))) = \textit{nustsu}$: the result of applying the sound change to each position, starting with the first postion on the left and ending with the last position on the right.

Why would this be the end result? The application of f_1, f_2 and f_3 to the sequence would not change anything. The first, second, and third positions do not match the environment for making the replacement. However, the application of f_4 would change the sequence since it does match the environment. Thus $f_4(f_3(f_2(f_1(\textit{nusssu})))) = \textit{nustsu}$. Applying f_5 to this output would yield *nustsu* again. The function f_5 does not change the input since the fourth position is not a mental representation of s and hence the fifth position does not satisfy the conditions for making the replacement. The application of f_6 also does not affect the string. Hence, the final output would be *nustsu*.

This result is completely different from section 12.2, where the result was *nusttu*. So, which interpretation is better? Within the confines of this example, there is no answer. However, for natural languages in general, there is, although it requires some investigation. As an empirical fact, phonological functions might be more akin to the one presented in this section or the one presented in section 12.2. Or perhaps neither. The important point is that there is a fact of the matter. There is a way of interpreting phonological rules so that they more accurately reflect what is going on in the mind.

Notice the interesting position we have gotten ourselves into. In considering how to interpret the formal rule systems precisely, we are forced to contemplate subtle distinctions in interpretations which can yield different types of functional results. Now, a question naturally crops up: Is our original interpretation of SPE rules correct, or instead is this alternative the one that we employ in our head? This is an interesting empirical question that could potentially be answered with a careful investigation of language data, but it is a question that might have remained obscured with the vague rule statements we were considering before.

In later units, we return to this issue of whether rule environments are exclusively represented in the input sequence or whether they should be updated segment by segment: a change at one segment potentially affecting the environment for a subsequent segment. For now, however, it is sufficient to note that a formal interpretation of the rule systems forces us to be precise about the functions the rules represent. We will not be able to provide a semantics for each iteration of our SPE system, but we hope we have increased your appreciation of the complexity of phonological computation with our preliminary attempts.

Exercises

12.1. Provide a global application intepretation for this rule: b → v / a ___ o

12.2. Provide a global application intepretation for this rule: b → v / a ___ a

12.3. Provide a general global application semantics for rules of the form $\alpha \rightarrow \beta / \gamma$ ___ δ

Part IV

The Logic of Neutralization

Unit 13

Introducing Neutralization

13.1 Taking Stock

Let's take stock of where we are. We have introduced a basic formalism—a syntax and semantics—used to specify a set of rules that map input strings to output strings. The syntax for the rules defines the range and limits of what is a possible rule in our theory. The semantics provides a precise and unambiguous way of mapping the symbols we use in our phonological theory to mental functions and mental representations.

We have also outlined how our phonological system might be integrated into the grammatical system as a whole. We provided a partial model of our language faculty, consisting minimally of a lexicon and phonological rules.[1] We have described how phonological rules allow us to push the idea of sound-meaning correspondences beyond what is immediately apparent just from looking at the surface form of words. Recall the Paramecian examples of *pota* 'the foot' and *posi* 'some foot' from Unit 7, where we hypothesized that the underlying phonological representation of the morpheme 'foot' was *pot* and the underlying form for the word 'some foot' was *pot-i*. A phonological rule—one that changes *t* to *s* before *i*—derives the surface form.

It is important to keep in mind that our theory is not static. As we proceed, we will make additions and adjustments to either increase or restrict its expressibility to model the empirical data we encounter. Sometimes these changes will affect the syntax (thus modifying our definition of a possible rule); sometimes they will affect the semantics

---

[1] We have also made reference to a morphological component that concatenates morphemes, yielding the strings that serve as URs for the phonology.

(thus changing how we map our theoretical symbols to actual mental functions and mental representations). Another important issue, but one we will not treat in this book, is the manner and extent to which the phonological system interacts with other modules of grammar, like syntax and morphology. Like all scientific theories, our model of phonology is dynamic, constantly evolving, hopefully towards the truth.

We can once again invoke Goldilocks as we work toward this goal. If an empirically well-established phonological pattern cannot be captured by our rules, or on the contrary, if the theory expresses rules that are clearly beyond our human capacity, we will need to tweak the model, looking for a theory that is "just right." Typically, we don't expect to get the whole thing right at once, so we isolate subdomains of phonology where getting things "just right" is a feasible goal. Every time we get closer to the truth in phonology, we get a better understanding of how the mind works.

One matter that we have not yet addressed concerns our choices after we have done our preliminary segmentation analysis, namely how to determine which phonological rules are in operation and which lexical forms are stored underlyingly. So far we have not justified our choices. We have just provided input forms and rules that "work"—rules that derive the output that constitutes the given data. However, as we will see in the next few units, we can make principled choices using some basic tools of reasoning. We introduce such reasoning tools through our investigation of a phenomenon called *neutralization*. Neutralization is typically defined in terms of segments. If two segments, say p and q, can sometimes occur in the same phonologically defined position in a language, say, before o, the segments are said to *contrast*. If there are environments where only one of them, say p, can occur, and a rule is posited turning q to p in that environment, then it is said that the contrast between p and q is *neutralized* in that environment. A potentially more complicated situation occurs when there is an environment in which neither p nor q appears, but a third segment r appears, and the appearance of r is assumed to be derived by rule from p's and q's in URs.

We will continue to talk about "neutralization of a contrast between p and q," or just "neutralization of p and q." However, since we have developed a theory of rules as functions whose domains are strings of segments, not individual segments, we will end up redefining neutralization in terms of rules applying to strings of segments. Later, this treatment of neutralization will provide insight into complicated data patterns. In the meantime, we will go back and forth between the segment and string perspective, but this should not cause any confusion.

13.2 Neutralization: A Dataset

As an introduction to neutralization, let's use our methods of segmentation to analyze the Yersinian dataset in (114).

(114) Yersinian

	Form	Meaning
a.	naču	'a dog'
b.	nači	'the dog'
c.	naku	'a hat'
d.	nači	'the hat'
e.	padu	'a foot'
f.	padi	'the foot'

By comparing [naču] and [nači], we can conclude that *nač* is the phonological representation of the morpheme meaning 'dog'. By comparing [padu] and [padi], we can conclude that *pad* is the form for the morpheme meaning 'foot'. By subtracting *nač* from [nači] and *pad* from [padi], we can conclude that *-i* is the form for the definite morpheme (meaning 'the'). Similarly, by subtracting *nač* from [naču] and *pad* from [padu], we can conclude that *-u* is the form of the indefinite morpheme (meaning 'a').

(115)   Some underlying representations (URs) for lexical items

a. *nač* is the UR for the lexical item meaning 'dog'

b. *pad* is the UR for the lexical item meaning 'foot'

c. *-i* is the UR for the lexical item meaning 'the'

d. *-u* is the UR for the lexical item meaning 'a'

So far, the segmentation methods are not yielding any inconsistencies. However, turning our attention to the morpheme meaning 'hat', things get a bit more difficult. By subtracting *i* from [nači], we can conclude that *nač* is the form for the morpheme meaning 'hat'. However, by subtracting *u* from [naku] we can also conclude that *nak* is the form of the morpheme meaning 'hat'.

(116)   Potential Contradiction

• *nač* is the UR for the lexical item meaning 'hat' (Subtraction of *-i*)

• *nak* is the UR for the lexical item meaning 'hat' (Subtraction of *-u*)

As mentioned in Unit 7, it is possible that there are two different lexical items that happen to have the same meaning, 'hat'. However, it is also possible that there is just one lexical item meaning 'hat'. The surface variation could be due to a phonological rule. If the latter explanation is right, a question arises as to which form is the correct underlying representation of the morpheme in the lexicon: *nač* or *nak*? This question of course entails a complementary one: What is the phonological rule at work here? Here are two obvious choices:

(117)   Two possible rules

      a. č → k / ___ u

      b. k → č / ___ i

Rule (a) says that *č* and *k* neutralize to *k* before *u*. Rule (b) says that *č* and *k* neutralize to *č* before *i*. Is there a way to determine which option is better?

In the next unit, we will argue that in such cases there is a simple method to determine which rule to posit, (117a) or (117b). The argument involves a standard type of reasoning we will refer to by the Latin name *modus tollendo ponens*. Such reasoning, when combined with another form of argument called *reductio ad absurdum*, proves to be a powerful tool for analyzing phonological patterns.

Unit 14

Choosing Lexical Forms

14.1   Implicit Assumptions

There are some implicit assumptions among phonologists about how to posit the underlying phonological representation of a morpheme. We typically make use of these assumptions as heuristics when we propose an analysis, and we also tend to assume that children apply similar reasoning in the course of language acquisition. Although we will ultimately have to reject these assumptions, for now it will be useful to outline how they work and why they are helpful.

The first assumption is often invoked in cases where our segmentation methods—comparison and subtraction—yield a single surface form of a morpheme:

(118)   **Non-alternation Assumption** (NAA). If there is one surface form of a morpheme in all environments, then the phonological representation of the lexical item is identical to that form.

To illustrate, recall the Yersinian data in (114), repeated here:

119

(119)   Yersinian (again)

	Form	Meaning
a.	nač̌u	'a dog'
b.	nači	'the dog'
c.	naku	'a hat'
d.	nači	'the hat'
e.	padu	'a foot'
f.	padi	'the foot'

Using our segmentation methods, we discovered only one form for the indefinite and definite markers, namely *-u* and *-i*, respectively. The non-alternation assumption tells us to posit in the lexicon a phonological representation consisting of just /-u/ for the indefinite morpheme and a phonological representation consisting of just /-i/ for the definite morpheme. The same reasoning applies to the lexical form of the morpheme meaning 'dog'. There is a single form *nač* that occurs in all surface forms and as a result, the non-alternation assumption tells us to posit the phonological representation /nač/.

The non-alternation assumption will not help us in the case of the morpheme meaning 'hat' since there are two alternants: [nak] and [nač]. In such cases, we will invoke a second assumption, the *surfacing lexical form assumption*:

(120)   **Surfacing Lexical Form Assumption** (SLFA). If there is more than one surface form, then the phonological representation of the lexical item is identical to one of those forms.

Since the meaning 'hat' corresponds to the two surface alternants—[nak] and [nač]—the surfacing lexical form assumption tells us that the underlying phonological representation must be *either* /nak/ or /nač/.

The careful reader will have noticed that our two assumptions are not independent. In fact, the non-alternation assumption (NAA) is just a special case of the surfacing lexical form assumption (SLFA): if the SLFA tells us that the lexical form must be identical to one of the surface forms, then when there is just a single surface form, that form will have to be chosen as the lexical form. We don't actually need the NAA as a separate assumption. However, we will continue to refer to the NAA for convenience, as a shorthand for "SLFA applies, but the choice is trivial since there is only one surface form."

It should be noted that the SLFA is not a logical necessity, which is fortunate, since we will eventually reject it in later units. However, it at least has the virtue of being simple enough to state explicitly. It will turn out to be a useful *heuristic*, a guide to making preliminary hypotheses that are subject to revision.

14.2   Modus Tollendo Ponens (MTP)

Working under these two assumptions, we still need to choose between /nak/ and /nač/ with respect to the morpheme meaning 'hat'. You should be warned from the outset to resist the temptation to choose /nak/ on the basis that it is different from /nač/, the underlying form of the morpheme meaning 'dog'. This is faulty reasoning. Although our methods of segmentation attempt to reduce each meaning to one underlying form, this does not mean that each segment sequence is uniquely associated with one meaning. Homophones are not only allowed, but are attested in many languages including English (e.g., the morpheme that is used to refer to the wooden stick in baseball games has the same lexical form as the morpheme used to refer to flying mammals, namely /bæt/). Furthermore, grammars can't be "allergic" to homophones, since the rules of phonology sometimes create identical SRs that derive from non-identical URs, via neutralization. In our dataset above, the words meaning 'the dog' and 'the hat' have the same surface form: [nači], but we will end up positing different URs for the two meanings.

As we will see, the conclusion that 'hat' should have the lexical form /nak/ *is* indeed correct, but not for the avoidance of homophony. The correct reasons lie rather with the establishment of our two hypotheses and the application of modus tollendo ponens or MTP for short. MTP is a valid form of reasoning that allows us to reason from an *or*-statement to a conclusion based on one member of that *or*-statement. The details are as follows.

(121)   **Modus Tollendo Ponens (MTP)**
For any two propositions p and q, if (p or q) is true and p is false, then it can be concluded that q is true.

Intuitively, this form of argument is easy to follow. If you know that it is true that either John is at school or he is at home but you also know that he is not at school, then you can validly conclude that he is at home. You can see that it does not matter which part you use as p and which as q—the order of elements in an *or*-statement does not matter. In other words, 'p or q' is equivalent to 'q or p'.

To establish a conclusion based on MTP, one only needs to construct a true *or*-statement and then demonstrate that one part of the *or*-statement (one of the *disjuncts*) is false. Luckily for us, we already have an *or*-statement in place, one that follows from the surfacing lexical form assumption.

(122) **Premise 1**: Either the phonological form of the morpheme meaning 'hat' is /nač/ or it is /nak/.

With this premise in place, the next step is to demonstrate that one part of the *or*-statement is false.

In the example above, we supposed that we knew that John was not at school, that it was false that he was at school. There are many ways in which we could have come to this conclusion. Maybe the school was locked and all the students had been sent home; maybe his teacher told us that he had left; maybe we had seen surveillance video showing him leaving. There are many ways to know that a statement is false, many of which involve the kinds of observations just mentioned. However, the phonological form of a lexical item stored in someone's brain is not accessible to direct observation using current neuroscientific methods, so we need to be clever to show that one part of our MTP statement is false. We will rely on an indirect method of reasoning called *reductio ad absurdum* (RAA), which is a valid form of reasoning in most logical systems:

(123) **Reductio Ad Absurdum (RAA)**
        For any proposition p, if assuming that p is true leads to a contradiction, then it can be concluded that p is false.

As with MTP, this form of reasoning is fairly intuitive. For example, let's say you assume that John is allergic to peanuts and you reason that if he ate peanuts he would have difficulty breathing, because everyone who is allergic to peanuts has difficulty breathing if they eat peanuts. But you see him eating peanuts and he is not wheezing. You can then conclude that he is not allergic to peanuts, contrary to your initial assumption. The initial assumption can't be true.

In our phonological case, we want to show that it is *false* that the phonological form of the morpheme meaning 'hat' is /nač/. To use RAA, we need to see what the consequences would be of assuming that something we think is false were true. So let's begin by assuming that it is *true* that the phonological form of the morpheme meaning 'hat' *is* /nač/. We can now reason as follows:

(124) Since /nač/ is (by assumption) the lexical representation of the morpheme meaning 'hat', we need the phonology to generate the alternant [nak]. In other words, we need a rule that turns *č* into *k* when it occurs before the segment *u*: we need a rule 'č → k / ___ u'. But it was already established that the

underlying phonological representation of the morpheme meaning 'dog' was /nač/ (by the non-alternation assumption in (118)). If this phonological rule were part of the grammar, then the surface form of the word meaning 'a dog' should be [naku]. But it is not. It is [naču]. Thus, assuming that the underlying form for 'hat' is /nač/ leads to a contradiction.

(125) **Premise 2 / Conclusion of RAA**: The assertion that the phonological form of the morpheme meaning 'hat' is /nač/ is false.

Taking Premise 1 and Premise 2 together and applying MTP, we get the following conclusion.

(126) **Conclusion of MTP**: The phonological form of the morpheme meaning 'hat' is /nak/.

From this, we can also conclude that the phonology must generate the alternant [nač] and hence that there must be a rule that turns k into $č$ when it occurs before i: formally $k \rightarrow č /$ ___ i.

Let's reiterate that RAA is just one method of arguing that something is false. If some future neuroscientist could determine by observing brain tissue that it is false that the phonological form of the morpheme meaning 'hat' is /nač/, then that neuroscientist could perform MTP reasoning without using RAA.

Another way to summarize the reasoning we used is this: The lexical form for 'dog' is /nač/. The lexical form for 'hat' is either /nak/ or /nač/, but it can't be /nač/ since the lexical form for 'dog' is also /nač/ and the two forms behave differently in the context of the indefinite suffix -*u*; one shows up as [naču], the other as [naku]. So the lexical form for 'hat' must be /nak/.

The combination of RAA and MTP provides us with the tools to make a principled choice between two phonological hypotheses. This form of reasoning is completely general, and should apply whenever there is a case of neutralization: a case where there is a single surface form that relates to two different underlying forms.

Let's reiterate that we did *not* appeal to functionalist reasoning to choose the underlying form for 'hat': we did not insist that the form must be /nak/ in order to avoid homophony. The rule that turns k to $č$ creates homophony in the definite forms; however, there is no reason to think that grammars "care about" avoiding homophony. In our (made up but realistic) example of Yersinian, the grammar generates surface homophony from distinct inputs.

It is also important to note that it is not enough to show that positing /nak/ for 'hat' and a '$k \rightarrow č$' rule works to generate the forms for 'hat', and does not lead to problems in forms for 'dog'. We also need to show that the alternative allowed by SLFA (i.e., positing /nač/ as the underlying form) does not work for the complete dataset. In brief, our aim is not just to find a solution that works, but, if possible, to find the *only* solution that works, given our assumptions.

14.3   Presenting a Phonological Solution

To keep track of your analysis of phonological datasets, it will be useful to follow a certain format in presenting a solution. Consider following our example presentation for Yersinian in (127). It is important not to skip steps in presenting an analysis. Students often resist taking the time to list the surface alternants for each morpheme, as we do in part A of the solution. Students tend to jump immediately into an analysis with rules before making it clear what the facts are that the analysis is to account for.[1] Sometimes, your initial hypotheses concerning the alternants may require revision as you work through a problem, because the subtraction and comparison methods are not foolproof.

(127)   Sample presentation for Yersinian

	Form	Meaning
a.	naču	'a dog'
b.	nači	'the dog'
c.	naku	'a hat'
d.	nači	'the hat'
e.	padu	'a foot'
f.	padi	'the foot'

A.   Morpheme alternants

- 'dog': nač
- 'hat': nak, nač
- 'foot': pad
- 'a': u
- 'the': i

---

[1]To encourage you, we appeal to your basest instincts: your teacher will probably give you partial credit for listing the morpheme alternants, typically an easy task, even if your subsequent analysis is misguided.

B. Lexical representation for each morpheme.

- 'dog': nač (by NAA)
- 'hat': nak (by SLFA, MTP, and RAA)
- 'foot': pad (by NAA)
- 'a': u (by NAA)
- 'the': i (by NAA)

C. Phonological rule: $k \rightarrow \check{c}$ / ___ i

D. Justification: The lexical form for 'dog' is /nač/. The lexical form for 'hat' is either /nak/ or /nač/, but it can't be /nač/ since the lexical form for 'dog' has to be /nač/ by NAA and the two *nač* forms behave differently when followed by *u*—one shows up as [naču] the other as [naku]. There is clearly no rule turning *č* to *k*, so the lexical form for 'hat' must be /nak/, and there must be a rule turning *k* to *č*.

E. Underlying representations and derivations for each word

UR	nač-u	nač-i
Effect of Rule	—	—
SR	naču	nači
Gloss	'a dog'	'the dog'

UR	nak-u	nak-i
Effect of Rule	—	nači
SR	naku	nači
Gloss	'a hat'	'the hat'

UR	pad-u	pad-i
Effect of Rule	—	—
SR	padu	padi
Gloss	'a foot'	'the foot'

F.   Comments: As derivations get more complex, you might want to include some comments here, like "The SRs for 'the dog' and 'the hat' are homophonous due to the neutralization of k and $č$ to $č$ before i."

In part B, it can be useful to briefly indicate the assumptions and forms of reasoning you used, as we have done here.

In part C, unless instructed otherwise, you should formulate the rule *in the most general form* that is compatible with the data. Given our limited Yersinian data, both rules in (128) will generate the desired result, but rule (a) is more general than rule (b).

(128)   Two rules that work for Yersinian

      a. $k \rightarrow č$ / ___ i

      b. $k \rightarrow č$ / a ___ i

There are arguments favoring each of these choices. Traditionally phonologists have favored choice (a), but they tend to be inconsistent in applying the principle of being as general as possible. In contrast, Hale and Reiss (2008) argue that acquisition considerations potentially favor (b), the idea being that child learners make the narrowest hypothesis compatible with the data, and expand, by loosening restrictions, only when new evidence allows them to do so. New data, like a paradigm *ziku* 'a plum', *ziči* 'the plum', would allow us to select (128a) over (128b) for Yersinian. Despite these complex issues, we encourage you in this book to follow the traditional approach by specifying as little as possible in the rule, under the premise that the dataset is complete in all relevant aspects.

In part D, we provide a summary of the reasoning used. As we have shown, the choice of lexical representations and the choice of rule are intimately related. You should discuss these in tandem in your justification of the analysis. In this example, we used a snippet from the discussion above.

Besides writing the SR in the appropriate box, it is *crucial* to provide the gloss. Here's why—we are looking at a lot of neutralization rules and these can generate homophones from distinct URs. We need to see which of the two words pronounced *nači* a given derivation corresponds to, for example. We need to see that the UR contains the right morphemes and that the rules are applied appropriately for the relevant derivation. This example will help you structure your solutions and keep track of your reasoning.

Exercises

In writing up phonological solutions, you are required to be as explicit as possible about the assumptions you are making and the kind of reasoning you are using in trying to convince a skeptical reader (your professor, peers, and colleagues) that your analysis is right, or at least on the right track. As a result, we believe that writing up phonology solutions will help you develop transportable skills for clear, persuasive writing in all domains, so you should embrace this aspect of your assignments.

For each dataset below, provide an analysis using the format specified in the previous section. For the first dataset, we have provided a skeleton for your answer. The same format should be used for the other datasets as well.

14.1. Martian Language

	form	gloss
a.	naka	'a dog'
b.	nači	'the dog'
c.	naka	'a hat'
d.	naki	'the hat'

  A. List all morpheme alternants

    a. 'dog':

    b. 'hat':

    c. 'a':

    d. 'the':

  B. Choose an underlying lexical representation for each morpheme:

    a. 'dog':

    b. 'hat':

    c. 'a':

    d. 'the':

  C. Posit a phonological rule:

  D. Justification:

E. Underlying representation and derivations for each word:

UR				
Rule				
SR	naka	nači	naka	naki
Gloss	'a dog'			

F. Comments:

14.2. Plutonian Language

	form	gloss
a.	pakus	'a dog'
b.	pagon	'the dog'
c.	pakus	'a hat'
d.	pakon	'the hat'

14.3. Uranian Language

	form	gloss
a.	pakus	'a dog'
b.	pagon	'the dog'
c.	pagus	'a hat'
d.	pagon	'the hat'

14.4. Venusian Language

	form	gloss
a.	torun	'a dog'
b.	tola	'the dog'
c.	torun	'a hat'
d.	tora	'the hat'

14.5. Saturnal Language

	form	gloss
a.	torun	'a dog'
b.	tola	'the dog'
c.	tolun	'a hat'
d.	tola	'the hat'

14.6. Now make up examples of your own using prefixes, instead of suffixes. Provide solutions to the problems you make up. Hint: You can just reverse the words of some of the datasets above to get started. You should try to make some problems in which the prefix or suffix has more than one alternant, and some in which the alternations show up on roots. For a challenge, you can make up some datasets where alternations show up both on roots and on affixes, as in Exercise 6 in Unit 7.

Unit 15

Nothing I:
No Morpheme versus
No Phonology in a Morpheme

This unit is the first of several that discuss various notions of *nothing* that are relevant to phonology. We start by introducing the possibility of morphemes—lexical entries—that have no phonological content. This is an old idea that is treated in depth by Benveniste (1966).

Consider the following forms in English,[1] given in orthography:

(129)   English singular and plural

	SG	PL
a.	*cup*	*cups*
b.	*pup*	*pups*
c.	*rat*	*rats*
d.	*mat*	*mats*

It seems reasonable to assume that the word *cups* has two parts, one at the beginning, with the form *cup* that seems to express the concept CUP, whatever that is, and another, at the end, that has the form *s* and seems to express the concept PLURAL, whatever

---

[1] As in every other language we cite, the usual disclaimers apply: English doesn't exist in any useful sense for scientific purposes. However, it gets pretty tedious using locutions like "English-type grammars."

that is. The other plural words would be analyzed in the same way by pretty much any person without any training in linguistics, and even linguists would have a hard time arguing with the analysis.

Things get more complex, however, when we look at the singular forms (even though singular forms look morphologically simple, not complex). Does the word *cup* consist of a single morpheme with the form *cup*[2] or is there a morpheme that expresses the concept SINGULAR in this word? The average person would probably not worry about the answer, and would consider the question to be uninteresting and pointless.

However, linguists do worry about such things, and we have reason to be a bit insecure about our judgement—like Socrates, the little knowledge we have lets us understand how far we are from being truly wise. Let's see if we can sow the seeds of Socratic self-doubt in you.

We linguists know about languages like Southern Barasano in (130):

(130) Southern Barasano singular and plural

	SG	PL	gloss
a.	kahea	kahe	'eye'
b.	bitia	biti	'bead'

In Southern Barasano, singular nouns have overt evidence of an additional morpheme, whereas the plural nouns look like they might contain only a root morpheme with a meaning like 'eye', 'bead', and so on.[3]

We also know about Swahili, which offers contrasts like the ones in (131):

(131) Swahili singular and plural

	SG	PL	gloss
a.	mtoto	watoto	'child'
b.	mtu	watu	'person'

Swahili singular nouns appear to have a prefix *m-* followed by a root such as *toto*, whereas plural nouns appear to have a prefix *wa-*.[4]

---

[2]The issue is not one of using a phonetic alphabet versus orthography—replace every token of *cup* (except for those in small capital letters) on this page with $k\Lambda p$ or $k^h\partial p$ or whatever you like, and the same questions arise.

[3]So much for the idea of *iconicity*, which would suggest that since plurals denote 'more' than singulars, they should have more phonological content. Such notions, attractive to the layperson, never end up providing insight into the nature of grammar. This undermining of "common sense" happens in all sciences.

[4]This is a tremendous simplification. Swahili has various noun classes with a range of singular and plural prefixes. These complexities do not affect our point that both singular and plural can be marked by overt morphemes.

Southern Barasano shows us that the singular can be marked overtly, and Swahili shows us that both singular and plural can be marked overtly. Pondering these facts, a linguist might wonder if singular nouns might actually be marked as such in *all* languages. Consider the sentence *The dog-catcher chased a dog*: the first token of *dog*, in *dog-catcher*, doesn't seem to contain the concept SINGULAR, since the word seems to mean something like 'person who regularly engages in catching dogs'. We may talk about a particularly obsessive dog-catcher who always pursues the same single dog, but that is not part of the meaning of *dog-catcher*. In contrast, the second token of *dog* in our sentence seems to be truly singular, so it is not implausible that this token of the surface form *dog* derives from a combination of morphemes, one of which has the semantic representation SINGULAR.

Fortunately, we don't need to solve this issue in a phonology book—it is a matter for syntacticians, semanticists, and morphologists to hammer out. They are still working on it.[5] We just want to introduce the idea that English, for example, might have a singular morpheme in words like *dog*.

Using our schematic diagram for morphemes, we can represent the singular morpheme of Southern Barasano as in (132), with informal descriptions of the content of each representation:

(132)   The singular morpheme in Southern Barasano.

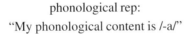
phonological rep:
"My phonological content is /-a/"

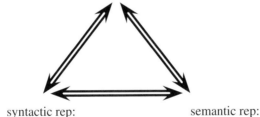

syntactic rep: semantic rep:
"I combine with nouns."   "I mean SINGULAR"

Typically, linguists would refer to the element in question as "the Southern Barasano morpheme /-a/". In other words, we use the phonological part of the morpheme as a

---

[5]See Link (1983); Krifka et al. (1995); Krifka (1987); Chierchia (1998); Harbour (2003); Sauerland (2003); Sauerland et al. (2005); Spector (2007); Bale (2009); Bale et al. (2011) and references therein.

label for the triplet of information. Of course, if there are homophonous morphemes with different semantics or syntax, we have to be more explicit. We see this in English when we refer to the "plural -*s*" as opposed to the "third person singular present verb suffix -*s*", the "reduced copula '*s*", and the "possessive -*s*", as in the following examples:

(133)   Four -*s* morphemes of English

      a.   Noun Plural: *The cats are playing.*

      b.   Verb suffix: *John walks to school each day.*

      c.   Copula: *Kate's an economist.*

      d.   Possessive: *Mike's son is painting the fence.*

Phonologically, the four suffixes are the same, but there are four distinct meanings, so there are four distinct morphemes. In this example, we have used orthographic representation, partly because of complications with this aspect of English, which we take up in Unit 60.

    Returning to singulars, we must consider the possibility that English has the morpheme shown in (134) that is *almost* identical to the singular marker of Southern Barasano:

(134)   The singular morpheme in English.

phonological rep:

"I have no phonological content"

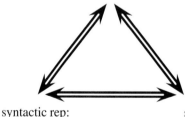

syntactic rep: semantic rep:

"I combine with nouns."   "I mean SINGULAR"

The difference between the two singular markers is that while the one in Southern Barasano has the phonological form /-a/, the one in English has no phonological form. Now, it is possible that the singular morpheme in English is not a suffix but rather a prefix, but we won't worry about that since it has no phonology to contribute to the UR of forms that it is part of.

Recall that when we introduced derivation tables in section 7.4, we decided to include hyphens to mark morpheme boundaries, even though this information is invisible to the phonology. We did that as a shortcut that allowed us to present the output of morphology and the input to phonology in a single structure. This issue takes on special importance here since we now have morphemes that have no phonological content at all.

In order to maintain our practice of showing the morphemes that enter into a UR, we can denote phonologically null morphemes with the symbol ∅. This symbol is only slightly different from the empty set symbol ∅ we use when discussing set theory, but the context should be clear enough to avoid any confusion, and you shouldn't feel obligated to keep them apart in your written assignments.

Let's make a few assumptions so that we can illustrate some issues that you need to be aware of. Let's assume that English has a SINGULAR morpheme with no phonological content, which we refer to as ∅. Of course, Southern Barasano also has a morpheme that we refer to as ∅, but that has the meaning PLURAL. Let's also assume, although it is kind of a strange thing to do, that the English ∅ under discussion is a suffix. Then we might represent the output of the morphology for the English word *dog* as /dɑg-∅/.

The only part of this form relevant to the *phonology*, under our current assumptions, is the string of phonological segments: /dɑg/. Given our discussion above, the word *dog-catcher* would *not* contain the morpheme ∅, since it does not mean 'catcher of one dog'.

There are many other arguments for phonologically null morphemes, depending on one's views of the lexicon, and agreement in morphology and syntax. For example, if you have a theory of binding of anaphors (reflexives like *herself* and *yourself*) that requires that an anaphor agree with its antecedent, then you might require a phonologically null plural morpheme on the subject in (135b) to agree with the plural form of the anaphor.

(135)   How many 2 PERSON pronouns in English?

     a.   You shot your**self** in the foot.

     b.   You shot your**selves** in the foot.

Of course, the question of whether there is a phonologically null singular morpheme on the anaphor in (135a) also arises. Fortunately, phonologists do not have to answer these questions.

If you feel strongly about the presence of a SINGULAR morpheme in the word *dog* in English, or the existence of any other phonologically null morpheme, you might

want to show that in your UR if you are generally showing which morphemes compose each word. The issue becomes important when we start talking about another
kind of *nothing* in the next unit, the nothing which follows the last segment in a word
or precedes the first segment in a word. In a nutshell, the only important point is that
whether you write /dɑɡ-∅/ or /dɑɡ/ as your UR, the segment ɡ is *at the end of the word*,
phonologically. It is the last segment in the word, and (for now) the only representations our phonological model cares about are strings of segments.

Unit 16

Nothing II: Enhancing Rule Environments for Nothing

16.1   Before and After Nothing

Modus tollendo ponens (MTP) provides us with a method for justifying a choice between two potential underlying forms. In this section, we will demonstrate how such reasoning also pushes us to change the type of symbols we use in specifying our environments for phonological rules. Thus far, we have assumed that the environment of a rule can be a single segment to the left and/or right of the target of the change. We will now discover that this assumption is too weak. Sometimes the trigger is not a segment at all.

We begin with the Chlorobian data in (136).

(136)   Chlorobian

	Form	Meaning
a.	nak	'a dog'
b.	nake	'the dog'
c.	nak	'a hat'
d.	nage	'the hat'
e.	git	'a foot'
f.	gite	'the foot'

In analyzing this data, we will make use of the idea introduced in the previous unit that there can be morphemes with no phonological content, which we refer to as ∅. With this in mind, we can provide the following segmentation analysis using our comparison method.

- By comparing [nak] with [nake], we can conclude that *nak* is the phonological representation for the morpheme meaning 'dog'.

- By comparing [git] with [gite], we can conclude that *git* is the phonological representation for the morpheme meaning 'foot'.

- By comparing [gite], [nake], and [nage], we can conclude that *e* is the phonological representation for the definite morpheme meaning 'the'.

We can also provide further analysis using our subtraction method.

- By subtracting the forms of the morphemes meaning 'dog' and 'foot', namely *nak* and *git*, from the forms of the words meaning 'a dog' and 'a foot', again *nak* and *git*, we can conclude that the phonological form for the indefinite morpheme meaning 'a' does not contain any segment. Thus, it is represented as ∅.

So far, there are no inconsistencies in our segmentation. This all changes when we focus our attention on the morpheme meaning 'hat'.

- By subtracting the indefinite morpheme (which has no phonological content) from the surface form for the word meaning 'a hat', namely [nak], we can conclude that *nak* is the phonological representation for the morpheme meaning 'hat.'

- By subtracting *e* from [nage], we can conclude that *nag* is the phonological representation of the morpheme meaning 'hat'.

After segmentation we have two potential phonological representations for the morpheme meaning 'hat': *nak* and *nag*. Correspondingly, there are two potential phonological rules: one that turns *k* into *g* and another that turns *g* into *k*.

Such observations, along with the *surfacing lexical form assumption*, leads to the *or*-statement in **Premise 1**:

(137) **Premise 1**: Either the phonological representation of the morpheme for 'hat' is /nak/ or it is /nag/.

Let's consider whether it is possible for the proposition in the first half of **Premise 1** to be true. In other words, could *nak* be the underlying form of 'hat'? As the following reasoning demonstrates, it cannot be.

(138) **Reductio ad absurdum (RAA)**: Suppose that *nak* is the underlying form of the morpheme meaning 'hat'. If it is, then there must be a phonological rule that produces the surface alternant *nag*. The rule must change *k* to *g* when it appears before the segment *e* (the definite marker): stated formally, k → g / ___ e. However, if this rule were in effect, then the surface form of the word meaning 'the dog' should be *nage*. But it is not. It is *nake*. We have reached a contradiction.

(139) **Premise 2—Conclusion of RAA**: The underlying form of the morpheme meaning 'hat' is NOT *nak*.

By application of MTP using Premises 1 and 2, we can reach the following conclusion.

(140) **Conclusion of MTP**: The phonological representation of the morpheme meaning 'hat' is /nag/.

Since the underlying form is *nag*, there must be a phonological rule that derives the surface form *nak* 'a hat'. However, what could this rule be? We are presently assuming that the changes reflected in our rules are triggered by the segments on the left or on the right of the rule target. In the case of *nak* vs. *nage* the segment on the left of *g* and *k* is the same. Thus, this segment cannot condition the change. In contrast, the environment to the right is different, but the difference is one of absence vs. presence of an *e*. The presence of *e* cannot trigger any structural changes since *nake* maintains the underlying form of 'dog'. This means that the absence of *e* must trigger the change. Yet, how can this be? The way we formally defined phonological rule syntax, the segment variables γ and δ must take values from the set ENV (the set of environment symbols) . Only these segments can trigger a change, and all of those elements are symbols for sound segments, not symbols for their absence.

16.2   Expanding Rule Environments

If we used natural language to express our rules, the change from underlying representations to surface representations would be easy enough to state. An example is given in (141).

(141)   The segment *g* becomes *k* when there is no segment to its right.

This is a common type of rule cross-linguistically. Our current problem is that our formal language is unable to express this rule. Recall our specification of the syntax of rules from 10.3, repeated below.

(142) **SPE rules**

Let SEG be the set of segment symbols. Let ENV be the set of symbols that specify the environment. Let α and β be any member of SEG. Let γ and δ be any member of ENV. The following are possible rules.

a. $\alpha \rightarrow \beta \,/$ ___ γ

b. $\alpha \rightarrow \beta \,/\, \gamma$ ___

c. $\alpha \rightarrow \beta \,/\, \gamma$ ___ δ

Nothing else is a possible rule.

According to this syntax, only members of ENV can serve as triggers. Thus far, we have only discussed examples where the set SEG is identical to ENV, both containing all and only the IPA symbols. In order to express rules like those in (142), IPA symbols will not be sufficient.

In this Goldilocks moment, one way to increase the power of the rule system, to increase expressibility, is to add a symbol to ENV that signifies the beginning and end of a word. You can think of it as a word boundary symbol, a symbol that appears between consecutive words in a sentence. There is a long phonological tradition that uses the symbol '#' for this purpose. In this tradition, the string #b denotes a b at the beginning of a word—a b preceded by no segment. Similarly, the string b# denotes a b at the end of a word—a b followed by no segment. For reasons related to other work of ours, but not justified here, we will distinguish these two possibilities by using '#' for the word-initial symbol, and '%' for the word-final symbol.

Now, although SEG will still be the set of IPA symbols, ENV will be the set of IPA symbols with the addition of '#' and '%':

(143) Revising ENV:

- SEG = IPA

- ENV = IPA $\cup$ {#,%}

Such an addition will allow us to state rules like the ones in (144). To help get an intuitive sense of what the rules mean, we have provided several English paraphrases.

(144)   Paraphrasing Rules

    a.   t → d / # ___

        • '*t* becomes *d* at the beginning of a word'
        • '*t* becomes *d* in word-initial position'
        • '*t* becomes *d* word-initially'

    b.   t → n / ___ %

        • '*t* becomes *n* at the end of a word'
        • '*t* becomes *n* in word-final position'
        • '*t* becomes *n* word-finally'

    c.   a → e / # ___ %

        • '*a* becomes *e* when it is both word-initial and word-final'
        • '*a* becomes *e* when it is the only segment in the word'

    d.   s → ʃ / # ___ u

        • 'word-initial *s* becomes *ʃ* before *u*'
        • '*s* becomes *ʃ* word-initially before *u*'

    e.   l → r / o ___ %

        • 'word-final *l* becomes *r* after *o*'
        • '*l* becomes *r* word-finally after *o*'

Note, for example, that '#' marks the beginning of the word, but we say that the symbol that follows '#' is 'in word-initial position' or occurs 'word-initially' or 'at the beginning of the word'. The terms *word-initial* and *word-final* are adjectives that refer to segments occurring next to '#' and '%', respectively.

Note also that phrases like "word-final *l*" in (144e), refer to the *input* to the rule. In the *output*, there is no word-final *l* anymore—instead there is word-final *r*. Make sure you understand these examples; things will become more complicated when we talk about insertion and deletion rules in the next unit.

Returning to our Chlorobian dataset, we need the rule in (145):

(145)   g → k / ___ %

This rule states that *g* becomes *k* when there is no segment to its right, that is, when *g* occurs at the end of a word. This is the rule we need in order to maintain the hypothesis that *nag* is the underlying form of the morpheme meaning 'hat', a hypothesis that was logically motivated by the paradigms in (136).

Here is an analysis of this language with derivations of all six surface forms:

(146)   Analysis of Chlorobian

1.   Data

	Form	Meaning
a.	nak	'a dog'
b.	nake	'the dog'
c.	nak	'a hat'
d.	nage	'the hat'
e.	git	'a foot'
f.	gite	'the foot'

2.   Morpheme alternants

   * 'dog': nak
   * 'hat': nak, nag
   * 'foot': git
   * 'a': ∅
   * 'the': e

3.   Underlying lexical representation for each morpheme:

   * 'dog': nak (by NAA)
   * 'hat': nag (by SLFA, MTP and RAA)
   * 'foot': git (by NAA)
   * 'a': ∅ (by NAA)
   * 'the': e (by NAA)

4.   Phonological rule: $g \rightarrow k /$ ___ %

5.   Underlying representations and derivations (see discussion below)

UR	nak	nak-e	nag	nag-e
Rule: $g \rightarrow k /$ ___ %	—	—	nak	
SR	nak	nake	nak	nage
Gloss	'a dog'	'the dog'	'a hat'	'the hat'

UR	git	git-e
Rule: g → k / ___ %	—	—
SR	git	gite
Gloss	'a foot'	'the foot'

These derivation tables are tools for us linguists to understand how phonology works, so we can put into them whatever we find helpful. As we mentioned in the previous unit, we could write *nak-∅, nag-∅, git-∅* as the URs for 'a dog', 'a hat', 'a foot', respectively, if we wanted to show that we think the forms contain a singular morpheme. However, even if we did that, it would still be the case that the *k, g, t* segments would be in word final position in those words. The phonologically null morphemes play no role in the phonology.

Leaving that issue aside, you may be wondering why we did not include the word boundary symbols in the URs, for example, *#nak%, #nak-e%* for 'a dog' and 'the dog'. This is a good question, since we have just proposed rules that can make reference to these symbols. We address this issue in the next section.

16.3   Interpreting the Environment

By adding new symbols, we can now state rules for cases in which the target segment is at the beginning or end of a word. However, it is not enough that we can state this new type of rule; we also must be able to interpret it. Such an interpretation will tell us what consequences the new symbol has for our mental representations.

There are two ways that this type of rule can be interpreted. One way treats the new symbols *syncategorematically*. In other words, although the new symbols influence how the rule is interpreted, there is no need to introduce a new type of mental representation. The other way treats the symbols *categorematically*, meaning that the new symbols directly relate to a new kind of mental representation. We discuss each type of interpretation below.

The syncategorematic treatment of the '#' and '%' symbols requires at least two new interpretation rules. These rules change the target segments that appear at the beginning or end of the input strings. Recall that the beginning of the input string is represented by the variable x_1, whereas the end is represented by x_n (see 12.2). Correspondingly, the beginning of the output string is represented by y_1, whereas the end is represented by y_n. Consider the following interpretation rules using a syncategorematic treatment of the word boundary symbols.

(147)   **Syncategorematic interpretation of the pattern**
$\alpha \to \beta / \underline{\quad} \%$

> If α and β, are members of SEG and $\%$ is a member of ENV, then $(\alpha \to \beta / \underline{\quad} \%)^M$ is the function f (a member of F) that maps any (finite) string of mental representations $x_1 x_2 \ldots x_n$ to the string of mental representations $y_1 y_2 \ldots y_n$ such that for each index i that is greater than or equal to 1 and less than or equal to n $(1 \leq i \leq n)$…
>
> (a)   If $x_n = \alpha^M$, then $y_n = \beta^M$.
>
> (b)   Otherwise $y_i = x_i$.

(148)   **Syncategorematic interpretation of the pattern**
$\alpha \to \beta / \# \underline{\quad}$

> If α and β, are members of SEG and $\#$ is a member of ENV, then $(\alpha \to \beta / \# \underline{\quad})^M$ is the function f (a member of F) that maps any (finite) string of mental representations $x_1 x_2 \ldots x_n$ to the string of mental representations $y_1 y_2 \ldots y_n$ such that for each index i that is greater than or equal to 1 and less than or equal to n $(1 \leq i \leq n)$…
>
> (a)   If $x_1 = \alpha^M$, then $y_1 = \beta^M$.
>
> (b)   Otherwise $y_i = x_i$.

The interpretation in (147) maps the phonological rule to a function that checks if the last segment in the input matches the target of the change. If it does, it outputs the desired change. The interpretation in (148) maps the phonological rule to a function that checks if the first segment in the input matches the target. If it does, it outputs the desired change. All other segments remained unchanged.

To understand this type of interpretation better, let's consider a concrete example:

(149) **Syncategorematic interpretation of the rule**

     $g \to k \,/$ ___ $\%$

        $(g \to k \,/$ ___ $\%)^M$ is the function f (a member of F) that maps any (finite) string of mental representations $x_1 x_2 \ldots x_n$ to the string of mental representations $y_1 y_2 \ldots y_n$ such that for each index i that is greater than or equal to 1 and less than or equal to n $(1 \leq i \leq n)\ldots$

        (a)   If $x_n = g^M$, then $y_n = k^M$.

        (b)   Otherwise $y_i = x_i$.

This rule is interpreted as a function that checks if the last segment in the input is g. If it is, it produces a k as the last segment of the output.

With the *syncategorematic* interpretation, the '#' and '%' symbols indicate how the rule-statement relates to a special type of function, but the symbols themselves do not have a corresponding mental representation. In this case, we do not need the boundary symbols in URs.

In contrast, the *categorematic* treatment of the '#' and '%' symbols provides a more direct interpretation. Such an option is simpler in that it does not require additional semantic machinery (like the additional interpretation rules above). Rather it only requires the following stipulation.

(150) **Categorematic Stipulation**

        $\#^M$ and $\%^M$ symbolize the mental representations corresponding to the non-segment symbols (the symbols for the beginning of a word and end of a word, respectively).

With this stipulation, we can interpret our new phonological rules using our old interpretation rule. Consider the following example.

(151) **Categorematic Interpretation of the pattern '$g \to k \,/$ ___ $\%$'**

        $(g \to k \,/$ ___ $\%)^M$ is the function f (a member of F) that maps any (finite) string of mental representations $x_1 x_2 \ldots x_n$ to the string of mental representations $y_1 y_2 \ldots y_n$ such that for each index i that is greater than or equal to 1 and less than or equal to n $(1 \leq i \leq n)\ldots$

        (a)   If $x_i = g^M$ and $x_{(i+1)} = \%^M$, then $y_i = k^M$.

        (b)   Otherwise $y_i = x_i$.

In this interpretation, $\%^M$ is treated as a mental representation of the end of a word. However, for this rule to work, we would need to add a bit more complexity to our mental representation of words. For example, the mental representation of *man* would no longer be the string *mæn* but rather *#mæn%*. Similarly, the mental representation of *walking* would no longer be *wɔkɪŋ* but rather *#wɔkɪŋ%*. All mental representations of words would need to begin and end with '#' and '%', respectively, so the boundary symbols should appear in the URs, in the input to the phonological rule system.

So which type of interpretation is right? It should be emphasized that this is an empirical matter. It all depends whether we really have mental representations that have special segments at the beginning and end of the strings. If we do, then the second option is a better model of our mind. If we don't, then the first option is better. At this point, we leave this as an open empirical question for future research. For the sake of simplicity, we will continue to use the categorematic interpretation, but to improve readability, we will not put the boundary symbols into URs.

So, let's make it clear that, under the categorematic interpretation of word boundaries, a combination of morphemes like *nak-∅* will appear as a UR in derivation tables as *nak*, but will be understood as *#nak%*. Note that even if you want to show the morphological structure of a UR by writing *nak-∅*, the *k* is still treated by the phonology as being word-final. The *k* immediately precedes %.

Exercises

16.1. State the rule that turns a word-initial *p* to *k* before *r*. Assuming the *categorematic* interpretation of such a rule, give some examples of inputs and outputs: one where the input is identical to the output and another where it is not.

16.2. State the rule that turns a word-final *t* to *n* after *r*. Assuming the *categorematic* interpretation of such a rule, give two example inputs and outputs: one where the input is identical to the output and another where it is not.

16.3. Why can't we express the following in SPE format?
     i. "p becomes g when the second segment to its left is k"
    ii. "p becomes q before a word-final y"
   iii. "k becomes g after a word-initial z"
    iv. "k becomes t before a word-initial m"
     v. "s becomes q after a word-final f"

Adopting the same assumptions and format we used for the exercises in Unit 14, provide analyses for the following datasets.

16.4. Neptunian Language

	form	gloss
a.	nač	'a dog'
b.	nači	'the dog'
c.	nak	'a hat'
d.	nači	'the hat'

16.5. Mercurian Language

	form	gloss
a.	pak	'a dog'
b.	pagon	'the dog'
c.	pak	'a hat'
d.	pakon	'the hat'

16.6. Jovian Language

	form	gloss
a.	pak	'a dog'
b.	obak	'the dog'
c.	pak	'a hat'
d.	opak	'the hat'

16.7. Erisian Language

	form	gloss
a.	tor	'a dog'
b.	tola	'the dog'
c.	tor	'a hat'
d.	tora	'the hat'

16.8. Haumean Language

	form	gloss
a.	tor	'a dog'
b.	tola	'the dog'
c.	tol	'a hat'
d.	tola	'the hat'

16.9. Makemakean Language

	form	gloss
a.	dol	'a dog'
b.	entol	'the dog'
c.	dol	'a hat'
d.	endol	'the hat'

16.10. Ceresian Language

	form	gloss
a.	ton	'a dog'
b.	toŋgi	'the dog'
c.	toŋ	'a hat'
d.	toŋgi	'the hat'

16.11. Eleninian Language

	form	gloss
a.	toŋ	'a dog'
b.	butoŋ	'the dog'
c.	toŋ	'a hat'
d.	budoŋ	'the hat'

Unit 17

Nothing III:
Something for Nothing and
Nothing for Something

"I see nobody on the road," said Alice.
"I only wish I had such eyes," the King remarked in a fretful tone. "To be able to see Nobody! And at that distance, too! Why, it's as much as I can do to see real people, by this light!"

Lewis Carroll, *Alice in Wonderland*

17.1   Insertion and Deletion

We have already discussed the use of the symbol $\varnothing$ to denote a morpheme that has no phonological content. We have also introduced the word boundary symbols that denote the beginning and end of a word (i.e., the *nothing* that occurs before the first segment and after the last segment). In this section, we introduce another kind of *nothing*: one that relates to the insertion and deletion of segments.

To understand this new type of nothing, consider the Trubanamanian data in (152):

(152)   Trubanamanian

	form	gloss
a.	to	'dog'
b.	tolgi	'the dog'
c.	to	'hat'
d.	togi	'the hat'

By comparing [tolgi] and [togi], we can conclude that -*gi* is the form for the morpheme that means 'the'. By comparing [to] in (c) with [togi] in (d) (or by subtracting -*gi* from [togi]), we can conclude that *to* is the form for the morpheme meaning 'hat'. For 'dog', however, there are two surface forms: one revealed by subtracting -*gi* from [tolgi], namely *tol*, and another revealed by comparing [to] in (a) with [tolgi], namely *to*.

The difference between these two forms for 'dog' is the presence versus absence of an *l*. We thus need a rule that either inserts or deletes *l*. Fortunately for us, this dataset has evidence against insertion. If the phonology inserted *l* between *o* and *g*, we would predict that the surface form for 'the hat' would be *tolgi* rather than *togi*. In other words, this rule is inconsistent with the data. In contrast, the data is consistent with a rule that *deletes l* at the end of a word. In other words, the underlying form of [to] 'dog' is /tol/. This is just our familiar MTP-RAA forced-choice reasoning, which applies to discover a deletion rule just as well as for the segment-changing rules we have seen previously.

However, given our rule syntax and the set of symbols we have proposed for SEG, we have no way to express such a rule. An expression like (153) is not well formed according to our syntax:

(153)   A non-rule: l → / ___ %

What we need is a new symbol that can be used to explicitly refer to the absence of a segment. We will use the mathematical symbol ϵ for this purpose, and formulate the relevant rule as in (154):

(154)   Good rule with ϵ added to SEG: l → ϵ/___%

We have once again tweaked our model, this time by adding to SEG:

(155)   Revising SEG

   - SEG = IPA ∪ {ε}

   - ENV = IPA ∪ {#,%}

Now that you see how to use ε for a *deletion* rule, you can probably figure out how to use it for an *insertion* rule, as well. Consider the Abutilonian data in (156):

(156)   Abutilonian

	form	gloss
a.	toj	'dog'
b.	toju	'the dog'
c.	to	'hat'
d.	toju	'the hat'

By comparing [toj] in (a) and [toju] in (b) we can conclude that the underlying form for 'dog' is *toj*. Similarly, by subtracting *toj* from [toju] in (b), we can conclude that the underlying form for 'the' is *-u*. However, we get two forms for 'hat': one by comparing [to] in (c) and [toju] in (d), leading us to the form *to*; and another by subtracting *-u* from [toju] in (d), leading us to the form *toj*.

   Unlike the previous example, it is not possible to hypothesize a rule that deletes *j* in word final position. If this rule were at play, then the form for 'dog' would be *to* instead of *toj*. However, we can hypothesize a rule that inserts a *j* between *o* and *u*.

(157)   An insertion rule: ε → j / o___u

This rule correctly predicts that 'dog' surfaces as *toj* but 'hat' only acquires a *j* when the *u* (from the morpheme *-u*) is added.

   Many issues arise with respect to the new element ε we have introduced. On the trivial side, we must be sure to not confuse this symbol with either the symbol for set membership, ∈, or with the IPA vowel symbol ɛ. They are all derived from the Greek letter epsilon, but our fonts differentiate the three versions. More interesting issues include dealing with the semantics of ε and with reasons why we don't use ε to replace # and %, which seem to mean something like 'nothing precedes me' and 'nothing follows me' respectively.

17.2   Expressing Insertion and Deletion in Words

It is fairly straightforward to express insertion and deletion rules in ordinary language. If a formal rule has ϵ on the left hand side of an arrow, then this indicates that the segment on the right side will be inserted in certain environments, whereas if a formal rule has ϵ on the right hand side, then this indicates that the segment on the left will be deleted in certain environments.

Here are some insertion examples with English translations.

(158)   Simple Insertion

    i. $\epsilon \rightarrow u$ / ___ l   'Insert u before l'

    ii. $\epsilon \rightarrow u$ / l ___   'Insert u after l'

    iii. $\epsilon \rightarrow u$ / o ___ l   'Insert u between o and l'

And here are some deletion examples with English translations.

(159)   Simple Deletion

    i. $u \rightarrow \epsilon$ / ___ l   'Delete u before l'

    ii. $u \rightarrow \epsilon$ / l ___   'Delete u after l'

    iii. $u \rightarrow \epsilon$ / o ___ l   'Delete u between o and l'

Remember, these English translations can be deceptive. Although they give you a sense of how the rule works, by their very nature they are vague and imprecise. Still, English translations are very useful to get an intuitive grasp of how a rule works.

An example of a potential confusion of the English translations concerns the use of the word *between* in (158iii) and (159iii). If you think about the insertion rule in (158iii), it targets substrings of the form *ol* and replaces that substring with *oul* in the output. If you think about the deletion rule in (159iii), it targets substrings of the form *oul* and replaces that substring with *ol* in the output. The everyday language statements can be confusing since they both refer to something happening 'between o and l', but the target substrings differ—*ol* as opposed to *oul*. In one case (deletion), 'between o and l' means find the segment between o and l in the input—there is nothing between the two segments in the output. In the other case (insertion), it means that the resulting output will have a new segment between o and l—there is nothing between the two segments in the input.

We have found that for some students, converting formal rules to everyday language gets a bit trickier when the word boundary symbols are involved. Compare the insertion rules in (160) to the deletion rules in (161).

(160)   Insertion at word edges

    i. $\epsilon \rightarrow$ r / ___ %   'Insert *r* word-finally' (or 'at the end of a word')

    ii. $\epsilon \rightarrow$ r / a ___ %   'Insert *r* word-finally, after *a*'

    iii. $\epsilon \rightarrow$ r / # ___   'Insert *r* word-initially'

    iv. $\epsilon \rightarrow$ r / # ___ a   'Insert *r* word-initially, before *a*'

(161)   Deletion at word edges

    i.   r $\rightarrow \epsilon$ / ___ %   'Delete *r* word-finally'

    ii.   r $\rightarrow \epsilon$ / a ___ %   'Delete *r* word-finally, after *a*'

    iii.   r $\rightarrow \epsilon$ / # ___   'Delete *r* word-initially.'

    iv.   r $\rightarrow \epsilon$ / # ___ a   'Delete *r* word-initially, before *a*'

The tricky aspect of the translations concerns the use of the terms *word-finally* and *word-intially*. For the insertion rules, the thing being inserted—the segment *r*—becomes *word-final* or *word-initial* in the *output*. Other segments are word-initial and word-final in the input. For the deletion rules, the thing being deleted—the segment *r*—is *word-final* or *word-initial* in the *input*. Other segments are word-initial and word-final in the output.

The semantics we provide for deletion and insertion rules in the next unit eliminates any confusion that could arise through the English translations. However, providing a precise and unambiguous interpretation of such rules is not as easy as it is for rules that simply substitute one type of segment for another. Deletion and insertion rules manipulate how segments are ordered in a string, so such rules may map a string of length n to a string of a different length. Thus, we will be forced to be more explicit about how such orderings are represented.

Exercises

17.1. Express the following rules in English. For rules involving word edges, give at least two English formulations. Use 'word-final' and word-initial' as adjectives; use 'word-finally' and 'word-initially' as adverbs; use 'at the beginning of a word' to refer to the position after '#'; and use 'at the end of a word' to refer to the position before '%'.

    i. $\epsilon \rightarrow g \,/\, o \,\_\_\_ f$

    ii. $m \rightarrow \epsilon \,/\, \# \,\_\_\_$

    iii. $\epsilon \rightarrow d \,/\, \_\_\_ \%$

    iv. $p \rightarrow \epsilon \,/\, a \,\_\_\_ x$

    v. $\epsilon \rightarrow q \,/\, g \,\_\_\_ \%$

    vi. $\epsilon \rightarrow h \,/\, m \,\_\_\_$

    vii. $\epsilon \rightarrow c \,/\, \# \,\_\_\_$

    viii. $\epsilon \rightarrow z \,/\, \# \,\_\_\_ n$

    ix. $\epsilon \rightarrow k \,/\, \_\_\_ r$

    x. $p \rightarrow \epsilon \,/\, \_\_\_ \%$

    xi. $k \rightarrow \epsilon \,/\, s \,\_\_\_ \%$

    xii. $t \rightarrow \epsilon \,/\, \# \,\_\_\_ b$

    xiii. $e \rightarrow \epsilon \,/\, \_\_\_ k$

    xiv. $f \rightarrow \epsilon \,/\, s \,\_\_\_$

17.2. Express the following rules in SPE format.

    i. "word-final h becomes p"

    ii. "k becomes j at the beginning of a word"

    iii. "k becomes j word initially"

    iv. "k becomes j in word-initial position"

    v. "k becomes j after the beginning-of-word symbol"

    vi. "insert q between d and z"

    vii. "delete m after j"

Unit 18

The Semantics of Segment Insertion and Deletion

18.1   Ordering of Segment Strings

We endorsed in Unit 8 the bottom-up approach to studying UG, which asks *How little can be attributed to UG while still accounting for the variety of I-languages attained?* In this light, we need to squeeze every possible benefit from our currently posited UG model before allowing ourselves to enhance it. Sometimes this means stating the obvious. It is obvious, for example, that our phonological representations encode some ordering. The phonological representation of a morpheme is not just a *set* of segments, it is an *ordered set*, a concept we introduced in Unit 4.8, since the segments occur in a particular sequence and the same segment can occur in different positions in the order. This ordering is typically represented implicitly in our writing. For example, with the same four segments, we can get *cats* [kæts] *tacks* [tæks], *stack* [stæk], *acts* [ækts], *task* [tæsk], *scat* [skæt], *sacked* [sækt], and *cast* [kæst].[1] We have been assuming ordering in representations all along, so now we are just recognizing this explicitly and relating this property to the concept of ordered sets. Obviously, the property of distinguishing morphemes by the ordering of segments, and not just by virtue of which segments

---

[1] Of course, it is not generally the case that *all* orderings of a set of segments will correspond to lexical items in a given language, and indeed these eight are only a third of the twenty-four logically possible orderings. Try to figure out why there are twenty-four. We will explain the reasoning in a different context in Unit 31. There are more than twenty-four if segments can be repeated.

they contain, contributes to the expressive capacity of our model. With a few atomic elements, a few segments, you can get a lot more ordered sets of a given size than simple sets (since $\langle a, b, c\rangle \neq \langle b, c, a\rangle$, but $\{a, b, c\} = \{b, c, a\}$).

We'll show you the math later to demonstrate that with 10 segments, you can get 2^{10} (which equals 1024) *sets* of segments, with each set ranging in cardinality from 0 to 10; and that, still with a mere 10 segments, you can define more than eleven billion *strings* or *ordered sets* of length 10 or less. We want to claim, nay, even celebrate, this combinatoric power of our humble model by acknowledging something as trivial as the fact that phonological representations are ordered.

In Unit 1, we asserted that we are interested in doing phonology as a form of theoretical neuroscience. We also mentioned scholars like Gallistel and King (2009), who point out that one way for cognitive scientists to contribute to neuroscience is to characterize in general mathematical and logical terms the nature of the data structures and computations that cognition requires in various domains. By stating the obvious, that phonological representations must be ordered sets of segments, rather than just sets, we identify a simple and precisely stated problem for neuroscientists: *Find out how these two types of data structure are distinguished in the brain's long-term memory*. We phonologists know that the brain has to be distinguishing these things. If you are used to reading in the newspaper grand claims about new neuroscientific insights concerning, say, brain activity involving cognition of social interaction or other high-level skills that humans—or dead salmon(!), see Bennett et al. (2011)—appear to have, you may be surprised that our type of humble problem is rarely explored by neuroscientists, and these simple issues are not understood at all at the level of the brain.

In the next section, we'll see that even within phonology, the handling of segment ordering presents challenges as we revise our semantics for insertion and deletion rules.

18.2   Ordering and Segment Tokens

The syntax of insertion and deletion rules is identical to that of rules in which segments are replaced. However, there is a fundamental difference in their interpretation due to the semantics of ϵ. Both deletion and insertion require the removal of certain precedence relations in the string, and the establishment of new relations. To represent the difference between the two types of rules, those with and without ϵ, we need to outline in more detail the nature of phonological strings as ordered sets. Consider the strings in (162), which represent the broad transcription of the English words *blast* and *popsicle*.

(162)   a. #blæst%

         b. #pɑpsəkəl%

It's intuitively obvious that strings are linearly ordered with a beginning and an end point, represented by the symbols '#' and '%', respectively. Furthermore, each segment (other than the beginning and end symbols), has a segment or symbol that immediately precedes it and a segment or symbol that immediately follows.

Another way to explicitly represent an ordered set of any length is to use a set of ordered pairs. Recall that we use the angled brackets '⟨ ⟩' for ordered sets. Thus, $\{a, b\}$ is equivalent to $\{b, a\}$, but $\langle a, b \rangle$ is not equivalent to $\langle b, a \rangle$. That is, $\langle a, b \rangle$ states that a is ordered before b, whereas $\langle b, a \rangle$ states the opposite. Ordered sets can be represented as a series of ordered pairs, where each pair states that one segment immediately precedes another segment (i.e., $\langle x, y \rangle$ and $\langle y, z \rangle$ mean that x immediately precedes y, and y immediate precedes z). Normally this type of representation is a bit cumbersome; however, such a representation will make it easier for us to understand the semantics of deletion and insertion processes. Let's reconsider the strings in (162) as such sets of ordered pairs.

(163)   a. $\{\langle \#, b \rangle, \langle b, l \rangle, \langle l, æ \rangle, \langle æ, s \rangle, \langle s, t \rangle, \langle t, \% \rangle\}$
         b. $\{\langle \#, p \rangle, \langle p, a \rangle, \langle a, p \rangle, \langle p, s \rangle, \langle s, ə \rangle, \langle ə, k \rangle, \langle k, ə \rangle, \langle ə, l \rangle, \langle l, \% \rangle\}$

The representations in (163) contain all the same information as the representations in (162) except that the ordering is explicitly stated. In plain words, the ordered pairs in (163a) state "the start symbol immediately precedes b, b immediately precedes l, l immediately precedes $æ$, $æ$ immediately precedes s, s immediately precedes t, and t immediately precedes the end symbol."

Note that the arrangement of the ordered pairs within the set makes no difference. The information about linear order is encoded by the (immediate) precedence[2] relationship (i.e., the ordered pairs) and not by where the ordered pairs appear within the set. Hence, all of the representations in (164) represent one and the same linear order, namely the transcription of *blast*.

---

[2]Immediate precedence is a special case of precedence. In the ordered set $\langle a,b,c \rangle$, a and b precede c, but only b immediately precedes c. This is an important distinction, in general, but not for our purposes, and from now on, for expository convenience, we will say *precedes* when we mean *immediately precedes*. Immediate precedence is the only precedence relationship that matters for us.

(164)   a. $\{\langle \#, b\rangle, \langle æ, s\rangle, \langle s, t\rangle, \langle b, l\rangle, \langle l, æ\rangle, \langle t, \%\rangle\}$

       b. $\{\langle l, æ\rangle, \langle \#, b\rangle, \langle æ, s\rangle, \langle b, l\rangle, \langle s, t\rangle, \langle t, \%\rangle\}$

       c. $\{\langle l, æ\rangle, \langle s, t\rangle, \langle t, \%\rangle, \langle \#, b\rangle, \langle æ, s\rangle, \langle b, l\rangle\}$

For example, the fact that $\langle t, \%\rangle$ is included in the set means that t is the last segment of the string—the segment before the word-final symbol. The fact that $\langle \#, b\rangle$ is included means that b is at the beginning. Similarly, the fact that $\langle s, t\rangle$ is included means that s immediately precedes t, no matter where the ordered pairs appear within the set.

The representations in (163) and (164) are not quite complete. Some information is missing that is necessary in terms of phonological rules and representations. For example, in the transcription of *popsicle* (repeated below), there are two instances of p, one at the beginning of the word and another in the middle.

(165) $\{\langle \#, p\rangle, \langle p, a\rangle, \langle a, p\rangle, \langle p, s\rangle \langle s, ə\rangle, \langle ə, k\rangle, \langle k, ə\rangle, \langle ə, l\rangle, \langle l, \%\rangle\}$

Phonological rules and processes need to distinguish these two instances. For example, most English speakers have phonological rules that aspirate the p at the beginning but not the p in the middle. Our ordered pair representation does not adequately distinguish that there are two p's. In fact, it only suggests that p begins the string, immediately precedes a, immediately follows a and immediately precedes s. This characterization of the string appears to contain a contradiction when we don't distinguish the different *tokens* of p.

For the sake of clarity, we will assign each segment in a string a token index. We will represent the token index with numerical subscripts, although it should be kept in mind that the subscripts are only meant to distinguish one token of a segment from another. With this convention in mind, the string in (165) is more accurately given in (166).

(166) $\{\langle \#_1, p_2\rangle, \langle p_2, a_3\rangle, \langle a_3, p_4\rangle, \langle p_4, s_5\rangle \langle s_5, ə_6\rangle, \langle ə_6, k_7\rangle, \langle k_7, ə_8\rangle, \langle ə_8, l_9\rangle, \langle l_9, \%_{10}\rangle\}$

To reduce confusion, we will often provide token indexes that correspond to the position of the segment in the string. However, it should be emphasized that this is not necessary. Token indexes do not necessarily reflect the order in which the segments appear. Thus, the representation in (166) is equivalent to the one in (167).

(167) $\{\langle \#_9, p_2\rangle, \langle p_2, a_8\rangle, \langle a_8, p_3\rangle, \langle p_3, s_7\rangle \langle s_7, ə_4\rangle, \langle ə_4, k_6\rangle, \langle k_6, ə_5\rangle, \langle ə_5, l_{10}\rangle, \langle l_{10}, \%_1\rangle\}$

The set still specifies that $\#$ immediately precedes a token of p regardless of the numerical values of their indexes (i.e., it doesn't matter that the index on $\#$ is greater than the index on p). The indexes are present to distinguish different tokens of the same sound. The p's with the same index tell us that they are one and the same instance/token, thus appearing in one and the same string position in (162b), while p's with different indexes mean that they are distinct instances/tokens, hence appearing in different string positions. The numerical value of the index serves no other purpose.

18.3   Deletion Functions

With a more accurate representation of strings, we can now provide an interpretation of deletion and insertion rules. Deletion and insertion processes do not involve replacing or modifying segments (as with other rules), rather they involve the removal and addition of immediate precedence relations.

Let's consider the interpretation of deletion rules first. It is probably easiest to understand the deletion rule as a two-step process (although technically it can be represented in one step). The two-step process will first involve marking segments for deletion, by replacing them with ϵ, something we will call ϵ-marking; the second step will involve removing the segments that have been marked for deletion.

To simplify the issue, let's consider a deletion rule where the trigger appears to the right of the segment to be deleted (i.e., the deletion rule is of the form $\alpha \rightarrow \epsilon$ / ___ γ). We will provide a more general interpretation at the end of this section. With this temporary simplification in mind, the function that marks the segments that are to be deleted can be specified as follows:

(168)   Let ϵ-MARK$(\alpha)($___$\gamma)$ be a function from a finite set of ordered pairs X to another set of ordered pairs Y, where Y is the smallest set such that each pair of tuples $\langle r_i, s_j \rangle$ and $\langle s_j, w_k \rangle$ in X maps to a corresponding pair of tuples $\langle x_i, y_j \rangle$ and $\langle y_j, z_k \rangle$ in Y and...

    (a)   if $r = \#^M$, then $x = \#^M$

    (b)   if $w = \%^M$, then $z = \%^M$

    (c)   if $s = \alpha^M$ and $w = \gamma^M$, then $y = \epsilon$, otherwise, $y = \alpha^M$.

In the definition above, we introduced two ordered pairs from the input string $\langle r_i, s_j \rangle$ and $\langle s_j, w_k \rangle$. The pairs contain variables, so these ordered pairs represent any ordered pairs in the input string. Critically though, the same variable, s, with the same index value, j, is used to specify the second member of one pair and the first member of the other. Thus, the two ordered pairs represent the position of a particular segment in the input string—what element appears to its left (r_i) and what element appears to its right (w_k). The function then specifies that the output string will have a corresponding ordered pair ($\langle x_i, y_j \rangle$ and $\langle y_j, z_k \rangle$) that is either identical to the input string or almost identical except that ϵ replaces instances of α^M when α^M appears to the left of γ^M in the input string.

Note that it is the third clause in the definition where the critical change is specified. According to this clause, the function marks (replaces) any segment that appears before the segment named by γ with ϵ although it leaves all other segments untouched. The first and second clause simply guarantee that the start and end symbols of the input are appropriately mapped to the start and end symbols of the output. Note that the input and output strings maintain the same indexing (i.e., the input pairs and output pairs have the exact same index variables, i, j and k).

Once the string has been ϵ-marked, the ϵ's can be removed. This can be done with the following function.

(169)   Let ϵ-DELETE be a function from a finite set of ordered pairs X (corresponding to a string) to another set of ordered pairs Y (also corresponding to a string), where Y is the smallest set such that for each tuple $\langle x_i, y_j \rangle$ in X ...

(a)   if neither $x = \epsilon$ nor $y = \epsilon$, then $\langle x_i, y_j \rangle$ is in Y

(b)   if $x \neq \epsilon$ and $y = \epsilon$, then $\langle x_i, z_k \rangle$ is in Y, where z_k is the first non-ϵ element that follows x_i in X

(c)   otherwise $\langle x_i, y_j \rangle$ is not in Y

This function keeps all the pairs that have no ϵ, removes all of the pairs that contain an ϵ and repairs the string so that segments that were paired with ϵ are now paired with the closest non-ϵ element.

Now that we have the functions ϵ-MARK and ϵ-DELETE, we can specify an interpretation of the rules of the form $\alpha \rightarrow \epsilon / \_\_\_\gamma$.

(170)   If α is a member of SEG and γ is a member of ENV, then $(\alpha \rightarrow \epsilon / \_\_\_\gamma)^M$ is the function f (a member of F) that maps any finite set of ordered pairs X to the finite set Y, such that $Y = \epsilon\text{-DELETE}(\epsilon\text{-MARK}(\alpha)(\_\_\_\gamma)(X))$.

The rule in (170) first replaces all α-segments that appear before a γ-segment with ϵ. It then removes all of the ϵ's and repairs the string. The resulting string will either be equal in size (if no ϵ's replaced any α-segments) or smaller.

The mechanics behind this type of interpretation are best understood with an example. Consider again the rule we introduced in (154), repeated here:

(171) $1 \rightarrow \epsilon / \_\_\_\%$

According to (170), this rule will have the following interpretation.

(172) $(1 \rightarrow \epsilon/\_\_\_\%)^M$ is the function f (a member of F) that maps any finite set of ordered pairs X to the finite set Y, such that $Y = \epsilon\text{-DELETE}(\epsilon\text{-MARK}(l)(\_\_\_\%)(X))$.

The function $\epsilon\text{-MARK}(l)(\_\_\_\%)$ substitutes an ϵ for all instances of l that occur word-finally. If we apply this function to the string in (173a), the result would be the string in (173b).

(173)   a. $\{\langle \#_1, t_2 \rangle, \langle t_2, o_3 \rangle, \langle o_3, l_4 \rangle, \langle l_4, \%_5 \rangle\} = \text{tol}$
        b. $\{\langle \#_1, t_2 \rangle, \langle t_2, o_3 \rangle, \langle o_3, \boxed{\epsilon_4} \rangle, \langle \boxed{\epsilon_4}, \%_5 \rangle\} = \text{to}\epsilon$

The segment token l_4 now appears as ϵ_4 in *both* tuples that previously contained l_4, as shown in the boxes. The $\epsilon\text{-DELETE}$ function removes any pairs with ϵ_4 from the string and adds the pair $\langle o_3, \%_5 \rangle$. Thus, applying $(1 \rightarrow \epsilon/\_\_\_\%)^M$ to the string in (173a) yields the string in (174).

(174) $\{\langle \#_1, t_2 \rangle, \langle t_2, o_3 \rangle, \langle o_3, \%_5 \rangle\} = \text{to}$

Other deletion rules have an interpretation similar to that in (172), but with the appropriate ϵ-marking functions. We give the two remaining ϵ-marking schemas in (175).

(175)   a.   Let $\epsilon\text{-MARK}(\alpha)(\gamma\_\_\_)$ be a function from a finite set of ordered pairs X to another set of ordered pairs Y, where Y is the smallest set such that each pair of tuples $\langle r_i, s_j \rangle$ and $\langle s_j, w_k \rangle$ in X maps to a corresponding pair of tuples $\langle x_i, y_j \rangle$ and $\langle y_j, z_k \rangle$ in Y and...
        (a)   if $r = \#^M$, then $x = \#^M$
        (b)   if $w = \%^M$, then $z = \%^M$
        (c)   if $s = \alpha^M$ and $r = \gamma^M$, then $y = \epsilon$, otherwise, $y = \alpha^M$.

        b.   Let $\epsilon\text{-MARK}(\alpha)(\gamma\_\_\_\delta)$ be a function from a finite set of ordered pairs X to another set of ordered pairs Y, where Y is the smallest set such that each pair of tuples $\langle r_i, s_j \rangle$ and $\langle s_j, w_k \rangle$ in X maps to a corresponding pair of tuples $\langle x_i, y_j \rangle$ and $\langle y_j, z_k \rangle$ in Y and...
        (a)   if $r = \#^M$, then $x = \#^M$
        (b)   if $w = \%^M$, then $z = \%^M$
        (c)   if $s = \alpha^M$, $r = \gamma^M$ and $w = \delta^M$, then $y = \epsilon$, otherwise, $y = \alpha^M$.

With these ϵ-marking functions, we can write a general schema for the deletion rules that works for any environment.

(176)   If α is a member of SEG and RULENV is a proper rule environment (as defined in the rule syntax), then $(\alpha \rightarrow \epsilon$ /RULENV$)^M$ is the function f (a member of F) that maps any finite set of ordered pairs X to the finite set Y, such that $Y = \epsilon\text{-DELETE}(\epsilon\text{-MARK}(\alpha)(\text{RULENV})(X))$.

Before leaving the issue of deletion, let's consider an example of deletion where more than one segment is deleted. In fact, the reason we have to be so careful with the interpretation of our rule is that it is possible that more than one segment deletes in a given word. Suppose we had the rule s $\rightarrow \epsilon$ / ___ t (i.e., s gets deleted when it appears to the left of a t). How would the steps in the deletion function work when applied to a string like *stosti* (i.e., a string where there are two instances of a segment that need to be deleted)? Such a string has the following representation in terms of ordered pairs.

(177) $\{\langle \#_1, s_2 \rangle, \langle s_2, t_3 \rangle, \langle t_3, o_4 \rangle, \langle o_4, s_5 \rangle, \langle s_5, t_6 \rangle, \langle t_6, i_7 \rangle, \langle i_7, \%_8 \rangle \}$ = stosti

The ϵ-marking function would yield the following string.

(178) $\{\langle \#_1, \epsilon_2 \rangle, \langle \epsilon_2, t_3 \rangle, \langle t_3, o_4 \rangle, \langle o_4, \epsilon_5 \rangle, \langle \epsilon_5, t_6 \rangle, \langle t_6, i_7 \rangle, \langle i_7, \%_8 \rangle \}$ = ϵtoϵti

All tokens of s that appear to the left of a t are replaced by ϵ. The ϵ-deletion function not only removes the pairs that have ϵ's from the string but also repairs the "gaps" by inserting the ordered pairs $\langle \#_1, t_3 \rangle$ and $\langle o_4, t_6 \rangle$.

(179) $\{\langle \#_1, t_3 \rangle, \langle t_3, o_4 \rangle, \langle o_4, t_6 \rangle, \langle t_6, i_7 \rangle, \langle i_7, \%_8 \rangle \}$ = toti

Thus, the function (s $\rightarrow \epsilon$ / ___ t)^M applied to *stosti* would yield the output *toti*.

18.4   Insertion Functions

The interpretation of insertion rules is similar to the interpretation of deletion. In both types of rules, old precedence relations are removed and new ones are added. The only difference is that insertion rules add more relations than deletion rules. Let's consider the interpretation of a basic insertion rule in more detail. As with the deletion rules, we will start by outlining the interpretation of a rule with only one kind of environment at first, providing a more general interpretation at the end of the section. We will start with rules of the form $\epsilon \rightarrow \alpha$ / γ ___ δ.

(180)   If α is a member of SEG and γ and δ are members of ENV, then $(\epsilon \rightarrow \alpha$ $/\gamma\_\_\_\delta)^M$ is the function f (a member of F) that maps any finite set of ordered pairs X to the finite set Y, where Y is the smallest set such that for each $\langle x_i, y_j \rangle$ in X,

(a)   if $x = \gamma^M$ and $y = \delta^M$, then $\langle x_i, y_j \rangle$ is not in Y but $\langle x_i, \alpha^M{}_k \rangle$ and $\langle \alpha^M{}_k, y_j \rangle$ are in Y, where k is a new and unique token index.

(b)   otherwise, $\langle x_i, y_j \rangle$ is in Y.

This rule looks for ordered pairs where tokens of γ^M precede tokens of δ^M (i.e., $\langle x_i, y_j \rangle$ where $x = \gamma^M$ and $y = \delta^M$). When the rule finds such a pair, it removes it (i.e., it gets rid of $\langle x_i, y_j \rangle$). It then inserts new precedence relations involving a new token of α^M. The segment γ^M becomes the new predecessor of α^M and α^M becomes the new predecessor of δ^M (i.e., the output includes $\langle x_i, \alpha^M{}_n \rangle$, $\langle \alpha^M{}_n, y_j \rangle$). Note that every insertion of α^M involves a new index that uniquely identifies the newly inserted token of α^M.

Let's consider a more concrete example. Consider the insertion rule in (181).

(181) $\epsilon \rightarrow$ d$/$ n___z

This rule is reminiscent of the rule in many dialects of English that inserts a *d* between an *n* and *z* (i.e., the plural form *cans* is pronounced as [kændz]). The interpretation of this rule, according to (180), would be as follows.

(182) $(\epsilon \rightarrow$ d $/$n___z$)^M$ is the function f (a member of F) that maps any finite set of ordered pairs X to the finite set Y, where Y is the smallest set such that for each $\langle x_i, y_j \rangle$ in X,

(a)   if $x = $n^M and $y = $z^M, then $\langle x_i, y_j \rangle$ is not in Y but $\langle x_i, d^M{}_k \rangle$ and $\langle d^M{}_k, y_j \rangle$ are in Y, where k is a new and unique token index.

(b)   otherwise, $\langle x_i, y_j \rangle$ is in Y.

This function maps the string in (183a) to the one in (183b).

(183)   a. $\{\langle \#_1, k_2 \rangle, \langle k_2, æ_3 \rangle, \langle æ_4, n_5 \rangle, \langle n_5, z_6 \rangle, \langle z_6, \%_7 \rangle\}$
          b. $\{\langle \#_1, k_2 \rangle, \langle k_2, æ_3 \rangle, \langle æ_4, n_5 \rangle, \langle n_5, d_8 \rangle, \langle d_8, z_6 \rangle, \langle z_6, \%_7 \rangle\}$

The addition of *d* includes the novel token index 8, which is guaranteed to distinguish it from all other tokens in the string.

The interpretations of the other two forms of insertion are almost identical to (180), except that the conditions for insertion change slightly. These interpretation schemas are given in (184).

(184)   a.   If α is a member of SEG and γ is a member of ENV, then $(\epsilon \rightarrow \alpha\, /\_\_\_ \gamma)^M$ is the function f (a member of F) that maps any finite set of ordered pairs X to the finite set Y, where Y is the smallest set such that for each $\langle x_i, y_j \rangle$ in X,

   (a)   if $y = \gamma^M$, then $\langle x_i, y_j \rangle$ is not in Y but $\langle x_i, \alpha^M{}_k \rangle$ and $\langle \alpha^M{}_k, y_j \rangle$ are in Y, where k is a new and unique token index.

   (b)   otherwise, $\langle x_i, y_j \rangle$ is in Y.

   b.   If α is a member of SEG and γ is a member of ENV, then $(\epsilon \rightarrow \alpha\, /\gamma\_\_\_)^M$ is the function f (a member of F) that maps any finite set of ordered pairs X to the finite set Y, where Y is the smallest set such that for each $\langle x_i, y_j \rangle$ in X,

   (a)   if $x = \gamma^M$, then $\langle x_i, y_j \rangle$ is not in Y but $\langle x_i, \alpha^M{}_k \rangle$ and $\langle \alpha^M{}_k, y_j \rangle$ are in Y, where k is a new and unique token index.

   (b)   otherwise, $\langle x_i, y_j \rangle$ is in Y.

18.5   Old Rules Revisited

Our interpretation of the new insertion and deletion rules look quite different from the other interpretations we gave for phonological rules in Unit 12. Some of this is unavoidable. There is something special about insertion and deletion because they manipulate precedence relations without changing or replacing segments. However, certain differences in the interpretations we presented are more notational than substantive. One of these differences is the use of the ordered pair notation rather than a string of variables $(x_1 x_2 \ldots x_n)$ with numerical indexes that represent different tokens of a symbol.

It is important to note that the interpretations for all the rules we have introduced can be rewritten using the ordered pair notation. In fact, the string notation could be thought of as short-hand for a more fundamental ordered pair representation. Let's reconsider one of the rules from Unit 12, repeated in (185).

(185)   **Interpretation of the pattern '$\alpha \to \beta / \gamma$ ___'**

If α and β are members of SEG and γ is a member of ENV, then $(\alpha \to \beta / \gamma$ ___$)^M$ is the function f (a member of F) that maps any (finite) string of mental representations $x_1 x_2 \ldots x_n$ to the string of mental representations $y_1 y_2 \ldots y_n$ such that for each index i that is greater than or equal to 1 and less than or equal to n $(1 \leq i \leq n)$...

(a)   If $x_i = \alpha^M$ and $x_{(i-1)} = \gamma^M$, then $y_i = \beta^M$.

(b)   Otherwise $y_i = x_i$.

This rule specifies a method of mapping strings to strings that does not use ordered pairs. However, it is easy to restate the exact same rule in a different notation. Consider the rule in (186).

(186)   **Interpretation of the pattern '$\alpha \to \beta / \gamma$ ___'**

If α and β are members of SEG and γ is a member of ENV, then $(\alpha \to \beta / \gamma$ ___$)^M$ is the function f (a member of F) that maps any finite set of ordered pairs X to another set of ordered pairs Y, where Y is the smallest set such that each pair of tuples $\langle r_i, s_j \rangle$ and $\langle s_j, w_k \rangle$ in X maps to a corresponding pair of tuples $\langle x_i, y_j \rangle$ and $\langle y_j, z_k \rangle$ in Y and...

(a)   if $r = \#^M$, then $x = \#^M$

(b)   if $w = \%^M$, then $z = \%^M$

(c)   if $s = \alpha^M$ and $r = \gamma^M$, then $y = \beta^M$, otherwise, $y = \alpha^M$.

In this rule, a set of ordered pairs is mapped to a set of ordered pairs. The ordered pairs in which a token of α^M is preceded by a token of γ^M are removed in the mapping. Instead, they are replaced by ordered pairs that specify that a token of γ^M precedes a token of β^M. It is no coincidence that this restatement of the segment-changing rule looks identical to the ϵ-marking function (with the adjustment that s is mapped to β instead of ϵ). In some ways, the deletion rules can be thought of as involving an extra step (i.e., ϵ-DELETE) on top of the segment-changing rules. Interestingly, the same cannot be said for insertion rules.

Exercises

18.1. Provide an interpretation of the rule 'f → v / m ___' using the ordered pairs notation.

18.2. Provide an interpretation of the rule 't → d / o ___ a' using the ordered pairs notation.

18.3. Provide an interpretation of the pattern '$\alpha \to \beta / \gamma$ ___ δ' using the ordered pairs notation.

Unit 19

Segment Mapping Diagrams

We have introduced derivations as mappings from underlying representations to surface representations via the application of phonological rules. In this unit, we present segment mapping diagrams that are useful for understanding the relations among segments that appear in URs and SRs. These diagrams are not themselves part of the theory of phonology developed in this book. They are not meant to model a component of the human phonological faculty, but we hope that they will be useful in developing *your understanding* of phonology.

In the simplest case, where there are no relevant phonological rules, the mapping between a segment in the input and a segment in the output is simple. Consider data such as the following:

(187) Segment mapping diagram (SMD) for Rapid Harsh Town Language

	SR	gloss	UR
a.	luš	'a dog'	/luš/
b.	luši	'the dog'	/luš-i/
c.	lus	'a hat'	/lus/
d.	lusi	'the hat'	/lus-i/

s   š   Underlying segments (present in lexicon, selected by MORPHOLOGY)

↓   ↓

s   š   Surface segments that show effects (if any) of the PHONOLOGY

167

The top row of the diagram shows segments that appear in URs (because they are present in lexical items that the MORPHOLOGY has put together). The bottom row shows segments that occur in SRs. The arrows show the relations between the segments. The diagram for (187) represents the very boring fact that underlying /s/ maps to surface [s] and underlying /š/ maps to surface [š]. Let's call such mappings *identity* mappings. We can imagine generalizing a diagram like (187) to the set of all segment symbols used in a language. The phonology of such a language would have no rules. We posit rules to account for alternations in morphemes, and there will be no alternations if there were only identity mappings of each segment in the URs to the identical segment in SRs.

19.1   SMD for Neutralization

Let's now introduce Dengue in (188), a language with forms similar to those in Rapid Harsh Town Language (187), but with a distribution pattern similar to what we saw in Yersinian (114).

(188)   Dengue: Neutralization of s and š: s → š / ___ i

		SR	gloss	UR
a.		luš	'a dog'	/luš/
b.		luši	'the dog'	/luš-i/
c.		lus	'a hat'	/lus/
d.		luši	' the hat'	/lus-i/

In contrast to (187), in (188) underlying input *s* can also surface (under some conditions) as *š*. This is illustrated in the diagram in (189):

(189)   Segment mapping diagram (SMD) for neutralization:

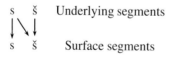

s   š   Underlying segments

s   š   Surface segments

This diagram shows the logical structure of a neutralization process—two inputs map to the same output. In the diagram, we show this in terms of individual segments. However, recall our analysis of rules as functions from strings to strings from Unit 10. Neutralization, then, is just the mapping of two (or more) input strings to the same output string. So, referring to the diagram, we can talk of the neutralization of *s* and *š*, but since rules apply to strings, this segment neutralization has a context. It is more precise to talk about neutralization of *si* and *ši*.

In some environments, /s/ neutralizes with /š/—they both show up on the surface as [š], whereas in other environments, each underlying segment maintains its underlying identity in the surface representation. Where an arrow connects an underlying segment to the identical surface segment, we assume that no rule has affected the segment in at least some environments. In other words, the vertical arrows in the diagram (189) represent the *absence* of a rule in the phonology. This apparently trivial point is worth pointing out in case you have been exposed to other phonological theories, such as Optimality Theory (OT) (Prince and Smolensky, 2004; Kager, 1999). In pretty much all versions of OT, there are constraints, called Faithfulness, Identity, or Correspondence constraints that have the effect of maintaining identity between input and output forms. So in our model, what is achieved by saying nothing, by the lack of a rule, is achieved in OT via a special kind of constraint.

The SMD in (189) does not indicate the environment in which a segment changes—where a rule applies—but we will sometimes enhance an SMD with an indication of the environment in which a rule applies as in (190):

(190)   SMD with rule environment: s → š / ___ i

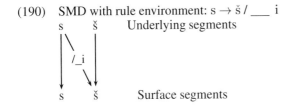

It is important to understand what the diagrams in (189) and (190) are intended to convey. Linear order of the segments on each row is irrelevant, so the diagram in (191) is equivalent to that in (189) in terms of informational content.

(191)   Order on rows is not important

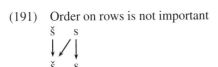

And if you have a perverse sense of layout, you could even draw the diagram as in (192), with non-vertical lines showing identity mappings.

(192)   No need to line up segments

The same information could also be represented by a set of *ordered pairs*, in which the first member of each pair is a segment in URs and the second member is a segment in SR, like this:

(193)   The same information as a set of ordered pairs:
        { ⟨s, s⟩, ⟨s, š⟩, ⟨š, š⟩ }

Of course, the order of listing the pairs is unimportant, since the pairs constitute a set; however, inside an ordered pair, the ordering does matter, as you know. The first member of each pair is a potential input segment to a rule and the second member is the output segment. As we get more complicated analyses with multiple rules, the diagram layout will prove useful.

    We should note that we are using these diagrams to focus on information that appears relevant to an observer trying to analyze phonological patterns. If the language in question also had forms like *lup, lupi* then we could present a diagram that showed the relationship between input and output *p*:

(194)   An SMD with interesting and uninteresting mappings

        s   š   p
        │╲│   │
        ↓ ╲↓   ↓
        s   š   p

The point of presenting the diagram in (194) is to help you see that an input š is as irrelevant to the rule in question 's → š / ___ i' as an input *p*. The neutralization of *s* and *š* confuses *us*, but it has no status from the perspective of the phonological computation.

19.2   SMDs Involving ε

You have probably already thought about how to draw an SMD for a deletion rule and an insertion rule. The tricky question of how to refer to 'nothing' arises again here, so let's consider two possibilities for the deletion of word-final *l* that we posited for a language in a previous unit.

    One approach would be to just show that input *l* is sometimes deleted, as in (195):

(195)   SMD for deletion, version 1

In some contexts, say, word-finally, an *l* is deleted and thus corresponds to no segment in the output, represented by ϵ.

Alternatively, we might want to highlight the difference between lack of a final *l* and presence of a final *l* in two URs and so we might draw an SMD that shows the continued 'non-*l*' nature of one of the lexical items in question, and thus draw an SMD like (196):

(196)   SMD for deletion, version 2

As we have already said, the SMD is a tool for our understanding and is not part of the model we are building, so the choice between these two versions is not a principled one. It is just a matter of what information we want to focus on.

The same distinction can be made for insertion rules. First, let's minimize our use of ϵ:

(197)   SMD for insertion, version 1

Now let's use ϵ as a placeholder in output forms:

(198)   SMD for insertion, version 2

As we proceed, we will refer to SMDs to show how complex the mapping between UR and SR can be.

Exercises

19.1. Examine the following Gan Gan data. Assume that there is a prefix *zi-*.

	form	gloss
a.	waka	'a dog'
b.	ziwaka	'the dog'
c.	waka	'a pig'
d.	ziaka	'the pig'

Give a full analysis, with an SMD of the mappings involving ϵ and one segment.

19.2. The closely related language Ang Ang has a different rule, but the same lexical items and the same underlying forms. Provide an analysis and an SMD for the alternations.

	form	gloss
a.	waka	'a dog'
b.	ziwaka	'the dog'
c.	aka	'a pig'
d.	zika	'the pig'

19.3. Another closely related language, Nag Nag, has two rules, but again the same lexical items and the same underlying forms as the related languages. Provide an analysis and an SMD for all the alternations.

	form	gloss
a.	waka	'a dog'
b.	ziwaka	'the dog'
c.	waka	'a pig'
d.	zika	'the pig'

Hint: You probably want to have two different ϵ's. Just use this idea mechanically without thinking too much about what it means.

Unit 20

Refining Neutralization

20.1 Neutralizations as Many-to-One Mappings

Recall from Unit 4.6 our function mapping from a set of children to a set of mothers, repeated here:

(199)   Extensional definition of a function

m :   Mary $\longrightarrow$ Ludmilla
        Kanguq $\longrightarrow$ Ludmilla
        Rolf $\longrightarrow$ Ludmilla
        Axochitl $\longrightarrow$ Ludmilla
        Öner $\longrightarrow$ Sigwan
        Taha $\longrightarrow$ Sigwan
        Giang $\longrightarrow$ Umakashte

We pointed out that two (or more) members in the domain of a function may map to the same member of the range. For example, both *Taha* and *Öner* map to *Sigwan*: $m(Taha) = Sigwan$ and $m(Öner) = Sigwan$. In mathematics one way of saying this is that the elements *Taha* and *Öner* have the same *image* under m. In our phonological rule, both *si* and *ši* have the same image *ši* under the rule 's → š / ___ i'.

Our analogy might confuse you a bit, because *Sigwan* is not identical to either of the inputs, *Taha* or *Öner*. So, instead think of the example in Unit 10.1, of a function that maps integers to the nearest 10. Both 9 and 11 get mapped to 10 by this function— 9 and 11 have the same image. So, the function can be said to *neutralize* the difference between 9 and 11, neither of which is identical to the output, 10. For 9 and 11, we can say that they are members of the domain that map to the same nearest 10 value, different from, say, 46, which maps to 50. Similarly, the m function neutralizes *Taha* and *Öner* as 'ones that have Sigwan as mother' or equivalently, 'children of Sigwan'.

The fact that 10 is *also* in the domain of the 'nearest 10' function is logically independent of the notion of neutralization of two or more inputs to a single output. We can say that 9, 10, and 11 (and others) *all* neutralize to 10. If we want, we can define the domain of our rounding function to exclude multiples of 10. The revised function would still neutralize 9 and 11 to 10. The presence or absence of 10 in the domain is irrelevant to the notion of neutralization.

This parallel to our SMD illustration of neutralization can perhaps be aided by more clearly illustrating the many-to-one mappings in our *mother* function, in parallel to the convention in SMDs:

(200)   Many-to-one mapping made clearer

The converging arrows show neutralization. Now that you understand these varied examples, we can formally define neutralization:

(201)   Definition of Neutralization Rule: A phonological rule R is *neutralizing* if there exist strings X and Y, $X \neq Y$ such that $R(X) = R(Y) = Z$; that is, the application of R to X has the same image as the application of R to Y.

More compactly, R is neutralizing if $R(X) = R(Y)$ for two distinct strings.
We can generalize the idea of neutralization to any function:

(202)   Generalized Definition of Neutralization: A function R is *neutralizing* just in case there exist X and Y such that X and Y are distinct ($X \neq Y$), and X and Y are in the domain R, and $R(X) = R(Y) = Z$. In other words, R is *neutralizing* just in case the application of R to X has the same image as the application of R to Y.

In mathematics, the technical term for neutralization is that a function is *many-to-one*. A function is many-to-one if there exist any members of the range that have more than one member of the domain mapped to them.

You can see that the actual value of the image does not matter. The image Z may be identical to either X or Y, as in the case of neutralization of *si* and *ši* to [ši] by the Dengue rule; or Z may be something completely different from X and Y, as in the mapping from both *Taha* and *Öner* to *Sigwan* under the *mother-of* function. Of course, in phonology, rules map strings to strings, so Z is always a string when functions are phonological rules. However, the string Z need not be identical to either X or Y.

20.2 Why Is the Analysis of Neutralization Challenging?

Our rule 's → š / ___ i' can be paraphrased thus:

(203)   If the sequence *si* occurs in a UR, then the corresponding segments will surface as *ši*

Let's break this down into parts:

(204)   • p = "the sequence *si* occurs in a UR"

   • q = "the corresponding segments will surface as *ši*"

   • If p, then q

We have already appealed to abstract forms of argument in our use of modus tollendo ponens (MTP) and reductio ad absurdum (RAA) in our analysis of neutralization. Conditional statements of the form in (204) are also common in discussions of basic logic. They are useful because they can guide valid reasoning, regardless of what is filled in for p and q. So, if we know that it is true that "If it is raining, Ulwazi will have her umbrella," then by confirming that it is raining, we are licensed to conclude that Ulwazi has her umbrella. This form of argument is known as *modus ponens*, and should not be confused with MTP:[1]

---

[1] Modus ponens says "If you accept p, then you accept q. So, if you know p is true, then you can conclude q is true." Recall that MTP says "If you accept that (p or q) is true, but you know p is false, then you can conclude that q is true."

(205)   Modus ponens

- I accept that "If p, then q" is true
- I know that p is true
- Therefore, I can conclude that q is true

Such inferences can also be thought of in terms of set theory. Call the set of days on which it is raining R; call the set of days on which Ulwazi has her umbrella B. To say it is true that "If it is raining, Ulwazi will have her umbrella" is to say that $R \subseteq B$—every rainy day is an umbrella-carrying day.

However, Ulwazi may carry her umbrella for other reasons besides protection from the rain. She may use it as a parasol or she may be auditioning for the part of Mary Poppins in the school play. Recall from our discussion of set theory in Unit 4.3 that there can be members of B that are not in R, so R may be a proper subset of B, $R \subset B$. This means that the fact that Ulwazi has her umbrella does not allow us to conclude that it is raining.

You probably see the logic now that we go through it carefully, but people are notoriously bad at this kind of reasoning in everyday life. The general error of reason is this:

(206)   A logical fallacy

- I accept that "If p, then q" is true
- I know that q is true
- Therefore, I can conclude that p is true

This logical fallacy is so common that it has several names, including the "fallacy of affirming the consequent" and "the confusion of necessity and sufficiency." In our opinion, a large part of the difficulty many people have with reasoning about neutralization is a reflection of the fact that human reasoning is plagued by this fallacy. Hale and Reiss (1998) discuss a case of the fallacy in the Optimality Theory literature on phonological acquisition. A famous psychological test that demonstrates, in part, the effects of this fallacy is the Wason Selection Test (Wason, 1968), which you can read about in numerous online sources.

So, just as Ulwazi may have her umbrella for a variety of reasons not related to rain, an SR can have the sequence *ši* for reasons unrelated to the phonological rule 's → š / ___ i'. Most simply, *ši* may occur in the SR because it was present in the UR. The cases of *ši* in SR from *si* UR are a proper subset of all the cases of *ši* in SR. Keep in mind that in analyzing phonology data you are given the SRs, and you have to *infer* the URs. If you infer that the UR has *si* because you know that the SR is *ši* and that there is a rule 's → š / ___ i', then you have committed a fallacy.

We discussed this common error of reasoning in terms of logical connectives like IF and THEN, and then we suggested the set-theoretic parallel for thinking about such matters. A course on mathematical logic would be a good place to look for more discussion of this sort if it interests you. Before moving on, let's add one more way to think about the fallacy.

Consider what happens if we reverse the mappings from children to their mothers in (199). We can do this by just reversing the arrows to show that the mothers are now the inputs, the elements of the domain:

(207)   Reversing the mapping from children to mothers

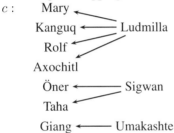

This set of mappings is *not* a function. Why not? Because each mother is not mapped to one particular child. The mapping *c* relates *Sigwan* both to *Taha* and to *Öner*. This reversal of the mappings in a function creates a set of mappings called the *inverse* of the function: *m* is a function and *c* is the inverse of *m*, but *c* is not a function. As we see, the inverse of a function is not necessarily itself a function.[2] For a mathematical example, consider the absolute value operation which is a function: $|7| = 7, |-7| = 7$, and so on. However, the inverse operation is not a function—if we ask you for a number whose absolute value is 7, you can choose 7 or -7.[3]

---

[2]The inverse of a function f will be a function too only if each element in the domain of f maps to a different element of the range of f. In other words, the inverse of f is a function if and only if f is a one-to-one mapping, or equivalently, if and only if each element of the domain has a unique image.

[3]It is worthwhile to realize that we can define a function from numbers to sets of numbers, where the domain is an absolute value and image of each element in the domain is a *set* of numbers. So, 7 maps to the set $\{7, -7\}$, and so on. Similarly, we can define a function that maps mothers to the *set* of her children, so that *Sigwan* maps to the *set* {*Öner, Taha*}.

A phonological rule *is* a function, since, given an input string (UR) like *si*, we know our rule will map that string to SR *ši*. However, the inverse mapping of this rule is *not* a function, because the rule is neutralizing—more than one input string can map to the same image. Given an SR [ši], we don't know whether it maps to UR /ši/ or /si/. So, the problem with reasoning that we discussed in terms of logic and set theory can also be understood in terms of the relationship between a function and its inverse. Given an SR there is not a deterministic way to decide what the UR is, and it is faulty reasoning to favor a non-identity mapping, say from SR [ši] to UR /si/.

Since children acquiring a language have evidence only from SRs, which are images (in the technical sense) of URs, the acquisition of phonological representations in the lexicon is not a trivial problem. Failure to recognize this basic logical point has undermined the work of some scholars working on phonological acquisition (see Hale and Reiss, 1998, 2008, for discussion). Our segment mapping diagrams will not only remind us that the complex mappings we will see later can be analyzed into several simple components, but they will also make salient the general non-invertibility of phonological functions. To summarize this section, we can say that the challenge in dealing with what we call *neutralization* in phonology, which is equivalent to many-to-one mappings by a function, is that neutralization *erases* information by *erasing* distinctions. As analysts, we need to recover that lost information, and we were able to do so using MTP-RAA reasoning. A great mystery of language acquisition by children is how they "recover" the lexical forms that their parents have.

20.3   Neutralization by a Set of Rules

We defined neutralization in (201) in terms of individual rules. In the neutralization rules we saw, there were two different input strings X and Y which map to the same output, say, X. In other words, the rule applies vacuously to X and non-vacuously to Y.

However, it can also happen that two or more rules all map different input strings to the same output string, with each rule applying non-vacuously. The phonology erases a difference in underlying forms, not by the effects of one rule, but by the effects of different rules working independently of each other. We can thus generalize the notion of neutralization beyond the level of the rule to the level of the grammar (i.e., to relationships among rules):[4]

---

[4]This is a mere terminological decision. We could frame the discussion in terms of homophony of SRs and reserve the term neutralization for homophony due to a single rule.

(208) Definition of a neutralizing set of two rules:

- If Q and R are distinct rules ($Q \neq R$), and there exist strings X and Y such that $Q(X) = Z$ and $R(Y) = Z$ (and $X \neq Y \neq Z$), then the set of rules $\mathcal{H} = \{Q, R\}$ is *neutralizing to Z*.

For example, consider the rules R_1: 'm $\rightarrow$ n / ___ %' and R_2: 't $\rightarrow$ ϵ / n ___ %'. If we apply these two rules to the URs /bam/ and /bant/, the output for both inputs will be [ban]. Each of these rules individually neutralizes one of those URs with a UR /ban/, as in (209).

(209) Neutralization by two different rules

UR	bam	bant	ban
m $\rightarrow$ n / ___ %	ban	—	—
t $\rightarrow$ ϵ / n ___ %	—	ban	—
SR	ban	ban	ban

The underlying distinction between the /bam/ and /bant/ is neutralized by the effects of the two rules. Each rule happens to be a neutralization rule because /bant/ and /ban/ are neutralized by one rule, and /bam/ and /ban/ are neutralized by the other. However, the two rules only form a neutralizing set by virtue of the /bam/ versus /bant/ distinction being neutralized to [ban] by the effects of the two separate rules. More generally, a set of rules $\mathcal{H}$ is neutralizing if there exists a string Z such that for each rule $H_i \in \mathcal{H}$ there is a distinct string X_i such that $H_i(X_i) = Z$ (and each $X_i \neq Z$).

This generalization of the concept of neutralization is useful for the discussion in the next unit of two situations. First, different rules may map distinct segments in URs to a single segment in SRs. Second, the combined effects of different rules may neutralize underlying differences in input strings, yielding identical outputs from inputs that may vary in several ways. As we illustrate these possibilities, we will see that a great variety of patterns arises as a natural consequence of our simple model.

Unit 21

Some Neutralization Patterns

In this unit we introduce various patterns of neutralization. The recurring point of all these examples will be that the simple mechanism of derivation by rule is sufficient to produce a wide range of apparently complex phenomena. This is exactly the kind of result we want from our bottom-up approach. We'll see that a simple system can generate phenomena that look very different to a naive observer. Of course, our goal is to turn *you* into a non-naive, phonologically sophisticated observer who can detect the simplicity beneath all the data.

21.1 Multiple Neutralization in One Context

Recall the data and analysis from Dengue in (188). Now in (210) consider another simple dataset showing neutralization:

(210) Kunjin

	form	gloss
a.	luš	'a dog'
b.	luši	'the dog'
c.	luṣ	'a pig'
d.	luši	'the pig'

At this point you should be able to analyze Kunjin in terms of rules and a set of underlying forms and to provide an SMD, as in (211).[1]

---

[1]In this discussion, we'll assume that there is no morpheme for the indefinite noun marker—if there is

(211)   Analysis of Kunjin (210)
        Lexicon:
         'dog':   luš
         'pig':   luş
         'the':   -i

        • Neutralization of ş and š: ş → š / ___i
        • SMD
           š   ş
           ↓ ╱ ↓
           š   ş

This analysis involves a rule with the same environment and the same output as for Dengue (188).

Now consider a language that is the union of Dengue and Kunjin. This language, Sindbisian, in (212), contains all the forms that occur in at least one of the other two languages.

(212)   Sindbisian = Dengue ∪ Kunjin

	form	gloss
a.	luš	'a dog'
b.	luši	'the dog'
c.	lus	'a hat'
d.	luši	'the hat'
e.	luş	'a pig'
f.	luši	'the pig'

Before we proceed, note that we have taken liberties with our definition of what a language is. By defining Kunjin and Dengue each as a set of forms, and Sindbisian as the union of those two sets, we are clearly not using an *intensional* definition of a language, in the I-language sense. Instead, we are using extensional definitions, treating languages as explicit lists of occurring forms. This is for expository convenience and to avoid awkward circumlocutions like this: "Sindbisian is a lexicon, morphology, and phonology that generate a set of surface forms which is the union of the sets of forms generated by the lexicons, morphologies, and phonologies of Kunjin and Dengue." Instead we just say informally that Sindbisian is the union of Kunjin and Dengue.

Sindbisian can be analyzed as in (213):

---

one, it has no phonological content and so would not bear on our phonological analysis, even if present.

(213) Analysis of Sindbisian with relations between UR and SR of segments

- Lexicon: /luš/ 'dog', /lus/ 'hat', /luş/ 'pig', /-i/ 'the'

- Phonological rules:

  – Neutralization of s and š: s → š / ___i
  – Neutralization of ş and š: ş → š / ___i

- SMD

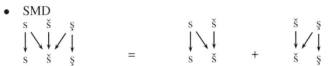

Note that for Sindbisian we posit the same lexical forms as we did in Kunjin and Dengue. Note also that we can use the two SMDs from above to see how the phonology is mapping underlying segments to surface segments. However, because the output of the rules is the same, we can also merge the two SMDs into a single one as shown. We see that it is possible to neutralize not just two, but three (and even more) underlying segments, here /s, š, ş/ to a single outcome, [š].

The point of this example is that multiple neutralization is *nothing special*. There are two neutralization rules and they happen to have the same output. This may make it initially difficult to see what is going on in Sindbisian, but we can see that this superficial complexity just arises from the combination of two instances of the "normal" neutralization we have been studying.

In Sindbisian, the output of the converging neutralization rules was [š]. In Armillarian in (214) we lead you to an analysis with a different set of rules that converge to an output of [s].

(214) Armillarian: Another case of multiple neutralization:

	form	gloss
a.	lus	'a dog'
b.	luši	'the dog'
c.	lus	'a hat'
d.	lusi	'the hat'
e.	lus	'a pig'
f.	luşi	'the pig'

The following SMD shows what's going on here:

(215) Relations between UR and SR of segments in Armillarian

- š → s / ___ %
- ṣ → s / ___ %

Sindbisian and Armillarian have been presented as containing two rules each. However, later when we break down segments into features, we'll see that it may be possible to collapse two or more rules affecting different segments into a single rule. This important issue is logically separate from our point about multiple convergent neutralizations.

21.2 Multiple Convergent Neutralization in Korean

Ask a Korean speaker how to say 'face' and he or she will say [nat⌐]. Ask a Korean speaker how to say 'day' and he or she will say [nat⌐]. Ask a Korean speaker how to say 'sickle' and he or she will say [nat⌐]. Ask a Korean speaker how to say 'piece' and he or she will say [nat⌐]. Ask a Korean speaker how to say 'grain' and he or she will say [nat⌐]. Now, before you start thinking that it would be really easy to learn Korean, even easier than Smurf, consider that as soon as you use these meanings in a sentence, things get complicated. Simplifying a bit, if we asked a Korean speaker to use each of these nouns as the object of a sentence, we would not get [nat⌐], [nat⌐], [nat⌐], [nat⌐], [nat⌐], but instead [načʰil], [najil], [nasil], [natʰil] and [nadil], respectively. The ending [-il] marks the ACCUSATIVE form of a noun, used as the object, but what happened to all the final [t⌐] consonants? Why do they now show up in five different forms?

(216) Korean multiple convergent neutralization[2]

	nominative	accusative
'face'	[nat⌐]	[načʰil]
'day'	[nat⌐]	[najil]
'sickle'	[nat⌐]	[nasil]
'piece'	[nat⌐]	[natʰil]
'grain'	[nat⌐]	[nadil]

---

[2]The NOMINATIVE is used for subject of a sentence and as a citation form.

A reasonable analysis is that the underlying form for each morpheme is identical to the alternant you see in the accusative, and that each of the distinct final segments in the various noun morphemes is mapped to [t˺] by a phonological rule.[3] The sequences č^h%, ǰ%, s%, t^h%, and d% all have the same outcome.

This example has two characteristics that we have not seen before. First, we have a five-way neutralization of underlying segments to a single surface segment. However, you should be able to see that this is just an extension of the multiple neutralization from the previous section, which in turn is just a combination of simple neutralizations. Second, in this Korean case, the surface segment that is the result of neutralization does not occur in underlying forms. We will discuss this later, when we consider what is traditionally called allophony, in Part V. For now, we can draw an SMD as in (217):

(217) Korean neutralization SMD

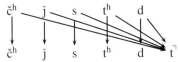

Let's see what lessons, old and new, we can extract from this example. First, note once again the recurring theme that superficial complexity can be reduced to combinations of simple patterns. We could easily break down the SMD in (217) into five separate ones, the one in (218) and four others:

(218) Korean neutralization SMD

Second, like all cases of neutralization, the Korean case reflects clearly the fact that languages are not best analyzed in functionalist terms. If languages "avoided confusion" or "didn't like" homophony, why would they contain rules like those we need to generate the Korean data? Why would a perfectly fine five-way contrast in lexical items be neutralized in some contexts? Whatever the answer is to such a question—and

---

[3] Again, we are not interested here in the question of whether one rule does all the work. Given the model of rules we have thus far, we need five distinct rules to handle Korean. But this will change later in the book.

we think this is a question best answered in the domain of language change, not grammar (see Hale, 2007)—it has nothing to do with communicative efficiency, avoidance of confusion or any other "commonsense" notion of what language is.

Third, we can reiterate what should by now be obvious: language learning involves quite a bit of abstraction from the data a child is exposed to. Korean learners can't just learn "the word for *sickle*" and then use it in various contexts, since the segments of morphemes are subject to variation based on their phonological environment. Learners can't even rely on the simple, unsuffixed form of a word to tell how it will always be pronounced. In this case, the unsuffixed forms are predictable in their pronunciation once you know the suffixed form, but the neutralizing rules are not invertible functions; a single surface segment corresponds to several underlying segments.

21.3   Overlapping Neutralizations

Consider the Baltraic forms in (219):

(219)   Baltraic Language

	form	gloss
a.	lus	'a dog'
b.	luši	'the dog'
c.	luša	'dogs'
d.	lus	'a hat'
e.	lusi	'the hat'
f.	lusa	'hats'
g.	luş	'a pig'
h.	luşi	'the pig'
i.	lusa	'pigs'

You can figure out the lexicon for this language—here are the rules:

(220)   Rules for Baltraic (219)

   Rule A: š → s / ___ %

   Rule B: ş → s / ___ a

Rule A is responsible for the homophony of 'a dog' and 'a hat', both *lus*, since the underlying /š/ of 'dog' is turned to *s* at the end of a word. Rule B is responsible for the homophony of 'hats' and 'pigs', both *lusa*, since the underlying /ş/ of the 'pig' morpheme is turned to *s* before *a*. So, we have rules turning two segments into *s*, but the rules have different environments.

We have added nothing to our simple SPE model to generate this overlapping pattern, but we can recognize that such datasets can be difficult to analyze. We predict the possibility of such patterns just by combining the elements of our simple system, but there is no aspect of the system that specifically was posited to generate such datasets.

Here are two SMDs for this language, with the environments of the rules shown:

(221)   Separate SMDs for Baltraic

And here are the two diagrams merged into one, again with the rule environments shown:[4]

(222)   A single SMD for Baltraic (219)

So, we have several neutralizations, several segments merging to one, but in different phonological contexts. According to (201), our definition of neutralization in Unit 20, these two rules do not constitute a single neutralization set, because we have defined neutralization in terms of strings, not segments. The loss of contrast between *š* and *s* happens in word-final position, so the neutralized output that corresponds to the *Z* of our definition is *s%* for one rule. Compare this with the loss of contrast between *s* and *ṣ*, which occurs before *a*, so the *Z* string in this case is *sa*.

When we see an [s] on the surface in this language, it can correspond to an underlying /s/ or an underlying /š/ if it is at the end of a word, or an underlying /ṣ/ if it is before *a*. The data looks complex, but it arises from the combination of simple patterns, two distinct neutralizations that just happen to overlap with respect to the segments involved.

---

[4]Later we will argue that rules are always ordered with respect to each other, so it is a bit misleading to combine the simple SMDs as we have done here. We'll address this when SMDs are revisited in the context of rule ordering.

21.4   Overlapping Neutralizations with ϵ

We saw in Unit 17 that deletion rules can be treated as neutralization with ϵ. For example, two input forms, /tol/ and /to/ might end up homophonous if the language has a rule deleting *l* at the end of a word. Given the existence of deletion and the existence of overlapping neutralization, it is not surprising that we can find overlapping neutralizations with ϵ. We don't need anything new to account for this phenomenon—it just combines things we have already seen.

Here is a case from a real language, Samoan:

(223)   Samoan data

simple	perfective	gloss
1. tau	tauia	'reach a destination'
2. tau	taulia	'cost'
3. taui	tauia	'repay'

Assume that the perfective suffix is *-ia*. We can then posit the following underlying forms for the verb roots:

(224)   Samoan verb roots

root	gloss
1. /tau/	'reach a destination'
2. /taul/	'cost'
3. /taui/	'repay'

The underlying form for each of the six words is then the following—the simple forms have no suffixes; the perfective forms have the suffix *-ia*.

(225)   Samoan underlying forms

simple	perfective	gloss
1. /tau/	/tau-ia/	'reach a destination'
2. /taul/	/taul-ia/	'cost'
3. /taui/	/taui-ia/	'repay'

In the surface form [tauia] from underlying /taui-ia/, it is not apparent which /i/ has been lost, but we can tell from other forms not given here. Just take our word for it that the second *i*, the one in the suffix, is the one that is deleted.[5] We can then posit the following rules:

---

[5] The deletion of *i* also occurs after *e*, and we will learn later how to cover these facts with a single rule referring to the environment 'after a front vowel'.

(226)   Samoan rules

Rule A: $l \to \epsilon$ / ___%   (Delete *l* at the end of the word.)

Rule B: $i \to \epsilon$ / i ___   (Delete *i* after an *i*.)

This analysis corresponds to the following SMD.

(227)   Samoan SMD

Both *l* and *i* are deleted, but in different contexts: the former at the end of a word, the latter after another *i*. This may seem a bit exotic, but there is nothing here that we haven't already seen, when we take the pieces apart.

The two context-sensitive deletion rules lead to neutralization with ϵ by two underlying segments, /i/ and /l/. The result is that the root /taul-/ ends up losing its *l* in the simple form, and thus is homophonous with the simple form of /tau/; and the suffix /-ia/ loses its *i* in the perfective form of the root (after the *i* of the root /taui/) and ends up homophonous with the perfective form of /tau/. The data itself looks complicated, but it just reflects a combination of simple rule applications.

This Samoan data reinforces two important points that may appear counterintuitive. The first point is that the lexical form of a root does not have to correspond to a pronounceable *word*. For example, the lexical form for 'cost' is /taul-/, but this could never be a word, since the word-final *l* will always get deleted in Samoan. The lexical forms of the two other roots appear to be identical to what occurs in the simple form, but this is not required, as shown by 'cost'.

Second, it is not necessarily the case that the lexical form consistently be apparent in a language from a single *morphological* category. In 'cost' the lexical form surfaces in the perfective form; in 'reach' and 'repay', the lexical form is apparent in the simple form, but you actually need both forms of 'reach' to be sure what the lexical form is. In practical terms, if you were taking a course in Samoan, you could not get away with learning the forms in one column in order to predict the forms in the other. You could predict all forms if you learned the appropriate abstract lexical form. More interesting to consider is the fact that a child learner must *infer* the lexical form—the child cannot just imitate words and use simple analogies. In fact, the child never hears a *word* [taul], yet that is what needs to be stored.

It follows from our simple system that there is no reason to expect the lexical form to show up consistently in one category. It would complicate our model to build in such a restriction, so we should not do so without good reason. It happens to turn out that we instead have evidence, like this Samoan data, that such restrictions are undesirable for a good model.

21.5   Reciprocal Neutralization

Thus far we have seen examples of neutralization in which two or more segments share just one of their realizations. However, other patterns are possible. Consider the following Cochliobolusian data:

(228)   Cochliobolusian

	form	gloss
a.	rat	'a penguin'
b.	radba	'the penguin'
c.	rad	'a polar bear'
d.	radba	'the polar bear'

Provide an analysis. You should end up with the following SMD:

(229)   SMD for (228)

Now consider further data from the same language.

(230)   More Cochliobolusian

	form	gloss
a.	rat	'a penguin'
b.	ratpi	'as a penguin'
c.	rad	'a polar bear'
d.	ratpi	'as a polar bear'

When you analyze this second dataset on its own, you should end up with this SMD:

(231)   SMD for (230)

Now, when you combine all the data and analyze it together you get the following. The morpheme meaning 'penguin' has alternants [rat] and [rad], and so does the morpheme meaning 'polar bear'. Applying the logic used thus far, it might appear that we are in trouble, since the two morphemes have the same set of alternants. Crucially, however, it is not the case that identical alternants show up in *every* environment. In particular, the two morphemes appear with non-identical alternants when each root is *not* followed by a suffix; that is, the final consonants of the two morphemes appear in a distinct form when they are also word-final. This allows us to set up 'penguin' as /rat/ and 'polar bear' as /rad/, with the combined SMD and rules shown in (232).

(232)   Reciprocal neutralizations:

- SMD

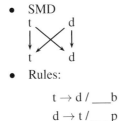

- Rules:

$$t \rightarrow d \ / \ \_\_\_ b$$
$$d \rightarrow t \ / \ \_\_\_ p$$

Because there is a rule neutralizing underlying /t/ to [d] and a rule neutralizing underlying /d/ to [t], we refer to such cases as *reciprocal neutralization*. The reciprocal neutralization pattern may make it difficult at first to see what is going on in such a dataset, but once again, there is no mechanism that is incompatible with our basic model.[6]

21.6   Non-surfacing Segments in URs

In Unit 2 we mentioned the Anishinaabemowin verb forms that Sigwan Thivierge found, in which one of the root vowels is always deleted. So, the segments of the lexical form have to be inferred from a combination of forms. Since the whole string occurring in the lexical form does not appear in any word, the lexical form is in some sense an abstract entity, not directly observable by a learner, or by a linguist. We also pointed out that all morphemes in all languages are stored as a representation that abstracts away from the intonation contour in which the morpheme happens to be encountered by a learner.

---

[6]We will see later how the two rules can be collapsed into one. This *will* require a new mechanism.

In this section, we present the possibility of yet another kind of abstractness. We suggest that some datasets lead us to posit lexical forms that contain *segments* that are never pronounced in a manner that contrasts them with other segments. Consider the Ustilago data in (233):

(233)   Ustilago: Non-surfacing URs

sg.	pl.	gloss
pak	pakla	'cat'
pag	pagla	'mat'
pag	pakla	'rat'

Our non-alternation assumption in (118) forces us to posit /pak/ for 'cat' and /pag/ for 'mat', since they each show a single surface alternant in all environments. This means that it is *not* possible to posit either of the analyses in (234) to account for the forms of 'rat'.

(234)   Analyses that won't work for Ustilago in (233)

A.   Lexical form of 'rat' is /pak/ and rule is k → g / ___%
     (This rule is problematic for the form *pak*, 'cat')

B.   Lexical form of 'rat' is /pag/ and rule is g → k / ___l
     (This rule is problematic for the form *pagla*, 'mats')

Faced with Ustilago, the surfacing lexical form assumption (SLFA) introduced in Unit 14 cannot be maintained. We need three different lexical forms, but we have only two surface forms shared among the paradigms. For the forms of 'rat', we have [pak-] and [pag-], but neither is available as the lexical form, since these will be assigned to 'cat' and 'mat', respectively, at the same time entailing that there are no 'k → g' or 'g → k' rules.

Notice that if we decide to apply the SLFA in analyzing 'rat', we will be forced to reject the non-alternation assumption (NAA) for one of the other two items. For now, we will maintain the NAA (which is, you will recall, just a special case of the SLFA). We will, however, later show that the NAA also runs into trouble.

So what do we do with Ustilago in (233)? Here is a suggestion: there is a segment at the end of the lexical form of 'rat' that surfaces sometimes as [k] and sometimes as [g], depending on the context. We can use an arbitrary symbol to represent it for now, say, H.[7] Here then is the analysis:

---

[7]We are treating 'H' here as an IPA symbol (which it isn't), just to avoid picking a random segment, and to avoid prejudicing the question of how to choose which real IPA symbol to use. The problem will

(235)   Analysis of Ustilago (233)

- Data

sg.	pl.	Root UR
pak	pakla	/pak/
pag	pagla	/pag/
pag	pakla	/paH/

- Rules:

  - $H \rightarrow k /$ ___l
  - $H \rightarrow g /$ ___%

- SMD

Recall that in our discussion of Korean in section 21.2, we already have seen that it may be the case that a surface segment, like the Korean [t˥] does not correspond to the identical segment in any input forms; we posited no underlying /t˥/ for Korean. In this Ustilago toy language, we have an underlying segment, H, that happens to have no identical correlates in surface forms, since H always surfaces as either *k* or *g*. But since *t˥* and H are in SEG, the set of segments that can appear as the input and output of rules, then the rules we have posited involving H are completely consistent with what we have seen before.

Solutions like that proposed in (235) gave rise to a discussion about "abstractness" in the early days of generative grammar (see Baković, 2009, for a useful overview), with many scholars arguing that such abstractness would be excluded by a psychologically realistic theory of phonology. However, given our current model, no further stipulation is needed to generate the possibility of non-surfacing segments. This "abstract" solution is once again just a particular manifestation of our simple model. There is no way for the phonology to "know" that it has two rules that together ensure that H is never realized on the surface. There is no mechanism in our model for rules to keep track of each other's effects. So we have reversed the traditional discussion of such issues. Instead of treating non-surfacing lexical forms as a complicated abstract

evaporate in Part VIII when we use features to define segments. We do not want to use a variable symbol like x (meaning a logical variable over IPA symbols, but itself a non-IPA symbol), since that would mean 'any segment'. By using H we mean 'a particular segment'.

phenomenon that we might need to exclude from the model, we have shown how the phenomenon is completely consistent with our stripped-down, bottom-up model building. We will later see data from real languages that calls out for this kind of analysis.

To reiterate, instead of justifying the existence of what is impressionistically complex, we show that such phenomena are expected results of our simple model—to stipulate against the possibility of such phenomena on the basis of an impression that they are complicated would violate the bottom-up approach we introduced in Unit 8, citing Chomsky (2007).

Unsurprisingly, there is also no reason to try to suppress the combination of non-surfacing segments in lexical forms with rules involving ϵ. These are two phenomena we accept, and we accept in principle their combination. Consider the Floreanan dataset in (236).

(236) Floreanan: Alternation with ϵ

sg.	pl.	gloss
pak	pakla	'frog'
pa	pala	'hog'
pa	pakla	'log'

We argue as before. The root in the forms for 'frog' should be set up as /pak/ according to the principles we have used so far (NAA). For 'hog', we might posit /pa/, since, again, there is no alternation. For 'log', there are two alternants, [pa-] and [pak-]. We can't posit /pak/ or /pa/ for this root, so we need to posit something else.

Parallel to what we did in Ustilago, let's posit that the root is /paH/, where H is some consonant other than k. We can propose the appropriate rules, as shown in (237).

(237) Analysis of Floreanan with a segment that never surfaces

sg.	pl.	Root UR
pak	pakla	/pak/
pa	pala	/pa/
pa	pakla	/paH/

Rules:

- $H \rightarrow k \,/\, \underline{\quad} l$
- $H \rightarrow \epsilon \,/\, \underline{\quad} \%$

So H either neutralizes with *k* (before *l*), or it neutralizes with ϵ (word-finally). Despite our discussion of Samoan in Unit 21.4, you may still find it counterintuitive that we can refer to ϵ as an entity with which another segment can neutralize. Perhaps rewriting the SMD in (237) will put you more at ease. But perhaps not. Maybe you feel a bit like Alice in the epigraph to Unit 17 when the King refers to "Nobody" as an individual who can be seen. The nice thing about formalization is that it doesn't matter how you feel! Our syntax and semantics mechanically allow for a pattern that our minds have a hard time grasping. That's exactly the kind of result we want from a scientific theory. Sure, it is strange that we are talking about the neutralization of nothing (ϵ) with something that never shows up (H), but our model has led us here. As Zenon Pylyshyn puts it in *Computation and Cognition*:

> [I]f you believe P, and you believe that P entails Q, then even if Q seems more than a little odd, you have some intellectual obligation to take seriously the possibility that Q may be true, nonetheless. (1984, p. xxii)

While you may or may not have balked at our suggested solution, you should take a moment to appreciate just how mind-blowing it actually is. We are proposing that the UR of the root can be a form containing segments that may never surface in any word. This may sound shocking, but it is a natural result of the model, and entirely expected given what we have developed thus far.

21.7   Combined Neutralization

Our discussion has been framed in terms of neutralization of underlying segmental differences by the phonology. To illustrate these phenomena, we have constructed datasets in which there exist pairs of corresponding forms in different paradigms (say, the plural of two nouns) that differ minimally, by a single segment, as well as corresponding pairs (say, in the singular) that do not differ at all—they are homophonous, due to the neutralizing effect of the grammar.

It is tempting, but wrong, to equate individual neutralization rules with the generation of homophonous forms from forms that are underlyingly distinct. To illustrate the independence of the two notions, consider the datasets below. Since we have already introduced the idea that languages may have more than a single rule, we will illustrate that homophony can arise from the application of two rules; obviously this result can be extended to more than two rules, as well.

21.7.1 Combined Neutralization within a Paradigm

We first consider two neutralizations that apply within a paradigm, within a set of forms that share a lexical root. The following forms are constructed with a prefix, a noun root, and a suffix in each word:

(238) Marchenan: Homophony via two rules affecting one form

form	gloss
vɪʁa	'with an ox'
vɪθon	'with oxen'
vɛθa	'with a sheep'
vɛθon	'with sheep (pl.)'
sɛʁa	'for an ox'
sɛθon	'for oxen'
sɛθa	'for a sheep'
sɛθon	'for sheep (pl.)'

We can account for this data with the lexical entries and rules in (239):

(239) Lexicon and rules for Marchenan (238)

    'with':   v-
    'for':   s-
    SINGULAR: -a
    PLURAL: -on
    'ox':   ɪʁ
    'sheep':   ɛθ

Rule A: ʁ → θ/___o

Rule B: ɪ → ɛ/ s ___

Constructing URs from the lexicon and applying the rules yields the following derivations:

(240) Derivations

UR	v-ɪʁ-a	v-ɪʁ-on	v-ɛθ-a	v-ɛθ-on
A: ʁ → θ/___o	—	vɪθon	—	—
B: ɪ → ɛ/ s ___	—	—	—	—
SR	vɪʁa	vɪθon	vɛθa	vɛθon
Gloss	'with an ox'	'with oxen'	'with a sheep'	'with sheep (pl.)'

UR	s-ɪʁ-a	s-ɪʁ-on	s-ɛθ-a	s-ɛθ-on
A: ʁ → θ/___o	—	sɪθon	—	—
B: ɪ → ɛ/s ___	sɛʁa	sɛθon	—	-
SR	sɛʁa	sɛθon	sɛθa	sɛθon
Gloss	'for an ox'	'for oxen'	'for a sheep'	'for sheep (pl.)'

You should confirm that the order in which we have applied the rules does not matter. We would get the same output for each input, even if Rule B were applied before Rule A.[8]

In this case of *combined neutralization*, we have two SMDs that are "independent" of each other, as in (241)—they don't show any overlap in the symbol mappings represented:

(241)   Independent SMDs in combined neutralization pattern

Note that the meaning 'ox' is realized in four different ways in this simple dataset: [ɪʁ, ɪθ, ɛʁ, ɛθ]. However, this complex surface set is accounted for by just two rules. In 'with an ox' neither rule has an effect; in 'with oxen' Rule A has an effect; in 'for an ox' Rule B has an effect; and in 'for oxen' both rules have an effect.

(242)   Deriving surface alternants of /ɪʁ/ 'ox' and relevant rules:

LEXICAL form: /ɪʁ/	ɪʁ	ɪθ	ɛʁ	ɛθ
Rule A has effect:	✗	✔	✗	✔
Rule B has effect:	✗	✗	✔	✔

It is important to note that the form [sɛθon] is ambiguous. It corresponds to two forms that are homophonous, 'for oxen' and 'for sheep', *not* because of a neutralization rule, but because of the combined effect of two rules. If grammars, or individual rules, were really sensitive to the generation of homophony, we might expect that one or both rules might be suppressed if a combination of rules were to lead to an ambiguous output. In other words, we could imagine that in the form meaning 'for oxen', either Rule A or

---

[8] As we will see later, this is not always the case; it is sometimes clear in what order a pair of rules must be applied.

Rule B would fail to apply, just to avoid homophony with 'for sheep'. Not only would this complicate tremendously our understanding of how derivations work, it would attribute to the grammar, a "dumb" computation system, sensitivity to whether the final grammatical output is somehow ambiguous. Empirically, rules do not seem to apply selectively depending on the effects of other rules, and we also know the language output is full of all kinds of ambiguity, including structural ambiguity (*I saw the man with the telescope*—Who had the telescope, me or the man?) and lexical ambiguity (*I saw the man with the telescope*—Do I regularly use a serrated telescope to cut the man into pieces?). Grammars do not care about ambiguity, and they have no means to be sensitive to it, even if they could care.

21.7.2   Combined Neutralization across Paradigms

In the previous example, both segmental alternations happened to occur in words containing the same root, 'ox'. Two two-way alternations led to a four-way surface alternation in the 'ox' words, but there was no alternation in the form of the 'sheep' morpheme.

We can also construct a situation in which each of two noun paradigms shows the effects of one of the rules, and homophony is thus generated. Here is one possibility, using the same lexicon as in Marchenan, above:

(243)   Pintan Language: Homophony via two rules affecting forms from different paradigms

form	gloss
vıʁa	'with an ox'
vıʁon	'with oxen'
vɛʁa	'with a sheep'
vɛθon	'with sheep (pl.)'
sɛʁa	'for an ox'
sɛʁon	'for oxen'
sɛʁa	'for a sheep'
sɛθon	'for sheep (pl.)'

We will model this language with the following lexical entries and rules:

(244)   Pintan lexicon and rules
       'with':   v-
       'for':   s-
       SINGULAR: -a
       PLURAL: -on
       'ox':   ɪʁ
       'sheep':   εθ
    Rules:

Rule A: θ → ʁ / ___a

Rule B: ɪ → ε / s ___

Constructing URs from the lexicon and applying the rules yields the following derivations.

(245)   Derivations

UR	v-ɪʁ-a	v-ɪʁ-on	v-εθ-a	v-εθ-on
A: θ → ʁ/ ___a	—	—	vεʁa	—
B: ɪ → ε/ s ___	—	—	—	—
SR	vɪʁa	vɪʁon	vεʁa	vεθon
Gloss	'with an ox'	'with oxen'	'with a sheep'	'with sheep (pl.)'

UR	s-ɪʁ-a	s-ɪʁ-on	s-εθ-a	s-εθ-on
A: θ → ʁ/ ___a	—	—	sεʁa	—
B: ɪ → ε/ s ___	sεʁa	sεʁon	—	—
SR	sεʁa	sεʁon	sεʁa	sεθon
Gloss	'for an ox'	'for oxen'	'for a sheep'	'for sheep (pl.)'

Try to draw the SMD for the Pintan data in (243). In this language, the two noun paradigms each show two surface forms of the root. In some of the words where a root surfaces, it is affected by only one of the rules. For example forms for 'ox' are affected by only Rule B. Homophony arises in the form [sεʁa], which means both 'for an ox' and 'for a sheep', but this is not due to the effect of a single neutralization rule. Instead the two rules take two underlying forms that differ in two ways, /sɪʁa/ and /sɛθa/, and act on them so as to make them end up identical. This is just an accidental result of what rules there are in the grammar and what morphemes are in the lexicon. It is hard to imagine how any kind of restriction against homophony could be built into our model of grammar. The empirical facts of known languages make it abundantly clear that we should not even want to model such a restriction, since lexical and derived homophony are both common.

In both of the examples in this unit, *combined neutralization* just refers to the situation in which sets of segments related by neutralization occur in paradigms some of whose members end up being homophonous due to the neutralizations.

To summarize this Part of the book, we have seen that from the simple mechanism of SPE rules we get to account for a massive amount of superficial diversity. The richness achieved by combining simple primitives is typical of scientific modeling. According to Chomsky (2000, p. 122), it is the "natural approach . . . to abstract from the welter of descriptive complexity certain general principles governing computation that would allow the rules of a particular language to be given in very simple forms".

We have devoted many pages to neutralization, but neutralization in all the variants we have seen is epiphenomenal. It arises as a byproduct of the model. Neutralization is not a thing, not a property of grammars. To use a fancy word, it is not part of the *ontology* of phonology. It is just a name for certain patterns of data that we can choose to lay out on a page. The lexical form of a morpheme is the best solution, in some sense, for generating the surface forms. We have seen that there is no requirement in our model that the lexical form be the same as a part of a surface form; sometimes, it is impossible to make it be so. Thus, in the end, we can't accept the surfacing lexical form assumption as reflecting a property of our model of phonology. We can continue to use the SLFA as a heuristic for analyzing datasets, but we need to be prepared sometimes to abandon it.

Unit 22

Neutralization Exercises

We present these exercises as a separate unit. In some questions, you will solve problems by providing the kind of analyses we have been presenting, and then in later questions you will have to construct your own datasets and provide analyses for those. Each student's responses will be idiosyncratic and will require discussion and evaluation by your peers or instructor.

Make sure that the rules needed conform to our SPE syntax. Be explicit in your solutions about when you are relying on the NAA or SLFA assumptions, as well as on MTP and RAA reasoning. If SLFA cannot be maintained, explain why.

Before beginning these problems, you should go back to some of the datasets we worked through earlier, such as Marchenan (238) and Pintan (243). See if you can solve them on your own, not by remembering our solution, but by reconstructing the arguments. This is a practice you should adopt as you see more and more complex datasets. At some point you will be able to apply the same forms of reasoning to completely novel data.

22.1. Four Tools: Match the name of each of the four tools we used for reasoning about neutralization with the correct definition: **modus tollendo ponens (MTP)**, **reductio ad absurdum (RAA)**, **surfacing lexical form assumption (SLFA)**, **non-alternation assumption (NAA)**.

   (a) _____ For any proposition p, if it is assumed that p is true and it can be demonstrated that with that assumption a contradiction can be reached, then it can be concluded that p is false.

(b) _____ If there is one surface form of a morpheme in all environments, then the phonological representation of the lexical item is identical to that form.

(c) _____ For any two propositions p and q, if (p or q) is true and p is false, then it can be concluded that q is true.

(d) _____ If there is more than one surface form, then the phonological representation of the lexical item is identical to one of those forms.

Provide a solution for the following. In order to get started, look for the paradigms that are easy to deal with, which typically means looking for morphemes with a single surface alternant. When you find morphemes with several alternants, try to derive some by combining the effects of multiple rules, rather than by formulating a new rule for each alternation you observe.

22.2. Diachean

	form	gloss
a.	nβɑd	'ox'
b.	nβɑf	'oxen'
c.	nβʕd	'sheep'
d.	nβɑf	'sheep (pl.)'

- List all morpheme alternants
  - 'ox':
  - 'sheep':
  - sg.:
  - pl.:

- Choose an underlying lexical representation for each morpheme:
  - 'ox':
  - 'sheep':
  - sg.:
  - pl.:

- Posit a phonological rule:

Now give an underlying representation for each word and show how it is derived by the rule. Remember that a given meaning has only one form in all URs. So the morpheme for 'sheep' should be the same in the UR for 'sheep' and 'sheep (pl.)'.

Underlying Rep				
Effect of Rule				
Surface Rep				
Gloss				

[Be sure to provide a gloss for each form and fill in all boxes with a form or a dash.]

22.3. Where did you appeal to each tool? **Give the first instance by placing a number above and explain.**

- Tool 1? *Tool 1 is* _____ *and as indicated above where I wrote* | *Tool 1* | *and gave its initials, I invoked it to determine . . .*

- Tool 2? *Tool 2 is* _____ *and as indicated above where I wrote* | *Tool 2* | *and gave its initials, I invoked it to determine . . .*

- Tool 3? . . .

- Tool 4? . . .

22.4. Trichian: (1) Provide a full analysis of the following data, as above, then (2) explain how it shows that one of our tools is not foolproof, that it sometimes fails. Which tool? Explain the failure.

sg.	pl.	gloss
ofh	ofhla	'cat'
ofs	ofsla	'mat'
ofs	ofhla	'rat'

For each of the following languages, provide a full analysis with (1) surface alternants, (2) lexicon, (3) rules, (4) derivations, (5) SMDs, and (6) a description of the neutralization pattern (multiple convergent, reciprocal, and so on).

22.5. Arcyrian

	form	gloss
a.	hjaš	'a dog'
b.	ihjaš	'the dog'
c.	ahjaš	'dogs'
d.	fjaš	'a hat'
e.	ihjaš	'the hat'
f.	afjaš	'hats'
g.	θjaš	'a pig'
h.	ihjaš	'the pig'
i.	aθjaš	'pigs'

22.6. Hemitrichian

	form	gloss
a.	fom	'a dog'
b.	fodba	'the dog'
c.	fomko	'dogs'
d.	fod	'a hat'
e.	fodba	'the hat'
f.	fomko	'hats'

22.7. Tubiferan: Combining simple patterns. Hint: First look for a paradigm where segmentation is easy.

	form	gloss
a.	dɔ	'ox'
b.	pʊqvɛ	'oxen'
c.	dɔqni	'the ox'
d.	pʊqso	'the oxen'
e.	dʊ	'sheep'
f.	pʊqvɛ	'sheep (pl.)'
g.	dʊqni	'the sheep'
h.	pʊqso	'the sheep (pl.)'
i.	dʊ	'dog'
j.	pʊvɛ	'dogs'
k.	dʊni	'the dog'
l.	pʊso	'the dogs'
m.	dɔ	'goose'
n.	pʊvɛ	'geese'
o.	dɔni	'the goose'
p.	pʊso	'the geese'

List morpheme alternants

- 'ox':
- 'sheep':
- 'dog':
- 'goose':
- sg.:
- pl.:
- indefinite in sg.:
- indefinite in pl.:
- 'the' in sg.:
- 'the' in pl.:

Lexical form

- 'ox':
- 'sheep':
- 'dog':
- 'goose':
- sg.:
- pl.:
- indefinite in sg.:
- indefinite in pl.:
- 'the' in sg.:
- 'the' in pl.:

• Posit two phonological rules:

Rule A:
Rule B:

Now give an underlying representation for each *word* and show how it is derived by the rules.

UR								
Rule A:								
Rule B:								
SR								
Gloss	a.	b.	c.	d.	e.	f.	g.	h.

UR								
Rule A:								
Rule B:								
SR								
Gloss	i.	j.	k.	l.	m.	n.	o.	p.

22.8. Loa Loa: Here is a similar problem for practice. Format your solution as you did for Tubiferan.

	form	gloss
a.	ifɑ	'a dog'
b.	tɑχʕ	'some dogs'
c.	ifɑʃɤ	'the dog'
d.	tɑŋɪʎ	'the dogs'
e.	ifɑ	'a sheep'
f.	tɑmχʕ	'some sheep (pl.)'
g.	ifɑmʃɤ	'the sheep'
h.	tɑmŋɪʎ	'the sheep (pl.)'
i.	ifɔ	'an ox'
j.	tɑmχʕ	'some oxen'
k.	ifɔmʃɤ	'the ox'
l.	tɑmŋɪʎ	'the oxen'
m.	ifɔ	'a goose'
n.	tɑχʕ	'some geese'
o.	ifɔʃɤ	'the goose'
p.	tɑŋɪʎ	'the geese'

22.9. Demonstrate that MTP-RAA logic works just fine for the case of reciprocal neutralization in Unit 21.5. It should be obvious that the non-alternation assumption will not be useful here.

Advanced Problems: For each of the following, use noun roots and *prefixes* to construct your forms. Provide the data and a full analysis in the format we have been using, along with a segment mapping diagram for each language. A *paradigm* refers here to a set of forms built from the same noun root.

22.10 Make up a set of forms that would lead to a simple neutralization analysis. Be sure that your data justifies positing two underlying segments that are neutralized on the surface.

22.11 Make up a set of forms that would lead to a multiple neutralization analysis in which two segments, a and b, neutralize with a third segment c, in the same environment.

22.12 Make up a set of forms that would lead to an overlapping neutralization analysis in which two segments, a and b, neutralize with a third segment c, in different environments.

22.13 Make up a set of forms that would lead to a reciprocal neutralization analysis.

22.14 Make up a set of forms that would lead to a combined neutralization analysis with two alternations occurring in the same paradigm.

22.15 Make up a set of forms that would lead to a combined neutralization analysis with two alternations each occurring in one of the paradigms.

Part V

The Logic of Allophony

Unit 23

Splits without Neutralization

In the segment mapping diagrams we have been using, we have focused on neutralizations, in which more than one segment in underlying representations have an arrow pointing to a single segment that shows up on the surface. For expository clarity, we have used the diagonal arrows to show the non-vacuous effects of rules. In the simplest cases, there was only one diagonal arrow and two vertical arrows. The vertical arrows represented identity mappings: a correspondence of a segment in URs with the same segment in SRs. The diagonal arrow represents the conversion of one underlying segment into a different surface segment.

To give a concrete example, consider the simple case of neutralization in Dengue repeated in (246):

(246)   Simple neutralization in Dengue, again

	form	gloss
a.	luš	'a dog'
b.	luši	'the dog'
c.	lus	'a hat'
d.	luši	'the hat'

As discussed in Unit 19.1, we can analyze this dataset as having an underlying /s/ that maps to both [s] and [š] on the surface, while also having an underlying /š/ that maps to itself on the surface. In cases like this, neutralization depends on a *split* in the mapping from UR to SR of at least one segment, just as much it depends on the *merger* of two or more segments in the mapping.[1] These two properties are illustrated in the two

---

[1]The terminology of *split* and *merger* is borrowed from historical phonology, where it means some-

211

versions of the same segment mapping diagram in (247).

(247)   "Merger and split" in neutralization

Note that the merger (dotted) and split (dashed) parts of the diagram are logically independent—they share the diagonal arrow, of course, but given our model so far, there is no reason why each of the two parts should rely on the existence of the other.

When we discussed the possibility of non-surfacing lexical forms in Unit 21.6, we represented the relevant neutralization pattern for a language like Ustilago (233) as in (248), with the symbol H representing a particular segment that surfaces sometimes as *k* and sometimes as *g*:

(248)   SMD with an underlying segment that has no vertical arrows

Since underlying H always surfaces as either [k] or [g], there is no vertical arrow from underlying H. Inputs with H are always affected by a rule that changes H into another segment. In this case, arrows from underlying H show not a split of a non-vertical arrow from a vertical arrow, but a split of two non-vertical arrows, one of which merges with a vertical arrow from underlying /k/ and the other with a vertical arrow from underlying /g/ depending on the environment. By hypothesis, H never surfaces at all.

Given that underlying representations do not need to surface, the SMDs in (249) should, in theory, be possible. We assume that these represent all the mappings of these segments in two languages.

(249)   "Merger and split" separately

---

thing quite different despite the notational and structural similarities used to describe the phenomena. See Hale (2007) for discussion of the dangers of not recognizing that sound changes and phonological rules are fundamentally different.

The left-hand side of (249) would be appropriate to describe a situation in which two underlying segments merge, yielding surface identity. Such a pattern is called *absolute neutralization* (Kiparsky, 1968). Although it may be hard to imagine why we would ever want to posit such an analysis for a real language, let's just note for now that nothing in our model precludes it.

For the time being, let's concentrate on the case of split without merger, the dashed diagram on the right-hand side in (249). This mapping could correspond to the rule we have used for neutralization cases:

(250)   s → š / ___i

This rule created the alternation that derived the difference between *lus* 'a hat' (246c) and *luši* 'the hat' (246d). With our neutralization dataset, a *merger* between *s* and *š* was needed because there was independent evidence for the existence of an underlying *š* segment, namely *luš* 'a dog' (246a) versus *lus* 'a hat' (246c). However, it is possible to have an alternation without any evidence for an underlying *š* segment. In fact, we just have to remove the (a) and (b) forms from (246), producing the data in (251). Assume that this is the complete set of relevant forms for a different language that we'll call Oxyurian:

(251)   Oxyurian: alternation without neutralization

form	gloss
lus	'a hat'
luši	'the hat'

With just this alternation and no non-alternating *š* forms, we may still be correct in positing a rule in Oxyurian that maps *s* to *š*.[2] We can do so in order to capture the idea that there is just one stored lexical form for 'hat' in the language. The relevant SMD has an underlying /s/ that splits to *s* and *š*, exactly what we saw on the right-hand side of (249), shown here in (252):

(252)   "Split" without merger in Oxyurian

---

[2]Assume that our morphological analysis is correct. Obviously, with just this data, it's possible that the rule is š → s / ___%.

Given the rule and SMD we propose for Oxyurian, there are tokens of the segment *s* which are sometimes mapped to *s* and sometimes to *š*. In the case of a language like Dengue (246), we are forced to select underlying /s/ to derive the *s~š* alternation according to our MTP-RAA forced-choice reasoning developed earlier, summarized here informally:

- We assume that the underlying segment at the end of the morpheme 'hat' should be identical to one of the surface variants, so it must be /s/ or /š/. This uses the surfacing lexical form assumption (SLFA).

- There are other lexical items, like 'dog' that only show *š* in the same environments where 'hat' alternates, so 'dog', by assumption, contains underlying /š/. This uses the non-alternation assumption. (NAA).

- Since 'hat' contains either /s/ or /š/, but this morpheme behaves differently from items that we know contain /š/, 'hat' must contain /s/. This uses modus tollendo ponens (MTP) and reductio ad absurdum (RAA).

In a language like Oxyurian (251), which by assumption has no non-alternating forms with *š*, we cannot use the identity of the segment in *other* lexical items to help us choose the form of the segment in the lexical items in question. Thus, a methodological question arises: What can we do? In the next unit, we will illustrate a method for choosing lexical forms, even in the absence of neutralization patterns.

In Oxyurian, the surface segments [s] and [š] are in a relationship traditionally called *allophony*: the two segments are referred to as ALLOPHONES of a single underlying segment called a PHONEME. In the following units we will explore the concepts of allophone and phoneme, and explore why modern phonology does not reserve an important role for these concepts. First, however, we make a digression to discuss some methodological and philosophical ideas concerning the relationship between observation and theory construction.

Unit 24

Rules as Generalizations

In this unit, we explore the relationship between our developing phonological theory and the empirical data we draw upon. We want to challenge the common misconception that theories just arise from a set of observations, and to suggest the importance of an alternative perspective: the idea that it is, in fact, the theory that determines what counts as data. This latter approach is sometimes referred to as the *rationalist* perspective on science, the idea that *reason* takes logical priority over observation in theory construction. The rationalist perspective, often associated with the ideas of the seventeenth-century philosopher and mathematician René Descartes, is often contrasted with the *empiricist* view that ideas and theories arise primarily from observation via the senses. Chomsky's 1966 *Cartesian Linguistics: A Chapter in the History of Rationalist Thought* (the term *Cartesian* is derived from the name Descartes) provides a partial history of the rationalist versus empiricist perspectives. Our use of toy grammars in this book is predicated on a strongly rationalist perspective—we want you to understand arguments and recognize patterns, and then ultimately apply your knowledge in understanding what is out in the world. We also want you to understand that accepting a broad role for rationalist, as opposed to empiricist, reasoning does not imply a rejection of *empirical* data as crucial in scientific reasoning.[1]

---

[1] The rationalist-empiricist distinction is not only relevant to doing science, but also to competing perspectives on children's cognitive development, including language acquisition. The notion of UG, which we presuppose in this book, reflects our rationalist perspective in this domain, too. The idea is that children come to the process of language acquisition with an innately determined toolkit common to all humans.

24.1   Simplicity and Generalizations

Let's back up, and suppose that we have not yet decided what the lexical forms should be in a language like Oxyurian. In (253) we have added a couple more items than we had in (251) in order to justify morpheme segmentation.

(253)   More Oxyurian

form	gloss
dar	'a potato'
dari	'the potato'
lus	'a hat'
luši	'the hat'

In the forms of 'hat' in (253), we have a single underlying segment that surfaces as either [s] or [š]. By appealing to the surfacing lexical form assumption (SLFA), we can assume that the underlying segment will be identical in form to either *s* or *š*. If this were a real language, we would need a principled way to choose which one.

Our limited dataset gives us no logical basis for choosing an underlying form. We could model the data in (253) by starting with underlying /s/ and mapping it to *š* in certain circumstances, say before the segment *i*. However, we could equally well posit underlying /š/ with a rule that maps *š* to *s* when it occurs at the end of a word. For a case like this, most phonologists would probably choose the first analysis, with underlying /s/ and a rule turning *s* into *š* before *i*. The reason has to do with an appeal to "naturalness." Such a rule is found over and over again in the languages of the world and is considered to be phonetically natural—it seems to follow from what we know about the vocal tract and the articulation of sounds. Whether or not such reasoning is valid (we don't think it is), we want to put such phonetic considerations aside and focus on the *logic* of the situation. This is important, since phonetic intuitions sometimes fail, in part because languages can end up with what have been called "crazy rules," rules that make no sense phonetically (Bach and Harms, 1972).

From the perspective of our rule system laid out in Unit 10, the two analyses appear to be equally good, and there is no obvious way to choose between them. This is sometimes the situation we are in—sometimes we just can't decide which analysis is better. However, let's enrich the dataset to learn how it may be possible to choose between two analyses on empirical grounds. Consider the dataset in (254):

(254) Yet more Oxyurian

form	gloss
dar	'a potato'
dari	'the potato'
dara	'potatoes'
lus	'a hat'
luši	'the hat'
lusa	'hats'

We now have evidence for a plural suffix /-a/. Crucially, the morpheme for 'hat' shows up as *lus* in [lusa], not *luš*. Now, if we let the underlying segment be /š/, we would need a rule like this:

(255) š → s / ___ (% or a)

That is, we would need to turn *š* into *s* if it occurs at the end of the word or before an *a*. However, our discussion of rule conditions in Unit 10 does not allow for the use of disjunctive conditions (i.e., those that make use of the notion *or* in rule environments). Thus, (255) is not a possible rule according to our theoretical assumptions.

This is a critical point and hence worth emphasizing. Our claim is *not* that we know that (255) is the incorrect rule for the language in question. Rather, the claim is that given the restricted model of rules we proposed, it is impossible to state (255). It is incompatible with the current theory. The statement in (255) *is not a rule* of the model we are using, so it cannot be the *correct rule* unless we change our model.

An alternative to (255) is to assume that the data justifies two separate rules:

(256) Two rules

    i.   š → s / ___ %

    ii. š → s / ___ a

In the case at hand, the left-hand side of the rules are exactly the same, but they are different rules because the environments are different. The possibility of a language with two or more rules is not precluded logically. In fact, we have seen cases where hypothesizing two or more rules is necessary. However, there is a simpler solution for modeling Oxyurian.

Consider what happens if we assume that the underlying segment is /s/. The data in (254) is compatible with this analysis if we combine it with a rule like (257):

(257) s → š / ___ i

This analysis works and it does not force us to posit two separate rules or fundamentally change our model of UG. This one rule solution is simpler (by virtue of having just one rule), and it captures a real generalization—*š* occurs only before *i*, and *s* occurs elsewhere. Just as individual data points— the words we observe—count as empirical data, so too do the generalizations that can be extracted from these data points.[2]

Science involves capturing generalizations, and it is a sophisticated kind of observation to notice that there is a single rule in (257) that describes the fact that *š* appears only before *i* in Oxyurian, a generalization which the two-rule analysis in (256) fails to capture. Although it is derived by looking at individual data points, this generalization is an empirical fact, in the context of our theory. Linguistics is an empirical science that aims to explain such facts, but what counts as a fact is theory dependent.

Note furthermore that the rule we formulated not only accounts for the observed facts, but also allows us to make predictions, which may or may not be borne out. For example, if rule (257) is correct—if it is an accurate model of an Oxyurian I-language—then we expect to find *s* not *š* before other segments, like *u, o, k, p*. If we don't, we'll have to revise our rule.[3]

We appealed to the notion of simplicity or elegance in settling on an analysis for Oxyurian. It is worth pointing out that we actually used two distinct notions of simplicity, and that the two can sometimes be in conflict. The argument for not allowing the potential disjunctive rule in (255) is based on a *universal* or general notion of simplicity in our model of the phonological faculty. The system defined in Unit 10 does not allow disjunctive environments ('before this *or* that'). The argument against the two-rule solution in (256) is based on *local* simplicity for Oxyurian. Each rule is allowable given the formal system, and we have seen that languages can have more than one rule, but the two-rule solution appears to be unnecessarily complex for this particular language, and it fails to capture a generalization. Implicit here is the claim that learners will develop a mental grammar consistent with phonological UG that contains fewer rules rather than one that contains more rules. They do not have the option of positing rules that are not consistent with phonological UG—so they can't posit rules

---

[2]If you find yourself resisting our claim that the generalizations can count as data, remember that even our "observations" of individual words are highly abstract. As simple inspection of the waveform will show, each token of someone pronouncing, say, *cat* is acoustically unique. Without a certain level of abstraction, we can't do linguistics, or science in general, since every event or region of the universe in space-time is unique!

[3]Or revise the model in some other way, as we will see later. Later, when we enrich our theory of phonological representations, we will be able to collapse what appear to be separate rules into one. In other words, what appear to be distinct rule targets or distinct rule triggers, may be expressible as elements of a single category, members of a what we will call a single *natural class*.

with disjunctions if the human language faculty does not provide for that.[4]

One could imagine a conflict between universal and local simplicity. For example, one could propose a mechanism that collapses several apparent rules into one for some particular language, but requires notions that never seem to be relevant in other languages. If we accept the existence of UG, then we are bound in principle to favoring universal simplicity over local simplicity. We can't posit tools for the UG toolkit on an ad hoc basis for a particular language. Recall that we want "to abstract from the welter of descriptive complexity certain general principles governing computation that would allow the rules of a particular language to be given in very simple forms" (Chomsky, 2000, p. 122). This means that the same kinds of rules are used in all languages. Accepting this is equivalent to accepting the idea that there is a human language faculty, a universal grammar.

In the actual phonological model developed in Chomsky and Halle's book, *The Sound Pattern of English*, disjunctive rules *are* allowed. In particular, curly brackets (braces) were used to indicate disjunction, so the statement in (255) can be expressed as a rule thus:

(258)   Disjunction with braces in Chomsky and Halle (1968)[5]

$$\text{š} \rightarrow \text{s} \; / \; \underline{\quad} \{\%, \text{a}\}$$

We will not make use of disjunctive rules, and in Part VIII, we use the braces for a different purpose as we revise our model.

24.2   Environments Define Equivalence Classes

The cognitive scientist Zenon Pylyshyn (1999) draws on linguistic notions to point out the abstractness of mental representations:

> The most remarkable property of human behavior involving intelligence (as well as similar behavior of certain other species) is that, in order to capture what is systematic about it, it is necessary to recognize **equivalence classes** [emphasis added—ab&cr] of causal events that cannot be characterized using the terms of existing natural sciences. The anthropologist [and linguist, mentioned in Unit 3—ab&cr] Kenneth Pike once made the

---

[4]See Chapter 11 of Isac and Reiss (2013) for an illustration of how UG determines the set of attainable languages.

[5]They would use '#' for our '%'.

astute observation that human behavior cannot be understood in terms of objective physical properties of the world, which he called *etic* properties, but only in terms of the way in which the world is perceived or represented in the mind, which he called *emic*, or internalized, properties. (p. 3)

The term *etic* is derived from *phonetic*, with the suggestion of being characterized by concrete acoustic (e.g., What is the waveform?) and physiological (e.g., Where is the tongue?) properties. The term *emic* is derived from *phonemic*, which is an older term relating to abstract phonological segments that must be posited to understand linguistic patterns, basically the segments we posit for lexical entries.[6]

Pylyshyn imports the term *equivalence class* from mathematics, where it has an intuitive meaning. If we collect into a set all and only those integers that leave a remainder of 0 when divided by 2, we get the equivalence class of *even numbers*. The number 4 is different from the number 1096, but with respect to the process of finding the remainder when dividing by 2, these numbers are equivalent, members of the same equivalence class. The odd numbers constitute another equivalence class. Similarly, we can divide a group of people by their month of birth. Those who are born in January are each different from each other, but they are equivalent in terms of all yielding a true statement 'x is born in January'. We can get twelve equivalence classes under the relation mapping people to months.

We've been using the idea of equivalence classes implicitly in our rule environments. In a rule like '$p \rightarrow q /$ ___ r', we intensionally define an equivalence class of segment strings in which p is replaced by q. This class includes *opri, opru, opropoprasi, lmjoilpkpipra* and infinitely more, but not *opku, fadtuh, orppu, juuuug* and infinitely more. The equivalence class of strings in which the rule has an effect, in which it applies non-vacuously, is defined by the rule syntax.

In this section, we make more explicit a few ideas that bear on the relationship between rule environments and input strings. In particular, we focus on how environments divide input strings into two equivalence classes: those in which there is a substring that triggers a non-vacuous application of the rule, and those in which there is no such substring. The notion of equivalence classes is actually ubiquitous in linguistics. In syntax the names of *categories* or *parts of speech* define equivalence classes. The nouns *dog*, *cat*, *virtue*, and so on, have *etic* differences (for example, they have different phonological representations), but they are all members of the same equiv-

---

[6]Similar points were made in the 1930s by another anthropologist/linguist, Edward Sapir (1949, translated into English in 1933), who pointed out that "no entity in human experience can be adequately defined as the mechanical sum or product of its physical properties" and that "it is notorious how many of these physical properties are, or may be, overlooked as irrelevant."

alence class, the class of nouns. Prepositions are members of a different equivalence class. Morphological rules may make reference to equivalence classes like *prefix*, *root*, *suffix*, and so on.

Returning to phonology, we discuss here the idea that rule environments define equivalence classes, but the notion will take on even greater importance as we develop our model of phonological representation to include syllable structure and sub-segmental features. In phonology, the notion of *equivalence class* is usually referred to as a *natural class*, and we will use the terms interchangeably, as we proceed.

In our SPE rule system, we describe the environments in which a rule applies (non-vacuously) using a long underscore symbol with other symbols appearing to the left and/or to the right. Not only does this environment-format limit what counts as a triggering environment, it also gives us information on what types of environments count as the "same" or "different." For example, consider the three rules in (259) and the three-segment input strings in (260):

(259)   Three rules

      a. s → š / u ___ i

      b. s → š / ___ i

      c. s → š / u ___

(260)   Some potential input strings
      (i) usi   (ii) asi   (iii) esi
      (iv) usa   (v) use   (vi) uso

The rules in (259) each divide up the input strings in (260) in different ways. For example, the environment specified in (259a) affects only the string in (260i). This is the only form that has an *s* segment between a *u* and an *i*. In contrast, the rule in (259b) affects all the strings in (260i-iii). All of these strings are "equivalent" in the sense that they each have an *i* segment appearing after an *s*.[7] Finally, the rule in (259c) affects only the string in (260i) and the strings in (260iv-vi). Once again, the rule treats these strings as equivalent in the sense that they each have a *u* segment appearing before an *s*.[8]

---

[7] Note that the lack of a symbol on the left side of the underscore signals that the segments to the left of *s* do not matter with respect to the application of the rule. With nothing specified there, the interpretation is that *anything* can occur there. This is a nothing that means 'everything'.

[8] Similar to the previous rule, the lack of a segment on the right side of the underscore signals that the segments to the right of *s* do not matter with respect to the application of the rule.

The idea that the rules define equivalence classes of strings can be expanded to strings of arbitrary length. For example, the same types of observations can be made about the strings in (261).

(261)   Additional potential input strings

      (i) busita   (ii) gimasi   (iii) sibonu
      (iv) trusan   (v) gratusena   (vi) rusotuna

With respect to (259a), any input string that contains the substring *usi* will be equivalent in terms of triggering a non-vacuous application of the rule. Similarly, with respect to (259b), any input string that contains the substring *si* will be equivalent, whereas for (259c) it will be any input string that contains the substring *us*.

When we start to break down segments into smaller elements called *features*, we will expand our notion of equivalence classes. Looking ahead, let's illustrate this with a simple example that you may have already seen in an introductory class.

The segments *m*, *n*, and *ŋ* are nasal consonants.[9] Suppose that in a given language, *L*, these are the only nasal segments, and that we find alternations that support the following rules:

(262)   Each nasal as a separate equivalence class/natural class

      • e → i / ___ m

      • e → i / ___ n

      • e → i / ___ ŋ

In our current model, each nasal consonant after an underscore defines a different equivalence class: '___m' defines the set of strings that contain the substring *em* as an equivalence class; '___n' defines the set of strings that contain the substring *en* as an equivalence class; and '___ŋ' defines the set of strings that contain the substring *eŋ* as an equivalence class. Later, we will have a way of collapsing these three rules into a single one that will define a single equivalence class that is general enough to include substrings that contain any one of the three nasals after the underscore.

---

[9]They are made with air flowing from the lungs out through the nose—while making a long *m* sound pinch your nose shut and see what happens.

(263) Informal rule treating nasals as a natural class:

     a. e → i / ___ ċ, where $c \in \{m,n,ŋ\}$

     b. e → i / ___ any nasal consonant

In (263a), the set of nasals is defined extensionally, and the variable c can be assigned the value of any member of this set. In (263b) we informally refer to the set of nasals intensionally. At this point, we cannot look *inside the segments* to find properties that allow us to define *sets of segments* intensionally, but that is where we are heading. Part VIII will outline the features that we will use to decompose segments. For the moment, we just want to prepare you to see that using descriptions like 'nasal consonants' is logically like referring to substrings to describe rule environments.

24.3   Counting Environments

Our discussion of Oxyurian has involved a very restricted dataset. It was trivial to see that in (254) š occurs before *i*, and that *s* occurs in two environments, before *a* and word-finally. Suppose we have more data, as in (264):

(264) Even more Oxyurian

form	gloss
dar	'a potato'
dari	'the potato'
lus	'a hat'
luši	'the hat'
lusa	'hats'
šišiɡ	'a bag'
šišiɡi	'the bag'
ɑšiɡan	'a book'
ɑšiɡani	'the book'

There are more *tokens* of š in the data, but that could just be an artifact of the words we happened to collect. Although a statistical approach to language may treat the prevalence of š as important, there is no role for such considerations in our model. Recall that in Unit 21.6 we even posited underlying segments that *never* surface as being present in lexical forms, so such superficial statistics cannot be relevant for us.

Let's move on to the distribution patterns that we have been concerned with. Even if we restrict ourselves to environments that obey our SPE three-segment window, we might come to the conclusion that š occurs in four different environments:

(265)   Environments where š occurs in Oxyurian

- #___
- i ___i
- ___i
- ɑ___

However, this is not a valid move. This is the beauty of commitment to a model. Our SPE syntax not only *lets* us see the generalization that š occurs only before *i*, it *forces* us to see things that way. The environments 'at the beginning of a word' and 'before *i*' cannot be treated as different if, in fact, all the word-initial cases are also before *i*. The model tells us what to collapse into one rule environment. In other words, our SPE model determines our observations about the data.

24.4   Another Peek at Natural Classes

We are now ready to synthesize four ideas:

- natural classes of segments

- the idea that environments define natural classes of strings

- universal versus local simplicity

- the rationalist approaches to doing science—theory precedes data

We introduced the natural class of nasal consonants above. Here we will make use of the class of all consonants, a class that you probably have some intuitions about, namely that it is in opposition to the class of vowels. Suppose you have a language L with an alternation between segments x and y, and you notice that x occurs only before *i, u, a,* and %; whereas y occurs only before *p, t, k, b, d, g, n, m, r, l, s, z, ʃ, ʒ*:

(266)   a. x appears /___i, u, a, %

          b. y appears /___p, t, k, b, d, g, n, m, r, l, s, z, ʃ, ʒ

Suppose that there are no other segments in L. Just counting symbols, it looks like x occurs in four different environments and y occurs in fourteen different environments. Since $14 > 4$, we might be tempted to choose y as the segment in the lexical form.

Then we would need just four rules to turn *y* into *x*, instead of fourteen rules to turn *x* into *y*.

Of course, you can see that *y* is the wrong choice as the underlying segment. Choosing *y* misses a generalization. On the surface, the segment *y* occurs before any *consonant*, whereas *x* occurs before any vowel *and* at the end of the word. So, there is a generalization about the occurrence of *y*, but not about the occurrence of *x*. In our current model, we cannot state this generalization, because we don't have a way to refer to some subset of ENV as 'consonants'. In other words, it takes a theory, one that we haven't yet given you, that treats the segments *p, t, k, b, d, g, n, m, r, l, s, z, ʃ, ʒ* as members of a single category, a single equivalence class, to make the observation that *y* occurs in a single environment, and that *x* does not.

Students are typically told to select as the underlying form in an allophony problem the segment that has a "more general distribution," that occurs in "more environments." What they are not typically told is that the decision about what counts as "more environments" is not just a matter of pure observation. The tools for describing and collapsing environments must be provided by a theory.

This relationship between data and theory is a general property of science. The theory often tells us what the relevant observations are. As Einstein famously put it, "It is the theory that decides what we can observe." Here is the context of Einstein's statement, in a conversation with Heisenberg (Heisenberg and Pomerans, 1971, p. 63):

(267)   Theory and Observation

> Heisenberg: "We cannot observe electron orbits inside the atom. . . Now, since a good theory must be based on directly observable magnitudes, I thought it more fitting to restrict myself to these, treating them, as it were, as representatives of the electron orbits."

> "But you don't seriously believe," Einstein protested, "that none but observable magnitudes must go into a physical theory?"

> "Isn't that precisely what you have done with relativity?" I [Heisenberg] asked in some surprise. . .

> "Possibly I did use this kind of reasoning," Einstein admitted, "but it is nonsense all the same....In reality the very opposite happens. It is the theory which decides what we can observe."

Similar issues were discussed, specifically with respect to speech segments, by Robert Hammarberg, the author of a paper called "The Metaphysics of Coarticulation" (1976, p. 354):

Chomskian linguistics is explicitly anti-empiricist, and all indications are that current philosophy of science is moving toward a rejection of the empiricist programme (Fodor 1968, pp. xiv *ff*). A key feature of the new programme is exactly a reevaluation of the concept of observation. Observations are now held to be judgments, and these judgments are made in terms of the criteria provided by the paradigm. Thus the taxonomy of a discipline is to be regarded as imposed from above, rather than emerging from below, i.e., rather than emerging in the form of brute facts before the unprejudiced eyes or ears of the researcher. The relevance of this to the study of phonetics and phonology should be obvious: the concept of the segment, which is indispensable to phonetics and phonology, is a creature of the paradigm, not of the raw data.

If you have spent any time trying to segment waveforms of speech on a computer, you will understand Hammarberg's point very well—there are generally no clearly defined boundaries between segments in the speech signal, as you saw if you did Exercise 3.3. Both as scientists and as speakers/listeners we impose segments on the signal we hear. Speech perception does not *find* segments in the signal, rather it *constructs* them from the signal. This is not the place to delve into such issues, but make sure you understand that Hammarberg's point is that Chomskyan linguistics is anti-empiricist, not anti-empirical. Failure to appreciate this distinction has led even prominent thinkers to misunderstand and mischaracterize the goals of theoretical linguistics, including Google's Peter Norvig (2011).

Unit 25

Allophones

25.1 Allophony versus Neutralization

In Dengue (246) in Unit 23 and Oxyurian (254) in Unit 24, we constructed two languages that had both s and $š$ in SRs, and we also argued in each language for a rule that converts s to $š$ before i. However, the justifications for the rule—modus tollendo ponens versus simplicity—were different. Given the similarity of the datasets, it might be fruitful to review why we used such different methods to choose the lexical forms and justify the choice of rule.

We enlarge the datasets for the two languages, and present them side by side in (268):

(268)   Different data yields the same rule in two languages

Dengue		Oxyurian		
root	SR	root	SR	gloss
/dar /	dar	/dar /	dar	'a potato'
	dari		dari	'the potato'
	dara		dara	'potatoes'
/pas/	pas	/pas/	pas	'a foot'
	paši		paši	'the foot'
	pasa		pasa	'feet'
/luš/	**luš**	/lus/	**lus**	'a dog'
	luši		luši	'the dog'
	luša		**lusa**	'dogs'
/lus/	lus	/lus/	lus	'a hat'
	luši		luši	'the hat'
	lusa		lusa	'hats'

As you can see in (268), if we consider the surface forms, the two languages are identical aside from the forms in boldface. Both languages have a definite suffix -*i* and a plural suffix -*a*. Furthermore, the underlying representations of the roots match almost completely, except for one critical discrepancy in the boxed forms: in Dengue, the root meaning 'dog' is distinct from the root meaning 'hat', whereas in Oxyurian the two forms are identical.

There is a tradition followed in some introductory texts of treating the rules of Dengue and Oxyurian as fundamentally different, because Dengue shows neutralization and Oxyurian does not. In Dengue, there are instances of š that are clearly not created by the rule, such as the one in *luš* ('a dog'). In fact, all the 'dog' forms in Dengue have š in the SR derived unchanged from the same segment in the UR. In Oxyurian, there are no such instances of underlying š.

Under the model we have developed, however, neutralization is just the name of a set of relations between underlying forms and surface forms—it is not actually part of the model. There are no principles of neutralization or constraints on neutralization in phonological UG. In fact, according to our model, the difference between these two languages is just a difference between their respective lexicons (i.e., the set of forms that a speaker of each language must memorize). In the case of Dengue, the lexicon happens to have some morphemes containing /š/, whereas in the case of Oxyurian, there are no such morphemes in the lexicon—the segment š doesn't appear in the underlying phonological form of any morpheme.[1,2]

This is not to say that there are not interesting descriptive differences between the two languages. Despite the fact that their phonological systems are identical, the distributional characteristics of their surface representations lead to distinct generalizations. For example, in the case Dengue, there are minimal pairs of words that on the surface differ just with respect to the segments [s] and [š]: *lus* vs. *luš*. If we know that a word begins with *lu* and then has one more segment in it, we cannot predict what that segment will be—it could be [s] or [š] (or something else, presumably). We can say that the two segments *overlap* in their distribution, since either can occur in the blank in *lu_*, and the choice between the two can signal a difference in meaning.

However, if we know that a word in this language has the form *lu_i*, and we know that in the position of the blank there is either [s] or [š], we can be sure that it is [š]. This is guaranteed by the existence of the rule that neutralizes the contrast between the two segments.[3] The two segments overlap in their distribution, but that does not mean that they occur in *all* the same environments. In some environments only [š] appears—and our rule provides an explanation for why that is the case.

The situation is different for Oxyurian, the language without neutralization. In this language, if we know that a word contains on the surface either [s] or [š], we can predict with complete confidence which it is, since [š] only occurs before *i*, and [s] never does; and [š] never occurs before % nor before *a*, whereas [s] does occur in these two environments. There is no overlap in the surface distribution of the two segments, as long as we define the environments correctly.

When the surface distribution of two, or more, segments is completely predictable according to the phonological environment in which they occur, we say that they are in *complementary distribution*. In the next section, we will explore this notion further.

---

[1] There are approaches to phonology that derive the absence of segments in the lexicon or in surface forms from other factors—for example, from ranked constraints that constitute the grammar in such frameworks (e.g., Kager, 1999 on Optimality Theory). We think it is an advantage of our approach that the idiosyncracies of segment distributions are nowhere directly encoded in the computational part of the grammar. This is an issue of ongoing controversy: Exactly what does a phonological theory have to account for? See the discussion of phonotactics in Unit 26.2.

[2] The classic discussion on rejecting a principled distinction between allophonic rules and neutralization rules is Halle 1959. Halle's argument, based on the elegance of the rule system, has a different focus from our reference to the lexicon, but the two arguments, we think, are equivalent, as discussed in Reiss 2017a.

[3] Guaranteed for now. Phonological life will get complicated later.

25.2 Set Complements and
Complementary Distribution

The members of a set can be anything, so {Alan, Charles, Mars, peace, 3, horse} is a set with six members. However, set theory is typically used to talk about a particular domain, such as the set of students in a university, or the natural numbers, $\mathbb{N} = \{1, 2, 3, \ldots\}$, or the segments that can appear in phonological rules. We refer to such a domain as the *domain of discourse*, or the *universe of discourse*, or the *universal set*, denoted U. So U refers to the set of everything we are interested in talking about for the moment.

If U is the set of small letters of the English alphabet, and $T = \{a, b, c, d, e, f, g, h, i, j, k, l, m, n, o, p, q, r, s, t, u, v, w, x\}$, then $U - T = T' = \{y, z\}$. As you can see, $U - T' = T$. You can also see that $T \cup T' = U$ and $T \cap T' = \emptyset$. These relations are always true, no matter what you select for U and T.

If we are interested in the natural numbers, then the members of U are all and only the natural numbers, since $U = \mathbb{N}$. If we are interested in the segment symbols that can appear in rules, then since $U = $ IPA, the members of U are all and only the IPA segment symbols. All empty sets are the same, but U varies by context. U can have a finite number of elements, for example if $U = $ IPA, or an infinite number of elements, for example if $U = \mathbb{N}$.

Suppose that $U = \mathbb{N}$, the set of natural numbers. Then P, the set of *prime numbers*, is a subset of U: $P \subseteq U$. We might want to refer to the rest of the natural numbers, the ones that have the property of being *non-prime*. We gave you a means to do this in Unit 4.4.4 with the *set subtraction* operation. The set of natural numbers that are *not prime* is just $\mathbb{N} - P$, the set of everything that is in $\mathbb{N}$, but not in P. Since we have assigned the value to the universal set $U = \mathbb{N}$, the set of non-primes is also expressed by $U - P$. When we subtract any set A from the universal set U, the result of $U - A$ is called *the (absolute) complement of A*, which we denote A'. Think of the word *complement* as being related to *complete*: together A and A' complete U, since $A \cup A' = U$. You should convince yourself that if $B = A'$, then $A = B'$.

If we define a set intensionally as consisting of all and only the members of U having some property, as we did for the set of primes, P, it may be the case that the members of P' also share some property or set of properties. For example, if $U = \mathbb{N}$, then P' is the set of natural numbers that are divisible by at least one other integer besides 1 and themselves: for example $6 \in P'$. However, if $U = \mathbb{Z}$, the set of all positive and negative integers, then $\mathbb{Z} - P$ will not be a 'natural class' since prime numbers are all positive, so in this case P' will include not only 6, but also the negatives of the primes (which are not called primes), like -2, -3, and so on. We can refer to the non-prime members of $\mathbb{Z}$, but they have to be defined by a disjunction—they are divisible by another number, or they are negative.

Let's return to phonology. The term *complementary distribution*, which we applied to the allophones of Oxyurian, derives from the set-theoretic notion of complement. In Oxyurian, if we consider the environment 'before i' we can find $š$ there. In other environments, we find s. In other words, call the set of environments that contains just the member 'before i' E, and call the set of all environments U. Then, we can find s only in the environments that are members of $U - E = E'$.

Note that given our dataset, the attested members of E' are just 'before a' and 'before %'. These two environments do *not* constitute a natural set of environments— just as the *non-prime members of* $\mathbb{Z}$ do not constitute a natural class of numbers. Since s occurs in a set of environments that are not a natural class, it cannot be the case that the appearance of s is dependent on a rule, because in our model, rule environments are *defined* by natural classes of strings.

As we suggested, U is actually to be understood as the set of *all* environments, not just environments where you might find either s or $š$. So, let's say that in Oxyurian, you never find either of these segments between p and k. This environment, '$p\_\_\_k$', is in U, nonetheless. There may be no lexical items or URs that could ever have $š$ between p and k, but the grammar has nothing to say about this. Only the environment of the rule, '$\_\_\_i$', is encoded in the grammar. The unspecified complement set of environments is not part of a rule, and it is sometimes referred to as the ELSEWHERE case—$š$ occurs before i, and s occurs elsewhere.

Figure 25.1 corresponds to the Oxyurian situation, where s and $š$ are in complementary distribution. Let's reiterate that complementary distribution refers to the distribution of segments over sets of environments, sets of environments that are complements of each other.

There are more complicated scenarios, in which there are more than two segments in a complementary distribution relationship, but the basic ideas remain. For example, consider the Dhori data in (269) showing distribution of s, $š$, and $ṣ$ and the distribution of segments, shown in Figure 25.2.

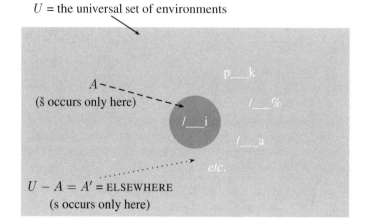

U = the universal set of environments

A
(š occurs only here)

p___k

/___%

/___i

/___a

etc.

$U - A = A' = $ ELSEWHERE
(s occurs only here)

Figure 25.1 Complementary distribution for Oxyurian.

(269)   Dhori three-way complementary distribution
         a. haš   'sugar'
         b. haški   'with sugar'
         c. haṣra   'in sugar'
         d. haṣruɡ   'for sugar'
         e. haspo   'under sugar'
         f. haspi   'before sugar'
         g. hašlum   'despite sugar'
         h. hasplar   'on account of sugar'

We could analyze Dhori with two rules:

(270)   Rules for Dhori

         • š → ṣ / ___ r
         • š → s / ___ p

In Dhori let's assume that ṣ appears only before r; s appears only before p; and š appears elsewhere. Now, the 'elsewhere' case is the complement of where the other two rule-governed segments appear, which is the union of those two sets of environments. The surface segment š occurs in $U - (A \cup B)$.

U = the universal set of environments

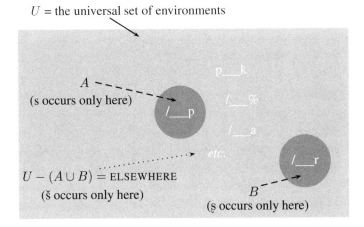

Figure 25.2 Complementary distribution for Dhori.

Let's note a few more things about Dhori. We chose the 'elsewhere form' *š* not because it occurred "the most" in the dataset. It occurs in three words in (269), but so does *s*. We don't count words but, rather, make our decision in terms of possible rule environments—that is, possible natural classes of strings. Also note that the elsewhere form, the one we posit as the underlying segment, is *š*. There should be nothing surprising about the fact that this symbol is more complex than the symbol *s*—such orthographic accidents should have no bearing on our analysis.

This brings us to another point. Sometimes, two (or more) segments are in complementary distribution, but we cannot tell which one should be posited as the lexical form, because each occurs in a natural class of environments. For example, just as the even and odd numbers divide ℕ into two "natural classes," we might find two segments, say *r* and *l*, where the first occurs at beginning of a word, '# ___', and the second occurs at the end of a word '___%' (but neither occurs in the middle of a word). We could posit either of the two analyses:

(271)   Two possible analyses

- r → l / ___ %
- l → r / # ___

In such a case, we should *not* pick one segment at random, or because it is simpler to type. This was sometimes the practice for field linguists who, in the old days, had to write up notes on a typewriter under difficult circumstances. Given the adverse circumstances under which they were working, we can forgive such practice. However, there are lingering effects from this practice when phonologists try to draw conclusions about trends involving underlying segment inventories. In other words, if field linguists are more likely to select as underlying the segment t over the segment θ, for typographic reasons, then phonologists surveying grammars may be thereby misled into thinking that underlying t is more common than θ in the languages of the world. Some typological claims in the literature are based on such basic errors. As a phonologist, when you have no principled way to select one analyis over another, to choose one underlying segment over another, the only principled solution is … no solution. Admit your inability to offer a principled solution.

25.3   Allophones Again

When complementary distribution is the result of a rule that maps one underlying segment to two (or more) surface forms without neutralization occurring, it is traditional to say that the two (or more) surface segments are *allophones* of a single underlying segment. The traditional term for the underlying segment that maps to one or more allophones is a *phoneme*.[4] So, a phoneme that splits in the mapping to the surface can have two (or more) allophones, whereas a phoneme that maps only to itself has only a single allophone.[5]

Despite the terminological conventions, it is important to remember that rules of allophony and neutralization are no different from the perspective of the phonology. With respect to our rule system, rules either apply vacuously, mapping underlying segments to themselves, or non-vacuously, mapping segments to other segments. An allophonic situation just combines these two primitive ideas, identity mapping (a → a) and non-identity mapping (a → b) as in (272).

(272)   Allophone mapping

---

[4]We will see later how two segments can be in complementary distribution without being allophones of a single phoneme.

[5]Typically phonemes with only one allophone are assumed to map to themselves, although in some cases this might not be true. The more typical association follows from our non-alternation assumption (118). We will see later that there are alternatives.

By combining this with another token of identity mapping that happens to overlap with the output of the previous example, we get neutralization as in (273):

(273)   Neutralization mapping

Thus, the apparent descriptive complexity that accounts for the difference between (272) and (273) can be derived from basic combinations of identity and non-identity mappings in the phonological rule system.

25.4   Korean and the Status of Allophones

Allophones, according to the traditional definition, are surface realizations of a *single* underlying segment. Thus, in both Dengue and Oxyurian from the previous sections, [s] and [š] are allophones of underlying /s/. However, it is not clear how useful this definition is since the phonology is only concerned with how rules apply to underlying representations. In the past, phonologists wanted to classify all surface forms as allophones of some underlying phoneme. Usually, such a classification falls out naturally from the analysis of the appropriate rules, but sometimes the desire to preserve the status of a surface form being an *allophone* led to needlessly complicated analyses.

For example, consider again the case of the Korean multiple convergent neutralization, as discussed in section 21.2.

(274)   Korean multiple convergent neutralization

	nominative	accusative
'face'	[nat$^\urcorner$]	[nač^{h}il]
'day'	[nat$^\urcorner$]	[naǰil]
'sickle'	[nat$^\urcorner$]	[nasil]
'piece'	[nat$^\urcorner$]	[nat^{h}il]
'grain'	[nat$^\urcorner$]	[nadil]

As shown in (274), [t$^\urcorner$] alternates with [č^h], [ǰ], [s], [t^h], and [d]. The obvious generalization that can be made with respect to this data is that č^h, ǰ, s, t^h, and d neutralize to t$^\urcorner$ word-finally. This generalization is represented by the SMD in (275).

(275)   Korean neutralization SMD

Note that, if we adopted the traditional definition by which an allophone corresponds to a *single* underlying segment, [tˀ] is not an allophone of any of the five segments that neutralize to it. This may seem arbitrary to you, and it is arbitrary. The only reason we mention this perspective is that we want to contrast the traditional use of the term *allophone*, which plays a role in various older approaches to phonology, with our perspective, which treats allophony and the various neutralization patterns as just surface manifestations of an underlying rule system. Such older approaches would analyze the Korean data quite differently from the SMD in (275). To understand their perspective, you first have to imagine a phonological system where multiple rules apply in a particular order. As we discuss in later units, natural languages often have more than one phonological rule active in their grammar, so eventually we will need to expand our model to include such a system. We won't go into any details of how to implement multiple rules for now, but the idea can be conveyed by the SMD in (276).

(276)   Possible Korean neutralization SMD

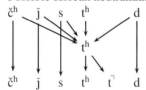

In (276), there are five rules from the URs to the next step in the derivation, one rule for each of the underlying segments, mapping underlying /čʰ/, /ǰ/, /s/, /tʰ/, and /d/ to t^h. Then there is another rule that maps t^h to [tˀ] when it appears at the end of a word. (It maps t^h to [tʰ] otherwise.) Such a system seems much more complicated than the simpler SDM given in (275). It requires more rules, and it requires rules that have no justification in terms of the surface distribution of segments in the language. However, these older phonological traditions favored the analysis in (276) over the one in (275) in order to preserve the classification of $t^ˀ$ as an allophone. In (276), $t^ˀ$ can be classified as an *allophone* since it is derived from a single *non-surface* segment, namely t^h.

In 1959, Morris Halle's *The Sound Pattern of Russian* pointed out that this approach exists merely to maintain an arbitrary distinction between rules of neutralization and rules of allophony. Furthermore, Halle showed that this distinction prevents us from collapsing rules applying to individual segments into a single rule applying to natural classes of sounds (something we'll see later when we discuss features). In other words, the maintenance of an arbitrary restriction on the definition of *allophone* prevents us from capturing generalizations. That's a good sign that the definition of allophones and allophonic rules should be rejected. We have made the same point as Halle by saying that the difference between the two putative rule types is irrelevant to the phonology of a language since reference to the distinction just reflects what happens to be in the lexicon.

Unit 26

More on Distributional Patterns and Phonotactics

26.1   Distributional Patterns

In the phonological representations found in the lexicon of each I-language there is some subset of IPA, the set of universally possible segments. This subset is sometimes called the "phoneme inventory" in older work, or the underlying segment inventory. Other segments may arise in the course of derivations and appear in SRs. For example, English has underlying /p/ but on the surface, we find [p] and [pʰ]. The contents of an English-type lexicon and the rule together account for the distribution of these two segments—where they occur and also where they do not occur. The situation is parallel for the segments š and s in Oxyurian—knowing the lexical entries and the rules allows us to know where each of the two will surface.

It is useful to contrast the distribution diagram we gave for Oxyurian with diagrams for two more toy languages, Dengue, which we have already seen, and Tocaribe, introduced with enriched datasets of the former languages in (277):

239

(277)   Three related (toy) languages with *s* and *š*

Dengue *neutralization*			Oxyurian *allophony*			Tocaribe *no rule*		
root	SR		root	SR		root	SR	gloss
/dar /	dar		/dar /	dar		/dar /	dar	'a potato'
	dari			dari			dari	'the potato'
	dara			dara			dara	'potatoes'
/pas/	pas		/pas/	pas		/pas/	pas	'a foot'
	paši			**paši**			**pasi**	'the foot'
	pasa			pasa			pasa	'feet'
/luš/	**luš**		/lus/	**lus**		/luš/	**luš**	'a dog'
	luši			luši			luši	'the dog'
	luša			**lusa**			**luša**	'dogs'
/lus/	lus		/lus/	lus		/lus/	lus	'a hat'
	luši			**luši**			**lusi**	'the hat'
	lusa			lusa			lusa	'hats'

As we have seen, Dengue has neutralization of *s* and *š* before *i*, and Oxyurian has complementary distribution of *s* and *š*. These two languages have the same rule, 's → š / ___ i'. Tocaribe has a much simpler pattern—you can get *s* and *š* in all the same environments, even before *i*. The distribution diagram for Tocaribe is pretty dull, as seen in Figure 26.1. We can, of course, describe environments where these segments do not appear, say 'p___k', but such statements play no role in the grammar. The grammar encodes only the environments that are used in rules, and there are no rules in Tocaribe.

The situation in Dengue is different from both Oxyurian and Tocaribe, as shown in Figure 26.2. In this case, with neutralization, there is one environment, *A*, where *s* does not occur, as shown. However, in *A'* both segments can appear. Here the two segments are not in complementary distribution, but rather in OVERLAPPING distribution.

In English, the distribution of the two segments *š* and *s* is like what we see in Tocaribe and Dengue, in the sense that there are minimal pairs that contrast with respect to the two segments. Just as Tocaribe has *lus* versus *luš*, English has *sign* versus *shine*. English, like Tocaribe, but unlike Dengue, does not have a rule neutralizing the two segments.[1] There are no morpheme alternations that would support positing such a rule.

---

[1] Some dialects might have a rule of *s* to *š*, for example in phrases like *Ki*[š] Charles. We are not concerned with such dialects.

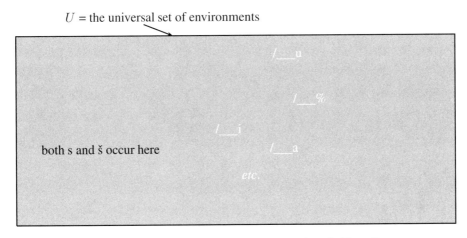

Figure 26.1 No rule; *s* and *š* occur everywhere in Tocaribe.

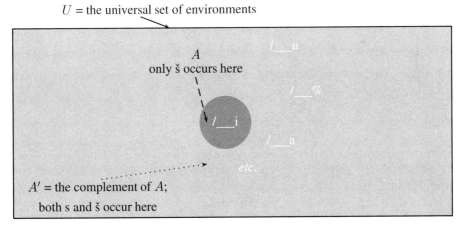

Figure 26.2 Neutralization by rule *s* → *š*/___*i* in Dengue.

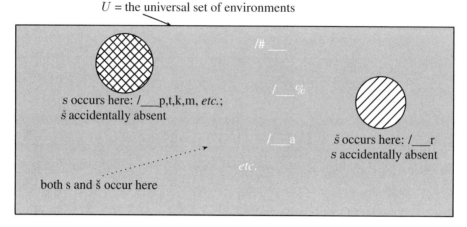

Figure 26.3 No rule; *s* and *š* occur aside from accidental gaps in English.

Nonetheless, there are environments where only one of the two segments appears. For many dialects of English, these generalizations hold at the beginning of a word:

(278)   Some distributional generalizations common in English dialects[2]

    a. *š* occurs before *r*, as in *shrimp*, but *s* does not occur before *r*

    b. *s* occurs before many other consonants, as in *sleep, small, spin, stint, skin*, but *š* does not occur before any consonants but *r*

It might be tempting to explain these facts by positing rules that turn *s* to *š* before *r*, and *š* to *s* before other consonants. However, such rules would not be justified since, in the dialects we are considering, there are no alternations involving the two segments. Of course, there is a history to the distributional patterns, but this history is not available to a child learning these dialects. We take the position that these distributional patterns are not encoded in the grammar—because only rule environment patterns are encoded.

Here is the important point of the previous discussion. Despite the fact that English *s* and *š* distribution is more precisely described by Figure 26.3 than by Figure 26.1, given the gaps in distribution we discussed (no *s* before *r*, *etc.*), the correct *grammatical* characterization of English is given by the same diagram we used for Tocaribe, Figure 26.1. The absence of *s* and *š* in certain environments in English is accidental

---

[2]Item (b) is not true of dialects that have incorporated borrowings from Yiddish like *shlep, shmooze, shtick* and many other words. It is also not true of dialects that have *š* in words like [š]*traw*, [š]*tream*.

and uninteresting.[3] Two segments that fully overlap in their distribution, aside from accidental gaps, are in PARALLEL distribution.

26.2 Phonotactics

Our position on the absence of *s* and *š* in certain contexts is certainly non-standard. Some approaches to phonology support the idea of such language-particular constraints on segment sequences. For another example, English has lexical items that contain sequences of a stop (like [p,t,k]) followed by a liquid, (like [l,r]). Examples would be *prince, play, tray, clean*. Note, however, that there are no morphemes beginning with sequences of *tl*. As we suggested, we assume that these gaps are either truly accidental, or else a reflection of historical factors—either way they are not encoded in the synchronic grammar. However, there are many serious arguments against our position, and the study of such combinatoric gaps in segment strings, known as *phonotactics*, plays a large role in most other approaches to phonology. The issues are quite complex, and we will restrict ourselves to a brief discussion.

A phonotactic explanation of the lack of a *tl*-sequence at the beginning of words (or syllables) maintains that there are language-specific, grammatical constraints on what are licit and illicit sequences of segments. There are two types of evidence that are often cited in support of such explanations. The first is the distributional gap, but as noted in the previous section, it is always possible that gaps are accidental and not a reflection of the current phonological system. The second piece of evidence relates to speaker intuitions: if we ask English speakers whether a certain sequence of segments sounds like a possible English word, they will often say no when it comes to sequences that begin with *tl*.

However, speakers' judgments are often unreliable. North American speakers, for example, take a lot of convincing to judge the consonants in the middle of *rider* and *writer* to be identical, but they are both so-called flaps. They will also emphatically deny that any English words begin with [pt] (other than ones like *pterodactyl*, which actually don't begin with [pt]). Yet in colloquial speech the word *potato* pretty clearly has no audible vowel between the [p] and the [t] for most speakers. Speaker's judgments about phonotactics are affected by the writing system, by their exposure to different dialects, and other non-phonological factors. In summary, it is unclear what the status of speakers' judgments is if their phonotactic judgments about their own language are

---

[3] If one is so inclined, one could argue that the borrowing of Yiddish words like *shmooze* or the pronunciation by some speakers of *Sri Lanka* with an *s* before an *r* provides evidence that the gaps described are not encoded in grammar.

often wrong.

This status about judgments becomes even cloudier when one considers that judgments about languages one definitely does *not* speak can be somewhat accurate. Consider the case of the Swedish chef of the Muppets. He speaks in nonsense words that kind of sound like Swedish. However, one's ability to enjoy the show and know that the Muppet is a Swedish chef, as opposed to Mandarin or French, does not depend on whether one speaks Swedish or not. Many audience members can correctly identify Swedish versus Mandarin or French words or sentences without speaking any of those languages. The conclusion of this simple thought experiment is that there is no reason to assume that strong, and often correct, phonotactic judgments indicate the presence of *grammatical* knowledge. People may have such judgments about languages for which they clearly have no grammar. Of course, one is unlikely to have good judgments about languages that one knows nothing about. On the other hand, one is likely to have very strong, accurate judgments about a language to which one has a lot of exposure, like one's native language. But these judgments are not necessarily based on *grammatical* knowledge.

Exercises

26.1. Consider the distribution of segments in the following forms in a toy language:

kɔfɔ	kɔvu	vunɔ	fɔnɔ	vuki	fɔki	lofɔ	lovu	miv
mɔv	muv	vuk	vik	fɔk	nivl	nuvl	mɔsv	mɔsfɔ
mɔsvi	tunvo	josfɔ	tunfɔ	kɔwɔ	kɔru	runɔ	wɔnɔ	ruki
wɔki	lowɔ	loru	mir	mɔr	mur	ruk	rik	wɔk
nirl	nurl	mɔsr	mɔswɔ	mɔsri	tunro	joswɔ	tunwɔ	sal

    a. If either [v] or [f] appears, can the environment to the left fully determine which of the two it will be? Explain.

    b. If either [v] or [f] appears, can the environment to the right fully determine which of the two it will be? Explain.

    c. If either [v] or [f] appears, can the environment on both sides fully determine which of the two it will be? Explain.

    d. If either [w] or [r] appears, can the environment to the left fully determine which of the two it will be? Explain.

    e. If either [w] or [r] appears, can the environment to the right fully determine which of the two it will be? Explain.

    f. If either [w] or [r] appears, can the environment on both sides fully determine which of the two it will be? Explain.

    g. Give some environments where neither [v] nor [f] appear.

    h. Give some environments where neither [w] nor [r] appear.

    i. Are [v] and [f] in complementary distribution?

    j. Are [v] and [w] in complementary distribution?

    k. Are [ɔ] and [u] in complementary distribution, parallel distribution, or partially overlapping distribution? Explain.

26.2. Consider the following data from a different language.

vasavalikobi	bnuk	mevago	blah	sonovahi	blong	tipabluka	van
sovabrimak	obuvag	vawkulits	bwig	obrabulo	kulb	daruvaki	kub

Based on the distribution of [v] and [b] in the data, answer these questions:

    • Do you expect to find minimal pairs based on the distinction between [b] and [v] in this language?

- What rule would account for the distribution of [b] and [v] in these forms? You'll have to make a decision about URs to answer this.
- Draw an SMD that shows what is going on:

Unit 27

Confused Use of Complementary Distribution in Syntax

Complementary distribution is one of the most basic heuristic notions used in phonology, predating the advent of Generative Phonology in the 1960s. As we have discussed, the term derives from the idea that the variant forms of a phoneme occur in a set of environments that is the complement of the set of environments in which other allophones appear. So, given an environment defined in some manner relevant to allophone distribution, only one variant can occur there. Of course, allophones of another phoneme can occur in the same environment.

If you've had a standard introduction to linguistics you have learned that there are aspirated and unaspirated versions of each of the voiceless stops in English, *p, t, k*. The unaspirated versions can occur after *s*, for example the [p] in *spot*, but the aspirated [pʰ], cannot occur there. Instead the aspirated version occurs word-initially, as in *pot*. Unaspirated [k] can occur in the same environment as unaspirated [p]. Of course, only one or the other, [p] or [k], can occur directly after an *s* in a given word. In this sense, the two are mutually exclusive. If there is a [p] after an *s*, then there can't be a [k], and if there is a [k], there can't be a [p].

Curiously, as pointed out to us by Peter Liem, a former undergraduate at our university, among syntacticians, the term *complementary distribution* is typically (or at least not infrequently) used in exactly the *wrong* way, to mean 'mutually exclusive'.

For example, a syntactician might say that the auxiliaries *will, must, should*, and so on, are in complementary distribution. What is meant is that only one of these auxiliaries can occur in a clause—if you have one, you can't have another.

It would perhaps not be a problem that syntacticians use the term to mean the opposite of the traditional phonological meaning, if it were not the case that syntacticians are inconsistent among themselves. For an example of the use of the term to mean 'mutually exclusive', consider this statement from the lecture notes posted online by a prominent syntactician:

> *According to this rule, the infinitival auxiliary,* to, *and the modal auxiliaries (*will, could, must, *etc.) are in complementary distribution. They cannot co-occur (* *for John to will go, *for John will to go*).*

The scholar is quite explicit that he used *complementary distribution* to mean *mutually exclusive*:

> *Words of the same class share the same distributional pattern. They exhibit (i) mutual substitutability, and (ii) complementary distribution.*

Such examples can be easily multiplied by a web search for *syntax* with *complementary distribution*.

One can also find many examples of the term being used in a manner inconsistent with this usage, but consistent with the set-theoretically coherent meaning in phonology involving complement sets of environments. For example, a pronoun like *him* and a reflexive like *himself* can be said to be in complementary distribution. The actual facts are complicated, but this use of the term is correct. In syntactic terms, *himself* can occur only when it is *locally bound*—don't worry about what this means if you have not studied binding theory. The regular pronoun *him*, in contrast, can occur only in contexts where it is *not* locally bound, the complement set of environments for *himself*.

Why, in a phonology textbook, are we discussing this inconsistency in the use of a term in the syntactic literature? Because complementary distribution is such a basic notion in phonology, one that every linguistics student is expected to master. We want to prepare you in case you are being presented with contradictory definitions. In our own experience, many excellent syntacticians have recognized their error immediately when it was pointed out, and careful evaluation of the use of the term should help you understand both syntax and phonology better.

Part VI

The Logic of Rule Interaction

Unit 28

Function Composition

28.1 Order (Sometimes) Matters

In Unit 12, we showed how our theory assigns a functional interpretation to a single phonological rule statement. For example, the rule 'p → b / m ___' is interpreted as a function that, when given a string of segments, produces an output string with all the p's that occur after an *m* converted to b's. Every attested I-language contains a variety of such rules, and so the question arises as to how such rules interact with one another.

There are several possibilities to explore for how rules might interact. For example, it is logically possible that all the rules work in parallel, each mapping a UR to a potentially different output. A complex algorithm might then integrate the set of outputs into one SR. It is also possible that the rules are applied in a random order each time a speaker maps a UR to an SR, thus providing a different possible SR at different points in time for the exact same UR. The hypothesis we will end up pursuing is that the rules of a given language apply in a fixed order, always yielding the same unique output for any given UR. In other words, the phonology is a complex function that maps a UR to an SR based on a certain arrangement of primitive functions, the individual phonological rules.

In this section, we characterize a phonology for a given language using the mathematical operation of functional composition, sometimes symbolized as $\circ$. A function f can compose with a function g (i.e.; $f \circ g$), if and only if the range of g is a subset of the domain of f. In other words, we need g's outputs to be possible inputs to f. If, say, g maps ID numbers to last names, and f maps integers to their square, neither $f \circ g$ nor

$g \circ f$ are functions.

When we treat a phonological rule as a function, the domain will be the set of all strings of segments. The outputs of rules are also strings, so the range of each rule will also consist of sets of segment strings. This means that we will be able to compose rules in the way we compose other functions, since all the members of the range of a rule will fall into the domain of all other rules.

(279) **Functional Composition**: For any two functions f and g, where the range of g is a subset of the domain of f, $f \circ g(x) = f(g(x))$.

If we think of a phonological derivation as the application of a complex function mapping a UR to an SR, then the rules we posit can be thought of as primitive functions that compose to give the full phonology. If we know the phonology, as mappings between UR and SR, we can try to decompose it into individual rules. If we know the individual rules, we can try to figure out how they compose to give the full phonology.

Applying rules in a given order corresponds to composing functions in a given order. If we have two functions to compose, f and g, we can, for example, apply f first to get a value $f(x)$. We can then use this value as the input to the other function, thus $g(f(x))$ which is equivalent to $g \circ f(x)$. Depending on the nature of the functions f and g, the order of composition will matter. That is, $g(f(x))$ will not always yield the same value as $f(g(x))$ and thus $g \circ f$ is not always the same as $f \circ g$.

A simple example where the order doesn't matter is a case where there is one function that adds two to a number and another that subtracts three. For example, for any number x, let $f(x) = x + 2$ and $g(x) = x - 3$. If we take a certain number, such as 5, and we apply f to 5, yielding 7, and then apply g to the result, the final output will be 4. Similarly, if we take 5 and apply g to it, yielding 2, and then we apply f to the result, the final output will be 4. In fact for any number x, $f(g(x)) = g(f(x))$ and hence $(g \circ f) = (f \circ g)$.

However, in many cases the order of composition is critical. Let's take the familiar example of a conversion algorithm between the Celsius and Fahrenheit temperature scales. If we have a number of degrees on the Celsius scale, we need to multiply that number by $9/5$ ($f(x) = 9/5 \times x$) and then add 32 ($g(x) = x + 32$) to the outcome of the first function to get the corresponding value on the Fahrenheit scale. For example, start with the boiling point of water on the Celsius scale, $100°$; multiply by $9/5$, giving 180; add 32 and we get $212°$ Fahrenheit, which is the boiling point of water on that scale. In this example the complex function $g(f(x))$ is evaluated for $x = 100$.

However, if we were to reverse the order of application of the two functions, we would not get the same result. Let's start again with 100, but first add 32 to get 132, then multiply by $9/5$ yielding 237.6. This temperature, $237.6°$, is not the boiling point of water on the Fahrenheit scale. To get the right conversion, we need to first multiply, then add—the addition function takes the output of the multiplication function as its input, as illustrated in (280):

(280)   Converting degrees Celsius to degrees Fahrenheit:

* First multiply, then add
* $F = (C \times 9/5) + 32$

Unsurprisingly, the order also matters for the conversion the other way around. A conversion from Fahrenheit to Celsius involves subtracting by 32 and dividing by $9/5$. We leave it as an exercise to figure out which function should apply first.

   Depending on which rules and inputs are involved, the order of function composition can also matter in the application of phonological rules. For the temperature conversion, we use functions that map numbers to numbers (values from the two temperature scales). In phonology, we use functions that map segment strings to segment strings (underlying forms and surface forms, so far). The principles of composition remain constant, however—that's a benefit of applying well-understood mathematical notions to a new domain like phonology. Changing the order of individual rule application sometimes changes the effect of the complex composed function, so we assume that there is always one actual ordering in an I-language phonology. Sometimes we cannot determine a single unique ordering that works, but the I-language perspective means that we believe that a phonological grammar *is* a particular ordering of rules into a complex function. So, when we say that two rules are *unordered* we mean that we cannot determine their order.[1] This lack of ordering is an *epistemological* issue, a reflection of our state of knowledge as linguists. It is important to distinguish this situation from a hypothetical model that allows unordered sets of rules. This latter situation would have a lack of ordering in its *ontology*, as part of the nature of the language faculty.

   A detail to keep in mind is that in many cases, the output of applying a phonological rule to a string will be identical to the input string. For example, a rule like 'i → e / q ___' will map the string *bogamiknos* to *bogamiknos*. In other words, the rule has no effect on the input string, since the sequence *iq* does not occur in the string *bogamiknos*. It is actually a mistake to say that the rule "does not apply" to the string under consideration, since a phonological rule applies to every input string that it gets—the

---

[1] This is similar to saying in historical linguistics that two languages are *unrelated*. That just means that they are *unrelatable* by the methods of historical linguistics. New data may allow us to relate previously unrelated languages.

domain of a rule is the set of phonological strings. The rule semantics make it clear that rules apply to all strings, but that in some cases a rule may map a string to itself. We call this situation called *vacuous* rule application. Pretty much all phonologists (including ourselves) sloppily say that a rule "does not apply," when they mean that application of the rule is vacuous.[2] Just be aware of this widespread bad habit. In fact, our attempts at precision will lead us to a point where this matters in a later unit when we treat ordered rules as composed functions.

28.2   Demonstration of Rule Ordering

To understand how function composition can affect the mapping between URs and SRs, let's imagine two closely related dialects, Choisyan and Petunian, with identical URs but a difference in rule ordering. We'll fill in some derivation tables using the same two rules with opposite ordering. These languages have the two rules in (281):

(281)   Two rules of Choisyan and Petunian

Rule A: $b \rightarrow \epsilon$ / ___ %

Rule B: $o \rightarrow u$ / ___ b

Rule A is a function from a string of segments to another string that deletes b's that appear word-finally. Rule B is a function from a string of segments to another string that converts all instances of o that occur before a b into a u. Probably just by looking at the rules you can see that there is a potential for them to interact with one another. Rule A sometimes deletes instances of b, whereas the conversion of o to u in Rule B is triggered by instances of b. However, the actual interaction of the two rules is determined by the order in which they apply.

   As usual, the values of cells in a table are *computed* by applying the relevant rule for a row to the form in the cell above. In Choisyan, Rule A applies to the UR and Rule B applies to the output of Rule A.

---

[2]There is another more restricted use of the term *vacuous application*: often phonologists use the term for cases where the rule has no effect on an input, but the form in question is already consistent with the output form. This only makes sense when we use features to formulate rules, so we will discuss this later.

(282)   Choisyan: Rules applied in order A,B

UR	fo	fo-b	fo-b-osi	na	na-b	na-b-osi
Rule A: $b \rightarrow \epsilon \, / \, \underline{\quad} \, \%$	—	fo	—	—	na	—
Rule B: $o \rightarrow u \, / \, \underline{\quad} \, b$	—	—	fubosi	—	—	—
SR	fo	fo	fubosi	na	na	nabosi
Gloss	'rat'	'the rat'	'the rats'	'hat'	'the hat'	'the hats'

In this table, the second to last row gives the output of applying the two rules. The intermediate rows give the result of the rule applications. The second row shows that Rule A applies vacuously to most of the URs, although it maps *fob* to *fo* and *nab* to *na*. The dashes represent instances where the input to the rule is identical to the output. The third row shows the output of Rule B, which in turn takes the output from Rule A as input. Rule B also applies vacuously to most forms, although it maps *fobosi* to *fubosi*. Thus, the final surface representations of the words are *fo, fo, fubosi, na, na, nabosi*, respectively.[3]

Now let's apply the rules in the opposite order to derive Petunian SRs.

(283)   Petunian: Rules applied in order B,A

UR	fo	fo-b	fo-b-osi	na	na-b	na-b-osi
Rule B: $o \rightarrow u \, / \, \underline{\quad} \, b$	–	fub	fubosi	–	–	–
Rule A: $b \rightarrow \epsilon \, / \, \underline{\quad} \, \%$	–	fu	–	–	na	–
SR	fo	fu	fubosi	na	na	nabosi
Gloss	'rat'	'the rat'	'the rats'	'hat'	'the hat'	'the hats'

---

[3] You should not be confused by the fact that the deletion of final *b* leads to homophony of different forms in the same paradigm. Of course, the data given makes it hard to see why we segmented the forms as we did, and why we posit a -*b* suffix in the definite singular forms. Think about what additional data would help you justify such an analysis. Indefinite plurals might be a good place to start. This is a toy language, but it is a good idea to make such thought experiments when thinking about real languages, too. It is also good, on the other hand, to understand how URs presented in scholarly articles are justified, and to be skeptical in some cases. See the footnote on Petunian, below, for further discussion.

In Petunian, Rule B applies to the URs first. For four of the items, the rule applies vacuously. However, it maps *fob* to *fub* and *fobosi* to *fubosi*. Note that the rule changes segments in the word meaning 'the rat' since the *b* has not been deleted. Rule A applies to the output of Rule B, deleting any *b*'s that appear word-finally. The final surface representations are *fo, fu, fubosi, na, na, nabosi*, respectively. Critically, the final SR for 'the rat' in Petunian is different from when Rule A applied first in Choisyan. All other SRs shown for the two languages are identical.[4]

Exercises

28.1. Consider the functions *mother-of(x)* and *father-of(x)*. Compute the value of the following composed functions, assigning to x the value of yourself

- *mother-of(father-of(x))*

- *father-of(mother-of(x))*

- *mother-of(mother-of(x))*

- *father-of(father-of(x))*

28.2. Show that order matters in applying two operations to a book lying on the table in front of you: (a) flip the book toward you $180°$, then (b) rotate the book $90°$ counterclockwise. If you reverse the order of operations, the book should end up in a different orientation. Draw the two different final orientations, starting from this image—assume the back cover just says "BACK":

28.3. Show that order matters in the composition of the function that squares an integer, $f(x) = x^2$, with the function that finds the smallest prime number larger than an integer, $p(x) =$ the smallest prime number larger than x. In other words,

---

[4]Note that in Petunian, unlike Choisyan, above, we do have indirect *phonological* evidence for the presence of an underlying difference between, for example, 'rat' and 'the rat'. The *o/u* difference has to come from *some* underlying difference. However, it is crucial to realize that we are not allowed to use this argument for Petunian as an argument for an underlying difference in the corresponding forms in Choisyan. We can look to UG to make arguments about individual languages, but we can't look to the idiosyncratic aspects of one language (the rule ordering, the particular rules in the grammar, or the accidental properties of morphemes) to understand another.

show that $p(f(x)) \neq f(p(x))$ in general. (It's pretty obvious that the two expressions can never be equal, since one describes a prime and the other a perfect square. You just need to give one case.)

28.4. Show that order matters in the application of the following processes: (a) 'reduplicate a phonological string' (concatenate it with itself) and (b) 'delete the final segment of a string'. What is the result of composing these two processes and applying them to the string *kapum*?

Unit 29

Rule Interactions I: FEEDING

29.1 FEEDING: The Basic Pattern

Now that we have some experience working with rule ordering, let's look at another dataset to see how we might go about discovering rule ordering effects. The first effect we explore is called a *feeding relationship*, or *feeding interaction*, between two rules. A feeding interaction occurs when the output of one rule creates an environment that allows non-vacuous application by another rule, which otherwise would not occur. To illustrate, let's consider the Begonian dataset in (284).

(284) Begonian

	form	gloss
a.	lup	'a dog'
b.	lupi	'the dog'
c.	lupo	'a hat'
d.	lupi	'the hat'
e.	lus	'a frog'
f.	luši	'the frog'
g.	luso	'a pig'
h.	luši	'the pig'
i.	luš	'a nut'
j.	luši	'the nut'

We've constructed the data so that it seems plausible that the indefinite forms like 'a dog' contain a single morpheme with phonological content, the root morpheme; and

259

the definite forms like 'the dog' consist of the root suffixed by -*i*. Looking only at forms (c) and (d) we appear to need either an insertion rule or a deletion rule to account for the *lup/lupo* alternation. However, when we also consider forms (a) and (b), it is clear by applying MTP-RAA reasoning that the lexical form for *dog* is /lup/ and the lexical form for *hat* is /lupo/, and that the correct rule is a deletion rule. Forms (e) and (f) demand a rule that either turns *s* to *š* or *š* to *s*, and forms (i) and (j) suggest that the former choice is correct, again by MTP-RAA reasoning, and that the lexical form for *frog* is /lus/, and the lexical form for *nut* is /luš/. So, the two rules in (285) appear to be justified:

(285)   Two rules for Begonian

R_1.   s → š / ___ i   (see e-f and g-h)

R_2.   o → ε / ___ i   (see c-d and g-h)

The only forms remaining to be explained are (g) and (h) 'a pig' and 'the pig'. We know from (g) that the root ends in /o/; and yet there is an alternation between *s* and *š* that seems to be consistent with the evidence for R_1. We know that this rule can't apply directly to a UR /luso-i/ to yield an SR with *š*, so we might be tempted to look for another, more complicated rule, perhaps even to expand our rule syntax to include something like '*s* becomes *š* when there is an *i* immediately after it, or two segments after it'. In other words, perhaps we need to allow the "optional" presence of an intervening *o* in the interaction between *s* and *i*.

This optionality is not a logical impossibility, and in fact, we will later have to abandon our SPE syntax to allow for some "long-distance" effects. However, for now, we do not need to take such drastic measures if we instead treat the rules as components of a composed function. In other words, by *first* applying R_2, the *o* of /luso-i/ will be deleted. We show this in (286), along with the vacuous application to some of the other forms:

(286)   Application of R_2 to URs

UR	lup	lupi	lupo	lupoi	lus	lusi	luso	lusoi
R_2	–	–	–	lupi	–	–	–	lusi
Gloss	'a dog'	'the dog'	'a hat'	'the hat'	'a frog'	'the frog'	'a pig'	'the pig'

Next, R_1 can apply to the outputs of R_2, which include two forms *lusi*, from different URs. These both have *s* directly followed by *i*. The strict ordering of the rules will derive the correct output for the word 'the pig' /luso-i/ ↝ [luši], for 'the frog' /lus-i/ ↝ [luši],[1] and for all the other forms, as we see in (287):

(287)   Application of R_1 to output of R_2

UR	lup	lupi	lupo	lupoi	lus	lusi	luso	lusoi
R_2	–	–	–	lupi	–	–	–	lusi
R_1	–	–	–	–	–	luši	–	luši
SR	lup	lupi	lupo	lupi	lus	luši	luso	luši
Gloss	'a dog'	'the dog'	'a hat'	'the hat'	'a frog'	'the frog'	'a pig'	'the pig'

The application of R_1 is non-vacuous in only two of the derivations—the ones for 'the frog' and 'the pig'. The latter form, the one for 'the pig', undergoes non-vacuous application by both rules. Hence, at least some of the URs in this language are affected by more than one rule in the course of a derivation. Critically, there is a sequence *si* that is created by R_2 that was not present in the UR. Such sequences are then affected by R_1 and surface as *ši*. As a result, R_1 is *surface true* in the sense that the existence of the rule is supported by the fact that no *si* sequences show up on the surface. To rephrase the same point, in the word 'the pig' the neutralization of s and š occurs only because of the effects of R_2.

It should be noted that we have fundamentally changed our initial assumption about how rule application works. Primitive rules no longer apply strictly to the UR—they compose with other primitive rules in ways that manifest interactions among their effects.

We illustrated the patterns in terms of the later rule applying to an intermediate form that is neither a UR or an SR. This is a natural way to talk about the composed function we just illustrated, but the step-by-step process with intermediate representations should not be taken literally as a description of how the mind computes derivations. Recall Exercise 28.2, which involved ordering a flip and a rotation of a book. We described different outcomes derived from ordering the two movements as discrete operations, but we could also move the book into the same final position by a single continuous twisting motion that ends up with the same result as the two separate motions.

---

[1] We use the symbol ↝ to compress the complete mapping of all ordered rules applied to a UR to derive an SR.

29.2   Defining FEEDING

Before we move on, let's attempt to formalize the notion of feeding. For the sake of simplicity, we will confine our attention to the case where two rules are composed, although the definitions below can be easily generalized to more complex functions.[2]

To formalize feeding, we first need to define what it means to be a minimal environment that serves as the "trigger" for a segment change in a given rule. Consider the definition in (288).

(288)   **Minimal Triggering Environment** (MTE): A sequence z is a minimal triggering environment for a rule R if and only if (i) $R(z) \neq z$ and (ii) there is no subsequence y of z such that $R(y) \neq y$.

The definition in (288) states that an MTE is the "smallest" subsequence that "triggers" a non-vacuous application of the rule.[3] For example, if the rule R were 'p $\rightarrow$ b / m ___' then an example of an MTE would be *mp*. The sequence *ma* would not be an MTE since this sequence would not be altered by the rule (R(ma) = ma), and neither would *emp* since this sequence is "too large" to be minimal. Note, it doesn't matter that the smallest sequence would never be a possible word, and hence an unlikely "real life" input to the rule R. The rule is defined for all sequences of segments independent of their plausible appearance as a word or morpheme in the language.

With the idea of an MTE fully defined, we can now try to characterize when a feeding relationship occurs between two rules.

(289)   **Feeding**: A rule R_j feeds a rule R_i in a composed function f if and only if the following conditions hold:

    a. In the composed function f, R_j appears to the right of R_i (i.e., $f = R_i \circ R_j$)

    b. There is a sequence of segments x such that the number of MTEs relative to R_i in x is less than the number of MTEs relative to R_i in $R_j(x)$.

Intuitively (and less precisely) stated, a feeding relationship exists between two rules R_i and R_j if and only if R_j applies first, and there is at least one (potential) input where

---

[2]Representations consist of strings of segments for now, although the definitions should work for representations that are more complex than strings, for example, when we introduce syllable structure.

[3]In many cases, there will be only one possible segment subsequence that is an MTE for a given rule. However, the definition of feeding is consistent with there being a set of minimal segment subsequences. This aspect of our definition will be critical when we talk in more detail about rules using features in Part VIII. With such rules, there are often several types of MTEs for a given rule.

R_j applied to that input creates new environments that lead to non-vacuous application of R_i.

Let's consider the rules discussed above, namely R_1 = s → š / ___ i and R_2 = o → ϵ / ___ i. The sequence *si* is an MTE for the rule R_1. Now consider the underlying form for 'the pig' in the Begonian dataset, namely /luso-i/. The number of MTEs in *lusoi* with respect to R_1 is zero. However, there is one instance of *si* in R_2(lusoi) = *lusi*. Hence, according to our definition, R_2 feeds R_1.

In this example, the string that establishes a feeding relationship increases the number of MTEs from zero to one. However it is not necessary that this always be the case. For example, consider the string *lusisoi*. This string has one MTE with respect to R_1. However, this string still establishes a feeding relationship between R_2 and R_1 since R_2(lusisoi), which is *lusisi*, contains two MTEs. What is necessary is that the number of MTEs for R_1 in $R_2(x)$ (the output of R_2 applied to x) be greater than that in the original string x itself. In other words, when R_2 feeds R_1, the application of R_2 to x creates a new MTE for R_1 to apply.

It would not be difficult to expand our definition of feeding so that it could account for complex functions where multiple rules compose; however, we won't go into further detail here. Our main point relates to the recurring theme about the relationship between our model and the data. What we call *feeding* makes for complicated patterns of data for the analyst (and learner), but such patterns arise from the interaction of the parts of our simple model. Given the idea that rules map inputs to outputs, and that the rules of a language compose into a single complex function, feeding patterns emerge. Even if we successfully fully formalize what we mean by *feeding*, we should not be fooled into thinking that we have thereby done something phonologically important. At most, we would have precisely defined a term that phonologists use, but in our view, from the perspective of phonology itself, feeding does not exist. It has no status whatsoever in the theory. When we have the simple mechanism of ordered rules, we predict that so-called feeding patterns will arise, but that is just a name we give to the patterns. The status of the rules as feeding is not represented in the grammar. Once again, we see that our simple model can give rise to a "welter of descriptive complexity." In other words, the data looks massively complex, but the model that generates this data is simple. This is one of the hallmarks of a successful theory.[4]

---

[4]Our colleagues Eric Baković and Lev Blumenfeld have done a lot of work on the formalization of different types of rule interaction effects, and we have benefited from discussion with them. We suggest that you seek out some of their handouts and other material on this topic.

29.3   A Non-ordering Solution:
The Free Reapplication Model

You may have considered a very different solution to Begonian. The rule ordering solution hypothesizes the existence of two primitive rules, $R_1 = s \rightarrow š /$ ___ i and $R_2 = o \rightarrow \epsilon /$ ___ i. We suggested that composing these two rules yields the correct empirical results, namely that $R_1 \circ R_2$ when applied to the URs produces the attested forms. However, there is an alternative solution, where the rules R_1 and R_2 are freely applied in any order, as often as possible until all instances of application are vacuous. We will call this the *free reapplication model*.[5] This method of unordered rule application is exactly what is used in phrase structure grammars to account for aspects of syntactic structure, so such a method of rule application is not without precedent.

Let's consider this type of freely-ordered, repeated rule-application in more detail by walking through an example using the Begonian URs posited above in (287), shown again in (290).

(290)   Begonian URs

UR	lup	lupi	lupo	lupoi	lus	lusi	luso	lusoi
Gloss	'a dog'	'the dog'	'a hat'	'the hat'	'a frog'	'the frog'	'a pig'	'the pig'

We could apply R_2 and then R_1, as we did above, yielding the same result as with our rule ordering solution. However, we could also first apply R_1, yielding the following results.

(291)   Application of R_1 to URs

UR	lup	lupi	lupo	lupoi	lus	lusi	luso	lusoi
R_1	–	–	–	–	–	luši	–	–
OP	lup	lupi	lupo	lupoi	lus	luši	luso	lusoi
Gloss	'a dog'	'the dog'	'a hat'	'the hat'	'a frog'	'the frog'	'a pig'	'the pig'

The second to last row of this table, labeled OP, represents the output of applying R_1. As shown in the table, R_1 would apply vacuously to every UR other than *lusi*. Since we can apply R_1 iteratively, we could apply it to the forms in the OP row; however, this would not change any of the forms. The rule would apply vacuously to every sequence. The only application of a rule that would be non-vacuous would be the application of

---

[5]This discussion of the free reapplication model and the direct mapping model below owes much to the treatment by Kenstowicz and Kisseberth (1979).

R_2. In this type of theory, if a rule can apply non-vacuously, then it must be applied. This would yield the following results:

(292)   Application of R_1 then R_2

UR	lup	lupi	lupo	lupoi	lus	lusi	luso	lusoi
R_1	–	–	–	–	–	luši	–	–
R_2	–	–	–	lupi	–	–	–	lusi
OP	lup	lupi	lupo	lupi	lus	luši	luso	lusi
Gloss	'a dog'	'the dog'	'a hat'	'the hat'	'a frog'	'the frog'	'a pig'	'the pig'

R_2 applies non-vacuously to two forms, *lupoi* and *lusoi*, yielding *lupi* and *lusi* respectively. Once again, we could apply R_2 again, but this would not change any of the forms. However, because we are free to apply any rule as often as possible, we could also choose to reapply R_1. This would yield a non-vacuous result, for 'the pig' as shown in (293).

(293)   Application of R_1 then R_2 then R_1 again

UR	lup	lupi	lupo	lupoi	lus	lusi	luso	lusoi
R_1	–	–	–	–	–	luši	–	–
R_2	–	–	–	lupi	–	–	–	lusi
R_1	–	–	–	–	–	–	–	luši
OP	lup	lupi	lupo	lupi	lus	luši	luso	luši
Gloss	'a dog'	'the dog'	'a hat'	'the hat'	'a frog'	'the frog'	'a pig'	'the pig'

If a rule can apply non-vacuously, then it must be applied. Hence, R_1 necessarily maps the newly created *lusi* to *luši*.

At this point, any application of either R_1 or R_2 to the forms in the OP would yield a vacuous mapping. Hence, the output in (293) represents the SR of this type of iterative rule application. As can be easily checked, this output is the same as the one we had when we first applied R_2 and then applied R_1.

We now have an alternative model to generate Begonian. In this simple case, at least, the ordering method and the free reapplication method appear to be extensionally equivalent—they generate the same dataset, so you might be wondering how we could ever choose between them. We will come back to the issue of deciding which is a better model of a real I-language in a later unit.

29.4   Neutralization and Homophony

Feeding patterns establish a new observation about neutralization (and resulting homophony), namely that neutralization of strings by one rule can depend on the effects
of another rule. For example, the Begonian words for 'the frog' and 'the pig' start out
as /lus-i/ and /luso-i/ respectively. The deletion of *o* before *i* leads to the two forms
becoming identical: both are mapped to *lusi*.

   The two forms are then subject to the rule turning *s* to *š* before *i*, resulting in
[luši]. Homophony arises from a combination of rules that are applied in a specific
order affecting a particular subpart of the input. Thus, neutralization of underlying
differences is not a property of a rule, but an effect that emerges from the grammar as
a whole.

   In the allophonic patterns we looked at, the absence of neutralization turned out to
be a fact about the lexicon. In this unit, neutralization of underlying differences derives
from the interaction of rules: /lus-i, luso-i, luš-i/ all end up homophonous: the first is
affected by one rule, the second by two rules, and the third by no rules.

   In order for a loss of underlying difference to occur, there must be the right configuration of lexical items, rules and ordering. In fact, we'll see in the next unit that *the
same rules* that resulted in homophony of /lus-i, luso-i, luš-i/ ↝ *luši* in this unit can
interact in other ways without yielding any homophonic forms via neutralization.[6]

29.5   Complex SMDs

Our segment mapping diagrams have helped us understand the mappings between input segments at UR and output segments at SR. We hinted at rule ordering in an SMD
in an earlier discussion of multiple convergent neutralization in Korean in (276). Now
that we have discussed ordered rule interactions explicitly, it is worth illustrating again
how SMDs can reflect such a situation. Here is an SMD for the feeding interaction
illustrated by the data in (284).

---

[6]This is important since it implies that there can be no phonological principles that refer to neutralization
or homophony, just as there are no syntactic principles that refer to structural ambiguity. It is useful to compare the model developed here to others, such as versions of Optimality Theory that incorporate constraints
that penalize neutralizations, such as the MAXIMIZE CONTRAST constraints of Flemming (2004). We reiterate that in our model, functionalist notions like contrast and neutralization play no role. See Hale and Reiss
(2000); Reiss (2017a,b) for discussion.

(294)   SMD for ordered *o*-deletion and *s/š*-neutralization

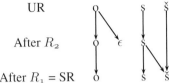

The mapping from the top line in this SMD to the second line affects only underlying /o/. There is no rule affecting /s/ at this stage, so every underlying /s/ survives intact, which is why there is only a vertical arrow between the /s/ in the UR and the *s* at the next level. However, the environment of some tokens of /s/ will change. The deletion of /o/ by R_2 will create additional strings in which *s* occurs directly before *i*, and thus these strings will meet the conditions for R_1 to apply. The input string /luso-i/ is an example that will undergo effects of both rules. The input string /lus-i/ will undergo effects of only R_1. The input string /lupo-i/ will undergo effects of only R_2. The input /lup-i/ will not show effects of either rule. We included in the Begonian data in (284) the forms with the meaning 'nut', whose lexical form is /luš/, so that we could justify positing the existence of underlying /š/, and thus a neutralization rule, but we don't show derivations of those forms in (295), for reasons of space.

(295)   SMD for ordered *o*-deletion and *s/š* -neutralization

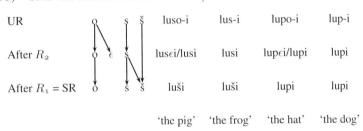

As the SMD makes clear, the deletion of *o* and the conversion of *s* to *š* are independent—it is just an accident that the input /luso-i/ happens to be affected by both of these rules.

Unit 30

Rule Interactions II:
COUNTERFEEDING

30.1 COUNTERFEEDING: The Basic Pattern

In the last unit we discussed and analyzed a feeding pattern. In this unit, we analyze the opposite type of phenomenon: a counterfeeding pattern. As we discuss at the end of this unit, a counterfeeding pattern will help us decide between the two theories presented in the last unit that accounted for Begonian, namely rule ordering versus free reapplication.

Before we get to these theoretical issues, let's first consider the Strelitzian dataset in (296), which is very similar to Begonian from the last unit, except that the form for 'the pig' is *lusi* instead of *luši*.

(296) Strelitzian

	form	gloss
a.	lup	'a dog'
b.	lupi	'the dog'
c.	lupo	'a hat'
d.	lupi	'the hat'
e.	lus	'a frog'
f.	luši	'the frog'
g.	luso	'a pig'
h.	**lusi**	'the pig'
i.	luš	'a nut'
j.	luši	'the nut'

We'll suppose in Strelitzian, as in Begonian, that the indefinite forms consist of just the root morphemes, and that the definite forms consist of the root plus the suffix *-i*. Furthermore, the same forms used to argue for the *o*-deletion rule in Begonian are present in Strelitzian (296 a-d). In addition, the forms (296 e-f) demonstrate that there is again a rule that either converts *s* to *š* or vice versa. Recall that in Begonian, only the rule that converts *s* to *š* was consistent with the data.

The *s*/*š*-alternation in Strelitzian is not as straightforward as Begonian. On the one hand, the Strelitzian forms (296 e,i) ([lus] 'a frog' and [luš] 'a nut', respectively) make it unlikely that there is a rule that converts *š* to *s* word-finally. On the other hand, the forms (h) ([lusi] 'the pig') and (f, j) ([luši] 'the frog', 'the nut') make it problematic to posit a rule that converts *s* to *š* before an *i*.

As we show in the next two sections, there are at least two possible solutions to this Strelitzian data: one again using rule ordering, and the other using a different way to combine rules.

30.2   Rule Ordering for Strelitzian

One possible way to account for the pattern in Strelitzian is to hypothesize the exact same rules that account for Begonian, namely $R_1 = o \rightarrow \epsilon / $ ___ i and $R_2 = s \rightarrow š / $ ___ i; however, instead of applying R_2 before R_1, we apply R_1 before R_2. Let's walk through this possibility in detail, spelling out each step of the analysis.

Consider the derivation table in (297). By applying rule R_1 to the underlying forms, we derive *š* from *s* when it appears before an *i*.

(297)   Apply R_1

UR	lup	lupi	lupo	lupoi	lus	lusi	luso	lusoi
R_1	–	–	–	–	–	luši	–	–
OP	lup	lupi	lupo	lupoi	lus	luši	luso	lusoi
Gloss	'a dog'	'the dog'	'a hat'	'the hat'	'a frog'	'the frog'	'a pig'	'the pig'

The only form that is affected by R_1 is *lusi* ('the frog') since this is the only form that has an *s* appearing before an *i*.

Now suppose we apply R_2 to the output of R_1. This is shown in (298).

(298)   Apply R_2 to the output of R_1

UR	lup	lupi	lupo	lupoi	lus	lusi	luso	lusoi
R_1	–	–	–	–	–	luši	–	–
R_2	–	–	–	lupi	–	–	–	lusi
SR	lup	lupi	lupo	lupi	lus	luši	luso	lusi
Gloss	'a dog'	'the dog'	'a hat'	'the hat'	'a frog'	'the frog'	'a pig'	'the pig'

R_2 applies non-vacuously only to two forms, *lupoi* ('the hat') and *lusoi* ('the pig'). The surface representations of this rule application generates the Strelitzian data. Critically, the form meaning 'the pig' has an *s* appearing before an *i* in its surface form. The reason for the surface form *lusi*, despite R_1 being part of the grammar, is that the *s* did not appear before an *i* when R_1 applied.

This type of rule interaction is called *counterfeeding* and can be defined as follows. Once again, for the sake of simplicity, we will restrict our definition to cases where the composed function consists of only two rules.

(299)   **Counterfeeding**: A rule R_j counterfeeds a rule R_i in a composed function f if and only if the following conditions hold:

    a.   In the composed function f, R_j appears to the left of R_i (i.e., $f = R_j \circ R_i$).

    b.   There exists a composed function f', such that R_j appears to the right of R_i in f' (i.e., $f' = R_i \circ R_j$) and R_j feeds R_i in f'.

Informally, R_j counterfeeds R_i if R_j applies after R_i, but if the order were the opposite, R_j would have fed R_i.

Strelitzian, with counterfeeding rule ordering, is harder to analyze than Begonian. However, this difficulty is a property of us, the analysts. The actual grammars are identical in their complexity. They have the same lexical items, the same rules, and an ordering of the rules.

In earlier discussions, distributional patterns gave us clues about the rules we needed to posit—for example, if s never appeared before i in a given dataset, but there were cases of $š$ before i alternating with cases of s, we took this as evidence that there was a rule in the phonology of the form s → š / ___ i. In other words, the effects of the rule were directly observable in the patterns in the surface forms. However, we have just constructed a situation where the grammar has a rule that appears to have exceptions: the data has cases of s appearing before i in SRs, despite there being a rule 's → š / ___ i'. If there is a rule turning s to $š$ before i, why would we find sequences of si? The answer is obvious from our construction of the language—the si sequence we find in Strelitzian is not present in the UR, but rather is created by a rule that applied after the rule changing s to $š$. Rules that do not correspond to a true surface generalization about the data, rules whose effects are not apparent in the surface forms, are called *opaque* rules (Kiparsky, 1973). A rule is only opaque by virtue of its interaction with other rules in a grammar. The rule 's → š / ___ i' is opaque in Strelitzian, but not in Begonian.

30.3   Direct Mapping for Strelitzian

You may have noticed that in the mapping from SRs to URs in Strelitzian in (298), each form is affected by at most one of the two rules, R_1 or R_2.[1] In such a situation, we could just as easily derive the same outputs by assuming that both rules apply simultaneously to the URs, and only those whose conditions are met have any effect.

A model in which rules are applied only directly to the UR is called the *direct mapping model*. This model has the intuitive appeal of simplifying the derivation. Since we only have two rules in our toy language, we can illustrate the direct mapping model by placing each rule directly adjacent to the UR, as in (300).

(300)   Direct mapping

R₁	–	–	–	–	–	luši	–	–
UR	lup	lupi	lupo	lupoi	lus	lusi	luso	lusoi
R₂	–	–	–	lupi	–	–	–	lusi
Gloss	'a dog'	'the dog'	'a hat'	'the hat'	'a frog'	'the frog'	'a pig'	'the pig'

---

[1]This discussion is a bit informal—consider the derivation of a hypothetical Strelitzian UR like this /peso-i-kas-ima/. This form would be affected by both rules in the course of the derivation, but we would still have counterfeeding ordering. The output would be [pesikašima].

In such a model, the SRs are the forms that have either undergone a change by one of the rules, or are equivalent to the URs if no rule applied to them non-vacuously. As illustrated in (300), the direct mapping model accounts for the counterfeeding pattern in Strelitzian.

Given this alternative analysis of the counterfeeding pattern, we may not need to hypothesize rule ordering in order to explain this type of dataset. We saw the same situation with the feeding pattern in the previous unit, where free reapplication was able to produce the same surface representations as rule ordering. At this point, we have not given any arguments to choose rule ordering over direct mapping and free reapplication, but you may have a sense of how our argument will proceed. Hold that thought...

30.4   Choosing a Model

If we do not adopt the I-language perspective on phonology, the view that grammars are components of individual minds, then it really does not make sense to ask which is a better model for generating Begonian or Strelitzian given our assumptions about the lexicon and the rules. For example, our grammatical accounts with rule ordering on the one hand and free reapplication on the other are extensionally equivalent with respect to Begonian—they generate the same data, and they even generate it from the same set of inputs, with the same UR-SR mappings. Either one would do for building a robot that pronounced words from Begonian based on the relevant morpheme combinations. In other words, if we adopt the artificial intelligence goal of *simulating* a speaker of the language, the choice between grammars does not matter, and as engineers we could implement whichever is simpler to program, or whichever uses less battery power to run.

However, once we adopt the I-language perspective, we are forced to recognize that grammars in the mind have certain properties, and they may be better modeled by rule ordering as opposed to free reapplication or vice versa. Similar considerations hold for the choice between rule ordering and direct mapping with respect to Strelitzian. In each case, we may not know which model is better, but we are forced to accept that there is a correct answer that more accurately reflects the way phonological systems are represented and implemented in humans.

We can go even further with the I-language perspective. Since each grammar in a particular human's mind is part of the human language faculty, it is reasonable to expect that such grammars are constructed from the same basic building blocks, despite their surface differences. In other words, the description of one language should be couched in the same terms as that of another. This type of consideration might help us to choose between rule ordering and the other accounts of the feeding and counterfeeding patterns.

Recall that we were able to generate Strelitzian with ordered rules or with the direct mapping model. However, it is important to note that the free reapplication model would fail—the form [lusi] would not be an SR since it is subject to the rule that turns *s* to *š* before *i*. In the free reapplication model, rules apply over and over again until all applications are vacuous.

Similarly, recall that we were able to generate Begonian with ordered rules or with the free reapplication model. But the direct mapping model would fail, since the form [luš] from underlying /luso-i/ could not be generated. With direct mapping the rule that turns *s* to *š* before *i* has to apply directly to URs, and the application of the rule to the UR /luso-i/ would be vacuous, as it does not contain the sequence *si*.

As the table in (301) summarizes, only rule ordering works as a way to combine rule applications in both Begonian and Strelitzian:

(301)   Only rule ordering works for both Begonian and Strelitzian

Pattern	Ordering	Direct Mapping	Free Reapplication
Feeding	✔		✔
Counterfeeding	✔	✔	

Rule ordering thus appears to be the best model of rule application for UG.

Of course, a demonstration that some data necessarily had to be modeled using direct mapping or free reapplication would undermine this argument. Such a demonstration would show that certain languages *cannot* consist of ordered rules, and thus the rule ordering model would not be a plausible model for all phonological systems. However, let's leave this possibility aside for the moment. For now, the important lesson is that the I-language perspective leads us to a hypothesis about the nature of the human language faculty that can have bearing on the analyses we posit for a given dataset, an idea clearly expressed by Chomsky in *Knowledge of Language*:

> Because evidence from Japanese can evidently bear on the correctness of a theory of [the initial state of the human language faculty], it can have indirect—but very powerful– bearing on the choice of the grammar that attempts to characterize the I-language attained by a speaker of English. (1986, p. 38)

As demonstrated by this quote, Chomsky, who has sometimes been maligned for being anti-empirical, clearly *expands* the range of empirical data that bears on, say, the grammar of "English" by showing us that "Japanese" data, or the data from any language for that matter, is also relevant.

30.5   More Complex SMDs

Before leaving the issue of counterfeeding, let's return to our discussion of segment mapping diagrams. In the previous unit we presented a complex SMD to illustrate the effects of rules in a feeding order. The same rules have been used in this unit, but in a counterfeeding order. Here's the relevant SMD:

(302)   SMD for s → š ordered before *o*-deletion

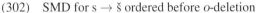
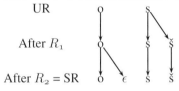

Since the deletion rule applies *after* the s → š / ___ i rule, the former cannot create environments in which the latter can apply.

Exercises

30.1. Consider these rules:

- Rule A: w → ε / u ___ u
- Rule B: o → u / # ___

a. Put the rules in the order A-B and compute the derivations in the table below.

b. What do we call this ordering?

c. Draw an appropriate SMD.

UR	o-wuka	pi-wuka	nu-wuka	o-kuli	pi-kuli	nu-kuli
Rule A:						
Rule B:						
SR						
Gloss	'a dog'	'the dog'	'dogs'	'a hat'	'the hat'	'hats'

a. Put the rules in the order B-A and compute the derivations in the table below.

b. What do we call this ordering?

c. Draw an appropriate SMD.

UR	o-wuka	pi-wuka	nu-wuka	o-kuli	pi-kuli	nu-kuli
Rule B:						
Rule A:						
SR						
Gloss	'a dog'	'the dog'	'dogs'	'a hat'	'the hat'	'hats'

Unit 31

Combinatorics of Rule Ordering

Recall that one of our goals is to create a simple model that nonetheless is able to cover a wide variety of phenomena. Once we have the mechanism of rule ordering as function composition, we can consider the combinatoric possibilities of such a system. We can take advantage of pre-existing results in basic combinatorics and apply them to phonology.

Suppose you have a bag containing a red ball and a blue ball. If you stick your hand in the bag and pull out a ball, it will be either red or blue. Assuming you do not replace the first ball, when you stick your hand in again for a second ball, there will be just a single possible outcome: if the first ball was red, the second is blue; if the first was blue, the second is red.

When another ball is added to the bag, the number of orderings increases. For the first choice there are three possibilities; once a first ball is pulled out, there remain two possibilities for the next selection. And finally, for the third selection, there is just a single choice. So, there are six possible sequences for pulling the three balls from the bag. Each series of choices shown in (303) corresponds to one of the sequences.

(303)   Balls from a bag: 3! = 6

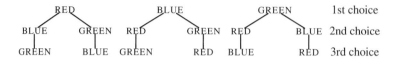

This reasoning obviously applies to other situations, such as lining up three people to buy tofu burgers, or the order in which you read three books. A crucial aspect of such examples is that the balls don't go back into the bag after they are selected, so the number of balls decreases with each selection. Similarly, if we place Laskarina at the front of the tofu burger line, she can't also be placed in the middle or the back.

Of course, the reasoning generalizes to higher numbers, so that if we add a yellow ball to the bag, there will be *four* choices for the first selection, then three for the second, two for the third and one for the last selection. Then the total number of sequences will be $4 \times 3 \times 2 \times 1 = 24$ distinct sequences. This is easy to see if you imagine placing a yellow ball into one of the sequences in (303), say the first one: you can place YELLOW just before RED, just before BLUE, just before GREEN, or at the end of the sequence. There are four places to place YELLOW for each sequence in (303), so adding one more ball, increases the number of sequences fourfold.

In general, if we start with n balls, the number of distinct sequences will be $n \times (n-1) \times (n-2) \ldots \times 1$. This expression is abbreviated in mathematics as $n!$, and it is pronounced "n factorial."

We adopt the position that the possibilities for ordering the rules in a language is analogous to the combinatorics of pulling balls from a bag without replacing them. The rules are in a strict order and they cannot be used more than once—they cannot be "placed back in the bag."

Let's see how this works out if we consider a set of three rules, $\mathcal{R}$. Recall that the set of rules in a language defines a set of correspondences between strings. Our job as phonologists is to figure out the actual correspondences between URs and SRs in a language. One way to restrict the set of correspondences defined by $\mathcal{R}$ is to propose that the phonology is a composition of the functions corresponding to each rule, with the condition that each rule enters into the phonology once and only once. In other words, given a language L_1 with rules r_1, r_2, r_3, the only possible phonologies of L_1 are the composed functions in (304), where ς_u is a UR and ς_s is an SR:[1]

---

[1] The symbol 'ς' is a variant of the Greek letter sigma. We use ς to denote a string. So, ς_u is a string corresponding to a UR, and ς_s is its corresponding SR string.

(304) All the orderings of a set of three rules $\mathcal{R}$

$\varsigma_s = r_1(r_2(r_3(\varsigma_u)))$	Apply r_3 to the UR; apply r_2 to that output; apply r_1 to that output; the final output is the SR.
$\varsigma_s = r_1(r_3(r_2(\varsigma_u)))$	...
$\varsigma_s = r_2(r_1(r_3(\varsigma_u)))$	...
$\varsigma_s = r_2(r_3(r_1(\varsigma_u)))$	...
$\varsigma_s = r_3(r_1(r_2(\varsigma_u)))$	...
$\varsigma_s = r_3(r_2(r_1(\varsigma_u)))$	Apply r_1 to the UR; apply r_2 to that output; apply r_3 to that output; the final output is the SR.

The *actual* phonology of the language L_1 will be one of these six. We can also say that each ordering corresponds to a different grammar, a different I-language. Note that some of these orderings may give identical outputs for any conceivable form. This means that we may not be able to determine which is the one correct ordering; but this does not mean that there is not a single ordering instantiated in the mind of a speaker of a given language. In fact, our theory now *defines* a phonology to be the composed function that is an ordered set of rules, so there has to be one correct ordering, according to the model. Our inability to determine this ordering in a particular case is an *epistemological* problem, a reflection of our limited knowledge as linguists, that has no bearing on the existence of a specific ordering in the mental grammar that is the object of study.[2]

Since one of our goals is to consider how a restricted model of phonology can account for the vast variety of human languages, it is worthwhile considering the combinatoric possibilities provided by rule ordering. With just three rules, we can define $3! = 6$ different languages (rule orderings). With a set of just ten rules, the number of logically distinct languages is $10! = 3,628,800$—the factorial function grows very fast!

The $n!$ orderings are relevant to our balls-in-a-bag example only under the assumption that we pull all the balls out, that we always get a sequence of length n. Of course, if we allow shorter sequences, there are more possibilities. With three balls, we have the six sequences of length three, plus six sequences of length two, plus three sequences of length one. In other words, we get more sequences by allowing omissions (of balls or rules). If we consider a set of just twenty possible rules and think of

---

[2]On this topic, see section 4.2 of Isac and Reiss (2013) for discussion of extensionally equivalent grammars. In the case of indistinguishable rule orderings, it may be that the temporal order in which a learner encounters relevant forms plays a role in the order of composition of rules.

each language as having just some subset of ten of the twenty, we can define over 670 *billion* (670×10^9) rule orderings, each defining a different language.[3]

So, you can see that for a learner, it is not enough to figure out the rules of the ambient language—the learner also has to figure out the order of composition of the rules. But this example also shows us that our simple model has the potential to account for a very large range of different languages. We've built up a simple system that has lots of power by virtue of its combinatoric nature—this is exactly what we want in a model of a computational module of the mind (Gallistel and King, 2009; Matamoros and Reiss, 2016).

If you followed our combinatoric argument concerning rule ordering, we advise you *not* to remember it. Don't *remember* that the number of orderings for, say, a set of seven rules is 7!. Instead, we encourage you to *understand* the argument and its premises so that you can reconstruct the reasoning on your own. This means appreciating, for example, that we restrict rules to applying only once in the course of a derivation. You need to keep such assumptions in mind so that you can evaluate their empirical validity as you encounter more complex phonological phenomena.

Exercises

31.1. If a language has 7 rules, R1, ..., R7, how many ways can they be ordered? First give a mathematical expression that corresponds to the answer, then calculate the exact number.

31.2. A group of n people are waiting to see a doctor. Mathematically, how many ways can the triage nurse order the group?

---

[3]We get this by calculating $20!/10! = 20 \times \times 18 \times 17 \times 16 \times 15 \times 14 \times 13 \times 12 \times 11$. We are computing the so-called *partial permutations* of 10 members of a set of twenty rules.

Unit 32

Minimal Pairs and Complementary Distribution

In Part V we discussed the traditional notion of allophones. Allophones are the variant realizations of a phoneme in different contexts. We made the point that allophonic rules are not fundamentally any different from neutralization rules—the classification is just a reflection of what segments happen to exist in the lexicon. If a grammar has a rule of the form 's → š / ___ i', then the rule is a neutralization rule if there are underlying tokens of š,[1] but it is an allophonic rule if the only source of š is from s before i.

One of the most basic skills typically taught in introductory linguistics courses is the use of a heuristic, a discovery procedure, for determining whether two sounds are in complementary distribution, and thus potentially allophones. In its simplest form, the procedure to demonstrate that two segments are *not* allophones is to show that they can occur in exactly the same environment—that they are *not* in complementary distribution.[2]

---

[1] It is also possible that there could be two underlying forms that surface as š (neither of which is š underlyingly) with two or more rules producing this effect: recall the Korean example where five underlying segments all neutralize to a single form that does not occur in the lexicon.

[2] In other words, assume they are in complementary distribution, then look for a so-called "minimal pair" of words that differ only by contrasting the two segments in question. This shows that the two *can* occur in the same in environment and thus are not in complementary distribution. This is a version of *proof by contradiction*, which is a particular form of *reductio ad absurdum* (RAA), which was presented in our discussion of neutralization.

281

In English, for instance, we can demonstrate that [s] and [š] cannot be allophones of a single phoneme since they can occur in the same environment. For example, they both appear at the beginning of a word and before a [u] and furthermore this contrast in sound signals a critical contrast in meaning, as in the words *shoe* [šu] and *sue* [su].[3] A reasonable conclusion, given this heuristic, is that *s* and *š* are *contrastive* or *distinctive*: their difference is *phonemic*. A pair of words from the same language, like English ⟨*shoe, sue*⟩, which differ minimally with respect to only a single segment, is called a *minimal pair*. So, the idea is that if two segments can be shown to distinguish a minimal pair, then the segments must be manifestations of different phonemes, different underlying segments in the language.

However, with the introduction of rule ordering, it is possible to demonstrate that this basic and commonly taught heuristic is not reliable. We can illustrate this by slightly modifying Begonian and Strelitzian from the discussion of Feeding and Counterfeeding. In those datasets, we included minimal pairs like *lus* 'a frog' and *luš* 'a nut', as well as homophonous pairs *luši* 'the frog' and *luši* 'the nut'. Such pairs helped to establish that there is neutralization of *s* and *š*. Thus, a given surface token of *š* could have come from either underlying *s* or underlying *š*.

In contrast, consider Zinnian, which is almost identical to Begonian and Strelitzian, except that it lacks the forms that would lead us to posit an underlying *š*.

---

[3]Traditionally, minimal pairs are pairs of *words* that differ in meaning. This focus on phonological differences that can signal a meaning difference is an example of implicit functionalism in earlier phonological approaches. The idea is that a segmental distinction can function to signal a difference in meaning, which is what language is "for" under a functionalist view. Our view is like that expressed by Morris Halle in "Confessio Grammatici":

> Since language is not, in its essence, a means for transmitting [cognitive] information—though no one denies that we constantly use language for this very purpose—then it is hardly surprising to find in languages much ambiguity and redundancy, as well as other properties that are obviously undesirable in a good communication code. (1975, p. 528)

.

(305)   Zinnian

	form	gloss
a.	lup	'a dog'
b.	lupi	'the dog'
c.	lupo	'a hat'
d.	lupi	'the hat'
e.	lus	'a frog'
f.	**luši**	'the frog'
g.	luso	'a pig'
h.	**lusi**	'the pig'

With Zinnian, we still need a rule of the form 's → š / ___ i' to account for the alternation in the forms for 'frog' (e) and (f) and a rule of the form 'o → ε / ___ i' to account for the alternation in the forms for 'hat' (c) and (d). However, the rule that converts *s* to *š* would be "allophonic" since there is no neutralization with an underlying segment.

A critical aspect of Zinnian is that we *do* find minimal pairs like *luši* 'the frog' and *lusi* 'the pig', but we *do not* need to posit an underlying difference in the two roots between the segments that surface as *s* and *š*. We can hypothesize that the form *lusi* 'the pig' has *s* because when the 's → š / ___ i' rule applied, the *s* was "protected" by a not-yet-deleted *o*. This assumes a counterfeeding analysis of the two rules, as in Strelitzian. As a result, we have a minimal pair that on the surface distinguishes *s* and *š*, but rule ordering shows that we can derive them from a single underlying source. The existence of the minimal pair, and hence the lack of complementary distribution, means that we can't call the rule *allophonic* in the traditional sense, and we can't treat *s* and *š* as allophones of a single underlying segment.

Such cases demonstrate that understanding phonological systems requires fairly sophisticated analysis, not just an examination of surface forms. Testing for minimal pairs or complementary distribution can be useful heuristics for developing hypotheses, but they do not lead us directly to an insightful analysis. They can fail, just as our use of the Surfacing Lexical Form Assumption (SLFA) can fail.

Note that there is a new implicit assumption embedded in our discussion of minimal pairs. In analyzing Zinnian, we implied that it is clearly desirable to *not* posit an underlying *š* since we don't need to do so. In Zinnian, there is a good reason to adopt this approach, since every morpheme that has an alternant with [š] also has an alternant with [s], and we are working with the assumption that each morpheme has a single phonological representation in the lexicon. (There is, in fact, only one [š] in this dataset, but you can imagine extending it with parallel cases.) So, the absence of lexical tokens of [š] follows from our assumptions about the uniqueness of phonological representations for morphemes.

But things could be different. Suppose we extend the Zinnian data to Zinnian′, where there are cases of [š] that do not alternate:

(306)   Zinnian′

	form	gloss
a.	lup	'a dog'
b.	lupi	'the dog'
c.	lupo	'a hat'
d.	lupi	'the hat'
e.	lus	'a frog'
f.	luši	'the frog'
g.	luso	'a pig'
h.	lusi	'the pig'
i.	**šip**	'a pail'
j.	**šipi**	'the pail'

In Zinnian′, there are two instances of š appearing at the beginning of a word and before an *i*. We obviously still need our 's → š / ___ i' rule to deal with the forms of 'frog', but does the existence of this rule mean that we *must* derive all cases of [š] from /s/ just because we can? In other words, should we hypothesize that the underlying form for 'pail' is /sip/ and that it surfaces as [šip] due to our rule? Note that from a learner's perspective, storing the morpheme for 'pail' as /šip/, with an initial underlying /š/, even though we have the machinery to derive it from /s/, would constitute a more straightforward learning path—the learner hears *šip* and the learner stores *šip*, and everything is fine. Why should the learner take the extra step of converting the stored form to /sip/?

Now consider yet another language that has tokens of non-alternating š that occur only before *i*, but has no morphemes with alternations. Salvian in (307) represents such a language:

(307)   Salvian

	form	gloss
a.	sap	'a dog'
b.	sape	'the dog'
c.	lus	'a hat'
d.	luse	'the hat'
e.	šik	'a mouse'
f.	šike	'the mouse'
g.	sok	'a pot'
h.	soke	'the pot'
i.	šip	'a pail'
j.	šipe	'the pail'

There is no evidence for a rule from alternations of *s* and *š* in Salvian; however, positing a rule that converts *s* to *š* before *i* would allow us to minimize the number of distinct segments in underlying forms. Despite the absence of alternations, it is the case that [s] and [š] are in complementary distribution and thus it is possible to derive all the cases of [š] from underlying /s/. Phonologists long assumed that this kind of efficiency was justified, but some recent work in phonology has suggested that minimizing the number of underlying segments might not constitute the most elegant account of phonological acquisition. This is an ongoing topic of discussion in the literature.

Looking back at Zinnian' (306), it is of course possible that the non-alternating cases of [š] are derived from underlying /š/ and the alternating ones are derived from underlying /s/. At this point, we do not have a means of choosing among these competing, extensionally equivalent analyses.

Unit 33

Rule Interactions III:
BLEEDING and
COUNTERBLEEDING

We adopted the name FEEDING for an ordering relation in which one rule *creates* an output that allows a subsequent rule to apply non-vacuously. We called an ordering COUNTERFEEDING if it was the opposite of a feeding ordering. Rules can also potentially interact in a manner in which one rule *destroys* the chance for another to apply non-vacuously. In such a case, we say the first rule BLEEDS the second. If the ordering is contrary to a bleeding ordering, we call it COUNTERBLEEDING.

33.1   Bleeding

Suppose there are two rules R_i and R_j that apply non-vacuously to a string x. If R_j applies before R_i and turns x into y, and y does not meet the conditions for R_i to apply to it non-vacuously, then we say that R_j *bleeds* R_i. This is because R_j did something to x that blocked the non-vacuous application of R_i. We can define this type of situation more generally as in (309). (In (308), we repeat for convenience the definition of a minimal triggering environment from (288); and as we did in the discussion of feeding, we limit our definition of bleeding to cases where the complex function consists of the composition of two rules.)

(308) **Minimal Triggering Environment** (MTE): A sequence z is a minimal triggering environment for a rule R if and only if (i) $R(z) \neq z$ and (ii) there is no
subsequence y of z such that $R(y) \neq y$.

(309) **Bleeding**: A rule R_j bleeds a rule R_i in a composed function f if and only if
the following conditions are met:

   a. In the composed function f, R_j appears to the right of R_i (i.e., $f = R_i \circ R_j$)

   b. There is a sequence of segments x such that the number of MTEs relative
       to R_i in x is greater than the number of MTEs relative to R_i in $R_j(x)$.

To illustrate this concept more thoroughly, consider the simple example of a bleeding
pattern given in (310).

(310) Chaetognatha manifests *bleeding*

N	on a N	for a N	on Ns
'fish'	pun	puk	tun
'knish'	pan	pak	tan
'dish'	pun	tok	tun

By employing our comparison method, we can conclude that -*n* is a suffix associated
with the meaning 'on X' (by comparison of forms in columns 1 and 3), -*k* is a suffix
associated with the meaning 'for X' (by comparison of the forms in column 2), and *t-*
is a prefix associated with indefinite plurality (by comparison of the forms in column
3).

The form associated with the singular morpheme is a bit more complicated. By
comparison of the forms in column 1 and the first two forms in column 2, it seems
reasonable to hypothesize that *p-* is the prefix associated with indefinite singular forms.
However, this is inconsistent with the last form in the second column, namely *tok* ('for
a dish'). It is a reasonable hypothesis that a phonological rule may be at play, perhaps
one that converts *p* to *t* when it appears before an *o*. Assuming such a rule, we would
have the following URs for the prefixes and the suffixes in (310).

(311) Chaetognatha morphemes

'on'	'for'	INDEF SG	INDEF PL
-n	-k	p-	t-

Turning our attention to the noun roots, comparison of the forms in rows 1 and 2 suggest that /u/ is the form of the underlying morpheme for 'fish' and /a/ is the form of the underlying morpheme for 'knish'. However, things get a bit more complicated with respect to the UR of the root meaning 'dish'. Subtraction of *-k* and *t-* (assuming the rule that converts *p* to *t* before *o*) from the second form in row 3 yields /o/ as the underlying form for 'dish', whereas comparison of the first and last forms in row 3 yields /u/ as the underlying form. Either there is a rule that maps *o* to *u* before an *n*, or there is a rule that maps *u* to *o* before a *k*. This second rule is unlikely since the form for 'for a fish' is *puk* and not *pok*. Thus, it is most likely the case that the morpheme associated with 'dish' is /o/ and there is a rule that maps *o* to *u* before *n*.

The analysis is summarized by the table in (312), where the morphological structure of the words is shown using hyphens.

(312) Lexical forms for the nouns of Chaetognatha

N	on a N	for a N	on Ns	UR of N
'fish'	p-u-n	p-u-k	t-u-n	/u/
'knish'	p-a-n	p-a-k	t-a-n	/a/
'dish'	p-u-n	t-o-k	t-u-n	/o/

According to our analysis, there are two rules at play, R_a = o → u / ___ n and R_b = p → t / ___ o. A quick inspection of the data reveals that the rules have to be composed in the following order: $R_b \circ R_a$ (i.e., R_a applies before R_b). If R_b applied before R_a then the surface form meaning 'on a dish' would have been *tun* instead of *pun*.

With this analysis of the data, let's walk through the derivations of the SRs using the derivation tables in (313).

(313) Chaetognatha derivations

UR	p-u-n	p-u-k	t-u-n	p-a-n	p-a-k
R_a: o → u / _ n	—	—	—	—	—
R_b: p → t / _ o	—	—	—	—	—
SR	pun	puk	tun	pan	pak
Gloss	'on a fish'	'for a fish'	'on fish'	'on a knish'	'for a knish'

UR	t-a-n	p-o-n	p-o-k	t-o-n
R_a: $o \rightarrow u /$ __ n	—	pun	—	tun
R_b: $p \rightarrow t /$ __ o	—	$\boxed{—}$	tok	—
SR	tan	**pun**	**tok**	tun
Gloss	'on knishes'	'on a dish'	'for a dish'	'on dishes'

In the form *pun* 'on a dish', the effect of 'o $\rightarrow$ u / ___ n' ensures that the /p/ surfaces unchanged by getting rid of the *po* sequence. We have placed a box in the table to see where R_b has been *bled* by R_a. We say that R_a BLEEDS R_b for this form, since R_a destroys the environment for the non-vacuous application of R_b. If R_a had not applied, then this word would have been affected by R_b. In *tok*, however, there is no rule to get rid of the *o*, and thus the *po* sequence of the UR becomes *to* via R_b.

33.2   Counterbleeding

If we keep the same rules and the same underlying forms, but apply the rules in a different order, some of the SRs will be different. This order of rule composition is an example of a counterbleeding order.

(314)   Counterbleeding

UR	p-u-n	p-u-k	t-u-n	p-a-n	p-a-k
R_b: $p \rightarrow t /$ __ o	—	—	—	—	—
R_a: $o \rightarrow u /$ __ n	—	—	—	—	—
SR	pun	puk	tun	pan	pak
Gloss	'on a fish'	'for a fish'	'on fish'	'on a knish'	'for a knish'

UR	t-a-n	p-o-n	p-o-k	t-o-n
R_b: $p \rightarrow t \, / \, \_\_\_ \, o$	—	~~ton~~ (boxed)	tok	—
R_a: $o \rightarrow u \, / \, \_\_\_ \, n$	—	tun	—	tun
SR	tan	tun	tok	tun
Gloss	'on knishes'	'on a dish'	'for a dish'	'on dishes'

You might think that R_b *feeds* R_a, but it does not. R_b does not create strings that R_a can apply to that it would not have otherwise applied to. Look at the form *ton* in the box. The first rule is R_b and it turns the underlying *p* to *t* before *o*. The 'o → u / ___ n' rule also applies non-vacuously to this form, but it would have applied whether *p* was converted to *t* or not.

Counterbleeding can be more formally defined as follows:

(315)   **Counterbleeding**: A rule R_j counterbleeds a rule R_i in a composed function f if and only if

   a.   In the composed function f, R_j appears to the left of R_i (i.e., $f = R_j \circ R_i$)

   b.   There exists a composed function f', such that R_j appears to the right of R_i in f' (i.e., $f' = R_i \circ R_j$) and R_j bleeds R_i in f'.

A useful analogy for understanding feeding and bleeding is to think about creation and destruction. Failing to create something is not the same as destroying it, just as failing to feed a rule is not the same as bleeding it. These terms are useful for recognizing data patterns, but once again, they are not actually part of the theory of phonology. Given our simple model of ordered rules, all four types of interaction that we have discussed are predicted to occur. It would actually be surprising if phonological UG prohibited, say, counterfeeding rule ordering since the possibility of such ordering is just an expected consequence of our understanding of rule ordering as functional composition. It is not even clear how one could formulate a UG ban on counterfeeding if it was deemed desirable to do so—such ordering has nothing to do with the form of individual rules or with the mechanism of ordering itself, but with accidental properties of certain derivations by certain grammars. Since the derivations themselves are not stored in memory, it is unclear how to prohibit them.

Exercises

33.1. Here are three rules and four different languages. Some languages use R1 and R2 and others use R1 and R3.

    R1: t → s/___i

    R2: e → i/___%

    R3: i → e/___%

Study the given derivations and state whether the rules are ordered in a *bleeding, counterbleeding, feeding,* or *counterfeeding* order.

A. Eenyan
    UR: /pot-ik-at-e/
    R1: posikate
    R2: posikati
    SR: [posikati]

B. Meenyan
    UR: /pot-ik-at-e/
    R2: potikati
    R1: posikasi
    SR: [posikasi]

C. Minyan
    UR: /pot-ik-at-i/
    R3: potikate
    R1: posikate
    SR: [posikate]

D. Moese
    UR: /pot-ik-at-i/
    R1: posikasi
    R3: posikase
    SR: [posikase]

33.2. Here is a list of possible rules for different languages. Study the data and derivations and answer the questions about each language. When asked to describe ordering relations use the terms *feeding, counterfeeding, bleeding,* or *counterbleeding,* for example "Rule$_A$ feeds Rule$_B$."

R_1: p → k / ___o

R_2: u → o / ___%

R_3: o → u / ___%

R_4: o → ε / k ___l

A. Jackieish
   UR: /tap-olip-o/
   R_1: takoliko
   R_3: takoliku
   SR: [takoliku]

   i. Describe the ordering of R_1 and R_3.

   ii. Why did the leftmost p change into k?

   iii. Why did the rightmost p change into k?

B. Titonian
   UR: /tap-olip-o/
   R_3: tapolipu
   R_1: takolipu
   SR: [takolipu]

   i. Describe the ordering of R_1 and R_3.

   ii. Why did the leftmost p change into k?

   iii. Why didn't the rightmost p change into k?

C. Jermainean
   UR: /ru-pup-olip-u/
   R_1: rupukolipu
   R_2: rupukolipo
   SR: [rupukolipo]

   i. Describe the ordering of R_1 and R_2.

   ii. Why didn't the leftmost p change into k?

   iii. Why did the p in the middle change into k?

   iv. Why didn't the rightmost p change into k?

D. Marlonian
  UR: /ru-pup-olip-u/
  R_2: rupupolipo
  R_1: rupukoliko
  SR: [rupukoliko]

  i. Describe the ordering of R_1 and R_2.

  ii. Why didn't the leftmost p change into k?

  iii. Why did p in the middle change into k?

  iv. Why did the rightmost p change into k?

E. Michaelese
  UR: /tap-olip-o/
  R_1: takoliko
  R_3: takoliku
  R_4: takliku
  SR: [takliku]

  i. Describe the ordering of R_1 and R_3.

  ii. Describe the ordering of R_1 and R_4.

  iii. What can you say about the ordering of R_3 and R_4? Don't just answer "nothing."

33.3. Consider these rules:

  • Rule A: delete [n] at the end of a word

  • Rule B: e → i before [n]

  • Put the rules in the order A-B and compute the derivations in the table below.

  • What do we call this ordering?_____

  • Draw an appropriate SMD.

Underlying Rep	ze	ze-n	ze-n-tim	pa	pa-n	pa-n-tim
Rule A						
Rule B						
Surface Rep						
Gloss	'rat'	'the rat'	'the rats'	'hat'	'the hat'	'the hats'

- Put the rules in the order B-A and compute the derivations in the table below.

- What do we call this ordering?_____

- Draw an appropriate SMD

Underlying Rep	ze	ze-n	ze-n-tim	pa	pa-n	pa-n-tim
Rule B						
Rule A						
Surface Rep						
Gloss	'rat'	'the rat'	'the rats'	'hat'	'the hat'	'the hats'

33.4. Consider this Cymothoan data:

SG	PL	
sɛ	sed	'leak'
se	sɪd	'peak'
sɪ	sid	'freak'
si	sid	'steak'

How many rules do you need to account for Cymothoan? Provide lexical forms for all morphemes. List the rules, provide an ordering, and name each of the orderings between pairs of rules that you have evidence for.

33.5. The relation *is-taller-than* is *transitive* since, if we know that A is taller than B, and that B is taller than C, then we know that A is taller than C. The relation *is-next-to* is not transitive since, if we know that Jorge is next to Jing, and that Jing is next to Sana, it does not follow that Jorge is next to Sana.

Is the precedence relation of rule ordering transitive or not transitive? Referring to the previous question on Cymothoan, explain how we might be able to order two rules, even if there are no direct arguments for the kinds of interactions we have described.

33.6. Here are two rules:

- R1: t → ϵ / n ___ %
- R2: n → ϵ / i ___

Consider these mappings by the phonology:

- /gopont/ ⤳ [gopon]
- /mapantak/ ⤳ [mapantak]
- /hukint/ ⤳ [huki]
- /holintuk/ ⤳ [holituk]

- What is the correct rule ordering?
- What do you call this ordering? Explain.
- What surface forms would you get from the opposite ordering?

33.7. Solve this Taenian dataset using two rules in a bleeding relation. Assume you can refer only to immediate left or right positions to define rule environments. Provide a full solution with presentation of alternants, a lexicon, and derivations for *all sixteen* forms.

	form	gloss		form	gloss
a.	ŋɹf	'a dog'	i.	ŋɹf	'a pen'
b.	ŋɹfnim	'the dog'	j.	ŋɹθnim	'the pen'
c.	qɹf	'some dogs'	k.	qɹf	'some pens'
d.	qɹfnim	'the dogs'	l.	qæθnim	'the pens'
e.	ŋæf	'a house'	m.	ŋæf	'a stone'
f.	ŋæfnim	'the house'	n.	ŋæθnim	'the stone'
g.	qæf	'some houses'	o.	qæf	'some stones'
h.	qæfnim	'the houses'	p.	qæθnim	'the stones'

33.8. Taenian's close relative Naeglerian has the same lexicon and rules, but the rules apply in the opposite order. How will Naeglerian SRs differ from those of Taenian? Give derivations for the sixteen Naeglerian forms corresponding to the Taenian forms above.

Unit 34

Alternative Analyses

When confronted with a new, unorganized dataset, we are often desperate to find an analysis that "works," a set of posited lexical forms and rules in an order that generates the observed surface forms. If we have no restrictions on the format that our lexical forms and rules can take, there are literally an infinite number of solutions to every dataset—we might have rules inserting and deleting segments over and over again with no observable effects on the output, for example. However, it is important to realize that, even with the restricted model we have developed, multiple solutions may be possible.

For the following Eisenian dataset there are at least seven different solutions that use licit rules. We provide two. See if you can find others.

(316) Eisenian, with multiple solutions

	form	gloss
a.	tʊʒ	'ox'
b.	ɔχon	'oxen'
c.	tɔχ	'sheep'
d.	ɔχon	'sheep' (pl.)

In the first solution we give, we'll make the two noun roots differ in two ways, and make the rules be unordered. This means that there will be no evidence for the ordering—either ordering works—but we will assume that in an actual phonology, all the rules are in some order.

First, let's deal with the affixes. Let's assume in all the solutions that there is a singular prefix /t-/ and a plural suffix /-on/. Since there is only one alternant meaning 'sheep', let's posit that form as the lexical form: /ɔχ/. Now, since we are constructing a solution in which the two noun roots differ in two ways, we can posit for the morpheme meaning 'ox' the alternant /ʊʒ/. With the lexicon we have proposed, it is simple to see that we can use the following two rules:

(317)   Rules for first solution (unorderable)

R_a ʊ → ɔ / # ___

R_b ʒ → χ / ___ o

You should be able to see that these rules will derive the right results if we set up URs using our posited lexical forms, and that the rules do not have any potential to interact since one (R_a) involves only material from the left edge of the root and the prefix, and the other (R_b) involves only material from the right edge of the root and the suffix.

It would really be more precise to say that we have just come up with two solutions, one with the rules ordered one way, R_a before R_b, and another with the reverse order, since a real mental grammar by hypothesis has to have the rules ordered.

In the second solution, using the same underlying forms for the noun roots and affixes, we can posit two rules in a feeding order:

(318)   Rules for second solution (feeding)

R_c ʊ → ɔ / # ___

R_d ʒ → χ / ɔ ___

You should see why there is feeding in this case. The first rule creates the ɔ, which determines the environment of the second rule.

In the Exercises, see if you can come up with a few more solutions according to the conditions given. Even if you can't come up with all of the solutions we refer to, you should appreciate the fact that this "freedom" is actually a problem. Our model allows *all* of these solutions. Perhaps more data would show that some of our solutions are untenable. Perhaps some aspect of the acquisition process determines which solution is the correct one—perhaps it depends on the order in which the data is encountered—but for now, we have to recognize that we do not know enough to choose among these solutions. In other words, the indeterminacy is epistemological, not ontological. We may not be able to decide on the correct description of a particular I-language, but that does not mean that it does not have specific properties.

Exercises

Provide new solutions for Eisenian, following the guidelines given. Show derivations and SMDs for each solution. All of your rules should be licit according to the model we have developed—referring to at most a single segment to the left and to the right.

34.1. Using the same exact lexical items as in the two solutions given in (317) and (318), first have a rule affecting ʒ and have that rule feed a rule affecting ʊ.

34.2. In another solution, make the noun roots differ with respect to just one segment. Use two rules, but make sure that no ordering argument is possible.

34.3. In the next solution, again make the two roots differ in a single segment, different from the previous one, and again make sure that no ordering argument is possible for the set of two rules.

34.4. In the next solution, make the two roots differ in a single segment (potentially like one of the preceding cases) and posit rules that must apply in a bleeding ordering.

34.5. Now make the lexical items differ in a segment different from the previous one, and provide another solution with a bleeding ordering.

Unit 35

Getting Ready to Expand SPE

We have gotten a lot of mileage from our SPE rule system (which, we remind the reader, is named after the system in Chomsky and Halle's 1968 book, *The Sound Pattern of English*, although ours is actually much less sophisticated than that system). Despite the fact that we restricted its representational apparatus to a set of segment symbols (along with the word boundary and null segment symbols) and we restricted its computational apparatus to the composition of rules with a very simple syntax, we were able to show that the system can still generate a lot of superficial complexity—we can describe a lot of phenomena using a very simple model. In fact, this very property, the ability to describe a lot using a simple model, is one of the standard ways of conceiving of scientific theories; a theory can be thought of as a form of data compression (Chaitin, 2006). By capturing generalizations, a good theory can describe a range of facts more succinctly than a bad theory or a mere catalog of observations.

Our insistence on SPE has been in large part driven by pedagogical aims. We want to show how to build an explicit model of phonology, with an explicit semantics of the rules and representations it uses, and show that it is plausible that the variety and apparent complexity of human language data could, in fact, arise from a system that itself is fairly simple.

However, we have known all along, and we have hinted to you, that our SPE model is woefully inadequate. There are many aspects of human language phonology that require more than our SPE-type rules containing segment symbols. In the rest of this book we will present some of these inadequacies and expose you to some further devices that phonology seems to demand.

The restricted model we have presented so far has not been a waste of time. On

303

a practical level, it will allow you to understand much of the published literature on phonology; our SPE system is interesting enough and useful for many discussions. More importantly, we hope you have come to understand some basic principles of scientific methodology in the course of our discussion. Finally, we cannot promise you that we will now present "the correct theory" of phonology, because that theory has not yet been discovered. Like all scientific endeavors, phonology is a work in progress with lots of steps forward, blind alleys, controversies, and confusion. You are hereby invited to participate in this undertaking.

Some of the topics we now turn to may have already occurred to you, depending on your background in linguistics. They include the following phenomena:

- phonological length (long versus short vowels and consonants)

- tone—pitch differences that can distinguish word meaning despite identity of segments

- featural analysis of segments into *natural classes*, such as *vowels vs. consonants* or *voiced vs. voiceless* sounds

- syllable structure

- long-distance rules like vowel harmony

- phonological stress

- metathesis—rules that appear to target a pair of segments and switch their relative order in the string

- rules that express relationships like identity between segments

Whole books have been written about each of these topics, and all of them remain challenging to phonologists. Aside from our discussion of the logic of featural analysis, our discussion of these topics will be fairly superficial. In more advanced courses, you will be able to apply the ideas we have introduced via SPE to these topics. When you do so, you will be at the cutting edge of current phonological research.

Part VII

Suprasegmental Phonology

Unit 36

Metathesis

In this unit, we briefly look at metathesis, a phenomenon that our SPE rule system is clearly incapable of handling. Metathesis is the first of several topics that force us to expand our rule system and to also develop a more sophisticated model of phonological representation. We need a model that contains more than just strings of segments as the phonological component of morphemes. Aspects of phonological representation that are not contained within a segment might be called extra-segmental, in the sense that they involve information that is external to the segments. Rather than *extra-segmental*, a traditional term is *suprasegmental*, the idea being that there are kinds of information that are superimposed on the segment string and that involve structures larger than individual segments. As we explore the suprasegmental phenomena of tone, syllable structure, and stress computation in the following units, we will have to significantly expand our model.

Recall our discussion of expressibility from Part III. Our precise formalization of SPE syntax restricts us to rules of the form in (319):

(319)   SPE rule format

      a. $\alpha \rightarrow \beta \,/ \underline{\quad} \; \gamma$

      b. $\alpha \rightarrow \beta \,/ \gamma \underline{\quad}$

      c. $\alpha \rightarrow \beta \,/ \gamma \underline{\quad} \; \delta$

Each of these rules involve the substitution of one kind of segment for another in a restricted set of environment types. No other type of rule is expressible in SPE. We now consider one attested phonological process that cannot be expressed in our SPE system.

There appear to be rules that involve switching the order of segments, a phenomenon called METATHESIS. An illustration of a metathesis pattern is given in (320):

(320)   Metathesis: UR: /kolp/ → SR: [klop]

Many apparent metathesis patterns turn out not to be part of the phonology of an I-language. Instead these examples show metathesis as a historical process. Suppose one generation of a speech community pronounces some words with an *ol* sequence, but a subsequent generation pronounces a historically related word with an *lo* sequence. This would be an example of historical or diachronic metathesis. It could be that the change happens only in words with certain properties. So, maybe the earlier generation has related forms *kolp* and *kolpa*, and the later generation has *klop* and *kolpa*. It is possible that the later generation has a phonological rule relating these forms, but it is also possible that alternate forms are stored separately in the lexicon. Good parallels might be the forms *were* and *was* or *wife* and *wives* in English, which contain historically related forms that can't be related by phonological rules in the synchronic grammar.

In a widely cited case from Hebrew, illustrated in (321), metathesis applies synchronically, but it appears to be sensitive to morphological structure, applying only in certain verb forms, so it may not be a purely phonological process.

(321)   Metathesis in Hebrew
        UR   SR
    a. /hi-t-nakem/   hitnakem   'he took revenge'
    b. /hi-t-kabel/   hitkabel   'it was accepted'
    c. /hi-t-sarek/   histarek   'he combed his hair'

As you can see by comparing (a) and (b) with (c), an underlying /ts/ sequence surfaces as [st].

Both historical and morphological metathesis patterns are beyond the scope of a purely phonological theory, and hence there is no need to modify our current theory to account for these types of patterns. However, other examples of metathesis seem to require a phonological explanation. For example, Faroese, the language of the Faroe Islands, is one of a few languages posited to have a fully productive phonological metathesis process. In this language, the underlying sequence /sk/ surfaces as [ks] when followed by a *t*, as you can see by comparing the masculine forms, with the ending -*ʊr*, to the neuter forms, with the ending -*t*, in (322). The sequence '*skt*' occurs in some verb forms, too, and metathesis is seen there, as well.

(322) Faroese metathesis

    Masc   Neut

    fɛskʊr   fɛkst   'fresh'

    raskʊr   rakst   'energetic'

We obviously cannot formulate such a process in our current system: SPE rules cannot affect the relative ordering of two segments in a string. Let's consider how metathesis challenges the current SPE model.

One approach to metathesis is to treat it as due not to a single rule, but to a sequence of rules. For the Faroese case, it is hard to see how this helps to maintain SPE rule syntax—you should give it a try.

Another way to deal with metathesis is to completely reject the SPE notation and adopt a new notation that transparently encodes the fact that rules map strings to strings. Sometimes this notation is called the *transformational notation* in phonology. In logic and theoretical computer science these systems are called *string rewriting systems* or, the label we adopt, *semi-Thue systems*, since they are a version of a formalism developed by the logician Axel Thue (1863–1922).

To formulate the Faroese pattern in (322) using a semi-Thue system, we just write a rewrite rule for strings like (323):

(323) skt → kst

Such a rule is interpreted as applying to all substrings of the form *skt* wherever they occur in a string.[1] So, the rule not only maps *fɛskt* to *fɛkst* and *raskt* to *rakst*, but also *usktaraskta* to *ukstaraksta*.

All of the SPE rule schemas in (319) can be expressed in semi-Thue format, as in (324):

(324) SPE and semi-Thue rules

SPE format	semi-Thue format
$\alpha \rightarrow \beta\ /\ \_\_\_\ \gamma$	$\alpha\gamma \rightarrow \beta\gamma$
$\alpha \rightarrow \beta\ /\ \gamma\ \_\_\_$	$\gamma\alpha \rightarrow \gamma\beta$
$\alpha \rightarrow \beta\ /\ \gamma\ \_\_\_\ \delta$	$\gamma\alpha\delta \rightarrow \gamma\beta\delta$

Each one of these rule schemas represents a rewrite system, where substrings that match the symbols to the left of the arrow are rewritten as the substrings to the right

---

[1] Just like the SPE rules, it is not specified by the syntax whether these rules are interpreted as functions that apply to strings left-to-right, right-to-left, or globally. A semantics for such a system would be needed to clarify which type of function was intended if we embedded it into a model of human phonology.

of the arrow. The "environment" is included on both sides of the arrow instead of appearing in its own separate section of the rule.

For a specific example, consider a rule we have used several times before, expressed in (325) as a semi-Thue rule:

(325)   SPE format: s → š / ___ i ⟹ Semi-Thue format: si → ši

This rule specifies that *si* substrings are rewritten as *ši* substrings. The effect is the same as the application of the SPE rule. Thus, not only can a semi-Thue system express metathesis rules, it can also express any rule that can be expressed in the SPE system—in other words, it is a more powerful notational system.

Beyond the ability to express metathesis rules, semi-Thue systems have other advantages. One of them is the simplification of insertion and deletion rules. In semi-Thue systems, it is unnecessary to introduce an empty segment symbol, ϵ. Rather, insertion and deletion rules can be expressed by the absence of certain symbols—deletion by the absence of a segment to the right of the arrow and insertion by the absence of a symbol to the left. For example, consider the SPE insertion and deletion rules in (326) and their translations into semi-Thue notation.

(326)   a. ϵ → a / b ___ c ⟹ bc → bac   "Insert *a* between *b* and *c*"

        b. a → ϵ / b ___ c ⟹ bac → bc   "Delete *a* between *b* and *c*"

Semi-Thue rules simplify our theory by reducing the number of symbols we need.

However, there are some potential disadvantages in using such a system. For example, the system allows for rules that are sensitive to environments larger than the three-segment neighborhood of the SPE system, including rules like the ones in (327).

(327)   a. abcd → abfd "Replace *c* with *f* if preceded by the sequence *ab* and followed by *d*."

        b. abcde → aecdb "Switch the position of *b* and *e* in the sequence *abcde*"

Furthermore, such systems allow for rules that have a "three-segment neighborhood" but that make changes to more than a single segment. For example, consider the two rules in (328).

(328)   a. arn → eln "Replace *ar* with *el* when followed by *n*."

        b. arn → nar "An *arn* subsequence is replaced by a *nar* subsequence."

On the one hand, our SPE system seems incapable of handling metathesis. On the other hand, adopting semi-Thue formalism provides no guidelines about what is a possible rule. Recall the goals we discussed in Part III. We want to develop a rule system that neither over- nor undergenerates—we want to be like Goldilocks and choose the porridge that is "just right" in the sense that it accurately captures the nature of our phonological capacities. In this case, it is hard to make a decision between SPE and the semi-Thue systems. One is too cold while the other is too hot; neither is "just right." We are still looking for the perfect theory (and we will still be looking at the end of the book).

It appears that natural languages need something stronger than SPE, something with greater expressive power. However, semi-Thue systems appear to be fairly unconstrained and do very little to provide a plausible theory of what is a possible phonological rule. Not only is this unsatisfying to linguists, but, more seriously, it does nothing to explain what Ray Jackendoff likes to call the *paradox of language acquisition*, the idea that, in contrast to the struggles of linguists to understand the structure of languages and language generally, young children acquire languages without any explicit instruction. The solution to the paradox is that for kids, the hypothesis space of languages is delimited by universal grammar. If children can only posit SPE-type rules to explain the alternations in the data they encounter, the space of possibilities is more constrained than if they have to consider any possible string-to-string mappings allowed by a semi-Thue system. Knowledge of universal grammar is not accessible to consciousness, so linguists can't benefit in their theorizing from the constrained hypothesis space that guides children in the course of acquisition.

Unit 37

Length

In Part V we made use of the concept of *minimal pairs* as a heuristic for demonstrating that two sounds are not in complementary distribution. Typically, minimal pairs of words are distinguished by a single segment, for example, English [sɪn] *sin* versus [ʃɪn] *shin*, and thus the words correspond to segment strings of the same length, with a different segment in just one position. When we find such a minimal pair we can conclude that the segment difference corresponds to a meaning difference: *sin* and *shin* have different meanings. Traditionally, the existence of minimal pairs based on a segment difference has been used to argue that these two surface segments derive from different underlying segments.[1] We can extend the notion of minimal pair to words that differ in length, with one member of the pair having one segment more than the other, in any position, as illustrated in (329):

(329) English minimal pairs based on absence versus presence of a segment

Final position	[bi] *bee*	[bin] *bean*
Initial position	[pɪn] *pin*	[spɪn] *spin*
Medially	[bæk] *back*	[bæsk] *bask*
Medially	[tæp] *tap*	[tɹæp] *trap*

In some languages, there exist minimal pairs based on absence or presence of a segment that is identical to an adjacent segment. For example, in Mi'gmaq, an Eastern

---

[1] Recall, however, that in Zinnian (305) in Unit (32) there is a minimal pair *lusi/luši*, but we don't need to posit two underlying segments. We were able to derive the minimal pair without an underlying segmental contrast of /s/ and /š/ via counterfeeding rule ordering.

Algonquian language spoken on the east coast of Canada, we find minimal pairs involving single segments versus double segments, as in (330):

(330)   Minimal Pairs in Mi'gmaq

    a.   [ebit] ('he or she is seated') *vs.* [eebit] ('woman')

    b.   [tebagan] ('car SG') *vs.* [tebagann] ('car PL')

We have single versus double *e* in (330a) and single versus double *n* in (330b). This contrast is represented in the transcriptions in (330) as being between one versus two (adjacent) tokens of a segment. It is common to also describe such a contrast as one of phonological quantity or LENGTH. The double *ee* is a long version of the single *e*, and the double *nn* is a long version of the single *n*.

Orthographic and phonetic transcription systems used for languages of the world have various ways of representing long segments. Mi'gmaq orthography uses an apostrophe after the vowel: *e* is short, whereas *e'* is long, just like the long *i'* in the name of the language. Many orthographies and transcription systems use the macron symbol: *a* is short, whereas *ā* is long. Some orthographies use the acute accent to mark length: *a* is short, whereas *á* is long. In the International Phonetic Alphabet (IPA) a colon is used to mark length: [a] is short whereas [aː] is long.[2] We will sometimes use a colon as in IPA transcription, but we will also represent length using repetition as we did in (330) above, the system also used in Finnish orthography, for example: *a* is short, whereas *aa* is long.[3] Such a representation more accurately reflects our phonological assumptions, namely that a long segment is underlyingly a sequence of two (short) segments.

Some languages have only long vowels, but not long consonants; some have long consonants, but not long vowels; some have long vowels and long consonants; and some have no length contrast in either vowels or consonants. Long consonants are sometimes called *geminates*, a term derived from the Latin word for 'twin' seen in the astrological sign *Gemini*. Geminate consonants and long vowels may be present in lexical forms, but they can also arise from the concatenation of morphemes.[4]

---

[2]Notice the special triangular colon in the IPA font. Many transcriptions don't distinguish this symbol from a regular colon.

[3]It is worth noting that in languages that are said to have length contrasts, it may be the case that various short-long pairs show a range of phonetic differences. For example, Hungarian short and long [o], written *o* and *ó*, respectively, differ mostly in duration; however, the Hungarian short and long vowels written *a* and *á* correspond to the IPA transcriptions [ɔ] and [æː], respectively. In Icelandic, most of the so-called short-long pairs differ along several phonetic dimensions, for example, several of the 'long' vowels are pronounced as diphthongs, a sequence of a vowel and a glide.

[4]These two sources of phonological length can be reflected in different behavior, but this is an advanced topic that we can't pursue here (see Schein and Steriade, 1986, for discussion).

37.1   The Abstractness of Phonological Length

If you did some of the transcription exercises in Unit 3, you have experienced firsthand the complexity of the relation between a speech signal and a representation of an utterance as a discrete string of segments. One might expect that the correlation between phonological length and temporal duration of an articulatory gesture or an acoustic pattern would be straightforward, but this is not the case. One of the simplest ways to appreciate this is to recognize that a so-called short vowel spoken slowly may actually take more time to utter than a long vowel spoken quickly.

Finnish is a language with long and short vowels and consonants. Suppose that Akbar, a native speaker of Finnish, wakes up, drinks a triple espresso, works hard all day, returns home exhausted in the evening, and enjoys a beer as he prepares his dinner. An hour after the morning coffee, Akbar might speak rather quickly; in the evening, as he relaxes and the alcohol enters his bloodstream, he may speak much more slowly. Akbar's "hyper" pronunciation of the long *uu*, *ll*, and *ee* of the Finnish word *tuulleen* (a form of the verb 'blow') spoken on the commute to work might be of shorter absolute duration than his mellow postprandial drawling of the phonologically short *u*, *l*, and *e* of the word *tulen* (a form of the verb 'to come'). There has been no change in Akbar's *phonological* representations or rules, but the relative durations of segment articulation do change throughout the day nonetheless. The temporal duration of segment articulation is dependent to some extent on speaking rate, not only on phonological length.

Intonation can also affect the duration of segments. Think about how you would pronounce the [o] in a sentence written like this: *He is* **so** *funny!* The [o] would probably be much shorter if you read this: *He is so* **funny***!*

Yet another factor is position: an [f] at the beginning of a word in English, as in *feel*, tends to be much shorter than an [f] at the end, as in *leaf*, but nobody analyzes English as having short and long versions of [f]. This positionally determined difference is just one of the factors that make words played backwards sound so funny. Record yourself saying *leaf-feel* in *Praat* and reverse the recording (use Modify > Reverse). Given the transcriptions [lif-fil] you might expect the reversed sound to be like the original, but the difference in duration of the two *f*'s is one of several factors that make the positional variants differ from each other. Such variation appears to be constant across languages, and thus it is grammatically irrelevant.

There are situations in which languages are described phonologically as having a length contrast, and the contrast does seem to correlate with a clear duration difference for *some* segments. But for other segments, the difference is realized acoustically in a different fashion, for example, by the strength of the burst of a stop consonant. So,

we might refer to a "length" contrast, but the realization of this *phonological* property might correspond to phonetic duration only for some single-double pairs. A good
example of such different realizations of phonological length is found in Malay, illustrated in the UCLA phonetic database (www.phonetics.ucla.edu) with recordings and
discussion from Abramson (1986). In brief, "long" sonorants like [l:] are significantly
longer than "short" ones, but "long" stops like [k:] may be distinguished only by having a greater burst than "short" ones at release of the oral closure. In (331) you can see
that the long [l:] at the beginning of the word lasts about as long as the *m* and each of
the two *a*'s, whereas the short [l] is barely visible:

(331)   Malay [l:] versus [l]

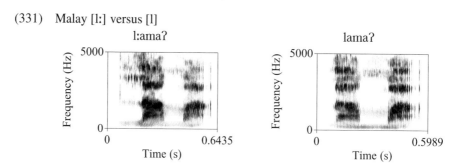

In comparison, the phonological length contrast of initial [k:] and [k] is not apparent
as a large difference in duration.

(332)   Malay [k:] versus [k]

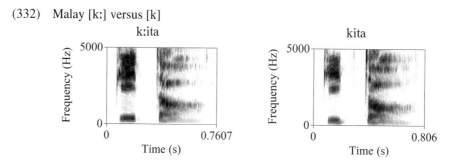

In fact the difference between the two bursts is hardly visible at all, and in keeping with
the abstract nature of phonological representations, may be most salient acoustically
on the following vowels. Note that the first vowel of *k:ita* appears to be louder and
longer than that of *kita*. Speakers treat the duration differences on /l/ versus /l:/ as the
same, phonologically, as the burst differences on /k/ versus /k:/, despite the fact that

the latter are completely different acoustically and are in fact realized on the following vowel segment. This is not an unusual state of affairs—segmental representations are abstract, and the phonological properties of a segment may have a salient phonetic correlate displaced from where we place the segment in a string.

These spectrograms raise another issue in the correlation between phonetic duration and phonological length: duration is partially dependent on segment type. So, in all languages that have [a] and [i] as segments, the articulation of the [a] is consistently longer than the articulation of [i] (factoring out speaking rate, of course). Each segment appears to have an *inherent* length that must be used as a baseline in comparing long and short versions, if the language has forms that make such distinctions. You can see that the single, phonologically short vowels in the Malay spectrograms in (331) and (332) are all significantly longer than both short, single [k] and long, double [k:].

To reiterate, there are at least five factors that show the complex relationship between what is called *length* in phonology and actual temporal duration, measured in milliseconds:

(333)   Factors relevant to phonetic realization of phonological "length"

- Speaking rate (syllables or segments per second)
- Intonation
- Position of a segment in the syllable
- Non-durational realization of length, e.g., force of consonant release
- Inherent duration of different kinds of segments

Each of these interacting factors can be studied as part of the phonetics of speech, and they lead to fascinating questions about the representation, perception, and production of speech. As a group, they probably provide good evidence that phonological length is the manifestation of an innately available representational distinction, since its phonetic correlates are so various. There is no articulatory or acoustic reason to group together the various correlates of phonological length, so the grouping is imposed by the human speech perception system. In this book, however, we will leave these important issues aside and adopt a fairly standard *phonological* view of segment "length" that treats long segments as sequences of short segments. In the following section, we focus primarily on long vowels, but similar arguments apply to consonants.

37.2   Representing Length

Given our SPE rule system, there are two immediate theoretical consequences that
stem from treating long vowels as a sequence of short vowels. First, it *allows* rules to
target the two halves of a long segment separately—for example, a rule could change
the second 'a' of an *aa* sequence without affecting the first. Additionally, this treatment
should *prevent* us from treating the two halves of a long segment as one. As we saw
in our discussion of metathesis, the SPE rule syntax does not allow us to target two
segments—for example, we cannot express changes like *aa→ ee* as a single rule.

Phonologists typically want to "have their cake and eat it, too"—they want a representation of long segments that allows the two halves to be targeted differentially, but
they also want to be able to treat long segments as unitary entities, not just as sequences
of two segments that just happen to be identical. There is an empirical justification for
this desire. Some rules, such as deletion, often target only one of the segments of a
long vowel, whereas other rules, usually those that affect the quality of the vowel—for
example, a rule that maps *e* to *i*—often affect both segments. The trick that phonologists use to get both the "two-ness" and the "one-ness" of a sequence like [ee] is to
treat the "two-ness" with respect to the number of positions it occupies in a string and
the "one-ness" with respect to a shared quality that is linked to both positions. This
subtlety is perhaps easiest to understand through a diagram. Consider the diagram in
(334).

(334)   A long vowel

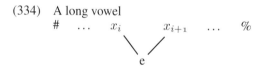

The *e* symbol on the lower line of the diagram represents the *quality* of the two segments. The x_i and x_{i+1} represent something that phonologists call the "timing tier."
The lines between the e-symbol and the x values are called *association lines*. The fact
that *e* is associated to two timing tier values signals that the vowel is long.

In contrast, a short vowel would be represented like this:

(335)   A short vowel

Of course, the diagram in (335) fails to specify that the segment is definitely short, that the *e* is *not* associated to another slot in the sequence, say x_{i-1} or x_{i+1}. This is actually a serious issue—how do we refer to a segment that is linked to one and only one position in the sequence?—but we will leave it aside.

Much of the phonological literature since the 1980s relies on representations of length like these, with the timing tier separate from the tier that shows the segment qualities. There are two main variants. One variant uses a capital X to refer to each position on the timing tier, and the order of those "X-slots" is represented as left-to-right linear order in a diagram. So, our long and short segments would look like this:

(336) A long vowel

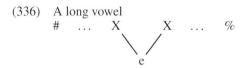

(337) A short vowel

So, we are now using the X's for the position markers of the timing tier.

The second variant of timing tier theory also uses the left to right order to show temporal order, but instead of X, it uses capital V and C to indicate a difference between vowels and consonants. The diagrams in (338) and (339) represent the difference between long and short vowels occurring between two consonants in this type of model.

(338) A long vowel between consonants in the CV model

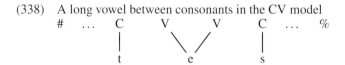

(339) A short vowel between consonants in the CV model

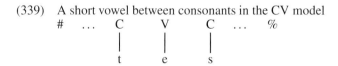

Now, suppose we had a rule of the form e → æ / ___ s. Given the rule semantics developed in Unit 12.2, this rule is interpreted as a function that maps underlying *e*'s to *æ*'s when they occur before an *s*. If we adjust our semantics so that we don't treat each *x* as a segment, but instead as a position to which a segment can be *associated*, we can have a semantics that can work for rules that refer to both long and short consonants.

We have hinted at some of the complications that arise when phonological length is treated as a many-to-one relation between positions on a timing tier and segmental symbols representing "qualities." Many details of what rules are possible in such a system need to be worked out. Part of the reason we are not presenting more detail is that the answers are not completely clear. In many cases, you will be able to provide informal analyses that work fairly well by treating long segments as unitary entities in your rules, for example, treating *o:* as a segment of the same status as *o*, *p*, or *s*. However, we urge you to be sensitive to both the advantages and challenges of the two-tier solution that phonologists have developed.

Exercises

37.1. The Kavols language has long and short vowels that contrast, as in the verb roots /pa:k/ 'think' and /pak/ 'drink'. A sequence of suffixes containing only long vowels can be added to each of these roots yielding the following derivations:

      UR   SR
      /pa:k-a:m-a:t-a:/   ⇝   [pa:k-am-at-a]
      /pak-a:m-a:t-a:/   ⇝   [pak-a:m-at-a]

These surface forms can be generated by a rule that shortens a long /a:/ to [a] after a long /a:/, something like 'a: → a / a ___'.

- If you apply this rule from right to left, does it yield the correct output?
- If you apply this rule from left to right, does it yield the correct output?
- Does this challenge our assumption for SPE that rules are always applied globally?

37.2. A language closely related to Kavols is Labadig,[5] which has the same lexicon and morphology as Kavols, but with the following derivations:

UR		SR
/pa:k-a:m-a:t-a:/	⤳	[pa:k-am-a:t-a]
/pak-a:m-a:t-a:/	⤳	[pak-a:m-at-a:]

As in Kavols, these surface forms can be generated by a rule that shortens a long /a:/ to [a] after a long /a:/.

- If you apply this rule from right to left, does it yield the correct output?

- If you apply this rule from left to right, does it yield the correct output?

- Does this challenge our assumption for SPE that rules are always applied globally?

---

[5]These toy languages are based on the discussion of Slovak and Gidabal in Kenstowicz and Kisseberth (1979, chap. 8).

Unit 38

Tone

In Yekhee, a language of Nigeria, the segment string in the word for 'ram' is *oke*. The word for 'one' has the string *okpa*.[1] To say 'one ram', the noun precedes the number, so you get the string *oke okpa*. Yekhee has a phonological process that affects inputs like this—the last segment of *oke* is deleted, so the output string is [okokpa]. We might say that a rule like (340) has applied:

(340)   e → ϵ / ___o

But there is more to the story. A more complete transcription of the morphemes we have seen would be /òké/ and /òkpá/. The symbol ò represents a different speech segment from the symbol ó. The former is pronounced with the mouth in the position of the sound in English *boat*, more or less, but with a relatively low pitch; the latter is pronounced with the mouth in the same position but with a relatively high pitch. Pitch differences that can distinguish word meanings are called *tones* in phonology. An example of a word with the segment /ó/ is *ówà* 'house'. There are high tone and low tone versions of other segments, such as /á/ versus /à/, /é/ versus /è/, and so on.

So, let's return to the phrase 'one ram', with the tones represented: /òké òkpá/. Given the deletion rule (340) we might expect that this would be pronounced as *[òkòkpá], but, as the asterisk indicates, this is not the case. Instead, the phrase is pronounced [òkôkpá]. The segment é appears to have disappeared, which is not surprising given

---

[1] Some details will be ignored, like the fact that the sequence *kp* represents a single labio-velar segment. Such segments are sometimes written with a tie bar either above or below the component symbols to show that both parts map to the same position on the timing tier k͡p or kp.

the deletion rule, but the low-toned ò of òkpá appears to be replaced by a new segment ô. This segment has the same mouth position as ó and ò, but the pitch starts relatively high and drops over the pronunciation to relatively low—we call it a *falling tone*.

One way to make sense of all this is to suppose that our compositional transcription system is actually a good representation of what is going on. In other words, there is a mental representation corresponding to 'o' and there is a mental representation corresponding to ' ´ ', and the combination of these symbols denotes the combination of these two mental representations. Similarly, ò is a combination of o and ` . The same holds for the other pairs of symbols: é is e combined with ´ and è is e combined with `. With this in mind, we can think of ô as the result of deleting the e from the sequence /é ò/ by rule (340), leaving ´ and ò. The ´ then combines with ò to yield an o with two tones, a high and a low, in that order. This explains the pronunciation with falling pitch, represented by the symbol ^ on [ô].

While this analysis may seem obvious to you, it actually contains a profound idea. Our compositional transcription system works so well because the objects we are modelling are also compositional. In other words, speech sounds are not atomic, primitive, unanalyzable entities. Instead they are structured combinations of more basic entities. In the case we just considered, a speech sound has been analyzed as consisting of a *tonal* part and another part, which is typically called the *segmental* part.

Let's look at another construction from the same language. Reduplicating a noun N gives the meaning 'every N', so the reduplication of ówà 'house' would be ówà-ówà 'every house'. The output of the phonology in this case is [ówŏwà] with the symbol 'ŏ' denoting an 'o' with a pitch rise, from relatively low to relatively high. This is called a *rising tone*. Note that the deletion of the a in the mapping from /ówà ówà/ to [ówŏwà] is not accounted for by rule (340). We need another rule—one deleting a before o, as in (341):

(341)   a → ε / ___o

Once again, we can account for the tonal pattern by assuming that the segment part of 'à' is a mental object separate from the tonal part. Suppose that, after deletion of the segment, the tone of 'à' remains and combines with the following 'ó' to produce 'ŏ' with a rising tone.

There is a lot to learn from these simple examples. First, note that our analysis has allowed us to avoid attributing to our model symbols for basic rising and falling tones. Instead of positing a set of four tonal elements (rising, falling, high, low) that combine with segments, we have a way of positing only two, just low and high, which we will denote L and H.

Second, we have a parallel to the analysis of length from the previous unit. Just as a single segment symbol can be associated to more than one X-slot position on the timing tier, a single segment symbol can be associated to more than one tonal element. The parallel to our treatment of length is obvious from the diagram in (342):

(342)   A vowel associated with two tones—rising pattern
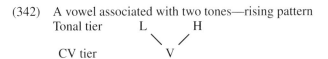

It has been argued that phonological representations also allow a single tonal element to be associated with more than one timing element as in (343):

(343)   A tone associated with two vowels
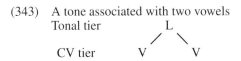

In sum, the mappings between segmental positions and tones is many-to-many: one tone can associate to more than one segment position; and one segment position can associate to more than one tone.

Third, we must remind ourselves that our intuitive account of rising tones as composed of a sequence of a low tone followed by a high tone still involves quite a bit of abstraction. The rising pitch pattern that we identify as the realization of a rising tone is not physically a sequence of the (relatively stable) physical pitch pattern of a low tone followed by the (relatively stable) physical pitch pattern of a high tone. Rising tones are *phonologically* a sequence of two basic tones, but the actual articulatory and acoustic correlates of a rising tone are not simple sequences of the correlates of the other tones. This is, or course, a normal situation in cognition; it is a simple case of what Ray Jackendoff (1994) calls "the construction of experience."

To conclude this brief unit on tone let's reiterate some key points. Tones appear to sometimes behave independently from the vowels they are associated to, so they provide evidence that speech sounds have some kind of internal structure. We have also seen evidence for the decomposition of tonal patterns themselves—in at least some cases, we can analyze rising and falling tonal patterns as sequences of high and low tones. Determining the exact number of basic tones needed to account for all languages is a matter of ongoing research, but the idea that we can reduce some complex patterns to combinations of basic elements is well established. Parallel to the abstractness of phonological length with respect to actual *duration*, pointed out in the previous unit, we should not forget the abstract nature of phonological tone relative to actual voice pitch. The realization of low tone by a small boy may be much higher than the realization of a high tone by his transgendered nanny, for example. Finally, the possibility of non-one-to-one mappings between tones and segments demonstrates that phonological representations must be much more complex than the simple strings we have worked with thus far.

Unit 39

Syllables I

39.1 Discovering Syllables

In this unit, we show that strings of segments sometimes appear to be organized into units called SYLLABLES, and further, that syllables have an internal structure consisting of different positions. To understand environments of rules, it is not enough just to know the sequence of segments. We sometimes need to know the syllable affiliation and syllable-internal position of segments, too.

Let's begin by examining the Bartican data in (344):

(344)   Bartican: Two environments or one?
       a. ɢat   'horse'   ɢat   'chipmunk'
       b. ɢatna 'with a horse'   ɢatna 'with a chipmunk'
       c. ɢato   'on a horse'   ɢado   'on a chipmunk'
       d. ɢati   'to a horse'   ɢadi   'to a chipmunk'

After our brief discussion of natural classes in Unit 24.4, you are ready to think about rule environments that are characterized by *sets* of segments—natural classes like the set of vowels in a language, or the set of consonants. So, you might be tempted, if you concentrate only on the forms containing the meaning 'chipmunk', to say that *t* becomes *d* when it appears before any vowel (*o* and *i* in our examples). However, the forms that contain the meaning 'horse' show that this cannot be correct, since the *t*'s in 'horse' do not show up as *d* before vowels.

It appears that we need to posit underlying /d/ and hypothesize a rule that changes /d/ to [t] in rows (a) and (b) for 'chipmunk'. In (a), the final segment of the root is at the end of a word, but in (b) it is before *n*. Given everything we have seen thus far, we are forced to posit *two* rules to account for this data, as in (345):

(345)   Two rules for Bartican (344)

       1.   d → t / ___ %

       2.   d → t / ___ n

But suppose we find even more environments where /d/ surfaces as [t], as in (346):

(346)   Further Bartican data

a. ɡat	'horse'	ɡat	'chipmunk'
b. ɡatna	'with a horse'	ɡatna	'with a chipmunk'
c. ɡato	'on a horse'	ɡado	'on a chipmunk'
d. ɡati	'to a horse'	ɡadi	'to a chipmunk'
e. ɡatlu	'under a horse'	ɡatlu	'under a chipmunk'
f. ɡatbak	'from a horse'	ɡatbak	'from a chipmunk'

The 'horse' forms still prevent us from positing a rule that changes /t/ to [d], but the 'chipmunk' forms don't force us to posit more than the two rules in (347) if we accept the existence of a natural class of segments: the consonants that can be referenced in a rule, as discussed in Unit 24.4.

(347)   Two rules for Bartican using the class of consonants (346)

       a.   d → t / ___ %

       b.   d → t / ___ any consonant

           •   d → t / ___ n

           •   d → t / ___ l

           •   d → t / ___ b

       •   etc.

In Part VIII we will formalize the use of natural classes of segments indicated in (347b).

Can we do better for Bartican than the two-rule analysis? It turns out that over and over again, we find that in a given language, the same phonological change occurs in the same two environments seen in the rules of (347). In other words, many languages show rules of these forms:

(348)   Recurring rule pairs schema

    a. $\pi \rightarrow \rho \,/\, \underline{\quad}\; \%$

    b. $\pi \rightarrow \rho \,/\, \underline{\quad}$ any consonant

It is important to understand that the symbols π and ρ are variables over the set of segments that are used here with scope over the *set* of rules in (348), not over each rule separately. In other words, we are considering the situation like Bartican where a language appears to have something like the rules in (347) that both turn /d/ to [t].[1]

So how can we explain the fact that over and over again we find identical phonological changes affecting consonants that are triggered by both a following consonant and the end-of-word symbol? This could be a coincidence, of course, or merely a reflection of some phonetic commonality that is not encoded in the phonological representation. However, phonologists have pursued another possibility, one that allows us to account for languages like Bartican with a single rule. The key is to propose that the elements of the timing tier, the X-slots we introduced in our discussion of length, are not just organized in a simple sequence, but also enter into structures called SYLLABLES. The idea is that in (347), the target segment actually occurs in both cases in a natural class of environments: in the coda of a syllable.

You probably have an informal understanding of syllables—enough to judge that the word *dog* consists of a single syllable and the word *experimental* consists of five syllables. Our sensitivity to the existence of syllables is reflected in our ability to compose and appreciate poetic structures from haiku to the limerick. As we will see in the next section, syllable structures are also the basis of stress computation in many languages.

There are many controversies about syllables and there appear to be differences in how languages syllabify—impose syllable structure on—the same sequence of segments, but let's assume that the words in Bartican (346) are syllabified as in (349), with the dot marking the end of each syllable.

(349)   Marking the ends of syllables

a. ɢat.	'horse'	ɢat.	chipmunk
b. ɢat.na.	'with a horse'	ɢat.na.	with a chipmunk
c. ɢa.to.	'on a horse'	ɢa.do.	on a chipmunk
d. ɢa.ti.	'to a horse'	ɢa.di.	to a chipmunk
e. ɢat.lu.	'under a horse'	ɢat.lu.	under a chipmunk
f. ɢat.bak.	'from a horse'	ɢat.bak.	from a chipmunk

---

[1] As we develop a model of syllable structure, we'll see that in actually attested rules, π and ρ will always refer to consonants, not vowels.

This type of syllabification is fairly common among the world's languages. Each vowel is the so-called *nucleus* of its own syllable. In these words, each syllable has a single consonant at the beginning, a vowel in the middle and sometimes a consonant at the end. As you can see, when a single consonant appears between vowels, it is grouped into a syllable with the following vowel. This seems to be the case in all languages.

With the syllable breaks explicitly represented, we can now write a unified rule that conforms to our SPE syntax, as long as we add the '.' syllable-end symbol to the set of environment symbols.

(350)   a. A new symbol: ENV = $\text{ENV}_{\text{old}} \cup \{\ .\ \}$
         b. General rule schema with syllable boundaries: $\alpha \rightarrow \beta\ /\ \underline{\quad}$.
         c. Bartican rule with syllable boundaries: $d \rightarrow t\ /\ \underline{\quad}$.

The rule in (350c) simply says that *d* becomes *t* at the end of a syllable.[2] In the rest of this unit, we introduce some of the terminological and theoretical tools linguists have developed to talk about syllables.

39.2   Syllables as Hierarchical Structures

SPE-style rules with syllable boundaries are used in phonological analyses, but linguists have also argued for an *internal* structure for syllables. Instead of just referring to the adjacency of a syllable boundary, this richer structure allows rules to make reference to a well-defined set of positions inside the syllable. As we introduce syllable-internal structure it should be obvious that the model requires a major departure from our SPE rule system, since we won't be able to state our rules in terms of simple sequences of segment symbols.

It is useful to compare syllable structure with similar ideas used from syntax. Sentences consist of strings of words pronounced in linear order, one after another. However, syntacticians have many reasons to believe that the words in a sentence are actually organized into constituents, higher level groupings of words. For example, in a sentence like *The boy quickly left*, syntacticians assume that the words *the boy* form a unit, to the exclusion of the other words.

One way to express constituency relations is by using a syntactic tree diagram, like the one in (351).

---

[2]The careful reader will be thinking about how to get purely word-final effects, since the input to rules will contain both kinds of symbols under the categorematic treatment of word boundaries adopted in Unit 16.3: Is the *t* of /kæt.%/ word-final? Don't worry about this—we are about to get a more sophisticated view of syllables.

(351)   Basic syntactic tree

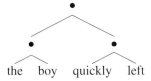

         the   boy   quickly   left

This diagram shows that *the* and *boy* form a constituent, since there is a node that dominates these two words and no others. This is not true for the words *boy* and *quickly*. On the other hand, *quickly left* is a constituent since there is a node that dominates all and only the words in that string. Similarly, the whole string *the boy quickly left* is a constituent. Syntacticians typically provide labels in their trees that indicate what kind of constituents are present:

(352)   Basic syntactic tree with labels

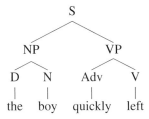

In (352) we use S to denote the *sentence*, NP to denote a *noun phrase* like *the boy*,[3] and VP to denote a *verb phrase* like *quickly left*. Each word also has a category label, D for *determiner*, N for *noun*, Adv for *adverb*, and V for *verb*.[4]

In phonology, it appears to be the case that strings are structured as well. For our purposes, the highest level of structure we will consider is one that is immediately

---

[3]We sometimes call this phrase a DP, for 'determiner phrase'. The word *the* is a determiner.

[4]Since we have spent so much time on set theory and related notions in this book, we will point out that such tree structures can also be represented in terms of nested ordered sets. The words *quickly* and *left* are members of an ordered pair, *<quickly, left>*. The words *the* and *boy* are members of another pair *<the, boy>*. The whole sentence can be represented as an ordered pair whose members are ordered pairs, thus: *<<the, boy>, <quickly, left> >*. This tuple representation shows the same relationships among words as the tree diagram—the two are just notational variants. We can add labels to the tuple representation, as we do in the tree: *< ₛ< ₙₚthe, boy>, < ᵥₚquickly, left> >*.

above the syllable, which we will denote W.[5] Our W corresponds to what is sometimes called a *phonological word*.

We will assume that the syllable is potentially divided into two constituents, called an ONSET and a RHYME. The ONSET consists of the consonants at the beginning of a syllable. The RHYME, in turn, can be divided into NUCLEUS and CODA—the NUCLEUS consisting of the vowel elements and the CODA any other consonants at the end of a syllable. These pre-terminal nodes, ONSET, NUCLEUS, CODA, contain X-slots that are linked to segments, which are the terminal elements, the "leaves" of a syllable tree. We typically will not represent the X-slot level in our syllables.

We assume that every syllable has a NUCLEUS, and thus a RHYME, but that other constituents may be absent. Thus, the least a syllable can contain is a single segment, as in the following, where the Greek letter sigma (σ) marks the syllable level in the hierarchy:

(353)   Minimal syllable with and without X-slot shown

On the other hand, a syllable can have more than a single segment dominated by each pre-terminal node:

---

[5]You might think that this level is obviously that of the *word*, but things are not so simple, since syllables can straddle word boundaries. This tells us that syllables are (at least sometimes) *computed* by the phonology, since the information about what word will follow a given word in a sentence is not information encoded in the lexicon. The same goes for syllabification across morphemes, of course. Syllables have to be computable because the strings that are syllabified may only come into existence by concatenation of separate morphemes.

(354)   Lush syllable tree

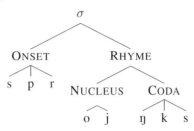

We will assume that the left to right ordering of elements in such a diagram corresponds to linear ordering in string—in other words, the onset of the syllable in (354) is the string *spr*. This is a divergence from a common assumption in syntax that trees do not encode precedence directly. Note that the consonants in (354) are all direct daughters of the ONSET or CODA node. There are alternative views about such sequences, but we won't consider them here.

We will assume that there are syllables, and that they contain internal structure—but we must recognize that some scholars do not believe that syllables are part of phonological representations (see Samuels, 2011, for a useful overview and original discussion). However, once we adopt syllables into our model, such structures can be referenced in the formulation of phonological rules, as we will soon see.[6]

39.3   Intrasyllable Relations in Rules

Once we have syllable internal structure, we expect it to play a role in defining the set of possible phonological rules. Consider the derivations of the Standard French forms in (355).[7]

---

[6]It is worth pointing out that there are limits to the parallel between syntactic structure and phonological structure. Words (or morphemes) are combined by the syntax to generate structure. In phonology, strings of segments are stored as strings in the lexicon, and syllable structure is imposed over pre-existing strings (as well as the strings that result from morpheme concatenation). Put simply, the segments of the word *cat* exist in a string in the lexicon, whereas the words in *the tall boy* are combined by the syntax into a particular structure and order. That is, *cat* is stored in long-term memory, whereas the phrase *the tall boy* is not.

[7]Unlike most examples in this book, these derivations involve phonology across a word boundary. We will use the node W (for *phonological word*) in syllable structure trees to group syllables that fall into the same domain for the application of rules. These Ws are larger than what we typically think of as words. It is also the case that, like all real data, the facts of French are quite complicated. Think of this as a "restricted"

(355)   French vowel nasalization

    a. /bɔn-o/ ⤳ bɔ.no⤳ [bɔno]   'good bone'

    b. /bɔn-tip/ ⤳ bɔn.tip ⤳ bõntip ⤳ [bõtip]   'good guy'

The UR for each form contains the morpheme meaning 'good' /bɔn/, and a noun, 'bone' /o/ in (a) or 'guy' /tip/ in (b). We assume that syllabification occurs and leads to a difference in where the n's are syllabified. In /bɔn-o/, the n is between vowels, so it ends up as the onset of the second syllable as in (356):

(356)   Syllabification of 'good bone' /bɔn-o/

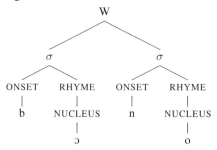

Notice that there is no necessary correlation between the location of syllable boundaries and the location of morpheme boundaries. This is consistent with our assumption in Unit 7.4 that phonology has no access to morphological structure during the derivation.[8]

    In contrast to the input /bɔn-o/, in the form /bɔn-tip/, the n ends up in the coda of the first syllable as in (357):

---

language in the sense that Pike (1947) used the term, as we discussed in Unit 3.

    [8]Once again, we are forced to simplify. There is a tremendous literature on apparent phonology-morphology interactions. Versions of Optimality Theory, for example, select surface forms with reference to the "alignment" of syllable edges and morpheme edges (Kager, 1999, chap. 3). Such a model obviously requires that the edges of syllables and morphemes be represented in surface forms. See Hale and Reiss (2008, chap. 6.3) for some critical discussion of this aspect of Optimality Theory.

(357)   Syllabification of 'good guy' /bɔn-tip/

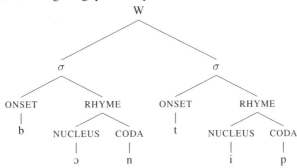

After initial syllabification, we posit a rule that turns ɔ into ɔ̃ when followed by *n*. However, a rule like (358) will give the right result for 'good guy' but not for 'good bone':

(358)   ɔ → ɔ̃ / ___ n

We need a rule that changes ɔ to ɔ̃ only before an *n* that is *in the coda of the same syllable*. Such a rule is given in (359):

(359)   A rule with sensitivity to syllable structure

ɔ → ɔ̃ /

RHYME

NUCLEUS   CODA

___   n

The underscore '___' in (359) is interpreted in the same way as before—this is where the target segment occurs in the input form. So, we have a rule 'ɔ → ɔ̃ / ___ n' with the added specification that the *n* is in the coda of the syllable. Another common way of describing this situation is that 'ɔ → ɔ̃ before a *tautosyllabic* n', which means 'an *n* in the same syllable'.

After this rule applies, the input form /bɔno/ is unchanged, and the input form /bɔntip/ is bɔ̃ntip. We need another rule to delete *n* of the latter form, so a rule like (360) that deletes *n* only in coda position:

(360)   Delete *n* in coda

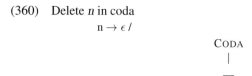

This rule will have no effect on the derivation of 'good bone' since there is no *n* in coda position in that form. We assume that all syllable structure is erased before the end of the derivation and the SRs are just strings. The two SRs are then [bɔno] and [bɔ̃tip].

You may wonder why we referred to coda position in the deletion rule in (360) instead of just a rule deleting *n* before *t*. The reason is that the *n* deletes even when there is nothing following it in a phonological word, for example in sentence final position we get /bɔn/ ⤳ [bɔ̃]. The syllabification of the relevant input is given in (361):

(361)   Syllabification of sentence final 'good' /bɔn/

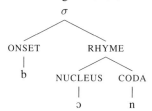

As desired, this form will be affected by the ɔ → ɔ̃ rule in (359) and then the deletion rule in (360)—the presence or absence of a following *t* is not relevant once the syllable structure has been assigned.

Our analysis of French contains (359), a rule that refers to the nucleus and the coda at the same time, as well as (360), which refers only to the coda. Other combinations are possible, such as a rule that references the onset and coda in the same syllable. Such a case is reported in Seri, an indigenous language of Mexico (Marlett and Stemberger, 1983):

(362)   Seri: Delete a coda glottal stop if there is a glottal stop in the onset

      a.   ʔa-a:ʔ-sanx ⤳ ʔ-a:-sanx   'who was carried'

      b.   ʔi-ʔ-a:ʔ-kašni ⤳ ʔi-ʔ-a:-kašni   'my being bitten'

      c.   koʔpanšx ⤳ koʔpanšx   'run like him!'

The rule applies to tautosyllabic glottal stops so the second glottal stop in (b) is not affected. In general, coda glottal stops can surface, as shown by (c).

We need a rule in which a glottal stop is deleted from a coda if the onset of the same syllable contains a glottal stop, as in (363):

(363)   Seri glottal stop

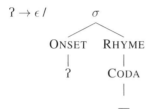

Notice that we need to refer to syllable structure and not just to glottal stops separated by a vowel to get the distinction between (362a) and (362b).

39.4   Intersyllable Relations in Rules

In addition to rules referring to positions within a syllable, it appears that rules can make reference to positions in adjacent syllables. We will see several cases in later units, but for now let's look at a simplified example based on vowel harmony in Finnish.

(364)   Finnish noun forms

Nominative	Partitive	
maa	maata	'earth'
sisar	sisarta	'sister'
pææ	pæætæ	'head'
kevæt	kevættæ	'springtime'

Note that the partitive ending consists of a *t* followed by a vowel that is either *æ* or *a*. In each case, the suffix vowel is identical to the preceding vowel. The vowel of the ending is always separated from the preceding vowel by either just the *t* (*maata* and *pæætæ*) or by the *t* and an additional consonant (*sisarta* and *kevættæ*). This means that the suffix vowel can't be determined by a rule that says 'look two segments to the left' or a rule that says 'look three segments to the left'. Let's assume instead that the rule relies on syllable structure. Further, we'll assume that the lexical form of the suffix is /ta/.

(365)   Finnish nucleus-to-nucleus vowel harmony rule

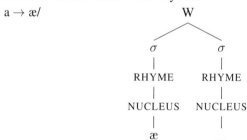

This rule turns underlying *a* to *æ* when the vowel of the preceding nucleus is *æ*. As we said, this is a very simplified version of what happens in Finnish, but it gives you a sense of how syllable structure can be used in rules that need to refer to relations between syllables.

There are a few important points to make now. First, we have gone far beyond our SPE model of rules that apply to segments with a context defined by at most one segment to the right and one to the left. We now have introduced some structure into rule environments, and so we will need a new syntax and semantics, too. We cannot provide these for you for the simple reason that linguists are not yet sure what the range of possible syllable structure relations are in phonological rules. We have given you a taste of what the notation can express, and we have selected examples that appear to correspond to attested phonological processes, but we have not provided a restrictive model that rules out certain relations. For example, can rules refer to the onset of a syllable and the coda of the following syllable? It is hard to see how to rule out such possibilities. So, as it stands, the model of syllable structure we have provided is fairly unrestricted. A second and related point is that some of the rules we have alluded to might be able to be reformulated in terms of operations that search through a string.

We discuss this possibility in more detail in Unit 56.

Exercises

39.1. Using IPA symbols, transcribe and syllabify the following English words. Show the syllable structure diagram. Assume that syllable onsets are maximized in the sense that you put as many consonants as possible into syllable onsets, assuming that possible onset clusters are the same as the clusters found at the beginning of words.

   (a) *bog*

   (b) *mouse*

   (c) *gecko*

   (d) *rhododendron*

   (e) *pesto*

   (f) *estimate*

   (g) Do the last two conform to your intuitions as a speaker of English?

39.2. Catalan is a Romance language spoken in and around the Autonomous Community of Catalonia in Spain. The vowels in this Catalan data are [i,e,a,o,u]; every other symbol denotes a consonant. Assume that vowel quality plays no role in the consonant alternations in the data. The nouns here are all of masculine gender. Adjectives agree with the gender and number of the noun they modify.

MASC SG	MASC PL	FEM SG	FEM PL	GLOSS
mal	mals	malə	males	bad
bo	bons	bonə	bones	good
ple	plens	plenə	plenes	full
sa	sans	sanə	sanes	sane
ultim	ultims	ultimə	ultimes	last
gram	grams			gram
gra	grans			grain
dulen	dulens	dulentə	dulentes	bad

   i. Look only at the forms for 'bad' (with a one-syllable root) in the first row. Assume that there is just one plural suffix and just one feminine suffix—so the feminine plural forms contain them both. Assume that ə is **not present** in underlying forms. Propose a rule to account for the form of the feminine singular and call it Rule A.

ii. Write out Rule A.

iii. What is the UR of the feminine marker?

iv. Once you posit this rule, is the form *ple* in the third row problematic? Looking only at the forms in the first seven rows, posit one more rule (B) and come up with a solution that makes use of rule ordering.

- Write out Rule B.
- Rule A is ordered before/after Rule B (choose one).
- This ordering is feeding/counterfeeding/bleeding/counterbleeding (choose one).
- Give URs for 'full', 'good, 'sane', and 'grain'.

v. Now look at the last row. There is a Rule C, deleting /t/. What syllable structure position do you think it happens in?

vi. How is this Rule C ordered with respect to Rule B?

- Rule C is ordered before/after Rule B (choose one).
- This ordering is feeding/counterfeeding/bleeding/counterbleeding (choose one).
- What is the UR for the (two-syllable) root meaning 'bad'? _____

vii. Do derivations for the following forms. List the rules in an order that works.

UR					
Rule ___					
Rule___					
Rule ___					
SR	bo	ple	plens	plenə	plenes
Gloss					

UR				
Rule ___				
Rule___				
Rule ___				
SR	dulen	dulens	dulentə	dulentes
Gloss				

viii. Apply the rules **in reverse** order to the UR of *dulen*. What is the output? It will be different from the attested form, so we mark it with an asterisk.

UR	
Rule ___	
Rule___	
Rule ___	
SR	*_____
Gloss	'bad'-M.SG.

This exercise is continued in Unit 58.

39.3. English is typically described as having an underlying /p/ that surfaces as [pʰ] at
the beginning of a stressed syllable. Ignoring stress and restricting ourselves to
words of one syllable, the data looks like this:[9]

pin   [pʰɪn]
spin   [spɪn]
print   [pʰɹɪnt]
sprint   [spɹɪnt]

Try to formulate the rule of aspiration, starting with '*p* → *pʰ*'. The target must be
in onset position, but what other conditions hold? Describe the problems you encounter. Some phonologists propose that in syllables beginning with consonant
sequences like *sp*, the *s* is not actually in the onset, but rather in an "appendix"
position directly attached to the σ node of a syllable tree. Does this help at all
with your rule formulation? There is no obvious solution, so focus on identifying
problems as you think about this.

---

[9]Aspiration in the word *print* is realized during the pronunciation of the *r*, making the *r* sound like a
voiceless *r*, but we typically transcribe the aspiration as belonging to the *p*. See the discussion in Unit 3
about how we decide on the "correct" transcription.

Unit 40

Syllables II

40.1 Syllable Types

As we have noted, pretty much everyone who uses syllables assumes that in a sequence consisting of a consonant followed by a vowel, the consonant will always, in all languages, be the onset of a syllable which has the vowel as its nucleus. In other words, a sequence of a consonant followed by a vowel does not contain a syllable boundary between the two segments. Consider the examples in (366):

(366)   A consonant syllabifies with a vowel to its immediate right

    a.   a.ra

    b.   a.pa

    c.   ap.ra OR a.pra

    d.   ar.pa

    e.   arp

    f.   a.o.pa

Forms (366a) and (366b) will be syllabified as *a.ra* and *a.pa* in all languages. Languages may differ in how they syllabify the cluster in (366c), so the syllabification of that form may be *ap.ra* or *a.pra*, depending on the language, but the *r* at least will definitely be in the onset of the final syllable.

343

In attested language data, the distribution of segments in syllables tends to be somewhat restricted, with various patterns recurring cross-linguistically and some patterns appearing to be universal. For example, languages that have syllables with two segments in the onset are much more likely (maybe 100 percent more likely!) to have *pr* and *pl* sequences than *rp* and *lp* sequences. As exemplified in (366d), *arpa* syllabifies as *ar.pa* with just *p* in the onset, rather than *a.rpa*. The reverse is true in codas, where *rp* and *lp* are common but *pr* and *pl* are perhaps unattested.[1] So, (366e) is a possible one-syllable form in many languages. We will not consider the reasons for these kinds of generalizations here; they may or may not be relevant to the theory of the phonological component of the language faculty. Many phonologists try to account for these generalizations in terms of a property of segments called SONORITY. Our own bias is that these generalizations are not encoded in the phonology, but this is the view of a very small minority.

There are two ways to get a syllable without an onset: (i) word-initial vowels will be the nucleus of a syllable with no onset, and (ii) a sequence of vowels inside a word, like *aopa* can yield a syllabification *a.o.pa*, as in (366f). The first and second syllables have no onset in this form.

The tree-like representations in the last unit depict two categorizations of syllables: open and closed, light and heavy. Many rules that are sensitive to syllable structure can be described by reference to these categorizations. If a syllable ends in a vowel—in other words, if the coda is empty—it is called an *open* syllable. In contrast, if there is a consonant in the coda, the syllable is *closed*. If a syllable has a branching rhyme or a branching nucleus—in other words if there are two (or more) segments in the rhyme—it is called *heavy*. Otherwise, the case where the rhyme contains just a single segment, the syllable is called *light*. Light syllables *must be* open, because any closed syllable will have at least two segments in the rhyme. Recall from our discussion of length that a long vowel, for example, the long version of *o*, is denoted as a sequence of identical segments, *oo*, and therefore it makes a syllable heavy. So, heavy syllables *can be* open. We can categorize syllables as open or closed, and as light or heavy, but the combination *closed* and *light* is not possible, given how the categories are defined.

Here are some examples of syllables categorized by heavy versus light and open versus closed. In (367), there is a branch in the rhyme, since there is a consonant in the coda. The consonant in the coda makes the syllable closed. The branching rhyme makes it heavy.

---

[1]We say "perhaps" because syllable structure is not directly observed, but must be inferred. Such inferences depend upon one's assumptions. Standard French words like *souple* 'supple' or *table* 'table' may be analyzable as containing a single syllable, even when the /l/ is pronounced, but this cannot be decided on the grounds of phonetic measurements, only on the grounds of phonological arguments we illustrate below.

(367) *poŋ* : heavy, closed

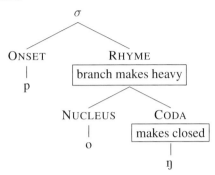

In (368), there is a further branch, since there are two segments in the coda, but this does not affect the status of the syllable—it is still closed and heavy.

(368) *poŋs* : heavy, closed

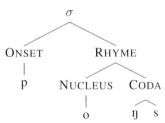

The difference between (367) and (368) can become relevant if a language syllabifies across word boundaries by using consonants at the end of one word in the onset of a following syllable.[2] Note that we are making use here of the assumption that syllables always get at least one onset segment, if available. For example, if the sequence of segments in (368) is followed by a word *ak*, we might end up with a sequence of syllables like this:

---

[2]Elsewhere in this book we have assumed that the word is the maximal domain in which rules apply. This simplifying assumption must be abandoned, not only for syllabification across word boundaries, but also for other common phenomena.

(369)   /poŋs ak/ → [poŋ.sak] :

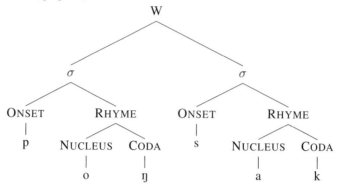

Note that the first syllable is closed and heavy. What happens if the form *poŋ* in (367) is followed by *ak* and syllabification applies across word boundaries? In this case, the final consonant of the first word again ends up as the onset of the second syllable, as shown in (370), but the first syllable is open:

(370)   /poŋ ak/ → [po.ŋak]

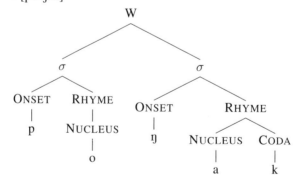

Here is another heavy, closed syllable:

(371) *po:ŋ* : heavy, closed

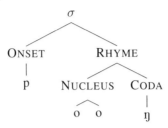

What happens if this word is followed by *ak* and syllabification applies across word boundaries? What will the syllabification be? Will the first syllable be open or closed? Light or heavy?

Here are two heavy open syllables, one with a long vowel in the nucleus, the other with a *diphthong* (i.e., a vowel followed by a glide like *j* or *w*) in the nucleus.

(372) *po:* : heavy, open

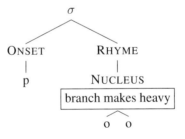

(373) *poj* : heavy, open

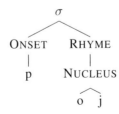

Of course, if the evidence suggests that *poj* acts like a closed syllable, we would conclude that the glide *j* is in a CODA.

Finally, here is a light, open syllable, with no branching, and thus a single segment, in the rhyme.

(374)   *po* : light, open

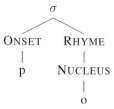

Keep in mind that whatever we add to the onset, we still have a light open syllable if the rhyme contains only *o*:

(375)   *splo* : light, open

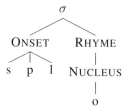

These two classifications of syllables, open/closed and light/heavy play a role in a wide variety of phonological phenomena. We'll see some examples in the next section.

40.2   Inferring Syllable Structure

We pointed out that the same string of segments can syllabify differently in different languages, as in the example of *ap.ra* and *a.pra* as possibilities in (366c). Different syllabifications do not necessarily correlate with a clear and consistent set of acoustic differences. In fact, *Acoustic Phonetics* (Stevens, 2000), a six-hundred-page volume, does not even have an index entry for "*syllable*". So how do we know which syllabification of a string is correct for a given language? The answer is that we linguists, just like learners of the language, must *infer* syllable structure. We do this by figuring out which syllable structure hypothesis leads to a more coherent rule system. This is quite abstract, so let's illustrate with some examples.

Consider the North American English pronunciation of the words *Atlantic* and *atrocious*. Both words are pronounced with primary stress on the second syllable, which we show with standard IPA transcription here.

(376)   • *Atlantic*: [æʔˈlænɪk]

        • *atrocious*: [əˈtʰɹowʃəs]

The first word, *Atlantic* is pronounced with a glottal stop corresponding to the first *t*. In addition, many speakers have no [t] in the last syllable, and for some speakers the [n] is a nasalized flap. The second word, *atrocious* is pronounced with an aspirated consonant for the *t*. The aspiration is realized during the ɹ, yielding something that sounds like a voiceless ɹ̥ or a voiceless fricative.

If we make the (non-trivial) assumption that the glottal stop of *Atlantic* and the aspirated stop of *atrocious* both correspond to underlying /t/, then we can propose that the different outcomes reflect a difference in syllabification. The glottal stop is in a coda, and the aspirated stop is in a complex onset with the following ɹ.

The idea is that in English, the underlying /t/ does not syllabify in an onset with a following /l/, but it can syllabify in an onset with a following /ɹ/. While this may seem like an ad hoc explanation, it is consistent with several observations. Note that English has *words* that begin with [tʰɹ], and so we know that it has *syllables* that begin with this sequence. But English has no words that begin with [tl] or [tʰl] or [ʔl], consistent with the idea that these segments don't form an onset sequence in English. Finally, note that segments that pretty clearly are derived from /t/ *do* surface as glottal stop in a coda position: *cat* is pronounced [kʰæʔ] in these dialects, but we hear the *t* in the plural *cats*. These additional observations make the syllable-based account plausible.

Similar reasoning can be applied to Italian. In this language, there are no minimal pairs that differ only in vowel length. However, stressed vowels are sometimes long. For example, in a word like *fato* 'fate', the *a* is long. In *molto* 'much', the first *o*, although stressed, is short. Speakers asked to break such words into syllables are likely to say *fa-to* and *mol-to*. There are no words in Italian that begin with *lt*, but many words begin with *t* followed by a vowel, so perhaps the explanation of vowel length contrasts is to be found in syllable structure. It looks like vowels in stressed *open* syllables like *fa* are lengthened, but vowels in stressed *closed* syllables like *mol* are not. Interestingly, there are some consonant clusters that can be preceded by a long vowel. A word like *sopra* 'above' has a long *o*. It turns out that speakers will break this word up as *so-pra*, and there are lots of words that begin with a *pr* cluster, such as *pronto, presto, prego*, and so on. This suggests that *pr* clusters syllabify in an onset with a following vowel, but *lt* clusters do not.

In both English and Italian, we are able to capture generalizations by making certain assumptions about the syllabification of clusters. For example, we hypothesize that in English the clusters *tl* and *tr* behave differently from each other—the first gets split between syllables, whereas the second goes into an onset. In Italian, the clusters *lt* and *pr* behave differently from each other. The first gets split between syllables, whereas the second goes into an onset.

Despite the fact that we are nativists, that we accept the idea that there is a nontrivial innate component of the human phonological faculty, we tend to be skeptical about many claims concerning universals of syllable structure. This is because, as we have just seen, some of the details of syllabification in a language can be inferred from surface patterns. If we assume that learners, not just linguists, can make such inferences, then learners can figure out *some* aspects of syllabification, given *some* other aspects as an innate toolkit. The grouping of nucleus and rhyme together into a constituent appears to be a universal property of syllable structure. The syllabification of consonant sequences appears to be variable and inferable from the data.

40.3   Reasoning about Syllable Structure

The English rule we just saw turns *t* to *ʔ* in codas. The Italian example involved vowel lengthening in open syllables. There are many other rules in the literature that are formulated in terms of syllable structure. Our goal for the remainder of this unit is to give you practice inferring syllable structure from morpheme alternations.

We will present several toy languages with a single rule needed for the analysis of the given data. In order to simplify the task, we limit the number of possible rules to two. Each of next two toy languages has a rule that neutralizes the vowels *a* and *a:* in certain syllables. Furthermore, we will assume that there are only two possible rules:

(377)   Two possibilities for the following languages

 • R1: a → a: in open syllables

 • R2: a: → a in closed syllables

We won't formulate the rules with syllable trees, but instead use the informal descriptions in (377). Our tasks are determine lexical forms for each morpheme, infer which syllables are open and which are closed, and to figure out which rule is present in each language, R1 (lengthening in open syllables) or R2 (shortening in closed syllables).[3] We will assume that sequences like [au] are in separate syllables.

(378) Questions for syllable structure

- Does the language have a lengthening rule (a → a: in open syllables) or a shortening rule (a: → a in closed syllables)?

- What is the lexical form for each morpheme?

- How do various consonant clusters syllabify? Use C for stops (*p, t, k*), R for liquids (*r, l*), and V for vowels, if this helps you express certain generalizations. Otherwise, use specific symbols where necessary, like *l*, *t*, and so on.

Let's begin with the analysis of Ferentarian in (379):

(379) Ferentarian

N-SG	N-PL	a N	the N	with N	for N	
na	nas	nako	naro	nalo	nau	'potato'
na:	**nas**	na:ko	na:ro	na:lo	na:u	'blouse'
nap	naps	napko	napro	naplo	napu	'mouse'
nap	naps	*napko*	na:pro	na:plo	na:pu	'spouse'
nat	nats	natko	natro	natlo	natu	'grouse'
nat	nats	natko	na:tro	na:tlo	na:tu	'house'
nar	nars	narko	narro	narlo	naru	'louse'
nar	nars	narko	narro	narlo	na:ru	'tomato'

When you first look at such a dataset, it is easy to become overwhelmed. A good strategy in phonology, and in solving any complex problem, is to ignore some of the data and see if you can make a testable hypothesis using just a subset of the forms. You might have to reject or refine your initial hypothesis, but that is a kind of progress.

Consider just the four boxed forms in the upper left corner of the table. With these forms alone, we can apply our MTP forced-choice reasoning. These forms suggest that the UR for 'potato' is /na/ by the NAA. Then the SLFA tells us that the UR for 'blouse' is either /na/ or /na:/. If we select the former, we need a rule that lengthens /a/ to [a:] in open syllables (given the restrictions we have given on possible rules). We know that [na] and [na:] are open syllables and [nas] (both tokens) are closed syllables. So, a lengthening rule will prove problematic in accounting for [na], the first form in the

---

[3]We have constructed the datasets so that [a] and [a:] occur only in non-final syllables.

table. Our RAA reasoning leads us to reject /na/ for 'blouse' and choose /na:/, with a rule of shortening in closed syllables. This rule yields [nas] in bold for 'blouses' from /na:-s/.

So, now that we know that 'blouse' has an underlying /a:/ and that there is a shortening rule, we can conclude that any syllable in which there is a short vowel alternant of 'blouse' must be a closed syllable. The only example is [nas].

Let's move to the next two rows in the table. The forms with the meaning 'mouse' all have a short vowel, so we will assume that the UR is /nap/. In contrast, the forms of 'spouse' have long and short vowel alternants. We know there is a shortening rule, so we can therefore conclude that 'spouse' has a UR with long /a:/, and that wherever there is a short vowel in a SR for 'spouse' the syllable must be closed. So, we can conclude that the forms of 'spouse' syllabify as follows:

(380)   Syllabification of forms of 'spouse' in Ferentarian
             nap   naps   nap.ko   na:.pro   na:.plo   na:.pu

It is obvious that the first two monosyllabic forms each contain one closed syllable. The third form, [napko], italicized in the table, contains a closed syllable, *nap*, since the vowel has been shortened. In contrast, the last three forms, [na:pro], [na:plo], [na:pu] all have an open initial syllable. The openness of the first syllable in the last form is obvious, since the *p* must syllabify with the following vowel, but we learn from the other two forms that *pl* and *pr* syllabify into the onset of the second syllable, leaving the long underlying vowel intact. These clusters behave differently from the *pk* cluster of *napko*.

Continuing in this vein, you should be able to see that *tk* behaves like *pk*, divided between coda and onset. You should also be able to see that *rk* and *rr* clusters also split across syllable boundaries, closing the first syllable. In contrast *tr* and *tl* in Ferentarian syllabify into onsets, allowing underlying long /a:/ to surface unchanged.

Let's apply the same kind of reasoning to another language, Tineretuluian in (381):

(381)   Tineretuluian

N-SG	N-PL	a N	the N	with N	for N	
na:	nas	na:ko	na:ro	na:lo	na:u	'potato'
na:	na:s	na:ko	na:ro	na:lo	na:u	'blouse'
nap	naps	napko	napro	naplo	na:pu	'mouse'
na:p	na:ps	na:pko	na:pro	na:plo	na:pu	'spouse'
nat	nats	natko	natro	natlo	na:tu	'grouse'
na:t	na:ts	na:tko	na:tro	na:tlo	na:tu	'house'
nar	nars	narko	narro	narlo	na:ru	'louse'
na:r	na:rs	na:rko	na:rro	na:rlo	na:ru	'tomato'

Once again we start out looking for an easy subset of the data to make an initial hypothesis. The four boxed forms in this language suggest that the lexical form for 'blouse' is /na:/, since there is only one alternant. We know that *na:s* definitely has a closed syllable, so the language can't have R2, the shortening rule. So it must have the lengthening rule, R1, and the lexical form of 'potato' must be /na/.

As we look through the data, we see some rows that always have long [a:], so that must be the underlying vowel, whereas others alternate, and thus have underlying short /a/. But the alternating vowels never surface as long before a sequence of two consonants followed by a vowel, whether the sequence is *tr, pr, rr, tk, pk, rk, tl, pl*, or *rl*. This means that no sequence of two consonants is syllabified together into an onset before a vowel. The first consonant closes the first syllable and the second is the onset of the second syllable. Tineretuluian has no "complex" onsets. So, although there is a lengthening rule, there are fewer open syllables than in Ferentarian. For example, the sequence *natro* is syllabified as *na.tro* in Ferentarian, but as *nat.ro* in Tineretuluian. You will practice this kind of reasoning on your own in the exercises that follow.

Exercises

40.1. Indicate whether each of the following syllables is heavy or light and open or closed:

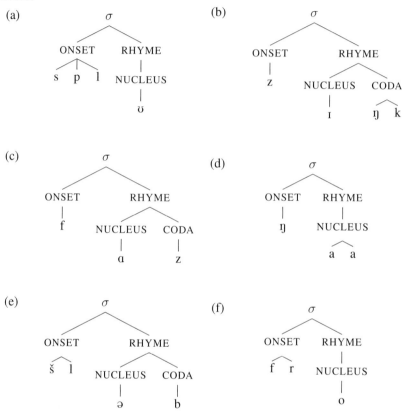

For the first two languages below, decide whether the language has R1 or R2 from (377), and describe how various clusters syllabify. Explain your reasoning and give lexical forms. We have rearranged the data so you'll need to look around for easy cases to start with.

40.2. Rahovan

N-SG	N-PL	a N	the N	with N	for N	
nap	naps	napko	na:pro	na:plo	na:pu	'mouse'
na:r	na:rs	na:rko	na:rro	na:rlo	na:ru	'tomato'
na:p	na:ps	na:pko	na:pro	na:plo	na:pu	'spouse'
na:	nas	na:ko	na:ro	na:lo	na:u	'potato'
nar	nars	narko	narro	narlo	na:ru	'louse'
na:	na:s	na:ko	na:ro	na:lo	na:u	'blouse'
nat	nats	natko	na:tro	na:tlo	na:tu	'grouse'
na:t	na:ts	na:tko	na:tro	na:tlo	na:tu	'house'

40.3. Bercenian

N-SG	N-PL	a N	the N	with N	for N	
na	nas	nako	naro	nalo	nau	'potato'
nat	nats	natko	na:tro	natlo	na:tu	'house'
na:	nas	na:ko	na:ro	na:lo	na:u	'blouse'
nap	naps	napko	napro	naplo	napu	'mouse'
nat	nats	natko	natro	natlo	natu	'grouse'
nar	nars	narko	narro	narlo	naru	'louse'
nap	naps	napko	na:pro	na:plo	na:pu	'spouse'
nar	nars	narko	narro	narlo	na:ru	'tomato'

So far we have used R1, a rule of vowel lengthening in open syllables, and R2, a rule of vowel shortening in closed syllables. But the logic you are learning can be generalized. In the following two languages there is one of the following rules:

- Ra: ɪ → i in open syllables

- Rb: i → ɪ in closed syllables

Provide the same kind of analysis as above, replacing R1 and R2 with Ra and Rb.

40.4. Vitanian

N-SG	N-PL	a N	the N	with N	for N	
nit	nits	nitko	nitro	nitlo	nitu	'house'
nip	nips	nipko	nipro	niplo	nipu	'spouse'
nɪr	nɪrs	nɪrko	nɪrro	nɪrlo	niru	'louse'
nir	nirs	nirko	nirro	nirlo	niru	'tomato'
ni	nɪs	niko	niro	nilo	niu	'potato'
ni	nis	niko	niro	nilo	niu	'blouse'
nɪp	nɪps	nɪpko	nipro	niplo	nipu	'mouse'
nɪt	nɪts	nɪtko	nitro	nɪtlo	nitu	'grouse'

40.5. Dristoran

N-SG	N-PL	a N	the N	with N	for N	
nɪr	nɪrs	nɪrko	nɪrro	nɪrlo	niru	'tomato'
nɪt	nɪts	nɪtko	nɪtro	nɪtlo	nɪtu	'grouse'
nɪ	nɪs	nɪko	nɪro	nɪlo	nɪu	'potato'
ni	nɪs	niko	niro	nilo	niu	'blouse'
nɪp	nɪps	nɪpko	nɪpro	nɪplo	nipu	'mouse'
nɪp	nɪps	nɪpko	nɪpro	nɪplo	nipu	'spouse'
nɪr	nɪrs	nɪrko	nɪrro	nɪrlo	nɪru	'louse'
nɪt	nɪts	nɪtko	nɪtro	nɪtlo	nitu	'house'

We are treating syllabification as a mapping of phonological structures to other phonological structures. This means that syllable structure can be built and destroyed in the
course of a derivation, as segments get inserted and deleted and changed by other rules.
Thus, syllabification rules must be ordered with respect to other rules. In the following
toy datasets, we again restrict the hypothesis space that you must consider, as follows:

- For all of the following languages, assume that stop-liquid clusters always go
  into a following onset. Stops are *p,t,k*; liquids are *l,r*. This is constant for all
  these languages.

- Each of the following languages has either R1, the lengthening rule above, or
  R2, the shortening rule.

- Each language also has either insertion or deletion of ə:

  - Rα: $\epsilon \rightarrow$ ə/ p ___k
  - Rβ: ə $\rightarrow \epsilon$ / a ___

- For each language, determine whether the language has R1 or R2, and whether it has Rα or Rβ.

- Name the ordering (feeding, bleeding, etc.) and explain your reasoning.

- Figure out the lexical forms for all morphemes in each language. You are given the UR for one of the suffixes.

40.6. Koliban: Assume there is a suffix /-k/

Hint: This language has the shortening rule, R2. It has Rα, insertion of ə. Rα bleeds R2, as shown by the form [na:pək].

V-PRES	V-PAST	V-FUT	V-PERF	V-FTPF	V-participle	V-DUB	
na	nas	nak	nato	naro	nalo	nau	'eradicate'
na:	nas	nak	na:to	na:ro	na:lo	na:u	'abdicate'
nap	naps	napək	napto	napro	naplo	napu	'evaporate'
nap	naps	na:pək	napto	na:pro	na:plo	na:pu	'bifurcate'
nar	nars	nark	narto	narro	narlo	naru	'masticate'
nar	nars	nark	narto	narro	narlo	na:ru	'date'

40.7. Kramárese: Assume there is a suffix /-k/

V-PRES	V-PAST	V-FUT	V-PERF	V-FTPF	V-participle	V-DUB	
na	nas	nak	nato	naro	nalo	nau	'eradicate'
na:	nas	nak	na:to	na:ro	na:lo	na:u	'abdicate'
nap	naps	napək	napto	napro	naplo	napu	'evaporate'
nap	naps	napək	napto	na:pro	na:plo	na:pu	'bifurcate'
nar	nars	nark	narto	narro	narlo	naru	'masticate'
nar	nars	nark	narto	narro	narlo	na:ru	'date'

40.8. Lamačese: Assume there is a suffix /-ək/

V-PRES	V-PAST	V-FUT	V-PERF	V-FTPF	V-participle	V-DUB	
na	nas	nak	nato	naro	nalo	nau	'eradicate'
na:	nas	nak	na:to	na:ro	na:lo	na:u	'abdicate'
nap	naps	napək	napto	napro	naplo	napu	'evaporate'
nap	naps	na:pək	napto	na:pro	na:plo	na:pu	'bifurcate'
nar	nars	narək	narto	narro	narlo	naru	'masticate'
nar	nars	na:rək	narto	narro	narlo	na:ru	'date'

40.9. Čunovese: Assume there is a suffix /-ək/

V-PRES	V-PAST	V-FUT	V-PERF	V-FTPF	V-participle	V-DUB	
na	nas	nak	nato	naro	nalo	nau	'eradicate'
na:	nas	na:k	na:to	na:ro	na:lo	na:u	'abdicate'
nap	naps	napək	napto	napro	naplo	napu	'evaporate'
nap	naps	na:pək	napto	na:pro	na:plo	na:pu	'bifurcate'
nar	nars	narək	narto	narro	narlo	naru	'masticate'
nar	nars	na:rək	narto	na:rro	na:rlo	na:ru	'date'

40.10. Vajnoryan: Assume there is a suffix /-k/

V-PRES	V-PAST	V-FUT	V-PERF	V-FTPF	V-participle	V-DUB	
na:	nas	nak	na:to	na:ro	na:lo	na:u	'eradicate'
na:	na:s	na:k	na:to	na:ro	na:lo	na:u	'abdicate'
nap	naps	na:pək	napto	na:pro	na:plo	na:pu	'evaporate'
na:p	na:ps	na:pək	na:pto	na:pro	na:plo	na:pu	'bifurcate'
nar	nars	nark	narto	narro	narlo	na:ru	'masticate'
na:r	na:rs	na:rk	na:rto	na:rro	na:rlo	na:ru	'date'

40.11. Ružinovan: Assume there is a suffix /-k/

V-PRES	V-PAST	V-FUT	V-PERF	V-FTPF	V-participle	V-DUB	
na:	nas	nak	na:to	na:ro	na:lo	na:u	'eradicate'
na:	na:s	na:k	na:to	na:ro	na:lo	na:u	'abdicate'
nap	naps	napək	napto	na:pro	na:plo	na:pu	'evaporate'
na:p	na:ps	na:pək	na:pto	na:pro	na:plo	na:pu	'bifurcate'
nar	nars	nark	narto	narro	narlo	na:ru	'masticate'
na:r	na:rs	na:rk	na:rto	na:rro	na:rlo	na:ru	'date'

40.12. Rusovcean: Assume there is a suffix /-ək/

V-PRES	V-PAST	V-FUT	V-PERF	V-FTPF	V-participle	V-DUB	
na:	nas	nak	na:to	na:ro	na:lo	na:u	'eradicate'
na:	na:s	na:k	na:to	na:ro	na:lo	na:u	'abdicate'
nap	naps	na:pək	napto	na:pro	na:plo	na:pu	'evaporate'
na:p	na:ps	na:pək	na:pto	na:pro	na:plo	na:pu	'bifurcate'
nar	nars	na:rək	narto	narro	narlo	na:ru	'masticate'
na:r	na:rs	na:rək	na:rto	na:rro	na:rlo	na:ru	'date'

40.13. Jarovcese: Assume there is a suffix /-ək/

V-PRES	V-PAST	V-FUT	V-PERF	V-FTPF	V-participle	V-DUB	
na:	nas	na:k	na:to	na:ro	na:lo	na:u	'eradicate'
na:	na:s	na:k	na:to	na:ro	na:lo	na:u	'abdicate'
nap	naps	na:pək	napto	na:pro	na:plo	na:pu	'evaporate'
na:p	na:ps	na:pək	na:pto	na:pro	na:plo	na:pu	'bifurcate'
nar	nars	na:rək	narto	narro	narlo	na:ru	'masticate'
na:r	na:rs	na:rək	na:rto	na:rro	na:rlo	na:ru	'date'

Unit 41

Stress

Another phonological phenomenon that requires us to look at units larger than segments is STRESS. Phonetically, stressed syllables are marked by some combination of extra loudness, raised pitch, and extra duration, which make them more salient. We will not worry about the cross-linguistic variability in the realization of stress, or the related question of whether stress is a single phenomenon. These are important questions that are the subject of much current research. Instead, we will take an idealized view based on a few simple cases that provide an overview of the kinds of stress systems found in the languages of the world.

We will consider four kinds of systems:

- Some languages have fixed stress, say on the final or on the initial syllable.

- Some languages appear to have totally unpredictable stress—the stress has to be memorized as an idiosyncratic aspect of pronunciation, just like the question of whether a given morpheme begins with, say, /t/ or /n/.

- Some languages show interactions of stress with syllable weight (light versus heavy) and/or syllable type (open versus closed).

- Some languages compute stress by dividing words into groups of syllables called *feet* and building from feet to a pattern of word stress.

These four types of systems are not mutually exclusive, and, in fact, the best model would probably show, for example, that fixed stress is just the result of a trivial version of a foot-based computation.

41.1   Fixed Stress

Languages that are described as having *fixed stress* manifest the same simple pattern in every word. For example, they might always stress the first syllable of every word, like Hungarian. Other languages, such as International (Standard) French, are described by some linguists as having no stress at all, or, by others, as having a fixed position of stress on the last syllable. This explains one aspect of a typical French accent when speaking English—it sounds like the speaker is always stressing the final syllable, no matter what the normal English stress is for a given word. It is this aspect of a French accent that is the basis of the gag in the movie *The Trail of the Pink Panther*, where the main character (Inspector Clouseau, played by Peter Sellers) neutralizes the difference between the English words *massage* and *message*.[1]

41.2   Lexical Stress

The accent marks added to the English words *masságe* and *méssage* indicate the difference in their stress pattern.[2] From such examples, English stress appears to be an idiosyncratic property of certain syllables in words. Given words of several syllables, we can't predict where the stress will fall, so this information needs to be part of the stored phonological representation of morphemes. This reinforces the point that our earlier treatment of phonological representations as just sequences of segments was too simple. Since the information is stored in morphemes in the lexicon, such a system is referred to as *lexical* stress.

It is less clear how to treat the pairs of related nouns and verbs in English that differ just in the location of stress, as shown in (382):

(382)   a. He will re**córd** the **ré**cord next year.

        b. She can con**vért** the **cón**vert back to his previous religion.

        c. He won't con**tráct** a disease by touching the **cón**tract.

Such examples suggest some level of systematicity, so we might be tempted to treat the alternation with some combination of phonological and morphological computation. However, this stress alternation between verbs and nouns is not completely regular, as seen in (383):

---

[1] Search "peter sellers message" or try https://youtu.be/dzbgpGuX6-s.
[2] This is not the standard IPA notation for stress.

(383) a. The chef will fi**lét** the fish into three fi**léts**.

   b. The reporter will **ín**terview the woman who once said she would never do an **ín**terview.

In (383a), the final syllable is stressed in both the verb and the noun; in (383b), the initial syllable is stressed in both the verb and the noun. Our dialect also has stress-based minimal pairs of the same syntactic category, like **Rám**bo and Rim**báud**, two names that consist of the exact same string of segments, *ræmbo*, but with a distinction based on the location of stress.

For the purposes of this basic overview, we will assume that languages like English have lexical stress, which requires a speaker to memorize the location of a stressed syllable. However, this obscures many interesting issues, including the question of how word stress is affected by stress in neighboring words. A famous example of this phenomenon is the difference in the stress on some words spoken in isolation and the stress pattern when the words are combined into a phrase. In (384), we once again use boldface and an acute accent to indicate the location of stressed syllables.

(384) Word stress and phrasal stress

   • Isolated words

     – twenty-s**é**ven

     – Mississ**í**ppi

     – l**é**gislators

   • Phrase: **twén**ty-seven **Mís**sissippi **lé**gislators.

In addition to the main stresses indicated, English words and phrases also have syllables that receive a secondary stress, marked with grave accents in (385). These syllables with secondary stress are less salient than the primary stressed syllables, but more salient than the totally unstressed syllables:

(385) **twén**ty-s**è**ven **Mís**siss**ì**ppi **lé**gisl**à**tors

Such examples show us that, even if English *word* stress is lexical, and thus directly reflects stored information, there is still a computational aspect to *phrasal* stress in an English grammar. Given the unbounded nature of phrasal syntax, the phrasal stress algorithm must be able to generate an unbounded set of forms.

41.3   Weight and Stress

The third type of stress system we consider makes reference to the distinction between heavy and light syllables introduced in the previous unit. In Latin, words with three or more syllables display two distinct stress patterns. If the second to last syllable of the word—the penultimate syllable—is heavy, then stress falls on this syllable. However, if it is not heavy, stress falls on the third to last syllable—the antepenultimate syllable.

For example, a Latin word like *di.vi:.nus* 'divine' has a long vowel in the second-to-last syllable, so the syllable is heavy, even though it is open. As a result, stress falls on this heavy penultimate syllable. In the Latin name *Au.**gus**.tus*, the penultimate syllable has a short vowel, but there is an *s* in the coda that makes that syllable heavy. So, again, stress falls on the heavy penult, as in *di.**vi:**.nus*. In contrast, *li*, the penult of the name ***Iu:**.li.us*, has a short vowel and no coda. So, the syllable is light and thus not stressed. Stress fails on the antepenult, the initial syllable ***Iu:***.

The appearance of stress on a syllable in Latin can thus be characterized by an algorithm, unlike the case of English, where stress is idiosyncratic. In English, stress information has to be stored in the lexicon, but in Latin it can be computed by the algorithm in (386):

(386)   a.   If a word has only one syllable, then stress falls on that syllable.

          b.   If a word has only two syllables, then stress falls on the first syllable.

          c.   If the second to last syllable in a word is heavy—in other words, if it has a rhyme with two elements (a long vowel, a diphthong, or a vowel with a coda consonant), then stress falls on this syllable.

          d.   Otherwise, stress falls on the third to last syllable in a word (the antepenultimate syllable).

Note that the algorithm captures two facts not mentioned above, namely that (i) Latin words with only one syllable have stress falling on that syllable and (ii) Latin words with two syllables have stress falling on the first syllable.

We said that the algorithm *can* compute the stress of Latin words; however, there are three pieces of evidence that suggest the stronger claim that Latin stress *must* be computed, rather than stored like English lexical stress. First, the algorithm accounts for the systematicity of the stress pattern—it appears to be completely regular. Second, borrowed words appear to have been subject to the same patterns as native words, so the algorithm appears to have been productive. Finally, there are shifts in stress when elements called *clitics* are incorporated into words. For example, the suffix *que* [kwe] 'and' in Latin attaches to the second of two words that are coordinated, as in (387):

(387)   a. *Iulius Augustusque* 'Julius and Augustus'

       b. *Augustus Iuliusque* 'Augustus and Julius'

Compare syllabification and word stress in the forms with and without -*que*:

(388)   a. *Au.**gus**.tus* : *Au.gus.**tus**.que*

       b. ***Iu**.li.us* : *Iu.li.**us**.que*

Adding -*que* to the end of a word changes the syllable count, so in *Au.gus.**tus**.que*, the syllable *tus* is the penultimate syllable; and it is closed and thus heavy, so it is stressed, instead of the syllable *gus* in the unsuffixed form. In *Iu.li.**us**.que*, *us* is the penultimate syllable; and it is closed and thus heavy, so it is stressed, instead of the syllable *Iu* in the unsuffixed form.

Since -*que* can be suffixed to any word and adjust the syllable count, it must be the case that Latin stress is assigned by an algorithm like the one in (386). The exact form of the algorithm is a topic of ongoing research in the context of a universal model of stress computation, but in any event, the correct algorithm for Latin will have to be extensionally equivalent to the one in (386).

Before moving on, let's point out that the Latin stress algorithm makes crucial reference to the light versus heavy distinction of the previous unit. Thus Latin stress supports our decision to treat open syllables with a long vowel as equivalent to syllables with a short vowel and a coda (and to syllables with both a long vowel and a coda). The Latin stress algorithm suggests that the category "heavy syllable" is a real element of phonological UG.

41.4   Computing Stress with Feet

The last kind of stress pattern we'll look at relies on algorithms that group syllables into larger units called FEET. Let's consider some simple cases adapted from the discussion in Idsardi 1992. In the following datasets, the symbols *i, e, a, o, u* correspond to vowels and we assume that each vowel corresponds to a separate syllable. As represented in previous sections, a vowel with an acute accent like *á* has primary stress; and a vowel with a grave accent like *à* has secondary stress. Unaccented vowel symbols bear no stress.

Let's look first at Weri, a language of Papua New Guinea. The following forms are representative of words with an odd number of syllables—the (a) cases—and those with an even number, like (b).

(389)   a. Odd number of syllables: àkunèpetál

         b. Even number of syllables: ulùamít

As we did for Latin, we will try to discover an algorithm that maps an input string without any stress assignment to an output string with stress markers. Thus, the algorithm should map /akunepetal/ to [àkunèpetál] and /uluamit/ to [ulùamít].

Like Latin, the secret to figuring out Weri stress is to start at the *end* of the word, the right edge. Stress in Weri falls on *every other syllable* counting from the right, with main stress falling on the rightmost syllable (the first from the right, the last in the word). In order to characterize this pattern correctly, the notion of "every other syllable" needs to be developed. One way to do this is by grouping pairs of syllables into feet. The algorithm in (390) correctly characterizes the stress assignment in (389).

(390)   An algorithm for Weri stress

   • Syllables are grouped into pairs, starting from the end of the word as follows. Each grouped pair is called a *foot.*

       a. a(kune)(petal)

       b. (ulu)(amit)

   • unmatched syllables—solo syllables—are grouped by themselves:

       a. (a)(kune)(petal)

       b. (ulu)(amit)

   • Stress is assigned to the syllable at the right edge of each foot:

       a. (à)(kunè)(petàl)

       b. (ulù)(amìt)

   • The rightmost stress in the word is given primary stress:

       a. (à)(kunè)(petál)

       b. (ulù)(amít)

This algorithm works for all words in Weri.

Now consider data from another language called Maranungku, spoken in Northern Australia:

(391)   a. tíralk

b. mérepèt

c. jángarmàta

d. lángkaràtefì

e. wélepèlemànta

In this language, like Weri, stress falls on every other syllable; however, this time it is every other syllable starting from the left, the beginning of the word. We can use an algorithm that is very similar to the one we used for Weri to compute Maranungku stress. We just need to change the direction in which we scan the word to build feet, as well as the side of each foot that gets stressed. Consider the algorithm in (392).

(392)   Maranungku stress

- Syllables are grouped into pairs, starting from the **beginning** of the word. Each grouped pair is called a *foot*.

    a. (mere)pet

    b. (jangar)(mata)

- unmatched syllables—solo syllables—are grouped by themselves:

    a. (mere)(pet)

    b. (jangar)(mata)

- Stress is assigned to the syllable at the **left** edge of each foot:

    a. (mère)(pèt)

    b. (jàngar)(màta)

- The **leftmost** stress in the word is made the primary stress:

    a. (mére)(pèt)

    b. (jángar)(màta)

This algorithm generates the correct stress assignment for all the words in Maranungku.

Having broken down the two algorithms into these parts, we could imagine the parts recombining in various ways. In other words, we can think of each of the four parts as varying independently. This allows us to come up with a language with a stress computation algorithm like the following:

(393)   Modified Maranungku

- build binary feet from left to right
- unmatched syllables **do not** form a foot of their own
- stress the leftmost member of each foot
- the leftmost stress is the primary stress

These settings are identical to those for Maranungku, except that unmatched syllables do not get a foot of their own, and thus they do not get a stress. It turns out that this is exactly what is needed to account for Pintupi, another Australian language, which has a pattern identical to Maranungku, except that final syllables, even if they are odd numbered, do not get stressed:

(394)   Pintupi manifests the stress rules in (393)

a.   pána

b.   ʧútaya

c.   málawàna

d.   púliŋkàlatʲu

e.   ʧámulùmpatʲùŋku

f.   tílirìŋulàmpatʲu

Finally, consider a language with yet another combination of settings:

(395)   Another combination of stress rules

- build binary feet from right to left
- unmatched syllables **do not** form a foot of their own
- stress the leftmost member of each foot
- the rightmost stress is the primary stress

This system ensures primary stress on the second to last syllable and alternating secondary stresses on every other syllable preceding the primary stressed one. The initial syllable will be stressed only in words with an even number of syllables. This is exactly the system needed to account for Warao, an indigenous language of South America, as shown by these representative words with even and odd numbers of syllables:

(396)   Warao manifests the stress rules in (395)

    a. yiwàranáe

    b. yàpurùkitàneháse

These examples help us to see how a well-defined system makes the idea of an innate toolkit plausible. Combinations of a relatively small number of choices allow for a wide variety of superficial patterns.

(397)   Stress rule parameters

    a. Build binary feet from left or right?

    b. Include unmatched syllables in a foot?

    c. Which member of a foot gets stressed?

    d. Which edge of the word gets primary stress?

The four parts of these stress rules combine to give rise to sixteen possible systems, and that number rises when we allow for sensitivity to weight, such as what we saw in Latin, and other factors. Once again, we return to our recurring theme: the idea that we can rely on simple combinatorics to generate a large amount of descriptive complexity from a simple system.

Exercise

41.1. Is the parameterized model of stress presented in (397) in conflict with our working assumption for the SPE model that rules always apply globally?

Part VIII

Features and Feature Logic

Unit 42

Substrings and Sets of Strings

A fundamental question for phonologists is *What is the set of entities that constitute phonological representations?* Implicit in this question is the idea that phonological representations are complex, that is, analyzable into simpler parts. We have to discover the simplest, atomic, non-complex parts and their manner of composition.

There is a nice payoff to understanding the component parts of representations. For example, by dissecting certain representations (such as segments like *p* and *m*) into their component parts, we can ask whether they share any of the same parts. We can then define sets or classes by collecting all the representations (e.g., all the segments) that share certain component parts. Sets of segments—or any other type of representation for that matter—that can be defined intensionally in terms of shared subparts are called *natural classes* in linguistics. Natural classes are usually discussed relative to segments, but we can also define natural classes relative to any linguistic representation.

As we pointed out in Unit 24.2, even our segment-based rules implicitly introduced the idea of natural classes of representations. For example, a rule like 's → š / ___ i' affects not just one form in one derivation, but rather it affects all strings that contain the substring *si*. We can think of the substring *si* as a description of a set (or class) of strings, the set of strings that contain *si* as a substring. Call this class Q. The class Q includes *posi, naposi, posinkultasi, krusi* and an infinite list of others that may or may not be possible URs in a given language. Using the symbol '$\lesssim$' to denote the substring relation and q to denote strings, we can define Q as the set of all strings that have *si* as a substring: $Q = \{q : \text{si} \lesssim q\}$.

Notice that a longer, *more specified* substring will define a set that is a *subset* of the class defined by a shorter substring. For example, the string *si* is a substring of *osi*, and the latter defines a subset of Q (an infinite one) that contains *posi, naposi, posinkultasi* but does not contain *krusi*, and infinitely many other members of Q. Let's use R to name this subset of Q.[1] In (398) we see an example of the inverse relation between the amount of information in a string and the size of the set of strings it characterizes:

(398)   *si* and *osi* as partial descriptions characterize sets of strings
      a. si $\lesssim$ osi   '*si* a substring of *osi*'
      b. $Q = \{q : si \lesssim q\}$ 'the set of all the strings that *si* is a substring of'
      c. $R = \{r : osi \lesssim r\}$ 'the set of all the strings that *osi* is a substring of'
      d. $R \subseteq Q$

The relations illustrated in (398) generalize to the sets defined by any two strings, α, β, that are in a substring relation:

(399)   Strings as partial descriptions characterize sets of strings
      If $\alpha \lesssim \beta$ and
      $A = \{a : \alpha \lesssim a\}$ and
      $B = \{b : \beta \lesssim b\}$ then
      $B \subseteq A$

We are sure that you understand these ideas intuitively, but since one of our goals is to study how we reason about phonology, we will illustrate how the notion of natural classes of strings plays a role in analyzing datasets. We will do this in the following unit. Then we will extend the notion of natural classes to segments.

---

[1]Notice how interesting things get when you talk about infinite sets. Both R and Q are infinite sets, and even though they have the same cardinality, R is a proper subset of Q. A good parallel is the relationship between the set of even positive integers $\{2, 4, 6, 8, \ldots\}$ and the set of all positive integers $\{1, 2, 3, 4, \ldots\}$. Both are infinite sets, yet the former is a proper subset of the latter.

Unit 43

Beyond Perfect Datasets: What Can We Ignore?

43.1 Equivalence Classes in Rules via Substrings

Most of the data in this book is made up. In addition to minimal pairs of words, like *lap* versus *lab*, we have studied minimal pairs of paradigms, like *ras, rasa* versus *ras, raʃa*. We used these artificial datasets for two reasons. First, our focus in the earlier parts of the book was on the logic of derivation, rule application, and rule ordering (and the resulting patterns of neutralization and allophony), and using artificial data allowed us to abstract away from issues that are logically independent of those. Second, real data from real languages is rarely as neat as the examples we have used.[1] However, we occasionally can find such perfect datasets.

Consider the following pair of paradigms from Russian:

(400)   Russian ideal data

	form	gloss
a.	porok	'vice' (NOMINATIVE)
b.	poroka	'vice' (GENITIVE)
c.	porok	'threshold' (NOMINATIVE)
d.	poroga	'threshold' (GENITIVE)

---

[1] It actually isn't clear what "real" means in these contexts. There is no such thing as "raw data," an under-appreciated point that is clearly discussed by Hammarberg (1981), and the I-languages we are interested in are not directly observable.

375

At this point, you should have no trouble positing that the lexical forms for 'vice' and 'threshold' are /porok/ and /porog/, respectively, and furthermore that the language has a rule that neutralizes underlying /g/ and /k/ word-finally by changing the /g/ to a [k]—something like 'g → k /___%'.[2]

In teaching you how to carry out these types of analyses, we introduced two types of simplifications with respect to rule environments: first, we provided a system that limits the kind of conditions you are allowed to posit with respect to rule application (i.e., the segments before and after the target); and second, we have taught you to ignore factors that do not distinguish the forms that do undergo the rule from those that do not undergo the rule. For example, recall the Dengue toy forms from Unit 19.1, repeated in (401):

(401)   Dengue neutralization data

	form	gloss	UR
a.	luš	'a dog'	/luš/
b.	luši	'the dog'	/luš-i/
c.	lus	'a hat'	/lus/
d.	luši	'the hat'	/lus-i/

The underlying *s* that changes to *š* in form (401d) is preceded by a *u*, but so is the *s* in form (c), which does not change. So, as far as we can tell, the presence of preceding *u* is not relevant to the rule application. Only the following *i* appears to matter. Of course, if we added to the data in (401) a paradigm like *los, losi*, we might have to consider that the rule environment is 'u___i', and not just '___i'.

We also insisted that your rule changing *s* to *š* *not* make reference to the initial *l* in form (d). The impossibility of referring to the *l* follows from the SPE rule syntax we are using. It is an empirical question whether such a restriction on rule formats provides the best model of human phonology. If we accept this restriction, then a form like [guši] can be treated as non-distinct from [luši] with respect to the rules under analysis. In other words, the forms are members of the same equivalence class, the set of strings that have *uši* as a substring.

When we look at data from actual languages, we rarely find minimally differing paradigms like the Russian one above, and we often find alternations between segments

---

[2]With just this data, it is not clear if the preceding segment is relevant, in other words if the correct rule is instead 'g → k / o___%'. This is a valid point that will be clarified as we proceed, both for the Russian case, and in general. We actually believe that a language learner should initially include the preceding vowel in the environment, but this is a minority view. Our view is also at odds with what linguistics students are told to do when writing rules—see below.

that occur in a range of environments. For example, here is a more typical kind of dataset from Russian, showing the same alternation as in (400):

(402)   Russian more typical data
      a.   vrak   'enemy' (NOMINATIVE)
      b.   vraga   'enemy' (GENITIVE)
      c.   urok   'lesson' (NOMINATIVE)
      d.   uroka 'lesson' (GENITIVE)

Since this data is also from Russian, we probably want to give it the same analysis as above. However, if we hadn't seen the data in (400), it would not be a logical necessity to posit the simple rule 'g → k / ___%'. We cannot know, based on this data alone, that the identity of the segment preceding the alternating segment is irrelevant. Perhaps the rule should be 'g → k / a___%', that is, *g* becomes *k* between an *a* and a word-boundary. Or even 'k → g / a ___a'.

Pretty much every phonologist would posit the rule that we chose above for (400), 'g → k / ___%', even without seeing additional data like (402).[3] This is true for several reasons, some of them good and some not so good. Phonologists have a lot of intuitions about what kinds of alternations happen in the languages of the world, and so when they are confronted with data like (400), they call on their intuitions to make an analysis. If one's primary concern is to make an analysis that works, one that can simulate a Russian speaker, then this use of intuition is often fine. These intuitions come from several sources, including knowledge of acoustic, articulatory, and perceptual phonetics; knowledge of diachronic linguistics; and the particular languages and theoretical frameworks the phonologist has been exposed to.

Sometimes the decision to choose a particular rule is based on a phonologist's intuitions about what is phonetically natural as a sound change. We know that in the course of language change, merger of *g* and *k* at the end of a word is a really common event. We also know that such language changes are a source of synchronic phonological rules. So, if rules reflect changes, then we might expect common changes to be more often reflected in rules than less common changes. So it is a good guess that this is what is going on in Russian: *g* → *k* at the end of a word is a likely rule, because it is a likely historical sound change. However, sometimes languages have rules that do not make sense in terms of the phonetics of language change—phonetic intuition can fail, as can all heuristics.

In addition to intuitions based on phonetics, phonologists also tend to have implicit theories of what can count as a condition on a rule. These implicit theories may be

---

[3]They would probably expect the g~k alternation to be part of a more general process that we will discuss later.

dependent on a scholar's research experience, such as the kind of rules that have been encountered previously because of the particular languages that were studied. A phonologist may call upon this implicit experience-based knowledge in making guesses in a particular case without formalizing a theory of what is a possible rule. In this book, we have been trying to address this shortcoming by starting our investigation with an overly strict view of what can be a rule. We expand the set of possibilities only when forced to. This is basic scientific methodology, a version of the principle known as Occam's razor. Our goal is to try to develop a formal model that chooses an analysis based neither on phonetic intuitions nor on a vague and implicit theory of rule formats. So, we *can* start our investigations by appealing to an intuition that the forms in (402) constitute a minimal set—that the vowel preceding the consonants of interest are irrelevant—and then we can see if further data is consistent with this view. However, following this tack relies implicitly on having a representational system that expresses the idea that certain differences are irrelevant—we need to develop a theory of what is relevant and what is irrelevant. In other words, we want a rule that will treat /porog/ and /vrag/ as equivalent.

The idea we are heading toward is this: our intuition might suggest that a single rule is at work turning *g* to *k* in both #*porog*% and #*vrag*%. Then we must answer this question: *Given all the data we have, when does our theory allow us to formulate a single rule?* The answer depends on the set of equivalence classes defined by the representations posited. Our theory of phonological representations determines the observations that we make about the data. You should review our earlier discussion of this point in Unit 24, as well as the discussion by Pylyshyn (1984, p. 16-21), who explains that a "theory never explains an entirely unique event, only an event viewed against a background of distinctions and equivalences defined by the vocabulary with which the events are described."

43.2 Natural Classes of Segments in Rule Environments

We'll come back to Russian after a detour discussing different types of natural classes. In the meantime, consider the Zafonian dataset in (403).

(403) Zafonian

N	with a N	to a N	for a N	after a N	gloss
lu	luk	lus	lur	lun	'cat'
lo	lok	los	lor	lun	'rat'

As a superficial observation, this dataset demonstrates an alternation between [o] and [u]: in the word for 'rat', [u] appears before [n], whereas [o] appears before other segments or at the end of a word—that is, [o] occurs elsewhere. The phonological rule and lexical entries in (404) model this surface pattern.

(404) • Rule: o → u / ___ n

       • Lexical entries: /lu/ = 'cat'; /lo/ = 'rat'; /-k/ = 'with'; /-s/ = 'to'; /-r/ = 'for'; /-n/ = 'after'

This rule changes underlying /o/ to [u] when it appears before a coronal nasal (and leaves underlying /u/ unchanged).

As we have done before, let's again note that implicitly, there is a certain degree of abstraction in the rule in (404). For example, consider the expanded dataset in (405).

(405) More Zafonian

N	w/ N	to N	for N	after N	N-accusative	gloss
lu	luk	lus	lur	lun	lunæ	'cat'
lo	lok	los	lor	lun	lunæ	'rat'

This expanded dataset has the morpheme -*næ*, which marks accusative case. This morpheme creates more underlying sequences of *on*, but now some followed by *æ*, instead of the end-of-word symbol %. However, the rule we posited in (404) still generates the alternations correctly. The environment '___n' specifies that the structural change applies when there is an *n* to the immediate right. The rule does not care whether the *n* is the final segment of a word or whether it precedes the vowel *æ*. The rule is obviously insensitive to syllable structure, too. In other words, the environment specification collapses '___n%' and '___næ%' into a single equivalence class. This collapse is actually a consequence of our rule syntax.

Another abstraction encoded in our rule in (404) is that we have ignored the preceding consonant *l*, which is present in each form. We have not provided data to justify doing so, but let's assume that the rule as stated is correct, so that a hypothetical input form /so-næ/ would show the effect of the rule and surface as [sunæ]. In other words, the segment preceding the target appears to be irrelevant to the rule, just like our Russian rule turning *g* to *k* word-finally.

Let's now consider the further expanded Zafonian dataset in (406).

(406) Even more Zafonian

N	w/ N	to N	for N	after N	under N	before N	w/o N	gloss
lu	luk	lus	lur	lun	lum	luŋ	lud	'cat'
lo	lok	los	lor	lun	lum	luŋ	lod	'rat'

There are three more suffixes in (406): /-m/ 'under', /-ŋ/ 'before', and /-d/ 'without'.
Notice that the underlying /o/ surfaces as [u] not only before [n], but also before [m]
and [ŋ]. To explain this pattern, we would have to adopt two more rules, making three
in total.

(407) Zafonian rules

- o → u / ___ n
- o → u / ___ m
- o → u / ___ ŋ

There are three things that are suspicious about these rules. First, they specify the same
structural change. We might hope that the same structural change should reflect to the
same rule—the "same thing" is happening in each case, $o \rightarrow u$. Second, not only
does the same structural change occur before n, m, and $ŋ$ in this language, but there
are many other languages where these segments all occur in the environment of rules
that affect other segments in a parallel fashion. Third, these three segments all involve
airflow through the nasal passage. They are all *nasal* segments, in phonetic terms. Let's
assume that these are the only such segments that are nasal in the language in question.
Then perhaps n, m, and $ŋ$ constitute an equivalence class in the grammar and the three
rules in (407) can be collapsed into one. That is, the separate cases of $o \rightarrow u$ really
involve *the same thing* happening *in the same place*! In words, it is easy to generalize
thus: 'o becomes u before any nasal segment in the language'. Our challenge is to
express this in a formal rule syntax.

43.3 Natural Classes of Segments in Rule Targets

The idea that we just introduced, the idea of rules as generalizations that abstract across
classes of segments, can apply not only to the environment of a rule, but also to the

target. In other words, rules can target all the members of a *set* of segments, not just individual segments. More clearly, the rule will affect forms that have any segment from a given set if that segment occurs in the correct environment. Let's go back to Russian for an example.

In the Russian data above, we saw that the identity of the segment preceding the alternating g/k element appears to be irrelevant—at least, it didn't matter if the g was preceded by *a* or *o*. In fact, the only relevant factor is that the segment in question (underlying /g/) occur at the end of the word, in which case, it surfaces as [k]. In order to define the natural class of forms that undergo the rule, we can treat strings like #*porog*% and #*vrag*% as equivalent. It is perhaps easy for us to extract the relevant commonalities in these strings, but formalizing how we do this is not so simple. How are we able to abstract away from the details of the rule *environment*? How can we be sure that the rule of '$g \to k$ / ___ %' doesn't just happen after *poro-*, but after any sequence whatsoever? The answer is that we can provide a partial description of a class of strings that undergo the rule that makes no reference to anything except the substring g%.

To continue with this line of reasoning, consider some more Russian data:

(408)   Russian more typical data

a.	trup	'corpse' (NOMINATIVE)
b.	trupa	'corpse' (GENITIVE)
c.	xlep	'bread' (NOMINATIVE)
d.	xleba	'bread' (GENITIVE)
e.	tˢvet	'color' (NOMINATIVE)
f.	tˢveta	'color' (GENITIVE)
g.	prut	'pond' (NOMINATIVE)
h.	pruda	'pond' (GENITIVE)

These patterns are quite general and there are many more examples of both kinds—paradigms of nouns in which the nominative (with no overt suffix) and the genitive (with suffix -a) show different root-final consonants, like [xlep, xleba]; and other paradigms in which the consonant does not vary according to the phonological context, like [trup, trupa]. Once we decide to abstract away from the preceding vowel, we know how to analyze a dataset containing forms of 'corpse' and 'bread'; or a dataset containing forms of 'color' and 'pond'; or a dataset containing forms of 'enemy' and 'lesson'. However, now we will develop a way to analyze all of the forms at once, with a single rule.

The three rules we would need at this point are the following:

(409)   Three rules

     a. ɡ → k / ___ %

     b. d → t / ___ %

     c. b → p / ___ %

Our model does not preclude the possibility of a language having three rules like this; however, these rules are surprisingly similar. In each case, the input target segment is made in exactly the same way as the output segment, except for the fact that the input segment involves vibrating the vocal folds, and the output segment does not. The input segments are called *voiced* and the output segments are called *voiceless*. The rules do not affect any other properties of the target consonants—the tongue position and lip positions for the pairs *g* and *k*, *d* and *t*, and *b* and *p*, respectively, are identical. We can describe the three rules with one statement thus: In Russian, the phonology maps a member of the set {b, d, ɡ} to the corresponding voiceless segment if it occurs word-finally. This can be stated even more abstractly. We'll assume that you have an intuitive understanding of the distinction between consonants and vowels, and we will further suppose that the generalization we just made applies to all consonants (we'll fine-tune this later). In other words, we can posit a single rule: In Russian, the phonology maps a consonant to its corresponding voiceless segment if it occurs word-finally.

When we use rules to refer to, say, word-final *g*, we don't care about what precedes the *g*. The reference to *g* followed by % denotes a natural class of strings that includes *og%*, *eg%*, *lg%*, and so on. In the same fashion, we will use a partial description, a symbol C to refer to the property of being a consonant, and use that property to define the natural class of consonants. The class contains all consonants—we won't care if the consonant involves closing the lips (like a *b* or *p*) or raising the back of the tongue to the velum (like a *g* or a *k*) or bringing the blade of the tongue to the back of the upper teeth (like a *d* or a *t*).

Notice that we have seen data in which *d* maps to *t* between a *u* and %, as in *prut*. We do not happen to have any cases in our dataset showing that the devoicing of *g* to *k* also happens after *u*, but our rule is useful in that it predicts that a hypothetical genitive like *luga* would correspond to a nominative *luk*. In fact, Russian turns out to have forms of the relevant type, such as *kruk/kruga* 'circle' and *druk/druga* 'friend'.

It is *very important* to understand that, if it turned out that word-final *g* did not become *k* after *u*, then we would have to conclude that the d∼t pattern and the ɡ∼k pattern **could not be due to a single rule**. The rule we are trying to express involves devoicing consonants in word-final position, abstracting away from the identity of the preceding segment. The point is that our theory determines what is a *possible* rule. We need to look at data to figure out what the *actual* rules are—it is not the case that the rules can be determined by just inspecting words in the absence of a theory. We will soon formalize our theory of natural classes in Unit 45.

We are now ready to state a new version of the Russian rule. In order to review, we'll give three equivalent formulations:

(410)   a.   In word-final position, a voiced consonant becomes its voiceless counterpart.

            b.   Voiced consonants become voiceless word-finally.

            c.   A voiced consonant surfaces as voiceless before %.

This will be be adjusted in various ways later, so let's throw in another issue while we are still using plain English to express the process. Consider a slight modification of the statements in (410). In (411) the "target" of the rule is more general than "voiced consonant." It is the class of consonants in general:

(411)   a.   In word-final position, only voiceless consonants surface.

            b.   Consonants become voiceless word-finally.

            c.   A consonant surfaces as voiceless before %.

Your intuition is probably that the overall effect of the statements in (410) and (411) is the same—consonants will be voiceless in word-final position. What we have done in (411) is to introduce a particular kind of *vacuous rule application*. This involves formulating a rule so that the set of targets includes segments that already conform to the changed output forms. In other words, the formulations in (411) include not only voiced consonants like *b,d,g* but also voiceless ones like *p,t,k* as targets of the rule. We'll elaborate on this kind of vacuous application later on in Unit 44.

Unit 44

Using Properties in Rules

We have shown that a string s can be used to characterize a set of strings, each member of which contains s as a substring. Now we will show how we can use a symbol like C, mentioned above, to characterize a set of segments. In order to do this, of course, we can no longer view segments as atomic, indivisible entities. Instead, we will view segments as sets of properties and this will allow us to characterize a set of segments Σ using a set of properties Q that is a subset of each member of Σ. Let's suppose that we have the property C, which is shared by consonants but not vowels, as well as a property V, shared by all vowels, but no consonants. In addition we have referred to the property of being voiced, which we will denote as D, and a property of being voiceless, which we'll denote as T. We need to distinguish segments made with the lips closed, like p and b for which we'll use P, from segments like k and g made with the body of the tongue raised to the back of the roof of the mouth, for which we'll use K. Finally, we'll use F to a characterize segments like t and d, made with the tongue raised in the front of the mouth near the upper teeth.

For the purposes of the following discussion, we will assume that these six segments p, b, t, d, k, and g are the only consonants in a hypothetical language L. So there is no m or s in L. We will also assume that the properties C, D, T, P, K, and F are the only properties provided by universal grammar for describing consonants.[1]

At this point, you might want to review your set theory, since we will be discussing sets that have sets as their members. We have in L a set of consonants $\{p, b, t, d, k, g\}$, and we can characterize each member of that set—each consonant segment—as a set

---

[1] We will assume that the property V, and perhaps some others, can be used to characterize vowels.

of properties rather than as an unanalyzable whole:

(412)   Segments as sets of properties
          p = {C,P,T}   b = {C,P,D}
          t = {C,F,T}   d = {C,F,D}
          k = {C,K,T}   g = {C,K,D}

Let's call the set of consonants $\mathcal{K}$. You can see how useful it is to abbreviate each segment with a single symbol, as oppposed to writing out each element of $\mathcal{K}$:

(413)   Segments as sets of properties that are elements of $\mathcal{K}$

        a. $\mathcal{K} = \{p, b, t, d, k, g\}$

        b. $\mathcal{K} = \{\{C,P,T\}, \{C,P,D\}, \{C,F,T\}, \{C,F,D\}, \{C,K,T\}, \{C,K,D\}\}$

You can think of $\{p, b, t, d, k, g\}$ in (413a) as an extensional characterization of the set $\mathcal{K}$, since it lists each element of $\mathcal{K}$ explicitly. The representation in (413b) extensionally characterizes both $\mathcal{K}$ and all elements of $\mathcal{K}$.

    Remember that we have said that we are considering a language L in which $\mathcal{K}$ is the set of all (and only) the consonants. You should now see that we can intensionally characterize $\mathcal{K}$ itself by reference to properties. $\mathcal{K}$ is the set whose elements are all the sets that contain the property C:

(414) $\mathcal{K} = \{\xi : C \in \xi\}$

This formulation can be replaced with the equivalent one in (415). If a set contains C as a member then {C} is a subset of that set:

(415) $\mathcal{K} = \{\xi : \{C\} \subseteq \xi\}$

Finally, it will turn out to be convenient to use the superset relation instead of the subset relation, so we can characterize $\mathcal{K}$ as the set whose members are all supersets of {C}:

(416) $\mathcal{K} = \{\xi : \xi \supseteq \{C\}\}$

We'll now generalize this notation to talk about rules in terms of properties.

    Using the extensional characterization of each segment, the three alternations expressed by the rules in (409) can be rewritten using properties as in (417):

(417)   Three rules with properties

      a. {C,D,K} → {C,T,K} /___%

      b. {C,D,F} → {C,T,F} /___%

      c. {C,D,P} → {C,T,P} /___%

Each rule changes a segment that has the property D to the corresponding segment that has all the same properties except for having T instead of D—the rules change voiced segments to voiceless ones.

The segments that are on the left side of the arrow, the targets of the rule, are all segments that contain the properties C and D—let's suppose that these are the only such segments in the language. All other segments don't contain C or they don't contain D or they contain neither C nor D. We can use this criterion, having *both* C *and* D, to intensionally characterize the segments of interest.

We'll use Greek letters like π here as variables for segments. Each segment is a set of properties. Another way to say that a set/segment π contains both C and D is to say that the set {C,D} is a subset of π, or that π is a superset of {C,D}.

Here is the intensional characterization of the segments we are interested in:

(418) $\Pi = \left\{\pi : \pi \supseteq \{C,D\}\right\}$

This is the set of all segments that are supersets of {C,D}. We can now express a rule using Π like this: "If a segment π is a member of Π and π occurs at the end of a word, then replace the D in π with T. Leave all other features of π unchanged." This rule in (419) will look strange if you are familiar with more standard notations, but bear with us as we unpack it and work our way back to a more familiar format.

(419)   Rule based on Π: $\Pi \to$ {T} /___%

There is a subtle difference between our use of the arrow '→' in (419) from how we used it in our earlier rules that have full segments on either side. The new type of rule targets members of a *set* of segments rather than a single segment, and so, the arrow means something like 'perform the specified replacement operation to *any* member of Π that appears in the relevant environment'.[2] If we think of rules as functions on strings, the old rules targeted a certain segment (such as *d*) in the string, whereas the new rules target sets of segments (such as *b, d, g*). As a result, the class of strings targeted by a rule is potentially much broader in the new format than the old one.

---

[2]Of course, this new interpretation of → is backward compatible with our earlier rules if we think of the earlier rules as targeting sets of segments with just a single member.

Using Π in our rule obscures the nature of the class of segments that are targets of the rule. So, let's go back to listing the properties, as we did in (418):

(420) Complete rule, showing what's in Π:
$$\{\pi : \pi \supseteq \{C,D\}\} \rightarrow \{T\} / \_\_\%$$

This is still pretty unwieldy, so let's introduce a new kind of bracket, different from our set braces:

(421) Square brackets for natural classes:
$$[C,D] \rightarrow \{T\} / \_\_\%$$

There are a few things going on here that need to be clarified, like the relationship between T and D—why does '$\rightarrow \{T\}$' mean 'replace D with T', and not something else? We'll come back to this.

For now, let's focus on one aspect of this rule: the target of the rule is in square brackets and we are using that notation to refer to a set of segments, that is, a set of sets of properties. Each of those segments is a potential target of the rule. The rule change, the right side of the arrow, uses plain set braces (curly brackets), because we are referring to a set of properties (a set with just one member, in this case). Traditional phonological discussions do not make this basic distinction in notation between sets of properties and sets of sets of properties, but we will continue to do so here. If you read other phonological literature, you should be aware; you will probably find rules that use only square brackets.[3]

Now that we have introduced the square brackets to represent natural classes in (421), let's turn our attention to the relationship between the D in the square brackets and the T in the curly brackets after the arrow, namely D and T in '$[C,D] \rightarrow \{T\}$'. In this rule, the D is part of the intensional description that specifies the natural class of voiced consonants. As we said before, the rule specifies that members of this natural class (if they appear in the right environment) have their D property replaced by the T property. However, we can simplify our rule even further as long as we include as a principle in our theory that no segment can have both the T and D properties—they are not compatible with one another. This makes sense phonetically. Recall that T refers to the property of voicelessness and D to the property of voicing. Something cannot be both voiced and voiceless at the same time. If this is the case, we can assume that by adding T to a segment we must first delete the D. However, if a consonant already has the T property, then "adding T" will have no effect (it is simply adding

___

[3]And curly brackets have a completely different meaning in such sources—they allow for the equivalent of logical OR in rules, something we exclude.

a property that the segment already has—remember, repetition of elements does not affect a set). In light of these considerations, we can simplify our representation of the rule by removing the D property from the set of targets.

(422)   Rule with vacuous application: [C] → {T} /___%

The rule in (422) says this: "If a consonant occurs at the end of the word, it has to end up containing T (and not D, since the two are mutually incompatible)."

Given a form in a derivation, we have three cases to consider. First, consider the case where a form ends in a vowel, that is, a segment that does not have the property C as an element. Formally we can say that the rule maps the input to an identical output. Typically, phonologists say in such cases that the rule "does not apply," but this is really just one version of vacuous rule application. The rule applies, it just doesn't change anything.

If a form *does* meet the conditions on rule inputs—if there is a segment that has C as a member, and the segment is in word-final position—then there are two cases to consider. Either the target consonant has the property D as a member, in which case the D gets replaced by T; or the consonant already has T as a member and the rule has no effect. This latter situation is what is usually called *vacuous rule application*, although it is just like an input with a word-final segment containing V as a member—both map an input to an identical output. The rule applies to a string with a word-final segment containing T, but with no effect—the string is mapped to itself.[4]

Coming back to our Russian data, note that with our new notation, an underlying form /urok/ would satisfy the structural description of the rule in (422), since the segment *k* is a superset of {C}. However, the rule will apply vacuously, since *k* already contains T.[5] You should be aware that in the phonological literature it is usually assumed, sometimes without explicit discussion, that rules should be formulated to ensure vacuous application, as in (422). However, our rule formalism will end up being a bit more complex as our representational system develops, and we will have to confront the issues more directly later on.

We have shown how to characterize sets of strings intensionally by giving a substring that each member of the set contains. The substring is a partial description of each string in the set. We have also shown how a partial description of a segment, consisting of a set of properties, can characterize a natural class of segments, each of

---

[4]Another possibility, that the word-final segment contains C, but contains *neither* D nor T, will be considered below.

[5]A mathematical analogy of such a function would be a mapping from integers to the nearest multiple of 5 that is no less than the original integer. So 6→ 10, 7→ 10 and 10→ 10. The function applies to all integers, but the output and the input are identical when the input is a multiple of 5.

which is a superset of the description. Such partial descriptions can characterize not only rule targets, as in (422), but also the environment of rules, as in (423):

(423)   Rule with natural class of segments in the environment:

[C] → {T} /___[C]

This rule converts any consonant (any property set containing C) to being voiceless (containing T) if it occurs before any other consonant. Note that the environment, like the target description, uses square brackets to denote a set of segments.

The use of partial descriptions of strings and the use of partial descriptions of segments can be combined. In fact, we have already done so in (423), where the environment means "immediately before a consonant, regardless of what follows that consonant and regardless of what precedes the target." We can make this a bit clearer with a rule like (424):

(424)   Rule with partial description of strings and segments:

[C] → {T} / ___[P]

This is a ridiculous rule from a phonetic perspective, and you'll never find a rule triggering such alternations in any language, but it is useful to illustrate our new property-based rule syntax. It means "Make a consonant voiceless if it occurs before any labial consonant (*p* or *b*)." We have a partial segment description that characterizes the set of labial consonants[6] and a partial string description that characterizes only the segment following the target. It does not restrict what precedes the target or what follows the labial.

---

[6]Recall that we are assuming the language *L*, which has no *m* or other labial.

Unit 45

More on Rules with Properties

45.1 Natural Classes Defined by Generalized Intersection

Recall the six consonant segments of the language L, which we discussed in the previous unit:

(425)   Segments as sets of properties
          p= {C, P, T}   b= {C, P, D}
          t = {C, F, T}   d = {C, F, D}
          k = {C, K, T}   g = {C, K, D}

Each segment is a unique set of properties. We have seen that we can refer to sets of segments by referring to subsets of properties: the set of properties {C,P} is a subset of the set characterizing p and of the set characterizing b, and no other segment. Similarly, the set {C,K} is a subset of the set characterizing k and of the set characterizing g, and no other segment in L.

We can also use a set with three properties: the set {C, K, T} is a subset of the set characterizing k and no other segment in L (recall that every set is a subset of itself). We can even use a set of properties with one member with useful results. On the one hand, the set {D} is a subset of the sets characterizing b, d, and g, and no other segment in L. On the other hand, the set {C} is a subset of the set characterizing each of the six segments we have discussed so far. This process of using properties and the subset (or,

391

alternatively, superset) relation to pick out classes of segments defines what it means to be a natural class. Natural classes can be formally defined as follows:

(426) **Natural Classes:** Suppose a language λ contains all and only the segments in a set S. N is a *natural class* of λ if and only if there exists a set of properties G such $N = \{n : n \in S \text{ and } n \supseteq G\}$.

The notation ensures that N contains all and only the members of a natural class, in the same way that the set $\{x : x \text{ is an apple}\}$ defines the set containing all things that are apples, and nothing else.

The definition in (426) tells us how to decide if a set of segments form a natural class, but it does not tell use how to find the set of properties that defines a natural class. This will be necessary in order to discover the rules of a language.

Intuitively, the set of properties that define a natural class that contains just two segments will be the set of properties shared by those two segments and no other segment. You already know that set intersection is an operation that finds elements shared by two sets, so you may have thought about using intersection to find the characterization of a natural class.

There are three issues to consider when we use intersection for natural classes. First, intersection of two segments will always give us a set of properties that can be used to define a natural class, but the class thus defined might contain other segments. Second, intersection will define the smallest natural class containing two segments, but it won't necessarily define that natural class in the most economical way. Third, we might want to define a natural class that contains more than two segments, but intersection, as we defined it, is an operation on pairs of sets.

Let's deal with the first issue. If we take the intersection of d and k, the result will be a set of properties that defines a class that contains more than just these two segments, given our inventory:

(427) The intersection of d and k

$$\begin{array}{ccc} d & & k \\ \{C, F, D\} & \cap & \{C, K, T\} & = \{C\} \end{array}$$

(428) The natural class defined by $d \cap k$

- $\Pi = \{\pi : \pi \supseteq \{C\}\}$
- $\Pi = \{p, t, k, b, d, g\}$

The natural class Π contains p, t, k, b, d, g, not just k and d. This turns out to be the outcome we want—the smallest natural class that contains d and k contains all the other consonants in the inventory of L—since all (and only) the consonants contain {C}.

Now let's turn to the second issue. If you take the intersection of two segments, you get a set of properties that characterizes the smallest natural class that contains them—but there may be a smaller *characterization* of the same class. For example, using the properties and segments we have, the intersection of k and g yields the set {C, K} :

(429)   {C, D, K} ∩ {C, T, K} = {C, K}

This set of properties defines the natural class that contains just k and g, since these are the only segments in the inventory of L that are supersets of {C, K}. However, this natural class can be characterized just using the feature set {K}, since, in L, only k and g are supersets of {K}.

In discussions of phonological rules, it is traditional to say that natural classes should be characterized as economically as possible, that is, in the most general terms and with the least specification that is compatible with the data. So this would favor the characterization with {K}, not {C, K}. However, this precept is often disregarded and, in practice, phonologists tend to be inconsistent about how much they generalize beyond the specific dataset they have on hand, and how much they leave out redundant features.[1]

We turn now to the third issue, how to compute natural classes for more than two segments. In Unit 4 we introduced the operations of set union and set intersection as taking two sets as inputs and yielding a set as output. We pointed out that the two operations are *commutative*, like normal multiplication and addition, which means that $A \cup B = B \cup A$ and $A \cap B = B \cap A$. Again like the arithmetic operations, these set operations are also *associative*, which means that we can perform, say, intersection over three sets, by grouping two of them together:

- $(A \cap B) \cap C = A \cap (B \cap C)$

These expressions are consistent with the property that intersection (and union) take two sets as input; however, given the associative property, it is also common to allow expressions that don't bother to show how the sets are grouped:

---

[1] See Hale and Reiss (2008) for discussion of why choosing the most general rule compatible with the data might not be the best strategy—part of the reasoning involves consideration of the acquisition process. One problem that arises is that it is sometimes possible to eliminate one feature or another, but not both, to make a natural class description more economical, and the choice is often arbitrary. This is undesirable if we want the learning process to be deterministic.

- $A \cap B \cap C$

So, you can imagine using such an expression to compute a natural class based on three segments, say $p \cap t \cap k$.

Of course, we sometimes need to define a natural class that consists of more than three segments, or a natural class containing just a single segment. In order to have a general method for computing natural classes from a set of segments, we will use the operation called *generalized intersection* (and while we are at it, we can introduce generalized union).

Instead of taking two sets as arguments, the generalized operations take a single argument, which must be a **set of sets**. The symbols for the generalized operations are just bigger versions of the regular symbols:

(430)   Symbols for generalized set operators

- Intersection $\cap$: Generalized intersection $\bigcap$

- Union $\cup$: Generalized union $\bigcup$

In plain English, the generalized intersection of a set of sets $\mathcal{Q}$ is the set of all elements that are common to all the member sets of $\mathcal{Q}$. Here's an example:

(431)   Example of generalized intersection

- $\mathcal{Q} = \left\{ \{a, b, c\}, \{b, c, d\}, \{a, b, c, d\} \right\}$

- $\bigcap \mathcal{Q} = \{b, c\}$

The generalized intersection of the set of segments $\{p, t, k\}$ is well defined, since each segment is a set of properties.

(432)   Generalized intersection with segments

- $\mathcal{A} = \{p, t, k\} = \left\{ \{P, T, C\}, \{F, T, C\}, \{K, T, C\} \right\}$

- $\bigcap \mathcal{A} = \{T, C\}$

As shown, generalized intersection yields a set of properties that defines all and only the voiceless consonants of L. We can define our general method of finding natural classes as follows:

(433) **Smallest Natural Class:** Given a language λ and a set of segments S' that is a subset of S (the set of all segments in λ), the smallest natural class containing every member of S' is $N = \{n : n \in S \text{ and } n \supseteq \bigcap S'\}$.

You can confirm that each of the three segments in (432) is indeed a superset of the set of properties $\{T, C\}$, and that no other segment of L is a superset of $\{T, C\}$. For example, the segment $d = \{C, F, D\}$ is not a superset of $\{T, C\}$. So, the smallest natural class containing all and only p, t, and k is the set of segments that contains exactly those three.

It is important to recognize that, given our assumed set of UG-given properties, and given the segment inventory of L, the smallest natural class containing just p and k is also the set that contains all three, $\{p, t, k\}$. In other words, under our current assumptions, p and k do not form a natural class to the exclusion of t. This is because $\bigcap\{p, t, k\} = \bigcap\{p, k\} = \{T, C\}$.

Notice that our definition of smallest natural class works even if S has just a single member.[2] Right now, you might think that this is obvious—the natural class computed over just one segment should be the class consisting of that segment, but we will get a surprising result later on.

We are not going to make use of generalized union, but you have probably figured out how it works. In plain English, the generalized union of a set of sets Q is the set of all elements that are in any of the member sets of Q. Here's an example:

(434) Example of generalized union

- $Q = \left\{ \{a, b, c\}, \{b, c, d\}, \{a, b, c, e\} \right\}$

- $\bigcup Q = \{a, b, c, d, e\}$

Obviously, if Q contains a single member set, R, then $\bigcup Q = R$.

The set of natural classes *for a given inventory* is determined by the property sets of all the segments. Given the inventory of six consonants we have introduced, there is no way to characterize the set of segments that includes exactly p, b, t, d and g (to the exclusion of k). This means that these five segments do not constitute a natural class in a language with all six segments.

It is important to note that we have *not* just demonstrated that a set of segments consisting only of the members p, b, t, d, and g can *never* define a natural class. As we pointed out in Unit 4.5, the same intensional definition of a set might correspond to a

---

[2]This result favors our definition of generalized intersection over definitions that treat generalized intersection as *iterated binary intersection*, since a binary operation cannot be applied if P has just one member.

different extension as circumstances change—the set of Seymour's favorite letters may be different this year from last year, for example. We have been discussing a language L, with the six consonants p, b, t, d, k, and g, and in a language with that inventory, excluding k does not yield a natural class. However, if we were to consider a different language, M, with a different consonant inventory, one that contains, say, just p, b, t, d, and g, then these five segments *do* constitute a natural class. They are all and only the segments in M that are supersets of $\{C\}$. The notion of natural class is thus relativized to a given segment inventory, since the inventory determines the universe of discourse, the universal set over which classes are defined extensionally.[3]

For a more homey example, consider that the set $A = \{$lime, blood orange, grapefruit$\}$ contains only three types of citrus fruit. In a large supermarket that sells these three, as well as tangerines, lemons, and navel oranges, A does not have the same extension as the natural class of citrus. However, if we look in your refrigerator and the only citrus fruit there are limes, blood oranges, and grapefruit, then, in the universe of your refrigerator A is the set of all and only the types of citrus. In other words, the set of "types of citrus" has a different extension in your refrigerator and in the supermarket.

45.2   Natural Classes and Epistemic Boundedness

The view that the target and trigger of a rule must be a natural class is at least implicit in most work in formal phonology. Yet it is surprising how rarely it is clearly stated that an expression can be considered a rule you might refer back to the discussion in Unit (4.5) of how a given intensional definition can correspond to different extensionally defined sets. if the set of targets and the environment constitute natural classes. For example, in the discussion of features and natural classes in his book *Mathematical Linguistics*, Kornai (2008, p. 29), says that "Phonologists would be truly astonished to find a language where some rule or regularity affects p, t, and d but no other segment." Similarly, a recent textbook (Hayes, 2009, p. 43) says that "in most instances, the segments that undergo a rule or appear in the environment of a rule form a natural class in the language in question." The point is reiterated later (p. 71) with reference to the "pervasive tendency of phonological rules to apply to natural classes."

We want you to understand that in the approach we are presenting here, if a lan-

---

[3]This notion of the domain or universe of discourse was introduced in Unit 25.2. You might also want to refer back to the discussion in Unit (4.5) of how a given intensional definition can correspond to different extensionally defined sets depending on the circumstances—the extension of the set of Seymour's favorite letters can change from year to year, as Seymour's tastes change.

guage with a typical stop inventory, including say, *p, b, t, d, k*, and *g*, deletes just *p*, *t*, and *d* in some context, we are *not able* to formulate a single rule to capture all the deletions—our theory prevents us from seeing the data as containing "some rule" because of the mechanics of generalized intersection. We are proposing a theory of rules, so natural classes are part of rules by definition, not as a "pervasive tendency" that holds in "most instances."[4]

As we suggested above, the role of natural class reasoning is often implicit in phonological work, and sometimes very eloquently laid out, as in texts like Odden (2013, p. 159), which refers to the "central claim that rules operate in terms of natural classes (conjunctions of properties)," and Spencer (1996, p. 135), which says that the "concept of a natural class allows us to sharpen up what we mean by a phonological rule."

The strong position we are taking here is partly a matter of focus and rhetoric, but it draws us into a discussion of some high-level issues. By defining phonological rules as functions that have targets and environments characterized by generalized intersection, we are simultaneously making the claim that human phonology *cannot* contain rules that have targets or environments that are *not* characterized by generalized intersection. In other words, we are limiting the expressibility of our model in a way that mimics a limitation we hypothesize for the phonological faculty. UG not only gives the phonological faculty the *power* to use generalized intersection, but it *prevents* it from not doing so. As Chomsky (1980, p. 45) puts it, "there is an inseparable connection between the scope and limits of human knowledge."

This idea—that our innate endowment grants us capacities, but at the same time limits the way we parse, conceptualize, and "know" the world—is known as *epistemic boundedness* (Fodor, 1983). While our general conscious reasoning capacities allow us to imagine and formulate rules applying to random collections of segments, such a rule is beyond the scope of our phonological faculty. The "scope and limits" of phonological rules are determined by the UG-given feature inventory, and the manner in which natural classes are defined. These properties allow our grammars to have phonological rules and representations, but also determine the bounds on what is a possible grammar. Just as a human grammar cannot contain a rule that refers to the deletion of segments in positions corresponding to prime numbers, a human grammar also cannot contain a rule that is not encoded in terms of natural classes.

---

[4]In Unit 60 a relevant subtlety, related to rule ordering, is discussed. It does not appear to be the case, though it is possible, that such complications are what led to the hedging about the status of natural classes in rules mentioned above.

45.3   Properties and the 'is-a' Relation

When we characterize segments as sets of properties, we need to use set-theoretic
terms and say things like "*b* has P as a member." However, it is more consistent
with linguistic tradition, and also consistent with the way such issues are discussed
in theoretical computer science, to say that "*b* is P" or "*b* is a P segment." There is
nothing complicated here—we can say that a tall person *has* the property TALL or we
can say that the person *is* TALL. In formal discussion, the relation we are interested in
is the "is-a" relation, as opposed to the "has-a" relation, used to express, for example,
part-whole relations, like "A sentence *has a* subject." We won't worry too much about
this—informally a segment may be said to "*be* Q," where Q is a property, but in set-
theoretic terms this means that the segment has Q as a member. One reason this is
confusing is that the extension of a set potentially shrinks as the set of properties used
to characterize the members grows. We'll look at this later.

45.4   Rules Refer to Natural Classes

The symbol C doesn't seem to be doing any work for us at this point. This is because
we have discussed only consonants. C is useful when contrasted with V, which we will
attribute to all and only vowels. The importance of C is that it can be used to define a
natural class that is disjoint from vowels, and hence rules can target consonants without
affecting vowels. For example, consider the rule '[C] $\rightarrow \epsilon /$___%', that is, 'Delete any
segment that is a member of the natural class characterized by the set of properties {C}
(any segment that is a superset of {C}), if that segment occurs at the end of a word'.
We will introduce a new notation for properties, but the symbol C is common in the
literature. Here are two things to keep in mind when you encounter rules using C and
V to stand for consonants and vowels, respectively.

Rule targets are sets of segments.   In most sources, the symbols C and V will not
occur in square brackets in a rule. This is a good time to review how our notation
differs from most sources. A rule that we would write as in (435a) will more typically
be written as in (435b):

(435)   Notational differences

    (a)   [C] $\rightarrow \epsilon /$___%

    (b)   C $\rightarrow \emptyset /$___#

We distinguish the word-final symbol from the word-initial symbol (for reasons that we have not made clear). For the empy segment symbol, we use 'ϵ' instead '$\emptyset$';[5] and we enclose the specification of our target in square brackets to show that it represents a set of segments.[6]

Variables are assigned a single value at a time. You might come across rules with environments like this: C___ C. The normal interpretation of this is 'between consonants', but there is a slight problem with this notation. It uses the symbol C as a variable whose domain is the set of consonants. However, in mathematical and logical expressions it is normal that the value assigned to a variable be unique when an expression is interpreted. So, if the variable x has the integers as its domain, then we can plug in an integer value for x in an expression like $y = 3x^2 + 2x + 4$. We can let $x = 7$ and compute the y-value: $y=3 \cdot (7^2) + 2 \cdot 7 + 4= 165$. We can't put in different values for the two occurrences of x. However, this is exactly what the traditional phonological notation can do—the environment refers to a position between any two consonants, not between identical consonants. Since we have been clear about the set-theoretic interpretation of our notation [C], it is not subject to the same lack of precision. In our notation the environment [C] ___ [C] means 'between any segment $x \supseteq \{C\}$ and any segment $y \supseteq \{C\}$'. The two segments, x and y might be, but don't have to be, identical.

Before we move on, note that we appear to need rules that *change* the properties of segments. For example, the Russian data we examined first suggested a rule like this: 'If a segment occurs at the end of a word and contains C and D as properties, then change the D to T'. We then introduced the idea of vacuous application as a way to simplify rules, ending up with something like 'If a segment occurs at the end of a word and contains C as a property, then make sure it has T as a property (and get rid of D, if necessary)'. We will soon see an alternative to allowing such rules. In brief we will use a sequence of two rules—delete D, and then insert T.

---

[5]Recall that we reserved $\emptyset$ for set theory, and we used a slight variant $\varnothing$ for phonologically null morphemes.

[6]The careful reader may be wondering if 'ϵ' is just the empty segment-set, a segment with no properties. It is not. It is the absence of a segment. See Bale et al. (2016) for discussion.

Exercises

45.1. Suppose that $\mathcal{A}$ is a set of sets: $\mathcal{A} = \Big\{ \{a, b, c\}, \{a, c, d\}, \{a, d, e\} \Big\}$

- What is $\bigcap \mathcal{A}$?
- What is $\bigcup \mathcal{A}$?

45.2. Suppose that $\mathcal{B}$ is a set of sets: $\mathcal{B} = \Big\{ \{a, b\}, \{c, d\}, \{e, f\} \Big\}$

- What is $\bigcap \mathcal{B}$?
- What is $\bigcup \mathcal{B}$?

Unit 46

A Binary Model of Segment Properties

In this unit, we'll introduce a slightly more complex model of the properties that segments (as sets) contain. The model we are developing proposes the existence of an innate, universal set of properties that can characterize human phonological segments. In fact, we adopt the position, recently under attack even by some generative phonologists, that it is a logical necessity that such a set of primitive mental building blocks exist (Hale and Reiss, 2003; Reiss, 2017b). The properties relate, via complex transduction processes, to phonetic substance—the details of articulation and speech perception. These properties are examples of what Chomsky (1965, p. 28) in *Aspects of the Theory of Syntax* calls *substantive universals*:

> It is useful to classify linguistic universals as *formal* or *substantive*. A theory of substantive universals claims that items of a particular kind in any language must be drawn from a fixed class of items. For example, Jakobson's [e.g., Jakobson et al. (1967)] theory of distinctive features can be interpreted as making an assertion about substantive universals with respect to the phonological component of a generative grammar. It asserts that each output of this component consists of elements that are characterized in terms of some small number of fixed, universal, phonetic features (perhaps on the order of fifteen or twenty), each of which has a substantive acoustic-articulatory characterization independent of any particular language.

...Substantive universals such as these concern the vocabulary for the description of language; formal universals involve rather the character of the rules that appear in grammars and the ways in which they can be interconnected.

In phonology, a formal universal would be the discovery that the phonology of all languages is a complex function—the composition of a strictly ordered set of rules of some well-defined class, or some alternative computational system. When we used segment-based rules, we assumed (contrary to what we now know) that the environment of all phonological rules was limited to the immediate left and immediate right of a target segment. That is, we adopted this three-position window as a formal universal of phonological processes, but then ultimately rejected it once we considered more complex phenomena like vowel harmony in Finnish in Unit 39.4.

In this unit we develop a model of the features Chomsky mentions that differs a bit from the properties we introduced above. The model is derived from the tradition of Jakobson and others, most notably Morris Halle, Chomsky's collaborator and by far the most important figure in the study of phonology as a cognitive science.

One point of potential disagreement with the quotation above is that we find no reason to believe that we can estimate the number of features needed for a universal phonological model to be around fifteen or twenty. If one assumes a small number of features, then it is probably necessary to assume that there are language-specific rules of phonetic implementation. Hale et al. (2007) take the position that it is more elegant to assume that UG provides *more* features, with a universal system of phonetic transduction between, say, feature representations and instructions to the articulatory system. On the other hand, we will also argue that there are reasons for thinking that the issue of how many features there are is of minor interest, because the combinatorics of even very small feature systems leads inevitably to astronomic combinatoric explosion—and this is a good thing! We will discuss this further in Unit 61.

Since we have no confidence in typical estimates of the *number* of features provided by UG, we have no idea what the *correct* features are. Our goals are, therefore, to teach you about the logic of reasoning with features, ideas that are meant to be flexible enough to generalize—not only to any number of features, but also to some extent to other systems of features than the one we present.

Earlier we noted a relationship between the properties T (voiceless) and D (voiced), namely that the two properties cannot belong to one and the same segment.[1] Before,

---

[1] We will just remind you here that any such description must be understood in terms of the relationship between mental representations and behavior. No two utterances, even two tokens of the same word spoken by the same person can have the exact same amount of vocal vibration on a given segment. Furthermore,

we merely stipulated that the two properties could not co-occur. However, we could also build such stipulation into the representational system itself. There are at least two ways of doing this:

Option 1:   Maybe we do not need to posit both T and D as substantive universals. Maybe only one exists. Let's arbitrarily propose that only D exists, and that some segments have the property D, whereas others lack D. For clarity, let's rename D "VOICED."

Option 2:   Instead of the properties T and D, there exists a single attribute VOICED, which combines with two different values. We could call these values '1' and '0' or anything else, but we'll stick with tradition and use '+' and '−'. Some segments have the *ordered pair* $< +, $ VOICED $>$ as a member and others have $< -, $ VOICED $>$, but a segment cannot have both. Following notational tradition in phonology, we will denote these ordered pairs without a comma or angle brackets: $+$VOICED and $-$VOICED.

You might feel like these two options are equivalent—in Option 1, we have segments that have the property VOICED and segments that don't; in Option 2, we have segments that have the property $+$VOICED and others with the property $-$VOICED. However, there is an important difference between the expressive power of the two systems. Option 1 is sometimes called a *privative* system, since a representation, a segment, either has or is de*prived* of a property. Option 2 is typically called a *binary*, or two-valued system, since a property like VOICED combines with one of two values in segments. Let us compare the logic of privative and binary systems. To do so, we will used the property VOICED and one other property. For now, it does not matter what that other property is or whether it is privative or binary. For simplicity, let's use the C and V properties introduced above.

Recall our definition of natural classes in (426) repeated in (436):

(436)   **Natural Classes:** Suppose a language λ contains all and only the segments in a set S. N is a *natural class* of λ if and only if there exists a set of properties G such $N = \{ n : n \in S \text{ and } n \supseteq G \}$.

In both Option 1 and Option 2, the representation [C] denotes the natural class of consonants (which contains no vowels, since C and V are incompatible, by hypothesis).

---

the amount or duration of voicing on, say, a *b* will not be on average the same as on a *g*, even if the two are produced at the same speaking rate. You are used to this kind of abstraction by now, and can see that the properties under discussion are mental symbols with complex relations to behavior.

Consider a *more* specified, and thus *smaller*, natural class under Option 2 specified as
[C, +VOICED]. This represents the class of segments that are supersets of the set {C,
+VOICED}—namely the set of voiced consonants. A different natural class is charac-
terized by the representation [C, −VOICED], namely the set of voiceless consonants.

Turning back to Option 1, we can again characterize the voiced consonants, in this
case by using the representation [C, VOICED]. Since the property VOICED is privative
in Option 1, there is no plus or minus value associated with VOICED. So far, Option
1 looks just like Option 2—both can characterize the set of voiced consonants as a
natural class. However, let's now try to use the privative system to refer to voiceless
consonants. There is no voiceless feature, so the best we could do is the following:
[C]. There are a couple of problems with this representation—the first is that it is
identical to what we used to refer to the set of *all* consonants above. So, this is a really
bad system if the same notation sometimes means "all the consonants" and sometimes
means "all the consonants that are not voiced." A related problem is that if we interpret
the absence of a feature here to mean "obligatorily absent," then we have introduced
two meanings for absence.

Once again, let's use some of the properties introduced above: P, K, F. If we
use [C] to mean "all the consonants lacking voicing," we are treating the absence of
D=VOICED differently from the absence of P, K or F. The absence of these properties
P, K, and F in '[C]' means "the presence of any of P, K, and F combined with C is
okay—we want *all* the segments that are supersets of {C}... except the ones that contain D=VOICED." So, D is obligatorily absent, whereas, say, P, may be present (as in
p) or absent (as in *k*).

These logical considerations lead us to reject privative properties and adopt the binary system of Option 2. Several issues remain to be explored, but we merely mention
them here.

• One might argue that, in fact, there are no rules, either attested or even possible
  for human phonology, that require reference to, say, −VOICED. In other words,
  there are rules that refer to all the consonants, and rules that refer to voiced
  consonants, but no rules that refer to just voiceless consonants. Hence, we can't
  refer to that natural class, and that is a good result. We will offer arguments later
  that this line of reasoning will fail empirically.

• We have argued against privative properties but not against multi-valued non-
  binary properties with, say, three or four values. In this book, we will *assume*
  that the representational system is uniform, and that all properties are binary.
  Each property can occur with a value '+' or '−'.

The common term in phonology for the properties that constitute segments is *features*. The term *feature* is used in a systematically ambiguous fashion. Sometime we refer to, say, the attribute VOICED as a feature, and sometimes we refer to the ordered pair of a value and an attribute, like −VOICED, as a feature. On the rare occasions that we need to make this distinction, we will call the ordered pairs like −VOICED *valued features*, but sometimes we will be sloppy in the traditional manner.

Unit 47

The Features We'll Use

> Mechanical and other detached methods of studying the phonetic elements
> of speech are, of course, of considerable value, but they have sometimes the
> undesirable effect of obscuring the essential facts of speech-sound
> psychology.

Edward Sapir, "Sound Patterns in Language"

We turn now to an illustration of a particular binary feature system and an exploration
of some of its properties. The feature inventory we will develop is similar to that found
in many phonology books, but you should always be on the lookout for the idiosyncracies of the system used in a particular resource. It is a topic of current research to
discover the correct set of features, and there is no question that the account offered
here is simplistic in many ways. However, our main concern is to teach some basic
feature logic, rather than to argue for a particular set of features. Another difficult
question, beyond our scope, is the relationship between articulatory gestures and features, and between acoustic traits and features. We will simply adopt one traditional
view that assigns primarily articulation-based names to the features, and leave these
very important issues aside. Strictly speaking, this issue is not part of phonology but
rather belongs to branches of phonetics and speech processing. From the perspective
of the phonology, features are just abstract symbols, neither acoustic nor articulatory.[1]

---

[1] If you crave a more concrete sense of what this means in terms of the brain, read the discussion of
symbols in Gallistel and King (2009).

407

We will assume that there is a single set of features that is used to characterize all segments, but that typically a certain subset of features is most relevant to distinguishing vowels and another set is most relevant to distinguishing consonants. For example, while some languages do have voiceless vowels, the feature VOICED more generally distinguishes among classes of consonants, so we won't include this feature in our discussion of vowels. This is just a matter of expository convenience.

47.1   Vowels

It is necessary to refer to the features with a name, and generative linguists usually use names based on somewhat reliable articulatory correlates of the features. However, the features are actually abstract mental entities that relate via transduction processes to complex articulatory and acoustic correlates (Poeppel and Idsardi, 2011; Volenec and Reiss, 2018). The grammar itself has no direct access to the acoustic or articulatory correlates of features. In this section, we introduce some of the features commonly associated with vowels. The features commonly associated with consonants will be discussed in the following section.

Syllabicity.   In our binary system, the V property used above corresponds to a feature SYLLABIC (SYLL). Vowels and syllabic consonants like the *l̩* and *n̩* in the final syllables of *bottle* and *button* are all +SYLLABIC. Typical consonants are −SYLLABIC. Some scholars do without this feature and instead refer only to syllable structure position. In other words, a syllabic *l̩* is a segment with a given set of features appearing in a syllable nucleus, whereas a "regular" consonantal *l* is the same set of features occurring in an onset or coda position.

Height.   From an articulatory point of view, vowel height corresponds approximately to the height of the tongue when the vowel is articulated. From an acoustic point of view, the higher the vowel, the lower the frequency of the first formant, in general. Since tongue height and formant frequency vary continuously, there would appear to be a potentially infinite range of vowel heights, or maybe as many as our auditory system can distinguish. Phonologically, however, it seems that vowels fall into three groups—there are three phonological equivalence classes imposed on the phonetics. These three categories are referred to as high, mid, and low vowels, and the three-way contrast is represented using a pair of binary features, HIGH (HI) and LOW (LO), as illustrated by the North American English words in (437):[2]

(437)   Vowel height in North American English

- {+HIGH, −LOW}: *i, ɪ, u, ʊ,* as in *beet, bit, boot, put*

- {−HIGH, −LOW}: *e, ɛ, ə, o, ɔ* as in *bait, bet, but, boat, bought*

- {−HIGH, +LOW}: *æ, a/ɑ* as in *bat, pot*

Given the phonetic interpretation of the features, the combination {+HIGH, +LOW} appears to be impossible. We will just accept this as an accidental property of the input and output transduction systems (speech perception and speech articulation) and continue working with a binary model. In other words, we might assume that a neuroscientist of the future could encode a vowel that is {+HIGH, +LOW} in the neural representation of a morpheme's phonology, but barring such a scenario, such vowels will never be attested. This is not a fact about grammar under our view.

Front-Back.   Phonetically, there are front, central, and back vowels, and within each category, there are finer distinctions—*i* is pronounced with the tongue further fronted than *ɛ*, for example. Phonology seems to ignore these distinctions, and appears to put vowels into just two categories that we will represent by +BACK and −BACK (±BK).[3] Note that we could just as well use FRONT, but we follow tradition in generative phonology in using BACK. The central vowels pattern with the back ones—they form a natural class with them—so this is how our inventory comes out:

(438)   Front and back vowels in North American English

- +BACK: *u, ʊ, ə, o, ɔ, a* as in *boot, put, but, boat, bought, pot*

- −BACK: *i, ɪ, e, ɛ, æ* as in *beet, bit, bait, bet, bat*

---

[2]The transcriptions here may disagree with what you find elsewhere due to dialect variation, to idiosyncracies of our choices, and to systematic simplifications, such as not transcribing the vowels of *bait* and *boat* as dipthongs, which they certainly are, phonetically. Other sources on basic phonetics and phonology will provide a much richer discussion of English vowel systems. A particularly egregious example of our disregard for IPA conventions is our failure to distinguish *a* from *ɑ*. We use the symbols interchangeably to denote something like the vowel of *pot*, which does not rhyme with *bought* in the Brooklyn, New York, dialect that one of us speaks. Our reasons are mostly practical, especially in light of the fact that the two symbols correspond to each other across various fonts, and in teaching, we inevitably end up carelessly mixing the symbols together in homework and exam problems.

[3]This is a standard view, but as we have suggested, there are lots of complications and lots of reasons to think that there might be more distinctions than typically recognized. The high vowels of Swedish and Norwegian are a particularly well-known problem for the limited set of features typically used by phonologists.

Although we are assuming no phonological contrast between back and central vowels, you should be aware that such distinctions exist phonetically. This is a good time to remind yourself that *central* means 'between front and back', whereas *mid* means 'between high and low'.

Rounding. Some vowels are pronounced with the lips rounded, denoted +ROUND (+RD), whereas others have the lips either in a neutral position or spread, denoted −ROUND. The symbols we typically use for English fall into these categories:

(439)   Round and unround vowels of North American English

- +ROUND: *u, ʊ, o, ɔ* as in *boot, put, boat, bought*

- −ROUND: *i, ɪ, e, ɛ, ə, æ, a* as in *beet, bit, bait, bet, but, bat, pot*

We are being a little evasive here because the facts are confusing. The symbol *ʊ* is typically said to represent a high, back, rounded, lax vowel; and it is typically used to represent the vowel of North American English *good*. However, in many dialects, the vowel in this word is not rounded,[4] whereas in British dialects it typically is. Ideally, we would want a single IPA symbol to correspond to a single set of features, regardless of the language under discussion. However, in practice, the symbols are used to denote a range of potentially distinct articulations.

Tense/Lax or ATR. In various languages, the mid and high vowels divide into two groups as follows: *i, u, e, o* versus *ɪ, ʊ, ɛ, ɔ, ə*. The first group is sometimes referred to as the tense vowels and the second group as the lax vowels. In more recent work, the tense/lax distinction is typically expressed with the feature ATR, an abbreviation for *advanced tongue root*, which suggests one of the articulatory correlates of the tense/lax distinction. Tense vowels are +ATR and lax vowels are −ATR.

It may help you to think about the fact that the tense vowels tend to appear in North American English with an off-glide: *ij, uw, ej, ow*, whereas the lax ones do not. In addition, the lax vowels, except ə, cannot end a word in North American English.[5] We'll assume that the low vowels are all −ATR:

---

[4]Despite the fact that many sources claim either that all non-low back vowels of English are +RD or that "markedness" considerations guarantee that a language won't have a back unrounded vowel without having its rounded counterpart in its inventory.

[5]At least this is what the books say. In fact, one of us has the vowel of [dæd] *dad* in his native version of this word, [dæ]. Also, given that *meh*, pronounced [mɛ] is a word for many speakers, we have evidence that a putative "ban" on final lax vowels is not a synchronic principle of grammar in at least some dialects in North America. Of course, the approach to phonology we are developing has no "bans" of any kind.

(440)   Tense vs. lax vowels of North American English

- +ATR: *i, u, e, o* as in *beet, boot, bait, boat*

- −ATR: ɪ, ʊ, ɛ, ɔ, ə, æ, a as in *bit, put, bet, bought, but, bat, pot*

Vowels can be specified with other features besides those we have given so far. For example, they can also contain specification for the features related to nasality or breathy voice. French has a distinction between a nasal vowel in [lõ] *long* 'long' and the non-nasal vowel in [lo] *lot* 'prize'. Since this book does not attempt an exhaustive catalog of the features provided by UG, we will introduce features relevant to a particular dataset as necessary. However, the following chart of vowel features, which includes some vowels that don't appear in English, will be useful for reference:

(441)   Chart of common vowel features

	i	y	ɪ	ʏ	e	ø	ɛ	œ	æ	ɑ	ə	ɔ	o	ʊ	ɨ	u
HIGH	+	+	+	+	−	−	−	−	−	−	−	−	−	+	+	+
LOW	−	−	−	−	−	−	−	−	+	+	−	−	−	−	−	−
BK	−	−	−	−	−	−	−	−	+	+	+	+	+	+	+	+
RND	−	+	−	+	−	+	−	+	−	−	−	+	+	+	−	+
ATR	+	+	−	−	+	+	−	−	−	−	−	−	+	−	+	+

So, the symbol *i*, for example, is just an abbreviation for the set {+HIGH, −LOW, −BACK, −ROUND, +ATR}.

As we pointed out in Unit 44, typical phonological notation does not distinguish between sets of features and natural class descriptions, which are sets of sets of features. In (442a), we see the features of the segment *i* in set braces. Note that we forgo commas when set elements are listed vertically.

This representation of a single segment is to be contrasted with something like (442b), which represents a natural class of segments, each of which is a superset of the set in (442a). Given the English inventory we just presented, this natural class has just one member, namely *i*. If we make the description less specific, as in (442c), we describe a natural class that contains both of the non-low, tense, unrounded front vowels, *i* and *e*.

(442)   Curly versus square brackets with valued features

segment i	natural class of just i	natural class of just i and e
a. $\left\{\begin{array}{l}+\text{SYLLABIC} \\ +\text{HIGH} \\ -\text{LOW} \\ -\text{BACK} \\ -\text{ROUND} \\ +\text{ATR}\end{array}\right\}$	b. $\left[\begin{array}{l}+\text{SYLLABIC} \\ +\text{HIGH} \\ -\text{LOW} \\ -\text{BACK} \\ -\text{ROUND} \\ +\text{ATR}\end{array}\right]$	c. $\left[\begin{array}{l}+\text{SYLLABIC} \\ -\text{LOW} \\ -\text{BACK} \\ -\text{ROUND} \\ +\text{ATR}\end{array}\right]$

We reiterate here that our distinction between curly and square brackets is not at all standard. In fact, curly brackets in phonology traditionally have a very different interpretation, namely *disjunction*, which is a fancy name for the meaning of the word *or*. For example, the rule in (443), in traditional generative phonology literature would be interpreted as 'change *g* to *k* if it follows a consonant or a word boundary':

(443)   Traditional use of brackets for disjunction:

$$g \to k \ / \left\{\begin{array}{c} -\text{SYLLABIC} \\ \# \end{array}\right\} \underline{}$$

Contrary to the actual rule system in Chomsky and Halle's book *The Sound Pattern of English*, we do not admit disjunction in our segment-based SPE system or any of our revisions of that system. Intuitively, the parts of *our* rules (target and environment) reflect natural classes of strings and segments, which are related to set intersections and the logical operator AND (and the word *and*). In contrast, the word *or* and its logical meaning OR are related to set-theoretic union, which does not relate to natural classes, but rather to arbitrary collections of elements.

47.2   Consonants

We now turn to features that most commonly figure in discussion of consonants.

Consonant constriction.   The most recognizable phonetic correlate of CONSONANTAL (CONS) is a constriction of the vocal tract that is significant in both degree and duration. Stops like *p, b, t, d, k, g* as in *pig, big, tie, dye, code, goad* have a full blockage of airflow at some point in the oral tract between the glottis and the lips. Other +CONS segments have a lesser degree of closure, some of which we'll discuss below.

A glide like *j* or *w* as in *year, wear* doesn't have enough of a constriction to count as a +CONS, and a flap or tap *ɾ*, as in American English *figh*[ɾ]*ing*, has a constriction that is too short, so these segments are −CONS, like vowels.[6] Sometimes CONSONANTAL is combined with SYLLABIC to distinguish glides or semi-vowels like *j* or *w* from other consonants. The semi-vowels are −CONSONANTAL and −SYLLABIC, whereas the other consonants are +CONSONANTAL and −SYLLABIC. Vowels are, of course, −CONSONANTAL and +SYLLABIC. The fourth logical possibility, the combination of +CONSONANTAL and +SYLLABIC is used by some authors to characterize syllabic consonants, like the syllabic [ɳ] at the end of *button* or the syllabic [l̩] at the end of *bottle*. Alternatively, the combination may be considered articulatorily impossible, and the syllabic consonants can be treated as −CONSONANTAL. As already mentioned, in some work, the feature SYLLABIC is not used—a glide like *j* and a vowel like *i* are distinguished merely on the basis of their syllable structure position. More accurately, since the segments don't exist as entities in the model anymore, these symbols abbreviate both a set of features and a syllable structure position.

Sonority. We misled you about Russian devoicing. It is not the case that *all* consonants undergo devoicing at the end of a word. The stops, affricates, and fricatives do so, but not sonorants like the nasals *m* and *n* or the segments *r* and *l*, which are characterized as +SONORANT (+SON). Because of the lack of a significant obstruction in airflow, nasals and approximants do not involve the big differences in air pressure inside versus outside the mouth that we see in stops, affricates, and fricatives. Stops, affricates, and fricatives, known as obstruents, are −SON. Vowels and glides, which also do not involve significant obstructions to airflow, are +SON.

Continuancy. Segments involving uninterrupted airflow through the oral tract are +CONTINUANT (+CONT). These include fricative consonants, like *f, v, θ, ð, s, z, ʃ, ʒ* as in *fine, vine, thin, this, sink, zinc, masher, measure*, and glides and *r*-type segments. Vowels are also +CONTINUANT. Stops and affricates are unsurprisingly −CONTINUANT, but nasals are also −CONTINUANT. This is because they involve blocking airflow *through the mouth* and diverting it through the nasal passage. Trills, taps, and flaps are sometimes argued to be +CONTINUANT.

---

[6] Despite the reasonable-sounding phonetic explanations we are offering, the featural analysis of segments is more typically decided on the basis of phonological patterning. In other words, we assume that the flap is −CONS because doing so yields more coherent phonological analyses (because the flap tends to pattern with other −CONS segments). Consistent phonetic correlates of features are notoriously difficult to identify. Philosopher Irene Appelbaum (1996) discusses this tenacious problem of *the lack of invariance*.

Nasality.   Segments that involve lowering the velum so that air passes through the nasal cavity and out the nose are +NASAL (+NAS). In English the +NAS segments are *m,n,ŋ*, the segments at the end of *swim, sin, sing.* The other consonants of English are −NAS. Many languages, such as French, have some vowels that are +NAS, but if no value is listed, a vowel is typically assumed to be −NAS.

Lateral.   The feature LATERAL (LAT) characterizes segments that involve airflow along at least one side of the tongue. English is typically described as having one +LAT, *l*, with variants that depend on syllable structure position. In codas, English *l* is typically described as back, velarized, or dark *ł*, which are equivalent terms related to the raising of the back of the tongue in the lateral pronounced in coda position. You can breathe in while you hold your tongue in the position for *l* and feel airflow along one or both sides, whereas the center of the tongue blocks airflow.

From lips to alveolar ridge.   The initial segment of *lock* has the front of the tongue, not the very tip, but the "blade," raised to the alveolar ridge, just behind the top front teeth. Any segment articulated at or in front of the alveolar ridge is +ANTERIOR (+ANT). This includes consonants with a primary restriction at the lips like *p, b, m, f, v*, as in *pie, buy, my, fie, vie.* It also includes interdentals like *θ, ð* and alveolars like *t, d, s, z* as in *thigh, thy, tie, dye, sink, zinc.* The front *l* that occurs in onsets in English is clearly +ANTERIOR, but it is not so clear whether the dark, velarized *ł* in codas always involves the tongue approaching the alveolar ridge.

   The segments *θ, ð, t, d, s, z* are also characterized as +CORONAL (+COR), because the consonant obstruction is made with the front part of the tongue, called the *corona* (Latin for 'crown'). Other +COR segments are *ʃ, ʒ, tʃ, dʒ*, sometimes transcribed as *š, ž, č, ǰ* respectively, as in *masher, measure, choke, joke* but these are articulated behind the alveolar ridge, so they are −ANT.

   Consonant segments that involve some level of obstruction at the lips are +LABIAL (+LAB). In English, these include *p, b, m, f, v.* Sometimes, LAB is collapsed with ROUND, but it may be necessary to distinguish the two, and in fact, there may be segments that are both +RD and +LAB in some languages. The labiovelar glide *w* is also +LAB (and +RD).

Fricatives.   Segments that are both −SON and +CONT are traditionally known as fricatives. The fricatives of English are *f, v, θ, ð, s, z, ʃ, ʒ.* The labiodental fricatives *f, v* are +LAB, −COR, while the others are −LAB, +COR.

Affricates.   The traditional category *affricate* is typically defined as a single segment consisting of a stop followed by a *homorganic* fricative part. There are various ways of arguing that, say, [atʃa] and [atʃa] are different, based on the duration of the parts or the effects on surrounding segments. The requirement that the parts be homorganic is problematic, partly for notational reasons. For example, in English *tʃ*, the symbol *t* in fact denotes a −ANT stop, at the same point of articulation as the *ʃ*, unlike the +ANT stop *t*. Many sources use the valued feature +DELAYEDRELEASE (+DELREL) to characterize all and only the affricates. Other treatments of affricates parallel the treatment of contour tones (rising and falling) introduced in Unit 38, but this topic is beyond our scope.

Further back in the mouth.   Segments that involve raising the back of the tongue to the velum are sometimes called *dorsal*, which refers to the mid, top surface of the tongue, or else *velar*, referring to the part of the top of the mouth that the dorsum approaches when it raises. We'll use +DORSAL (+DORS) for *k, g, ŋ*, as in *pick, pig, ping*. Since the dorsum can also raise up to the palate, we'll further specify these as +BACK (+BK), using the same feature we introduced for vowels. A consonant that is +DORS and −BK is what is typically called *palatal*. The glide *j* of *yes* and *you* is the only palatal of English.

Glottal.   Two consonants of English have their greatest obstruction down in the glottis, with a fairly open oral tract from above the glottis to the lips. One of these is the glottal stop *ʔ* which shows up as a segment derived from *t* in some positions: compare the (North American) pronunciation of *cat* in *I saw a ca*[ʔ] and *I saw two ca*[t]*s*. The glottal stop may also be present in the phonological representation of morphemes like *button* [bəʔn̩], in some dialects. The other glottal segment of English is *h*, a glottal fricative, as in *hat*. The segments *ʔ, h* are +GLOTTAL (+GLOT). Some of the values of the other features of glottals are easily deduced. For example, the primary vocal tract constriction for glottals is at the glottis, so they are −LAB, −ANT, −COR. Other feature values are not so obvious, so use the chart below as a guide.

As we pointed out in Unit 3, when you pronounce English words beginning with *h*, the articulation of the *h* differs greatly in, say, *hip* as opposed to *hop*, which we would probably transcribe as [hɪp] and [hɑp], respectively. From a phonetic perspective, the *h* in each word has the same articulation as a voiceless version of the following vowel, and so, an equally good phonetic transcription might be [ɪ̥p] and [ɑ̥p]. This example provides a good illustration of the fact that the "relation between a phonemic system and the phonetic record . . . is remote and complex" (Chomsky, 1964, p. 38). Neither segments nor rules are directly observable. They are instead the outcome of an analysis (by linguist or learner) in which the "essential properties underlie the surface form" (Katz and Bever, 1976, p. 12). We favor the transcriptions with [h] because the words pattern with other consonant-initial words, for example in the form of a preceding article: *a cat, a hip,* **an** *emu, a hop,* **an** *uncle*.

Voicing. We introduced the feature VOICED (VOI) earlier. Typically, this feature distinguishes only among obstruents, but there are cases of voiceless sonorants, even voiceless vowels, in some languages. As an example of the complex relationship between feature values and articulation, note that both *h* and *ʔ* are −VOI, but for very different reasons. In *ʔ* the vocal folds are held so tightly together that no air passes between them and they do not vibrate; in *h*, the folds are held so far apart that the air flows freely, and there is no opening and closing of the glottis. In voiced fricatives like *z* the vocal folds vibrate throughout the articulation of the segment,[7] but in a voiced stop like *d*, the voicing may cease during closure and the correlate of +VOI is the relatively fast restarting of vocal vibration after the closure release in comparison with the relatively slow restarting in a voiceless segment like *t*. You can learn more about this phenomenon of *voice onset time*, which involves voicing and aspiration, in a phonetics book.

Stridency. Some of the segments we need to distinguish differ slightly in their place of articulation, but phonological behavior across languages has led phonologists to encode these distinctions along a different dimension. For example, using features we have seen so far, there is no way to distinguish a voiced labiodental fricative like *v* from a voiced labial fricative *β* found in many languages, including Spanish. Instead of distinguishing these two places of articulation, the feature STRIDENT (STRID) is used. The labio-dental *v* and its voiceless counterpart *f* are +STRID, whereas the labial fricatives *β* and *ɸ* are −STRID. The labio-dentals involve more turbulent airflow and are louder than the labials. The interdentals *θ, ð* are −STRID, which distinguishes them from the otherwise featurally identical +STRID *s, z*. Despite the fact that *s, z* and *ʃ, ʒ* differ with respect to the feature ANT, these fricatives can be grouped together as the English fricatives that are +COR and +STRID.

A summary of the previous discussion of consonant features is provided in Table 47.1, below. This table will prove useful as we proceed; however, our main goal is to allow you to learn to manipulate and learn the logic of some feature system—we do

[7]Well, that's what you would expect, but English 'z' is often partially voiceless. We did warn you that the correlation of features to speech is complex.

not pretend to have discovered the "correct" inventory that our genes provide as part of universal grammar.

	p	t	k	b	d	g	f	v	θ	ð	s	z	ʃ	ʒ	h	ʔ	m	n	ŋ	r	ɹ	l	j	w	tʃ	dʒ
CONSONANTAL	+	+	+	+	+	+	+	+	+	+	+	+	+	+	−	−	+	+	+	−	+	+	−	−	+	+
SONORANT	−	−	−	−	−	−	−	−	−	−	−	−	−	−	−	−	+	+	+	+	+	+	+	+	−	−
CONTINUANT	−	−	−	−	−	−	+	+	+	+	+	+	+	+	+	−	−	−	−	+	+	−	+	+	−	−
NASAL	−	−	−	−	−	−	−	−	−	−	−	−	−	−	−	−	+	+	+	−	−	−	−	−	−	−
LATERAL	−	−	−	−	−	−	−	−	−	−	−	−	−	−	−	−	−	−	−	−	−	+	−	−	−	−
ANTERIOR	+	+	−	+	+	−	+	+	+	+	+	+	−	−	−	−	+	+	−	+	−	+	−	−	−	−
CORONAL	−	+	−	−	+	−	−	−	+	+	+	+	+	+	−	−	−	+	−	+	+	+	−	−	+	+
LABIAL	+	−	−	+	−	−	+	+	−	−	−	−	−	−	−	−	+	−	−	−	−	−	−	+	−	−
DELAYED REL	−	−	−	−	−	−	−	−	−	−	−	−	−	−	−	−	−	−	−	−	−	−	−	−	+	+
DORSAL	−	−	+	−	−	+	−	−	−	−	−	−	−	−	−	−	−	−	+	−	−	−	+	+	−	−
GLOTTAL	−	−	−	−	−	−	−	−	−	−	−	−	−	−	+	+	−	−	−	−	−	−	−	−	−	−
VOICED	−	−	−	+	+	+	−	+	−	+	−	+	−	+	−	−	+	+	+	+	+	+	+	+	−	+
STRIDENT	−	−	−	−	−	−	+	+	−	−	+	+	+	+	−	−	−	−	−	−	−	−	−	−	+	+

Table 47.1 Some feature values for common consonants.

Unit 48

Natural Classes with Features

48.1 Rules with Natural Classes of Features

In Unit 43.2, we discussed a language that we called Zafonian. In this language, there was evidence that underlying /o/ became [u] before the nasal consonants. The critical dataset is repeated below.

(444) Zafonian again

N	w/ N	to N	for N	after N	under N	before N	w/o N	gloss
lu	luk	lus	lur	lun	lum	luŋ	lud	'cat'
lo	lok	los	lor	lun	lum	luŋ	lod	'rat'

In our previous discussion we wrote three rules for the *o/u* alternation:

(445) A rule for each nasal

- o → u / ___ m
- o → u / ___ n
- o → u / ___ ŋ

We then discussed the possibility of collapsing these into a single rule by defining the environment in terms of a natural class, the class of nasal consonants in the language. Now we know that we can get this class by taking the generalized intersection of the set of segments {m,n,ŋ}

419

(446) Generalized intersection of the Zafonian nasals

$$
\bigcap \left\{
\begin{array}{c}
\text{m} \\
\left\{
\begin{array}{l}
+\text{Son} \\
-\text{Cont} \\
+\text{Voi} \\
+\text{Ant} \\
+\text{Lab} \\
-\text{Cor} \\
+\text{Nas} \\
\ldots
\end{array}
\right\}
\end{array}
,
\begin{array}{c}
\text{n} \\
\left\{
\begin{array}{l}
+\text{Son} \\
-\text{Cont} \\
+\text{Voi} \\
+\text{Ant} \\
-\text{Lab} \\
+\text{Cor} \\
+\text{Nas} \\
\ldots
\end{array}
\right\}
\end{array}
,
\begin{array}{c}
\text{ŋ} \\
\left\{
\begin{array}{l}
+\text{Son} \\
-\text{Cont} \\
+\text{Voi} \\
-\text{Ant} \\
-\text{Lab} \\
-\text{Cor} \\
+\text{Nas} \\
\ldots
\end{array}
\right\}
\end{array}
\right\}
=
\left\{
\begin{array}{l}
+\text{Son} \\
-\text{Cont} \\
+\text{Voi} \\
+\text{Nas} \\
\ldots
\end{array}
\right\}
$$

We'll assume that these are the only nasal segments in the language and so, we can dispense with the other features, at least for expository purposes. The natural class that defines the environments of the rule is $\{x : x \supseteq \{+\text{Nas}\}\}$, which we abbreviate with square brackets thus: [+Nasal].

Now consider the following extended paradigm of Zafonian:

(447) Yet more Zafonian

N	w/ N	to N	for N	after N	under N	before N	w/o N	gloss
lu	luk	lus	lur	lun	lum	luŋ	lud	'cat'
lo	lok	los	lor	lun	lum	luŋ	lod	'rat'
li	lik	lis	lir	lin	lim	liŋ	lid	'squat'
le	lek	les	ler	lin	lim	liŋ	led	'knot'
læ	læk	læs	lær	læn	læm	læŋ	læd	'robot'

Notice that in our extended Zafonian dataset there is another set of alternations, involving [e] and [i]. You can see that the rule must involve 'e → i before a nasal', so we tentatively have two rules:

(448) Parallel rules for *o* and *e* in Zafonian

- o → u / ___[+Nasal]

- e → i / ___[+Nasal]

You can see that the change from /o/ to [u] replaces the value −High with +High, and that the change from /e/ to [i] does the same. So, the rules involve identical changes. Finally, note that Zafonian appears to have only five vowels *i, e, a, o, u*, and the two vowels that are targets of our rules form a natural class:

(449)   *e* and *o* form a natural class:

$$\bigcap \left\{ \left\{ \begin{matrix} e \\ -\text{Back} \\ -\text{Round} \\ -\text{High} \\ -\text{Low} \\ +\text{Atr} \\ \cdots \end{matrix} \right\}, \left\{ \begin{matrix} o \\ +\text{Back} \\ +\text{Round} \\ -\text{High} \\ -\text{Low} \\ +\text{Atr} \\ \cdots \end{matrix} \right\} \right\} = \left\{ \begin{matrix} -\text{High} \\ -\text{Low} \\ +\text{Atr} \\ \cdots \end{matrix} \right\}$$

This class can be characterized as follows: $\{x : x \supseteq \{-\text{High}, -\text{Low}, +\text{Atr}\}\}$. So, extensionally, the natural class is just {e,o}, since these are the only two mid vowels in the language.

Now we can formulate a single rule that has a natural class for the targets and a natural class defining the environment and a single featural change. We'll ignore +Atr, as well as all the features that we are assuming to be irrelevant to vowels:

(450)   One rule for *o* and *e* in Zafonian (version 1)

• $[-\text{High}, -\text{Low}] \rightarrow \{+\text{High}\} / \_\_ [+\text{Nasal}]$

If we assume that the rule is formulated to vacuously target vowels that are already +High we get this final version.

(451)   One rule for *o* and *e* in Zafonian (final version)

• $[-\text{Low}] \rightarrow \{+\text{High}\} / \_\_ [+\text{Nasal}]$

The rule in (451) has two important properties: first, its target is a natural class and second, the environment also constitutes a natural class. However, it is important to remember that this type of rule still represents a function from strings to strings (leaving aside information about syllable structure). The rule takes an input string (a linearly ordered set of segments, where each segment is now a set of properties) and maps them to a corresponding output string. Any segment in the input string that either doesn't have the feature −Low or doesn't appear to the left of a segment that has the feature +Nasal will be mapped to an identical segment in the output string. However, if a segment, call it β, has the feature −Low ($-\text{Low} \in \beta$ and hence $\beta \in [-\text{Low}]$) and appears to the left of a segment that has +Nasal as a member, then that segment β maps to a corresponding segment γ in the output such that $\gamma = ((\beta - \{-\text{High}\}) \cup \{+\text{High}\})$ (i.e., γ is identical to β except for the addition of a +High feature and the removal, if necessary, of the −High feature). In the next unit, we will generalize a method for interpreting processes that change feature values, but we will separate such processes into two separate steps, deletion (for example of $-$HIGH) and addition (for example of $+$HIGH). We will provide justification for breaking down phonological processes in this way.

48.2   More on Features and Segments

Our goal of understanding phonological UG involves characterizing the basic phonological toolkit provided by our human genetic endowment, and figuring out how the elements of the toolkit combine and interact. In other words, we want to understand the hierarchy of data structures (Gallistel and King, 2009), such as sets, ordered sets, trees, and so on, that are relevant to phonology. We have already introduced valued features like $+$VOICED, but we should be explicit about the logical structure of such an entity.

We have assumed for UG one set containing two values, '$+$' and '$-$', and another set **F** containing features, including VOI, NAS, RD, SON, CONT, and others. The actual content of the set of features **F** is a topic of ongoing research. For the following discussion of feature logic, we'll sometimes make use of a set of four features whose members we'll refer to abstractly: $\{F_1, F_2, F_3, F_4\}$. The points we are interested in here do not depend on the actual number of features or their particular phonetic correlates.

Our simple model looks something like this:

(452)   A UG of two values (W) and four features (**F**)

- $W = \{+, -\}$
- $\mathbf{F} = \{F_1, F_2, F_3, F_4\}$

Given this formalization, the set of possible valued features can be represented as $W \times$ **F**. The cross symbol '$\times$' represents the Cartesian product, which is defined in (453):

(453)   If A and B are sets, then the Cartesian product of A and B (i.e., $A \times B$) is the set of all possible ordered pairs where the first member of the pair is a member of A and the second member of the pair is a member of B. In other words...

- $A \times B = \{\langle x, y \rangle : x \in A \;\&\; y \in B\}$

For example, the Cartesian product of $\{1, 2\}$ and $\{a, b\}$, that is, ($\{1, 2\} \times \{a, b\}$) is the set $\{\langle 1, a \rangle, \langle 1, b \rangle, \langle 2, a \rangle, \langle 2, b \rangle\}$, shown in the table in (454.i).

(454)   Two Cartesian products from two sets

$$\{1,2\} \times \{a,b\}$$

i.

	a	b
1	$\langle 1,a \rangle$	$\langle 1,b \rangle$
2	$\langle 2,a \rangle$	$\langle 2,b \rangle$

$$\{a,b\} \times \{1,2\}$$

ii.

	1	2
a	$\langle a,1 \rangle$	$\langle a,2 \rangle$
b	$\langle b,1 \rangle$	$\langle b,2 \rangle$

You can see that the set of *ordered* pairs you get from $\{1,2\} \times \{a,b\}$ is not the same as what you get from $\{a,b\} \times \{1,2\}$, shown in (454.ii). Unlike normal multiplication, the Cartesian product is not *commutative*. In other words, $A \times B$ is not, in general, equal to $B \times A$. In fact the two expressions are equal only if $A = B$ or if one of the sets is $\emptyset$.

More relevant for us, the Cartesian product of $\{+,-\}$ and $\{\text{NASAL}, \text{LABIAL}\}$ is the set given is (455), as you can see from the included table:

(455) $\{+,-\} \times \{\text{NAS}, \text{LAB}\} = \{\langle +, \text{NAS} \rangle, \langle +, \text{LAB} \rangle, \langle -, \text{NAS} \rangle, \langle -, \text{LAB} \rangle\}$

	NAS	LAB
$+$	$+$NAS	$+$LAB
$-$	$-$NAS	$-$LAB

It is not necessary for the two sets for which we compute the Cartesian product to have the same cardinality, so we can also compute the set of valued features if UG gives four features, say, $\{\text{NAS}, \text{LAB}, \text{RD}, \text{BK}\}$ instead of just two:

(456) $\{\langle +, \text{NAS} \rangle, \langle +, \text{LAB} \rangle, \langle +, \text{RD} \rangle, \langle +, \text{BK} \rangle, \langle -, \text{NAS} \rangle, \langle -, \text{LAB} \rangle, \langle -, \text{RD} \rangle, \langle -, \text{BK} \rangle\}$

	NAS	LAB	RD	BK
$+$	$+$NAS	$+$LAB	$+$RD	$+$BK
$-$	$-$NAS	$-$LAB	$-$RD	$-$BK

To review, UG provides the primitive sets of values and features, and the elements of these sets are combined to provide a set of valued features:

(457)   i.   The set of values: $W = \{+,-\}$

    ii.   The set of features: $\mathbf{F}$

    iii.   All valued features $\langle \alpha, F \rangle$ are members of $W \times \mathbf{F}$.

Given these definitions, we define a segment as a set of valued features, which we now present in terms of W and $\mathbf{F}$:

(458) **Segments as Sets**: All segments ς are sets such that $\varsigma \subseteq (W \times \mathbf{F})$

You can see how we have built increasingly complex data structures from the initial sets W and $\mathbf{F}$—first, valued features as **ordered pairs** of these primitives; then segments, as **sets** of valued features. Next of course, we can define strings of segments, corresponding to the phonological representations of morphemes. So we end up with strings of sets of ordered pairs of primitive elements. Only the most primitive elements (values and features) are specific to the domain of phonology. Everything else is built on simple mathematical structures.

Again, each segment is a set of valued features. Note that this does *not* mean that *every* set of valued features is a possible segment. In particular we adopt the assumption that segments are *consistent*. In plain language, a set of valued features is consistent if it does not contain conflicting or *opposite* values for a feature. If a consistent set contains the valued feature $+F_k$, then it does not contain the valued feature $-F_k$; and if a consistent set contains the valued feature $-F_k$, then it does not contain the valued feature $+F_k$.

(459) **Consistency**: A set of features ρ is consistent if and only if there is no feature $F \in \mathbf{F}$ (the universal set of features) such that $+F \in \rho$ and $-F \in \rho$.

Consistency is one way of formalizing the ideas outlined in our earlier discussion of the mutual incompatibility of certain properties, like T and D in the privative system. For example, with *consistency* defined as above, we can hypothesize that natural language segments do not contain both $+$VOICED and $-$VOICED, or any other conflicting pair of features:

(460) **Segment as Sets**: All segments ς are sets such that $\varsigma \subseteq (W \times \mathbf{F})$ and ς is consistent.

This hypothesis that segments are consistent is meant as a descriptive generalization about segments as natural objects in human grammars. It is not meant as a constraint or a condition in a formal system that 'generates' segments. Segments are somehow acquired or perhaps constructed in the course of language acquisition, but in an adult I-language, segments are not constructed. They are stored as part of the phonological representation of morphemes, and they may be inserted or changed by rules, but they are not 'built' in the sense that sentences are built in syntax. It is important to keep this in mind, because later we *will* use consistency as part of the specification of certain rules.

We have said that every segment is a consistent subset of $W \times \mathbf{F}$. Given our modest UG model in (452), the sets $\{+F_1, -F_2, -F_3, +F_4\}$ and $\{-F_1, +F_2, +F_3, +F_4\}$

are examples of segments. These segments each contain exactly one valued pair corresponding to each UG-given feature in $\mathbf{F}$. We will call such segments *complete*.

Notice that the sets $\{+F_1, -F_2,\}$, $\{+F_2, -F_3, +F_4\}$ and $\{-F_2\}$ also are consistent with our characterization of segments: each is consistent and each is a subset of $W \times \mathbf{F}$. We will call segments corresponding to such sets *incomplete segments*. These segments lack valued features corresponding to one or more members of $\mathbf{F}$. We formalize completeness in (461):

(461) **Completeness**: Let α be a variable with the domain $\{+, -\}$. A set of features ρ is *complete* if and only if, for each $F \in \mathbf{F}$ there is a valued feature $\alpha F \in \rho$. If ρ is not complete, it is incomplete.

To summarize, according to our definitions, segments are consistent, but they can be either complete or incomplete. The cardinality (see Unit 4.7) of a complete segment will be equal to $|\mathbf{F}|$—the cardinality of the universal set of features. The cardinality of an incomplete segment will be less than $|\mathbf{F}|$.

Exercises

48.1. Fill in values for these vowels. Treat TENSE as a synonym for ATR, which follows common practice (even if some scholars object to it). *You should learn these by heart.*:

	BACK	ROUND	HIGH	LOW	TENSE
i					+
u					+
ɪ					−
ʊ					−
e					+
o					+
ɛ					−
ɔ					−
ə					−
ɑ					−
æ					−

48.2. Give the bracket notation and the extensional characterization of the following natural classes of segments. Assume the vowel inventory in the chart in the previous exercise. We go back to using ATR here.

	w/ brackets	segments
$W = \{w : w \supseteq \{-\text{BK},+\text{ATR}\}\}$	ex. $[-\text{BK}, +\text{ATR}]$	ex. $\{\text{i,e}\}$
$W = \{w : w \supseteq \{+\text{RD},-\text{LO}\}\}$	▷	▷
$W = \{w : w \supseteq \{-\text{BK},+\text{RD}\}\}$	▷	▷
$W = \{w : w \supseteq \{+\text{LO}\}\}$	▷	▷
$W = \{w : w \supseteq \{-\text{LO}\}\}$	▷	▷
$W = \{w : w \supseteq \{-\text{LO},-\text{ATR}\}\}$	▷	▷

48.3. Assume the vowel inventory in the chart above. Rewrite the expression in the first column as a generalized intersection, then give the relevant set of **features**, and then add the segments from the inventory necessary (if any) to make a natural class. List **all** the segments in the class as a set of IPA symbols (in braces $\{\dots\}$).

	gen. intersection	feature set	natural class
▷ i ∩ ɔ =	$\bigcap\{\text{i, ɔ}\}$	$\{-\text{LO}\}$	$\{\text{i,ɪ,e,ɛ,ə,ɔ,o,ʊ,u}\}$
▷ ɑ ∩ ɔ			
▷ ə ∩ ɛ			
▷ ɪ			
▷ ɛ ∩ o			
▷ ɔ ∩ ɛ			
▷ ɑ ∩ ʊ			
▷ (ɑ ∩ ʊ) ∩ o			
▷ æ ∩ u			
▷ ə ∩ o			

48.4. For the following, refer to the feature chart in Table 47.1. You should **not** assume that the language in question has all the consonants in the chart. Instead assume the following segment inventory: [p, t, k, b, d, g, f, v, s, z, ʃ, ʒ, m, n, ŋ] . Only make use of these features in your answers: SONORANT, CORONAL, ANTERIOR, LABIAL, VOICED, NASAL, CONTINUANT.

(a) The following lists of segments are natural classes. Ignoring the feature +CONSONANTAL, define each class using as few features as possible. Here's how you do this: express each segment as a set of valued features; take the generalized intersection of the set of segments; express the natural class using that set of features; then get rid of any features you can without letting the class become larger. The first on has been done for you.

   i. p, b, m [+LABIAL, −CONTINUANT]
  ii. p, b, m, v, f
 iii. p, f
  iv. z, ʒ
   v. m, n, ŋ
  vi. b, d, g, m, n, ŋ
 vii. f, v, s, z, ʃ, ʒ
viii. s, z, ʃ, ʒ
  ix. f, s

(b) The following lists of segments are not natural classes. What is the minimum you can add to make a natural class, and how would that class be defined in features? Do this by taking a generalized intersection, then seeing what segments end up in the resulting natural class. The first on has been done for you.

   i. b, p, d   {b,p,d,t}
  ii. f, s, z
 iii. ʃ, ʒ, k
  iv. m, ŋ, g

(c) Define the following classes using features:

   i. [p, t, k]
  ii. [p, t, k, b, d, g]

(d) List the segments in these classes:

    i. $[-\text{SON}, +\text{LAB}]$

    ii. $[+\text{SON}]$

    iii. $[+\text{COR}, -\text{ANT}]$

    iv. $[+\text{VOI}, +\text{LABIAL}]$

48.5. Here are the features for some vowels in the Sacculina language:

$$
\text{i:} \left\{ \begin{array}{l} +\text{HIGH} \\ -\text{BACK} \\ -\text{ROUND} \\ +\text{ATR} \end{array} \right\} \quad
\text{u:} \left\{ \begin{array}{l} +\text{HIGH} \\ +\text{BACK} \\ +\text{ROUND} \\ +\text{ATR} \end{array} \right\} \quad
\text{y:} \left\{ \begin{array}{l} +\text{HIGH} \\ -\text{BACK} \\ +\text{ROUND} \\ +\text{ATR} \end{array} \right\}
$$

$$
\text{I:} \left\{ \begin{array}{l} +\text{HIGH} \\ -\text{BACK} \\ -\text{ROUND} \\ -\text{ATR} \end{array} \right\} \quad
\text{ʊ:} \left\{ \begin{array}{l} +\text{HIGH} \\ +\text{BACK} \\ +\text{ROUND} \\ -\text{ATR} \end{array} \right\} \quad
\text{Y:} \left\{ \begin{array}{l} +\text{HIGH} \\ -\text{BACK} \\ +\text{ROUND} \\ -\text{ATR} \end{array} \right\}
$$

Assume that there is a rule R_a in the language that affects the vowels /i/ and /Y/.

- It is guaranteed that R_a also affects two other vowels. What are these vowels?

- Show the natural class characterization of the target of R_a, assuming it affects only these four vowels:
$\{x : x \supseteq \{\underline{\hspace{6cm}}\}\}$

- *Clearly* explain in one or two sentences how this characterization is derived from knowing that /i/ and /Y/ are targets.

48.6. Ancient Sacculina had the same segment inventory as the modern language. If we find out that in Ancient Sacculina, only two of the vowels, /u/ and /Y/, were lengthened before nasals, we must conclude that the language had two distinct lengthening rules, not one. Explain.

48.7. Recall the Cymothoan data from Exercise 33.4:

Sɢ	Pʟ	
sɛ	sed	'leak'
se	sɪd	'peak'
sɪ	sid	'freak'
si	sid	'steak'

When we first looked at this data, we had access to rules referring only to segments, so we needed one rule for each alternation: ɛ → e, e → ɪ, and ɪ → i.

- Now that we have features, how many rules do you need? Refer to the vowel chart in (441) if necessary. Start by writing a rule for each alternation and expressing the target in terms of features. Which rules can be collapsed via generalized intersection and yield a valid result?

- Each alternation involves a change to a phonetically higher vowel, but we can't capture all the alternations with a single rule. Explain why not.

- Explain how this example relates to the idea that our theory, to an important extent, determines what our observations are. Is it a weakness of our theory that it does not allow us to formulate a single rule for Cymothoan (and real languages with similar patterns)?

48.8. In Koromfe (Odden, 2013), a language of Burkina Faso and Mali, there are two alternants of the singular ending: *-re, -rɛ*. The choice is conditioned by the root vowel, similar to the vowel harmony process we saw in Finnish in Unit 39.4:

nɛbrɛ	'pea'
ɡɪbrɛ	'hatchet'
koirɛ	'bracelet'
selre ⤳ selle	'space'

What determines whether the suffix vowel is +Aᴛʀ or −Aᴛʀ? How does this bear on our failure to formulate a single rule for Cymothoan in the previous question?

48.9. Fazonian looks a lot like Zafonian in (447), aside from the last line in the dataset. Analyze Fazonian with a rule R_A, a more general, less specific version of the rule we used for Zafonian, followed by two additional rules R_B and R_C, changing values of ROUND and LOW, respectively. Assume all Fazonian vowels appear in this data.

- Fazonian:

N	w/ N	to N	for N	after N	under N	before N	w/o N	gloss
lu	luk	lus	lur	lun	lum	luŋ	lud	'cat'
lo	lok	los	lor	lun	lum	luŋ	lod	'rat'
li	lik	lis	lir	lin	lim	liŋ	lid	'squat'
le	lek	les	ler	lin	lim	liŋ	led	'knot'
læ	læk	læs	lær	lin	lim	liŋ	læd	'robot'

48.10. Nozafian has one more vowel than Fazonian, the low, back, round [ɒ]. Otherwise, the languages are quite similar. Compare R_A that you formulated for Fazonian in the previous exercise, to a rule $R_{A'}$ that you would posit for Nozafian. Comment on the intensional characterization of the target of each rule and on the extensional characterization of the set of target segments in each language. (Don't worry about rules affecting BK and RD.)

- Nozafian:

N	w/ N	to N	for N	after N	under N	before N	w/o N	gloss
lu	luk	lus	lur	lun	lum	luŋ	lud	'cat'
lo	lok	los	lor	lun	lum	luŋ	lod	'rat'
lɒ	lɒk	lɒs	lɒr	lun	lum	luŋ	læd	'pangolin'
li	lik	lis	lir	lin	lim	liŋ	lid	'squat'
le	lek	les	ler	lin	lim	liŋ	led	'knot'
læ	læk	læs	lær	lin	lim	liŋ	læd	'robot'

Unit 49

Building, Then Deconstructing, a Feature-Based Rule

49.1 Using Features with '→ '

Recall the Russian rule that devoiced consonants word-finally, yielding alternations like [porok, poroga]. It turns out that Russian has more consonants than just *b, d, g, p, t, k,* but not all the consonants participate in this devoicing process. Every voiced consonant that is −SON is mapped to its voiceless counterpart word-finally, so in addition to the mappings we have seen, $b \rightarrow p$, $d \rightarrow t$, *and* $g \rightarrow k$, we also see $v \rightarrow f$, $z \rightarrow s$, and so on. However, voiced consonants that are +SON are not mapped to a voiceless counterpart. Segments like *n, m, r, l* do not undergo devoicing at the end of a word, so we get nominative-genitive pairs like like [vagon, vagona] 'wagon' with voiced *n* word-finally.

Before we show you how to formalize such a rule, it is important to note that voiceless sonorants do exist in the languages of the world. Burmese, for example, has voiceless nasals. The failure of Russian nasals to devoice word-finally is not a phonetic impossibility of the type we invoked, say, to account for the non-existence of vowels that are +HIGH and +LOW. Furthermore, we can't explain the failure of sonorants to devoice by invoking the general absence of voiceless sonorants in Russian.[1] If this

---

[1]For reasons that we do not fully understand, such arguments do appear in the literature under the name *structure preservation*. Structure preservation appears to be invoked opportunistically, when a rule is stated in a form that is general enough to create "allophones," but the allophones do not appear.

431

argument had any weight, there would be no so-called allophone rules. As we have seen, phonological rules can create surface segments that do not occur underlyingly.[2]

It is just a phonological fact of Russian that voiced obstruents undergo devoicing word-finally, but Russian sonorants do not. Phoneticians might want to explain why devoicing tends to affect obstruents more than sonorants, and more generally why different classes of consonants behave differently with respect to a given feature in terms of speech production and perception, and how these differences might lead to language changes that are biased in a certain direction. Our job as phonologists, however, is just to show how the relevant rule can be formulated in a manner consistent with our model of grammar. Keeping in mind our discussion of (valued) features, segments (sets of valued features), and natural classes (sets of sets of valued features), consider the following rule for Russian word-final devoicing:

(462)   Russian devoicing again

$$\begin{bmatrix} -\text{SON} \\ -\text{SYLL} \end{bmatrix} \rightarrow \{-\text{VOICED}\} / \_\_\% $$

We have included $-\text{SYLL}$ as a replacement for the property C in the earlier discussion. It may be the case that all valued features that are members of the sets that are consonants should be listed in the rule, valued features such as $-\text{LAT}$. This would yield a rule with more information, as in (489):

(463)   Russian devoicing yet again

$$\begin{bmatrix} -\text{SON} \\ -\text{SYLL} \\ -\text{LAT} \\ \dots \end{bmatrix} \rightarrow \{-\text{VOICED}\} / \_\_\% $$

However, it is more typical to write rules using the minimum information necessary, more like in (464), although we remain agnostic about whether or not this is how rules are encoded in grammars.

(464)   Russian devoicing one more time

$$[-\text{SON}] \rightarrow \{-\text{VOICED}\} / \_\_\% $$

---

[2]In fact, Russian has a voicing assimilation rule that is both neutralizing and allophonic, in the sense discussed in Part V. The rule voices *t* to *d* in certain environments, and underlying /d/ also exists; but it also voices *x* to *ɣ*, which is a segment that does not exist in the lexicon. Morris Halle's (1959) *Sound Pattern of Russian* discusses this example in detail to argue against having a principled distinction between neutralization rules and allophone rules. Some implications of Halle's discussion are presented in Reiss (2017a).

We can leave out the specifications of features SYLLABIC, because all the −SONORANT segments in Russian are −SYLLABIC. As a matter of expository convenience, we will typically write rules in the most general form consistent with the data.

Given what we said so far, and how we treated the → in previous units, the rule in (464) represents a function from strings to strings (again abstracting away from information about syllable structure). Each segment in the input string has a corresponding segment in the output string. If the input segments either (i) don't have the feature −SON or (ii) aren't at the end of the string, then the corresponding segments in the output string are identical to those in the input string. If the input segments already have the feature −VOICED, then the corresponding output segments are also identical. However, every other input segments β has a corresponding output segment γ such that γ is identical to β except that $+$VOICED $\notin \gamma$ and $-$VOICED $\in \gamma$. In the next section we will formalize the process of removing $+$VOICED from a target and the process of adding −VOICED.

49.2   Deconstructing '→ ': Two Steps to Devoicing

In this section we propose a different way to model the devoicing of word-final obstruents in Russian from the rule in (464). We won't justify our apparent complication right away, but as we proceed, you will see how some of the ideas we introduce here account for a wide range of empirical phenomena. The simple rule in (464) suggests that the phonology can change the valued feature $+$VOICED on a word-final obstruent to −VOICED. In contrast to this idea, we will assume that the phenomenon of final devoicing in Russian is really a two-step process. First, the phonology must *delete* $+$VOICED from a target segment. Second, the phonology must *insert* −VOICED into the same segment position.[3]

The two-step approach to devoicing has many implications. First, it is clear that we are using two very different operations, and so a single rule symbol '→ ' cannot suffice. Second, if deletion of a valued feature is possible, then there are stages in the derivation, at least as we implement the rules, in which a segment can be missing a value for some feature. We will assume that in such cases, the feature is absent from the segment altogether. In other words, the two-step approach to Russian implies that segments do not have to be *complete*, in the sense of having a valued feature for every member of the universal set of features, as defined in (461) in the previous unit. Third, if the target segments end up with a valued feature for a feature that was not previously

---

[3]This is an old idea, dating at least to Harris (1984), and adopted by many other scholars (such as Poser, 1993, 2004; Wiese, 2000; McCarthy, 2007; Samuels, 2011).

present, there must be a way to add valued features to segments. Fourth, since we are breaking the process into two parts, we are suggesting that each part can potentially occur independent of the other.

Since we have formalized segments as sets, we can immediately make use of well-understood operations from set theory in our phonology. A simple way of deleting elements from a set is to use the operation of set subtraction, introduced in Unit 4. Here are some examples of set subtraction to remind you how it works:

(465)   Examples of set subtraction

- $\{a,b,c\} - \{a,b\} = \{c\}$

- $\{a,b,c\} - \{a,b,d\} = \{c\}$

- $\{a,b,c\} - \{d\} = \{a,b,c\}$

- $\{a,b,c\} - \{a,d\} = \{b,c\}$

- $\{a,b,c\} - \emptyset = \{a,b,c\}$

- $\{a,b,c\} - \{a,b,c\} = \emptyset$

Examining these examples, you will recall that for two sets A and B, $A - B = C$, where C is the set of all members of A that are not members of B. So, to delete the valued feature $+$VOICED from a segment like b, we just need to set-substract $\{+$VOICED$\}$ from the set of valued features that represent b. This will yield something like (466):

(466) $\{+$VOICED$, +$LABIAL$, -$SON$, -$CONTINUANT$, \dots\} - \{+$VOICED$\} =$
         $\{+$LABIAL$, -$SON$, -$CONTINUANT$, \dots\}$

The outcome of this subtraction is a segment (a set of valued features) that lacks a specification for the feature VOICED. Note that there is no IPA symbol for such a segment—it is neither voiced nor voiceless. We will denote it B.

The formula in (466) demonstrates how set subtraction works on a single segment. However, to make a feature-deletion rule that applies to a string, we need a format that is similar to the one that we used for the arrow. Consider the following rule, where the arrow has been replaced by the symbol for the set subtraction operator:

(467) $[-$SON$, +$VOICED$] - \{+$VOICED$\} /$ ___%
         Interpretation: Map a word-final segment-set that is $-$SON$, +$VOICED to the same segment-set minus $\{+$VOICED$\}$

Like the rule with the arrow, we will use this rule to represent a function from strings to strings (as usual, ignoring information about syllable structure). Also as with the arrow rule, the features in the square brackets represent a natural class of segments rather than a particular set of features. Similarly, the information after the slash represents the environment that the feature will be deleted in (word-final position). The only difference between this rule and the arrow version is that instead of both deleting $+$VOICED and inserting $-$VOICED, this rule only performs the deletion of $+$VOICED.

A more formal and precise interpretation of this rule is given in (468). Recall that the superscript ^{M} maps our theoretical symbols to mental functions or mental representations. The mental representation of the features in the square brackets will be the natural class of voiced sonorants: i.e., $[-$SON$, +$VOICED$]^M = \{x : \{-$SON$, +$VOICED$\} \subseteq x\}$. In contrast, the mental representation of the features in the curly brackets is just the set of features themselves. When our symbolic representations straightforwardly mirror the mental representations, we will often leave off any superscript: i.e., $\{+$VOICED$\} = \{+$VOICED$\}^M$.

(468)   **Interpretation of a feature deletion rule:** $([-$SON$, +$VOICED$] - \{+$VOICED$\}$ / ___%$)^M$ is the function f that maps any (finite) sequence of mental representations $\langle x_1, x_2, \ldots, x_n \rangle$ to the sequence of mental representations $\langle y_1, y_2, \ldots, y_n \rangle$ such that for each index i that is greater than or equal to 1 and less than or equal to n $(1 \leq i \leq n)$...

    (a)   If $x_i \in [-$SON$, +$VOICED$]^M$ and $x_{(i+1)} = \%^M$, then $y_i = x_i - \{+$VOICED$\}$.

    (b)   Otherwise $y_i = x_i$.

This function maps strings to strings, where a $+$VOICED feature that occurs in a word-final segment in the input string is removed from the output string.

The next step in our devoicing process is to insert the $-$VOICED feature (e.g., turning B into p). A simple way to add an element to a set is via set union, so, we can get the desired result, as in (469):

(469) $\{+$LABIAL$, -$SON$, -$CONTINUANT$, \ldots \} \cup \{-$VOICED$\} =$
    $\{-$VOICED$, +$LABIAL$, -$SON$, -$CONTINUANT$, \ldots \}$

For reasons that will become clear later, we will not use set union, but instead a closely related operation called *unification*. Unification is what is called a *partial operation*, which means that it can sometimes fail to yield an output. Our definition of unification '$\sqcup$' is the following:

(470)   Unification: If A and B are sets, then $A \sqcup B = A \cup B$ if $A \cup B$ is consistent. Otherwise, $A \sqcup B$ is undefined.

It is tempting to refer to consistency in a definition like (470) as a *condition* on the application of rules that use unification. However, that makes it sound like there can exist a rule upon which consistency is a condition or constraint enforced from outside the rule. We suggest, instead, that you think of consistency as a part of rules, one possible component of their specification. Our model allows rules to contain consistency requirements. Our phonological computation module contains only ordered rules.

Given this definition in (470), here are some examples of unification applied to sets of valued features:

(471)   Unification of sets of valued features

- $\{+F, +G\} \sqcup \{+F, +G\} = \{+F, +G\}$
- $\{+F, +G\} \sqcup \{+F, +H\} = \{+F, +G, +H\}$
- $\{+F, +G\} \sqcup \emptyset = \{+F, +G\}$
- $\{+F\} \sqcup \{+G\} = \{+F, +G\}$
- $\{+F, +G\} \sqcup \{+F, -G\}$ is undefined

The very last example demonstrates a condition where unification is undefined. This is because the union of the two sets is not consistent, since it contains both +G and −G.

Parallel to our deletion operation, for insertion we want to specify a rule that maps strings to strings by inserting a −VOICED feature in the word-final position using the unification operator. Like we did with the set subtraction symbol, we will use the unification symbol in our representation of such rules, even though, strictly speaking, unification is an operation between sets. Our first attempt at a rule for Russian unification is given in (472), soon to be revised.

(472)   Russian insertion (first version):
        $[-\text{SON}] \sqcup \{-\text{VOICED}\}$ / ___%
        Interpretation: Unify an obstruent in word-final position with $\{-\text{VOICED}\}$

This rule maps strings to strings, inserting −VOICED into the word-final segment in the output as long as that segment does not have a +VOICED feature. This can be outlined more precisely as follows, keeping in mind that $[-\text{SON}]^M = \{x : \{-\text{SON}\} \subseteq x\}$ (i.e., the natural class of sonorants).

(473)   **Interpretation of a unification rule:** $([-\text{SON}] \sqcup \{-\text{VOICED}\} / \_\_\%)^M$ is the function f that maps any (finite) sequence of mental representations $\langle x_1, x_2, \ldots, x_n \rangle$ to the sequence of mental representations $\langle y_1, y_2, \ldots, y_n \rangle$ such that for each index i that is greater than or equal to 1 and less than or equal to n $(1 \le i \le n)\ldots$

(a) If $x_i \in [-\text{SON}]^M$, $x_{(i+1)} = \%^M$ and $x_i \sqcup \{-\text{VOICED}\}$ is defined, then $y_i = x_i \sqcup \{-\text{VOICED}\}$.

(b) Otherwise $y_i = x_i$.

In our Russian example, this rule applies after the deletion rule. As a result, when the rule applies, there are three kinds of segments in word-final position. First, there may still be some forms with a $+\text{VOICED}$ segment in word-final position. However, these segments must be $+\text{SON}$, since the $(-\text{SON})$ obstruents have already lost $+\text{VOICED}$ by the deletion rule. With respect to these segments, rule (472) applies vacuously in the sense of being irrelevant to these inputs: a word-final sonorant $(+\text{SON})$ does not fit the requirements of the rule target. The second kind of segment in word-final position will be obstruents that are $-\text{VOICED}$ (because they were thus specified in the lexicon). According to the rule in (472), these will unify vacuously with $\{-\text{VOICED}\}$, so the rule applies vacuously. The third kind of word-final segment are obstruents that started out $+\text{VOICED}$, but lost that value by the deletion rule (467). These now lack any valued feature containing VOICED, so they will be able to unify with $\{-\text{VOICED}\}$—i.e., rule (472) will apply non-vacuously in such cases.

The unification rule in (472) works in the sense that it accounts for the Russian data, but David Ta-Chun Shen (p.c.) pointed out that we can make such a rule even more elegant, as in (474), which can be interpreted as in (475):

(474) Russian insertion (final version):
[   ] $\sqcup \{-\text{VOICED}\}$ / __%
Interpretation: Unify any segment in word-final position with $\{-\text{VOICED}\}$

(475) **Interpretation of a minimal unification rule:** $([\quad] \sqcup \{-\text{VOICED}\} / \underline{\quad}\%)^M$ is the function f that maps any (finite) sequence of mental representations $\langle x_1, x_2, \ldots, x_n \rangle$ to the sequence of mental representations $\langle y_1, y_2, \ldots, y_n \rangle$ such that for each index i that is greater than or equal to 1 and less than or equal to n $(1 \leq i \leq n)$...

(a) If $x_i \in [\quad]^M$, $x_{(i+1)} = \%^M$ and $x_i \sqcup \{-\text{VOICED}\}$ is defined, then $y_i = x_i \sqcup \{-\text{VOICED}\}$.

(b) Otherwise $y_i = x_i$.

In this version of the rule, we use square brackets with nothing in-between. Because the empty set is a subset of every set, these empty brackets represent the natural class of all segments: i.e., $[\quad]^M = \{x : \emptyset \subseteq x\}$. With this formulation of the rule, word-final (voiced) sonorants will not lead to vacuous application due to a segment not meeting the target specifications, since the new version targets all segments. Instead, these sonorants will lead to vacuous application via unification failure, since all the +SONORANT segments in Russian are +VOICED.

The combination of the rules in (467) and (474), in that order, accomplishes the same input-to-output mapping as the rule with the arrow. An important difference is that with the two-step process, there is an intermediate stage where some word-final segments lack any specification for voicing. With the arrow rule, there is never any point in the derivation where a string has a segment that is underspecified in this way. As we will see later on with other languages, there are some empirical advantages to having such intermediate stages in the derivation.

49.3   Segment Mapping Diagrams and the Two-Step Process

The two-step process we have developed here corresponds to what is typically called a *feature-changing rule*. In our discussion of SMDs, starting in Unit 19, we adopted the convention that each non-vertical arrow in a SMD corresponds to a rule. Things have become more complicated now. Our feature-changing processes now are modeled with two rules, one that deletes a valued feature and one that inserts the feature with the opposite value. This means that a single arrow of an old feature-changing process now corresponds to two separate rules. For example, the final devoicing of d is achieved as a sequence $d \rightarrow D \rightarrow t$, where D represents the segment that is not specified for voicing (i.e., the segment that has neither +VOICED or −VOICED). This can be represented with a more precise SMD as follows:

(476)   Two-step SMD for final devoicing of d in Russian:

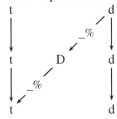

A useful aspect of this more explicit SMD is that it reinforces the independence of the two parts of the feature-changing process. In this case, the first rule creates D, then the second changes *D* to *t.* In subsequent units, we will see that it is not necessary for the two parts of such a process to occur together. In particular, we will posit the equivalent of underlying /*D*/.

Besides unification and feature deletion, there are other basic operations to be wrung out of the traditional arrow of phonological notation, for example, the deletion and insertion of full segments from a string, and maybe even the metathesis processes discussed in Unit 36. Since we will not be able to provide a full inventory of such operations, we will continue to use the arrow for some rules in the remainder of the book, with a view to a more thorough treatment in the future. In addition, as we proceed, it will often be convenient to ignore the details of two-step feature-changing processes, and not separate the steps of deletion and insertion either in rules or in SMDs. In such cases, we will sometimes refer to a *process* rather than a *rule*, and we will use the arrow, '→ ', to abbreviate the sequence of operations (first delete and then unify).

Unit 50

Failure of Minimal Pairs

In Unit 32, we showed that rule ordering can give rise to minimal pairs that can give a misleading view of which segments are present underlyingly. Specifically, we showed that the existence of a minimal pair of words contrasted by two segments, is not necessarily evidence that both segments have to be present in the lexicon, contrary to how minimal pair reasoning is first introduced to beginning students.

In the earlier discussion, there was a rule 's → š / ___ i' that occurred *before* a deletion rule 'o → ϵ / ___ i'. With this counterfeeding ordering, we get the mappings /lusi/ $\rightsquigarrow$ [luši] and /lusoi/ $\rightsquigarrow$ [lusi]. The minimal pair *luši~lusi* suggests, wrongly, that there must be an underlying contrast between *s* and *š*. We will now examine a similar situation using segment changing rules instead of a deletion rule in a series of toy languages, with the goal of preparing you to extend the reasoning to analyze Polish in Exercise 50.5, where you will have to make use of features to describe natural classes of segments.

We first present a dataset where two underlying contrasts and two neutralization rules interact to create a complex surface pattern. We first account for the *p/b* and *u/o* alternations in the Shilop data in (477):

(477)   Shilop

	SG	PL	gloss
a.	nop	nopi	'dog'
b.	nup	nupi	'cat'
c.	nup	nobi	'frog'
d.	nup	nubi	'rat'

In Shilop, there seems to be no overt morpheme marking the singular and there seems to be a suffix -*i* marking the plural. The morphemes meaning 'dog' and 'cat' show a single surface alternant each, whereas 'frog' and 'rat' each show two alternants:

(478)   Shilop morpheme alternants

alternants	gloss
a. [nop]	'dog'
b. [nup]	'cat'
c. [nup, nob]	'frog'
d. [nup, nub]	'rat'

The alternants of 'rat' show a *p*/*b* alternation that also shows up in the forms of 'frog'. In addition, 'frog' has a vowel alternation involving *o*/*u*. By applying MTP-RAA reasoning to the forms of 'frog' and 'rat', you should be able to see that we need a rule that changes *b* to *p*, let's say when it is in a coda (or maybe word-finally). We'll use the syllable boundary symbol '.' to avoid having to draw a syllable diagram:

(479)   b → p / ___ .

This rule takes care of the consonant alternation in 'frog' and 'rat'.

   Let's turn to the vowels. We have morphemes like 'dog' with non-alternating *o*; we have morphemes like 'cat' and 'rat' with non-alternating *u*; and we have morphemes like 'frog' with an *o*/*u* alternation. Thinking about our heuristics like the surfacing lexical form assumption (SLFA), this data may remind you of the discussion of non-surfacing segments in URs, proposed for Ustilago (233) in Unit 21.6. In other words, we might be tempted to posit the following analysis of Shilop:

(480)   Shilop analysis with /o,u,O/

- Lexical forms
    a. /nop/   dog
    b. /nup/   cat
    c. /nOb/   frog
    d. /nub/   rat
- Rules:
    R_1:   b → p/ ___.
    R_2:   O → o/ ___b
    R_3:   O → u/ ___p
- Ordering: R_1 precedes and feeds R_3

This analysis works, but it requires us to posit three underlying vowels, /o,u,O/. Note that the data lacks a paradigm showing non-alternating *o* with a root ending in underlying /b/. In other words, there are no paradigms like this—[nop, nobi], which we would posit to be underlying /nob/.

Suppose that this absence of non-alternating *o* before *b* is systematic—we find non-alternating *o* in roots with underlying final /p/ but not in roots with underlying /b/. An alternative to positing three distinct underlying vowels presents itself. Instead of the analysis in (480), we can propose an analysis with just two vowels and two rules:[1]

(481) Revised Shilop analysis with /o,u/

- Lexical forms

lexical forms	gloss
a. /nop/	'dog'
b. /nup/	'cat'
c. /nob/	'frog'
d. /nub/	'rat'

- Rules:

  R_A: o → u / ___ b.

  R_B: b → p / ___ .

  - Ordering: R_B follows and counterbleeds R_A

If R_B were ordered before R_A, then R_B would bleed R_A, since the former would turn *b*'s in codas into *p*'s, and R_A would not be able to apply. So, R_A must apply first—we have a counterbleeding order.

The derivations of all eight forms are as follows:

(482) Derivations

UR	nop	nop-i	nup	nup-i	nob	nob-i	nub	nub-i
R_A	–	–	–	–	nub	–	–	–
R_B	–	–	–	–	nup	–	nup	
SR	nop	nopi	nup	nupi	nup	nobi	nup	nubi
gloss	'dog'	'dogs'	'cat'	'cats'	'frog'	'frogs'	'rat'	'rats'

Here is the segment mapping diagram for this analysis (with the rule environments provided on the arrows):

---

[1]R_A is an illicit SPE rule since it requires two symbols after the environment symbol. However, the intended rule is '*o* becomes *u* before a *b* in the coda of the same syllable', which is consistent with the rules developed in Unit 39.3 that allow reference to syllable structure.

(483)   SMD for Shilop

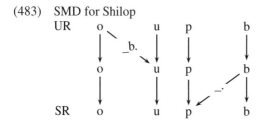

You should confirm that the contrast between the SRs [nop] 'dog' and the [nup] meaning 'cat' corresponds to an underlying *vowel* distinction. This is different from the pair [nop] 'dog' and [nup] 'frog', which does *not* correspond to an underlying vowel contrast, but rather to an underlying *consonant* contrast! This superficially confusing situation has arisen via the same kinds of processes we have seen over and over again— there is a split of underlying /o/ to [o] and [u], and a merger of underlying /b/ with [p] from /p/.

Given the lexicon and rules of this language, we get a set of three homophones via two neutralization rules. The /o/ of 'frog' changes to [u] before the following coda /b/; then the coda /b/'s of both 'frog' and 'rat' are devoiced to [p]. These two derivations converge with the unchanged [nup] from /nup/ 'cat'. To reiterate a point made in Unit 21.7, we see here that homophony can arise from the effect of a single rule, or from the effects of two rules. Thus it is hard to imagine that grammars could in some way encode constraints or principles limiting homophony. Homophony just happens to arise from certain rule interactions.

Recall that we began this unit with reference to minimal pairs. Comparing the Shilop SR [nop] 'dog' with the SR [nup] 'cat', we might conclude that the minimal pair shows that the lexicon must distinguish /o/ and /u/. That seems to be consistent with our analysis which posited two distinct underlying vowels.

But what if we chose to compare [nop] with the SR [nup] meaning 'frog'? Minimal pair reasoning would lead us to posit an underlying vowel contrast again, but in this case, we have decided that the underlying vowel is /o/ in both words! The existence of a minimal pair cannot guarantee the presence of an underlying distinction.

So what?, you may ask—there *is* a distinction in Shilop and so the minimal pair test gives the right result. Let's show that the test can actually fail us, by imagining a language that has a subset of the forms in Shilop, but the same exact rules.

(484)   Lopshi: No underlying /u/

SG	PL	gloss
nop	nopi	'snake'
nup	nobi	'ladder'

For Lopshi, assuming that this is representative data, we can posit the same rules as for Shilop, and apply them in the same order. In this case, we find a minimal pair [nop] versus [nup] that falsely suggests that *o* and *u* must be underlyingly distinct.

Here are the derivations for Lopshi:

(485)   Lopshi derivations

UR	nop	nop-i	nob	nob-i
R_A	–	–	nub	–
R_B	–	–	nup	–
SR	nop	nopi	nup	nobi
gloss	'snake'	'snakes'	'ladder'	'ladders'

The two roots differ from each other in one way but they can surface with two differences.

The segment mapping diagram in this case is the same as (483), but without any underlying /u/:

(486)   SMD for Lopshi: "non=phonemic" minimal pairs

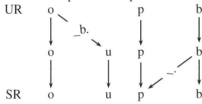

Lopshi has a split of underlying /b/ and merger of /b/ with /p/, like Shilop. However, it has a split of underlying /o/ but there is no underlying /u/ in this language. Once again, it is appropriate to point out that the "relation between a phonemic system and the phonetic record ... is remote and complex" (Chomsky, 1964, 38). Minimal pairs can be useful heuristics for figuring out a phonological system, but like all heuristics, the minimal pair test can fail.

Exercises

50.1. Lipsho: Provide an analysis that has a total of only two underlying vowels in these four roots (parallel to Shilop):

	SG	PL	gloss
a.	næʃ	næʃo	'parsley leaf'
b.	nɛʃ	nɛʃo	'sage leaf'
c.	nɛʃ	næso	'rosemary leaf'
d.	nɛʃ	nɛso	'thyme leaf'

50.2. Psholi: Provide an analysis that has a total of only three underlying vowels in these six roots (parallel to Shilop). Hints: There is a singular marker with two alternants and a plural marker with one alternant. You will need a rule with a two-sided environment. Finally, note that there are two rules, A and B, where A feeds B and B counterbleeds A.

	SG	PL	gloss
a.	mœʃ	bœʃ	'onion'
b.	nɛʃ	bɛʃ	'bunion'
c.	nɛs	bœs	'stallion'
d.	nɛs	bɛs	'scallion'
e.	mos	bos	'goat'
f.	moʃ	boʃ	'moat'

50.3. Pshoil:

	SG	PL	gloss
a.	dʊʔkra	dʊʔok	'mango'
b.	dɔʔkra	dʊfiok	'tango'

    a. Provide an analysis **assuming that the same underlying vowel is in the two roots** (parallel to Lopshi). Use /dʊʔ/ and /dʊfi/. Make any assumptions you need about syllable structure.

    b. Now provide a different analysis, assuming that the roots are /dʊʔ/ and /dɔfi/.

    c. Advanced: Now make up some additional data that forces you to adopt the analysis in (a).

50.4. Shoilp: Provide an analysis **assuming that the same underlying *consonant* is in the two roots**. Use /lab-/ and /lub-/ as the roots.

	SG	PL	gloss
a.	labik	lab	'igloo'
b.	lubik	lam	'palm tree'

50.5. Polish (Kenstowicz and Kisseberth, 1979): The toy languages we have been looking at were inspired by a well-known dataset based on Polish. The situation in modern Polish is not as clear as this data suggests, but we'll assume that at some point a purely phonological account of these forms worked for Polish generally. You only need two rules/processes to solve this problem, but the challenge is to get the natural classes right for targets and environments. Do not posit any other root vowels than /o/ and /u/. Provide ordered rules, a lexicon and derivations of all forms.

Singular	Plural	gloss	Singular	Plural	gloss
klup	klubi	'club'	trup	trupi	'corpse'
dom	domi	'house'	snop	snopi	'sheaf'
žwup	žwobi	'crib'	trut	trudi	'labor'
dzvon	dzvoni	'bell'	kot	koti	'cat'
lut	lodi	'ice'	grus	gruzi	'rubble'
nos	nosi	'nose'	vus	vozi	'cart'
wuk	wugi	'lye'	wuk	wuki	'bow'
sok	soki	'juice'	ruk	rogi	'horn'
bur	bori	'forest'	vuw	vowi	'ox'
sul	soli	'salt'	buy	boyi	'fight'
šum	šumi	'noise'	žur	žuri	'soup'

50.6. Most North American dialects of English have the following pronunciations for *rider* and *writer*: [rɑjɾɚ]/[rəjɾɚ]. Assume that the underlying representations of the roots are /rɑjd/ and /rɑjt/ respectively. Treat [ɑj] and [əj] each as a single segment. Assume rules ordered sequentially that turn /t/ and /d/ into [ɾ]. With all these assumptions, see if you understand why the data demands a counterbleeding rule ordering.

Unit 51

Reciprocal Neutralization Revisited

51.1   Hungarian Voicing Assimilation

In Unit 21.5 we introduced a pattern we called reciprocal neutralization in which two underlying segments neutralize to each other—for example, underlying /t/ sometimes surfaces as [d], and underlying /d/ sometimes surfaces as [t]. In that earlier discussion, we had to use two separate rules, one to turn /d/ to [t] and one to turn /t/ to [d]. The relevant SMD from Unit 21.5 is repeated in (487):

(487)   Reciprocal neutralization SMD:

Now, consider the following data from Hungarian:[1]

---

[1]Unsurprisingly, the Hungarian story is more complicated than what we present here. We present the Hungarian in a mixture of orthographic and phonetic transcription. The symbols ö and ü are, respectively, mid and high front rounded vowels, as in the orthography. The colon is used to mark length here, unlike in the orthography.

(488)   Reciprocal neutralization in Hungarian

Noun	In N	From N	To N	
kalap	kalabban	kalapto:l	kalapnak	'hat'
rab	rabban	rapto:l	rabnak	'prisoner'
ku:t	ku:dban	ku:tto:l	ku:tnak	'well'
ka:d	ka:dban	ka:tto:l	ka:dnak	'tub'
ʒa:k	ʒa:gban	ʒa:kto:l	ʒa:knak	'sack'
meleg	melegben	melektö:l	melegnek	'warm'
re:s	re:zben	re:stö:l	re:snek	'part'
vi:z	vi:zben	vi:stö:l	vi:znek	'water'
sem	semben	semtö:l	semnek	'eye'
bü:n	bü:nben	bü:ntö:l	bü:nnek	'crime'
fal	falban	falto:l	falnak	'wall'
ö:r	ö:rben	ö:rtö:l	ö:rnek	'guard'

You should ignore the vowel alternations in the data—they are examples of a phenomenon called *vowel harmony*, which we will look at later. Note that the root of the words for 'hat' ends in a [p] when there is no suffix, and when the suffix begins with /n/. Before a [t], we again see [p], but before a suffix that begins with /b/, the root final consonant is [b]. In the words for 'prisoner', we also get [p] before [t] and [b] before [b]. However, word-finally, the root ends in a [b], and [b] also shows up before [n].

Since the final consonants of the two roots behave differently, they must be different underlyingly. A simple analysis is that 'hat' is underlyingly /kalap/ and the phonology turns *p* to *b* before a *b*; and 'prisoner' is underlyingly /rab/ and the phonology turns *b* to *p* before *t*. In fact these alternations are representative of a more general pattern: *p* becomes *b* before any voiced obstruent, any sound that is −SON and +VOICED; and *b* becomes *p* before any voiceless obstruent, any sound that is −SON and −VOICED. The segment *n*, like other sonorants, does not trigger voicing assimilation, even though sonorants are voiced.

Looking down the list, we see that the first two examples also represent a more general pattern with respect to the rule targets: the coronal stops *t/d*, the coronal fricatives *s/z* and the dorsal stops *k/g* behave in a parallel fashion. Ignoring some interesting details, let's just say that the data suggests the presence of a voicing rule, 'voiceless obstruents become voiced before voiced obstruents', and a devoicing rule, 'voiced obstruents become voiceless before voiceless obstruents'. Assuming vacuous application, we can simplify these statements: 'obstruents become voiced before voiced obstruents' and 'obstruents become voiceless before voiceless obstruents'.

For a moment let's forget the two-step approach to changing features we developed for Russian in Unit 49 and go back to using the arrow '→'. We can write two rules thus:

(489)   Two rules for Hungarian voicing

a. $\left[\begin{array}{c} -\text{Son} \end{array}\right] \rightarrow \{+\text{Voiced}\} \, / \, \underline{\quad} \left[\begin{array}{c} -\text{Son} \\ +\text{Voiced} \end{array}\right]$

b. $\left[\begin{array}{c} -\text{Son} \end{array}\right] \rightarrow \{-\text{Voiced}\} \, / \, \underline{\quad} \left[\begin{array}{c} -\text{Son} \\ -\text{Voiced} \end{array}\right]$

Notice that a natural language translation of these rules might be something like 'an obstruent becomes $+\text{Voiced}$ before an obstruent that is $+\text{Voiced}$', and 'an obstruent becomes $-\text{Voiced}$ before an obstruent that is $-\text{Voiced}$'. These two statements can be combined: 'an obstruent ends up with the same value on Voiced as the following segment, if that following segment is also an obstruent'. Or yet again, 'If two obstruents end up next to each other, they end up with the same value for Voiced as the one on the right.'

51.2   Expressing "The Same Value"

One way to formalize this combined statement is to use a variable whose domain is the set of values $\{+, -\}$. It is traditional in phonology to use Greek letters for such variables, and in fact, variables that range over $\{+, -\}$ are often called α, *alpha variables*, or *Greek letter variables*. Using α as a variable, we can combine the two rules in (489) as in (490):

(490)   One rule for Hungarian voicing

$$\left[\begin{array}{c} -\text{Son} \end{array}\right] \rightarrow \{\alpha\text{Voiced}\} \, / \, \underline{\quad} \left[\begin{array}{c} -\text{Son} \\ \alpha\text{Voiced} \end{array}\right]$$

Note that there are two tokens of α in (490). The interpretation of rules with Greek letter variables is that all tokens of a variable must have the same value for a given application of the rule. This is consistent with general logical and mathematical practice—in a formula like $y = x^2 + 2x + 1$ values of y correspond to expressions where the same value is filled in for x in both places where it occurs. The rule in (490) does just what we want—it assigns to the left-hand obstruent *the same* value ('+' or '−') for Voiced as the value of α on the right-hand obstruent. Let's call this use of α the *identity* use.

51.3   Expressing "The Opposite Value"

The definition of consistency in Unit (48) is repeated in (491).

(491)   **Consistency**: A set of features ρ is consistent if and only if there is no feature $F \in \mathbf{F}$ (the universal set of features) such that $+F \in \rho$ and $-F \in \rho$.

In this definition, we explicitly refer to the valued features $+F_i$ and $-F_i$. Another way to define consistency is to explicitly define the notion of *opposite* value, such that '+' and '−' are opposites, and, say, $+\text{ROUND}$ is the opposite valued feature of $-\text{ROUND}$. The tools we develop to do this will prove useful later on.

Let's assume that $+$ and $-$ are opposites of one another.[2] Given this assumption, we can define a function that maps each value to its opposite, thus mapping $+$ to $-$ and mapping $-$ to $+$. Thus, the domain and range of the function are both $W = \{+, -\}$.

We can give the generic name f to this function and give the extensional definition in (492).

(492) $\begin{aligned} f\colon \quad + &\longrightarrow \quad - \\ - &\longrightarrow \quad + \end{aligned}$

Thus, $f(+) = -$ and $f(-) = +$. This function is reminiscent of how '−' affects negative and positive values in mathematics—for example, $-(-4) = +4$ and $-(+4) = -4$.

Note that the symbol $-$ is used ambiguously in mathematics. In an expression like '$-(-4)$', one token of '−' is used to mark the value of the number, either positive or negative, while the other '−' is used as a function that switches values to their opposite—that is, the function that multiplies numbers by -1.[3] We will adopt the same ambiguity in our phonological theory for two reasons. First, it is standard in the literature. Second, the analogy to the mathematical function should help you remember the effects of the f function.

We can combine the notion of *opposite* with Greek letter variables to express consistency in a new way:

---

[2] This relation of opposites has the property of being *symmetric*. If x is the opposite of y, then y is the opposite of x. Another example of a symmetric relation is SIBLING-OF: if x is a sibling of y then y is necessarily a sibling of x. A relation like MOTHER-OF is not symmetric. Why isn't BROTHER-OF symmetric?

[3] And of course, in math, the same symbol is used to denote subtraction, a third, distinct meaning. We also used this symbol for set subtraction. All three meanings show up below in (494).

(493) **Consistency**: A set of features ρ is consistent if and only if it is the case that there is no feature $F \in \mathbf{F}$ (the universal set of features) such that $\alpha F \in \rho$ and $-\alpha F \in \rho$.

Since segments are consistent, this means that features do not appear with opposite values within a segment.

51.4 A Two-Step Analysis of Hungarian Reciprocal Neutralization

Now that we have introduced Greek letter variables, we can use them to get a two-step account of the feature-changing process of Hungarian reciprocal neutralization. The first step will be to delete the voicing value on an obstruent that occurs before an obstruent with the opposite value for VOICED:

(494) Deletion for Hungarian reciprocal neutralization

$$\left[\, -\text{SON} \, \right] - \{\alpha\text{VOI}\} \, / \, \underline{\qquad} \left[\begin{array}{c} -\text{SON} \\ -\alpha\text{VOI} \end{array} \right]$$

This rule shows an identity use of α combined with the opposite function. The rule deletes any value of VOICED that is on an obstruent that precedes another obstruent with the opposite value of VOICED. Make sure that you understand each of the three different uses of the '$-$' symbol in this rule.

The next rule we need assigns a value for VOICED to obstruents that are followed by another obstruent. The value assigned is "copied" from the one on the right to the one on the left by using a Greek letter variable:

(495) Insertion for Hungarian

$$\left[\, -\text{SON} \, \right] \sqcup \{\alpha\text{VOI}\} \, / \, \underline{\qquad} \left[\begin{array}{c} -\text{SON} \\ \alpha\text{VOI} \end{array} \right]$$

Rule (495) shows the identity use of α to ensure that the obstruent on the left ends up with the same value for VOICED as the obstruent on the right.

Note that we used the same Greek letter α in both rules, (494) and (495). This is valid, since the alpha-variables appear in two separate rules and thus their values are assigned independently. There is no relationship between the value assigned to α in (494) and that assigned in (495).

We can now see that Greek letter variables complicate our SMDs. We showed in the previous unit that the arrows of our early SMDs sometimes correspond to two rules, two parts of a feature-changing process. Now we can see that a single rule can require two different arrows in an SMD, because of the two possible values for a Greek letter variable.

In (496) we provide an SMD that reflects the rule system we have posited, a system that neutralizes *t* and *d* to a segment lacking VOICED, which we denote D. Both *t* and *d* become D before an obstruent; then D becomes *t* or *d* depending on the voicing of the following obstruent (represented by *p* and *b* here).

(496)   Revised reciprocal neutralization SMD:

$$
\text{Rule (494): } \begin{bmatrix} -\text{SON} \end{bmatrix} - \{\alpha\text{VOICED}\} / \underline{\quad} \begin{bmatrix} -\text{SON} \\ -\alpha\text{VOI} \end{bmatrix}
$$

$$
\text{Rule (495): } \begin{bmatrix} -\text{SON} \end{bmatrix} \sqcup \{\alpha\text{VOICED}\} / \underline{\quad} \begin{bmatrix} -\text{SON} \\ \alpha\text{VOICED} \end{bmatrix}
$$

Compare this SMD to the one in (487), which does not break down the two steps of feature changing, and the one in (476) for Russian final devoicing, which just has deletion of VOICED from one member of a voiced/voiceless pair. Soon, we will see that the mappings shown between the bottom two rows of (496) are independent of what happened between the top two rows. In other words, we will find evidence for *underlying* segments like /D/.

51.5   No "Existential" α

Before we proceed, we should point out another use of Greek letter variables in the phonology literature that we can call the *existential* use. An existential α occurs alone, so it does not convey identity of the value on two tokens of a feature, but just existence or presence of a feature in a set. For example, consider the expression in (497) from Kiparsky (1985, p. 92):

(497)   Kiparsky's marking condition on English sonorants

$$
* \begin{bmatrix} \alpha\text{VOICE} \\ +\text{SON} \end{bmatrix}
$$

The asterisk '*' means 'not allowed'. This expression is intended as a constraint, a ban, against the presence in the lexicon of a sonorant with either value of VOICE—there is no agreement or identity encoded in this use of α. The phonological model we are developing does not contain constraints or bans of any kind, and we do not make use of the existential single α.

Exercises

51.1. The following forms from Hungarian suggest that voicing assimilation is not limited to clusters of two obstruents, and that the rightmost member of a sequence of obstruents determines the voicing of the whole sequence.

Noun	In N	From N	To N	
teʃt	teʒdben	teʃttöːl	teʃtnek	'body'
ʃmaragd	ʃmaragdban	ʃmarakttoːl	ʃmaragdnak	'emerald'

Our current rule formalisms cannot account for such effects. Propose three different extensions to our model that could yield the desired result. One proposal should refer to how rules are applied (left-to-right, right-to-left, or globally); one should refer to how rules are ordered and applied in the derivation; and one should refer to how segment relations are expressed in rules—in other words, get rid of the adjacency requirement. Your suggestions may include ideas that we rejected earlier for our simple model.

51.2. Do we really need to specify the target of the rule in (495) as −SONORANT? Discuss.

Unit 52

Nothing IV: Non-surfacing URs Revisited

We have seen Russian final devoicing, which involved changing voiced obstruents to voiceless ones by deleting a particular valued feature and then inserting its opposite. We have also seen Hungarian voicing assimilation, a reciprocal neutralization process that we analyzed by deleting both values of VOICED on an obstruent before another obstruent, and then inserting a new value of VOICED that is identical to that of the right-side obstruent.

One implicit claim of the two-step analysis of such feature-changing rules is that the two parts are logically independent, an idea we suggested with the detailed SMD in (496). In this section, we provide evidence for this independence by introducing feature-filling processes. These are processes that make use of insertion (via unification) without a preceding deletion process. We will illustrate this phenomenon with data from Turkish based on discussions by Inkelas and Orgun (1995).

Recall the Ustilago toy language we discussed in Unit 21.6, repeated in (498):

(498) Ustilago: Non-surfacing URs

sg.	pl.	gloss
pak	pakla	'cat'
pag	pagla	'mat'
pag	pakla	'rat'

Something with exactly this structure appears in Turkish. Turkish has roots ending with a non-alternating [t] as in (499a); it has other roots ending with a non-alternating [d] as in (499b); and it also has roots that alternate on the surface between a root-final [t] and a root-final [d], as in (499c).

(499)   a.   Non-alternating voiceless:
                sanat 'art', *sanatlar* 'art-plural', *sanatım* 'art-1sg.poss'

         b.   Non-alternating voiced:
                etüd 'etude', *etüdler* 'etude-plural', *etüdüm* 'etude-1sg.poss'

         c.   Alternating:
                kanat 'wing', *kanatlar* 'wing-plural', *kanadım* 'wing-1sg.poss'

You can ignore for now the difference between the two forms of the plural suffix *-ler/-lar*, and the two forms of the first person possessive *-ım/-üm*.

If you analyzed just the (a) and (b) forms using our forced-choice MTP reasoning, you would posit underlying /t/ and /d/, respectively, for the final segments of the roots. But if you analyzed just the (a) and (c) forms, you would posit underlying /t/ in *sanat-* and underlying /d/ in *kanad/kanat-*, with rules that devoice /d/ to [t] in coda position. However, the forms in (b) show that these rules do not work since *etüd* has a [d] in coda.[1]

Similarly, if you analyzed just the (b) and (c) forms, you might posit underlying /t/ for *kanat/kanad-* with rules voicing /t/ to [d] in onsets. However, the forms in (a) show that these rules do not work since *sanatım* has [t] in onset. The final consonant of the root meaning 'wing' can be neither /t/ nor /d/. It seems to be a coronal stop, but neither value for voicing seems to work. We can solve this dilemma by again realizing that segments can be incomplete and assuming that the segment in question is underlyingly a coronal stop without a voicing specification—it is an incomplete segment. Let's call it /D/. Compare the SMD in (500) to the one we gave the toy language example back in (235):

---

[1]This data comes from Orhan Orgun (Inkelas and Orgun, 1995), a native speaker of Turkish, who is also a phonologist. Markus Pöchtrager, an Austrian phonologist who has worked in Turkey for ten years, reports (p.c.) that he cannot find anyone who pronounces *etüd* with a final [d]. This situation is not at all unusual. The descriptions of even widely discussed phenomena in well-studied languages including Turkish, French, Japanese, English, Russian, and German are often controversial, for a variety of reasons ranging from dialect variation to disagreement about the phonetic analysis of the exact same recordings. This issue bears on what "real" data is. There are definitely wrong analyses of datasets, but the correct analysis may end up being quite theory dependent. Luckily for us, we are most interested in the logical structure of the problems as presented.

(500) Segment Mapping Diagram for Turkish /t,D,d/

If we adopt this analysis, we are committed to adding two rules to the grammar. One rule ensures that /D/ surfaces as [d] in onset position, and the other rule ensures that /D/ surfaces as [t] in coda position:

(501) Rules for underlying /D/

      a.   /D/ → [d] in onset

      b.   /D/ → [t] in coda

Since stops always appear in either a coda or an onset, there is no environment where underlying /D/ emerges unchanged.

But there's a problem when we try to formulate the target for the rules in (501). Since we want the target to be only D, we need to calculate a natural class based on the generalized intersection of the set that contains only D, shown in (502):

(502) $\bigcap\{\mathrm{D}\} = \bigcap\{\{+\text{CORONAL}, -\text{CONTINUANT}\}\}$

Of course, as we pointed out in the discussion (433), generalized intersection of a set with just one member set is that member itself (that is, for any set X, $\bigcap\{X\} = X$). Therefore, the generalized intersection of the set that contains only the set D = {+CORONAL, −CONTINUANT} is {+CORONAL, −CONTINUANT}. The set $\Pi = \{\pi : \pi \supseteq \{+\text{CORONAL}, -\text{CONTINUANT}\}\}$ is the smallest natural class of segments defined by this set of features. The problem is that this natural class Π contains t and d as well as D. In (503) we summarize the reasoning that led us here.

(503) *D* can't define a natural class alone

- D = {+Cor, −Cont}
- ⋂{D} = {+Cor, −Cont}
- Smallest natural class containing just *D*:

  $\Pi = \big\{\pi : \pi \supseteq \{+\textsc{Cor}, -\textsc{Cont}\}\big\}$
- Extensional characterization in features:[2] Π =

  $\big\{\{-\textsc{Cor}, +\textsc{Cont}\}, \{+\textsc{Voi}, -\textsc{Cor}, +\textsc{Cont}\}, \{-\textsc{Voi}, -\textsc{Cor}, +\textsc{Cont}\}\big\}$
- $D, d, t \in \Pi$

So now we see that it is impossible for a rule to target just *D*, without targeting both *t* and *d* as well. This is because any natural class that contains *D* also contains these other two segments.

So, how can we make rules that affect *D* without affecting *t* and *d* if we can't make rules that target *D* without targeting *t* and *d*? More specifically, how can we add +Voiced to *D* in onsets, without also adding it to *t* in onsets? And how can we add −Voiced to *D* in codas without also adding it to *d* in codas?

Fortunately, we already have the tool to do this, namely unification. Recall that there are three different ways that this rule can apply vacuously with respect to a segment in a string: i) the segment might not be a member of the natural class specified in the target, ii) the segment might be a member of the natural class specified in the target but it already has the feature that the rule inserts, and iii) the segment might be a member of the natural class specified by the target, but it contains a feature that is inconsistent with the feature that the rule inserts.

For example, our rule for adding +Voiced in onsets will target three types of segments: *D and d and t*. In the first case, the rule will apply non-vacuously, and *D* will surface as [d]. In the second case, unification succeeds but is vacuous, since *d* is already +Voiced, so the rule applies vacuously and *d* surfaces as [d]. In the third case, unification of {+Voiced} with voiceless *t* fails, so the rule applies vacuously, mapping *t* to [t]. Parallel reasoning applies in codas, with *D* surfacing as [t], *d* surfacing as [d], and *t* surfacing as [t].

The addition of features via unification is exactly what we did in the second step of our two-step feature-changing processes of Russian devoicing and Hungarian reciprocal neutralization. For the Turkish, there is no feature-deletion rule that precedes the insertion rule.

So, the root-final segments will be analyzed as follows:

---
[2]We are still leaving aside "irrelevant" features like Lateral and Nasal.

(504)   a.   Non-alternating voiceless: −VOICED /t/
             sanat 'art', *sanatlar* 'art-plural', *sanatım* 'art-1sg.poss'

        b.   Non-alternating voiced: +VOICED /d/
             etüd 'etude', *etüdler* 'etude-plural', *etüdüm* 'etude-1sg.poss'

        c.   Alternating: (no specification for VOICED) /D/
             kanat 'wing', *kanatlar* 'wing-plural', *kanadım* 'wing-1sg.poss'

Our rule for turning *D* into *d* in onsets is (505):

(505)   Feature-filling of +VOICED:
        [+CORONAL, −CONTINUANT] ⊔ {+VOICED} / in ONSET

The intensionally defined target of the rule has the set of segments {t, d, D} as its extension.

We can make a parallel move for the rule that supplies −VOICED in codas. This rule neutralizes *t* and *D* to *t* in that environment:

(506)   [+CORONAL, −CONTINUANT] ⊔ {−VOICED} / in CODA

Once again, the target of the rule is the set of segments {t, d, D}, but now the output of the rule is defined only for inputs *t* and *D*, since unification of *d* with {−VOICED} fails.

The underspecification approach we have adopted avoids positing the possibility of referring to segments like *D* as 0VOICED, where 0 is a third possible value other than − or +. If we had a third possible value for the coefficient, then we could represent the difference between *t*, *d* and *D* using this third value: $t = \{−\text{VOI}, +\text{COR}, −\text{CONT}\}$; $d = \{+\text{VOI}, +\text{COR}, −\text{CONT}\}$; and $D = \{0\text{VOI}, +\text{COR}, −\text{CONT}\}$.

With such a representation, rules could target *D* to the exclusion of *t* and *d* using the natural class {0VOI, +COR, −CONT}. This would be problematic for two reasons. First, allowing reference to 0VOICED would allow us to have rules that affect segments with respect to a feature F, only if they are underspecified[3] with respect to a different feature G. In other words, it would be possible, say, to turn *D* into a fricative, changing its −CONTINUANT to +CONTINUANT, without doing so to *t* and *d*. This seems like something that does not happen in real languages—rules that appear to target only underspecified segments actually target the corresponding fully specified ones, but the rule either affects them vacuously, like when we unify *t* with {−VOICED}; or else

---

[3] We will use *unspecified* and *underspecified* interchangeably, contrary to the practice in some sources. We do not need the distinction that is sometimes, but inconsistently, made in the literature.

the output is undefined, like when we unify d with $\{-\textsc{Voiced}\}$. While our model definitely allows some kinds of rules that do not occur in attested languages, there is nothing gained by gratuitously allowing rules that refer directly to underspecification.

Second, allowing a third value opens the door to *four* possibilities: $+$, $-$, 0, and absence—the possibility of incompleteness (a segment with no value for some features) remains. There seems to be no reason to introduce a new member to the set of values and also increase the possibilities for segment-sets when we can achieve the same empirical coverage in a more economical fashion.

In Unit 46 we already argued against a privative feature system, one that allows a single value, along with underspecification. Now we have argued against allowing for three (and by implication, more) overt values, along with underspecification (absence of any mention of a feature). In other words, we have presented data and arguments, as well as an explicit model, that allows for two overt values, our '$+$' and '$-$', as well as underspecification. With this "three-for-two" model,[4] we suggest that we have found the sweet spot for phonological modeling—in this small domain, the porridge appears to be "just right".[5]

It is worthwhile to step back and consider the implications of our analysis of Turkish. Let's note again that such data tells us that the SLFA, which we used in our discussions of neutralization as a heuristic for positing lexical forms, is going to fail sometimes. The Turkish root meaning 'wing' surfaces as [kanat-] or [kanad-], but we need to posit something else as the lexical form. Such analyses further reinforce the idea that language acquisition cannot be a matter of imitating what is heard—the child has to posit a lexical form that *never* surfaces. The segment D never surfaces as such in Turkish.[6]

You will surely have realized that our posited D is just like the D of the previous unit, the segment derived by deletion of underlying voicing values in Russian. In

---

[4]This "trick" is not limited to phonology. See, for example, Andrej Bauer's discussion "How many is two?" at http://math.andrej.com/2005/05/16/how-many-is-two/.

[5]Note that by excluding the existential use of Greek letter variables in Unit 51.5 we avoid the possibility of defining a natural class $[\alpha F]$ that includes segments that are either $+F$ or $-F$, but not those that are unspecified for F. So we avoid the possibility of targeting D without targeting t and d because we can't refer to "absence"; and we also avoid the possibility of targeting t and d without targeting D because we can't use α to characterize a natural class.

[6]In the examples we discuss in this book, unspecified features are always filled in during the course of a derivation. However, Keating (1988) and Choi (1992) have shown that the output of the phonology may also contain segments that are unspecified for some features. For examples, Marshallese has surface vowels that are neither $+\textsc{Back}$ nor $-\textsc{Back}$. The existence of surface underspecification suggests that the view (e.g. Nevins, 2010, p. 193) that segments *must* receive missing values from the phonology "in order to be interpreted by the articulatory component of language and perceived by the interlocutor" is on the wrong track.

Russian *D* is only derived; in Turkish, there are morphemes that contain *D* in the lexical form. Both patterns are allowed by the possibility of incomplete segments. The data might look complex to us, but the analyses are straightforward.

The use of underspecification in phonological analyses is widespread, not only in cases like the Turkish consonants we just looked at, where we used a single binary feature to account for a three-way split in behavior, but also in cases where there is no principled way to select an underlying form that matches a surface form. In the case of *t, d, D, neither* of the fully specified segments could be chosen as the underlying form of the underspecified one. In other cases, the problem is that *either* of the two would work, but there is no way for a linguist (or a learner) to choose between them. Instead of just being happy that we can get a working solution, we recognize the impossibility of choosing between competitors and we propose a principled third way. We'll see this pattern in the next unit.

Exercise

52.1. Halle (1964, p. 328) says "We shall say that a set of speech sounds forms a *natural class* if fewer features are required to designate the class than to designate any individual sound in the class." This definition is widely adopted, for example, by Harms (1968, p. 26), but it fails in two (related) ways in comparison with our use of generalized intersection. First, explain why this definition fails for the class that contains just [t]. Then explain why it fails for the class that contains [t, d, D].

Unit 53

Turkish Vowel Harmony I

Examine the forms in (507) that show the eight surface vowels of Turkish in a list of words. These forms are written in normal Turkish orthography with the IPA version of the vowel provided in the next column. We will use the orthographic vowels, not the IPA symbols, in the following discussion.

(507)   The eight Turkish Vowels
        a.   ip   [i]   'rope'
        b.   ek   [e]   'joint'
        c.   gül   [y]   'rose'
        d.   öç   [œ]   'revenge"
        e.   kıl   [ɯ]   'body hair'
        f.   sap   [ɑ]   'stalk'
        g.   pul   [u]   'stamp'
        h.   son   [o]   'end'

The eight different vowels in these words can be described and distinguished from each other using three features as in (508): BACK, HIGH, and ROUND. You can see in the table that the vowels [i, e, ü, ö] are −BACK whereas [ı, a, u, o] are +BACK, and so on.

(508)   Feature analysis of Turkish vowels

	−BACK		+BACK	
	−ROUND	+ROUND	−ROUND	+ROUND
+HIGH	i	ü	ı	u
−HIGH	e	ö	a	o

465

We have already introduced the idea that each segment symbol is actually an abbreviation for a set of properties, and specifically, in our model, the properties are valued features. These sets are *consistent*, that is, they cannot contain incompatible values: for a given feature F, a segment cannot contain both $-$F and $+$F.

Representations of the sets corresponding to the vowels *i* and *u* are given in (509), which is just another way of representing some of the information in (508).

(509)   Sets of valued features corresponding to *i* and *u*

$$i = \left\{ \begin{array}{l} -\text{BACK} \\ -\text{ROUND} \\ +\text{HIGH} \end{array} \right\} \quad u = \left\{ \begin{array}{l} +\text{BACK} \\ +\text{ROUND} \\ +\text{HIGH} \end{array} \right\}$$

There are other features relevant to vowels across languages but the three features shown in (509) are sufficient for our discussion of Turkish.

To understand the usefulness of the featural analysis of segments, and to understand why we think of features and values as basic symbols, as building blocks for segments, let's see how they allow us to understand vowel harmony, which we present with some simplifications for expository purposes. In (510) we give the singular and plural nominative forms of some Turkish nouns. There are nouns whose roots contain *e*, and there are nouns whose roots contain *a*. Notice that the vowel of the suffix *-ler/-lar* is identical to the preceding vowel, suggesting that the vowel in the suffix is just a copy of the set of features from the vowel immediately before it.

(510)   Some Turkish singular/plural noun pairs

SINGULAR	PLURAL	MEANING
dev	devler	'giant'
kek	kekler	'cake'
ters	tersler	'contrary'
can	canlar	'soul'
tarz	tarzlar	'type'
kap	kaplar	'receptacle'

There are at least two ways to think about what is going on here. Following the patterns seen so far in this book, we might posit an underlying plural suffix *-lar* and a rule that turns the *a* into an *e* under appropriate conditions. Let's think about several potential versions of such a rule:

(511)   Potential versions of a Turkish rule

     i.   '*a* becomes *e* when the vowel of the root is *e*'

    ii.   '*a* becomes *e* when the third segment to its left is *e*'

   iii.   '*a* becomes *e* when the preceding vowel is *e*'

   iv.   '*a* becomes *e* when the nucleus of the preceding syllable is *e*'

Let's comment on each of these:

(512)   Comments on each version

     i.   This is not a pure phonological rule since it makes reference to the root. We will see later that this reference to non-phonological information makes the wrong prediction.

    ii.   This is clearly a false statement. Which data shows that this kind of counting of segments is incorrect?

   iii.   This seems to work, but we haven't formalized the idea of 'the preceding vowel' yet.

   iv.   This seems to be basically equivalent to the option (iii), but it uses syllable structure to define the environment of the rule.

We could also try to reverse the direction of the alternation in our rule by starting with underlying *-ler* and having rules that turn *e* to *a*. Given our limited dataset, this appears to work just as well, and is also consistent with the approach to alternations we have developed throughout the book.

In contrast to rules that have a fully specified underlying vowel, there is another possible approach. Suppose that the rule is basically a formalization of the idea that the final vowel (the one in the plural suffix) must be identical to the preceding vowel (descriptively, the one in the root). In other words, the phonology imposes a relation of identity or equality between the vowels. This strong hypothesis predicts that when we look at other words, we'll get even more forms of the plural suffix. For example, we predict that the plural of *ip* 'rope' is *iplir*. Like any good scientific hypothesis, this one is falsifiable. In fact, it turns out to be false! The plural of *ip*, in fact, is *ipler*.

So have we been wasting your time? Look at the plurals for all the forms we used to illustrate the eight Turkish vowels (and accept our word for it that they are representative).

---

(513) More Turkish plurals

SINGULAR	PLURAL	MEANING
ip	ipler	'rope'
ek	ekler	'joint'
gül	güller	'rose'
öç	öçler	'revenge'
kıl	kıllar	'body hair'
sap	saplar	'stalk'
pul	pullar	'stamp'
son	sonlar	'end'

We *don't* always find the same vowel in the plural as the vowel that occurs in the preceding syllable. But if you look at the set of features contained by each segment, in (508), you see that the suffix vowel is not copying or agreeing with the whole set of features from the preceding vowel, but only the information relevant to the BACK feature.[1]

Descriptively, then, we see that the suffix vowel always agrees with the preceding vowel with respect to the feature BACK. Note how this observation is consistent with our move to split up segments, to analyze them into smaller components. If segments did not *have* components, then we could not talk about them agreeing with each other with respect to their components! The existence of phenomena like Turkish vowel harmony supports the decomposition of segments into features.

The behavior of Turkish also supports a point we made when we introduced discrete values for features. The acoustic and articulatory correlates of frontness (−BACK) in *i* is different from that in *ö*, for example. Yet the two vowels behave the same with respect to the rule—they are members of an equivalence class. Recalling the discussion in Unit (24.2), we can say that this class is defined in terms of *emic* properties, as opposed to *etic* properties.

In addition to the alternation in the BACK values of its vowel, we know some other things about the plural suffix. For example, there is no reason to assume that it begins with anything other than *l* and ends with anything other than *r*. We also know that the vowel that it contains may be *a* or *e*, but that it is never a high vowel, *i, ü, ı, u*, or a round, non-high vowel, *o, ö*. Therefore, it seems reasonable to assume that the vowel of

---

[1] As we have pointed out before, in the IPA, *a* is a low front vowel and *a* is a low back vowel. However, this distinction gets complicated when using various fonts in a document, since fonts vary in which version of a small 'A' they use. We will just assume that a lowercase letter 'A' is always a +BACK vowel, no matter which IPA symbol it looks like. In our own dialect, this low vowel contrasts only with the only low front vowel *æ*.

the suffix is $-$HIGH and $-$ROUND; that is, these features are in the segment-set—the set that specifies the vowel.[2]

The only two vowels that appear in Turkish that are supersets of { $-$HIGH, $-$ROUND} are *e* and *a*, so we might be tempted to choose one of them as the vowel of the plural suffix. However, there is an alternative. We have said that a segment is a set of valued features. Recall that we have posited the property of *consistency* for segment-sets—if a feature is present in a segment-set with one value, it is not present with the other value. However, as we discussed using the Turkish *t/D/d* distinction, we have not stipulated that a segment-set must have a valued feature for each feature that UG provides—we have not stipulated that a segment be *complete*. The segment *D*, posited as a derived segment for Russian and an underlying segment for Turkish, is an example of an incomplete segment lacking a value for VOICED. We can now propose that the vowel of the plural suffix is analogous to the *D*.

We have said that we can make our derivations work by positing either /a/ or /e/ in the plural suffix, with a rule generating the other form. However, there are some complications that arise from doing so. First, there are other morphemes, like the temporal suffix *-ken*, that always surfaces with [e], even when the suffix is attached to a root with a back vowel: *yürüyorken* 'while walking'. So, there is not a general rule causing all underlying suffix /e/'s to harmonize. There are also disharmonic roots like *keman* 'violin' that suggest that there is not a rule making all underlying /a/'s harmonize with a preceding front vowel. There are ways to deal with such cases as *-ken* and *keman*, ways that appeal to morphological structure, and are thus not fully phonological. However, we will pursue an alternative.

Instead of making a choice between /-ler/ and /-lar/ for the plural, the solution we adopt is to ignore the Surfacing Lexical Form Assumption, yet again, and assume that the lexical form has neither of these vowels, but instead has an incomplete vowel, denoted as *A*. This will always surface as either [e] or [a], depending on the context. This situation is represented graphically in (514), where we have not shown that the same surface vowels may also correspond to underlying /e/ or /a/.

---

[2] Of course, what we are doing here is applying the *non-alternation assumption* (NAA) not to the whole morpheme but to segments, like the *l* and *r* of the plural, and also to *part* of the vowel. As obvious as this is, it is worthwhile to note that we can apply such reasoning to pieces of structure—features, segments, strings of segments in the phonological part of morphemes—only because we assume that linguistic representations *really are* complex data structures built from small discrete units. Such reasoning is not available to anyone who denies this property.

(514)   SMD: The underlying −HIGH and −ROUND vowel /A/ has no specification
        for BACK, and surfaces as [e] or [a] depending on context

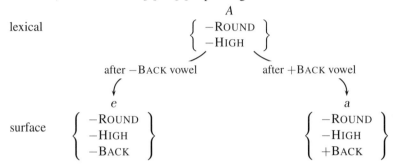

Like *D*, *A* is a segment that lacks specification for some feature *F*, and which surfaces
as the unification of its underlying form with either {−*F*} or {+*F*}. In the case of /D/,
we were driven by forced-choice reasoning—for some roots, neither surface form, [t]
or [d], could be chosen. In the case of /A/, we noted that similar problems arose given
suffixes like non-harmonizing *-ken* and disharmonic roots like *keman*. There is an
additional justification for choosing /A/, however. If we assumed underlying /-lar/ for
the plural suffix, we would need a deletion rule that turns *a* to *A*, and then a unification
rule to turn *A* to *e* in front vowel contexts. However, if we start with underlyng /-lAr/,
a single *α*-rule allows us to derive *e* and *a* where appropriate. The underspecification
analysis gives us a more concise, more elegant rule system, which we must favor, just
as we did in our discussion in Unit 24.1.

    The discussion above, including the diagram in (514), probably gives you a good
sense of our proposal for Turkish, but some details need to be laid out. Note that if
the lexical form of the plural is *-lAr*, then it appears that we need *two* rules in Turkish
phonology, one to turn /A/ to [e] and one to turn /A/ to [a], just as we needed two rules
to turn /D/ into [t] or [d], depending on the context:

(515)   Two informal rules for Turkish *e/a* vowel harmony

        i.   *A* → *e* when the preceding vowel is {−BACK}

        ii. *A* → *a* when the preceding vowel is {+BACK}

We can formalize this a bit more using unification, features, and syllable structure:

(516) Two rules for Turkish *e/a* vowel harmony

i. *A → e* after a front vowel

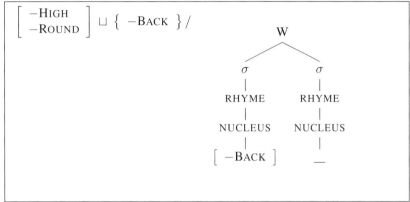

ii. *A → a* after a back vowel

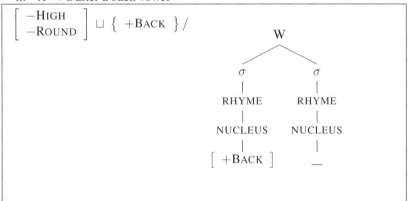

An ordinary language version of what is going on suggests an alternative to using two rules, and you already have the tools to formulate this alternative. As we have seen, the vowel of the suffix *agrees* with the preceding vowel with respect to the value associated with the feature BACK. Whatever value is present on the preceding (root) vowel, shows up on the following (suffix) vowel. The two values are linked somehow. We can achieve this by using the α variables introduced in our discussion of Hungarian reciprocal neutralization in Unit 51. If the root vowel has α as the value associated with BACK then the suffix vowel also ends up with α. With a Greek letter variable, we can state a single rule for Turkish that looks like this:

(517) One rule for Turkish *e/a* vowel harmony

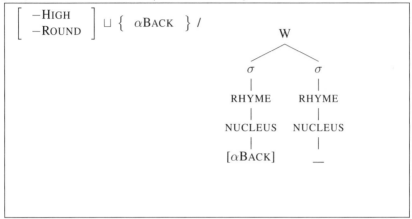

This rule assigns to a vowel the same value for BACK as the preceding vowel.

Let's review a bit. This analysis in (517) of the vowel of the Turkish plural with underlying *A* is like the analysis in (490) of Hungarian reciprocal neutralization, in that it uses a Greek letter variable. The Turkish vowel analysis with *A* is also like the analysis of the Turkish *D* in (505) and (506) in positing an underlyingly incomplete or underspecified segment. However, the vowel harmony with *A* differs from the case of *D* in that we are able to use a single rule to get context-dependent outcomes of *A* as *a* or *e* using the Greek letter variable; whereas we need two separate rules to turn *D* into *t* and *d*. This difference between the two Turkish examples is obscured a bit by the structural similarity of the SMDs in (500) and (514), since in the former, there are two non-vertical (non-vacuous) mappings and two rules, whereas in the latter, there are two non-vertical mappings corresponding to a single rule that uses a Greek letter variable. We'll come back to comparing these various situations in the next unit.

Our analysis of the Turkish plural suffix illustrates the idea that the elements we posit in a lexical form should be *unpredictable* or *idiosyncratic*. These two words are used interchangeably in phonology, and they are used in a potentially confusing way. Let's illustrate with a simple example from English. If you are asked "What is the missing segment in the following word: [___æk]?" you would not be able to answer, unless you were told the meaning. If we are looking for a word that means something like 'pin', then the missing segment would be a voiceless coronal stop, and the word would be *tack*; but if the meaning is something like 'storage framework', then the missing segment would be a non-lateral liquid, and the word would be *rack*. So, even though the word *tack* always starts with *t*, and the word *rack* always starts with *r*, these are arbitrary properties of those words. In this sense, despite being constant, these properties are idiosyncratic, unpredictable. Such properties have to be stored in long-term memory in the lexicon.

Contrast your inability to select the missing segment above with the following questions. "The missing segment in the following word is a voiceless coronal stop; is it aspirated or unaspirated?: [___æk]. How about in this word?: [s___æk]". If you know that English voiceless stops are aspirated in initial position, then you know that *tack* begins with t^h and *stack* has unaspirated *t* after the *s*. The aspiration is *predictable* even if you are not sure which exact word is intended: "The initial consonant of [___ɪk] is a voiceless stop, but I won't tell you which one. Is it aspirated?" You know that the stop will be aspirated, whether the word is *pick, tick*, or *kick*.

In phonology, idiosyncratic information *must* be stored in the lexicon if it is to play a role in how morphemes surface. There is no other way for information to enter in derivations other than by being brought from the lexicon (stored, constant information) or by being added by rules (predictable information).

Returning to Turkish, there is no principle or rule that tells us that the plural suffix should begin with *l*. Instead, this is inferred by a learner from the fact that the suffix always shows up with initial *l*, and then this constant information must be stored. Similarly, there is no principle that the suffix should end with *r*. And there is no principle that tells us that the vowel should always be −HIGH and −ROUND. Yes, you can predict that every time a Turkish speaker utters a noun in the plural, there will be an *l*, a −HIGH and −ROUND vowel, and an *r* in the suffix, because you know that those are constant properties of the plural, but that is not what we mean by phonological predictability—that's just knowing what is in the lexicon.

In contrast, it *is* predictable whether the vowel shows up as −BACK or +BACK. You don't need to memorize the *exact* plural of *ip*, only the idiosyncratic parts. We can leave the specification of −BACK or +BACK out of the lexical entry. The view we are pursuing is not only that we, the linguists, can do so, but that this is in fact what a learner does in constructing a Turkish grammar.

If this view is correct, we have, once again, an argument against the view that language learning involves imitation in any simple sense. In Unit 2, we pointed out that children always hear words with some intonation, but they have to store an abstract representation that can be plugged into any intonation pattern. Here we claim that despite the fact that Turkish learners always hear *-ler* or *-lar*, they store in long-term memory the underspecified vowel *A*, which is never pronounced.

Exercises

53.1. Which is a better representation of the Turkish plural suffix?

$$\text{(a) } l \left\{ \begin{matrix} -\text{HIGH} \\ -\text{ROUND} \end{matrix} \right\} r \qquad \text{(b) } l \left[\begin{matrix} -\text{HIGH} \\ -\text{ROUND} \end{matrix} \right] r$$

53.2. In footnote (2) of this unit we compared our reasoning for selecting the lexical form of the Turkish plural as /-lAr/ to application of the *non-alternation assumption* to the *parts* of morpheme alternants, instead of looking at complete morpheme alternants as we originally did. Perhaps we could formulate a principle for choosing lexical forms based on this idea, something like this:

The Constancy Assumption: Any phonological information present in *all* surface alternants of a morpheme must be present in the morpheme's lexical form.

Phonological information would include factors like the number and sequence of segments in a morpheme, but the feature content of segments might be partial. For example, we posited the *A* vowel for the Turkish plural, a vowel which is underspecified for BACK.

The constancy assumption is appealing, but it is difficult to apply when, for example, a morpheme has alternations involving deletion. Suppose a language has surface forms such as [kiral-, kral-], which alternate according to stress conditions. A simple-minded approach that looks at the first segment of each alternant, then the second, and so on, would miss the fact that both alternants contain *k, r, a,* and *l* with constant precedence (not immediate precedence) relations among them, so a more sophisticated approach is needed.

Whether or not the constancy assumption can be made to work for such cases, we want you to consider some simpler questions:

A. How is traditional reasoning about lexical forms, what you were taught in introductory linguistics, inconsistent with the constancy assumption? As a point of departure for your discussion, consider the English word *cap*, which is typically pronounced [kʰæp], and is typically assumed to be underlyingly /kæp/.

B. Can you think of any justification for the traditional view?

C. If we try to apply the Constancy Assumption for cases like *cap*, what (else) would change about our views of English phonology? Anything about the grammar? The lexicon? The course of acquisition?

Unit 54

Discussion: Surface Segments and SMDs

In this unit, we review some of the neutralization patterns we have discussed by comparing the relevant segment mapping diagrams (SMDs). Remember that SMDs have no status in our theory but are just tools that help us understand various data patterns that arise in languages. We can use simple SMDs if we are just interested in mappings between segments in UR and SR.

However, now that we have deconstructed the arrow '$\rightarrow$' of phonological rules into separate parts, it may be useful to revisit some of the SMDs we have seen. To narrow the discussion, while at the same time abstracting from particular languages, let's assume that ϕ and ψ are segments, like t and d, that differ only in the value of one particular feature F, so that if ϕ is $+F$, then ψ is $-F$, or else if ϕ is $-F$, then ψ is $+F$. Furthermore, assume that $\Delta = \phi \cap \psi$; in other words, Δ is identical to ϕ and ψ, except for being underspecified for feature F, like D with respect to t and d.

Here in (518) are SMDs that show several of the patterns we have discussed:

(518) Six Different Segment Mapping Patterns

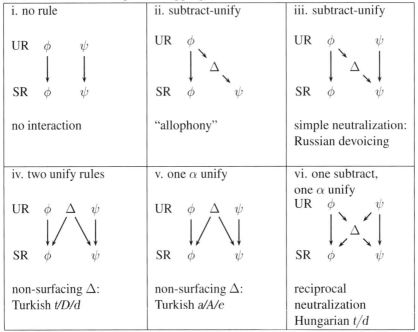

Pattern (i) corresponds to a case where there are no phonological rules relating the segments ϕ and ψ. Pattern (ii) shows a simple split of an underlying segment into a form generated by a rule, and a default form. The two forms would be in complementary distribution, if no other rules interfere with this pattern, and traditionally we would call this a case of allophony, like the cases introduced in Unit 23. Pattern (iii) is simple neutralization, like the pattern of final devoicing discussed in Russian in Unit 49. Given our two-step approach to feature-changing, patterns (ii) and (iii) both involve feature deletion (via set subtraction) and feature insertion (via unification).

Pattern (iv) corresponds to the Turkish stops discussed in Unit 52, where the underlying underspecified D is neutralized with t in one environment by one rule and with d in another environment by another rule. Pattern (v) looks like (iv), and it also has an underlying underspecified segment. In this case, however, a single rule with a Greek letter variable generates two different outcomes in different environments. This corresponds to the Turkish vowel harmony example involving a /A/ e that we discussed in Unit 53.

Finally, pattern (vi), like (ii) and (iii) involves feature deletion, resulting in an underspecified segment, followed by a rule with a Greek letter variable, like pattern (v), that yields different outcomes depending on the environment. This corresponds to the reciprocal neutralization of Hungarian *t/d*, and other pairs like *p/b* and *s/z* discussed in Unit 51.

We present these SMDs to once more illustrate our attempt "to abstract from the welter of descriptive complexity certain general principles governing computation that would allow the rules of a particular language to be given in very simple forms" (Chomsky, 2000, p. 122). By recombining computational and representational tools like Greek letter variables, underspecification, rule ordering, and the status of unification as a partial function, we are able to get a wide range of phenomena, a "welter of descriptive complexity," from a fairly simple model.

Exercises

54.1. Look at pattern (v) in (518). Why do we assume that Turkish has underlying /a/ and /e/ in addition to the surface [a] and [e] derived from /A/?

54.2. Consider the following SMD:

Assume that this is a mapping between UR segments and SR segments with the feature characterizations given in this unit. Describe this situation in a brief paragraph. What kind of data might lead you to such an analysis? You might have to refer to phonetic factors in answering this.

54.3. Consider the following SMD:

$$
\begin{array}{ccc}
\text{UR} & & \Delta \\
& \swarrow & \searrow \\
\text{SR} & \phi & \psi
\end{array}
$$

Assume that this is a mapping between UR segments and SR segments. Describe this situation in a brief paragraph. What kind of data might lead you to such an analysis?

54.4. Hungarian, like Turkish and Finnish, has vowel harmony involving the features ROUND and BACK. Unlike Turkish, Hungarian does not have on the surface a +HIGH, +BACK, −ROUND vowel like *ɪ*. For most roots with a front vowel, harmonizing suffixes surface with a front vowel like *e*. Roots with a back vowel surface with a suffix alternant containing a back vowel like *a*:

> "Regular" harmony
>
> | N | N-DATIVE | gloss |
> |------|----------|-----------|
> | vi:z | vi:znek | 'water' |
> | sem | semnek | 'eye' |
> | rɑb | rɑbnɑk | 'prisoner' |
> | ku:t | ku:tnɑk | 'well' |

However, there are some roots that always surface with the front vowel *i*, but nevertheless occur with back vowel forms of the suffixes:

> "Exceptional" harmony
>
> | N | N-DATIVE | gloss |
> |------|----------|----------|
> | hi:d | hi:dnɑk | 'bridge' |

Such patterns have nothing to do with the consonants in the word.

Construct a hypothesis about what is going on in Hungarian. Your solution should be purely phonological, so you can't refer to exceptions to rules or stored exceptional forms. Your solution should be based on an SMD with this structure for UR and SR (with intervening levels as well).

Schematic SMD for Hungarian

You should provide the following in your analysis:

i. The lexical form for the roots 'water' and 'bridge' and the dative suffix.

ii. A simple vowel harmony rule that works for *all* the dative forms, stated in words.

iii. Another rule of the form '$a \rightarrow b$' with *no environment*, in violation of our SPE rule typology laid out in unit 10.

iv. A description of the type of rule interaction.

v. A richer SMD using features, with at least one level between UR and SR.

vi. Derivations for the two forms containing 'water' and the two containing 'bridge'.

vii. A brief discussion of what such an analysis implies for the process of acquiring the language. Is the analysis plausible? What are some alternatives?

Unit 55

Turkish Vowel Harmony II

The analysis we developed for the −HIGH harmonizing vowels in Turkish is potentially more general than we have indicated. Consider the following forms of the genitive suffix on the same eight nouns we saw above:

(519)   Natural class of root vowels and their corresponding genitive form

NOM. SG.	GEN.SG	GLOSS	ROOT VOWEL CLASS
ip	ipin	'rope'	[−BACK, −ROUND]
ek	ekin	'joint'	
kıl	kılın	'body hair'	[+BACK, −ROUND]
sap	sapın	'stalk'	
pul	pulun	'stamp'	[+BACK, +ROUND]
son	sonun	'end'	
gül	gülün	'rose'	[−BACK, +ROUND]
öç	öçün	'revenge'	

Note that the genitive suffix has four alternants [in, ın, un, ün]. It is a constant fact, but arbitrary and thus unpredictable, that the suffix should have an *n* at the end, and it is similarly unpredictable (that is, a constant, idiosyncratic fact about the lexical form) that the vowel should always be +HIGH. These idiosyncratic properties must be stored in long-term memory, in the morpheme's phonological representation. Note, however, that the values for BACK and ROUND are completely predictable phonologically—they are identical to those on the preceding vowel, the root vowel. For example, [ek] has a vowel that is −BACK, −ROUND, and the genitive form of this word is [ekin], with a −BACK, −ROUND suffix vowel [i]; in contrast [son] has a vowel that is +BACK,

+ROUND, and the genitive form of this word is [sonun], with a +BACK, +ROUND suffix vowel [u]. The form [ip] takes the same suffix form as [ek], because their respective vowels are members of same natural class, as shown in (519).

Applying the same logic we used for the plural suffix, we can posit a genitive suffix with a vowel that is incomplete, but now with respect to *two* features, BACK and ROUND. We will continue to ignore all the features that seem to play no role in Turkish and work with the representation in (520):

(520)   Representation of the Turkish genitive suffix
      (a)   { +HIGH } n   (b)   I n

In (520a) we give the featural representation of the vowel segment in the suffix (restricted to the features under discussion), and in 520b), we continue the practice of using capital letters to denote underspecified segments, as we did with *D* and *A* in earlier discussion. So *I* denotes a vowel that is +HIGH but unspecified for BACK and ROUND.

One option for generating the correct alternants of the genitive suffix from underlying /In/ is to posit a single unification process that supplies two valued features at a time:

(521)   One rule for Turkish *i, ı, u, ü* vowel harmony

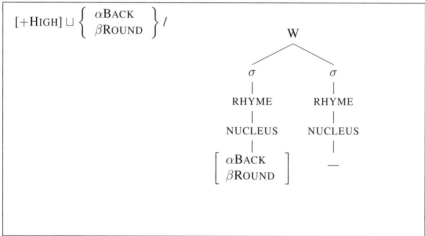

Let's call this the *two-at-a-time* analysis, since both missing features are filled in at the same time, by a single unification.

An alternative is to have one rule that fills in values for ROUND, and another that fills in values for BACK. Our theory demands that the two rules be ordered, but we have no basis for choosing an order, so we must admit our ignorance. Here are the two rules:

(522) Two rules for Turkish *i, ı, u, y* vowel harmony[1]

    i. BACK harmony

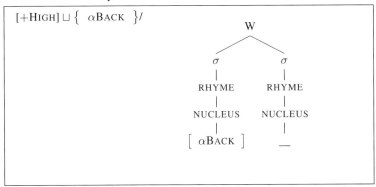

    ii. ROUND harmony

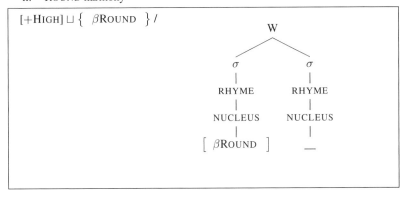

---

[1]We use α and β for expository clarity in these rules to avoid the impression that the two rules making up the harmony process share a variable. Of course, we are not obliged to use two different variables here, since the scope of variable assignment is a single rule—in other words, our theory does not countenance transderivational Greek letter variables, variables that can maintain an assigned value through a sequence of rules. Phonology seems not to need such power.

Note that the effect of rule (522i) is to fill in a value for BACK on a +HIGH vowel that is unspecified for BACK. We can actually collapse this rule with rule (517) to fill in a value on *any* vowel that is underspecified for BACK.

(523)   One rule for Turkish BACK vowel harmony

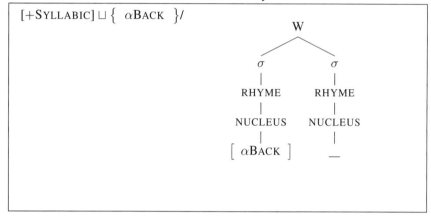

Note that we have supplied the value +SYLLABIC to the natural class of targets in this rule, just to have something to refer to here, but this feature is potentially present in the preceding harmony rules as well, such as (522.ii).[2]

Once we generalize the BACK harmony rule, as in (523) to cover *e/a* harmony and *i, ı, u, y* harmony, we still need a separate rule for ROUND harmony. You may be tempted to maintain the rule developed above in (522ii), revised here with a +SYLLABIC specification (which is actually redundant, since the rule environment specifies the target should be in nucleus position):

---

[2]This issue will be handled more thoroughly below.

(524)   ROUND harmony formulated for +HIGH vowels

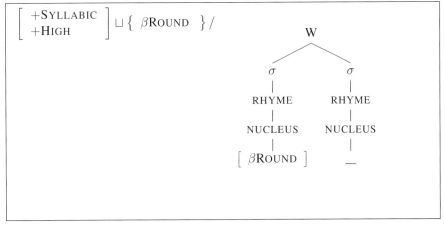

However, you should now see that the more general rule in (525) would work just as well:

(525)   ROUND harmony formulated for all vowels

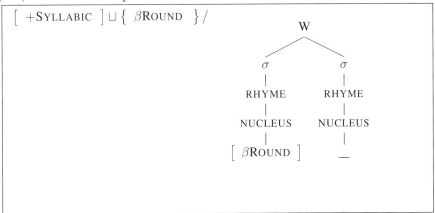

This works, given the information we have thus far, since the other underspecified vowel we have seen, the *A* of the plural suffix is already specified as −ROUND. And of course, the other vowels we have seen, the vowels in roots, are fully specified. So, an attempt at unification of any of these vowels that have an underlying value for ROUND with a set containing either +ROUND or −ROUND will result in either vacuous unification, when the values agree, or failed unification, when the values disagree. In other words, this ROUND harmony rule, as stated in (525) will give us exactly the desired result for all vowels lacking a value for ROUND, whether the vowel is +HIGH or −HIGH.

The strategy that we just invoked for collapsing the ROUND harmony rules for all vowels can be pushed even further. Suppose that the only segments in Turkish that are lacking specifications for BACK and ROUND are the two vowels we have been discussing. Suppose that all other vowels, and all consonants, bear a value for those features. In such a case, we can make our rules even more general, yet still have them give the desired output. As before, we can use empty square brackets [ ] to refer to the natural class of *all* segments—by requiring nothing, we characterize everything. Remember that, in our notation, if $X, Y,$ and Z are properties of segments, then $[X, Y, Z]$ denotes the natural class of segments $R = \{r : r \supseteq \{X, Y, Z\}\}$. Each member of the class is a superset of the set of properties $\{X, Y, Z\}$. You recall that the empty set $\emptyset$ is a subset of *every* set. This means that *every* set is a superset of the empty set. Therefore, the notation [ ] means $R = \{r : r \supseteq \{\}\} = \{r : r \supseteq \emptyset\}$, which is the set of *all* segments.

We can get the same effect by performing generalized intersection over the set of all segments. If you take the generalized intersection of all the segments in a language, including both consonants and vowels, it is likely that you will end up with the empty set—there are probably no features shared by all the segments.[3]

Let's use this result to update our rules. Here is the "minimalist" version of our rule for BACK harmony:

---

[3]There could be some shared valued features. For example, if a language L has no laterals, it may be the case that every segment is specified −LAT. Then, instead of using the empty set to characterize the natural class of all segments, we would use $\{-\text{LAT}\}$. Extensionally, the resulting natural class would be the same—it would include all the segments in L. Using the empty set gives you all universally possible segments, but only a subset of these will be in L.

(526)   BACK harmony (re-)formulated for all vowels

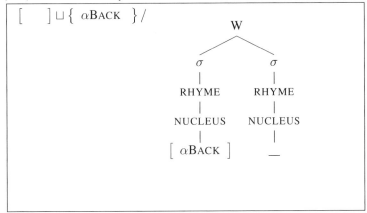

And here is the "minimalist" version of our rule for ROUND harmony:

(527)   ROUND harmony (re-)formulated for all vowels

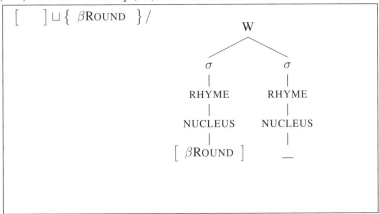

Although the empty brackets signal that the rule targets all segments, the environment restricts the set of targets to those that are in the nucleus position. Since only vowels appear in nucleus position, the rule will in fact only target vowels.

Exercise

55.1. Some languages are claimed to have rules that delete the final segment from a word, whether it is a vowel or a consonant. Your tasks are (a) to formulate such a rule, under the assumption that there is no valued feature shared by all segments in the language, and (b) to provide a set of forms that could plausibly lead to such an analysis. There has to be evidence that something is in the UR if you want to delete it by rule. Note that for (a), you are not allowed to make use of a feature ±SEGMENT.

Unit 56

Turkish Vowel Harmony III

We have looked at Turkish plural forms like *ipler* and *saplar*. These forms have no overt case marking, but they are used as nominative forms, for example as the subject of a sentence. We have also looked at genitive singular forms, which have a genitive suffix, but no marker of singular. Consider now forms that combine the meaning of a root like *ip* with the meanings PLURAL and GENITIVE. Examples of these forms are shown in the third column of table (528).

(528) Turkish genitive plural forms

	NOM PL	GEN SG	GEN PL	
a.	ip-ler	ip-in	ip-ler-in	'rope'
b.	ek-ler	ek-in	ek-ler-in	'joint'
c.	kıl-lar	kıl-ın	kıl-lar-ın	'body hair'
d.	sap-lar	sap-ın	sap-lar-ın	'stalk'
e.	pul-lar	pul-un	pul-lar-ın	'stamp'
f.	son-lar	son-un	son-lar-ın	'end'
g.	gül-ler	gül-ün	gül-ler-in	'rose'
h.	öç-ler	öç-ün	öç-ler-in	'revenge'

Note that while there are four forms of the genitive singular suffix, [in, ın, un, ün], there are only two forms of the genitive suffix that surface in the plural, [in, ın]. Do we have to posit separate suffixes for genitive singular and genitive plural? We can see that the vowels of the genitive suffix forms that show up in the plural are never +ROUND, so perhaps we need a singular genitive suffix with a vowel that is unspecified for ROUND and a plural genitive suffix with a vowel that is specified −ROUND:

(529)   Are there two genitive suffixes in Turkish?

	GENITIVE SINGULAR	GENITIVE PURAL
Alternants	[in, ın, un, ün]	[in, ın]
Lexical form	{ +HIGH }n	{ +HIGH −ROUND }n

Recall our discussion of alternative accounts of the plural suffix in (511). One possibility we considered was a solution that was not purely phonological, the possibility
that vowel harmony involves copying features from the *root* vowel. This is contrasted
with the possibilities that harmony involves purely phonological conditioning by either
the preceding vowel or the vowel of the preceding syllable. Notice that the root-based
solution won't allow us to treat the genitive forms of the singular and plural in a unified manner. For example, in the singular, the root *gül* bears a suffix alternant [-ün],
but in the plural, the same root combines with a suffix alternant [-in]. However, the
genitive plural forms are completely consistent with the genitive singular forms, not
with respect to the exact range of attested forms, but with respect to the phonological
conditioning—the genitive plural forms always agree with the preceding vowel in both
ROUND and BACK.

Here's a problem: we have already decided that the plural suffix is -*lAr* with a vowel
unspecified for BACK, so how can the genitive suffix copy a value for BACK that is not
there? There are two obvious ways to deal with this problem. The first approach is
a kind of ordering solution, but it is not a matter of ordering among different rules.
Instead the idea is to apply the same rule of BACK harmony *twice*. First, the plural
suffix copies a value for BACK from the preceding (root) vowel; then the genitive
suffix copies the value for BACK from *its* predecessor vowel, namely that of the plural
suffix.

This solution contradicts an assumption we made in Unit 11, namely that rules
are not applied iteratively right-to-left or left-to-right, but rather globally in one fell
swoop. Our assumption about global application is just that, an assumption that may
be unjustified and maybe should be rejected. However, instead of rejecting global
application outright, we will briefly sketch an alternative.

Our alternative also constitutes a radical revision to the kinds of rules we have
been using, rules that have been fairly restricted in the range of environments that can
be used. Suppose we allowed a relativized notion of *locality* that includes the capacity
of rules to search through the phonological string for a particular terminating element.
Concretely, assume an underlying representation for the genitive plural of *öç* as in
(530):

(530)   Underlying representation of *öçlerin*

$$\left\{\begin{array}{l} +\text{SYLLABIC} \\ -\text{BACK} \\ +\text{ROUND} \\ -\text{HIGH} \end{array}\right\} \quad \text{çl} \quad \left\{\begin{array}{l} +\text{SYLLABIC} \\ -\text{ROUND} \\ -\text{HIGH} \end{array}\right\} \quad \text{r} \quad \left\{\begin{array}{l} +\text{SYLLABIC} \\ +\text{HIGH} \end{array}\right\} \quad \text{n}$$

Instead of a rule assigning αBACK to an underspecified vowel by copying αBACK from the first vowel to the left, we will allow a rule to search from an underspecified vowel to the first vowel to the left that has an αBACK value.

The difference between these conditions can be clarified with a non-linguistic example. Consider the potential differences between the results of these sets of instructions to a group of people living in a building, one per floor:

(531)   Searching for a middle name: Adjacent or as far as necessary

A.   If you have a middle name, write down your middle name. If you don't have a middle name,

-   SEARCH: find the first person above you, and
-   COPY: write down that person's middle name.
-   DEFAULT: If either the person immediately above you has no middle name or there is nobody immediately above you, write X.

B.   If you have a middle name, write down your middle name. If you don't have a middle name,

-   SEARCH: find the first person above you *that has a middle name*, and
-   COPY: write down that person's middle name.
-   DEFAULT: If either there is nobody at any distance above you with a middle name, or there is nobody at all above you, write X.

In each scenario, the third clause provides a default value 'X' when no other middle name is available. Under scenario (A), you might end up with no middle name to write down in case neither you nor your immediate upstairs neighbor has one. Under scenario (B), you have a greater chance of ending up with a middle name to write down, since you can look beyond your immediate upstairs neighbor to more remote ones, up to the top floor of the building.

Let's assume that Turkish BACK harmony works like scenario (B). What this means is that both of the underlying incomplete vowels in *öçlerin* can "look for" a value for

BACK *at the same time*. In other words, we can save global application by sacrificing the immediate neighbor requirement. In one derivational step, each vowel searches for the first αBACK to its left, and the vowel from which each search initiates "attempts" to unify with the $\{\alpha$BACK$\}$ it finds. Vowels that underlyingly have a value for BACK will either unify vacuously, or else unification will fail, also leading to vacuous application of the rule in the relevant substring. The only "visible" effects of the rule will be on the underlyingly incomplete vowels.[1]

We will be fairly informal in our description of vowel harmony processes, but we will use the terms SEARCH and COPY to indicate the kind of specific rule components that we have in mind. Ultimately, we should provide a full semantics of such rules as functions mapping strings to strings, as with our earlier formalizations. Here is our first semi-formal SEARCH and COPY rule in (532) with a sketch of an interpretation in (533):

(532)   Turkish BACK harmony:
        SEARCH leftward from each vowel ς for the first segment γ bearing αBACK;
        $\varsigma \sqcup \{\alpha$BACK$\}$ (that is, COPY αBACK to ς).

(533)   Sketch of interpretation: Map each string $x_1 x_2 \ldots x_n$ to the string $y_1 y_2 \ldots y_n$, such that for each i that is greater than 1 and less than n:

        i.   if the following three conditions hold:

             a. $+$SYLL $\in x_i$ (x_i is a vowel)
             b.   there is an x_j, such that x_j is the first segment to the left of x_i such that αBACK $\in x_j$ (there is a preceding segment that has a specification for BACK)

---

[1]Returning to our middle name search, you can confirm that it is still possible for a search to turn up empty and for an "incomplete" name to remain incomplete (that is, lacking a middle name). It turns out that there is evidence that incomplete segments in some languages sometimes surface without receiving values for some features (Keating, 1988). This is a situation that we won't worry about here for phonology, since in Turkish, at least, it seems that incomplete vowels occur only in the lexical forms of suffixes. Therefore, there is always a value to copy from in the root, somewhere to the left of the suffix.

It is also possible to provide a mechanism to fill in a default value. For names, instead of the X used in (531), we can assign a default middle name by replacing the third clause of each scenario with the following:

• Default middle name assignment: If you complete your search and don't find a middle name to copy, write down 'Ada'.

We don't need this kind of default assignment for Turkish, but default assignment does seem to be necessary when this kind of SEARCH and COPY algorithm is more widely applied in phonology. In other words, we might have harmony filling in both $+$BK and $-$BK, but with a further default assignment for BK when harmony does not provide a value.

  c. $x_i \sqcup \{\alpha\text{BACK}\}$ is defined,   (unification does not fail)

  then $y_i = x_i \sqcup \{\alpha\text{BACK}\}$ (COPY αBACK to x_i)

 ii. Otherwise $y_i = x_i$

Of course, if unification fails, ç maps to ç, as we discussed earlier. Here is the result of applying this rule (532) to the UR in (530):

(534) Output of SEARCH and COPY for αBACK to UR of *öçlerin*

$$
\left\{
\begin{array}{l}
+\text{SYLLABIC} \\
-\text{BACK} \\
+\text{ROUND} \\
-\text{HIGH}
\end{array}
\right\}
\; \text{çl} \;
\left\{
\begin{array}{l}
+\text{SYLLABIC} \\
\boxed{-\text{BACK}} \\
-\text{ROUND} \\
-\text{HIGH}
\end{array}
\right\}
\; \text{r} \;
\left\{
\begin{array}{l}
+\text{SYLLABIC} \\
\boxed{-\text{BACK}} \\
+\text{HIGH}
\end{array}
\right\}
\; \text{n}
$$

Each suffix has an underlying vowel that has no value for BACK. When the rule applies, both suffix vowels receive their value for BACK, shown in a box, in a single global application.

 Note that the final vowel, the vowel of the genitive suffix, is still missing a value for ROUND. We still can't strictly order ROUND harmony with respect to BACK harmony, but we will just apply it second here to yield the SR of *öçlerin*. The rule and interpretation for ROUND harmony work exactly the same as those for BACK harmony in (532) and (533), as shown in (535) and (536)

(535) Turkish ROUND harmony:
  SEARCH leftward from each vowel ç for the first segment γ bearing αROUND;
  ç $\sqcup$ $\{\alpha\text{ROUND}\}$ (that is, COPY αROUND to ç).

(536) Sketch of interpretation: Map each string $x_1 x_2 \ldots x_n$ to the string $y_1 y_2 \ldots y_n$, such that for each i that is greater than 1 and less than n:

 i. if the following three conditions hold:

  a. $+\text{SYLL} \in x_i$ (x_i is a vowel)

  b. there is an x_j, such that x_j is the first segment to the left of x_i such that $\alpha\text{ROUND} \in x_j$ (there is a preceding segment that has a specification for ROUND)

  c. $x_i \sqcup \{\alpha\text{ROUND}\}$ is defined,   (unification does not fail)

  then $y_i = x_i \sqcup \{\alpha\text{ROUND}\}$ (COPY αROUND to x_i)

 ii. Otherwise $y_i = x_i$

Again, if unification fails, there is vacuous application and ç maps to itself. There is only one vowel, the vowel of the genitive suffix, that is incomplete with respect to ROUND. That vowel ends up as −ROUND because the first value for this feature to the left is the −ROUND on the vowel of the plural suffix.

(537)   Output of SEARCH and COPY for αROUND yields SR *öçlerin*

$$
\left\{ \begin{array}{l} +\text{SYLLABIC} \\ -\text{BACK} \\ +\text{ROUND} \\ -\text{HIGH} \end{array} \right\} \text{ çl } \left\{ \begin{array}{l} +\text{SYLLABIC} \\ -\text{BACK} \\ -\text{ROUND} \\ -\text{HIGH} \end{array} \right\} \text{ r } \left\{ \begin{array}{l} +\text{SYLLABIC} \\ -\text{BACK} \\ \boxed{-\text{ROUND}} \\ +\text{HIGH} \end{array} \right\} \text{ n}
$$

You could compare this derivation with that of *öçün*. The UR of this word is as in (538), with the suffix lacking values for BACK and ROUND:

(538)   Underlying representation of *öçün*

$$
\left\{ \begin{array}{l} +\text{SYLLABIC} \\ -\text{BACK} \\ +\text{ROUND} \\ -\text{HIGH} \end{array} \right\} \text{ ç } \left\{ \begin{array}{l} +\text{SYLLABIC} \\ +\text{HIGH} \end{array} \right\} \text{ n}
$$

Again, we will apply BACK harmony first, yielding (539):

(539)   After application of BACK harmony to UR of *öçün*

$$
\left\{ \begin{array}{l} +\text{SYLLABIC} \\ -\text{BACK} \\ +\text{ROUND} \\ -\text{HIGH} \end{array} \right\} \text{ ç } \left\{ \begin{array}{l} +\text{SYLLABIC} \\ \boxed{-\text{BACK}} \\ +\text{HIGH} \end{array} \right\} \text{ n}
$$

Next, ROUND harmony derives the SR:

(540)   Application of ROUND harmony yields *öçün*

$$
\left\{ \begin{array}{l} +\text{SYLLABIC} \\ -\text{BACK} \\ +\text{ROUND} \\ -\text{HIGH} \end{array} \right\} \text{ ç } \left\{ \begin{array}{l} +\text{SYLLABIC} \\ -\text{BACK} \\ \boxed{+\text{ROUND}} \\ +\text{HIGH} \end{array} \right\} \text{ n}
$$

You can now confirm that a single representation for the genitive suffix, a single BACK harmony rule and a single ROUND harmony rule will yield the difference in alternant sets in the genitive singular [in, ɪn, un, ün] versus the genitive plural [in, ɪn]. To sum up, in the singular, the genitive suffix gets values for both missing features from the root vowel, because in the singular the root vowel is the first vowel to the left that has values for those features. In contrast, in the plural, the genitive suffix gets its back feature from the root vowel but its round feature from the plural suffix. It is important to note that in the genitive plural forms there is a structural similarity between the root vowel and the plural suffix value: each is the first vowel to the left of the genitive suffix with a specified αF, for some feature F. The root vowel is the first vowel to the left that has a value for BACK, while the plural suffix vowel is the first vowel to the left that has a value for ROUND.

In the plural, the first "donor" to the left of each suffix vowel for the feature BACK is the root vowel. The plural suffix has an underlying $-$ROUND, which is the value that gets copied by the genitive suffix in the plural.

As we noted, using the kind of SEARCH-based rule sketched here is a major enhancement to our evolving view of phonological rules. However, SEARCH saves us from having to apply harmony rules iteratively from left to right. You can find more explicit developments of these ideas in a variety of recent work, including Samuels (2011) and Shen (2016).

Recall our discussion of metathesis in Unit 36, in which we were forced to admit that the SPE model is inadequate to model such phenomena. Now that we have broken down feature-changing processes into deletion and insertion components and have also introduced the possibility of SEARCH algorithms, you can see that our rules and representational systems are subject to further enhancement. You might be able to imagine developing a specific method for dealing with metathesis without opening the door to the full power of semi-Thue rules. Unfortunately, we will say no more about this challenging problem here.

Exercises

The first few questions below involve variations on the middle name search algorithms discussed in (531). You should confirm that the six sets of instructions given below (A, B, C, D, E, F) lead to six different results.

In each scenario, there will be some people who end up without a middle name to write down. We have simplified here by leaving out the clauses about default behavior—you should be able to figure out when to write X denoting that no middle name has been found by the specified SEARCH and COPY parts of each algorithm. For example, Harriet Tubman, never gets a middle name in any of the six scenarios since she lives on the top floor and all searching is upwards. Always mark X for her middle name.

For each of the six algorithms, the first step is always "If you have a middle name, write down your middle name." For each algorithm, we just list the instruction to follow if the first step fails—if a person has no middle name of his or her own.

56.1. First, consider the two sets of instructions from (531) for people living one per floor in a building, repeated in simplified form in (541):

(541)   Searching for a middle name: Adjacent or as far as necessary

    A.   If you don't have a middle name,

       – SEARCH: find the first person above you, and

       – COPY: and write down that person's middle name.

    B.   If you don't have a middle name,

       – SEARCH: find the first person above you *that has a middle name*, and

       – COPY: write down that person's middle name.

Fill in the results of these two middle name search algorithms applied to the following list of building tenants, from the roof down to the ground floor. Each person's gender is noted in the left column; we will use this information later. Mark any differences you find in the two columns. A few answers have been provided using just the appropriate middle initial to denote a middle name.

NAME	Immediate (541.A)	First (541.B)
(F) Harriet Tubman	X	
(M) Franklin Delano Roosevelt		
(F) Maryam Mirzakhani		
(F) Rosalind Elsie Franklin		
(M) Edvard Munch		
(M) George Washington Carver	W	
(M) Akira Kurosawa	W	
(F) Jane Austen	X	W
(M) René Descartes		
(F) Caroline Lucretia Herschel		

56.2. Repeat the previous exercise, but add the following condition: write down (COPY) a middle name only if the donor has the same gender as the SEARCH-er. In other words, SEARCH terminates as in A and B, but there is a condition of identity of gender on COPY. This gives the following two algorithms:

(542) Searching for a middle name: Gender as a condition on COPY

    C. If you don't have a middle name,

        – SEARCH: find the first person above you, and,

        – COPY: **if that person has the same gender as you**, write down that person's middle name.

    D. If you don't have a middle name,

        – SEARCH: find the first person above you *that has a middle name*, and,

        – COPY: **if that person has the same gender as you**, write down that person's middle name.

NAME	Immediate (542.C)	First (542.D)
(F) Harriet Tubman		
(M) Franklin Delano Roosevelt		
(F) Maryam Mirzakhani		
(F) Rosalind Elsie Franklin		
(M) Edvard Munch		
(M) George Washington Carver		
(M) Akira Kurosawa		
(F) Jane Austen		
(M) René Descartes		
(F) Caroline Lucretia Herschel		

56.3. Now, instead of using identity of gender as a condition on whether to write down (COPY) a middle name, we'll use it as a condition on how far upstairs to look (where SEARCH terminates). Here, in E and F, the gender identity condition is added to the conditions on SEARCH seen in A and B, respectively.

(543) Searching for a middle name: Gender as a condition on SEARCH

    E. If you don't have a middle name,

        – SEARCH: find the first person above you **that has the same gender as you**, and

–   COPY: write down that person's middle name.

F.   If you don't have a middle name,

–   SEARCH: find the first person above you *that has a middle name*, and has **the same gender as you**, and

–   COPY: and write down that person's middle name.

NAME	Immediate (543.E)	First (543.F)
(F) Harriet Tubman		
(M) Franklin Delano Roosevelt		
(F) Maryam Mirzakhani		
(F) Rosalind Elsie Franklin		
(M) Edvard Munch		
(M) George Washington Carver		
(M) Akira Kurosawa		
(F) Jane Austen		
(M) René Descartes		
(F) Caroline Lucretia Herschel		

56.4.   Invent a set of toy grammars and datasets involving vowel harmony that parallel each of the six SEARCH and COPY algorithms you used for middle names in the previous questions. For each case, invent a simple example with a small dataset based on the vowels of Turkish. Sharing the same gender could be analogous, say, to having the same vowel height, which you can express using Greek-letter variables. Treat the lack of a middle name as analogous to underspecification. We do not know if all the versions we gave correspond to possible languages, but once you explore the space of possibilities, you can look for real-language examples.

56.5.   Find some papers that discuss *parasitic harmony* or *parasitic assimilation*, for example, Jurgec (2013). Can you find any analogs in such work to the various SEARCH and COPY algorithms above? Are the analogies perfect? Explain.

56.6.   How might the SEARCH approach be generalized to deal with rules that require that trigger segments be immediately adjacent to targets? Hint: How can you get a SEARCH to terminate at the first segment to the left (or right)? In other words, how can you get adjacency to be just a special case of long-distance SEARCH?

Unit 57

Greek Letter Variables and Quantification in Rules

57.1 Further Thoughts on Greek Letters

There are two distinct positions that one could take about our use of rules that contain Greek letter variables in, say, Hungarian reciprocal neutralization discussed in Unit 51.

(544) Two views of Greek letters

> **Position 1.** It is a matter of fact that the Hungarian-type I-languages we are modeling contain two rules, but in the scientific language that we use to describe the Hungarian grammar, Greek letter variables serve as a convenient way of summarizing the existence of two distinct rules that share some parallel structure.

> **Position 2.** It is a matter of fact that the Hungarian-type I-languages we are modeling contain, as part of their primitive symbol inventory, variables that range over the set of feature values, the set of coefficients $\{+, -\}$. Thus, the harmony patterns we looked at *do* reflect a single rule.

Position 1 involves no new claims about phonological UG. Under this view, championed by McCawley (1971), α is just a variable in the *metalanguage* that we use to describe phonological systems, but there is no claim that such variables exist in the *object* language, the object of study, which in this case is the set of Hungarian-type

I-languages. Under Position 1, the relevant rules[1] are those given in (489), repeated in (545):

(545)   Greek letter variables in metalanguage: Two rules in Hungarian

a. $[\ -\text{SON}\ ] \rightarrow \{+\text{VOICED}\} / \underline{\quad} \begin{bmatrix} -\text{SON} \\ +\text{VOICED} \end{bmatrix}$

b. $[\ -\text{SON}\ ] \rightarrow \{-\text{VOICED}\} / \underline{\quad} \begin{bmatrix} -\text{SON} \\ -\text{VOICED} \end{bmatrix}$

In contrast, Position 2 makes the claim that UG actually provides variables that range over the set of feature coefficients, the values $\{+,-\}$, and that the rules of Hungarian-type grammars make use of these variables. This constitutes a stronger claim about language, one that requires an update to the inventory of symbols we accept as part of UG. So, under Position 2, something like the single rule given in (490), repeated in (546) is a component of a Hungarian I-language.

(546)   With Greek letter variables—One rule for Hungarian voicing:

$[\ -\text{SON}\ ] \rightarrow \{\alpha\text{VOICED}\} / \underline{\quad} \begin{bmatrix} -\text{SON} \\ \alpha\text{VOICED} \end{bmatrix}$

Later in this unit we will provide a fairly strong argument that we should attribute Greek letter variables to phonological UG, and thus favor the one-rule approach to Hungarian voicing assimilation in (546). For now, let's just explore the implications of accepting Greek letter variables, and see how they fit in with our "big picture" concerns.

Recall our discussion in Unit 43 concerning the kinds of abstractions UG equips us to make in grammars. Substrings are partial descriptions that characterize sets of strings, and sets of features can serve as partial descriptions that characterize sets of segments. In the same way, a rule that makes use of Greek letter variables is a partial description of two more highly specified formulas, each of which could be a rule in some language.[2] In other words, Greek letter variables, if they are really part of grammar, are another example of the fundamental ideas of partial descriptions and equivalence classes that characterize all aspects of linguistic representation and computation, as well as other cognitive systems.

---

[1]We'll use the '$\rightarrow$', and call them rules in this discussion, but they are really feature-changing processes consisting of a deletion rule and an insertion rule.

[2]We won't say that the α rule is a partial description of two rules in a language, because at issue is the very question of what the set of rules are!

This point does not constitute an argument for Greek letter variables, but it does put the discussion into the larger context of the categories of cognition. If we were not able to abstract in this way, there would be no categories whatsoever, and every experience would be completely distinct from every other experience. Equivalence classes allow us to have categories and make generalizations. Of course, the fact that we are innately endowed to parse the world using particular features means that we are *not* able to parse it in other ways. If you recall the discussion of epistemic boundedness and natural classes in Unit 45.2, you will see that we are faced with similar questions about Greek letter variables. Our general cognitive capacities obviously allow us to consciously understand concepts like this: "Adjacent obstruents in Hungarian end up having the same value for voicing as the rightmost one," so as humans we are capable of such abstraction. If Greek letter variables are part of our language faculty, then the language faculty also can encode this abstract notion of *agreement*. If the language faculty does not have Greek letter variables, the notion of feature agreement is beyond its bounds. It is perhaps interesting, as we consider whether or not to accept Greek letter variables in phonology to keep in mind the fundamental role that feature value agreement plays in other linguistic domains, such as syntax. Agreement certainly appears to be within the scope of the syntactic module, where verbs agree with their subjects, pronouns agree with their antecedents, and so on.

57.2   Identity Conditions in Rules

In phonology, the term *assimilation* is used to refer to processes in which segments become more like other segments in their environment. A simple case of assimilation would be a rule that makes vowels end up with the feature $+$NASAL before a nasal consonant. We have seen the identity use of Greek letter variables to express two-direction assimilations, for example, voiced obstruents becoming voiceless and voiceless obstruents becoming voiced, before voiceless and voiced obstruents, respectively.

In such an assimilation rule, a target segment takes on features of a segment in the environment, so we have one token of α in the environment, and one in the expression of the change. For example, the feature-filling part of the process of reciprocal neutralization in Hungarian developed in Unit (51) is given again in (547):

(547)   Insertion for Hungarian

$$[\ -\text{SONORANT}\ ]\ \sqcup\ \{\alpha\text{VOICED}\}\ /\ \underline{\quad}\ \begin{bmatrix} -\text{SONORANT} \\ \alpha\text{VOICED} \end{bmatrix}$$

The α value that unifies with a target is determined by the value on the following obstruent.

It is also possible to use α to express identity within the part of the rule that characterizes the environment. If α is assigned the value '+' anywhere in a given rule, then it must have the identical value everywhere it appears in that rule (in a particular derivation). Suppose we wanted to state a rule that makes a consonant agree with the voicing of its left and right neighbors, in case they agree in voicing. We could do that as follows:

(548)   Three tokens of a variable in a rule

$$\begin{bmatrix} -\text{SYLLABIC} \end{bmatrix} \rightarrow \left\{ \; \alpha\text{VOICED} \; \right\} / \begin{bmatrix} -\text{SYLLABIC} \\ \alpha\text{VOICED} \end{bmatrix} \text{---} \begin{bmatrix} -\text{SYLLABIC} \\ \alpha\text{VOICED} \end{bmatrix}$$

This rule means 'If a consonant occurs between two consonants that agree with each other in voicing, then the middle one will get that same value.' In addition to illustrating the use of three tokens of a variable, this example illustrates an identity relation within the environment. The segments on each side of the target must agree with respect to the value on VOICE for the rule conditions to be met.

Given our system thus far, we could imagine a requirement in the environment for an even higher degree of identity, say for two features. Let's use NASAL for illustration. We are not aiming for phonetic realism here, and we don't need to continue using three tokens for each variable—just make sure you understand the intention of the following rule:

(549)   Identity for two features

$$\begin{bmatrix} -\text{SYLLABIC} \end{bmatrix} \rightarrow \left\{ \; \alpha\text{VOICED} \; \right\} / \begin{bmatrix} -\text{SYLLABIC} \\ \alpha\text{VOICED} \\ \beta\text{NASAL} \end{bmatrix} \text{---} \begin{bmatrix} -\text{SYLLABIC} \\ \alpha\text{VOICED} \\ \beta\text{NASAL} \end{bmatrix}$$

This rule means 'Make a consonant have the same value for voicing as its left and right neighbors, but only if they agree with each other in voicing *and* they agree with each other in nasality'. This is a totally unnatural rule, but you get the idea.

Let's do one more:

(550)   Identity for three features

$$\begin{bmatrix} -\text{SYLLABIC} \end{bmatrix} \rightarrow \left\{ \; \alpha\text{VOICED} \; \right\} / \begin{bmatrix} -\text{SYLLABIC} \\ \alpha\text{VOICED} \\ \beta\text{NASAL} \\ \gamma\text{CONT} \end{bmatrix} \text{---} \begin{bmatrix} -\text{SYLLABIC} \\ \alpha\text{VOICED} \\ \beta\text{NASAL} \\ \gamma\text{CONT} \end{bmatrix}$$

This rule means 'Make a consonant have the same value for voicing as its left and right neighbors, but only if they agree with each other in voicing, nasality, *and* continuancy'.

We'll stop at three. Obviously, our system allows us to continue to use a Greek letter variable for as many features as we want. Before considering whether we need such power, let's return to the question of whether Greek letter variables are in the grammar or just in the metalanguage we use to describe grammars.

Under the metalanguage variable view, Position 1 in (544) of Unit 57.1, a formula with just one Greek letter variable is an abbreviation for two "real" rules in the object language, the mental grammar under analysis. There's the '+' version of the rule, and the '−' version. If we have two variables, as in (549), the statement abbreviates four possibilities:

(551)   Combinations of α and β

i. $[\ -\text{SYLLABIC}\ ] \rightarrow \{\ +\text{VOICED}\ \} / \begin{bmatrix} -\text{SYLLABIC} \\ +\text{VOICED} \\ +\text{NASAL} \end{bmatrix} \underline{\quad} \begin{bmatrix} -\text{SYLLABIC} \\ +\text{VOICED} \\ +\text{NASAL} \end{bmatrix}$

ii. $[\ -\text{SYLLABIC}\ ] \rightarrow \{\ +\text{VOICED}\ \} / \begin{bmatrix} -\text{SYLLABIC} \\ +\text{VOICED} \\ -\text{NASAL} \end{bmatrix} \underline{\quad} \begin{bmatrix} -\text{SYLLABIC} \\ +\text{VOICED} \\ -\text{NASAL} \end{bmatrix}$

iii. $[\ -\text{SYLLABIC}\ ] \rightarrow \{\ -\text{VOICED}\ \} / \begin{bmatrix} -\text{SYLLABIC} \\ -\text{VOICED} \\ +\text{NASAL} \end{bmatrix} \underline{\quad} \begin{bmatrix} -\text{SYLLABIC} \\ -\text{VOICED} \\ +\text{NASAL} \end{bmatrix}$

iv. $[\ -\text{SYLLABIC}\ ] \rightarrow \{\ -\text{VOICED}\ \} / \begin{bmatrix} -\text{SYLLABIC} \\ -\text{VOICED} \\ -\text{NASAL} \end{bmatrix} \underline{\quad} \begin{bmatrix} -\text{SYLLABIC} \\ -\text{VOICED} \\ -\text{NASAL} \end{bmatrix}$

And of course, if we add a third variable, γ, we get twice again as many rules—all of those in (551) combined with γ assigned the value '+' and all of those in (551) combined with γ assigned the value '−'. Each variable added to a formula doubles the number of rules the formula abbreviates. If there are, say, twenty features, then a formula with twenty Greek letter variables abbreviates over a million different rules: $2^{20} = 1,048,576$.

You may wonder if there is any reason to think we would ever have a rule with a significant number of Greek letter variables? Yes, there is. It turns out that there are rules that occur in environments defined as being between fully identical segments.

While we can say in a simple phrase "identical segments," the system we have built up, thinking of segments in set-theoretic terms, leads us to think of identical segments as those that have identical segment-sets. In other words, segment ς_1 and segment ς_2 are identical only if they correspond to exactly the same set of valued features.

To determine that two segments are identical, you need to check each feature in the two sets and make sure that they have the same coefficient associated with them. If feature F has the value + in the first segment, then feature F must have the value + in the second segment. And so on.

This operation of checking all the members of a set for a given property is called *universal quantification*. In this case, we need to check that every element (each valued feature) in a set occurs in another set (the other segment), and we need to reverse the direction of comparison as well—everything in A is in B, and everything in B is in A. Let's try to formalize this using a standard symbol for universal quantification, $\forall$, pronounced "for all":

(552)   Expressing identity

   • Let $\mathbf{F} = \{F_i : F_i$ is a feature$\}$

   • Segment ς_1 and segment ς_2 are identical if and only if

     $\forall F_i \in \mathbf{F} \ (\alpha F_i) \in \varsigma_1$ if and only if $(\alpha F_i) \in \varsigma_2$

This just says that two segments ς_1 and ς_2 are identical whenever they are exactly the same set of features.[3] For each feature, the coefficient of that feature has to be the same on ς_1 and ς_2. The subscripted F_i is a variable over the UG-given set of features.

Now that we know how to express identity, let's demonstrate that such rules are necessary. Bowern (2013, p. 120) tells us that in the Australian Aboriginal language Bardi "clusters of identical consonants are simplified to a single consonant across a morpheme boundary. They are pronounced without lengthening. (Clusters of identical consonants never appear within roots.)" In other words, when a sequence of identical consonants arises from the concatenation of morphemes, one of the two is deleted. For example, there is a noun *aalin* meaning 'sea eagle' and an ergative suffix *-nim*. When combined, the surface form is *aalinim*, with just one *n*. We will assume that it is the first of the two *n*'s that is deleted.

---

[3]Notice that our definition requires not just that the segments not disagree with respect to some feature. Fully specified d and underspecified D do not disagree with respect to any feature—it is just the case that d is +VOICED and D lacks a specification for that feature—yet d and D do not satisfy our identity condition. In some earlier discussions in generative phonology, d and D would be called *non-distinct*, but we do not make use of this notion directly (see section 1 of Reiss, 2003, for discussion).

Saying that the first of two identical segments[4] is deleted involves establishing the identity of the two segments in the input string. We need something like the rule in (553):

(553)   Delete first of adjacent identical consonants (version 1)

$$
\begin{bmatrix}
+\text{CONSONANTAL} \\
\alpha_1\,\text{VOICED} \\
\alpha_2\,\text{NASAL} \\
\ldots
\end{bmatrix}
\rightarrow \epsilon\,/\,\underline{\quad}
\begin{bmatrix}
+\text{CONSONANTAL} \\
\alpha_1\,\text{VOICED} \\
\alpha_2\,\text{NASAL} \\
\ldots
\end{bmatrix}
$$

The ellipsis '...' is meant to suggest that for each feature we have the same coefficient on its tokens in the two segments. We can make this a bit more abstract, assuming that F_1 to F_n are the rest of the features supplied by UG, in addition to CONSONANTAL.[5]

(554)   Delete first of adjacent identical consonants (version 2)

$$
\begin{bmatrix}
+\text{CONSONANTAL} \\
\alpha_1\,F_1 \\
\alpha_2\,F_2 \\
\ldots \\
\alpha_n\,F_n
\end{bmatrix}
\rightarrow \epsilon\,/\,\underline{\quad}
\begin{bmatrix}
+\text{CONSONANTAL} \\
\alpha_1\,F_1 \\
\alpha_2\,F_2 \\
\ldots \\
\alpha_n\,F_n
\end{bmatrix}
$$

Now, we can make use of the quantifier to express the identity condition more elegantly:[6]

(555)   Delete first of two adjacent identical consonants (version 3)

$\varsigma_1 \rightarrow \epsilon\,/\,\underline{\quad}\varsigma_2$
If $+$CONSONANTAL $\in \varsigma_1$ and
$\forall F_i \in \mathbf{F}$ $+$CONSONANTAL $\in \varsigma_2$ and $(\alpha F_i) \in \varsigma_1$ if and only if $(\alpha F_i) \in \varsigma_2$

We can make the rule a bit more readable:

---

[4]The careful reader will note that the deletion rule applies to sequences of identical consonants, not vowels, as the *aa* of *aalinim* shows.

[5]Note that we have to introduce yet another index, on the Greek letter variables. Using such indices is the same as using a unique Greek letter, α, β, and so on. We need to do this because there is no dependency between values across features. For example, the value on VOICED is in no way dependent on the value on NASAL in rule (553).

[6]This version also fixes a problem with the previous two versions. Those two do not give the right result if there is underspecification, since they require that all features in $\mathbf{F}$ appear in all the segments that are compared. This third formulation, and the subsequent ones, just compare the value of features that are present.

(556)   Delete first of two adjacent identical consonants (version 4)

$$\begin{matrix} \varsigma_1 \\ [\text{+Consonantal}] \end{matrix} \rightarrow \epsilon \, / \, \underline{\quad\quad} \begin{matrix} \varsigma_1 \\ [\text{+Consonantal}] \end{matrix}$$

If $\forall F_i \in \mathbf{F}$, $(\alpha F_i) \in \varsigma_1$ if and only if $(\alpha F_i) \in \varsigma_2$

We can simplify the notation a bit further by indexing the natural class descriptions in the rule, thus:

(557)   Delete first of two adjacent identical consonants (version 5)

$$[\text{+Consonantal}]_1 \rightarrow \epsilon \, / \, \underline{\quad\quad} [\text{+Consonantal}]_2$$

If $\forall F_i \in \mathbf{F}$, $(\alpha F_i) \in \varsigma_1$ if and only if $(\alpha F_i) \in \varsigma_2$

Part of this rule maintains the *SPE* syntax we used in the beginning of the book. However, we have clearly complicated things by appealing to the identity condition. As far as we can tell, this is a necessary move—phonology seems to make use of such relations among segments. If the reasoning is correct, we need Greek letter variables in the grammar, and we need to be able to use them in quantificational statements. In other words, we have argued in favor of Position 2 in (544) of Unit 57.1, the idea that UG provides variables that range over the set of feature values, the set of coefficients $\{+,-\}$.[7]

In (555) through (557) we quantified over $\mathbf{F}$, the set of all features. However, it is also possible to find rules with conditions of *partial* identity in which segments must agree, but only with respect to the features in some subset of $\mathbf{F}$.

In Lithuanian, the vowel *i* is inserted in consonant clusters like *td* or *pp* but not in clusters like *tk* or *pm*:[8]

(558)   Lithuanian

ati-teisti	'to adjudicate'	api-puti 'to grow rotten'
ati-duoti	'to give back'	api-berti 'to strew all over'
at-ko:pti	'to rise'	ap-kalbeti 'to slander'
at-rasti	'to find'	ap-mo:ki:ti 'to train'

The prefixes *at* and *ap* surface with an inserted [i] before a root beginning with a consonant that is fully identical to the *t* or *p*, or else differs from the *t* or *p* only in voicing. Note that [i] is inserted between *t* and *t* and between *t* and *d*, but not between

---

[7]UG must also provide variables that range over the set of features in $\mathbf{F}$.

[8]We have simplified the data and discussion by not marking palatalization on Lithuanian consonants. The substance of our point concerning partial identity is not affected by this simplification. See Baković (2006) for a different take on the Lithuanian pattern.

t and *k* or between *t* and *r*. Similarly, [i] is inserted between *p* and *p* and between *p* and *b*, but not between *p* and *k* or between *p* and *m*. The set of features over which identity is computed is the set of all features, except for VOICE.

Let's refer to the set of features over which the rule quantifies as **G** and assume that the features are the following: **G**={LABIAL, NASAL, CORONAL, SONORANT, LATERAL, DORSAL}. The rule can be written[9] by listing all the features in **G**, making sure that the coefficient that appears with a given feature is the same in each segment:

(559)   Lithuanian insertion with partial identity condition

- Insert an *i* between two identical consonants, ignoring voicing.

$$\epsilon \rightarrow [\text{i}] / \begin{bmatrix} +\text{CONSONANTAL} \\ \alpha_1\text{LABIAL} \\ \alpha_2\text{NASAL} \\ \alpha_3\text{CORONAL} \\ \alpha_4\text{SONORANT} \\ \alpha_5\text{LATERAL} \\ \alpha_6\text{DORSAL} \end{bmatrix} \underline{\quad} \begin{bmatrix} +\text{CONSONANTAL} \\ \alpha_1\text{LABIAL} \\ \alpha_2\text{NASAL} \\ \alpha_3\text{CORONAL} \\ \alpha_4\text{SONORANT} \\ \alpha_5\text{LATERAL} \\ \alpha_6\text{DORSAL} \end{bmatrix}$$

Before we develop the quantificational version of this process, let's remind ourselves of the implication of the position that Greek letter variables are just metavariables, and not part of the grammar itself. With six features, there are $2^6 = 64$ different rules that the formula in (559) abbreviates. Here are just two of them:

(560)   Two (of sixty-four) cases of rules without using Greek letter variables

a. $\epsilon \rightarrow [\text{i}] / \begin{bmatrix} +\text{CONSONANTAL} \\ +\text{LABIAL} \\ -\text{NASAL} \\ -\text{CORONAL} \\ -\text{SONORANT} \\ -\text{LATERAL} \\ -\text{DORSAL} \end{bmatrix} \underline{\quad} \begin{bmatrix} +\text{CONSONANTAL} \\ +\text{LABIAL} \\ -\text{NASAL} \\ -\text{CORONAL} \\ -\text{SONORANT} \\ -\text{LATERAL} \\ -\text{DORSAL} \end{bmatrix}$

---

[9]This version can't handle underspecification, but that problem will disappear in our quantificational version of the rule, below.

b. $\epsilon \rightarrow [i] /$ $\begin{bmatrix} +\text{CONSONANTAL} \\ -\text{LABIAL} \\ -\text{NASAL} \\ +\text{CORONAL} \\ -\text{SONORANT} \\ -\text{LATERAL} \\ -\text{DORSAL} \end{bmatrix}$ ___ $\begin{bmatrix} +\text{CONSONANTAL} \\ -\text{LABIAL} \\ -\text{NASAL} \\ +\text{CORONAL} \\ -\text{SONORANT} \\ -\text{LATERAL} \\ -\text{DORSAL} \end{bmatrix}$

So, rejecting Greek letter variables would preclude treating these two formulas in (560) as manifestations of the same rule, and would require us to list a large number of individual rules in the grammar.[10] This is a potential argument for including Greek letter variables as an actual property of language. Simply put, denying that Greek letter variables are part of the grammar itself is tantamount to denying that our natural language generalization "insert a vowel between two identical consonants, ignoring voicing" constitutes a real property of the grammar. Keep this in mind in the next section.

If we accept the Greek letter variables, we can now use them to quantify over sets of valued features as follows:

(561)   Lithuanian insertion with quantifier

- $\mathbf{G}=\{\text{LABIAL}, \text{NASAL}, \text{CORONAL}, \text{SONORANT}, \text{LATERAL}, \text{DORSAL}\}$
- $\epsilon \rightarrow i / [+\text{CONSONANTAL}]_1 \underline{\quad\quad} [+\text{CONSONANTAL}]_2$
  if $\forall F_i \in \mathbf{G}$, $\alpha F_i \in \varsigma_1$ if and only if $\alpha F_i \in \varsigma_2$

Full identity is just a special case of partial identity. In full identity, $\mathbf{G} = \mathbf{F}$.

The identity conditions we introduced are just like any other information in a rule—they specify the conditions under which the rule has a non-vacuous application. Sometimes in the phonology literature, a stipulation like an identity condition is described as a constraint on the rule's application, but we see no use in treating such conditions as any different from all the other "stipulations" that just constitute the statement of the rule. Identity conditions are "inside" rules. Recall that we applied the same argument to the notion of consistency in Unit 49.2.

---

[10]It is clear that not every one of the sixty-four would be attestable. For example, we assume that nasal segments are all sonorants—but this is an accidental fact of the phonetics that maps to the features and not an inherent property of the computational system. In addition, the literature suggests that all the examples we can find in Lithuanian involve underlying voiceless stops as the first consonant, reflecting the prefixes found in the lexicon. In any case, as the size of the set of features over which identity must be computed grows, the number of individual rules expands, potentially exponentially.

57.3 Non-identity Conditions in Rules

We have seen that we can express identity by writing out a list of many rules, each a particular case of identity. We can make progress toward compressing our account by listing features in two or more places in a rule and using identical coefficients on the tokens of a given feature, as in (559). We also saw that we can express such a rule using the universal quantifier and quantifying over some set of features, as in (561).

Yet another way of indicating identity in the phonological literature is to use a single token of a feature and indicate in a diagram that it is shared by two segments.[11]

(562) Identity via linking

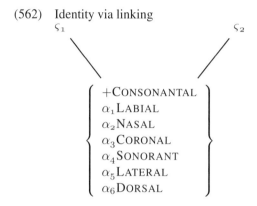

$$
\begin{cases}
+\text{CONSONANTAL} \\
\alpha_1 \text{LABIAL} \\
\alpha_2 \text{NASAL} \\
\alpha_3 \text{CORONAL} \\
\alpha_4 \text{SONORANT} \\
\alpha_5 \text{LATERAL} \\
\alpha_6 \text{DORSAL}
\end{cases}
$$

This represents any sequence of two segments such that both are +CONSONANTAL and they agree with respect to all the other listed features, LABIAL, NASAL, and so on. For any features not in the doubly linked set, like VOICED, the two segments can disagree. In (563) the first is specified as −VOICED and the second as +VOICED:

---

[11]There is a slight inconsistency in this diagram, since we have said that segments *are* sets of features, but here we show segments as being *associated with* sets of features. Please let this slide, as it is not crucial to the point under discussion.

(563)   Identity via linking with some disagreement specified

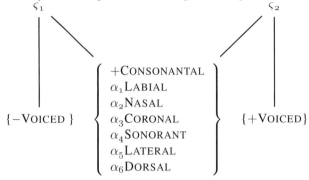

This representation shows that ς_1 and ς_2 have specific different values for VOICED but the same value for all the members of the set to which they are both associated. Obviously, we could also switch the values of VOICED on the two segments, so that ς_1 would be +VOICED and ς_2 would be −VOICED.

An interesting situation arises with the use of a feature to show obligatory *disagreement*:

(564)   Disagreement specified with Greek letters

$$\varsigma_1 \qquad\qquad \varsigma_2$$
$$| \qquad\qquad\qquad |$$
$$\{\alpha\text{VOICED}\} \qquad \{-\alpha\text{VOICED}\}$$

Such a representation corresponds to sequences such as *pb, pd, dp, dt, nt*, but not sequences like *pt, nd, bd*. Is there any reason to believe that our phonological system allows us to combine Greek letter variables with negation in this way? Is there any reason to think that such representations are needed to capture real linguistic generalizations?

One possible situation where this is needed is explored in Exercise 57.1 at the end of this unit. For now, we'll turn to a type of condition that combines negated Greek letters with quantification, where *not* using a quantifier is extremely unwieldy. These are cases where linking diagrams like (563) won't work, and the listing approach—sketched in (560) where all the combinations of values are listed is awkward—even more so than in the identity conditions we saw above. In other words, these examples will support the idea that Greek letter variables and quantificational logic really are part of phonology.

Sometimes a rule's effects can be described as something like this: 'Do Q *unless* segments x and y are identical'. This is equivalent to saying 'Do Q only if segments x and y are *not* identical'. Note that determining that two segments are *not* identical does not require universal quantification. We don't need to check every member of **F**, or every member of some subset of features **G**, to ensure that the coefficients match— we just need to find *at least one* feature for which there is a mismatch. Crucially, that *one* feature can vary from case to case. If two segments disagree with respect to LABIAL, they are non-identical. If they disagree with respect to CORONAL, they are non-identical. And so on. So, there is no way to represent non-identity with the kind of linking diagram we see in (562), because any one, or more, of the features in the relevant set, might disagree on the two segments—maybe they disagree with respect to LABIAL; maybe with respect to NASAL; maybe with respect to both LABIAL and NASAL; maybe with respect to some other combination of features.

Let's stick with the set of features **G** that we used above. There are six features in this set: **G**={LABIAL, NASAL, CORONAL, SONORANT, LATERAL, DORSAL}. Since each feature is binary, there are two possible values for each feature[12] and so, there are two choices for LABIAL, namely +LABIAL and −LABIAL, and two choices for NASAL, namely +NASAL and −NASAL, and so on. So there are $2 \times 2 \times 2 \times 2 \times 2 \times 2 = 2^6 = 64$ possible ways to assign values to the features in **G**. That means that for each of the 64, there are 63 that are non-identical to it. So, there are $64 \times 63 = 4032$ ways to assign pluses and minuses to the features in **G** for two segments and ensure that they disagree somewhere, that they are non-identical.

In such cases, instead of the universal quantifier, we need the *existential quantifier*, which looks inside a set for *at least one* element that satisfies a condition: Is there at least one feature for which the two segments disagree? The symbol for the existential quantifier in logic is '∃'. It is pronounced "there exists."[13]

In terms of model building, *not* using quantifiers is more costly in general for non-identity cases than for identity cases. This is because, with n features in **G**, a rule with a universal quantification version of identity corresponds to 2^n cases; whereas a rule with an existential quantification version of non-identity corresponds to $2^n \times (2^n - 1)$

---

[12]Let's not worry about "incomplete" segments here.

[13]If you have done some basic quantificational logic before, you are probably aware that a logical system can get away with just one of these quantifiers, since the other can be combined with negation to express the meaning of the one left out. For example, "It is not the case that all men are not green" is logically equivalent to "There exists at least one man who is green."

cases.[14] For example, if $n = 6$, then a universal quantification identity rule stands for 64 cases, but an existential quantification non-identity rule stands for $64 \times 63 = 4032$ cases. This is because for each of the 64 definable segments, there are 63 that are not identical to it.

As an example of a non-identity condition, consider a rule in Iraqi Arabic that deletes medial vowels under certain conditions (which we ignore here) but only if the flanking consonants are non-identical:

(565) Vowel deletion in Iraqi Arabic (from Odden, 1988)
       a. xaabar   'he telephoned'   xaabr-at   'she telephoned'
           ħaajaj   'he argued'   ħaajij-at   'she argued'

A syncope (vowel deletion) rule applies non-vacuously in the form *xaabrat*, but it has no effect in *ħaajijat*, because the consonants flanking the targeted vowel *i* are identical.

Rule (566) shows how to express the condition that vowel deletion occurs unless the flanking consonants are identical, that is, only when the consonants are non-identical.

(566) Iraqi rule with non-identity condition:

$$[-\textsc{Consonantal}] \to \epsilon \,/\, [+\textsc{Consonantal}]_1 \underline{\quad} [+\textsc{Consonantal}]_2$$
If $\exists F_i \in \mathbf{F}$ such that $\alpha F_i \in \varsigma_1$ and $-\alpha F_i \in \varsigma_2$

The rule deletes a vowel between two consonants if the consonants disagree with respect to the value on some feature.[15]

In (566) we apply existential quantification over $\mathbf{F}$, the set of all features. Given the system we have developed, it is also possible to formulate rules that require non-identity within a restricted subset of features. An example would be a rule that applies only if two segments are *not* homorganic, in other words, they are not made in the same place of articulation.[16] So, disagreeing with respect to Voice might be irrelevant, but features like Labial, Coronal, Anterior, and Dorsal would be relevant.

In earlier units, we spent a lot of time showing how the simple SPE system can generate a vast amount of descriptive complexity. In this unit we have made a complementary point: it is easy to express an identity or non-identity condition in words,

---

[14]We are assuming fully specified segments here—the number of cases increases if underspecification is allowed (see Unit 61). In other words, the elegance of using quantification becomes even more apparent when there is underspecification.

[15]As formulated, non-identity requires disagreement in values, not just presence of a value versus absence (see Exercise 59.1).

[16]Recall that *homorganic* means 'made with the same articulatory organs', in the same place of articulation.

yet formalization requires some sophisticated logico-mathematical notions. Since we advocate a realist view of our theory, we attribute quantificational logic to our object of study, the human phonological faculty.

Exercises

57.1. You may have heard of so-called *dissimilation* processes, which make input segments *less* alike to each other. While it is tempting to model dissimilation using a negated Greek letter variable, it is hard to find cases of full two-way dissimilation, for example, *l* dissimilating from another *l* in the environment to become *r*, and also *r* dissimilating from another *r* to become *l*. Here is a toy example of the kind of data we have in mind. Provide an analysis with a single rule.

Srirachayan I

PRESENT	PAST	gloss
latuno	nosuno	'dance'
latfilo	notfilo	'enhance'
laspika	nospika	'prance'
latxomi	notxomi	'glance'
laskuda	noskuda	'lance'
latipuk	nosipuk	'dig'
lateluri	noseluri	'carbonate'

Now make your rule *less* general to account for the following:

Srirachayan II

PRESENT	PAST	gloss
latmasa	nosmasa	'pinch'
latrugo	nosrugo	'winch'
latlogu	noslogu	'bounce'
latnoki	nosnoki	'trounce'
latwosa	noswosa	'cure'

57.2. We are obviously epistemically bounded in a fairly uninteresting sense by performance factors. For example, we can't have any thought that would take up more memory than our brains make available or take more time than our allotted lifetime. However, a more interesting sense of epistemic boundedness relates to thoughts or ideas for which we just lack necessary representational apparatus. Give an example of such a thought or explain why you cannot.

57.3. Characterize your conception of God, whether or not you believe in God. Is the God of your conception epistemically bounded? Supposing that *that* God exists, could anyone know if that God is epistemically bounded? If humans are created in God's image, how does God's status with respect to epistemic boundedness bear on that of humans?

57.4. Imagine you were asked to contribute a chapter on phonology and epistemic boundedness for an expanded second edition of *Dr. Seuss and Philosophy: Oh, the Thinks You Can Think!*, Rider et al. (2011). Prepare a one-page abstract of your chapter. You might want to review some of Dr. Seuss's work before answering this question.

57.5. Tagalog:[17] Here are two columns of forms from Tagalog. The forms in column A contain one morpheme. Those in column B contain the root that occurs in A and a suffix -*in*. Look through the data and answer the questions that follow. **Hint:** There is no interaction among the vowels.

	A	B	Root Alternant 1	Root Alternant 2	Underlying root
a.	bukas	buksin		buks	
b.	kapit	kaptin		kapt	
c.	tubos	tubsin			
d.	opos	upsin			
e.	posod	pusdin			
f.	bata	bathin			
g.	bili	bilhin			
h.	dipa	diphin			
i.	polo	pulhin			
j.	puyo	puyhin			
k.	banig	baŋgin			
l.	damit	damtin			
m.	ganap	gampin			
n.	putol	putlin			
o.	atip	aptin			
p.	tanim	tamnin			
q.	laman	lamnin			

i. Fill in the third and fourth columns (not the fifth) in the table above.

[17]See Halle (2001) for a discussion of an extravagant phonological claim based on a misanalysis of standard Tagalog orthography.

ii. The forms in A all contain a vowel that does not appear in B. In a clear sentence or two, explain why those vowels must be part of the underlying representation of the roots. Use the word *predictable* or *unpredictable* in your answer.

iii. Since the vowels must be part of the UR, we need a rule of vowel deletion to account for the forms in which column?

iv. Assume the rule says "Delete a vowel in an open syllable preceded by an open syllable." Call this rule R1. Are there any forms (in column A or B) that look problematic given this formulation of the rule? List one and explain.

v. Look at the forms in (d), (e), and (i). There is an alternation in the inital vowel of the root in each case. Give the two vowels that alternate: _____ _____.

vi. In order to choose one of these as the underlying vowel, you need to look at more data. Which rows tell you what to choose as the UR for the vowels in (d), (e), and (i)? Use MTP forced-choice reasoning.

vii. What distributional fact confirms your hypothesis? Hint: Look at which vowels occur before sequences of two consonants.

viii. Write a feature-changing process using '→' to capture what is happening. Use syllable structure to state the environment. **Hint:** You will have to refer not only to the syllable of the target, but also to the existence of a following syllable. Explain why. Call this R2.

Assume that these are the features for Tagalog vowels.

	i	e	a	o	u
HIGH	+	−	−	−	+
LOW	−	−	+	−	−
BACK	−	−	+	+	+
ROUND	−	−	−	+	+

ix. Circle the correct ordering:

- R1 before R2
- R2 before R1

Explain why that ordering is necessary.

x. Assume that consonant interactions occur between adjacent consonants.

- Explain in words what is going on in row (k).

- Do the same for row (m).

xi. State a single process **in words** that covers both cases. Call the process R3.

xii. How should R3 be ordered?

- Can it be ordered with respect to R1? Explain.
- Can it be ordered with respect to R2? Explain.

xiii. Express R3 using '→ ' and features. Use Greek letter variables. You can use as few features as possible, but don't overgeneralize by using too few.

xiv. Account for (f), (g), (h), (i), and (j):

- Assume that all roots in this language end with a consonant underlyingly. Write a process to account for (f), (g), (h), (i), and (j). Call your process R4.
- Does R4 have to be ordered with respect to any of the other rules/processes? Look back at any unresolved problems that you may have had related to syllables.

xv. Now look at the order of consonants in the two forms in (o).

- Without positing a solution, say what needs to be accounted for.
- Call the pattern of ordering of consonants you see in column A 'X', and call the pattern you see in column B, 'Y':
  - ⋆ X =
  - ⋆ Y =

xvi. Now look at (b).

- What pattern, X or Y, shows up in the two columns of row (b)?
- So, what is the underlying pattern for (b), X or Y? _____
  - Give the underlying representation of the root:
- What is the underlying pattern for (o), X or Y? _____
  - Give the underlying representation of the root:

xvii. What rule would account for forms like (o)?

- Write the process in words and call it R5.
- Why is this rule different from those we have expressed in our rule format?
- What do we call processes like this?

- In addition to (o), what other forms does R5 apply to?
- Give the underlying form for the root in (o) and for one other form affected by R5.

xviii. Why isn't row (l) affected by R5?

- Explain.
- Give the underlying form for the root in (l):

xix. Where does R5 get ordered with respect to R1? Explain.

xx. • What is the underlying form of the root in (m)?

- Does R5 apply to (m)?
- Does (m) meet the structural description for R5?
- Explain how it is possible that the two previous answers are both correct. What do you need to specify? Explain.

xxi. Give the underlying form of the other root that has a form that shows the effects of R5.

xxii. Why isn't this form unaffected by R5? Why isn't it like the form in (m)? Hint: Make the *environment* of R3 specific enough to provide a solution. Explain and write out the new version of R3.

xxiii. Fill in the last column of the data table with underlying forms for all the roots.

xxiv. List all five rules/processes in a column and draw arrows to show which ones we have crucial ordering arguments for. Start by listing any rules that have no explicit ordering relations. Your final list should show an order that works, read from top to bottom.

xxv. Provide underlying representations (consisting of roots and suffixes) for the following surface forms. Start by filling in numbers for your rules in an order that works. Just write a dash in a box if a rule does not have any effect.

UR								
R___								
R___								
R___								
R___								
R___								
SR	tubos	tubsin	opos	upsin	polo	pulhin	kapit	kaptin

UR								
R___								
R___								
R___								
R___								
R___								
R___								
SR	atip	aptin	ganap	gampin	banig	baŋgin	laman	lamnin

    xxvi. Give an example of a root that shows that the surfacing lexical form assumption is sometimes false—that the UR need not be realized in any surface form. In other words, show that it may be the case that, for a particular root, there is no single word that will show all the segments in the root.

57.6. Rewrite the Lithuanian rule in (561) with a quantifier, but instead of defining **G** extensionally, quantify over a set description that uses **F** and makes use of the irrelevance of VOICE. In other words, using set-theoretic operations, quantify over the set of 'all the features except for VOICE'.

57.7. Yapese, a language spoken on the Micronesian island of Yap, deletes vowels in initial syllables between homorganic consonants, consonants made with the same place of articulation. As you see in the following data, features like NASAL, SONORANT, and VOICE are not relevant to determining whether consonants are homorganic. Assume that only CORONAL, LABIAL, and DORSAL are relevant.

Underlying	Surface	Gloss
ba-puw	bpuw	'it's a bamboo'
ni-te:l	nte:l	'take it'
rada:n	rda:n	'its width'

Formulate a rule that deletes the vowels (ignore the initial syllable condition in your rule) using a quantificational statement.

57.8. Express the identity condition in (552) without using quantification. Just use set-theoretic relations among segments.

57.9. Come up with a new Srirachayan rule to account for the data in Exercise (1) as well as the following. This pattern is probably unattestable, but it allows you to practice playing with rule formalism:

Srirachayan III

PRESENT	PAST	FUTURE	INFINITIVE	gloss
latuno	nosuno	pikuno	moxuno	'dance'
laspika	nospika	pixpika	moxpika	'prance'
latxomi	notxomi	pikxomi	moxxomi	'glance'
laskuda	noskuda	pikkuda	moxkuda	'lance'
latsuma	nossuma	piksuma	moksuma	'flout'
lattiko	nostiko	pixtiko	moxtiko	'doubt'

Unit 58

Applying What We Have Learned—Lamba

In this unit you will work, with some guidance, through a dataset from Lamba, a Bantu language spoken mostly in Zambia. This problem allows us to review many aspects of our discussion thus far. You will see that our toy data and our modular approach to developing a theory can be fruitfully applied to more naturalistic datasets.

Here are some of the topics we will be revisiting:

(567) Lessons from Lamba

- reasoning about neutralization
- two ways of finding the underlying form
- rule ordering
- natural classes as building blocks of rules
- the partial indeterminacy of our analyses
- syllable structure in rules

Keep these all in mind as you analyze the data below. For the purposes of this problem, we will collapse the deletion and insertion parts of feature-changing processes and express them in a single statement using the traditional arrow '→' of phonological notation.

We will treat the final -*a* of each form as part of a single suffix on each verb. For example, the passive marker will be assumed to be just -*wa*. Assume that the symbol *ň* denotes a palatal nasal consonant, equivalent to IPA *ɲ*. Here is some useful (partial) information about the segments in the data:

(568)   Some features of Lamba segments

- *s* is +ANTERIOR, +CONTINUANT, −VOICED
- *š* = ʃ is −ANTERIOR, +CONTINUANT, −VOICED
- *č* = *tˢ* = *tʃ* is −ANTERIOR, −CONTINUANT, +DELAYEDRELEASE, −VOICED
- *t* is +ANTERIOR, −CONTINUANT, −DELAYEDRELEASE, −VOICED
- *k* is −ANTERIOR, −CONTINUANT, −DELAYEDRELEASE, −VOICED
- *l* is +ANTERIOR, +LATERAL, −NASAL, +SONORANT, −LABIAL
- *n* is +ANTERIOR, −LATERAL, +NASAL, +SONORANT, −LABIAL
- *i* is +HIGH, −LOW, −BACK, −ROUND
- *u* is +HIGH, −LOW, +BACK, +ROUND
- *e* is −HIGH, −LOW, −BACK, −ROUND
- *o* is −HIGH, −LOW, +BACK, +ROUND
- *a* is −HIGH, +LOW, +BACK, −ROUND

And here is the data we will study:

(569)   Lamba data

PAST	PASSIVE	NEUTER	APPLIED	RECIPROCAL	Gloss	SRs	URs
masa	maswa	mašika	mašila	masana	'plaster'		
soŋka	soŋkwa	soŋkeka	soŋkela	soŋkana	'pay tax'		
kosa	koswa	koseka	kosela	kosana	'be strong'		
lasa	laswa	lašika	lašila	lasana	'wound'		
fisa	fiswa	fišika	fišila	fisana	'hide'		
tula	tulwa	tulika	tulila	tulana	'dig'		
pata	patwa	patika	patila	patana	'scold'		
česa	česwa	česeka	česela	česana	'cut'		
šika	šikwa	šičika	šičila	šikana	'bury'		
seka	sekwa	sekeka	sekela	sekana	'laugh at'		
kaka	kakwa	kačika	kačila	kakana	'tie'		
fuka	fukwa	fučika	fučila	fukana	'creep'		
ima	imwa	imika	imina	imana	'rise'		
puma	pumwa	pumika	pumina	pumana	'flog'		
fweňa	fweňwa	fweňeka	fweňena	fweňana	'scratch'		
pona	ponwa	poneka	ponena	ponana	'fall'		
ŋaŋa	ŋaŋwa	ŋaŋika	ŋaŋina	ŋaŋana	'snigger'		
mena	menwa	meneka	menena	menana	'grow'		

Work through the following questions by referring to the forms above.

1. In the second column from the right, list all the surface alternants of each verbal root—leave the last column empty for now.

2. List the **surface variants** of each suffix (assume that there is a single suffix marking each verb form—in other words, assume that the final *-a* is part of each suffix):

   1. *-a*   PAST
   2. _____PASSIVE
   3. _____NEUTER
   4. _____APPLIED
   5. _____RECIPROCAL

3. There are only two segment alternations in roots. In other words, some roots show a single surface form, and others show two alternants. There are two pairs of alternating segments. What are the two pairs of alternating segments?

   • Segment alternation in 'wound':

   • Segment alternation in 'creep':

4. For each of these pairs, choosing one form allows you to state a rule whose trigger is a natural class. The two rules have the same environment. State the two rules using segment symbols, not features:

   • Rule A to account for alternation in 'wound':

   • Rule B to account for alternation in 'creep':

5. Now that you have those rules, you should be able to posit the underlying form for all the verb roots. List them in the last column of the data table.

6. Now you should account for the alternations in the suffixes. There are four alternants of the APPLIED suffix. You will account for the four forms using two rules. The rule you will need to account for the alternation between [l] and [n] is not sensitive to any properties of adjacent vowels, so the rule does not conform to our original SPE syntax. You'll need something analogous to the rules we developed for Turkish vowel harmony. Formulate a rule in words that mentions syllable structure positions (like ONSET, NUCLEUS, CODA). Use MTP forced-choice reasoning to decide whether the underlying consonant in the suffix is *l* or

n. You will have to look outside of the APPLIED column to do this. Treat *l* and *n* as differing with respect to the features NASAL and LATERAL. Deal with both features in a single rule. Hint: Figure out the RECIPROCAL suffix first.

- RECIPROCAL suffix UR:

- Consonant of APPLIED suffix UR: /-V___a/

- Rule C to account for alternation (in words and segment symbols):

7. The last alternation to account for is in the vowel of the APPLIED suffix. This alternation occurs also in the NEUTER. You won't be able to use forced-choice MTP reasoning here. Once again, you'll need a rule that does not refer to adjacent segments, so make reference to syllable positions. Natural class reasoning will be crucial.

- Vowel of APPLIED suffix and NEUTER suffix UR:

- Rule D for vowel alternation:

- Full APPLIED suffix UR:

- Full NEUTER suffix UR:

8. You have now posited four rules, A, B, C, and D. Draw an independent segment mapping diagram for each rule.

9. There is some crucial ordering (ordering for which there is evidence). There is one rule that comes before two of the others. Describe:

- Rule _____ must come before Rule _____ and Rule _____

- Are these orderings *feeding* or *bleeding* or something else? Explain your answer.

10. Draw an SMD that shows rule interactions for just *s/š* and the vowel change.

11. Draw an SMD that shows rule interactions for just *k/č* and the vowel change.

12. We do not have enough information to fully determine the rule ordering. List *all* the orderings that work.

13. Using one ordering that works, provide derivations for the forms listed.

UR					
R_					
R_					
R_					
R_					
SR	fišika	koseka	fweňena	poneka	imina

UR				
R_				
R_				
R_				
R_				
SR	imana	fweňana	fučika	sekela

14. Indeterminacy I: Redo the derivations using a different ordering that also works.

15. Indeterminacy II: What is your underlying form for 'bury'? Is there a reasonable alternative? Is the traditional notion of allophony relevant? Explain.

16. Indeterminacy II: What is your underlying form for 'cut'? Is there a reasonable alternative? Is the traditional notion of allophony relevant? Explain.

17. It may be tempting to collapse two of your rules. Which two? Explain why it cannot be done. These two processes would be called *palatalization* in a typical treatment, and in fact, they are collapsed into a single rule by some phonologists. We have avoided such terms in favor of mechanical application of our formalism, and the model we developed tells us that the two rules *cannot* be collapsed for simple set-theoretic reasons. Explain. Forms like *patika* should play a role in your discussion. Remember that all the parts of a rule (target, change, environment) must have simple set-theoretic characterizations.

Now return to (567) and make sure you see how each issue listed arose in the solution to Lamba.

Exercises

58.1. More on Lamba

a. Which Lamba root shows that the *l* → *n* rule has to be triggered by a nasal in the immediately preceding onset, and not in just any preceding onset?

b. Which Lamba root shows that the *l* → *n* rule has to be triggered by the immediately preceding onset, and not any nasal that is separated by just one vowel from the target?

c. Reformulate the Lamba *l* → *n* rule without referring to onsets, but just to types of segments, such as consonants and vowels. You can do this in words.

58.2. Like Lamba, another Bantu language, Tshiluba (Odden, 1994; Johnson, 1972) shows an *l* → *n* rule whose effects show up in the applicative suffix:

INFINITIVE	APPLICATIVE	gloss
kutoota	kutootila	'harvest'
kukina	kukinina	'dance'
kukinisa	kukinisina	'make dance'
kudumuka	kudumukina	'jump'
kudumukisa	kudumukisina	'make jump'

As you can see, the *l* → *n* rule in this language can be triggered by a nasal that is further away than in the previous onset. Let's assume that it can be arbitrarily far away. Formulate a rule to account for Tshiluba that combines the reasoning we used in Lamba with the SEARCH idea we used for the Turkish genitive plural. You can make a single rule using just '→' instead of a two-step feature-changing process.

58.3. Read through *all* of these instructions before you begin answering any of the questions. In your analysis of Catalan in Exercise 39.2, your Rule C should have been something like this:

Rule C: t → ∊/ in CODA

This rule accounted for mappings like UR /dulent/ ⤳ SR [dulen].

Consider now the forms of an adjective meaning 'small':

MASC SG	MASC PL	FEM SG	FEM PL	GLOSS
petit	petits	petitə	petites	'small'

Revise Rule C to Rule C′ by adding an additional condition on the environment (one that does not refer to particular vowels).

- Write Rule C′ using a syllable structure diagram.

Now make sure your rule is consistent with the following data (and the data from Exercise 39.2) by making the target and environments more general (less specific):

MASC SG	MASC PL	FEM SG	FEM PL	GLOSS
al	als	altə	altes	'tall'
profun	profuns	profundə	profundes	'deep'
for	fors	fortə	fortes	'strong'

- Write the new Rule C″.

If necessary revise Rule C″ to a new version Rule C‴ to account for the following:

MASC SG	MASC PL	FEM SG	FEM PL	GLOSS
blaŋ	blaŋs	blaŋkə	blaŋkes	'white'

You will probably have to revise the rule yet again to Rule C‴′ to account for the following data.

MASC SG	MASC PL	FEM SG	FEM PL	GLOSS
kork	korks			'termite'
kalk	kalks			'copy'
eskerp	eskerps	eskerpə	eskerpes	'sharp'
serp	serps			'snake'
	alps			'the Alps'
polp	polps			'octopus'
palp	palps			'touch'

It may be useful to know that *l* and *r* are +CORONAL. Assume that the other features relevant to place of articulation are LABIAL and DORSAL.

- Write out C‴′.

The final segment of the adjective meaning 'married' must be different from the final segment of the adjective meaning 'small':

MASC SG	MASC PL	FEM SG	FEM PL	GLOSS
kazat	kazats	kazaðə	kazaðes	'married'

If we were to assume that this root ended in /d/, how many additional rules would be need? Write them out and show the derivations for [kazat] and [kazaðə].

- Write out the two rules for the /d/ → [t] process. Call them D1 and D2.
- Write out the two rules for /d/ → [ð] process. Call them D3 and D4.
- Propose a different underlying segment, not /d/, for the final segment of this root meaning 'married'. Use features.
- Write out the rules you would need to make your solution work. You should need a total of only two feature-filling rules. Call them E1 and E2.
- Provide derivations for the four forms of 'married'. You should use the E rules, not the D rules.

Compare the following data to the forms for 'strong' above:

MASC SG	MASC PL	FEM SG	FEM PL	GLOSS
kla	klas	klarə	klares	'plain'
du	dus	durə	dures	'hard'

- Why is it problematic to propose a single deletion rule to derive the masculine singular and masculine plural forms for 'plain' and 'hard'?
- Can you account for the masculine singular forms by generalizing an earlier rule? Explain and rewrite the rule, calling the new version Rule F.
- Write a Rule G to account for the masculine plural forms.
- Provide derivations using your final set of rules for all the forms of 'strong', 'hard', 'sharp', 'married', 'small', 'deep'. You will need to look back to Exercise 39.2 for some of the rules and data.

Unit 59

High Quality Ignorance

In the Lamba discussion in the previous unit we encouraged you to admit when you could not fully determine all aspects of the analysis. We could not fully determine the rule ordering, and there were reasonable options concerning some aspects of URs. We hope that we have made it clear throughout this book that phonology is in its infancy, and that so little is well understood. If we can claim any progress, perhaps it is just that we now can ask better questions, that our explorations lead to "higher quality ignorance," as neuroscientist Stuart Firestein puts it in his TED talk, "The Pursuit of Ignorance". In this vein, let's consider a pattern that is simple to describe but that can lead us to widely divergent accounts, even within the narrow theoretical framework we have developed in this book.

We will analyze the distribution of aspiration in Sierra Popoluca, a language spoken in Veracruz, Mexico. We will demonstrate that there are at least two distinct analyses consistent with the data and consistent with the model we have been developing. Of course, scientific research aims for constrained models and rich datasets that lead to a single, explicit analysis of some phenomenon. In science, it is not better to have two explanations than one. At the end of our discussion, we will not be able to choose between the two analyses. We will have to acknowledge our uncertainty, yet we will argue that we find ourselves in a better position than if we had not applied scientific rigor at all.

59.1   Overview of the Data

Sierra Popoluca has aspirated and unaspirated oral voiceless stops in complementary distribution, but in a pattern very different from English:[1]

(570)   Some Sierra Popoluca forms
  pet^{h}pa?   'he sweeps'
  pet^{h}kuy   'broom'
  petta:p^h 'it is being swept'

The forms in (570) appear to contain a root 'sweep' with the alternants pet/pet^h. Note that the root-final consonant is in the coda in all three forms, and it is aspirated before k and p, but not before t.

   Let's look at some more forms with voiceless coronal stops:

(571)   More forms with coronal stops
  ti:ttit^h 'mestizo'
  mak^{h}ti?   'ghost'

Both these forms contain onsets with voiceless coronal stops, and they are not aspirated. The word for 'mestizo' also has two such stops in coda position. The word-final t^h fits a general pattern of final voiceless stops—they are always aspirated. The consonant in the coda of the first syllable is unaspirated and it occurs before t. This is consistent with the data in (570) where we found aspirated t^h in coda, except before t.

   Let's turn to velar stops:

(572)   Sierra Popoluca forms with velar stops
  kek^{h}pa?   'it flies'
  kekgak^{h}pa?   'it flies again'
  ikka?   'he killed it'
  mak^{h}ti?   'ghost'
  mok^h 'corn'

In the first two forms in (572) there appears to be a root with alternants kek/kek^h. Aspirated k^h appears before p in the first form, but not before g in the second form. In the next form, 'he killed it', the coda k is unaspirated, before an onset k. However, in the word for 'ghost' we see aspirated coda k^h before t in the following onset. In the

---

[1]Oral voiceless stops don't include the glottal stop ?, which is never aspirated. In the rest of this discussion we always mean 'oral voiceless stops' when we refer to 'voiceless stops'.

word for 'corn' we see that final coda velar stops are aspirated. The dataset also shows us that onset velar stops are unaspirated.

We have seen that coronal voiceless stops are unaspirated in onsets, and aspirated in word-final codas. They are also aspirated in medial codas, as long as the following onset does not contain *t*. We have also seen that velar voiceless stops are unaspirated in onsets, and aspirated in word-final codas. They are also aspirated in medial codas, as long as the following onset does not contain *g* or *k*.

If you remember that *g* and *k* are identical aside from voicing, you may be able to see a generalization emerging: it looks like voiceless stops are aspirated in codas, as long as they are *not* followed by a homorganic consonant, a consonant made at the same place of articulation. The available data for labial voiceless stops is consistent with this generalization:

(573)   Sierra Popoluca forms with labial stops
        nip^h   'mouth'
        ho:ppaʔ   'it rolls'

The final labial stop in the first form is aspirated p^h, but in the second form, there is no aspiration of a coda labial stop before a labial stop.

This data seems to need an analysis in terms of identity conditions. As Elson (1947, p. 15) says, "The stops *p*, *t*, t^y and *k* are aspirated in syllable-final position, if not followed by a phoneme of the same point of articulation." However, Elson's statement is difficult to handle since it suggests that word-final position and coda before a non-homorganic consonant superficially group together as one environment.

59.2   First Analysis: Two Aspirating Rules

One solution to the apparent parallel treatment of voiceless stops that are word-final and those that precede a non-homorganic consonant is to assume that consonants are unspecified for aspiration underlyingly. We then need to posit two separate aspiration rules. One rule aspirates word-final codas; another rule aspirates those word-internal codas that do get aspirated (the ones that are not following by homorganic onsets).

Here's one rule that unifies a consonant with {+SPREADGLOTTIS}, which is the featural correlate of aspiration.

(574)   Word-final aspiration
        [+CONSONANTAL] ⊔ {+SPREADGLOTTIS} / ___%

Rule (574) of course only aspirates word-final consonants that are underspecified for aspiration. We'll assume that voiceless stops are not specified for aspiration, and that other consonants are specified as $-$SPREADGLOTTIS underlyingly. The unification in (574) would thus fail with word-final consonants that are not voiceless stops, and the rule would leave strings containing such consonants unchanged, by our conventions on vacuous application.

We can formulate the next rule with a non-identity condition. Let's assume that the features relevant to place of articulation, those that determine whether segments are homorganic, are LABIAL, CORONAL, and DORSAL. Here's a possible rule:

(575)   Coda aspiration before non-homorganic onset

$$\begin{bmatrix} +\text{CONSONANTAL} \\ -\text{CONTINUANT} \\ -\text{VOICED} \\ \cdots \end{bmatrix}_1 \sqcup \{+\text{SPREADGLOTTIS}\}/\underline{} \begin{bmatrix} +\text{CONSONANTAL} \\ \cdots \end{bmatrix}_2$$

If $\exists F_i \in \{$LABIAL, CORONAL, DORSAL$\}$ such that $\alpha F_i \in \varsigma_1$ and $-\alpha F_i \in \varsigma_2$

This rule adds the aspiration feature, $+$SPREADGLOTTIS to a voiceless stop that occurs before another consonant which has the opposite value for some place of articulation feature, LABIAL, CORONAL, or DORSAL. We can simplify by not giving features to describe voiceless stops as in (576), since the unification would fail when the first consonant is specified $-$SPREADGLOTTIS:

(576)   Coda aspiration before non-homorganic onset (version 2)

$$\begin{bmatrix} +\text{CONSONANTAL} \\ \cdots \end{bmatrix}_1 \sqcup \{+\text{SPREADGLOTTIS}\}/\underline{} \begin{bmatrix} +\text{CONSONANTAL} \\ \cdots \end{bmatrix}_2$$

If $\exists F_i \in \{$LABIAL, CORONAL, DORSAL$\}$ such that $\alpha F_i \in \varsigma_1$ and $-\alpha F_i \in \varsigma_2$

Since we are assuming that the voiceless stops are underlyingly underspecified for aspiration, we need another rule that follows the rules in (574) and (576). This rule will make the voiceless stops that have not become aspirated ($+$SPREADGLOTTIS) become instead unaspirated ($-$SPREADGLOTTIS). The segments that will be affected by this rule are either onset voiceless stops or non-final coda voiceless stops that occur before homorganic consonants.

(577)   Default non-aspiration

$$\begin{bmatrix} +\text{CONSONANTAL} \end{bmatrix} \sqcup \{-\text{SPREADGLOTTIS}\}$$

Since this rule in (577) follows the rule that aspirates word-final codas and the one that aspirates internal codas before non-homorganic consonants, we formulate the third rule in (577) to target all voiceless consonants for unification with $\{-\text{S}\text{PREAD}\text{G}\text{LOTTIS}\}$.[2] Unification will fail exactly where aspiration (unification with $\{+\text{S}\text{PREAD}\text{G}\text{LOTTIS}\}$) has previously applied via one of the two preceding rules (574, 576), and the correct pattern will be generated.

Using capital letters for underspecified segments, we have derivations as in (578):

(578)   Derivations using rules: R1=(574), R2=(576), R3=(577)

UR	moK	KɛKgaKPaʔ
R1. Word-final aspiration	mokʰ	–
R2. Coda aspiration before non-homorganic	—	KɛKgakʰPaʔ
R3. Default non-aspiration	—	kɛkgakʰpaʔ
SR	mokʰ	kɛk.gakʰ.paʔ

For the solution in (578) to work, R1 bleeds R3, and R2 bleeds R3. The relative ordering of R1 and R2 cannot be determined from the available data.

59.3   Second Analysis: One Aspirating Rule

The solution above generates the observed patterns of Sierra Popoluca aspiration. However, our goal is to understand the power of our framework and to understand what is in the mind of a speaker of Sierra Popoluca, not just to mimic the patterns seen in the data. Therefore, we need to recognize that other solutions are possible. We now present one possible alternative.

Again, assume that all voiceless stops are underspecified for the feature SPREAD-GLOTTIS, and that the other consonants are specified as $-\text{S}\text{PREAD}\text{G}\text{LOTTIS}$. We'll assign aspiration via unification with $\{-\text{S}\text{PREAD}\text{G}\text{LOTTIS}\}$ to voiceless stops in onset position (we'll express this as the position before a vowel):

(579)   Default non-aspiration in onset
$$[+\text{C}\text{ONS}] \sqcup \{-\text{S}\text{PR}\text{G}\text{LOT}\} / \text{\_\_\_}[+\text{S}\text{YLL}]$$

This is a feature-filling rule. It targets all consonants since unification will either fill in the feature $-\text{S}\text{PREAD}\text{G}\text{LOTTIS}$ (for voiceless stops) or be vacuous (for other consonants that are underlyingly $-\text{S}\text{PREAD}\text{G}\text{LOTTIS}$).

---

[2]Note that we did not consider such default rules, rules with no environment, when we developed the SPE rule system. We did not allow rules of the form 'a → b / ____'. We can now see that such rules can be useful, and should probably be allowed by our rule syntax.

The next rule incorporates an identity condition to capture the fact that the first member of a cluster is unaspirated only if the second member is homorganic. The rule's effect is to unify a coda consonant with the set containing the value of SPREAD-GLOTTIS on the following onset consonant just in case the coda consonant is identical in place of articulation features with the onset consonant.[3]

(580) Copy (non-)aspiration from a homorganic onset

$$
\begin{bmatrix} +\text{CONS} \\ -\text{CONT} \\ -\text{VOI} \\ \ldots \end{bmatrix}_1 \sqcup \{\alpha\text{SPRGL}\} / \underline{} \begin{bmatrix} +\text{CONS} \\ \alpha\text{SPRGL} \\ \ldots \end{bmatrix}_2
$$

If $\forall F_i \in \{\text{LAB}, \text{COR}, \text{DOR}\}, \alpha F_i \in \varsigma_1$ if and only if $\alpha F_i \in \varsigma_2$

The onset consonant is either underlyingly $-$SPREADGLOTTIS (if it is, say, /g/) or else, if it is a voiceless stop, it will have received the value $-$SPREADGLOTTIS by the previous rule (579) (the one making sure onsets are unaspirated). Therefore, the current rule, if it effects any change, will always unify the coda consonant with $\{-\text{SPREADGLOTTIS}\}$ if it is homorganic to the following onset segment.[4]

A further rule then applies that unifies $\{+ \text{SPREADGLOTTIS}\}$ with all coda consonants (with no further conditions).

(581) General coda aspiration

$$
\begin{bmatrix} +\text{CONS} \end{bmatrix} \sqcup \{+\text{SPRGL}\} / \text{in CODA}
$$

Unification will fail with consonants that are not voiceless stops, since they are underlyingly $-$SPREADGLOTTIS, and it will also fail with voiceless stops that have previously copied the value $-$SPREADGLOTTIS from a following homorganic onset consonant.

Here in (582) is the derivation using the three rules:

(582) Derivations using rules: R4=(579), R5=(580), R6=(581)

UR	moK	KɛKgaKPaʔ
R4. Default non-aspiration in onset	—	kɛKgaKpaʔ
R5. Coda (non-)aspiration from homorganic onset	—	kɛkgaKpaʔ
R6. General coda aspiration	mok^h	kɛkgak^{h}paʔ
SR	mok^h	kɛk.gak^h.paʔ

---

[3]We'll assume that consonant clusters in this language always straddle a syllable boundary, so the second consonant is in an onset.

[4]Of course, this means that we did not have to express this rule as involving copying of an α value. We could have just used unification with $\{-\text{SPREADGLOTTIS}\}$ when the following onset is homorganic. If we had done so, the rule ordering would not be fully determined.

In this solution in (582), the first two rules, R4 and R5, bleed R6, but the relative ordering of R4 and R5 cannot be determined.

59.4 The Benefits of Commitment

Our discussion of Sierra Popoluca is vague in at least two ways. First, we presented two distinct sets of rules to generate the data (and hinted that there are more possibilities). Second, within each of our two solutions, there was some indeterminacy concerning rule ordering. Despite this vagueness, we maintain that the discussion is preferable to an apparently straightforward statement like this:

(583)   Informal statement of Sierra Popoluca pattern: "Coda voiceless stops are aspirated unless they precede a homorganic consonant."

The plain language statement in (583) seems simple, but it suffers from the lack of precision and formalization discussed in the epigraph to Unit 9 from the preface of Chomsky's *Syntactic Structures* (1957, p. 5): "Obscure and intuition-bound notions can neither lead to absurd conclusions nor provide new and correct ones, and hence they fail to be useful in two important respects." The statement in (583) makes no hypothesis about the nature, or even the existence, of an underlying form in the lexicon for voiceless stops. In contrast, the formalizations that we provided posit underlying voiceless stops underspecified for aspiration. This assumption may be incorrect, but at least it is explicit enough to be tested and debated. In other words, despite our incapacity to fully determine what is going on in Sierra Popoluca, we have achieved "higher quality ignorance" compared to what we had before.

It is also important to note that the statement in (583) turns out to be misleading. It looks like an observation, a description of the data, but the terms of the description obscure what we understand to be going on once we have the analytic toolbox provided by a theory. The condition "unless they precede a homorganic consonant" is meaningless in terms of our theory of rules. Possible analyses in terms of rules and the possible correct descriptions of the data *follow from* the theory.

The word *unless* in (583) obscures the fact that the statement treats word-final voiceless stops and those that precede a non-homorganic consonant in parallel, as if these environments constitute a natural class. The model we have built up does not treat these environments as a natural class, and we have to derive the surface pattern from an interaction of three separate rules. Instead of introducing the concepts that we build into rules on an ad hoc basis, we made a commitment to a certain model of rules and stuck with it to see where it would take us. It led us to discover, for example,

that even relations among segments like identity and non-identity require the power
of quantificational logic. More generally, this example illustrates Chomsky's (1957,
p. 14) statement that "each grammar is related to the corpus in a manner fixed in advance by a given linguistic theory." Without this methodological constraint, linguistic
analysis of various corpora can make no claims to universal relevance.

To reiterate, it is preferable to present several analyses that are constrained by some
set of theoretical commitments, even if we do not have the means to choose between
the competitors, than to just provide an informal, unconstrained description of the
phenomena in plain English. Such a natural language formulation can just mask complexity at several levels, whereas the mere attempt to honor the constraints of a theory
leads to "high quality ignorance."

Exercises

59.1. Notice that our formulation of non-identity conditions, as in (576) requires that
the two segments have opposite values for some feature—it is not sufficient that
one be specified and one be underspecified for a feature. Formulate a version
of the rule in (576) that would allow two segments ϕ and ψ to count as non-
identical if they have opposite values for some feature in a given set or if $\phi \subset \psi$
or $\psi \subset \phi$ (note the *proper subset* symbol). Do this with one simple condition.

59.2. On the surface, the Mayan language Tzutujil (Dayley, 1985) has four pairs of
aspirated and unaspirated voiceless stops p/p^h, t/t^h, k/k^h, q/q^h, and two pairs of
aspirated and unaspirated voiceless affricates t^s/t^{sh}, $t^ʃ/t^{ʃh}$. Like Sierra Popoluca,
the distribution of aspirated and unaspirated stops is very different from what
we see in English. However, just as in English and Sierra Popoluca, each pair in
Tzutujil, like p and p^h, is derived from a single underlying segment. In traditional
terms, p and p^h appear to be in complementary distribution and we might call
them *allophones of a single phoneme*. Examine the following forms.

a.	pɔjp^h	'mat'	g.	saq^h	'white'
b.	tap^{h}qiij	'albino'	h.	piːm	'thick'
c.	tʊt^h	'palmera'	i.	saq^{h}bat^{ʃh}	'hailstone'
d.	laq^h	'cup'	j.	kapɛ	'coffee'
e.	kuːk^h	'squirrel'	k.	t^{ʃh}paan	'in it'
f.	qas	'very'	l.	t^{h}kami	'that he die'

a. Based **only** on forms (a-j) select an underlying form for each pair of surfacing voiceless stops and affricates, and describe in words a rule to generate the derived forms. Refer to syllable structure in your rule.

b. Explain why forms (k-l) undermine your hypothesis.

c. The source for this data offers a rule that basically says 'Make a −VOICED, −CONTINUANT consonant become +SPREADGLOTTIS if it occurs either before a consonant or at the end of the word'.[5] Our theory of rules demands that the target and environment of a rule each correspond to a natural class, so we are not allowed to use disjunctive conditions like 'either before a consonant or at the end of the word'.

One might be tempted to conclude that we need to translate Dayley's rule into two separate processes, one that aspirates in the environment ___C, and another that aspirates in the environment ___%. How might we select an underlying form that avoids the conclusion that Tzutujil has two processes of aspiration, one for each environment, ___C and ___%? You must maintain the principle that targets and environments are natural classes.

Provide two solutions:

Version 1. Don't use underspecification, and collapse your rules into a single feature-changing process using '→'

Version 2. Posit an underspecified form for each underlying segment, for example, derive p and p^h from underlying /P/, which will denote a voiceless labial stop that has no value for SPREADGLOTTIS. You'll need two rules; make the second rule as general as possible.

d. Are the surface segments [p^h] and [q] in complementary distribution?

e. Why would you not derive [p^h] and [q] from a single underlying segment?

- Give one argument based on the form [saqiil] 'whiteness', which has a suffix *-iil*.

- Give another argument.

---

[5]Dayley (p. 14) uses the curly brackets of standard generative phonology to denote disjunction, a practice we mentioned in (258) in Unit 24.1. Dayley's rule is also formulated to exclude the voiceless glottalized consonants, which do not have aspirated versions.

59.3. The Greenlandic Eskimo data below is often used as an example of a simple allophone problem. The symbols used here can be assumed to have their IPA values, aside from *r*, which has the value of IPA [ʁ], a voiced uvular fricative. So, *q* and *r* are the only uvular consonants in the language. From published descriptions, the actual phonetic realizations of the vowels appear to be quite complicated, even within particular dialect areas, but we will take the transcriptions below to be accurate for the purposes of discussion. It is not uncommon for teachers to expect students to come up with an analysis of this data that treats the language as having three underlying vowels /i,u,a/, with [e] as an allophone of /i/ and [o] as an allophone of /u/. Here is the final sentence of an instructor's solution we found online:

> "The whole real rule: [i] becomes [e], and [u] becomes [o], when they occur before uvulars or word-finally."

(a) Explain why this solution is untenable given the model we have developed in this book.

(b) Provide a solution that is consistent with our view of rules and natural classes, maintaining the traditional analysis of /i,u,a/ as the underlying vowels.

(c) Suppose that uvulars, but no other consonants, are +LOW. If you try to make a single rule and assume that the underlying vowels are /e,o,a/, there is one form in the data that is problematic.

   i. Write the rule using features.

   ii. Identify the problematic form and explain why it is problematic.

ivnaq	'bluff'	qasaloq	'bark'	iperaq	'harpoon strap'
ikusik	'elbow'	imaq	'sea'	qilaluvaq	'white whale'
tuluvaq	'raven'	qatigak	'back'	itumaq	'palm of hand'
sakiak	'rib'	sava	'sheep'	ugsik	'cow'
nuna	'land'	orpik	'tree'	ine	'room'
nerdloq	'goose'	nanoq	'bear'	marraq	'clay'
iseraq	'ankle'	iga	'pot'	isse	'eye'
igdlo	'house'	sermeq	'glacier'	sako	'tool'

Unit 60

The Remote and Complex Phonology of the English Plural

There is a vast literature demonstrating that the "relation between a phonemic system [the underlying segments in morphemes] and the phonetic record ... is remote and complex" (Chomsky, 1964, p. 38). Neither segments nor rules are directly observable. They are instead the outcome of an analysis (by both the linguist and the child language learner) in which the "essential properties underlie the surface form" (Katz and Bever, 1976, p. 12). This means that we (again, both the linguist and the child language learner) must have a theory of rules and representations to impose on stimuli and generate observations and generalizations.

Using a familiar example from English, we will see in this unit that surface patterns may appear not to conform to the equivalence classes that constitute rules, such as natural classes of segments, or syllable structure positions. In other words, the *intensional* characterizations of rules in a grammar must involve natural classes of segments, defined set-theoretically; but the actual set of forms extensionally manifesting the non-vacuous application of a rule might not reflect the rule's formulation, because of the effects of other rules. (Here, as elsewhere, we may refer to *a rule*, where a more careful discussion would distinguish rules from multi-rule processes.)

60.1 The Extension of the Target: A Toy Example

Let's illustrate this abstract idea with a toy language before illustrating with the phonology involved in the English plural. The Katajanokkan roots in (584) show that the language has three underlying +HIGH vowels, /i, y, u/ and four underlying −HIGH vowels /e, a, ə, o/:

(584)   Katajanokkan

SG	PL	gloss	Root
pik	pikra	'hammock'	pik
pikɪ	pikira	'hummock'	piki
pikʊ	pikura	'cassock'	piku
pika	pikara	'hassock'	pika
piko	pikora	'hillock'	piko
pik	pikyra	'haddock'	piky
pike	pikera	'bannock'	pike
pikə	pikəra	'mattock'	pikə

The +HIGH vowels have the features in (585):[1]

(585)   The +HIGH vowels of Katajanokkan

$$
\begin{array}{ccc}
i & y & u \\
\left\{ \begin{array}{c} +\text{HI} \\ -\text{BK} \\ -\text{RD} \end{array} \right\} &
\left\{ \begin{array}{c} +\text{HI} \\ -\text{BK} \\ +\text{RD} \end{array} \right\} &
\left\{ \begin{array}{c} +\text{HI} \\ +\text{BK} \\ +\text{RD} \end{array} \right\}
\end{array}
$$

One natural class in this language is [+HIGH], with *i, y, u*, since we have constructed the language so that no other vowels are supersets of {+HIGH}. The high front vowels *i, y* constitute another natural class [+HIGH, −BACK], and the high round vowels *y, u* form yet another [+HIGH, +ROUND]. However, the vowels *i, u* do not form a natural class to the exclusion of *y*, since the intersection of *i* and *u* is the set {+HIGH}, and y is a superset of this set of features.

Suppose that Katajanokkan has a rule, R1, that deletes word-final *y*, and another rule (or process) R2, which laxes word-final *i, u* to *ɪ, ʊ*. The rules (or processes) are given in (586) in the order in which they apply, R1 before R2:

---

[1] Since all the high vowels are underlyingly +ATR, we can ignore that feature for the moment.

(586)   Rules of Katajanokkan

      R1: $[+\textsc{High}, +\textsc{Round}, -\textsc{Back}] \rightarrow \epsilon\ /\ \_\_\_\%$

      R2: $[+\textsc{High}] \rightarrow \{-\textsc{Atr}\}\ /\ \_\_\_\%$

These rules provide one possible analysis of the data in (584).[2]

If you examine the data for effects of the laxing rule, R2, you'll see that the extensional characterization of the segments affected by this rule is {i,u}. Underlying /i, u/ have lax counterparts in SRs (*pikɪ, pikʊ*), but underlying /y/ has no lax counterpart on the surface. However, as we have explained, these two segments do not form a natural class to the exclusion of *y*. So how can we make a single rule that targets *i* and *u* but not *y*? Do we need separate rules for *i* and *u*? No, we do not need separate rules for the two vowels, as long as we understand that the natural classes in our rules are characterized *intensionally*.

Consider the derivation of the relevant forms:

(587)   Katajanokkan Derivations

UR	/piki/	/piki-ra/	/piku/	/piku-ra/	/piky/	/piky-ra/
R1: Deletion	–	—	—	—	pik	–
R2: Laxing	pikɪ	—	pikʊ	—	–	–
SR	[pikɪ]	[piki-ra]	[pikʊ]	[piku-ra]	[pik]	[piky-ra]
Gloss	'hummock'	–PL	'cassock'	–PL	'haddock'	–PL

Notice that the boxed form shows no effects of the second rule–R2 has been bled in this derivation by R1, which deleted word-final *y*.

As you can see, the target of the laxing rule is a natural class that *does* contain *y*, and the language has the segment *y*, yet there are no instances on the surface of an underlying /y/ that has been changed into [ʏ]. Given our model, it is not only *possible* to have such a situation where the overt manifestations of a rule's effect do not constitute a natural class, but it is *necessary*...if we want to make the claim that the laxing of *i* to *ɪ* and the laxing of *u* to *ʊ* reflect *the same* feature-changing process. But the intensional characterization in terms of natural classes is [+High], a natural class that contains *i, y, u*. This natural class contains *y*, but there is no lax version of this vowel,

---

[2] Given the data we have presented, the lax vowels *ɪ, ʊ* only arise from underlying /i, u/ as "allophonic" conditioned variants, but this plays no role in the following discussion—our points would remain valid even if R2 were neutralizing.

no ʏ, word-finally, because word-final *y* has been deleted.[3] Given our theoretical commitment to rules that refer to natural classes, the correct version of the rule target class is more general than the set of observable forms suggests. This result follows simply from the interaction of natural class logic and rule ordering, but it illustrates the profound observations cited above—the relationship between the underlying segments and the phonetic record is "remote and complex" (Chomsky) because "essential properties underlie the surface form" (Katz and Bever).

At this point, you should go back to Units 4.5 and 45.1, to see how we prepared you for this result by ensuring that natural classes are defined *intensionally*. In the course of the derivation, circumstances change: initially, in URs, all three +HIGH vowels occur word-finally, so there is a perfect match between an intensional characterization of word-final high vowels and an extensional listing of word-final high vowels in words. However, the effects of R1, which deletes word-final *y*, change the *extension* of the set of word-final high vowels during the course of a derivation. Crucially, the *intensional* characterization of the set targeted by R2 does not change.

60.2 The Extension of the Environment: The English Plural

The toy Katajanokkan data has provided all the concepts we need to understand the slightly more complex case of the regular English plural. In Katajanokkan we considered intensional and extensional characterizations of rule targets. In English, we look at intensional and extensional characterizations of segments in a rule's environment. We will not be considering nouns like *child/children* or *foot/feet*. We also will not be considering nouns like *leaf/leaves* or *moth/moths* which, in standard dialects at least, have an alternation in the voicing of the root-final consonant. We will be concerned only with nouns whose stems are constant in the singular and plural. Here is a representative sample:

---

[3]Of course, the deletion rule could be a deletion of ʏ occurring after the other rule, but this does not change our main argument.

(588)   English nouns with each alternant of the regular plural suffix

a. [-s]	b. [-z]	c.[-ɨz]
cup	cub, head, rug	bus
mat	farm, son, song	bush
rack	car, hill	match
cliff	hive	whiz
myth	bow, bee, clue	garage
	pickle, burger	judge

You see that there are three different endings, which we transcribe as [-s], [-z] and [-iz]. The exact value of the vowel in this last form, transcribed here with the +HIGH, +BACK, −ROUND *i* may be different from what you have in your dialect—maybe ə?—but don't worry about that.

If we assume that the underlying form of the plural marker is /-z/, that is, a morpheme consisting of just one segment, then the forms in column (b) manifest the underlying form unchanged. Consistent with this analysis, we see that the stems in this column end in segments that do not form an obvious natural class—we have vowels, sonorant consonants (nasals, liquids, glides) and some obstruents (stops and some fricatives). All of these root-final segments are voiced; however, there are some voiced segments at the end of the roots in column (c), such as the final consonants of *judge, garage, buzz*. Hence, the alternant [-z] does not occur after *all* voiced segments.

If we look at the segments that end the roots in column (c), we see that they *do* form a natural class. Let's first take the generalized intersection of these six segments:

(589) $\bigcap\{s, \int, t^\int, z, ʒ, d^ʒ\} =$

$$
\bigcap \left\{
\begin{matrix} s \\ \begin{bmatrix} +\text{COR} \\ +\text{STRID} \\ -\text{NAS} \\ -\text{LAB} \\ -\text{SON} \\ -\text{LAT} \\ -\text{DEL} \\ +\text{CON} \\ +\text{ANT} \\ -\text{VOI} \end{bmatrix} \end{matrix} ,
\begin{matrix} \int \\ \begin{bmatrix} +\text{COR} \\ +\text{STRID} \\ -\text{NAS} \\ -\text{LAB} \\ -\text{SON} \\ -\text{LAT} \\ -\text{DEL} \\ +\text{CON} \\ -\text{ANT} \\ -\text{VOI} \end{bmatrix} \end{matrix} ,
\begin{matrix} t^\int \\ \begin{bmatrix} +\text{COR} \\ +\text{STRID} \\ -\text{NAS} \\ -\text{LAB} \\ -\text{SON} \\ -\text{LAT} \\ +\text{DEL} \\ -\text{CON} \\ -\text{ANT} \\ -\text{VOI} \end{bmatrix} \end{matrix} ,
\begin{matrix} z \\ \begin{bmatrix} +\text{COR} \\ +\text{STRID} \\ -\text{NAS} \\ -\text{LAB} \\ -\text{SON} \\ -\text{LAT} \\ -\text{DEL} \\ +\text{CON} \\ +\text{ANT} \\ +\text{VOI} \end{bmatrix} \end{matrix} ,
\begin{matrix} ʒ \\ \begin{bmatrix} +\text{COR} \\ +\text{STRID} \\ -\text{NAS} \\ -\text{LAB} \\ -\text{SON} \\ -\text{LAT} \\ -\text{DEL} \\ +\text{CON} \\ -\text{ANT} \\ +\text{VOI} \end{bmatrix} \end{matrix} ,
\begin{matrix} d^ʒ \\ \begin{bmatrix} +\text{COR} \\ +\text{STRID} \\ -\text{NAS} \\ -\text{LAB} \\ -\text{SON} \\ -\text{LAT} \\ +\text{DEL} \\ -\text{CON} \\ -\text{ANT} \\ +\text{VOI} \end{bmatrix} \end{matrix}
\right\}
$$

$$
= \left\{ \begin{bmatrix} +\text{COR} \\ +\text{STRID} \\ -\text{NAS} \\ -\text{LAB} \\ -\text{SON} \\ -\text{LAT} \end{bmatrix} \right\}
$$

These six segments are the only ones (in English) that are supersets of the set of features in the generalized intersection in (589). As a result, the six segments *s, ∫, t∫, z, ʒ, d∫* do indeed constitute a natural class, the class represented in (590):

(590)   Natural class defined by intersection of final segments in (588c)

$$\Pi = \left\{ \pi : \pi \supseteq \left\{ \begin{matrix} +\text{COR} \\ +\text{STRID} \\ -\text{NAS} \\ -\text{LAB} \\ -\text{SON} \\ -\text{LAT} \end{matrix} \right\} \right\} = \left[\begin{matrix} +\text{COR} \\ +\text{STRID} \\ -\text{NAS} \\ -\text{LAB} \\ -\text{SON} \\ -\text{LAT} \end{matrix} \right]$$

For expository convenience, we will use a smaller set of features to characterize this natural class, just referring to CORONAL and STRIDENT:

(591)   Stripped down natural class for final segments in (588c)

$$\left[\begin{matrix} +\text{COR} \\ +\text{STRID} \end{matrix} \right]$$

It is an open question which characterization is actually in a speaker's grammar, but we'll stick with this more compact one and refer to the relevant natural class as *coronal stridents* in our discussion. Note that English has other coronal segments, like *t, d, l, r,* and *n* and other stridents like *f* and *v,* but the natural class we want are all and only the segments that contain *both* +CORONAL and +STRIDENT, the ones that are a superset of {+CORONAL, +STRIDENT}.

Given the UR /-z/, we can generate the form in column (588c) with the rule in (592):[4]

(592)   Insertion rule: $\epsilon \rightarrow i$ / $\left[\begin{matrix} +\text{COR} \\ +\text{STRID} \end{matrix} \right]$ ___ z

For ease of discussion we have not represented *i* and *z* in terms of features. The rule can be paraphrased as 'Insert *i* between a coronal strident and *z*'.[5]

Now let's turn to column (a) of the English data in (588). Once again, we need a rule to affect the underlying form of the plural, specifically one that devoices the *z* to *s.* All the stem final consonants in column (a) are voiceless, but these are not *all* of the voiceless segments. Specifically, *s, ʃ, tʃ* are not among the segments we find stem-finally in column (a), yet these segments are supersets of {−VOICED}.

If you mechanically compute the generalized intersection of the final segments from column (a), you'll end up defining a natural class that includes the voiceless

---

[4]This rule still uses the "un-deconstructed" arrow of our early rules.

[5]You might be tempted to formulate the rule to insert *i* between any two coronal stridents. How does a word like *mischief* bear on this idea, given the internal consonant cluster *stʃ*.

coronal stridents. Intuitively, the fact that f and p are in the column (a) set tells us that neither value of STRIDENT will be in the intersection. And the fact that p and t and k are in the column (a) set tells us that neither value of CORONAL, LABIAL, or ANTERIOR will be in the intersection. Let's explicitly calculate the generalized intersection of the segments at the end of the forms in column (a):

(593) $\bigcap\{\text{p, t, k, f, } \theta\} =$

$$
\bigcap \left\{
\begin{array}{c}
\text{p} \\
\left\{\begin{array}{l}
-\text{COR} \\
-\text{STRID} \\
-\text{NAS} \\
+\text{LAB} \\
-\text{SON} \\
-\text{LAT} \\
-\text{DEL} \\
-\text{CON} \\
+\text{ANT} \\
-\text{VOI}
\end{array}\right\}
\end{array},
\begin{array}{c}
\text{t} \\
\left\{\begin{array}{l}
+\text{COR} \\
-\text{STRID} \\
-\text{NAS} \\
-\text{LAB} \\
-\text{SON} \\
-\text{LAT} \\
-\text{DEL} \\
-\text{CON} \\
+\text{ANT} \\
-\text{VOI}
\end{array}\right\}
\end{array},
\begin{array}{c}
\text{k} \\
\left\{\begin{array}{l}
-\text{COR} \\
-\text{STRID} \\
-\text{NAS} \\
-\text{LAB} \\
-\text{SON} \\
-\text{LAT} \\
-\text{DEL} \\
-\text{CON} \\
-\text{ANT} \\
-\text{VOI}
\end{array}\right\}
\end{array},
\begin{array}{c}
\text{f} \\
\left\{\begin{array}{l}
-\text{COR} \\
+\text{STRID} \\
-\text{NAS} \\
+\text{LAB} \\
-\text{SON} \\
-\text{LAT} \\
-\text{DEL} \\
+\text{CON} \\
+\text{ANT} \\
-\text{VOI}
\end{array}\right\}
\end{array},
\begin{array}{c}
\theta \\
\left\{\begin{array}{l}
+\text{COR} \\
-\text{STRID} \\
-\text{NAS} \\
-\text{LAB} \\
-\text{SON} \\
-\text{LAT} \\
-\text{DEL} \\
+\text{CON} \\
+\text{ANT} \\
-\text{VOI}
\end{array}\right\}
\end{array}
\right\}
=
\left\{\begin{array}{l}
-\text{NAS} \\
-\text{SON} \\
-\text{LAT} \\
-\text{DEL} \\
-\text{VOI}
\end{array}\right\}
$$

Notice that the voiceless coronal stridents, s, $\int$, and t' are all supersets of the set of features we just calculated. Let's look at s for example:

(594) A natural class problem?

$$
\begin{array}{c}
\text{s} \\
\left\{\begin{array}{l}
+\text{COR} \\
+\text{STRID} \\
-\text{NAS} \\
-\text{LAB} \\
-\text{SON} \\
-\text{LAT} \\
-\text{DEL} \\
+\text{CON} \\
+\text{ANT} \\
-\text{VOI}
\end{array}\right\}
\end{array}
\supseteq
\left\{\begin{array}{l}
-\text{NAS} \\
-\text{SON} \\
-\text{LAT} \\
-\text{DEL} \\
-\text{VOI}
\end{array}\right\}
$$

So, there is no way to write a rule that devoices z to s after p, t, k, f, and θ but not after s, $\int$, and t', because the smallest natural class containing the former group necessarily contains the latter group.

We have adopted the principle that it is a defining property of rules that their targets and environments are natural classes, so it looks like we would have to abandon the idea that there is a single rule devoicing z to s in English, just as we had to abandon the possibility in Lamba (Unit 58) that a single rule palatalized k to $\check{c}$ and s to $\check{s}$. However, there is an alternative, which you can probably see if you recall how we managed to have a single rule in Katajanokkan at the beginning of this unit.

What we see in the English plural is that the *extensionally* defined set of segments that trigger devoicing of z to s is not a natural class. However, it does not follow that the *intensionally* defined natural class consisting of all the segments that are supersets of the set of features computed in (593) cannot serve to define a rule environment.

Before we explain further, let's adopt a pared-down version of the set computed in (593), again to aid our exposition:

(595)   Natural class of devoicing rule environment: [−Voi]

This natural class obviously contains all the segments *p, t, k, f, θ, s, ʃ,* and *tʃ,* and yet we want to use the representation in (595) to define the environment of a rule whose effects are seen only after *p, t, k, f,* and *θ.* How is this possible? You have all the tools required for the solution. Here's what we can do: we can use a rule that is intensionally (that's intensionally, with *s*!) more broad than the evidence suggests it should be, but we manipulate the set of potential inputs to the rule by using rule ordering.

After rule (592) applies, there will be no sequences of *s-z, ʃ-z,* or *tʃ-z,* because they will have been broken up by vowel insertion. We could then apply the devoicing process to the output of rule (592). The devoicing process—deletion by set subtraction and insertion by unification—would turn *z* to *s* after any voiceless segment.

(596)   Devoicing rule: z→ s / [−Voi] ___

At the point in the derivation when the devoicing rule (596) applies, the only voiceless segments before *z* will be ones that are NOT coronal stridents. We'll get *s* as the plural marker of noun stems ending in any one of {p, t, k, f, θ}.[6]

This result demonstrates again the importance of intensional definitions of natural classes. In the course of the derivation, circumstances change: initially coronal stridents may be adjacent to the *-z* of the plural marker, but after the vowel-insertion rule, no coronal stridents occur adjacent to the *-z.* So the extension of the set of root-final segments that trigger devoicing has changed, but the rule formulated in terms of natural classes defined intensionally refers to *all* voiceless obstruents. Here are some derivations:

---

[6]You can think of the situation thus: the set of voiceless segments is a natural class, and the set of coronal stridents is a natural class, but the subtraction of the latter from the former, the so-called *relative complement* of the former with respect to the latter, namely {p, t, k, f, θ}, is *not* a natural class.

(597)   English Plural Derivations

UR	/mæt-z/	/klɪf-z/	/hɛd-z/	/bʊʃ-z/	/dʒədʒ-z/
Rule (592): Insertion	—	—	—	bʊʃiz	dʒədʒiz
Rule (596): Devoicing	mæts	klɪfs	—	—	—
SR	[mæts]	[klɪfs]	[hɛdz]	[bʊʃiz]	[dʒədʒiz]
Gloss	'mats'	'cliffs'	'heads'	'bushes'	'judges'

The vowel insertion rule (592) bleeds certain instances of the devoicing rule.

This is a simple and well-known example,[7] but it has profound consequences. Think about this example from the perspective of a child acquiring language. Once again, we need to see the child as positing a grammar that is not directly detectable in the signal. The learner must posit a rule that is patently false—it is *not* the case that all root-final voiceless segments trigger devoicing of the plural marker, and yet that is what the grammar encodes. Once again we see that the relationship between the underlying segments and the phonetic record is "remote and complex" because "essential properties underlie the surface form."

We believe that such examples provide evidence that acquiring an I-language phonology is possible only because the space of possibilities for a learner is highly constrained by an innate feature set and a format for rules (based on natural classes defined by generalized intersection). This view is to be contrasted with recent suggestions (such as Mielke, 2008) that features are not innate but rather are discovered by observing the rules in a language. We think it is fairly obvious that such an approach is a dead end (but see Archangeli and Pulleyblank 2015 for different view). It is hard to imagine how rules could be observed in the absence of features with which to parse their target and environment classes. How can a process be described if the learner has no features with which to describe it? And given our example, how can rules be learned if the body of direct data available to the learner contradicts the correct formulation of the rule: it is just not observable that all voiceless segments cause *z* to become *s*, and yet that is the content of the rule that a learner must posit. The potential for interaction of rules guarantees that some surface patterns will be inexpressible in terms of natural classes. It is only our theoretical commitment that guarantees that rules are expressed in terms of natural classes.

To reiterate, it seems like we need features to learn rules since they are not directly observable, and we would need rules to learn features, since the rules can tell us what

---

[7]For some reason Kiparsky (1985) selects underlying /-s/ for the English plural, but the analysis appears to be deeply flawed.

segments form natural classes. We get out of this vicious cycle by assuming that we don't learn features—they are innate. We use these innate features, along with innate knowledge of the format of rules, to learn the specific rules of the language of our environment.[8]

Exercises

60.1. Switch the order of the rules for Katajanokkan in (586) and provide the derivation for the same underlying forms as in (587). Are the surface forms the same? Are the derivations the same?

60.2. Demonstrate that the phonological rule we developed to account for the variants of the English plural suffix also accounts for the possessive suffix (like *Jack*'s *book*) and the third person singular verbal ending (like *Mary shoot*s *a three-pointer*) by making a table for each morpheme parallel to that in (588).

60.3. Draw tripartite morpheme diagrams for each of the three morphemes in the previous question, showing syntactic, semantic, and phonological information for each.

60.4. (i) Make a table like (588) to illustrate the alternants of the past tense ending seen in *walked, jogged, treated*. (ii) Make a *single rule* that accounts for the vowel insertion rule discussed in this unit and the vowel insertion in forms like *treated*. Don't make your rule too general. Discuss any problems you encounter.

60.5. Suppose you wanted to reject our view of innate features and propose that, based on observed patterns, a learner of English somehow posits an ad hoc feature F, shared by *p, t, k, f, θ,* and no other English segments. How would you explain the fact that *kick* and *kiss* both take a past tense marker pronounced [t]? Would such facts make your rejection of innate features untenable? Inelegant? Stronger? Or are such facts irrelevant?

---

[8]For further discussion on why features have to be innate, see Hale and Reiss (2003); Reiss (2017b); for discussion of the myth of 'raw' phonetic data, see Hammarberg (1981, 1976).

Unit 61

Combinatorics and the Plausibility of Universal Grammar

[T]he number of symbols that might have to be realized in a representational system [like the brain–ab&cr] with any real power is for all practical purposes infinite; it vastly exceeds the number of elementary particles in the universe, which is roughly 10^{85} (or 2^{285}), give or take a few orders of magnitude. This is an example of the difference between the infinitude of the possible and the finitude of the actual, a distinction of enormous importance in the design of practical computing machines. A computing machine can only have a finite number of actual symbols in it, but it must be so constructed that the set of possible symbols from which those actual symbols come is *essentially infinite*. (By 'essentially infinite' we will always mean greater than the number of elementary particles in the universe; in other words, not physically realizable.) This means that the machine cannot come with all of the symbols it will ever need already formed. It must be able to construct them as it needs them—as it encounters new referents.

C. R. Gallistel and A. P. King, *Memory and the Computational Brain: Why Cognitive Science Will Transform Neuroscience*

A recurring theme of this book has been how much descriptive power, how many different languages, we can model with even the simple systems we have developed. Of course, we know that the correct theory of phonology is more complex than what we have presented. But the very richness that we can model with even a relatively simple theory of phonology constitutes an indirect, yet powerful, argument for the plausibility of a universal grammar for phonology, and for language more generally.

As we went through various neutralization patterns and the types of rule interactions like feeding, bleeding, counterfeeding, and counterbleeding, we repeatedly made the point that a wide variety of languages could be generated by the simple computational system we developed using our restricted SPE rules. We contrasted the apparent complexity and variety of phenomena we could account for with the simplicity of the model itself. Just because the phenomena look complicated to a naive human observer, it does not follow that the phenomena are due to a complicated underlying system. We ended up showing that the SPE model was too restrictive, since the original rule syntax could not express rules involving syllable structure, metathesis, and other phenomena that appear in human languages. However, in this unit, we will revert to a fairly simple model, built on the binary feature system and basic SPE rules.

We will perform some basic combinatoric calculations based on this very conservative view of UG in order to consider the question of how many languages can be described in principle, from various perspectives. After we lay out a basic model of UG with just four features and show that it allows us to describe eighty-one different segments, we will illustrate how these eighty-one segments can be used to characterize languages. First we will think of a language as just a segment inventory, then we will think of a language as an ordered set of phonological rules, and next we will think of a language as a lexicon, a list of morphemes. In each case, the number of different languages we can define using our modest UG is quite large, maybe not what Gallistel and King (2009) call "for all practical purposes infinite," but astronomical, nonetheless.

We'll also explore how minimally enriching a representational system can make the possibilities of a computational system explode using models called cellular automata. In addition to our phonological points, you will also get a review and extension of the informal survey of basic combinatorics we started in earlier units, such as the discussion of the combinatorics of rule ordering in Unit 31. Recall that we pointed out there that a set of just ten rules can be ordered in three-and-a-half million ways. We'll now apply similar reasoning to other aspects of our simple phonological model.

61.1 Power Sets

We need one more idea from set theory for our discussion of combinatorics. Given a set S, the power set of S, denoted $\mathcal{P}(S)$, is the set of all subsets of S. Here is a concrete example:

(598)   A set and its power set

- $A = \{x, y, z\}$

- $\mathcal{P}(A) = \left\{ \emptyset, \{x\}, \{y\}, \{z\}, \{x,y\}, \{x,z\}, \{y,z\}, \{x,y,z\} \right\}$

Note, first of all, that power set is a set and not just a list of subsets. That's why we have the outer brackets in (598). Next, note that the power set of a set contains *all* the subsets, including the empty set $\emptyset$ and the whole, original set, in this case A itself, which is $\{x, y, z\}$.

We have listed the members of $\mathcal{P}(A)$ in an order that probably seems sensible to you: we started with the $\emptyset$, moved to the subsets with one member, then to those with two members, and finished with A itself, with three members. This is a useful way to proceed when you have to catalog a power set, but we'll show you an alternative below.

Recall that the *cardinality* of a set is just the number of elements in the set, so for the set A above, $|A| = 3$, since A has three members, x, y, and z. What is the cardinality of $\mathcal{P}(A)$, that is, $|\mathcal{P}(A)|$? You can just count and see that there are eight members in this set, so the $|\mathcal{P}(A)| = 8$.

Let's look at B, a smaller set than A, and compute its power set:

(599)   Another set and its power set

- $B = \{x, y\}$
- $\mathcal{P}(B) = \{\emptyset, \{x\}, \{y\}, \{x,y\}\}$

So $|B| = 2$ and $|\mathcal{P}(B)| = 4$.

Let's look at an even smaller set C:

(600)   Yet another set and its power set

- $C = \{x\}$
- $\mathcal{P}(C) = \{\emptyset, \{x\}\}$

So $|C| = 1$ and $|\mathcal{P}(C)| = 2$.

The next smallest set is the empty set, $\emptyset$:

(601)   The empty set $\emptyset$ set and its power set

- $\emptyset = \{\}$
- $\mathcal{P}(\emptyset) = \{\emptyset\}$

So $|\emptyset| = 0$ and $|\mathcal{P}(\emptyset)| = 1$. You have probably figured out the pattern: $2^0 = 1$; $2^1 = 2$; $2^2 = 4$; $2^3 = 8$, so if a set Q has cardinality n (i.e. $|Q| = n$), then $|\mathcal{P}(Q)| = 2^n$. Why is this the case?

Let's go back to the set A, which has three members: $A = \{x, y, x\}$. For each subset of A, that is, each member of $\mathcal{P}(A)$, we need to ask, *Is the element x in this subset?*, *Is the element y in this subset?* and *Is the element z in this subset?* Thus we have a two-way question for each element of A—the answer to each question is YES or NO. With three segments, x, y, z, that gives us $2 \times 2 \times 2 = 2^3 = 8$ sets of answers corresponding to the eight subsets in $\mathcal{P}(A)$, as shown in (602):

(602) $\mathcal{P}(A)$ where $A = \{x, y, z\}$

	Is x an element?	Is y an element?	Is z an element?	
Subset 0	no	no	no	$\emptyset$
Subset 1	no	no	yes	$\{z\}$
Subset 2	no	yes	no	$\{y\}$
Subset 3	no	yes	yes	$\{y, z\}$
Subset 4	yes	no	no	$\{x\}$
Subset 5	yes	no	yes	$\{x, z\}$
Subset 6	yes	yes	no	$\{x, y\}$
Subset 7	yes	yes	yes	$\{x, y, z\}$

If you are wondering why we ordered the subsets like this, and numbered them from 0 to 7 instead of 1 to 8, it is because we can easily replace "no" with 0 and "yes" with 1, and make each subset correspond to a *binary number*[1] from 0 to 7, as in (603):

---

[1] In normal decimal numbers, the rightmost column is *ones*, the next is *tens*, the next is *hundreds*, and so on. In binary numbers, the columns correspond to powers of two, instead of powers of ten. We won't further explain binary numbers here, but you can find a clear discussion on Wikipedia or elsewhere online. The main thing you need to keep in mind is that $2^0 = 1$, and in fact, for any number n, $n^0 = 1$. Also note that leading zeros do not affect a number: just as in decimal numbers 99 is the same as 099 or 00099; in binary, 1 and 01 and 000000001 all write the same number.

(603)   Ordering elements of $\mathcal{P}(A)$ with binary numbers

| | | *binary number* | | |
| | 2^2 | 2^1 | 2^0 | |
	fours	*twos*	*ones*	
0= 0+0+0	0	0	0	$\emptyset$
1= 0+0+1	0	0	1	$\{z\}$
2= 0+2+0	0	1	0	$\{y\}$
3= 0+2+1	0	1	1	$\{y, z\}$
4= 4+0+0	1	0	0	$\{x\}$
5= 4+0+1	1	0	1	$\{x, z\}$
6= 4+2+0	1	1	0	$\{x, y\}$
7= 4+2+1	1	1	1	$\{x, y, z\}$

Using binary numbers like this gives us a simple way to order the members of a power set and refer to them. Note that we assigned x to the *fours* column, y to the *twos* column and z to the *ones* column, but any consistent order works. Given a system like this, we can agree that, say, the fourth member of $\mathcal{P}(A)$ is Subset 3, $\{y, z\}$.[2] With this understanding of power sets, we can turn back to phonological issues.

61.2   Combinatorics of the Universal Segment Inventory

61.2.1   Assuming Two Choices per Feature

In Unit 53 we listed the eight surface vowels of Turkish, repeated in (604):

(604)   Feature analysis of Turkish vowels

| | $-$BACK | | $+$BACK | |
	$-$ROUND	$+$ROUND	$-$ROUND	$+$ROUND
$+$HIGH	i	ü	ı	u
$-$HIGH	e	ö	a	o

Note that these eight vowels correspond to the eight possible choices for three features $\pm$BACK, $\pm$ROUND, $\pm$HIGH. Replacing these three features with abstract ones

---

[2]Since A has three members, the cardinality of $\mathcal{P}(A)$ is $8 = 2^3$. The members of $\mathcal{P}(A)$ correspond to the binary version of numbers from 0 to 7—there are eight of them, but the highest is 7. This illustrates a general pattern: labeling items from 0 to $2^n - 1$ yields 2^n items. You already know this for decimal numbers: 100 $= 10^2$, but you can label one hundred items by labeling them from 0 to 99, which is $10^2 - 1$.

(F_1, F_2, F_3), we can give the set Σ of all eight complete segments that could be defined if these were the only three features made available by UG:

(605) Σ with three features and only complete segments: $|\Sigma| = 8$

$$\left\{ \begin{array}{l} \{-F_1, -F_2, -F_3\}, \{-F_1, -F_2, +F_3\}, \{-F_1, +F_2, -F_3\}, \{-F_1, +F_2, +F_3\}, \\ \{+F_1, -F_2, -F_3\}, \{+F_1, -F_2, +F_3\}, \{+F_1, +F_2, -F_3\}, \{+F_1, +F_2, +F_3\} \end{array} \right\}$$

Each set of valued features inside a pair of brackets corresponds to a segment. Here, each feature occurs with either a '+' or a '−', so there are $2^3 = 8$ possible segments. There are three features and the cardinality of each segment-set is 3, since each segment has three value-feature specifications.[3]

In general, discussions of phonological features assume, as we just did, that if UG provides n features, then it is possible to define 2^n segments, since each segment contains n value-feature specifications. You can think of it this way: a segment is a string of answers to these questions 'Plus or minus for F_1?', 'Plus or minus for F_2?', ... 'Plus or minus for F_n?'. There are $2 \times 2 \times 2 \ldots \times 2 = 2^n$ ways to answer these questions.

61.2.2   Assuming Three Choices per Feature

However, we did not restrict ourselves to two answers for each feature when we introduced *incomplete* segments in our discussion of Turkish vowel harmony in Unit 53. The third possibility we allowed was that a feature can be completely absent from a segment. For the plural suffix of Turkish, we posited the underlying vowel A which has the values −HIGH and −ROUND, but lacks a value for BACK. And for the genitive suffix in Unit 55, we posited a vowel I which has a value +HIGH, but lacks values for both ROUND and BACK. We used similar reasoning in our discussions of Turkish stops in Unit 52, where we posited lexical items containing the *incomplete* segment D which is identical to t and d aside from its lack of a valued feature for VOICE.

Allowing incomplete segments changes the relevant combinatoric computations. There are now three possible answers to each question about the feature specification

---

[3]Notice that you can replace each $-F_i$ with '0' and each $+F_i$ with '1' to convert the segments to a list of binary numbers from 0 to 7. This gives us a convenient way to order the set of possible segments, just as we used the same technique to order the members of a power set above. In fact, the segments are listed here in order from 0, $\{-F_1, -F_2, -F_3\}$, to 7, $\{+F_1, +F_2, +F_3\}$.

in a segment: 'plus', 'minus', or 'absent'. This means that a set of three features can define $3 \times 3 \times 3 = 3^3 = 27$ segments.

In (606) we list the 27 possibilities for segments as sets of valued features if there are three features given by UG, and if incomplete segments are allowed.

(606) Σ with three features and underspecification: $|\Sigma| = 3^3 = 27$

$$\Sigma = \left\{ \begin{array}{l} \emptyset, \\[4pt] \{+F_1\}, \{-F_1\}, \{+F_2\}, \{-F_2\}, \{+F_3\}, \{-F_3\}, \\[2pt] \{+F_1, +F_2\}, \{+F_1, -F_2\}, \{+F_1, +F_3\}, \{+F_1, -F_3\}, \\[2pt] \{-F_1, +F_2\}, \{-F_1, -F_2\}, \{-F_1, +F_3\}, \{-F_1, -F_3\}, \\[2pt] \{+F_2, +F_3\}, \{+F_2, -F_3\} \\[2pt] \{-F_2, +F_3\}, \{-F_2, -F_3\} \\[2pt] \{+F_1, +F_2, +F_3\}, \{+F_1, +F_2, -F_3\}, \{+F_1, -F_2, +F_3\}, \{+F_1, -F_2, -F_3\} \\[2pt] \{-F_1, +F_2, +F_3\}, \{-F_1, +F_2, -F_3\}, \{-F_1, -F_2, +F_3\}, \{-F_1, -F_2, -F_3\} \end{array} \right\}$$

The first item listed in this set of segments is a segment that is completely underspecified. It lacks a value for all three of the features given by this version of UG. The next item is $\{+F_1\}$. This item has no value for $+F_2$ and $+F_3$. The last item is specified as $\{-F_1, -F_2, -F_3\}$.[4]

Underspecification, the possibility of incomplete segments, is typically treated as an advanced idea in phonology, and you might be under the impression that it corresponds to an added complexity to our basic model. It turns out that the opposite is in fact true: recognizing underspecification, the possibility of incomplete segments, is a *simplification*. To avoid underspecification, we would have to *stipulate* that segments must be complete. By streamlining our theory, by stripping away this stipulation, we get a simpler model that also happens to solve some problems by making underspecified segments available (see Chomsky, 2007; Reiss, 2012, for discussion).

It is obvious that the universal segment inventory with 27 segments based on 3 features in (606) will correspond to *at least* as many phonetic realizations as the in-

---

[4]Just as we can order the segments as binary numbers when there are two choices for each feature, $+$ or $-$, we can now order them as ternary numbers, by, say, letting 0='absent', 1= '$-$', and 2 = '+'. This would give us the ternary numbers from 0 to 26, corresponding to the 27 segments. Ternary numbers use columns corresponding to powers of 3. So, the ternary number $000 = 0 \times 3^2 + 0 \times 3^1 + 0 \times 3^0$, which is equal to the decimal ("normal") number 0. Thus the first of our 27 segments (actually, the zeroth one) is the one that corresponds to the segment-set with the values "absent for F_1", "absent for F_2", and "absent for F_3", which yields the set $\{\ \} = \emptyset$. In contrast, the ternary number $222 = (2 \times 3^2) + (2 \times 3^1) + (2 \times 3^0) = 18 + 6 + 2$. This is the decimal number 26. Thus the last segment in our numbering scheme, the twenty-seventh (counting from 1), corresponds to the segment-set specified $\{+F_1, +F_2, +F_3\}$. If F_1 is HI, F_2 is BK, and F_3 is RD, what is the number (from 0 to 26) corresponding to the Turkish vowel /A/ of Unit 53?

ventory with 8 segments in (605), since every member of the latter is a member of the former—the set in (605) is a subset of the set in (606).

One might be concerned that the massive increase in combinatorial power entailed by underspecification presents a problem for the learner since it appears to increase the size of the hypothesis space for learning lexical items. It is not clear that this is so, and in fact, the 3^n view has at least two arguments to commend it.

First, let's assume that each feature must be learned separately for each segment in each stored lexical item. Suppose the number of possible segments is actually around one billion, just to choose an arbitrary number for illustration. Without underspecification, we need the cardinality of $\mathbf{F}$, the set of UG-given features, to be around 30, since 2^{30} is just over a billion. However, if we allow the underspecification approach, we get to a billion with the cardinality of $\mathbf{F}$ to be equal to just nineteen, since 3^{19} is over a billion, as shown in Figure 61.1.

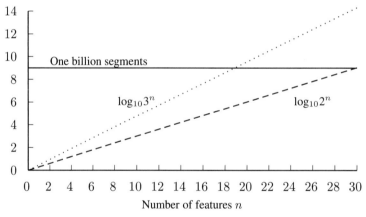

Figure 61.1 Comparison of $y = log_{10}2^n$ and $y = log_{10}3^n$.

One billion is 10^9. This is denoted by the horizontal line at height 9. The dotted and dashed curves cross that line at the x-value for which 2^n and 3^n, respectively, are equal to one billion. Those values are around 30 and 19, respectively.

As Chomsky (2007) says, "The less attributed to genetic information (in our case, the topic of UG) for determining the development of an organism, the more feasible the study of its evolution." It is simpler to study the evolution of a system with 19 features than one with 30. The simplicity and generality of our proposals for innate knowledge can be contrasted with the very rich proposals of models like Optimality Theory (e.g., Kager, 1999), which in some versions proposes innate constraints against front rounded vowels, voiced obstruents in codas, and other highly specific phonological representations.

61.3 Combinatoric Explosion of the Set of Segment Inventories

Let's arbitrarily assume that UG provides exactly four features and two values, and so we posit just the following six primitives:

(607)   A UG offering a modest four features

- $W = \{+, -\}$
- $\mathbf{F} = \{F_1, F_2, F_3, F_4\}$

We have a model with just six elements, but it allows us to define a set of $3^4 = 81$ segments. To review, this is because each segment is a set of valued features, where each feature is "specified" '+', '−' or 'absent'.

One measure of a good scientific theory is its capacity to describe a domain compactly. In some sense, theory building is a kind of data compression. If a theory is just a restatement of observations, it is not much of a theory. However, if a theory allows for an economical account of a wide range of observations, it is a good theory—it captures generalizations. By exploiting the power of combinatorics, our six primitives serve as a useful form of data compression, in contrast with just listing a set of 81 unanalyzable symbols. This is an abstract argument for analyzing segments into features, one that complements the empirical generalizations we got by referring to natural classes.

Let's take this data compression view further. We have been talking about a model of Σ, the universal segment inventory provided by a particular model of UG. Now we want to consider how many *particular* segment inventories this *universal* inventory Σ provides for.

Obviously, the inventory of each particular language must be a subset of Σ. If we focus just on this aspect and think of a language as a segment inventory, then the set of languages is just the set of subsets of the universal set of segments. In other words, if Σ is the set of segments that UG allows, then we can use the notion of power set again: $\mathcal{P}(\Sigma)$ is the set of possible inventories, possible languages in this narrow sense.

How big is this set of possible languages? Recall that for any set T, the cardinality of its power set, $|\mathcal{P}(T)|$ is $2^{|T|}$, that is 2 to the power of the cardinality of T.

Now, let's stick to the situation in (607) with a UG with just four features. As we have seen, the cardinality of Σ is 81 in this case, so the cardinality of $\mathcal{P}(\Sigma)$ is $2^{|\Sigma|} = 2^{81}$. This number is about 2.4×10^{24}, or 2.4 *septillion*. One estimate puts this at ten thousand times the number of grains of sand on earth. This is the descriptive power we get from our six little primitives in (607)—four features and two values. With those six primitives we intensionally define a set of languages that has 2.4 septillion members. One language has all 81 segments; another language has the first 64 segments in the list; another language has only the fourteenth and thirtieth segment; and so on.

This number, 2.4 septillion, is a bit unwieldy, so just for fun, let's suppose that **F** has just one feature, F.

(608)   A super modest UG offering just one feature

- $W = \{+, -\}$
- $\mathbf{F} = \{F\}$

Now let's see what we get for Σ, the set of segments: As we see in (609), there are *three* possible segments ($3^1 = 3$) in Σ:

(609) $\Sigma = \left\{ \varsigma_0\colon \{\}, \varsigma_1\colon \{-F\}, \varsigma_2\colon \{+F\} \right\}$

One segment is ς_2, which is just the set of valued features $\{+F\}$; another segment is ς_1, which is just the set of valued features $\{-F\}$; and the last segment, ς_0, is the empty set of valued features, $\{\ \}$ or $\emptyset$.[5]

Given this universal set of segments, let's calculate $\mathcal{I}$, the set of *inventories* we can define based on our super modest UG with a single feature. Since we are thinking of a language as just a segment inventory, each language is one subset of Σ, and the set of languages is just the power set of Σ. Since $|\Sigma| = 3$, the cardinality of the power set of Σ is 2^3: $|\mathcal{P}(\Sigma)| = 8$.

Here are the eight possible inventories:

(610)   Inventories definable with a single binary feature $\pm F$

- Set of features: $\mathbf{F} = \{F\}$ (just one feature)

- Set of segments: $\Sigma = \left\{ \varsigma_0\colon \{\}, \varsigma_1\colon \{-F\}, \varsigma_2\colon \{+F\} \right\}$ (three segments)

---

[5]Of course, there is just one empty set: the empty set of valued features is identical to the empty set of frogs.

- Set of inventories: $\mathcal{I} = \mathcal{P}(\Sigma)$ (eight inventories)

$$\begin{array}{lll}
\iota_0 = \emptyset & 000 & \text{no segments} \\
\iota_1 = \{\varsigma_2\} & 001 & \\
\iota_2 = \{\varsigma_1\} & 010 & \\
\iota_3 = \{\varsigma_1, \varsigma_2\} & 011 & \\
\iota_4 = \{\varsigma_0\} & 100 & \\
\iota_5 = \{\varsigma_0, \varsigma_2\} & 101 & \\
\iota_6 = \{\varsigma_0, \varsigma_1\} & 110 & \\
\iota_7 = \{\varsigma_0, \varsigma_1, \varsigma_2\} & 111 & \text{all possible segments}
\end{array}$$

If the set of features is $\mathbf{F}$ with a cardinality of n, then the general formula for the number of languages we can define is 2^{3^n}. We annotate the parts of this formula in the table in (611):

(611)   Segment inventory combinatorics for phonological UG

$\mid\mathbf{F}\mid$ = number of features in $\mathbf{F}$, given by UG	
$3^{\mid\mathbf{F}\mid}$ = number of segments in Σ, definable via $\mathbf{F}$ and the three possibilities '+', '−', and 'absent'	$2^{3^{\mid\mathbf{F}\mid}}$
$2^{3^{\mid\mathbf{F}\mid}}$ = cardinality of $\mathcal{P}(\Sigma)$, the number of inventories definable via Σ	

This result sometimes confounds those (professional linguists) who first see it. A typical reaction is that this is an argument *against* the idea of universal grammar. Another reaction is that this is a bad result if we want to understand how children acquire a particular language. How can they search such a tremendous space of possibility and find the language of the environment? However, both these views are confused. The combinatoric explosion we get from a simple system demonstrates the plausibility of universal grammar, since it shows that we can in fact get a massive amount of descriptive variety from a small set of primitives. With a fairly spare UG, we can account for what Chomsky calls the "welter of descriptive complexity" we see when we look at the languages of the world. This result in turn makes the study of the evolution of language more tractable, since the less we need to attribute to UG, to the genome, the simpler it is to study its evolution.

On the issue of acquisition, it should be clear that if UG and particular grammars are defined *intensionally*, not extensionally, children do not actually search an astronomically large space. Viewing language as a combinatoric system built from a small number of primitives reduces the search space significantly. These issues are further discussed in Reiss (2012) and Matamoros and Reiss (2016).

61.4   Combinatoric Explosion via Rule Syntax

Recall the variety of rules that can be formulated using our simple SPE rule syntax. In Unit 10 we showed that with just two segment symbols for inputs and outputs, as well as for defining environments, we can define thirty-two rules. Let's not consider "useless" rules of the form 'a → a / …'. Doing so reduces the possibilities to just sixteen rules if we have only two segments. If we have, say, fifty possible segments, then the cardinality of SEG will be fifty-one, since we can add the insertion and deletion null symbol ϵ to the set of symbols that occur before the '/' in a rule. The size of ENV will be fifty-one as well, since we have the two boundary symbols, '#' and '%', each restricted to one position. So considering our rule possibilities there are $51 \times 50 = 2550$ possibilities for the left side of the '/'. For the right side there are fifty-one possibilities for γ if the environment has the form 'γ ___', and fifty-one if the environment has the form '___ γ'. If the environment has the form 'γ ___ δ', there are fifty-one possibilities for both γ and δ, so, $51 \times 51 = 2601$ possibilities. So, the number of possible rule environments is $51 + 51 + 2601 = 2703$. Multiplying the number of pre- and post-'/' possibilities yields $2703 \times 2550 = 6892650$, or about seven million possible rules. The number would of course be much greater if we allowed syllable structure, tonal phonology, quantificational conditions, and so forth into our rules.

In principle, a language can have any subset of the seven million or so rules if it has the relevant segments for the rules. Let's simplify and assume each language has exactly ten rules. How many ways are there to choose ten rules from seven million choices? This number is expressed in combinatorics as "seven million choose ten" and it is approximately 8×10^{61} or 80 novemdecillion.[6] Of course, the n rules of a language can be ordered in $n!$ ways.[7] Now 10! is about 3.5 million, so the number of languages you can describe if each language has ten ordered rules is about 3.5 million $\times$ 80 novemdecillion, or about 2.9×10^{68}, also known as 2.9 unvigintillion. Even with our fairly conservative assumptions we are inching toward Gallistel and King's "essentially infinite" realm, greater than the number of particles in the universe. Once we formulate rules in terms of features, instead of in terms of segments, the combinatoric growth is even greater—each segment is equivalent to a natural class with one member, so

---

[6]We won't teach you how to calculate this number. To learn more, read about the *binomial theorem* online.

[7]Look back at Unit 31 if you need to review the factorial function.

we will have to consider rules referring to larger natural classes as defined by sets of segments.

These informal calculations involve some arbitrary decisions, some of which increase the results, but some of which massively decrease the results. For example, two languages could have exactly the same rules in exactly the same ordering, but contain partially different segment inventories. Our off-the-cuff calculations ignore such possibilities. In any case, it should be clear that with just our SPE rules (based on segments, not features), we can derive a lot of variety, even if we accept a universally defined segment inventory with just fifty members.

61.5   Combinatoric Explosion of the Lexicon

Another source of richness is the lexicon. Let's think of the set of possible languages now as the set of possible lexicons, given that our UG contains just four features in (607). The four features give us 81 segments, as we have seen. How many lexicons can we get with 81 segments? Let's suppose that each lexicon has 1000 morphemes, each of which has a phonological representation consisting of a string of one to five segments from the inventory of 81 segments. Of course, it is probably the case that no existing human language has a morpheme whose phonology is /ppprp/, but this is not a *linguistic* fact—it does not follow from properties of UG (see Hale and Reiss 2008, chapter 1, and Isac and Reiss 2013, chapter 11, for discussion).

In some respects, our assumptions about the lexicon are quite conservative. For example, many languages have lexical items that consist of more than five segments; it is trivial to find morphemes in our own grammars that are longer, like /morfim/. So, if we assume a universal inventory of 81 segments, then there are 81 possible phonological representations for a morpheme of length 1. There are $81 \times 81 = 6561$ possible representations for a morpheme of length 2, since there are 81 choices for the first segment and 81 for the second segment. And so on up to length 5. Therefore the number of possible segment strings for morphemes up to length 5 is $81 + 81^2 + 81^3 + 81^4 + 81^5 = 3,530,369,205$. If we conservatively restrict the size of every lexicon to 1000 members, then we need to compute how many ways we can take 1000 elements from a set of cardinality 3,530,369,205. This number, expressed as "3,530,369,205 choose 1000" is about 1.6×10^{6980}. That is well into the realm of Gallistel and King's "essentially infinite."

61.6 Cellular Automata Illustration of Tone Combinatorics

One of the purposes of this unit is to undermine your confidence, to make you realize just how bad your intuitions will be about the computational and representational toolkits you consider in modeling phonology. Your intuitions will be bad, because everyone's intuitions are bad about such matters. We'll provide in this section one more example of a basic calculation that deals with the combinatorics of the interaction of representation and computation.

In Unit 38, we introduced tonal phonology using a widespread representational system involving the symbols 'L' and 'H' for low and high tones. Just like other phonological entities, tones can interact with each other in rules. Let's assume that tonal rules are restricted in their syntax in the same way as our early SPE rules, with sensitivity to only the immediate left or right neighbor. Let's consider rules like the following:[8]

(612)   Some tone rules

L → H / H___H   'A L tone becomes H between two H's'
H → L / L___H   'A H tone becomes L between a L and a H'

How many such rules can be formulated? Let's start with a simpler question: How many three-tone windows are there? The answer is eight, as we can see by enumerating them: LLL, LLH, LHL, LHH, HLL, HLH, HHL, HHH. Of course you know that we get these eight possibilities because there are two choices for the first position (L or H), two choices for the second position, and two choices for the third position; and so $2 \times 2 \times 2 = 2^3 = 8$. We have eight rule environments.[9]

For each environment, we can change the middle segment or leave it alone. In other words, for each window, we either have a rule that changes the tone, or we don't—we are going to count "useless" rules in this discussion. Let's treat these two options as two separate rules, recognizing that they are mutually exclusive, since a language can have only one of the rules for a given environment: no language can have both 'L → H / H___H' and 'L → L / H___H'. So there are sixteen possible rules defined by the system, but a given language can have only eight rules, one for each window.

---

[8]We are making several simplifications here in our analogy. These simplifications don't affect the order of magnitude of our typologies, and they allow us to parallel a simple discussion of a set of formal systems called *cellular automata*, on which the following discussion is based (Wolfram, 2002).

[9]And you also realize that we can replace 'L' by '0' and 'H' by '1', and the list of "windows" will correspond to the binary numbers from 0 to 7: 000, 001, 010, 011, 100, 101, 110, 111.

How may languages can be defined by this system? Well, for each of the eight three-tone windows, there is a binary choice: replace the central tone or leave it alone. Equivalently, for each window, the output for the central tone will be L or H.

(613)

Window	LLL	LLH	LHL	LHH	HLL	HLH	HHL	HHH
Choice:	L/H	L/H	L/H	L/H	L/H	L/H	L/H	L/H

One language might have these choices for each window:

(614)

Window	LLL	LLH	LHL	LHH	HLL	HLH	HHL	HHH
Choice:	L	H	L	L	L	L	H	H

And another language might have these choices:

(615)

Window	LLL	LLH	LHL	LHH	HLL	HLH	HHL	HHH
Choice:	H	L	H	L	L	L	H	L

So there are eight windows/environments, and each language consists of a set of eight corresponding settings: choose L or H, for the first environment; choose L or H for the second environment; and so on. In other words, there are $2 \times 2 \times 2 \times 2 \times 2 \times 2 \times 2 \times 2 = 2^8 = 256$ possible languages definable using our simple tone rule system.

Of course, we could use our trick of replacing 'L' with 0 and 'H' with 1 once again and have a handy system for referring to these languages. If a language replaced all of its central tones with L, it could be represented like this:

(616)

Window	LLL	LLH	LHL	LHH	HLL	HLH	HHL	HHH
Choice:	L	L	L	L	L	L	L	L

Replacing L with 0 and H with 1 yields this:

(617)

2^7	2^6	2^5	2^4	2^3	2^2	2^1	2^0
128s	64s	32s	16s	8s	4s	2s	1s
0	0	0	0	0	0	0	0

So, (616) is Language 0.

Here is Language 13:

(618)

Window	LLL	LLH	LHL	LHH	HLL	HLH	HHL	HHH
Choice:	L	L	L	L	H	H	L	H

Replacing L with 0 and H with 1 yields this:

	2^7	2^6	2^5	2^4	2^3	2^2	2^1	2^0
(619)	128s	64s	32s	16s	8s	4s	2s	1s
	0	0	0	0	1	1	0	1

We get this since $2^3 + 2^2 + 2^0 = 8 + 4 + 1 = 13$.

Finally, here is Language 245:

(620)	Window	LLL	LLH	LHL	LHH	HLL	HLH	HHL	HHH
	Choice:	H	H	H	H	L	H	L	H

Replacing L with 0 and H with 1 yields this:

	2^7	2^6	2^5	2^4	2^3	2^2	2^1	2^0
(621)	128s	64s	32s	16s	8s	4s	2s	1s
	1	1	1	1	0	1	0	1

We get this since $2^7 + 2^6 + 2^5 + 2^4 + 2^2 + 2^0 = 128 + 64 + 32 + 16 + 4 + 1 = 245$.

Things become interesting when we consider what happens if there are more than just two tones. Many actual human languages appear to have three distinct tones. It doesn't matter if we think of them as L, H, and M (for 'mid') or as L, H, and the absence of a tone. We are interested in how this additional representational possibility affects the space of tone rules, the number of different languages, conceived as a set of tone rules.

Without thinking about it very hard, write down an estimate: if a UG with two tone possibilities yields 256 languages, how many do you get with three tone possibilities? Write down your estimate...

Now let's do the calculation. We are assuming that nothing else changes, so we are still dealing with three-tone windows, and we can have rules like the following:

(622)   •   H → M / L ___L

        •   M → M / L ___H

First, how many windows are there? For each window, the first position can be L/M/H, so there are three possibilities for that position. The same holds for the second and third positions. In total, there are $3 \times 3 \times 3 = 3^3 = 27$ windows, instead of just eight (as when there were only two tones to choose from). One window is LLL, another is LMM, another is HLM, and so on.

We can use L/M/H or colors like white/gray/black or digits like 0/1/2 to represent the three tones. In any case, we get 27 windows, as illustrated in (623). Instead of binary numbers, we will need *ternary* numbers, in which each column corresponds to a power of 3. For example, the ternary number 211 corresponds to $2 \times 3^2 + 1 \times 3^1 + 1 \times 3^0 = 18 + 3 + 1 = 22$.

(623)   Tonal, ternary, and decimal representation of nine of the 27 three-color, three-cell neighborhoods

L	L	L	L	L	M	L	L	H
□	□	□	□	□	▨	□	□	■
0	0	0	0	0	1	0	0	2
	0			1			2	
L	M	L	L	M	M	L	M	H
□	▨	□	□	▨	▨	□	▨	■
0	1	0	0	1	1	0	1	2
	3			4			5	
				⋮				
H	H	L	H	H	M	H	H	H
■	■	□	■	■	▨	■	■	■
2	2	0	2	2	1	2	2	2
	24			25			26	

We are finally ready to return to the burning question of how many more languages we can describe using three tones, rather than two. Recall that with two tones and eight windows, there were $2^8 = 256$ possible combinations of rules, so 256 distinct languages. Well, with three tones and twenty-seven windows, there are 3^{27} possible languages. This number is equal to more than seven and a half *trillion*, 7,625,597,484,987 to be precise. This means, if our analogy is any good, that you get over seven trillion additional languages if you go from a UG with L and H to one with L, M, and H. If we consider the possibility that M just denotes the absence of L and H, then allowing vowels with no tone is the mechanism that leads to this explosion. As we like to phrase it, you get *seven trillion languages for nothing*!

61.7   The Bright Side of Combinatoric Explosion

These examples of combinatoric explosion from a modest toolkit are reminiscent of a discussion in Gallistel and King (2009, p. 82) who discuss the "picture space" of a digital camera:

> The camera constructs a symbol for an image during the interval when the shutter is open. If it is a six-megapixel camera, the symbol consists

of 6 million 24-bit binary numbers. The number of different symbols of this kind (the number of different pictures that may be taken with a 6-megapixel camera) is infinite[10] just as is the number of possible images. But, of course, the number of different pictures that even the most avid photographer will take is finite. ...The camera can represent an infinite range of possibilities with finite resources, because it constructs its symbols on demand. The possibilities are infinite, but the actualities are finite.

This camera example suggests that the number of data strings needed for cognition, even for purposes like insect navigation, Gallistel's domain of expertise, is so great as to be considered infinite, for all practical purposes. However, the resources required for realizing and storing these strings are clearly limited in brains. A biologically plausible computational system must therefore start with a small number of simple symbols and be able to combine them and store relevant combined symbols in response to received stimuli—the system does not store all the possibilities, only those that are actually encountered:

> What is needed is an architecture that combats combinatoric explosions with combinatorics. ...It must be possible to store sequences that actually occur in a memory capable of storing a great many... sequences, drawn from the essentially infinite number of possible such sequences, and to compare those stored sequences to whatever sequences may prove to be relevant. This architecture uses memory and combinatorics to cope with the finitude of the actual. (Gallistel and King, 2009, p. 136)

This is exactly the model we have proposed—UG gives us a toolkit to parse input into features, segments, and segment strings that can be stored or compared to ones that were previously stored. This toolkit is itself compact, but combinatoric explosion gives it tremendous power. In simple terms, UG characterizes *intensionally* a set of languages whose extension is essentially infinite.

---

[10]It is actually $2^{24^{6,000,000}}$ which is way more than Gallistel and King's definition of "essentially infinite," meaning 'more than the number of elementary particles in the universe', which is something like a mere 2^{285}.

Exercises

61.1. Review the definitions of generalized intersection and generalized union from Unit 45.1. Given an arbitrary set T, what are the following? Explain.

- $\bigcap \mathcal{P}(T)$
- $\bigcup \mathcal{P}(T)$

61.2. Letting $\{F_1, F_2, F_3\}$= {BACK, ROUND, HIGH} and assuming no underspecification, provide the *binary* number corresponding to the eight Turkish surface vowels: [i, ü, ı, u , e, ö, a, o].

61.3. Letting $\{F_1, F_2, F_3\}$= {BACK, ROUND, HIGH} and assuming that underspecification *is allowed*, provide the *ternary* number corresponding to the following Turkish lexical vowels: /i, ü, ı, u , e, ö, a, o, A, I/.

61.4. (i)Referring to (610), rewrite inventories $\iota_1 - \iota_7$ using just set brackets and valued features—don't use ς. (ii) Which inventory is the empty set of segments? (iii) Which inventory has one segment which is the empty set of valued features?

61.5. How many hands of size 0-52 can you have from a deck of cards? Explain.

61.6. How many hands can you have of size 13, where you have *exactly* one ace, one two, one three, . . ., one ten, one jack, one queen, and one king? Explain.

61.7. How many hands can you have of size 13 or less, where you have at most one of each value? So, zero or one aces, zero or one twos, and so on.

61.8. If UG provides no features at all, $\mathbf{F} = \emptyset$, then what is Σ, the set of possible segments, and what is $\mathcal{I}$, the set of possible inventories/languages?

61.9. How many segments do you get if UG provides five features and underspecification is allowed? How many segment inventories? Just give mathematical expressions and explain. You can then feed the expressions into http://wolframalpha.com/ and report the result.

61.10. Power sets: Let A be the set $\{x\}$: What is $\mathcal{P}(A)$? We *don't* mean "What is the cardinality of $\mathcal{P}(A)$." We want you to write down $\mathcal{P}(A)$ with all the necessary brackets. The power set is a set. Next answer these two questions: What is $|A|$? What is $|\mathcal{P}(A)|$?

61.11. Natives of the planet Shandy have an innate language faculty that gives them three different segments $\{\otimes, \propto, \odot\}$. Each Shandian language has some subset of these segments, and each subset corresponds to a particular Shandian language. In other words, each language can be thought of as a segment inventory. How many logical choices for Shandian languages are there? Explain your answer, and arrange the Shandian languages using a sensible binary numbering system. Don't forget the particularly taciturn Shandians.

61.12. Explain how the discussion of infinitude in section 61.7 differs from the well-known statement by the nineteenth-century thinker Wilhelm von Humboldt that language "makes infinite use of finite means," which is usually quoted in the discussions of syntax. Do the differences derive from the nature of phonology versus syntax? In each case, what is infinitude a property of?

Unit 62

Postscript

> Everyone engaged in research must have had the experience of working with feverish and prolonged intensity to write a paper which no one else will read or to solve a problem which no one else thinks important and which will bring no conceivable reward—which may only confirm a general opinion that the researcher is wasting his time on irrelevancies. The fact that rats and monkeys do likewise [*sic*] is interesting and important to show in careful experiment.

Noam Chomsky, Review of Skinner's *Verbal Behavior*

We were inspired to write this book after our former undergraduate student Maxime Papillon, who is now (in 2018) working towards his PhD at the University of Maryland, described what we were trying to do in class on the social media site *reddit*. The feedback online, as well as the email requests for materials, suggested that our ideas of using phonology to teach basic math and logic, and of seeing how the math and logic could give insight into human phonology, were potentially exciting to an admittedly small—but passionate—audience.

Here's a review of some ideas that we presented by building on basic mathematical and logical notions:

- A theory of rules depends upon generalizing the use of partial descriptions to define natural classes of strings, segments, and structures.

- Natural classes are defined by generalized intersection.

- The traditional '→' of phonological rules can be deconstructed into various basic operations including segment insertion and deletion involving strings, and valued feature insertion (via unification) and deletion (via set subtraction) at the segmental level. Future work should discover further fundamental operations by continuing to deconstruct the arrow and thus contribute to the theory of possible rules.

- Simple formal systems can have rich descriptive power because of combinatoric explosion.

- The "relation between a phonemic system and the phonetic record ... is remote and complex" (Chomsky, 1964, p. 38), and the "essential properties underlie the surface form" (Katz and Bever, 1976, p. 12)—in part due to mathematical properties of phonological systems like rule ordering.

These ideas are either explicitly or implicitly stated in much of the work we drew on, but we hope that our discussion will inspire students to think more often and more deeply about fundamental concepts, perhaps for the purposes of showing where they remain vague and even to reject and replace them with better formulations.

The book is obviously still a work in progress. There are many, many areas of phonology and approaches to phonology that we have not treated. Some of the book's flaws reflect our own ignorance or the need to make arbitrary choices; others surely reflect errors in our reasoning, some of which we are vaguely but naggingly aware of; still others reflect the state of the art. If our humble attempts here inspire some readers to continue and improve our scientific project of understanding phonology, and our pedagogic project of teaching basic mathematical and logical reasoning, then we will consider the undertaking to have been worthwhile.

At the beginning of this book we quoted Gallistel and King (2009, p. vii): "The truths the cognitive scientists know about information processing, when integrated into neuroscience, will transform our understanding of how the brain works." We hope to have conveyed to you at least some truths about phonological information processing that can play a role in this transformation.

Exercises

62.1. Watch the 1973 lecture by conductor Leonard Bernstein about "musical phonology." You can find a few versions on YouTube, such as https://youtu.be/8fHi36dvTdE. The lecture is entertaining, and it is interesting to see how much Bernstein was influenced by Chomsky's ideas. Some things that Bernstein says about phonology seem imprecise, false, or downright wacky from the perspective of this book. Discuss two points he makes that fall into one of those categories, and then discuss two interesting ideas that he raises about parallels between phonology and music. There are other lectures in the series, relating music to syntax and semantics.

62.2. Discuss the various notions of *nothing* that played a role in our analyses. Review the symbols we introduced, and summarize our justifications for each one. If you think we left any out, be sure to include those in your discussion.

Bibliography

Abramson, Arthur S. 1986. The perception of word-initial consonant length: Pattani Malay. *Journal of the International Phonetic Association* 16 (1): 8–16.

Anderson, Stephen R. 1992. *A-morphous morphology*. Cambridge: Cambridge University Press.

Appelbaum, Irene. 1996. The lack of invariance problem and the goal of speech perception. In *The 4th International Conference on Spoken Language Processing*, 1541–1544. http://www.asel.udel.edu/icslp/cdrom/vol3/435/a435.pdf.

Archangeli, Diana, and Douglas Pulleyblank. 2015. Phonology without universal grammar. *Frontiers in Psychology* 6.

Bach, Emmon, and Robert T. Harms. 1972. How do languages get crazy rules. In *Linguistic change and generative theory*, ed. Robert P. Stockwell and Ronald Macaulay, 21. Bloomington: Indiana University Press. 1C21.

Baker, Mark. 1985. The mirror principle and morphosyntactic explanation. *Linguistic Inquiry* 16 (3): 373–416.

Baković, Eric. 2006. Antigemination, assimilation and the determination of identity. *Phonology* 22 (3): 279–315.

Baković, Eric. 2009. Abstractness and motivation in phonological theory. *Studies in Hispanic and Lusophone Linguistics* 2 (1): 183–198.

Bale, Alan. 2009. Yet more evidence for the emptiness of plurality. In *Proceedings of the North East Linguistic Society (NELS) 38*, 75–88. University of Massachusetts, Amherst: Graduate Linguistic Student Association.

Bale, Alan, Michaël Gagnon, and Hrayr Khanjian. 2011. On the relationship between morphological and semantic markedness: the case of plural morphology. *Morphology* 21 (2): 197–221.

Bale, Alan, Charles Reiss, and David Ta-Chun Shen. 2016. Sets, rules and natural classes: { } *vs.* [ ]. Ms. Concordia University.

Bennett, Craig M., Abigail A. Baird, Michael B. Miller, and George L. Wolford. 2011. Neural correlates of interspecies perspective taking in the post-mortem atlantic salmon: An argument for proper multiple comparisons correction. *Journal of Serendipitous and Unexpected Results* 1: 1–5.

Benveniste, Émile. 1966. Différentes formes de la composition nominale en français. *Bulletin de la Société de linguistique de Paris* 61 (1): 82–95.

Berko, Jean. 1958. The child's learning of English morphology. *Word* 14: 150–177.

Bowern, Claire. 2013. *A grammar of Bardi*. Berlin: De Gruyter Mouton.

Chaitin, Gregory. 2006. The limits of reason. *Scientific American* 294 (3): 74–81.

Chierchia, Gennaro. 1998. Plurality of mass nouns and the notion of "semantic parameter." In *Events and grammar*, ed. Susan Rothstein, 53–104. Dordrecht: Kluwer Academic Publishers.

Choi, John D. 1992. Phonetic underspecification and target interpolation: An acoustic study of Marshallese vowel allophony. PhD diss, UCLA, Los Angeles.

Chomsky, Noam. 1957. *Syntactic structures*. The Hague: Mouton.

Chomsky, Noam. 1964. Formal discussion in response to W. Miller and S. Ervin. In *The acquisition of language*, ed. Ursula Bellugi and Roger Brown, 35–39. Chicago: University of Chicago Press.

Chomsky, Noam. 1965. *Aspects of the theory of syntax*. Cambridge, MA: MIT Press.

Chomsky, Noam. 1966. *Cartesian linguistics*. New York: Harper & Row.

Chomsky, Noam. 1980. *Rules and representations*. New York: Columbia University Press.

Chomsky, Noam. 1982. *Some concepts and consequences of the theory of government and binding*. Cambridge, MA: MIT Press.

Chomsky, Noam. 1986. *Knowledge of language : Its nature, origin, and use*. Westport, CT: Praeger.

Chomsky, Noam. 2000. Language as a natural object. In *New horizons in the study of language and mind*, 106–133. Cambridge: Cambridge University Press.

Chomsky, Noam. 2007. Approaching UG from below. In *Interfaces + recursion = language?: Chomsky's minimalism and the view from syntax-semantics*, ed. Uli Sauerland and Hans-Martin Gärtner, 1–24. Berlin: Mouton de Gruyter.

Chomsky, Noam, and Morris Halle. 1968. *The sound pattern of English*. New York: Harper & Row.

Dayley, Jon Philip. 1985. *Tzutujil grammar*. Berkeley and Los Angeles: University of California Press.

Elson, Ben. 1947. Sierra Popoluca syllable structure. *International Journal of American Linguistics* 13 (1): 13–17.

Fant, Gunnar. 2006. *Speech acoustics and phonetics: Selected writings*. Springer.

Flemming, Edward. 2004. Contrast and perceptual distinctiveness. In *Phonetically based phonology*, ed. Bruce Hayes, Robert Martin Kirchner, and Donca Steriade, 232–276. Cambridge: Cambridge University Press.

Fodor, Jerry A. 1983. *The modularity of mind: an essay on faculty psychology*. Cambridge, MA: MIT Press.

Gallistel, C. R., and Adam Philip King. 2009. *Memory and the computational brain: why cognitive science will transform neuroscience*. Chichester, West Sussex, UK: Wiley-Blackwell.

Hale, Mark. 2007. *Historical linguistics: theory and method*. Malden, MA: Blackwell.

Hale, Mark, Madelyn Kissock, and Charles Reiss. 2007. Microvariation, variation and the features of Universal Grammar. *Lingua* 117: 645–665.

Hale, Mark, and Charles Reiss. 1998. Formal and empirical arguments concerning language acquisition. *Linguistic Inquiry* 29: 656–683.

Hale, Mark, and Charles Reiss. 2000. "Substance abuse" and "dysfunctionalism": Current trends in phonology. *Linguistic Inquiry* 31 (1): 157–169.

Hale, Mark, and Charles Reiss. 2003. The subset principle in phonology: Why the *tabula* can't be *rasa*. *Journal of Linguistics* 39: 219–244.

Hale, Mark, and Charles Reiss. 2008. *The phonological enterprise*. Oxford: Oxford University Press.

Halle, Morris. 1959. *The sound pattern of Russian*. The Hague: Mouton & Company.

Halle, Morris. 1964. On the bases of phonology. In *The structure of language*, ed. Jerrold J. Katz and Jerry Fodor, 324–333. Englewood Cliffs, NJ: Prentice-Hall. Chap. 9.

Halle, Morris. 1975. Confessio grammatici. *Language* 51 (3): 525–535.

Halle, Morris. 2001. Infixation versus onset metathesis in Tagalog, Chamorro, and Toba Batak. In *Ken Hale: A life in language*. Vol. 36 of *Current studies in linguistics*, 153–168. MIT Press.

Halle, Morris, and Alec Marantz. 1993. Distributed morphology and the pieces of inflection. In *The view from building 20*, ed. Kenneth Hale and Samuel Jay Keyser, 111–176. Cambridge, MA: MIT Press.

Halle, Morris, and Alec Marantz. 1994. Some key features of distributed morphology. *MIT working papers in linguistics* 21 (275): 88.

Halmos, P. R. 1960. *Naive set theory. The university series in undergraduate mathematics*. Van Nostrand.

Hammarberg, Robert. 1976. The metaphysics of coarticulation. *Journal of Phonetics* 4: 353–363.

Hammarberg, Robert. 1981. The cooked and the raw. *Journal of Information Science* 3 (6): 261–267.

Harbour, Daniel. 2003. The Kiowa case for feature insertion. *Natural Language and Linguistic Theory* 21: 543–578.

Harms, Robert T. 1968. *Introduction to phonological theory*. Englewood Cliffs, NJ: Prentice-Hall.

Harris, James W. 1984. Autosegmental phonology, lexical phonology and Spanish nasals. In *Language sound structure*, ed. Mark Aronoff and Richard T. Oehrle, 67–82. Cambridge, MA: MIT Press.

Hayes, Bruce. 2009. *Introductory phonology*. Malden, MA: Wiley-Blackwell.

Heisenberg, Werner, and Arnold J. Pomerans. 1971. *Physics and beyond: Encounters and conversations*. New York: Harper & Row Publishing Group.

Idsardi, William. 1992. *The computation of prosody*. Cambridge, MA: MIT dissertation.

Inkelas, Sharon, and Orhan Orgun. 1995. Level ordering and economy in the lexical phonology of Turkish. *Language* 71: 763–793.

Isac, Daniela, and Charles Reiss. 2013. *I-language: an Introduction to Linguistics as Cognitive Science*, 2nd edn. Oxford: Oxford University Press.

Jackendoff, Ray. 1994. *Patterns in the mind: Language and human nature*. New York: Basic Books.

Jakobson, Roman, Gunnar Fant, and Morris Halle. 1967. *Preliminaries to speech analysis*. Cambridge, MA: MIT Press.

Johnson, C. Douglas. 1972. *Formal aspects of phonological description*. The Hague: Mouton.

Jurgec, Peter. 2013. Two types of parasitic assimilation. *Nordlyd* 40 (1).

Kager, René. 1999. *Optimality Theory*. Cambridge: Cambridge University Press.

Kaplan, Ronald M. 1987. Three seductions of computational psycholinguistics. In *Linguistic theory and computer applications*, ed. P. Whitelock, M. M. Wood, H. L. Somers, R. Johnson, and P. Bennett, 149–188. London: Academic Press.

Katz, Jerrold J., and Thomas G. Bever. 1976. The fall and rise of empiricism. In *An integrated theory of linguistic ability*, ed. Thomas G. Bever, Jerrold J. Katz, and D. Terence Langendoen, 11–64. New York: Thomas Y. Crowell.

Keating, Patricia. 1988. Underspecification in phonetics. *Phonology* 5: 275–292.

Kenstowicz, Michael, and Charles Kisseberth. 1979. *Generative phonology: description and theory*. New York: Academic Press.

Kiparsky, Paul. 1968. Linguistic universals and linguistic change. In *Universals in linguistic theory*, ed. Emmon Bach and Robert T. Harms, 171–204. New York: Holt, Rinehart & Winston.

Kiparsky, Paul. 1973. *Three dimensions of linguistic theory.* Tokyo: TEC.

Kiparsky, Paul. 1985. Some consequences of Lexical Phonology. *Phonology Yearbook* 2: 85–138.

Kornai, András. 2008. *Mathematical linguistics.* London: Springer.

Koster, Jan. 2006. Is linguistics a natural science? In *Organizing grammar: Linguistic studies in honor of Henk van Riemsdijk*, ed. Hans Broekhuis, Norbert Corver, Riny Huybregts, Ursula Kleinhenz, and Jan Koster, Vol. 86, 350–358. Walter de Gruyter.

Krifka, Manfred. 1987. An outline of genericity. *Technical Report of the Seminar für Natürlich-sprachliche Systems* 87 - 25.

Krifka, Manfred, Francis Jeffrey Pelletier, Greg N. Carlson, Alice ter Meulen, Gennaro Chierchia, and Godehard Link. 1995. *The generic book.* Chicago: Chicago University Press.

Lenneberg, Eric H., Noam Chomsky, and Otto Marx. 1967. *Biological foundations of language.* New York: Wiley.

Link, Godehard. 1983. The logical analysis of plurals and mass terms: A lattice-theoretical approach. In *Meaning, use and interpretation of language*, ed. R. Baeuerle, C. Schwarze, and Arnim von Stechow, 302–323. DeGruyter.

Marantz, Alec. 1997. No escape from syntax: Don't try morphological analysis in the privacy of your own lexicon. In *University of Pennsylvania working papers in linguistics vol. 4.2*, ed. Alexis Dimitriadis, Laura Siegel, Clarissa Surek-Clark, and Alexander Williams, 201–225. University of Pennsylvania.

Marlett, S., and J. Stemberger. 1983. Empty consonants in Seri. *Linguistic Inquiry* 14: 617–639.

Marr, David. 1982. *Vision: a computational investigation into the human representation and processing of visual information.* San Francisco: W.H. Freeman.

Matamoros, Camila, and Charles Reiss. 2016. Symbol taxonomy in biophonology. In *Biolinguistic investigations on the language faculty*, ed. Anna Maria Di Sciullo, 41–54. John Benjamins.

McCarthy, John J. 2007. Slouching toward optimality: Coda reduction in OT-CC. *Phonological Studies (Journal of the Phonological Society of Japan)* 7: 89–104.

McCawley, James D. 1971. *On the role of notation in generative phonology.* Indiana University Linguistics Club.

Mielke, Jeffrey. 2008. *The emergence of distinctive features.* Oxford: Oxford University Press.

Moravcsik, Julius. 2017. *Meaning, creativity, and the partial inscrutability of the human mind* Palo Alto: Center for the Study of Language and Information.

Nevins, Andrew. 2010. *Locality in vowel harmony.* Cambridge, MA: MIT Press.

Newmeyer, Frederick J. 2005. *Possible and probable languages: a generative perspective on linguistic typology.* New York: Oxford University Press.

Norvig, Peter. 2011. On Chomsky and the two cultures of statistical learning. http://norvig.com/chomsky.html.

Odden, David. 1988. Anti antigemination and the OCP. *Linguistic Inquiry* 19 (3): 451–475.

Odden, David. 1994. Adjacency parameters in phonology. *Language* 70 (2): 289–330.

Odden, David. 2013. *Introducing phonology*, 2nd edn. Cambridge: Cambridge University Press.

Pike, Kenneth L. 1947. *Phonemics: A technique for reducing languages to writing. University of Michigan publications: Linguistics.* Ann Arbor: University of Michigan Press. Bosch

Pinker, Steven. 1994. *The language instinct.* New York: W. Morrow.

Poeppel, David. 2012. The maps problem and the mapping problem: Two challenges for a cognitive neuroscience of speech and language. *Cognitive Neuropsychology* 29 (1-2): 34–55.

Poeppel, David, and William Idsardi. 2011. Recognizing words from speech: the perception-action-memory loop. In *Lexical representation: a multidisciplinary approach*, ed. Gareth Gaskell and Pienie Zwitserlood, 171–196. New York: De Gruyter Mouton.

Port, Robert. 2007. How are words stored in memory? Beyond phones and phonemes. *New ideas in psychology* 25 (2): 143–170.

Poser, William J. 1993. Are strict cycle effects derivable? In *Studies in lexical phonology*, ed. Sharon Hargus and Ellen M Kaisse, Vol. 4. San Diego: Academic Press.

Poser, William J. 2004. On the status of Chumash sibilant harmony. Ms., University of Pennsylvania.

Prince, Alan, and Paul Smolensky. 2004. *Optimality theory: constraint interaction in generative grammar*. Malden, MA: Blackwell Pub..

Pylyshyn, Zenon. 1984. *Computation and cognition: Toward a foundation for cognitive science*. Cambridge, MA: MIT Press.

Pylyshyn, Zenon. 1999. What's in your mind? In *What is cognitive science?*, ed. Ernest LePore and Zenon W. Pylyshyn, 1–25. Malden, MA: Blackwell.

Reiss, Charles. 2003. Deriving the feature-filling/feature-changing contrast: An application to Hungarian vowel harmony. *Linguistic Inquiry* 34 (2): 199–224.

Reiss, Charles. 2012. Towards a bottom-up approach to phonological typology. In *Towards a biolinguistic understanding of grammar: Essays on interfaces*, ed. A. M. Di Sciullo, 169–191. Amsterdam: John Benjamins.

Reiss, Charles. 2017a. Contrast is irrelevant in phonology: A simple account of Russian /v/ as /V/. In *Arguments of substance: Beyond markedness*, ed. Bridget D. Samuels, 23–45. Amsterdam: John Benjamins.

Reiss, Charles. 2017b. Substance Free Phonology. In *Handbook of Phonological Theory*, ed. S. J. Hannahs and Anna R. K. Bosch, 425–452. Routledge.

Rider, Benjamin, Matthew F. Pierlott, Randall E. Auxier, Ron Novy, Tanya Jeffcoat, Eric N. Wilson, Dean A. Knowalski, Thomas M. Alexander, Anthony Cunningham, Aeon J. Skoble, et al.. 2011. *Dr. Seuss and philosophy: Oh, the thinks you can think!* Rowman & Littlefield.

Sadock, Jerrold M. 1985. Autolexical syntax: a proposal for the treatment of noun incorporation and similar phenomena. *Natural Language and Linguistic Theory* 3 (4): 379–439.

Samuels, Bridget D. 2011. *Phonological architecture: a biolinguistic perspective*. Oxford: Oxford University Press.

Sapir, Edward. 1925. Sound patterns in language. *Language* 1: 37–51.

Sapir, Edward. 1933. *La réalité psychologique des phonèmes*. Presses universitaires de France.

Sapir, Edward. 1949. The psychological reality of phonemes. In *Selected writings of Edward Sapir*, ed. D. Mandelbaum, 46–60. Berkeley and Los Angeles: University of California Press.

Sauerland, Uli. 2003. A new semantics for number. In *Proceedings of SALT 13*, 258–275. Cornell University, Ithaca, NY: CLC Publications.

Sauerland, Uli, Jan Andersen, and Kazuko Yatsushiro. 2005. The plural is semantically unmarked. In *Linguistic evidence*, ed. S. Kepser and M. Reis. Berlin: Mouton de Gruyter.

Schein, Barry, and Donca Steriade. 1986. On geminates. *Linguistic Inquiry* 17 (4): 691–744.

Shen, David Ta-Chun. 2016. *Precedence and Search: Primitive concepts in morpho-phonology*. Taipei: National Taiwan Normal University dissertation.

Sklar, Lawrence. 2000. *Theory and truth: Philosophical critique within foundational science*. Oxford: Oxford University Press.

Spector, Benjamin. 2007. Aspects of the pragmatics of plural morphology: On higher-order implicatures. In *Presuppositions and implicatures in compositional semantics*, ed. U. Sauerland and P. Statev, 243–281. London: Palgrave-Macmillan.

Spencer, Andrew. 1996. *Phonology: Theory and description*. Oxford: Blackwell.

Stevens, Kenneth N. 2000. *Acoustic phonetics*. MIT Press.

Volenec, Veno, and Charles Reiss. 2018. Cognitive Phonetics: The transduction of distinctive features at the phonology-phonetics interface. *Biolinguistics* 11.

Wason, Peter C. 1968. Reasoning about a rule. *The Quarterly Journal of Experimental Psychology* 20 (3): 273–281.

Wiese, Richard. 2000. *The phonology of German*. Oxford: Oxford University Press.

Wolfram, Stephen. 2002. *A new kind of science*. Champaign, IL: Wolfram Media.

Index

583

lexical form, *see also* morpheme, 189, 191

lexical item, *see also* morpheme, 66, 73

lexicon, 53, 73, 85, 228, 239

linguistic universal, 401
    substantive, 401
    formal, 402

Lithuanian, 506

locality, 490

logical fallacy, 176

Malay, 316

Maranungku, 366

mental grammar, 10

mental model, *see* model of the mind

mental representation, 104, 105

merger, 211, 212n1, 212, 213, 444, 445

metathesis, 308

Mi'gmaq, 314

minimal pair, 229, 282n3, 282, 283, 313, 363, 444

minimal triggering environment (MTE), 262, 263, 287

model of the mind, 104

modus ponens, 175

modus tollendo ponens (MTP), 121, 123, 137, 139, 214

morpheme, 52–54, 66, 73
    alternants, 66, 191

morphology, 54, 65–67, 74, 86

natural class, 24, 32, 218n3, 221, 231, 237, 327, 373, 392–394, 396, 403, 459, 460, 539, 541, 542, 546n6, 546, 547

naturalness, 216

neuroscience, 3, 156

neutralization, 116, 123, 126, 168, 174, 176, 178, 183, 184, 187, 200, 229, 234–236, 240, 266, 281–283, 453, 476
    absolute, 213
    combined, 197, 200
    reciprocal, 191

non-alternation assumption (NAA), 119, 120, 123, 192, 214

non-surfacing segment, 193, 194

Optimality Theory (OT), 91n10, 169, 176, 229n1, 266n6, 334n8, 556

ordered pair, *see* set

ordered set, *see* set

phoneme, 214, 234, 235, 281, 282

phonological acquisition, 285

phonological analysis, 62

phonological category, 20

phonological derivation, 252

phonological functions,
    non-invertibility of, 178

phonological length, 315–317

phonological predictability, 473

phonological representation, 54, 156, 239, 362
    uniqueness of, 284

phonological rule, 65, 66, 73, 84–86, 115, 397
    domain, 84
    environment, 86, 87, 220, 225, 310, 380, 501
    elsewhere, 231, 232
    feature-changing rule, 438, 457
    functional interpretation of, 108